Introduction

to Media

Studies

A Reader

Boulou Ebanda de B'béri,

Pierre C. Bélanger,

Mohamed Eid,

Mark Lowes,

and Evan Potter

OXFORD

UNIVERSITY PRESS

UNIVERSITY PRESS

70 Wynford Drive, Dons Mills, Ontario, M3C 1J9
www.oup.com/ca

Oxford University Press is a department of the University of Oxford.
It furthers the University's Objective of excellence in research, scholarship, and education
by publishing worldwide in

Oxford   New York
Auckland   Bangkok   Buenos Aires   Cape Town   Chennai
Dar es Salam   Delhi   Hong Kong   Istanbul   Karachi   Kolkata
Kuala Lumpur   Madrid   Melbourne   Mexico City   Mumbai   Nairobi
Sào Paolo   Shanghai   Tapei   Tokyo   Toronto

Oxford is a trade mark of Oxford University Press
in the UK and in certain countries

Published in Canada
by Oxford University Press

Cover Design: Brett Miller

to mammy, my best love!

About the Editors

Dr Boulou Ebanda de B'béri is the Director and Principal Investigator of the University of Ottawa's *Audiovisual Media Lab for the studies of Cultures and Societies* (AMELC&S). He has been a Visiting Scholar and Professor at the University of California, Santa Barbara and Northeastern University, Boston. He is the winner of various prizes and scholarships, including a *2006-New Opportunities Fund* awarded by the Canada Foundation for Innovation (CFI). He teaches Film and Cultural Studies, Intercultural Communication, and Media Studies.

Dr Pierre C. Bélanger is a Full Professor at the University of Ottawa's Department of Communication and the Institute of Canadian Studies. He specializes in Canadian media industries and the psycho-sociology of technological innovations. From 1998 to 2001, he was on secondment at CBC/Radio-Canada where he worked as Head of New Media for French radio and as Chief Advisor-New Media Development. He is a member of the Board of Directors of TV-Ontario.

Dr Mahmoud Eid is an Assistant Professor at the Department of Communication, University of Ottawa. He previously taught in the University of Regina's School of Journalism in Saskatchewan, and in Carleton University's School of Journalism and Communication in Ontario. His professional expertise lies in quantitative and qualitative research regarding the effects of mass media and social development. His research interests concentrate on international communication, media ethics, communication research methods, terrorism, crisis management and conflict resolution, modernity, and the political economy of communication.

Dr Mark Lowes is an Associate Professor in the Department of Communication. He has been researching and publishing for several years on the role that mega-sport events play in the economic and cultural growth strategies of world-class cities. His current work examines the viability of sport tourism for fostering economic and social development in Canada's rural and northern communities.

Dr Evan Potter is an Assistant Professor at the Department of Communication. His research program focuses on the projection of Canada's image in the international arena and the use of communications technologies in diplomacy. His other interests are communication planning, political communication, public opinion towards foreign policy and international communications.

Contents

Preface and Acknowledgements / ix

Part 1   **The Engaging New World of Traditional Media** / 1
         Section Editor: Pierre C. Bélanger
         Introduction / 1

         Radio / 3
         Radio in Canada: An Industry in Transition / 3
                 Pierre C. Bélanger
         The Tribal Drum / 21
                 Marshall McLuhan

         Television / 29
         The End of Television as We Know It: A Future Industry Perspective / 29
                 Saul J. Berman, Louisa A. Shipnuck and Niall Duff
         Introduction: Where in the World Are We? / 59
                 Samuel Weber
         Television: Set and Screen / 64
                 Samuel Weber

Part 2   **Old/New Media** / 79
         Section Editor: Boulou Ebanda de B'béri
         Introduction / 79

         Science, Technology, and the Human / 81
         Thinking about Technology / 81
                 George Grant
         Communications Technology and Society: Theory and Practice / 86
                 Mike Gasher and Rowland Lorimer

         Technology, Intellectual Property, and the End-of-Privacy? / 123
         Master of My Domain: The Politics of Internet Governance / 123
                 Daniel Paré
         Digital Resources: Content and Language / 143
                 Mark Warschauer

Part 3   **Media Theories and Communication Research** / 167
Section Editor: Mahmoud Eid
Introduction / 167

Theories of Media and Communication / 169
Communication and Media / 169
Stephen W. Littlejohn
Approaches to Theorizing International Communication / 207
Daya Kishan Thussu

Schools of Communication Research / 235
*Paul Lazarsfeld's Ideational Network and Contribution
to the Field of Communication Research* / 235
Mahmoud Eid
*On Introducing Ideology: Critical Theory and the Critique
of Culture* / 266
Hanno Hardt

Media Studies and Communication Research in Canada / 305
Considering Critical Communication Studies in Canada / 305
Sheryl N. Hamilton
New Communication Research from Canada / 327
John D.H. Downing

Part 4   **From Theory to Practice** / 335
Section Editor: Mark Lowes
Introduction / 335

Manufacturing the Agenda / 337
*Sports Page: A Case Study in the Manufacture of Sports News
for the Daily Press* / 337
Mark Douglas Lowes
*Differential Accounts of Race in Broadcast Commentary
of the 2000 NCAA Men's and Women's Final Four
Basketball Tournaments* / 355
Bryan E. Denham, Andrew C. Billings and Kelby K. Halone

Manufacturing the 'Others' / 374
*Opinion Discourse and Canadian Newspapers: The Case
of the Chinese "Boat People"* / 374
Joshua Greenberg
A Hazardous Profession: War, Journalists, and Psychopathology / 396
Anthony Feinstein, John Owen, and Nancy Blair

The 'Others' as Commodities / *408*
"I Don't Want Them Living Around Here": Ideologies of Race
  and Neighborhood Decay / *408*
    Timothy A. Gibson

Socio-Cultural Discourse in Mass Media Text:
  An Analytical Sample / *423*
Intermedial Location of Meaning in Muna Moto: *A Metalanguage*
  of Cultural Discourse / *423*
    Boulou E. de B'béri

Part 5 **Media, Culture, and Society** / *435*
    Section Editor: Boulou Ebanda de B'béri
Introduction / *435*

Language, Representation, Meaning Production,
  and Reception / *437*
Language / *437*
    Ronald B. Adler and George Rodman
Encoding, Decoding / *469*
    Stuart Hall

Meaning and Race Matter / *480*
The Matter of Whiteness / *480*
    Richard Dyer
Representations of Whiteness in the Black Imagination / *485*
    bell hooks

Meaning and Gender Matter / *490*
Women and Race in Feminist Media Research: Intersections,
  Ideology and Invisibility / *490*
    Linda Aldoory and Shawn J. Parry-Giles
Pictures, Porno, and Pop: Gender and Mass Media / *511*
    Diana K. Ivy and Phil Backlund

Part 6 **Media and Politics in Canada** / *557*
    Section Editor: Evan Potter
Introduction / *557*

Framing Political Discourse / *559*
Democracy, Technology, and Communication in Canada / *559*
    Daniel Barney
From Experience to Editorial: Gatekeeping, Agenda-Setting,
  Priming, and Framing / *573*
    Paul Nesbitt-Larking

Mass Media Politics / *604*

*Boundaries Blurred: The Mass Media and Politics
in a Hyper-Media Age* / *604*
Jonathan Rose and Simon Kiss

The Politics of Advertisement / *618*

*The Liberals Reap What They Sow: Why Their
Negative Ads Failed* / *618*
Jonathan Rose

Permission Credits / *627*

Preface and Acknowledgements

I conceived the idea of this reader after numerous discussions with several professors and students from diverse universities in Canada and the United States. I retained two paradoxical ideas from these discussions. First, most of my colleagues—including myself—were by some means frustrated about the lack of a critical mind-set among our undergraduate students. We all noted a specific kind of trend within the students at all levels of university scholarship. Most of us believe that undergraduate students prefer to have ready-made-recipe courses—the genre *how-to*—in lieu of critical analyses. On the other side, the diverse body of undergraduate students I spoke to have similar questions and concerns opposed to the professor's views. For example, many of them do not know what professors do besides teaching. More often they ask me: *when are we going to read a book or an article written by you?* Furthermore, if they have had a chance to read a text from one of their professors, they end up asking why professors write texts that are not comprehensible to the common students.

As a result of these discussions, I began to think about how to critically engage my students by means of instrumental teaching. In other words, how could we solve the paradox of balancing our sometime highly abstractive scholarships with illustrative everyday life objects or events without necessarily becoming simplistic? That most of our undergraduates are not at first interested in *understanding* what makes things what they are, but instead prefer to *learn* how to replicate things as they appear, shows the dilemma of this paradox. At the same time, the ways in which professors write, teach, and expose critical thinking to the students must constantly remain a question mark, hanging like a monkey on professor's shoulders. To help to solve this issue each section of this reader combines practical, straightforward texts with essays or edited chapters engaging epistemological thinking. The central idea behind this combination of texts is to disengage the hidden, critical talent of our undergraduate students and to help us to efficiently bridge theory with practice.

The second observation I made is that most undergraduates, especially those in third- and fourth-year media and communication studies, are not well served with appropriate reading material. Evidently, the good news is that there are, and will continue to be, many introductory books in media and communication studies. However, students are not often exposed to the important body of foundational critical materials available in this interdisciplinary field of study. For example, in my advanced level and directed study courses, I ask students to write a report mobilizing the notion of 'articulation' from Stuart Hall's 'Encoding/Decoding' article (which, I should here point out, is representative of student's remarks on professor's incomprehensible writing) and his audiovisual lecture, *Representation and the Media*. Surprisingly, a great number of students have never heard about, much less read, Hall's paper. Indeed, an important number of Art, Social Science, and Humanity graduates I met throughout four different universities in Canada and the United States had never read a text from Stuart Hall, bell hooks, or Cornell West, to name a few. I pick these names with a specific ideology in mind, to make a point, because the remaining question to pose is why?

This second observation permits me to conclude that there is not another place that is as ideologically driven as universities. For me, universities are made of various professors following specific academic agenda/discipline—what I term to be an ideology. Nonetheless, how could it be conceivable that in the dawn of the twenty-first century many of our graduating students, in North America particularly, still lack essential knowledge about the concept of power, culture, politics, identity, and representation/articulation? Why are the students in Media and Communication Studies not exposed to these essential key concepts that make this field of study such an interesting and powerful panel? Why don't they investigate these concepts and learn to illustrate how the concepts are related to the headlines of the prime-time news, to the front page of the newspaper, to the content of the Internet?

Introduction to Media Studies: A Reader was conceived with all of these questions and concerns in mind. With a specific focus on the Canadian context, students reading this will not only learn how to think critically, but also how to link critical media studies with our everyday life, overloaded as it is with mass-mediated texts. The central objective is to expose students to various conceptual frameworks that will allow them to comprehend and 'problematize' their everyday life experience with mass media texts. The Section Editors cautiously organized their selection of texts to meet this central goal. Each section includes insightful classics, carefully selected texts from various scholars and institutional productions, an introduction, and a study guide. With this specific design, the co-editors wanted to make sure that new students in the field of media and communication will be able to develop 'critical reading' and 'critical learning' skill by being exposed to a wide variety of texts. We picked each selection by taking into account one important level of conjunction: the articulation of theory *with* practice. We believe that advanced-level students will not be surprised anymore; they could use this reader to move into new, systematic levels of investigation. Indeed, the variety of the texts of this reader will stimulate the interest of third- and fourth-year students and guide them into thorough lines of investigation.

Sections One and Two focus attention on the impending impact of traditional and new technology in societies, and the overall complexity of mass media technology. The texts of these sections navigate between old and new media—newspapers, radio, magazines, and television—to outline the ways in which any sort of technology progressively creates a new social environment, new communicational and cognitive habits, and certainly a new way to comprehend and analyze the relationship between mass media's business model and societal transformation.

Sections Three and Four deal with communication theories, research perspectives, and methodology. In Section Three, the central focus is the debate between the major schools of thought in the field of communication research; Section Four deals with the process by which, methodologically, researchers move from theoretical frameworks to practical research designs for the study of media, culture, and society.

Sections Five and Six focus on the questions of representation, or framing, at the centre of mass media's texts. It is crucial to understand the corollary of this notion in mass media, because the process by which human beings make sense of the world is extremely complex, and mass media texts tremendously contribute to this meaning-making process. The last section of this reader concludes with an analysis of political communication in democratic societies. Indeed, Section Six exposes the struggling ethical relationship between the politicians, media makers, and the public interest.

Acknowledgments

I want to thanks Lisa Meschino, Acquisitions Editor at Oxford University Press, for helping me clear the copyrights of this collection and especially for keeping the production cost of this reader at its lowest possible level. I also want to acknowledge the works of my University of Ottawa colleagues, Bélanger, Eid, Lowes, and Potter who made the necessary arrangements to have their section done in time, despite short notice.

Boulou Ebanda de B'béri
University of Ottawa

Part 1

The Engaging New World of Traditional Media

Section Editor: Pierre C. Bélanger

Introduction

In the Western world, every country is experiencing a major media upheaval brought about by the impacts that emerging technologies are having on traditional broadcasting. This disquieting zone of turbulence is provoking significant changes in the way people use the 'old' media. Whether it is newspapers, radio, magazines, the music industry as a whole or television, no one is immune to the powerful technological *tsunami* that is forcing every major media group in Canada to revisit its business model.

To be sure, the youth segment of the public is exhibiting a media consumption behaviour that is raising many questions. The growth of user-produced content among the young, along with the phenomenal pace at which it is shared among users is creating a parallel media universe in which traditional linear media are all but excluded. Pod-casting only accentuates the personalization of media content even more. The coming of third generation wireless communication systems and devices will open up a whole new world of content, applications, and services. The much heralded merging of television and mobile telephony is but the latest iteration of a constant wave of change that is keeping many a media executive up at night. According to the Pew Internet and American Life Project, 57 per cent of young American Internet users between the ages of 12 and 17 years old, 'create digital content, from building Web pages to sharing original artwork, photos and stories to remixing content found elsewhere on the Web' (*New York Times,* November 3, 2005, p. C1). This type of relationship with media content reshapes our culture, directly challenges the legal definition of 'rights' and literally shatters the economic foundations on which our media institutions have been built.

In this fast developing digital melting pot, media lose their specificity. The Internet is turning out to be the great leveler, an online space where content from all corners of the worlds collide and compete for the attention of the users. The rules of this new game appear to have little connection with those of the previous regime. The texts of this section combine policy issues and futur-ist perspectives with ontological and epistemological reflections about mass media technology. Pierre C. Bélanger looks at the process of 'Canadianizing' the airwaves. He concludes that despite all the excitement surrounding novel forms of digital distribution, the traditional radio remains a stalwart of the Canadian media landscape; despite the fact that new types of customization continue to have 'a profound impact on the ways traditional radio conducts its business'. Marshall McLuhan's text, first published in the early 1960s, remains the classic analysis of the relationship between mass media and social change. This text opens up a different way to look at and analyze media's content and the structural change taking place in modern societies. For McLuhan, all mass media engage specific forms, which involve 'an intense visual organization'. To understand the constitutive materiality of the media, e.g. the ontological reflec-tion about television introduced by Samuel Weber, one needs to analyze the social structure shaped by the medium. From a Canadian identity perspective, the stakes have never been greater. Indeed, Weber moves the reflection of this section into the questioning of the materiality of television technology. Unlike McLuhan who once qualified television to be the 'timid giant', Weber argues that television set and screen does not simply allow us to overcome the dis-tance and separation, an attribute related to the illusion of 'global village'. Rather, television technology is a kind of Trojan horse that allows us to be far-sighted; and thus 'to see things that are distant more clearly that those that are close at hand', because the spatial connotation suggested by 'far' is converted into purely a measure of space and time. Looking at the evolution of multiple generations of television technology and media consuming practices, Saul J. Berman, Louisa A. Shipnuck, and Niall Duff project that we are moving toward a world of platform-agnostic content, fluid mobility of media experiences, indi-vidualized pricing schemes and an end to the traditional concept of television. They conclude that for the next five to seven years, on both the industry and consuming fronts, television 'experience will go far beyond traditional "lean back" behavior and constrained content access channels'. The industry will 'be stamped by consumer bimodality, a coexistence of two types of users with dis-parate channel requirements. While one consumer segment remains passive in the living room, the other will force radical change in business models in a search for anytime, anywhere content through multiple channels.'

Students are strongly urged to read the *Broadcasting Policy Monitoring Report 2005* in order to gain an insight into the industry's perspective. This document is available online at http://www.crtc.gc.ca/eng/publications/reports/ PolicyMonitoring/2005/bpmr2005.pdf.

Radio

Radio in Canada: An Industry in Transition

Pierre C. Bélanger[1]

Radio, or *wireless,* was perfected in 1895 by Italian physicist Guglielmo Marconi. However, a name that may merit wider exposure is that of Canadian inventor and Marconi competitor Reginald Fessenden. Indeed, when Marconi could still only transmit Morse code, Fessenden was already able to broadcast music and the sound of the human voice. On Christmas Eve, 1906, startled radio operators on ships at sea heard Fessenden's voice and some musical selections.

In 1912, the sinking of the *Titanic* underlined the value of radio as major newspapers found themselves dependent on wireless reports for news of the tragedy. Following the sinking, all ships at sea were required to maintain continuous wireless operations.

In 1918, the Department of Naval Service granted Marconi the first radio licence ever, for station XWA (later CFCF) in Montreal. XWA only began broadcasting in 1919. By 1923, CKAC Montreal became the first French-language station to go to air.

In 1924, the newly formed Canadian National Railways (CNR) installed *radio cars* on some of its trains so that passengers could enjoy highbrow musical programming consisting of opera, orchestras, and drama. By 1932, the CNR had a national and regional network comprising some 20 radio stations constructed alongside its tracks. That network would eventually become the basis of the CBC.

Events moved rapidly as radio enjoyed unprecedented social diffusion. The 1920s were the era of the "radio craze." Canada's Diamond Jubilee celebration highlighted the growing importance of radio: On July 1, 1927, the telephone and telegraph lines that made up the CNR network were interconnected so that orchestras located in its 23 cities from West to East could simultaneously play the national anthem. As they played, the network switched seamlessly from orchestra to orchestra. An estimated five million Canadians and Americans tuned in that day. Radio was now firmly implanted in the national consciousness of

Canadians. The Toronto *Globe* called radio "a democratic science, ready to instruct and entertain all manner and conditions of humankind who prepare to receive its blessings" (Nash, 1995, p. 49).

"Canadianizing" the Airwaves

However, a typical pattern emerged with radio, as with film and magazines. Canadian listeners turned in great numbers to American radio. Approximately 80 percent of their listening time was devoted to programs originating from south of the border.

This worried many who feared that exposure to American radio would damage the cultural fabric of Canada. As a result, the federal government struck the first of many royal commissions on broadcasting in 1928. The Aird Commission, named for its chairman Sir John Aird, was mandated to study the state of Canadian broadcasting; to recommend how it should be administered, managed, and monitored; and to provide an informed assessment of its financial needs and its responses to the Canadian audience. The Commission's final report concluded that American networks were, predictably, a threat to our airwaves and our culture.

The Aird Commission, however, also recommended the creation of a public broadcasting network and, after three years of debate, the federal government formally enacted the Canadian Radio Broadcasting Act (1932). The Act stated that Canada would have a *mixed* broadcasting system, consisting of both public and private radio stations. The Act also authorized the creation of the Canadian Radio Broadcasting Commission (CRBC), which went to air in 1933. The CRBC's mandate was twofold: (1) to regulate and control all broadcasting activities in the country; and (2) to provide a national broadcasting service.

One of the most fervent supporters of public broadcasting in Canada was Graham Spry whose slogan was "the State, or the United States!"[2] The CRBC, however, proved to be a failure. It angered some listeners by broadcasting in both French and English on the same channel, and other listeners by airing content deemed to be politically biased and socially insensitive. Consequently, in 1936, the Broadcasting Act was amended and the CRBC was replaced by the Canadian Broadcasting Corporation (CBC).

The CBC took over the CRBC's staff and facilities as well as its regulatory authority. Indeed, it is worth noting that the CBC was not only a broadcaster in competition with private stations but also the regulator of the entire system, able to grant or deny licences to its private competitors. This fact provoked much criticism from the private radio industry. As a result, in 1958, the federal government revised the Broadcasting Act again and transferred regulatory power away from the CBC to an independent regulatory body, the **Board of Broadcast Governors (BBG).** The BBG would regulate *both* the private broadcasters *and* the CBC. In 1968, the BBG itself was replaced by the Canadian Radio-Television Commission (CRTC).

The Radio Regulatory Environment

The CRTC[3] grants, renews, and denies broadcasting licences, and sets standards and quotas for both radio and television. It is an independent public agency whose members are appointed by the Prime Minister and that reports to Parliament through the Minister of Canadian Heritage. It is governed by the Broadcasting Act of 1991 and the **Telecommunications Act** of 1993. It attempts to balance the cultural, social, and economic goals of broadcasting and **telecommunications** legislation in the public interest. In the case of radio, this is accomplished chiefly by requiring programming to reflect Canada's linguistic duality, its multicultural diversity, and the special place of Aboriginal people in Canadian society.

The most definitive aspect of Canadian broadcasting regulation concerns Canadian content requirements or **CanCon**. Although specific CanCon requirements change over time, they always embody the same basic objectives: to ensure that the Canadian public is exposed to the work of Canadian artists and producers.

As of August 31, 2003, there were some 515 commercial AM and FM radio stations in Canada, of which 80 percent broadcast in English (CRTC, 2003). The CRTC requires that at least 35 percent[4] of popular music selections played by commercial AM and FM radio stations between 6 a.m. and 6 p.m., Monday through Friday, be Canadian. (An exception applies to stations whose playlists consist of at least 35 percent instrumental music, because the music pool from which they draw is more limited.) (CRTC, 2004a)

The CBC must abide by slightly more stringent conditions. On a weekly basis, at least 50 percent of its general popular music and 20 percent of its traditional and special interest selections between 6 a.m. and midnight must be Canadian. Nowhere is the contribution of public broadcasting to the promotion of Canadian talent more apparent than in the number and diversity of music styles played on its regional stations and national networks. For example, CBC Radio One and Radio Two air a weekly average of 4800 different musical selections. Of these, approximately 60 percent (roughly 2900 different musical selections) qualify as CanCon, thereby exceeding the CRTC requirement of 50 percent. Moreover, the CBC doubles the CRTC's 20 percent quota for special interest and classical music, since 40 percent of its average of 2500 weekly musical selections also qualify as CanCon.

The approximately 100 French-language private stations are subjected to even more demanding criteria. They are required to ensure that at least 65 percent of the popular vocal music selections they broadcast each week are in French. If taken literally, however, this requirement could result in a radio station playing only artists from France, Belgium, or another French-speaking country, since the French Canadian market could hardly meet the demand without an annoying degree of redundancy. In order to prevent the exclusion of French-language vocal music produced in Canada, the CRTC further specifies that no less than 35 percent of popular music selections aired weekly by French-language commercial AM and FM stations be Canadian and that at least 55 percent of the popular French vocal music selections be played between 6 a.m. and 6 p.m., weekdays.

Just as the CBC meets stricter criteria than private English-language radio stations, so too must Radio-Canada (the French-language wing of the CBC) meet stricter requirements than private French-language radio stations. Radio-Canada's *Première chaîne* (the equivalent of Radio One) must air 95 percent French-language content, of which 50 percent must be by Canadian artists. No more than 5 percent of its playlist may be devoted to English-Canadian vocal selections. *La chaîne culturelle* (renamed, in September 2004, *Espace musique*—the equivalent of Radio Two) must guarantee a minimum 20 percent airplay to Canadian traditional and special-interest music. Finally, every song must be played in its entirety in order to be counted toward the CanCon quota.

How Far Can the CRTC Go in Regulating Radio?

Not only does the CRTC set the licensing conditions by which the various radio broadcasters must abide, it also overlooks the daily operations of the various licensees. Far from being a complacent observer, the CRTC does, occasionally, react negatively. A well-publicized recent instance occurred in the summer of 2004 when the CRTC cancelled the licence of CHOI-FM in Quebec City. A brief outline of the debate and decision follows.

Genex Communications Inc. acquired CHOI-FM in 1997. Between then and 2004, 92 complaints concerning the "conduct of the hosts and the spoken word" were received. Already in 2002, the CRTC had notified Genex that it was running afoul of the Radio Regulations of 1986 and of the Broadcasting Act. At that time, the CRTC renewed the CHOI-FM licence for two years only, whereas licences are usually renewed for seven years. The CRTC also imposed a set of conditions (including an eight-second delay) intended to prevent the broadcasting of material that would lead to further complaints.

The content of CHOI-FM did not change, and in February 2004, the CRTC called Genex to a public hearing in Quebec City. The offending comments cited included statements about African students at Laval University, a rival radio host involved in a juvenile prostitution ring, and the desirability of euthanizing psychiatric patients. Most of the complaints dealt with spoken-word content that seemed to constitute a pattern of behaviour that was not only repeated but even grew worse. Genex denied there was a problem or that it was failing to comply with its conditions of licence.

When a licensee is judged as failing to meet its licence obligations, the CRTC has three options: it can (a) issue a short-term licence renewal; (b) issue a mandatory order; or (c) suspend, revoke, or not renew the licence.

The third option would be applied only exceptionally, but that was the CRTC's decision. As a result, for only the sixth time since 1968, the CRTC did not renew a licence. All previous non-renewals also involved radio stations from Quebec. More significant, though, is the fact that the CHOI-FM decision was the first time that the CRTC refused to renew a licence because of on-air views.

Genex immediately launched an appeal to the Federal Court, and the CRTC's decision generated unprecedented waves of protest in Quebec, including expressions of support from Quebec Premier Jean Charest, NDP Leader Jack Layton, and Conservative Leader Stephen Harper. By August 26, 2004, however, Genex and the CRTC had agreed to ask the Federal Court to allow CHOI-FM to remain on air until its appeal was finally heard.

What Qualifies As Canadian Content?

The CRTC (2001) goes to great lengths to define what qualifies as a "Canadian selection." The definition was conceived with two goals in mind: (1) a cultural goal of increasing audience exposure to Canadian performers, lyricists, and composers; and (2) an industrial goal of supporting the Canadian music and recording industry. This definition is critical to the entire radio industry and has given rise to a typically Canadian acronym, **MAPL.**

The letters in MAPL stand for *M*usic (is the selection composed entirely by a Canadian?), *A*rtist (is the selection performed principally by a Canadian?), *P*roduction (does the selection consist of a live performance that is (a) recorded entirely in Canada or (b) performed entirely in Canada and broadcast live in Canada?), and *L*yrics (are the lyrics written entirely by a Canadian?).

Some exceptions apply. If the selection was recorded before 1972 or if it is an instrumental performance of a musical piece written or composed by a Canadian, it need not conform to the MAPL standard.

Despite the fact that the MAPL system appears to be fairly efficient and reasonable, it has attracted very harsh criticism. Critics argue that CanCon is a bad solution to a structural problem inherent in the music industry. The public tends to develop a strong attachment to a limited number of artists. For example, Alanis Morissette, Shania Twain, the Tragically Hip, Céline Dion, Amanda Marshall, Brian Adams, the Barenaked Ladies, and Sarah McLachlan have been able to generate very strong followings over the last few years. But scores of other artists have not. Nonetheless, the successful artists are icons not just of the Canadian music scene, but of the international music scene. That so many Canadian artists have garnered international acclaim may be a cause for celebration. But, the critics ask, should we not be concerned about the impact of so few big names on the entire music industry?

These critics, therefore, argue that CanCon merely magnifies the dominance of a small group of stars to the detriment of promising new artists who simply cannot generate the same kind of bonding with audiences. As Larry LeBlanc, Canadian editor of *Billboard* magazine says: "The negative impact of CanCon regulation is very simple. If you're releasing a record today at the same time as Shania Twain or Nelly Furtado, you're going to have a lot of trouble" (cited in Everett-Green, 2001). Critics do not hesitate to point an accusing finger at radio stations that have become part of a sophisticated marketing system in which only those artists capable of producing and promoting a CD and a video receive airtime. Furthermore, many accuse commercial stations of not giving fair consideration to artists who are not distributed by one of the four major multinational conglomerates that dominate the entire music industry. Should the current regulations be amended, then, in order to force radio stations to increase the diversity of the artists who make up their daily playlists?

Canadian Public Radio

CBC/Société Radio-Canada is a major architect of the Canadian radio industry, and it maintains a unique connection for most Canadians. Public radio provides a unique style within the industry, and its non-commercial nature allows it to explore unorthodox programming styles and hence reach audiences that are not targeted by other stations. CBC Radio provides a wide range of programming in both French and English that, consistent with the Broadcasting Act, informs, enlightens, and entertains while reflecting Canada and its regions to themselves.

For most listeners, CBC Radio is easily identifiable. It has a distinctive sound and mode of delivery and, above all, is commercial-free. What is less apparent is its deep presence in every province of the country, which makes it unique in the international broadcasting community. According to its 2002–2003 annual report, Radio One consists of 36 owned and operated stations, whereas Radio Two consists of 14 stations. Additionally, several hundred rebroadcasting stations relay their signals. Statistics Canada estimates that more than 50 percent of Canadians use at least one of the four CBC radio services weekly. This translates into an average weekly unduplicated Radio One and Radio Two audience reach of some 3.8 million Canadians for English-language radio, while French-language radio is currently at an all-time record high with over one million listeners each week.

Over the last few years, CBC Radio has explored new delivery platforms, including satellite radio, digital radio, Internet applications, external syndication, and after-market distribution. Already the CBC's news headlines are distributed to wireless telephone users by most major Canadian cellular phone providers. Its digital pay audio service, Galaxie, available through satellite, cable, and microwave distribution systems offers 45 continuous, commercial-free music channels to a subscriber base of some 3.25 million. In addition, through its Rising Stars Program, it contributes about $500,000 annually to young Canadian artists and music organizations.

One of CBC's most technologically innovative ventures for reaching younger audiences is Radio Three, an award-winning service dedicated to the promotion of independent art and culture. Despite its name, Radio Three is available only on the Internet, at http://www.cbcradio3.com. Created in 2000, Radio Three currently draws a monthly average of about half a million unique visitors in the much sought-after 18-to-34 demographic, although the Web site creators prefer to speak of a common "psychographic" that connects their audience members. The site consists of four interconnected sections catering to different musical and artistic genres. Thus, while the main CBCradio3.com site features articles, essays, and videos on artists and youth culture, for example, 120seconds.com features individual musical contributions, NewMusicCanada.com features bands, Just-Concerts.com features recordings of live concerts, and RootsMusicCanada.com showcases country, folk, and world music.

Radio Types, Formats, and Listening Preferences

The Canadian radio environment is multi-tiered. There are four main types of licences granted to mainstream stations: (1) AM licences; (2) FM licences; (3) digital licences (spread over Montreal, Toronto, Windsor, and Vancouver); and (4) pay-audio licences (DMX Music and CBC Galaxie, available via satellite, cable, or wireless system). Licences are also granted to community stations, campus stations, Native stations, ethnic stations, and religious content stations (CRTC, 2004a).

The province with the most commerical stations (see Table 1) is Ontario (171), followed by British Columbia (104, including the Territories), Quebec (100), Alberta (74), Manitoba (29), New Brunswick (24), and Nova Scotia (22). The station ownership situation remains fluid because of ongoing transactions and a converging marketplace.

The CRTC also uses over two dozen different content categories to describe the various programming styles available. Whereas radio was a unifying force in its

Table 1 Number of commercial AM and FM stations in Canada, all languages, 2004

Province/Territory	AM	FM
Newfoundland & Labrador	11	7
Prince Edward Island	2	2
Nova Scotia	9	13
New Brunswick	5	19
Quebec	23	77
Ontario	51	120
Manitoba	14	15
Saskatchewan	18	21
Alberta	26	48
British Columbia (includes Yukon Territory, Northwest Territories, and Nunavut)	40	64
Networks	19	18
Total	218	404

Source: CRTC 2004b, Broadcasting Policy Monitoring Report 2004.

early days, the proliferation of niche stations has seen a fragmentation of audiences that cuts radically into the common experience of listeners. The original mass media nature of radio has given way to a form of localized **walled garden** programming that caters to highly specialized tastes and preferences.

The vast majority of Canadian radio listening (see Table 2) falls into 13 main formats. According to Statistics Canada (2004c), the most popular format is adult contemporary (AC) music (also known as light or adult rock), which captures 24.2 percent of all listeners. However, AC is not as dominant as it once was, having fallen 3.9 percent since 1999 and 7.3 percent since 1998.

Adult contemporary is followed by golden-oldies/rock at 18.6 percent of listeners. CBC is third with 10.9 percent (up from sixth place five years ago). The sudden growth in the popularity of public broadcasting can be explained by an aging population as well an increasing number of people with a postsecondary education. News/talk radio is fourth with 10.6 percent. Of Canada's 31 news/talk stations, 19 are concentrated in the four largest markets. Country ranks fifth at 9.7 percent, but since 1993, it has lost almost half of its listeners. Nowhere in

Table 2 Percentage share of radio listening by format, Fall 2003

Format	Canada	NL	PE	NS	NB	QC	ON	MB	SK	AB	BC
Adult contemporary	24.2	8.0	6.5	34.3	32.9	27.2	29.1	9.7	24.0	13.1	14.7
Album-oriented rock	2.5	13.8	0.0	0.0	0.1	3.6	1.2	3.6	1.3	3.6	3.3
CBC	10.9	13.4	20.8	16.0	13.1	11.6	9.3	10.6	10.8	7.7	15.0
Contemporary	7.9	31.8	26.0	3.2	4.0	18.9	1.3	7.8	0.2	7.6	6.7
Country	9.7	14.3	25.9	23.1	13.9	0.9	8.3	15.8	35.3	23.3	7.2
Dance	1.8	0.0	0.0	0.0	0.0	0.4	3.7	0.1	0.0	0.0	2.2
Easy listening	2.9	0.0	0.0	0.0	0.0	3.7	4.2	6.7	0.0	0.9	0.0
Golden-oldies/rock	18.6	12.8	20.0	19.7	13.2	14.6	18.6	23.6	19.3	22.5	23.1
Middle-of-the-road	2.7	0.0	0.0	0.0	0.0	0.9	4.4	1.3	0.0	1.7	4.2
Other	4.4	6.0	0.9	3.4	17.3	4.2	3.1	4.8	2.4	8.5	3.7
Sports	0.9	0.0	0.0	0.0	0.0	0.3	1.6	0.0	0.1	1.1	0.7
Talk	10.6	0.0	0.0	0.0	0.0	12.3	10.5	15.4	6.1	9.8	14.3
U.S. stations	3.0	0.0	0.0	0.2	5.6	1.5	4.7	0.7	0.3	0.2	5.0
Total listening	**100.0**	**100.0**	**100.0**	**100.0**	**100.0**	**100.0**	**100.0**	**100.0**	**100.0**	**100.0**	**100.0**

Source: Statistics Canada. (2004, July). *Radio Listening: data tables, Fall 2003*, catalogue no. 87F0007.

Canada does country succeed in winning a market, and in the two largest markets, Toronto and Montreal, there are no country music stations at all.

The growth of FM stations over the last dozen years has been spectacular. Indeed, Canadians now spend 74 percent of their total listening time with FM stations. Overall, Canadians listen to radio on average 19.5 hours per week, one hour less than in 1999. Also, radio appears to be losing ground with 12- to 17-year-olds as their listening has fallen from 11.3 hours per week in 1999 to 8.5 hours per week in 2003. A similar pattern is observed with young adults aged 18 to 24, although the reduction in their listening time is not as marked as with teenagers (Statistics Canada, 2003, 2004c).

The Corporate Structure of Canadian Radio

The role of the CRTC is not limited to allocating broadcasting licences and setting content quotas. From an economic standpoint, recent changes in the CRTC's commercial radio policy have significantly modified the Canadian radio landscape.

The most important change concerns ownership rules. Since the spring of 1998, in markets with eight or more *commercial* stations broadcasting in a given language—this calculation excludes public, community, campus, Native, religious, or ethnic stations—a person or company may own or control as many as two AM and two FM stations in that language. In markets with fewer than eight commercial stations operating in a given language, one can own as many as three stations, with a maximum of two stations in any one frequency band (AM or FM). Those hoping to acquire more than one AM and one FM station in a given language in the same market are asked to assess the likely impact of their ownership on the following issues: (1) the diversity of news voices, (2) the level of competition in the market, (3) the benefit to the local community and the furtherance of the objectives of the Broadcasting Act as a result of the programming they will typically broadcast, and (4) any other issues that may arise in the case of applicants who already own other media or have an interest in other radio stations in the same market.

The CRTC introduced this change as a result of the bleak financial situation faced by many commercial stations in the mid-1990s. Pressures for relaxation of ownership rules also mounted as consolidation (to achieve economies of scale, for example) similar to the American trend became economically sensible. Although never perfect, the CRTC's new regulation was perceived by many as an acceptable compromise.

Essentially, the post-1998 policy encourages consolidation. Radio station owners may solidify their financial situation, attract much-needed new investment, and—particularly important in the era of convergence—compete more effectively with other media.

However, in exchange for softening the ownership rules, the CRTC obtained two concessions: (1) the percentage of CanCon that private radio stations must play rose from 30 to 35 percent; and (2) purchasers of profitable stations must contribute at least 6 percent of the value of the transaction to support Canadian musical talent. The 6 percent contributions are to be distributed as follows:

a) 2 percent to either FACTOR in English Canada or MusicAction in French, at the discretion of the purchaser, to support talent development and the record industry;

b) 3 percent to the newly created Radio Starmaker Fund and its French-language counterpart, Le Fonds RadioStar, for the promotion of new artists and new recordings over the next decade;

c) 1 percent, at the discretion of the purchaser, to either (a) or (b) above or to any other eligible third party directly involved in the development of Canadian musical and artistic talent.

The CRTC wishes to encourage closer collaboration between the radio and music industries. As a result of the changes in ownership, approximately $26 million has been injected into the radio broadcasting system. Le Fonds RadioStar and the Radio Starmaker Fund received 48 percent of the new money, FACTOR and MusicAction received about 33 percent, and various discretionary projects received the remaining 20 percent.

As with most media businesses nowadays, the ownership and total number of Canadian stations vary as key players revisit their strategic priorities, partnerships,

Table 3 Ten largest radio operators, radio revenue, and national share, 2003

Operator	Number of Radio Undertakings	Radio Revenue ($ 000's)	Share of National Revenue (%)
Corus Entertainment Inc.	50	210,529	18
Standard Broadcasting Corp.	51	164,966	14
Rogers Communications Inc.	43	158,264	13
Astral Media Inc.	36	126,627	11
CHUM Limited	30	116,968	10
Newcap Inc.	41	55,509	5
Jim Pattison Industries Ltd.	18	33,365	3
Rawlco Radio Ltd.	12	27,020	2
Elmer Hildebrand (Golden West Broadcasting)	21	25,221	2
Maritime Broadcasting System Ltd.	21	23,593	2
TOTAL	323	942,062	79
TOTAL Canada (Private Radio Revenues)	532	1,189,483	100

Note: *Radio undertakings include networks.*

Source: CRTC. (2004b). Broadcasting Policy Monitoring Report 2004.

and market positions. If we exclude the CBC and its 79 radio stations, then only eight commercial operators dominate the Canadian radio scene. They own 330 of the country's 622 stations and generate 79 percent of the industry's total revenue, up significantly from 1998 when they held 148 stations and collected 61 percent of the revenue. Likewise, their share of tuning or listenership has also risen between 1998 and 2002, from 53 percent to 64 percent of the total radio listening time.

Corus Entertainment, a division of Shaw Communications Inc., is the leading station owner; it holds 50 stations and captures 18 percent of the total national radio revenue (see Table 3). Standard Broadcasting Corp. Ltd., with 51 stations, and Rogers Communications, with 43 stations, respectively take in 14 percent and 13 percent of the total radio revenue. Astral, CHUM, and Newcap Broadcasting respectively rank fourth, fifth, and sixth in terms of revenues generated.

The Economics of Radio

Year after year, experts predict that an aging population, satellite radio, the Internet, and music downloads will eventually bring radio to its knees. And year after year, they are proven wrong. After a period of deep losses in the 1980s and 1990s, caused partly by ownership rules that prevented the development of networks, 2003 brought much needed optimism: advertising reached $1.2 billion, an increase of 8.4 percent over the previous year. This was the best sales level since 1975 and the year-over-year increase was the second largest in the previous 15 years. What explains such an improvement? Why has private radio generated a higher profit margin than private television in the past six years?

Statistics Canada (2004a) reports that radio's profitability is chiefly attributable to cost-containment measures. These include operating efficiencies, a direct consequence of the 1998 decision allowing consolidation, which mean smaller staffs and increased reliance on computers and automated broadcast technologies. A healthier economy also contributed. Indeed, while FM revenues grew by 8.4 percent, their expenses rose by only 3.7 percent. Additionally, airtime sales grew by almost 10 percent in 2003, which translated into a 25.2 percent profit margin before interest and taxes. By comparison, AM advertising revenues grew by 4.5 percent while their profit margin grew by 1.6 percent. As Statistics Canada explains, "modest as they may appear, the 2003 results represent a significant turnaround for AM radio."

With a profit margin slightly over 23 percent, radio stations in Canada's 5 largest metropolitan areas continue to outperform those in smaller markets by 8 percent. The two most profitable markets are Calgary and Ottawa-Gatineau. Finally, the Canadian radio industry employed approximately 9000 people in 2003.

The Death Knell of AM Radio?

In small and mid-sized markets, AM radio is slowly fading. The migration of AM stations to the FM dial continues unabated. There were 19 signal shifts from AM to FM in 2001, and another 9 in 2002. Between 1998 and 2000, some 33 stations moved to the FM band. It may not be long before the same trend occurs in bigger cities.

Naturally, the desertion of the AM dial by young listeners who obtain their music from TV, the Internet, and P2P file sharing has severely affected the financial health of AM radio. Furthermore, pop music is nowadays segmented into so many sub-genres and categories that it is very difficult for AM radio to generate an audience large enough to appeal to potential advertisers. But that is only part of the equation. There is a more concrete, pragmatic, dollars-and-cents issue at stake: the cost of broadcasting an AM signal.

AM transmitters are expensive, with a capital cost of about $100,000. They require tall towers on large plots of land, thereby generating property taxes and high energy costs. It is estimated that the cost of setting up an AM station in a major city runs close to $1 million. An FM station, however, might cost only $250,000 to set up. The economics speak for themselves.

Additionally, AM radio simply cannot compete with the sound quality of FM. CDs and high-fidelity sound systems have accustomed listeners to high-quality sound, and people therefore avoid the tinny, monaural sound of AM radio. This is one reason for the transformation of AM radio into all-talk formats where sound quality is less evident.

In the mid 1990s, Rogers Communications gambled by switching the formats of its main AM stations in Toronto and Vancouver from music to all-news. Not only has the concept successfully spread to other major centres such as Victoria, Winnipeg, Edmonton, and Montreal, but 680 News in Toronto generates more revenue than any other AM station in the city. Corus has jumped on the talk-radio bandwagon by introducing "guy-talk" Mojo sports in Toronto and Vancouver. Others are trying their luck with "memory music" from the 1940s and 1950s, hoping that older audiences won't be so demanding in terms of sound quality.

However, if profits are so hard to generate and with so few viable formats, why are operators keeping their AM licences? The answer can be seen by looking to the future.

The Morphing of Radio

Technological developments are currently forcing radio into one of the most profound transformations since the arrival of stereo FM signals in the 1960s.

Digital Pay Audio Services

The two main providers of digital pay audio are Galaxie, with over 4 million residential and commercial subscribers, and DMX Music, with some 9000 commercial customers. These services offer approximately 50 commercial-free, uninterrupted, no-talk channels of music covering a range of styles including rock, urban, contemporary, jazz, classical, nostalgia, and various niche genres that receive limited airplay on conventional channels.

Despite this substantial subscriber base, most traditional radio operators believe that digital pay services compete with CDs or audiocassettes, not local radio. Local radio operators might be right for now, but what will happen once people discover the added value of getting their favourite music in a streamlined, seamless fashion? Might they then treat radio as they already treat television and start turning to specialty channels? The main limitation on mass adoption of digital pay audio is the fact that such services still depend on fixed appliances; that is, they plug into a home television or stereo and are therefore stationary devices. Fortunately for traditional radio, mobile listening, whether in the car or on a Walkman, is a strongly ingrained habit that is not about to change.

Digital Audio Broadcasting

It is a well-known fact that the FM band is saturated and that the scarcity of available frequencies makes launching new stations highly problematic. As a result, many see digital audio broadcasting (DAB) as the ideal solution for new services.

Often referred to as "high-definition radio," DAB is a digital radio system that operates in the L-Band. If popularized, DAB would create a level playing field for AM and FM radio by equalizing their sound quality. DAB offers CD-quality sound, interference-free reception, program-associated data, and graphics and text (including lyrics). A display window attached to the receiver provides dynamic labels describing the artist, song title, serial number of the album, and so on. Traffic and news briefs scroll in a text format while listeners enjoy their music. As DAB matures, services such as maps, visual traffic reports, pictures, and real-time stock market information will become available in both free and subscription formats. Furthermore, as they drive across Canada, listeners will be able to stay tuned to the same station with no signal fade and without changing frequency.

To this day, some 36 countries have adopted DAB or introduced legislation to test it. Over 500 DAB services are currently offered, reaching 300 million people around the world. In Canada, DAB reaches over 15 million people in places as diverse as Vancouver, Chilliwack, Calgary, Red Deer, Edmonton, Windsor, Toronto, Hamilton, Kitchener, London, Guelph, Cornwall, Ottawa, Montreal, Quebec, and Trois-Rivières. Some 70 radio stations are broadcasting in DAB and operators such as Astral Radio, CBC/Radio-Canada, Corus, Rogers, CHUM, and Standard Radio are all onboard.

However, DAB is an innovation that has generated more skeptics than supporters. Despite the deployment of DAB services in Canada and abroad, the technology faces a major roadblock: in order to enjoy its benefits, listeners must purchase a special DAB receiver. While the price has fallen from $1000 to about $100, DAB is still a long way from reaching a critical mass of users. Unless DAB enters the car market, it prospects remain uncertain.

Furthermore, the CRTC has decided that Canada will adopt a European DAB standard known as Eureka, which will be incompatible with the US IBOC (in band on channel) standard. Meanwhile, people are becoming more comfortable using

MP3 players, CD and DVD burners, iPod, streaming media, and satellite radio. DAB, therefore, seems caught in a vicious circle: while receiver manufacturers claim innovative broadcasting will drive consumer demand for their devices, broadcasters say they are waiting for greater consumer demand before launching DAB services. Hence, digital radio has all the allure of a missed rendezvous.

Subscription Satellite Radio

The year 2004 marked the 75th anniversary of the first car radio, the "Motorola." It was also the year in which the CRTC heard applications from three groups vying to provide satellite radio services to Canadians. Available in the United States since 2001, satellite radio is intended primarily for automobile use, although residential listening is possible, provided one purchases a specialized receiver. Two players control the American satellite radio market: XM Satellite Radio Inc., the current leader with over 2 million monthly subscribers and projections to reach 20 million by 2010; and Sirius Satellite Radio which, in the summer of 2004, reached the half-million subscriber mark. Together, XM Radio and Sirius own 5 satellites beaming a combined total of 200 channels of CD-quality music, information, weather, traffic, sports, and entertainment, as well as original comedy and kids' shows.

In order to establish a sound business model, both American firms struck agreements with auto manufacturers, who now offer $350 (U.S.) satellite receivers as an option in over 100 model lines. XM has partnered with General Motors, and Sirius with BMW, DaimlerChrysler, Ford, Mazda, and Audi. For the moment, the devices are not interoperable, although the companies are working on a solution to this irritant. They also intend to add video signals to cater to families wishing to keep their kids entertained in the back seat with over 500 channels of satellite TV.

Because the service was not licensed in Canada until 2004, Canadians wanting satellite radio would drive to the United States, obtain an American billing address, purchase a $100 (U.S.) receiver and become part of the so-called "grey market" of subscribers. The licensing of this service in Canada may direct some of those subscription fees toward Canadian operators. At the November 2004 hearings, the CRTC examined contiguous questions such as CanCon requirements, how much licensees should contribute to Canadian talent development, the number of providers that should be authorized, and the probable impact of satellite on existing radio broadcasters and congruent digital broadcasting services. In June 2005, the CRTC licensed three subscription radio services, SIRIUS Canada Inc., Canadian Satellite Radio, and CHUM/Astral.

Subscription radio is likely to have a substantial impact on the entire Canadian radio industry. Until now, traditional radio operators have paid little attention to satellite radio because subscription has been low relative to the pool of people who can listen to "free" radio, and because it has been available only on specialized receivers. But that complacency may soon give way to a different attitude when satellite radio providers ramp up their marketing strategies. For example, when people start to realize that their "free" listening is actually a type of payment (they give their time away for exposure to advertising), many listeners might find their time worth more and begin to look favourably on satellite radio.

Internet Radio

Of all the new technologies, none has had a greater impact on conventional radio than the Internet. Today, home Internet connections are closing in on cable television as 55 percent of Canadian homes have at least one member who regularly uses the Internet from home (Statistics Canada, 2004b). Clearly, Internet users develop habits, preferences, and expectations toward on-line content that are significantly different from the ones they express vis-à-vis traditional media. The "my content when I want it" mantra is creating a mindset that many conventional media are scrambling to catch up to. Many people are discovering the pleasures of being their own music and entertainment programmer or webcaster. As a result, media content is increasingly dissociated or disconnected from its traditional mode of distribution. Niche content also acquires a much larger role in the media diet of Internet users. With streaming audio, MP3 players, P2P file transfers, and so on, our former mass-media consumption becomes characterized by a behavioural triad based on (1) asynchronous listening (i.e., I choose the time that best suits me to listen), (2) personalization of content, and (3) mobility (i.e., I choose *where* to listen).

Just a few years ago, on-line radio was the domain of geeks experimenting with choppy, low-quality sound. In the spring of 2004, however, Arbitron estimated that in the United States alone some 19 million people turn to on-line radio at least once a week—a stunning 12 million more people than in 2000 ("The Revolution in Radio," 2004). Fuelled by a significant upswing in **broadband** connections, on-line listenership to the top five Internet broadcasters—AOL's Radio@Network, Yahoo's Launchcast, Live365, Musicmatch, and Virgin Radio—is up 32 percent between June 2003 and February 2004 ("Forget Radio," 2004). For example, Live 365, the self proclaimed largest Internet network with over 5000 stations available, reports that its listeners spend an average of 50 minutes per session and 32 hours a month tuned in.

Many critics contend that AM/FM radio has laid the groundwork for its own demise with its coast-to-coast homogenized, repetitive, ads-and-promo "McRadio" offerings that have become both politically conservative and aseptic. Despite packaging their stations with cool monikers like BOB, JACK, DAVE, and JOE, radio stations are having the hardest time retaining the younger segments of their audiences. Indeed, 13 percent of Americans aged 12 to 24 now declare they listen to on-line radio on a weekly basis, up from 6 percent in 2001 ("The Revolution in Radio," 2004). Many believe that if on-line radio could launch a popular "shock jock" like Howard Stern, the market would explode.

With thousands of stations available worldwide, Internet radio makes AM and FM stations with their limited range and choice look like throwbacks to another era. The great disadvantage of Internet radio is that it mostly requires a sedentary mode of listening. However, recent developments are about to expand the number of options. Replay Radio, a computer program available for under $50, allows the capture of scheduled radio programs as MP3 sound files that can be transferred to a portable MP3 player. In addition, many cellular phone manufacturers are working to provide Internet and traditional radio reception. Nokia's Visual Radio service is designed to help users purchase songs they hear on their phone's radio. In synchrony with a radio broadcast, Visual Radio is capable of displaying pictures during the news, weather, sports, and so on. Nokia estimates that about 75 percent of consumers who have an FM receiver on their handset typically use it about once a week. Other players such as Intel and Sony are forging ahead with innovations of their own.

In Canada, pay-per-content is gaining acceptance. The country's second-largest radio operator, Standard Broadcasting Corp., has launched Puretracks, a pay-for-music site that sells songs on-line from all record labels, much as Apple's iTunes, Roxio's **Napster,** RealNetworks, and Wal-Mart do. In the spring of 2004, Telus Corp. unveiled Pureradio, a customizable on-line music service—with 75 commercial-free stations—that also lets subscribers purchase songs. At $4.99 a month, Pureradio and the like hope to capitalize on a growing demand for on-line services where music **fans** look for legitimate outlets to buy their favourite music.

A Cloudy Future

Despite all the excitement surrounding novel forms of digital distribution, traditional radio remains a stalwart of the Canadian media landscape. The industry's recent financial results indicate that at least for the time being, the main operators seem to have found ways to stem the tide of losses. As a group they are fully cognizant of the challenges that lie ahead and are sparing no effort to extend the love affair that listeners have had with radio since its inception.

However, the industry cannot afford to turn a blind eye to the fact that nontraditional radio listening behaviour is bound to grow by leaps and bounds in the foreseeable future. The most popular Christmas presents in the United States in 2003 for people under the age of 40 were Apple iPods and satellite radio subscriptions. In 2004 alone, it is estimated that 10.8 million next-generation players will be sold, bringing the total installed base to 21.5 million ("Digital Music Player Marker," 2004). A walk around any Canadian university campus should indicate just how pervasive listening to music from non-radio sources has become. The recent epidemic proportions of music downloading and/or pirating illustrates clearly a drastic change in philosophy: people no longer want to "own" entertainment, they merely want to be connected to it wherever they go. As such, Internet radio and other peripheral digital devices are steadily undermining the last great advantage of broadcast radio, portability.

But there is more to consider. Our current rating systems such as **ACNielsen** and **BBM** present a somewhat distorted picture of the radio audience. By measuring listeners who use radio as background, ratings tend to measure the behaviour of people who are not really passionate about music. True music fans have flocked massively to Internet-based radio with its myriad of genres. In the words of Guy Zapoleon (2004), this has created a situation in which "radio studies the listeners that are left; and as it programs to those existing listeners, it becomes a 'self-fulfilling prophesy,' and no longer appeals to the passionate music listeners who no longer consume a lot of radio." Zapoleon fears that the upcoming widespread adoption of Internet radio, digital jukeboxes, and satellite subscription systems might turn broadcast radio into the next media "dinosaur." As emerging broadcasting standards such as WiFi and WiMax take root, they will make it easier for people to connect to the Web and choose their own type of radio. When this happens, the perennial force-fed programming mentality will give way to one of requests. Unquestionably, this type of customization is bound to have a profound impact on the ways traditional radio conducts its business.

Questions

1. What is CanCon and what are the arguments for and against it?
2. What is MAPL?
3. "CBC Radio plays an important role in solidifying Canadian identity." Discuss.
4. Should the amount of Canadian music played on radio be linked to the sales of Canadian music?
5. Is the success of radio bound up with the intimacy of the human voice, or is it the result of some other factor(s)?
6. How will the delivery and consumption of radio be transformed?
7. Based on the CHOI-FM case in Quebec City, is the CRTC justified in not renewing a licence for an entire station when the vast majority of the complaints concerned only a specific program and one or two hosts? Are there limits to freedom of expression in broadcasting?

Notes

1. The author wishes to acknowledge the assistance provided by Philippe Andrecheck during the research phases of this chapter.
2. Graham Spry (1900–1983) was a journalist, diplomat, and activist who campaigned tirelessly on behalf of public broadcasting in Canada. In 1930, he cofounded the Canadian Radio League, which was instrumental in orchestrating support for public broadcasting.
3. The CRTC's name was changed in 1975 to the **Canadian Radio-television and Telecommunications Commission,** although its acronym (CRTC) remained unchanged.
4. Prior to the spring of 1998, the requirement stood at 30 percent.

References

CRTC (Canadian Radio-television and Telecommunications Commission). (2001). Fact Sheet: The MAPL System. Retrieved from http://www.crtc.gc.ca/eng/ INFO_SHT/R1.htm

_____. (2003). Broadcasting Policy Monitoring Report 2003: Radio, Television, Broadcasting Distribution, Social Issues, Internet. Retrieved from http://www.crtc .gc.ca/eng/publications/reports/PolicyMonitoring/2003/bpmr2003.htm

_____. (2004a). Fact sheet: Canadian content for radio and television. Retrieved from http://www.crtc.gc.ca/eng/INFO_SHT/G11.htm.

_____. (2004b). Broadcasting Policy Monitoring Report 2004: Radio, Television, Broadcasting Distribution, Social Issues, Internet. Retrieved from http://www.crtc.gc.ca/eng/publications/reports/PolicyMonitoring/2004/bpmr2004.htm

Digital music player market set to double in 2004. (2004, July 21). *USA Today.* Retrieved from http://www.usatoday.com/tech/news/2004-07-21-digital-music-players_x.htm

Everett-Green, Robert. (2001, March 1). Why Nelly became a radio star. *The Globe and Mail,* p. R1.

Forget radio, tune in to net. (2004, June 28). *Wired.* Retrieved from http://www.wired.com/news/digiwood/0,1412,63982,00.html

Nash, Knowlton. (1995). *Microphone wars: A history of triumph and betrayal at the CBC.* Toronto: McClelland and Stewart.

The Revolution in radio. (2004, April 19). *Time,* 38–39.

Statistics Canada. (2004a, July 5). Private radio broadcasting, 2003. *The Daily.* Retrieved from http://www.statcan.ca/Daily/English/040705/d040705b.htm

_____. (2004b, July 8). Household Internet use survey, 2003. *The Daily.* Retrieved from http://www.statcan.ca/Daily/English/040708/ d040708a.htm

_____. (2004c, July 28). Radio listening, Fall 2003. The Daily. Retrieved from http://www.statcan.ca/Daily/English/040728/d040728b.htm

Zapoleon, Guy. (2004). Online radio will cater to music fans abandoned by AM and FM. Retrieved from http://www.kurthanson.com/archive/news/052504/ index.asp

The Tribal Drum
Marshall McLuhan

England and America had had their "shots" against radio in the form of long exposure to literacy and industrialism. These forms involve an intense visual organization of experience. The more earthy and less visual European cultures were not immune to radio. Its tribal magic was not lost on them, and the old web of kinship began to resonate once more with the note of fascism. The inability of literate people to grasp the language and message of the media as such is involuntarily conveyed by the comments of sociologist Paul Lazarsfeld in discussing the effects of radio:

> The last group of effects may be called the monopolistic effects of radio. Such have attracted most public attention because of their importance in the totalitarian countries. If a government monopolizes the radio, then by mere repetition and by exclusion of conflicting points of view it can determine the opinions of the population. We do not know much about how this monopolistic effect really works, but it is important to note its singularity. No inference should be drawn regarding the effects of radio as such. It is often forgotten that Hitler did not achieve control through radio but almost despite it, because at the time of his rise to power radio was controlled by his enemies. The monopolistic effects have probably less social importance than is generally assumed.

Professor Lazarsfeld's helpless unawareness of the nature and effects of radio is not a personal defect, but a universally shared ineptitude.

In a radio speech in Munich, March 14, 1936, Hitler said, "I go my way with the assurance of a somnambulist." His victims and his critics have been equally somnambulistic. They danced entranced to the tribal drum of radio that extended their central nervous system to create depth involvement for everybody. "I live right inside radio when I listen. I more easily lose myself in radio than in a book," said a voice from a radio poll. The power of radio to involve people in depth is manifested in its use during homework by youngsters and by many other people who carry transistor sets in order to provide a private world for themselves amidst crowds. There is a little poem by the German dramatist Berthold Brecht:

> You little box, held to me when escaping
> So that your valves should not break,
> Carried from house to ship from ship to train,
> So that my enemies might go on talking to me
> Near my bed, to my pain
> The last thing at night, the first thing in the morning,
> Of their victories and of my cares,
> Promise me not to go silent all of a sudden.

One of the many effects of television on radio has been to shift radio from an entertainment medium into a kind of nervous information system. News bulletins, time signals, traffic data, and, above all, weather reports now serve to enhance the native power of radio to involve people in one another. Weather is that medium that involves all people equally. It is the top item on radio, showering us with fountains of auditory space or *lebensraum*.

It was no accident that Senator McCarthy lasted such a very short time when he switched to TV. Soon the press decided, "He isn't news any more." Neither McCarthy nor the press ever knew what had happened. TV is a cool medium. It rejects hot figures and hot issues and people from the hot press media. Fred Allen was a casualty of TV. Was Marilyn Monroe? Had TV occurred on a large scale during Hitler's reign he would have vanished quickly. Had TV come first there would have been no Hitler at all. When Khrushchev appeared on American TV he was more acceptable than Nixon, as a clown and a lovable sort of old boy. His appearance is rendered by TV as a comic cartoon. Radio, however, is a hot medium and takes cartoon characters seriously. Mr. K. on radio would be a different proposition.

In the Kennedy-Nixon debates, those who heard them on radio received an overwhelming idea of Nixon's superiority. It was Nixon's fate to provide a sharp, high-definition image and action for the cool TV medium that translated that sharp image into the impression of a phony. I suppose "phony" is something that resonates wrong, that doesn't *ring* true. It might well be that F.D.R. would not have done well on TV. He had learned, at least, how to use the hot radio medium for his very cool job of fireside chatting. He first, however, had had to hot up the press media against himself in order to create the right atmosphere for his radio chats. He learned how to use the press in close relation to radio. TV would have presented him with an entirely different political and social mix of components and problems. He would possibly have enjoyed solving them, for he had the kind of playful approach necessary for tackling new and obscure relationships.

Radio affects most people intimately, person-to-person, offering a world of unspoken communication between writer-speaker and the listener. That is the immediate aspect of radio. A private experience. The subliminal depths of radio are charged with the resonating echoes of tribal horns and antique drums. This is inherent in the very nature of this medium, with its power to turn the psyche and society into a single echo chamber. The resonating dimension of radio is unheeded by the script writers, with few exceptions. The famous Orson Welles broadcast about the invasion from Mars was a simple demonstration of the all-inclusive, completely involving scope of the auditory image of radio. It was Hitler who gave radio the Orson Welles treatment for *real.*

That Hitler came into political existence at all is directly owing to radio and public-address systems. This is not to say that these media relayed his thoughts effectively to the German people. His thoughts were of very little consequence. Radio provided the first massive experience of electronic implosion, that reversal of the entire direction and meaning of literate Western civilization. For tribal peoples, for those whose entire social existence is an extension of family life, radio will continue to be a violent experience. Highly literate societies, that have long subordinated family life to individualist stress in business and politics, have managed to absorb and to neutralize the radio implosion without revolution. Not so, those communities that have had only brief or superficial experience of literacy. For them, radio is utterly explosive.

To understand such effects, it is necessary to see literacy as typographic technology, applied not only to the rationalizing of the entire procedures of production and marketing, but to law and education and city planning, as well. The principles of continuity, uniformity, and repeatability derived from print technology have, in England and America, long permeated every phase of communal life. In those areas a child learns literacy from traffic and street, from every car and toy and garment. Learning to read and write is a minor facet of literacy in the uniform, continuous environments of the English-speaking world. Stress on literacy is a distinguishing mark of areas that are striving to initiate that process of standardization that leads to the visual organization of work and space. Without psychic transformation of the inner life into segmented visual terms by literacy, there cannot be the economic "take-off" that insures a continual movement of augmented production and perpetually accelerated change-and-exchange of goods and services.

Just prior to 1914, the Germans had become obsessed with the menace of "encirclement." Their neighbors had all developed elaborate railway systems that facilitated mobilization of manpower resources. Encirclement is a highly visual image that had great novelty for this newly industrialized nation. In the 1930s, by contrast, the German obsession was with *lebensraum.* This is not a visual concern, at all. It is a claustrophobia, engendered by the radio implosion and compression of space. The German defeat had thrust them back from visual obsession into brooding upon the resonating Africa within. The tribal past has never ceased to be a reality for the German psyche.

It was the ready access of the German and middle-European world to the rich nonvisual resources of auditory and tactile form that enabled them to enrich the world of music and dance and sculpture. Above all their tribal mode gave them easy access to the new nonvisual world of subatomic physics, in which long-literate and long-industrialized societies are decidedly handicapped. The rich area of preliterate vitality felt the hot impact of radio. The message of radio is one of violent, unified implosion and resonance. For Africa, India, China, and even Russia, radio is a profound archaic force, a time bond with the most ancient past and long-forgotten experience.

Tradition, in a word, is the sense of the total past as *now*. Its awakening is a natural result of radio impact and of electric information, in general. For the intensely literate population, however, radio engendered a profound unlocaliz-able sense of guilt that sometimes expressed itself in the fellow-traveler attitude. A newly found human involvement bred anxiety and insecurity and unpredictability. Since literacy had fostered an extreme of individualism, and radio had done just the opposite in reviving the ancient experience of kinship webs of deep tribal involvement, the literate West tried to find some sort of compromise in a larger sense of collective responsibility. The sudden impulse to this end was just as subliminal and obscure as the earlier literary pressure toward individual isolation and irresponsibility; therefore, nobody was happy about any of the positions arrived at. The Gutenberg technology had produced a new kind of visual, national entity in the sixteenth century that was gradually meshed with industrial production and expansion. Telegraph and radio neutralized nationalism but evoked archaic tribal ghosts of the most vigorous brand. This is exactly the meeting of eye and ear, of explosion and implosion, or as Joyce puts it in the *Wake,* "In that earopean end meets Ind." The opening of the European ear brought to an end the open society and reintroduced the Indic world of tribal man to West End woman. Joyce puts these matters not so much in cryptic, as in dramatic and mimetic, form. The reader has only to take any of his phrases such as this one, and mime it until it yields the intelligible. Not a long or tedious process, if approached in the spirit of artistic playfulness that guarantees "lots of fun at Finnegan's wake."

Radio is provided with its cloak of invisibility, like any other medium. It comes to us ostensibly with person-to-person directness that is private and intimate, while in more urgent fact, it is really a subliminal echo chamber of magical power to touch remote and forgotten chords. All technological extensions of ourselves must be numb and subliminal, else we could not endure the leverage exerted upon us by such extension. Even more than telephone or telegraph, radio is that extension of the central nervous system that is matched only by human speech itself. Is it not worthy of our meditation that radio should be specially attuned to that primitive extension of our central nervous system, that aboriginal mass medium, the vernacular tongue? The crossing of these two most intimate and potent of human technologies could not possibly have failed to provide some extraordinary new shapes for human experience. So it proved with Hitler, the somnambulist. But does the detribalized and literate West imagine that it has earned immunity to the tribal magic of radio as a permanent possession? Our teenagers in the 1950s began to manifest many of the tribal stigmata. The adolescent, as opposed to the teenager, can now be classified as a phenomenon of literacy. Is it not significant that the adolescent was indigenous only to those areas of England and America where literacy had invested even food with abstract visual values? Europe never had adolescents. It had chaperones. Now, to the teenager, radio gives privacy, and at the same time it provides the tight tribal bond of the world of the common market, of song, and of resonance. The ear is hyperesthetic compared to the neutral eye. The ear is intolerant, closed, and exclusive, whereas the eye is open, neutral, and associative. Ideas of tolerance came to the West only after two or three centuries of literacy and visual Gutenberg culture. No such saturation with visual values had occurred in Germany by 1930. Russia is still far from any such involvement with visual order and values.

If we sit and talk in a dark room, words suddenly acquire new meanings and different textures. They become richer, even, than architecture, which Le Corbusier rightly says can best be felt at night. All those gestural qualities that the printed page strips from language come back in the dark, and on the radio. Given only the *sound* of a play, we have to fill in *all* of the senses, not just the sight of the action. So much do-it-yourself, or completion and "closure" of action, develops a kind of independent isolation in the young that makes them remote and inaccessible. The mystic screen of sound with which they are invested by their radios provides the privacy for their homework, and immunity from parental behest.

With radio came great changes to the press, to advertising, to drama, and to poetry. Radio offered new scope to practical jokers like Morton Downey at CBS. A sportscaster had just begun his fifteen-minute reading from a script when he was joined by Mr. Downey, who proceeded to remove his shoes and socks. Next followed coat and trousers and then underwear, while the sportscaster helplessly continued his broadcast, testifying to the compelling power of the mike to command loyalty over modesty and the self-protective impulse.

Radio created the disk jockey, and elevated the gag writer into a major national role. Since the advent of radio, the gag has supplanted the joke, not because of gag writers, but because radio is a fast hot medium that has also rationed the reporter's space for stories.

Jean Shepherd of WOR in New York regards radio as a new medium for a new kind of novel that he writes nightly. The mike is his pen and paper. His audience and their knowledge of the daily events of the world provide his characters, his scenes, and moods. It is his idea that, just as Montaigne was the first to use the page to record his reactions to the new world of printed books, he is the first to use radio as an essay and novel form for recording our common awareness of a totally new world of universal human participation in all human events, private or collective.

To the student of media, it is difficult to explain the human indifference to social effects of these radical forces. The phonetic alphabet and the printed word that exploded the closed tribal world into the open society of fragmented functions and specialist knowledge and action have never been studied in their roles as a magical transformer. The antithetic electric power of instant information that reverses social explosion into implosion, private enterprise into organization man, and expanding empires into common markets, has obtained as little recognition as the written word. The power of radio to retribalize mankind, its almost instant reversal of individualism into collectivism, Fascist or Marxist, has gone unnoticed. So extraordinary is this unawareness that *it* is what needs to be explained. The transforming power of media is easy to explain, but the ignoring of this power is not at all easy to explain. It goes without saying that the universal ignoring of the psychic action of technology bespeaks some inherent function, some essential numbing of consciousness such as occurs under stress and shock conditions.

The history of radio is instructive as an indicator of the bias and blindness induced in any society by its pre-existent technology. The word "wireless," still used for radio in Britain, manifests the negative "horseless-carriage" attitude toward a new form. Early wireless was regarded as a form of telegraph, and was not seen even in relation to the telephone. David Sarnoff in 1916 sent a memo to the Director of the American Marconi Company that employed him, advocating the idea of a music box in the home. It was ignored. That was the year of the Irish Easter rebellion and of the first radio *broadcast.* Wireless had already been used on ships as ship-to-shore "telegraph." The Irish rebels used a ship's wireless to make, not a point-to-point message, but a diffused broadcast in the hope of getting word to some ship that would relay their story to the American press. And so it proved. Even after broadcasting had been in existence for some years, there was no commercial interest in it. It was the amateur operators or hams and their fans, whose petitions finally got some action in favor of the setting up of facilities. There was reluctance and opposition from the world of the press, which, in England, led to the formation of the BBC and the firm shackling of radio by newspaper and advertising interests. This is an obvious rivalry that has not been openly discussed. The restrictive pressure by the press on radio and TV is still a hot issue in Britain and in Canada. But, typically, misunderstanding of the nature of the medium rendered the restraining policies quite futile. Such has always been the case, most notoriously in government censorship of the press and of the movies. Although the medium is the *message,* the controls go beyond programming. The restraints are always directed to the "content," which is always another medium. The content of the press is literary statement, as the content of the book is speech, and the content of the movie is the novel. So the effects of radio are quite independent of its programming. To those who have never studied media, this fact is quite as baffling as literacy is to natives, who say, "Why do you write? Can't you remember?"

Thus, the commercial interests who think to render media universally acceptable, invariably settle for "entertainment" as a strategy of neutrality. A more spectacular mode of the ostrich-head-in-sand could not be devised, for it ensures maximal pervasiveness for any medium whatever. The literate community will always argue for a controversial or point-of-view use of press, radio, and movie that would in effect diminish the operation, not only of press, radio and movie, but of the book as well. The commercial entertainment strategy automatically ensures maximum speed and force of impact for any medium, on psychic and social life equally. It thus becomes a comic strategy of unwitting self-liquidation, conducted by those who are dedicated to permanence, rather than to change. In the future, the only effective media controls must take the thermostatic form of quantitative rationing. Just as we now try to control atom-bomb fallout, so we will one day try to control media fallout. Education will become recognized as civil defense against media fallout. The only medium for which our education now offers some civil defense is the print medium. The educational establishment, founded on print, does not yet admit any other responsibilities.

Radio provides a speed-up of information that also causes acceleration in other media. It certainly contracts the world to village size, and creates insatiable village tastes for gossip, rumor, and personal malice. But while radio contracts the world to village dimensions, it hasn't the effect of homogenizing the village quarters. Quite the contrary. In India, where radio is the supreme form of communication, there are more than a dozen official languages and the same number of official radio networks. The effect of radio as a reviver of archaism and ancient memories is not limited to Hitler's Germany. Ireland, Scotland, and Wales have undergone resurgence of their ancient tongues since the coming of radio, and the Israeli present an even more extreme instance of linguistic revival. They now speak a language which has been dead in books for centuries. Radio is not only a mighty awakener of archaic memories, forces, and animosities, but a decentralizing, pluralistic force, as is really the case with all electric power and media.

Centralism of organization is based on the continuous, visual, lineal structuring that arises from phonetic literacy. At first, therefore, electric media merely followed the established patterns of literate structures. Radio was released from these centralist network pressures by TV. TV then took up the burden of centralism, from which it may be released by Telstar. With TV accepting the central network burden derived from our centralized industrial organization, radio was free to diversify, and to begin a regional and local community service that it had not known, even in the earliest days of the radio "hams." Since TV, radio has turned to the individual needs of people at different times of the day, a fact that goes with the multiplicity of receiving sets in bedrooms, bathrooms, kitchens, cars, and now in pockets. Different programs are provided for those engaged in divers activities. Radio, once a form of group listening that emptied churches, has reverted to private and individual uses since TV. The teenager withdraws from the TV group to his private radio.

This natural bias of radio to a close tie-in with diversified community groups is best manifested in the disk-jockey cults, and in radio's use of the telephone in a glorified form of the old trunk-line wire-tapping. Plato, who had old-fashioned tribal ideas of political structure, said that the proper size of a city was indicated by the number of people who could hear the voice of a public speaker. Even the printed book, let alone radio, renders the political assumptions of Plato quite irrelevant for practical purposes. Yet radio, because of its ease of decentralized intimate relation with both private and small communities, could easily implement the Platonic political dream on a world scale.

The uniting of radio with phonograph that constitutes the average radio program yields a very special pattern quite superior in power to the combination of radio and telegraph press that yields our news and weather programs. It is curious how much more arresting are the weather reports than the news, on both radio and TV. Is not this because "weather" is now entirely an electronic form of information, whereas news retains much of the pattern of the printed word? It is probably the print and book bias of the BBC and the CBC that renders them so awkward and inhibited in radio and TV presentation. Commercial urgency, rather than artistic insight, fostered by contrast a hectic vivacity in the corresponding American operation.

Television

The End of Television as We Know It: A Future Industry Perspective

Saul J. Berman, Louisa A. Shipnuck and Niall Duff

Executive Summary

Television (TV) has an inspiring past, ripe with milestones back to 1831, when British physicist and chemist Michael Faraday discovered electromagnetic induction.[1] The medium came of age in the 1950s, with popular shows like *I Love Lucy*, the 1954 World Soccer Championship, color broadcasting and the beloved remote control. For several generations, the TV audience happily embraced scheduled programming. For the industry, making a connection with consumers was a pretty straightforward, one-to-many experience . . . until recently.

Today, audiences are becoming increasingly fragmented, splicing their time among myriad media choices, channels and platforms. For the last few decades, consumers have migrated to more specialized, niche content via cable and multichannel offerings. Now, with the growing availability of on demand, self-programming and search features, some experiencers are moving beyond niche to individualized viewing. With increasing competition from convergence players in TV, telecommunications and the Internet, the industry is confronting unparalleled levels of complexity, dynamic change and pressure to innovate.

> "The industry is confronting unparalleled levels of complexity, dynamic change and pressure to innovate."

To hone our point-of-view of the mid-term future circa 2012, from both a demand and supply perspective, IBM conducted extensive industry interviews across the value chain and commissioned Economist Intelligence Unit (EIU) primary research in the U.S., Europe and Asia.

Our analysis indicates that market evolution hinges on two key market drivers: openness of access channels and levels of consumer involvement with media. For the next five to seven years, there will be movement on both of these fronts— but not uniformly. The industry instead will be stamped by consumer bimodality, a coexistence of two types of users with disparate channel requirements. While one consumer segment remains largely passive in the living room, the other will force radical change in business models in a search for anytime, anywhere content through multiple channels. The tech- and fashion-forward consumer segment will lead us to a world of platform-agnostic content, fluid mobility of media experiences, individualized pricing schemes and an end to the traditional concept of release windows.

> "Companies must get in front of change . . . or consumers threaten to leave them behind."

Given the influence of both segments in the 2012 forecast period, strategists must today work amid fragmentation, divergence and opposition in the market to optimize across nascent and long-standing business models; across new and traditional release windows; with old and new content programmers; and with both Internet Protocol (IP) and traditional supply chains. Given new market imperatives and heightened operating complexities, we expect value to shift throughout the industry, creating new winners and losers.

Today is the beginning of "the end of TV as we know it" and the future will only favor those who prepare now. Here, we enumerate six priority actions for executives: Segment, Innovate, Experiment, Mobilize, Open and Reorganize.

- *Segment:* Invest in divergent strategies and supply chains for bimodal consumer types. Identify, develop and continually refine data-driven user profiles in order to optimize product and service development, distribution, marketing messaging and service migration. Dynamically tailor content, advertising, pricing and reach.
- *Innovate:* Innovate business models, pricing, windows, distribution and packaging by creating—not resisting—wider consumer choice. Take risks today to avoid losing position over the long term.
- *Experiment:* Develop, trial, refine, roll-out. Repeat. Conduct ongoing market experiments, alone and with partners, to study "real life" consumer preferences. Invest in new measurement systems and metrics for the on demand world of tomorrow.
- *Mobilize:* Create seamless content mobility for users who require on-the-go experiences. Help ensure easy synchronization across devices and without required user modification.
- *Open:* Drive open and standards-based content delivery platforms to optimize content and revenue exploitation, and to create high business flexibility and network cost-efficiency. Position open capabilities to bolster digital content protection with consumer flexibility, and for plug-and-play business upgrades necessary in the fast-changing marketplace.
- *Reorganize:* Reassess your business composition against future requirements. Identify core competencies needed for future competitive advantage. Isolate non-core business components for outsourcing, consolidation or partnering.

From an external perspective, reconfigure the business to leverage market and financial levers to buy, build or team for future competitiveness.

Research Methodology

IBM conducted more than 65 one-hour interviews with "C-level" and senior industry executives. Wall Street analysts, economists and technology visionaries inside and outside IBM. Further, IBM commissioned primary research by the Economist Intelligence Unit (EIU). The EIU surveyed 108 industry executives from three constituencies: 1) cable, broadcast and Pay TV networks, 2) multiple system operators (MSO) and direct broadcast satellite (DBS) providers, and 3) new entrant video telecommunications companies. Respondents were evenly split among three geographical regions. Europe, Asia and North America.

A Future Scenario

This executive brief begins with a glance at a future consumer experience. For an advanced user in 2012, the TV experience will go far beyond traditional "lean back" behavior and constrained content access channels. Here we provide a look ahead . . .

My Gadget-Lover's Dream Realized

I am in digital-electronics-gadget nirvana. And, I am not afraid to boast. My home sports a fully wireless broadband (WIMAX) Internet environment, where content moves freely among the home server, several multiple high definition (HD) screens, the office PC and the mobile devices that I continually upgrade.

I regularly acquire favorite TV shows (new and old) either from Internet search engines such as Google Video, the video/telecommunications provider's on demand archive or fully-loaded Internet video destinations. I can't remember the last time I made "appointment TV," since I download or watch on replay from my multi-room digital video recorder (DVR) every important program or episode. A Bluetooth-like signal on my cell phone triggers the logon for my media center system. When ready to watch TV. I am greeted with a mosaic screen with tiles of favorite TV channels, suggested programs from the last 24 hours, season's passes and tailored on demand choices.

(Continued)

My home network offers different on demand pricing packages, dependent on the number of times I plan to watch, copy or download—and whether the content is a preview. When not skipping through. I am more amused than ever by advertising, particularly since it is tailored for me and comes with relevant links, add-ons and a variety of purchase options within the commercial itself. While all of these options can feel overwhelming to some. I view them as a challenge with a large pay-off. I will continue to put in the energy to be first on the block with the latest "gadget-lover's dream realized."

This scenario represents one key group of consumers who lead the market. While the future will deliver these gadget-lovers' dreams and more, it will be some time before leading-edge users inspire the mass audience. Suppliers are laying the foundation of change with infrastructure upgrades and service experimentation, but ultimately consumers will drive the multifaceted adoption schedule. At this important industry juncture, this paper profiles a TV industry whose relationships with both consumers and suppliers are undergoing significant and complex change.

Unparalleled Levels of Complexity and Dynamic Change

Significant changes in both demand and supply are driving the industry to unparalleled levels of complexity and dynamic change. This section of the paper explores current trends and challenges impacting the future prospects for participants within the TV industry. Key issues to appraise include strong consumer demand; audience fragmentation; misaligned business models; converged competition; and burgeoning market experiments.

The Picture Is Bright for Consumers

TV content is more popular than ever with consumers despite the availability of myriad alternatives, including digital music subscriptions, film DVD rental services, satellite radio and massively multi-player video games. Total TV consumption hours have continued to grow, with the average U.S. household estimated to spend 1826 hours with its TV in 2005 (the equivalent of more than five hours per day).[2] Hours viewed from content downloads and TV DVDs can be added to this traditionally measured consumption.

> "TV consumption is expected to rise, in part due to the appeal of new technologies which allow increased control over when, how and where content is viewed."

Many once predicted that broadband media platforms would be the greatest risk to TV viewership, but thus far, broadband seem to be without significant cannibalization effects. For example, before broadband reached mass adoption in the U.S.—defined as 25 percent of U.S. households–TV consumption grew at a

1.6 percent compound annual growth rate (CAGR) for the period 1996–2003.[3] Even after the point of mass broadband adoption, viewership increased year-to-year in 2005 by 2.5 percent.[4] Going forward, analysts predict TV usage to grow by an average of 1.7 percent per annum through 2008.[5]

Even the youth audience, ever experimental with new forms of media, continues to log in 3 hours and 51 minutes of TV hours per day.[6] A 2005 survey by the Kaiser Family Foundation reported that TV garners three to four times as many minutes per day as either computers (at one hour and two minutes, on average) or video games (boys at one hour and thirty-four minutes; girls at forty minutes, on average).[7] While there will surely be some movement to video games and other media, overall TV consumption is expected to rise, in part due to the appeal of new technologies which allow increased control over when, how and where content is viewed.

Audiences Become Finer and Finer

Consumers love content, but are having their attention more finely fragmented by over-choice and evermore proliferating channels and platforms. In days of yore, a consumer had only a few broadcast channels from which to choose. Today, the average U.S. household has 91 TV channels[8] and, in both the U.S. and abroad, the number of offered channels ranks in the hundreds.[9]

In the face of explosively expanding choices across all media (for example, tens of thousands of podcasts,[10] more than 43,000 magazines worldwide,[11] over 350 million Internet domains[12] and multicasting TV streams), viewers have trended toward targeted, niche content and messages. In 2005, 57 percent of U.S. TV viewership was on cable content networks versus broadcast.[13] Similarly, viewership in other countries has tracked away from broadcast, free-to-air channels to more specialized, targeted content. Demand is going niche and beyond, yet business models lag.

Consumers Change . . . Models Lag

One of the key revenue sources in TV, advertising (which funds approximately 50 percent of the market[14]), should theoretically be most elastic to audience changes. And to some degree, revenues have adjusted. From 2000 to 2004, niche advertising CAGRs for U.S. and European cable/multichannel networks were 74 percent and 6.2 percent respectively compared to a 2 percent CAGR for broadcast/terrestrial advertising.[15] Yet, cable in the U.S. collects only 30 percent of advertising revenues today, despite garnering almost double that percentage of viewership (see Figure 1).[16]

"Misalignment between performance and revenues primes the market for correction."

This may be due to lagging perceptions about the reach and effectiveness of broadcast messages, or the complexity involved with any alternative, non-broadcast media placement. Regardless of the causes, today's misalignment between performance and revenues primes the market for correction.

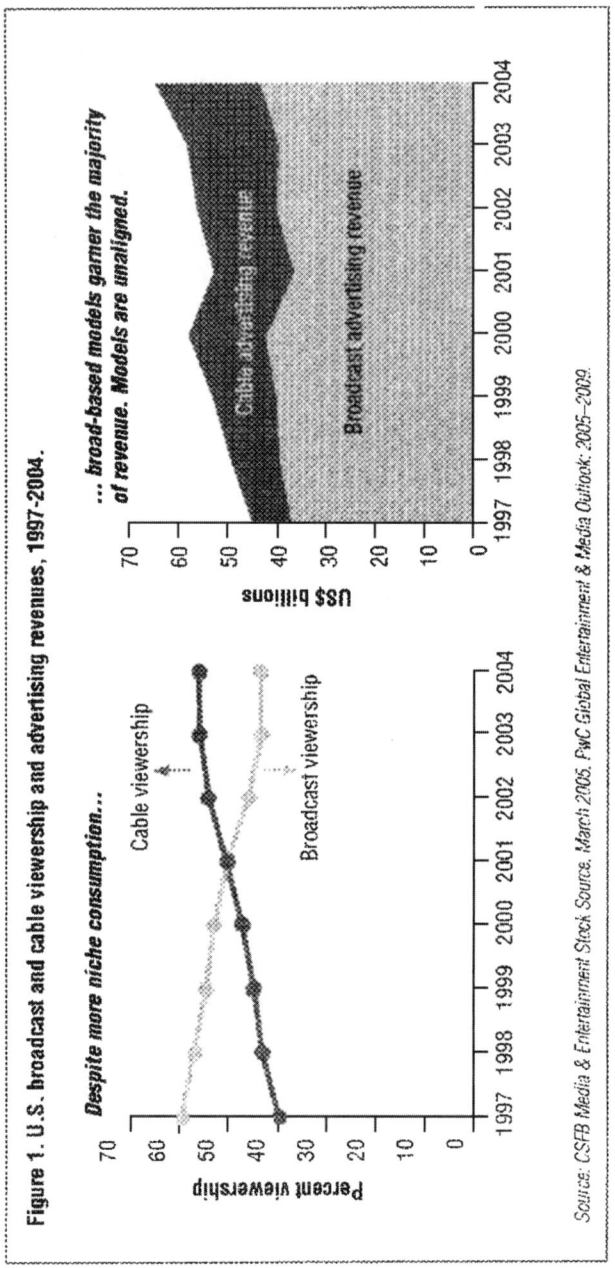

Figure 1. U.S. broadcast and cable viewership and advertising revenues, 1997-2004.

Despite more niche consumption...

Percent viewership

Cable viewership

Broadcast viewership

... broad-based models garner the majority of revenue. Models are unaligned.

US$ billions

Cable advertising revenue

Broadcast advertising revenue

Source: CSFB Media & Entertainment Stock Source, March 2005, PwC Global Entertainment & Media Outlook: 2005–2009.

Further, with today's growing availability of self-programming, search and on demand, some users are moving from a niche orientation (targeted content on cable and multichannel networks) to individualized services. Increasingly, viewers are becoming audiences of one, with individual power to determine specifically when, how and what they watch.

"The IBM/EIU survey revealed that 70 percent of MSO, DBS and Telco executives said 'on demand content' is a chief motivation in consumer purchase decisions, next to price."[17]

As the DVR makes advances—not just in the U.S., but also the U.K., Germany, France, Spain and Italy—ad-skipping is also taking off as, one by one, viewers opt out of advertising content. Ad-skipping is expected to lead to losses of 6 percent in U.S. TV annual advertising revenues in 2009.[18] Even with a slower roll-out in other regions, DVRs are still expected to have a material impact on advertising, with depressed annual revenues ranging from 2.4 percent in Germany to 6 percent in the U.K. in 2012 (see Figure 2).[19]

Overall advertising is expected to rise (in part because DVRs inspire more content consumption), but its potential will be mitigated by the DVR impact. It is noteworthy that in addition to the DVR, there might also be a negative impact on the advertisement model from on demand TV. Consumers may opt to buy episodes without advertising or skip through on demand content where allowable. Unlike the DVR, the on demand model is being heavily managed by content owners and networks. The bottom line is that as these new technologies move from the early adopter stage to the mass audience, we expect continued downward pressure on TV advertising (and the traditional 30-second spot), as even the most passive viewer enjoys ad-skipping and time-shifting (choosing *when* a TV program is viewed).

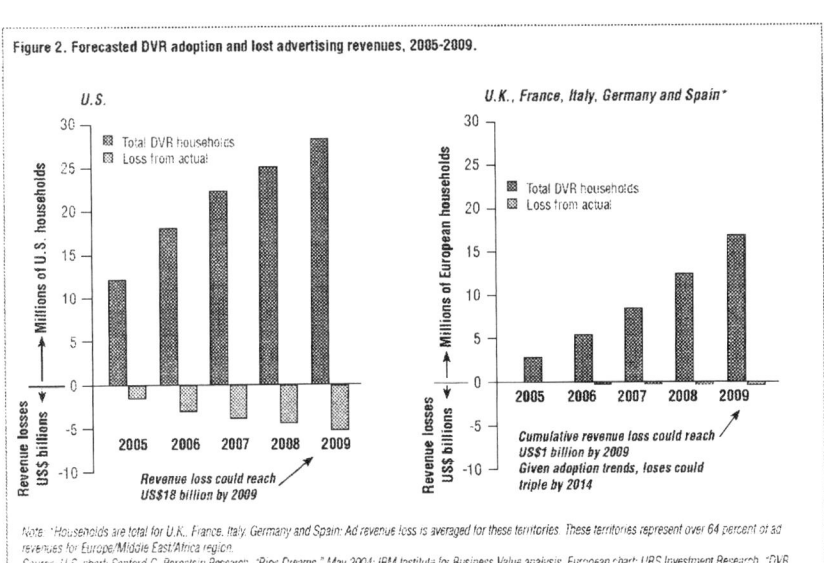

Figure 2. Forecasted DVR adoption and lost advertising revenues, 2005-2009.

Note: *Households are total for U.K., France, Italy, Germany and Spain; Ad revenue loss is averaged for these territories. These territories represent over 64 percent of ad revenues for Europe/Middle East/Africa region.
Source: U.S. chart: Sanford C. Bernstein Research. "Pipe Dreams," May 2004; IBM Institute for Business Value analysis. European chart: UBS Investment Research. "DVR – Broadcasters' nemesis?" October, 2004; PwC, "Global Entertainment and Media Outlook: 2005-2009," June, 2005. IBM Institute for Business Value analysis.

As consumers continue to move away from broad-based experiences, broad-based business models will be challenged as never before. And, advertising is merely the first revenue category to adjust to this trend. Content models, today sold in bulk or bundles among major institutional players, will also go in search of more user-driven, on demand opportunities on a widespread basis.

Industry Perspectives:

"In ten years, mass market will stop always trumping niche market."
—*Global Software Executive* [20]

The IBM and EIU research with executives across the TV value chain confirm this trend to individualized services from broad-based models. Most surveyed executives, regardless of company origin, placed the least confidence in TV advertising compared to user-driven, on demand revenue streams (see Figure 3).

While there is industry consensus about impending revenue transition, the EIU survey revealed a lack of agreement regarding replacement revenues. With uncertain return on investment in TV and lagging metrics, advertisers may simply move dollars to the Internet, where metrics are individualized. Arguably, this—a double-whammy coupled with the DVR—is happening already. Though Internet revenues start with a smaller base, its advertising growth rate is forecast to be almost triple that of TV advertising by 2009. [21]

Convergence Has Finally Arrived

Convergence in TV, telecommunications and the Internet is pitting the giants of industry against one another. Two key aspects of converged competition are video distribution and content aggregation.

"Convergence pits industry giants against one another."

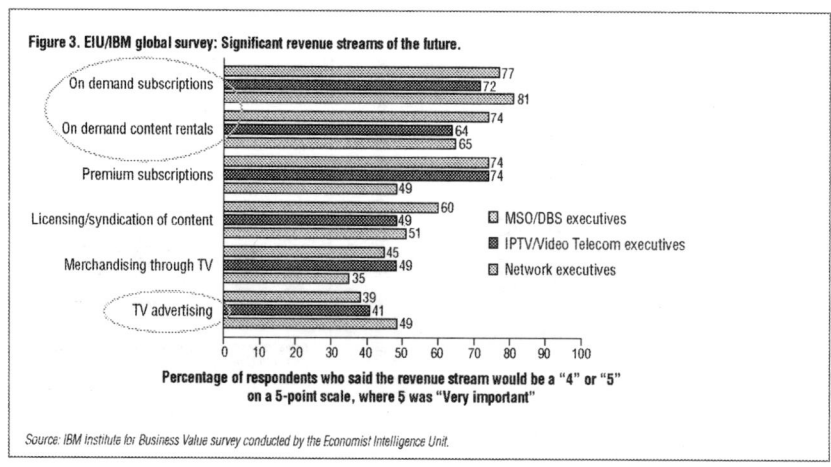

Figure 3. EIU/IBM global survey: Significant revenue streams of the future.

Legend:
- MSO/DBS executives
- IPTV/Video Telecom executives
- Network executives

On demand subscriptions: 77, 72, 81
On demand content rentals: 74, 64, 65
Premium subscriptions: 74, 74, 49
Licensing/syndication of content: 60, 49, 51
Merchandising through TV: 45, 49, 35
TV advertising: 39, 41, 49

Percentage of respondents who said the revenue stream would be a "4" or "5" on a 5-point scale, where 5 was "Very important"

Source: IBM Institute for Business Value survey conducted by the Economist Intelligence Unit.

First, we look to convergence in distribution and assess how the "triple play" (offering video, voice and high-speed data) and "quad play" bundles (triple play plus mobile) may evolve. In the video distribution marketplace, incumbents and new entrants alike are battling to provide TV and other services to the living room. In doing so, players have been engaged in a network upgrade cycle to win consumer loyalty and higher average revenues per unit. Between 1996 and 2004, the U.S. cable industry spent over US$95 billion on upgrades to move to two-way plant, with its potential for High Definition television (HDTV), digital cable, video on demand and digital phone.[22] With more than 90 percent of U.S. households passed by activated two-way infrastructure by the end of 2004,[23] the foundation was laid to convert 28.5 million households to digital cable and 23.9 million for video on demand by year-end 2005.[24] In Europe, while digital TV is estimated to be in 52 million homes (37 percent of total TV households),[25] video on demand is slower to be offered.[26]

Internet Protocol Television (IPTV) Reroutes Competition

Internet Protocol (IP) for video distribution. IPTV is the use of an IP broadband network to deliver quality TV content. IPTV is not open Web TV, as it is commonly mistaken. Most IPTV systems involve conditional access and set-top box equipment, similar to current services provided by digital satellite or cable companies. However, as broadband speeds to the home increase, consumers may begin receiving quality TV directly over the Internet—without the need for designated "pipes." For now, however, delivering even standard definition TV is challenged over residential high-speed data connections.

IPTV and the changing competitive landscape. IPTV is the moniker often used to connote the entry of telecommunications providers into video distribution. However, even within the telecom community, the term is often ill-fitting. In the U.S., for example, AT&T (formerly SBC Communications) is introducing video service over IP, while competitor Verizon Communications is not—instead using cable's quadrature amplitude modulation (QAM) scheme over fiber. Both AT&T and Verizon Communications, like their peers around the globe, are using new proprietary fiber networks to compete directly with traditional cable and digital satellite companies.

New entrant telecommunications providers around the world are also doing network upgrades in order to move into the video distribution business. With their core voice businesses under attack, telecom providers are investing heavily in fiber-to-the-home or curb and next generation networks for video services.

Often, the roll-outs are pure IP-based distribution of video, though some more closely resemble cable's QAM scheme over fiber. Whatever the technical transport mechanism, the borders of competition are falling between telecommunications companies and traditional video providers.

Most advanced IPTV roll-outs to date are found in Europe and Asia: China Netcom Group, Hong Kong's PCCW, Taiwan's Chungwa Telecom and Italy's FastWeb are all global examples of functioning, pilot IPTV networks. In select countries, like China and France, partnerships with municipalities are helping to speed upgrades and usage. In the U.S., Verizon Communications, Bell South Corporation and AT&T (formerly SBC Communications) have announced plans to pass more than 34 million homes by 2009 with fiber.[27] Accordingly, these three major U.S. entrants aim to convert up to 5 million video households by 2009, taking share equally from DBS and cable incumbents.[28]

> "If upgraded TV features don't prove new value to consumers, competition will devolve to price alone, placing pressure across the value chain."

With triple play or quad play bundles, competition is expected to be fierce in the forecast period of this paper. As the EIU research shows, the new entrant telecom providers seem poised to buy share (see Figure 4).

The growing popularity of triple and quad play bundles brings the possibility of a protracted price war. If upgraded features cannot prove new value to consumers, competition may devolve to price alone—placing pressure not just on distribution players downstream, but other value chain players as well. Greater profitability is expected to lie with those competitors who can manage the value-added play and not fall prey to discussions of price alone.

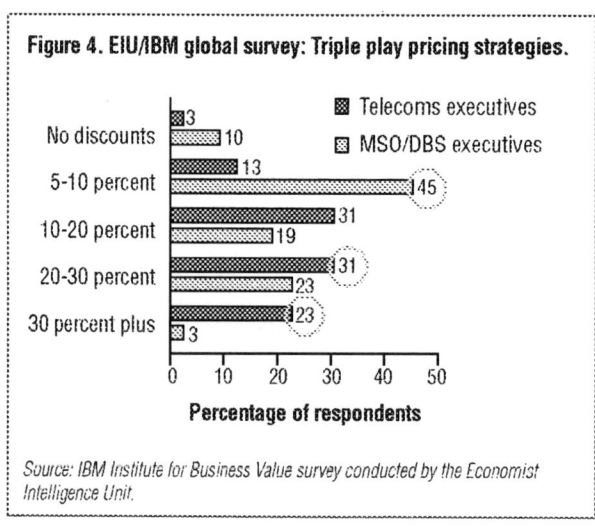

Figure 4. EIU/IBM global survey: Triple play pricing strategies.

Source: IBM Institute for Business Value survey conducted by the Economist Intelligence Unit.

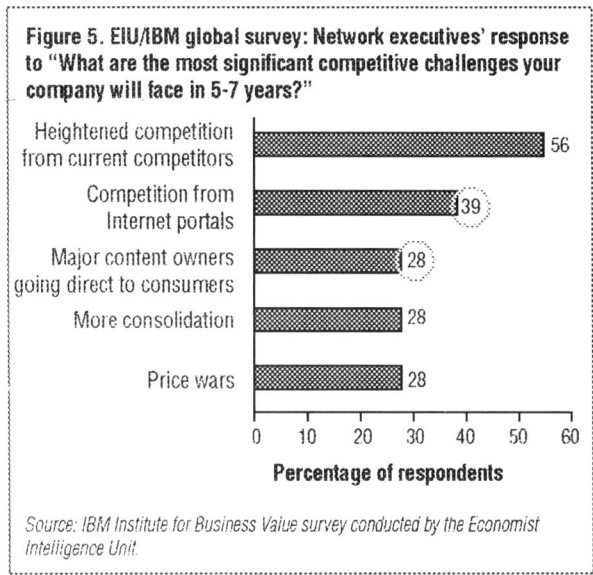

Figure 5. EIU/IBM global survey: Network executives' response to "What are the most significant competitive challenges your company will face in 5-7 years?"

Heightened competition from current competitors 56
Competition from Internet portals 39
Major content owners going direct to consumers 28
More consolidation 28
Price wars 28

Percentage of respondents

Source: IBM Institute for Business Value survey conducted by the Economist Intelligence Unit.

Besides convergence pressures in distribution, there is a second dilemma: Will Internet content aggregators circumvent traditional programmers? The Internet channel creates a potential bypass to traditional content packaging and programming, a function previously owned by networks for program line-up and scheduling. The EIU research indicates that today's programmers—the TV content networks—rank Internet services among the top areas of concern (see Figure 5).

When asked which competitive challenges they expect to be most significant in five to seven years, network executives worldwide cited nontraditional threats like Internet portals (such as Google, Yahoo! and AOL), and content owners going direct. While the degree to which mainstream users will watch Internet TV is debatable, it is clear that more "lost eyeballs" translates into further weakening of the traditional media network model. It is feasible that networks without consumer brand identities will effectively be squeezed from the market.

Industry Perspectives:

"Networks will be extinct in fifteen years."
—*European Public Broadcaster*[29]

The Beginning . . . But Not Nearly the End . . . of Market Experimentation

Market changes in supply and demand are triggering trials of new business models (see Figure 6). As Entertainment economist Harold Vogel explained. TV networks and content owners are "trying to find a model that enables them to

Figure 6. Examples of emerging business models.

	Akimbo	BBC "My BBC Player"	CBS and Comcast	Disney and Apple	MTV "Overdrive"	NBC-Universal and DIRECTV	Time Warner Cable "Start Over"	Warner Bros. and AOL "In2TV"	Yahoo and TiVo
Consumer device	TV	PC	TV	iPod	PC	TV	TV	PC	TV, PC
Revenues at launch	Monthly user fee of $9.99	No user fee	$0.99/episode Advertisements (but can be skipped)	$1.99/episode No advertisements	Skip-resistant advertisements	$0.99/episode No advertisements	Free access with TV cable subscription Skip-resistant advertisements	No user fee Skip-resistant advertisements	Access with TiVo subscription
Attributes	• Proprietary set top box required for on demand • Content includes Turner Classic Movies, BBC and Discovery	• P2P media player for BBC content • Most shows available for seven days after first run • To launch 2006	• CBS owned content to Comcast subscribers in markets with CBS owned and operated stations • To launch 2006	• Episodes of select ABC content one day after airdate on video iPod • PC playback with QuickTime	• Five genre-driven video channels • Music videos, trailers, news, behind-the-scenes footage	• NBC owned shows on demand to DIRECTV subscribers • To launch 2006	• Program restart anytime during its broadcast window • No ability to save programs	• 14,000 episodes available • Six thematic channels • One minute of advertising inserted into show • To launch 2006	• TiVo functionality for Yahoo content (Launch) and video search • To launch 2006

Source: Company Websites; IBM Institute for Business Value analysis.

recapture some of the profitability that goes away when people watch television differently than they have historically."[30]

In 2005, public broadcaster the British Broadcast Corporation (BBC) began piloting "My BBC Player," a technology that allows consumers to use broadband to download and share programs. With a public charter to "drive the market for free-to-air digital TV, digital radio and new media, focusing on improvements in awareness, availability and take-up,"[31] the BBC has launched a trial to make content freely available for seven days with peer-to-peer (P2P) software. Without conflicts from affiliates or network advertisers (that constrain its commercial counterparts), the BBC has experimented farther than most others in the global marketplace.

In November 2005, the Walt Disney Company, Disney ABC Television Group and Apple created another on demand landmark with their partnership to enable access to day-old episodes of popular shows via iTunes Music Store. In the first nineteen days, this major, first-of-kind launch tracked over 1 million downloads, purchased at US$1.99 per episode.[32] Content does not expire and is portable on the Apple Video iPod. Soon thereafter, competitors such as NBC, CBS and Warner Bros, released similar on demand announcements of their own.

Much like the various alliances in the early online forays of the music industry, these solutions are only the beginning—"placeholders" which do not yet allow for the ubiquitous access to content anytime, anywhere. The TV market will continue to evolve literally day-by-day, as industry participants keep seeking new, profitable models that serve consumer needs. As all of this activity leads to greater industry learning, as well as disruption, the riskiest option now seems to be that of inaction.

Music Industry Experience Offers Lesson for TV

At the turn of the 21st century, the music industry had seen five years of relatively stable CD sales growth.[33] However, as Napster gained momentum and CD sales started to slip, the industry was slow to react.

Napster quickly swelled and at its peak had 80 million users who traded over 15 billion songs.[34] In two years, the percentage of North American online households downloading music illegally had jumped from practically nonexistent, to just under 30 percent.[35] With downloads skyrocketing and artists crying foul, the music industry's lawsuit shut down the P2P Napster service in early 2001.[36] However, this effort did not stop copycat global networks which launched with new technology impervious to worldwide court or regulatory oversight. The U.S. music industry saw unit sales fall 21 percent between 2000 and 2003, the largest technology related revenue loss of any media business in the last two decades.[37]

The release of the iPod, followed by the iTunes launch in 2003, finally proved that embracing new technology could boister revenue. With hip design and fluid user interfaces, iTunes dominated the market and enticed users back from P2P file sharing. Apple has now sold half a billion songs online and digital music accounts for 4 percent of the US$13.4 billion global music market.[38] Following four consecutive years of declines, the music industry experienced solid growth in 2004, up 5.7 percent globally, fueled by digital distribution and mobile music.[39]

The key lesson from Music is to *get out in front of a changing marketplace.*

Views of the Future

Given the trends in motion, great disruption to the value chain appears nearly inevitable for the long-term. However, analysis shows that radical upheaval may be outside the forecast period of this paper, as the mainstream user takes time to catch up to the tech-optimists and fashion-forward users. This section of the paper outlines our view of the long-term future, as well as assumptions on the evolutionary mid-term and impending value shifts for 2012.

The Next Great "Earthquake" Is Coming (But Not Today)

Looking beyond the year 2012, we believe two key drivers will define long-term TV industry disruption: Open *content access* and highly involved *media consumers* (see Figure 7). The blue arrows show the expected movement to the upper right quadrant over time, as many mainstream users become more involved with their TV experiences and enjoy greater access to content through new platforms and channels.

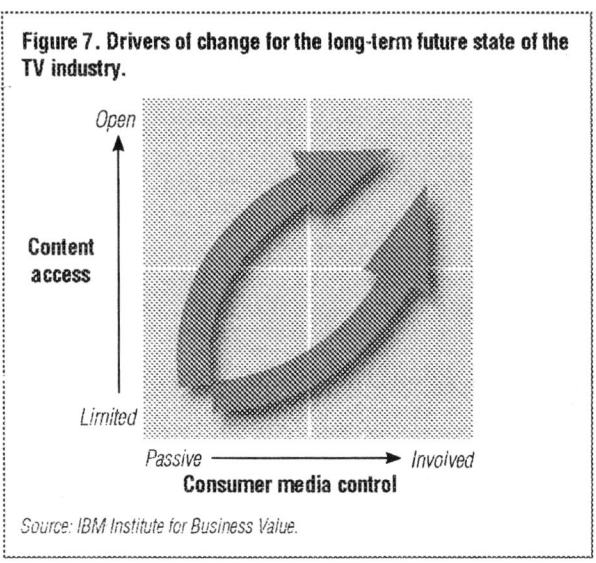

Figure 7. Drivers of change for the long-term future state of the TV industry.

Source: IBM Institute for Business Value.

The spectrum for consumer media control ranges from *Passive* to *Involved*. At one end, the historical and still predominant passive experience represents a "lean back" mode in which consumers do little more than flip on the remote and scan programming. At the other end are consumers who want to "lean forward," for a PC-like experience. Involved users will self-navigate, toggle, search and self-author content—and, this interactive group is willing to invest heavily in its TV and media experiences.

> "We believe two key variables will define long-term disruption: Open content access and highly involved media consumers."

The content access axis describes the channels for obtaining content, whether limited by a service provider in a safe haven or accessible through a more open. Internet-like state. The *Limited* end of the spectrum represents the predominant current state—a controlled environment like a "walled garden." Here, just a few distributors (namely MSOs. DBS and telecommunications providers) clear conditional access hurdles and aggregate content. By contrast, the *Open* end depicts a model where both protected and unprotected content is readily available through multiple platforms, channels and distributors (including mobile and Internet).

The matrix framework predicts disruptions across the market. While some tech-forward consumers can immediately force change, the tipping point will not be reached until the mass audience adopts behavioral shifts. Changes might include:

- Content bundles are "de-bundled" by consumer demand
- Internet content distributors take significant share from broadcast, cable or satellite networks

- Media networks without a consumer brand identity suffer the consequences of consumers "going around" them
- Search and self-programming reduce the value of content adjacencies (the time slot before or after a hit show), fundamentally changing marketing and promotions.

Media Consumers: A "Generational Chasm"

Massive Passive. Just beginning retirement. Sharon, age 61, and Ken, age 65, plan certain types of entertainment into their daily routine. Along with Ken's regular golf and bridge outings and Sharon's various social clubs, they both look forward to certain favorite prime-time and news magazine programs. Like many of their friends, they splurged last year on a large flat-screen TV, where Ken especially loves to watch live Dallas Cowboys football and golf tournaments. Sharon checks the TV Guide to stay informed about the movies-of-the-week and network specials. Her grandson is trying to teach her to use the built-in DVR, though she often forgets about the device's live-pausing or ad-skipping potential. Definitely part of the "lean back" category, Ken and Sharon haven't greatly modified their TV viewing habits in the last twenty years.

Two distinct sub-groups. Gadgetiers and Kool Kids, comprise the more involved, "lean forward" consumer segment:

Gadgetiers, Helene, age 29, is married to Franz, age 33. These on-the-move, working parents have set up a surround-sound home theater, enjoy downloads on the hottest portable devices, and transfer content and data via their WiMAX Internet connection. Helene and Franz have no preferred service provider for video service (cable, satellite or telecommunications provider), as long as they get top quality bundles at a value. Given their schedules for work-related travel, neither minds paying for certain content or services to accommodate their lifestyle. They have a particular fondness for convenience-oriented service like TiVoToGo and iTunes, which make their portable lives more flexible and fun. They also selectively use P2P resources for missed programming that is not available through on demand systems. Feeling great ownership over their media experiences. Helene and Franz enjoy showing friends and family their Gadgetier ways—even sharing information with other technophiles on various video blogs.

Kool Kids. Marcus, age 13, and Semana, age 15, are brother and sister. Both were exposed to high bandwidth networks as very young children and they experiment unflinchingly with media and platforms. While they have little disposable income, they follow all the latest gadget crazes. The mobile

(Continued)

device is the centerpiece of their lives and they text message while doing one, two or three other tasks. Though their parents refuse to allow it in their presence, Semana and Marcus even do instant messaging on the TV set while watching favorite shows. Marcus uses his tech-savvy to try to bypass network blocks and content encryption in order to rip and share content. Likewise, Semana doesn't worry about piracy warnings as she trades copies of CDs with her friends. Without thinking about it, both are heavily invested in media experiences and spend much time seeking TV episodes, current films and hard-to-find, cool niche content. Like practically all their friends, these teenagers have posted detailed profiles to several social networking sites, relying on those connections for media recommendations and most other aspects of their lives.

Bimodal Consumers Until 2012: It's All in How They Lean

Suppliers lay the foundation of change with network upgrades and converged service roll-outs. However, the industry tipping point ultimately depends on the mix of users and their acceptance of new services and pricing. For the short- and mid-term future, the TV industry will be marked by a bimodality among consumers: those who are mainly passive viewers and those who demand a more interactive media experience. This future state is described as the "Generational Chasm" because there is a rough correlation between a consumer's age and whether that person is more likely to be a passive or active viewer of TV content.

Today, the Massive Passives far outnumber the influential, fashion-forward, early adopters personified by the Gadgetiers and Kool Kids. Though the mass audience is indeed dwindling, it will take time for technology fluidity, education and customer service to take hold. As a result, the Generational Chasm is the expected state of the TV industry for the coming five to seven years, featuring the coexistence of these two distinct audience types (see Figure 8).

> "The Massive Passives, the largest group today, represent the annuity to fund the industry's future growth."

Massive Passives are generally content with their traditional TV experiences and uninspired to change viewing habits drastically in our forecast period. These device followers are expected to keep the TV as the media centerpiece for the near term and watch scheduled programming, with growing time-shifting.

By contrast, the Gadgetiers and Kool Kids seek more experiential interactive video experiences, with heightened control of aggregation, content sources, space-shifting (choosing *where* video content is viewed), time-shifting, user contribution of content and device interoperability. These early adopters are leading the way toward open distribution models.

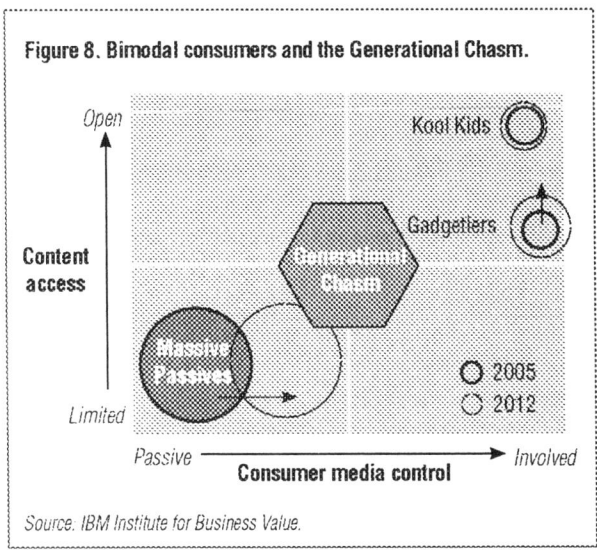

Figure 8. Bimodal consumers and the Generational Chasm.

Source: IBM Institute for Business Value.

Gadgetiers spend as much time with their PCs for media experiences as their TVs, often time-shifting and space-shifting with PCs and other devices. As this group grows over time, it can represent revenue growth opportunity for industry incumbents—if compelling content and device/platform extensions can be offered.

"If you don't get in front of Gadgetiers, they will leave you behind."

Kool Kids are distinct in their reliance on content sharing. This group has more time available than other groups, but fewer funds. As a result, they are device aspirants, using mobile devices as the centerpiece of their social and media experiences. Time-shifting and space-shifting are both prevalent with mobile, physical copies. Kool Kids represent revenue cultivation opportunities as the industry works to mitigate or prevent Napster-like propensities.

Analog Switch-Off Will Most Affect the Massive Passives

Digital TV switch-over hits mid-forecast period. Within a few years—the exact date is still being determined by the FCC and Congress for 2008/2009—broadcasters in the U.S. will suspend traditional analog transmissions and switch over to all-digital signals. The transition will free up valuable spectrum which the FCC will reallocate, some to public services, such as fire and police bands. Furthermore, when inevitably combined with HDTV, digital

(Continued)

TV offers better picture quality, richer digital sound and available digital data for many interactive purposes. Similar transitions are going forward in most major markets, with Japan, South Korea and the U.K. leading the way for transformations between 2008 and 2012.

Complex transition for consumers and companies alike. The analog-to-digital transition will be complex for several reasons. The analog shut-off is unique, in that past industry transformations (such as the start of FM radio) have typically been additive, not substitutive, and have been backward compatible. When the analog signal is ceased in the U.S. analysts predict that 200 million of the 300 million sets will not be digital-ready.[40] With cost upgrades estimated at approximately US$50-60 per TV set, the total cost is monumental and no full payer has been identified.[41] In Europe, even fewer households are digital than the U.S., illustrating the immense cost to be borne out in each global region for the transition. Any way you split the spectrum, digital TV is going to offer consumers more choice and greater interactivity— but it will entail transitional discomfort (particularly for Massive Passives, who are likely to be less comfortable with environmental change) in combination with vast industry expense.

Value Shifts in a Bimodal World

Due to the growing complexity and bimodality of the market, we expect value shifts in the industry as new and old participants fight for new relevance and prominence. In Figure 9, we have outlined possible scenarios for winners and losers in 2012 (as an extension of trends afoot in 2005).

For example, given the move of some advanced users to new screens, such as PC and mobile, and away from traditional broadcast schedules and advertising, it is conceivable that traditional programmers will weaken in the years ahead. Hence, the graph shows a downward arrow for that group, indicating loss of position from 2005. Furthermore, as Gadgetiers and Kool Kids actively seek new IP-based

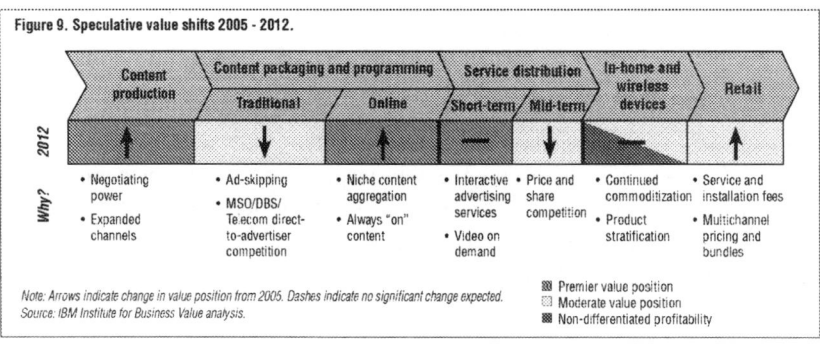

Figure 9. Speculative value shifts 2005 - 2012.

video experiences, it is fathomable that online packaging and programming providers—such as internet portals or search engines—will extend their position with users by adding TV and video offerings. In doing so, they can capture advertising and service revenues. The marriage of consumers and content aggregation may place the portals into a high-margin, high-value position within the TV business. An arrow pointing upward indicates that strengthening position between 2005 and 2012.

While the scenarios discussed above are only speculative, what is certain is that new winner and losers will rise up in the next five to seven years, given the degree of change ahead. Competing and maintaining value in the marketplace will be at least partially dependent on each company's ability to adapt, reset strategies proactively and prioritize action steps.

Priority Actions for Future Success

Providers of content creation, packaging, programming and distribution must act quickly to develop and implement complex strategies for a complex marketplace. Six key priority actions are essential to prepare for success in the TV industry of the future: Segment, Innovate, Experiment, Mobilize, Open and Reorganize.

1. *Segment: Invest in divergent strategies and supply chains for bimodal consumers.* Successful companies of the future will segment the market to serve both the "lean back" Massive Passives and the "lean forward" Gadgetiers and Kool Kids. To both protect current and grow future revenues, leading companies will need to:

- Dynamically profile consumer groups
- Tailor services and products by segment
- Cost-effectively operate tandem channels
- End the "one size fits all" marketing approach.

The first step is to perfect a process for acquiring and analyzing consumer data. Data will be crucial to profitably discriminating among user groups on pricing, bundles, technology integration, content form and function, release windows and advertising formats, among others. By constantly honing data-driven psychographic segmentation, a company will be armed with necessary information to pre-empt and meet market needs. To systematize information flow, continuous data mining and predictive modeling, technologies like customer relationship management systems are in order.

Just as product and service development must be reoriented by segment, so too must delivery supply chains. To deliver to bimodal demand, providers will need to develop and operate tandem supply chains and channels. In other words, while preserving status quo processes and systems for the Massive Passives, there must be initiatives to develop and upgrade nontraditional channels on behalf of the demanding Gadgetiers and Kool Kids.

To maintain the bottom line in this complex environment, executives will have to achieve significant cost savings from the traditional supply chain in order to invest in new delivery channels. While each company along the value chain targets users from a different vantage point, none will be exempt from the tremendous cost pressures arising from bimodal demand—and its associated requirements for multifaceted supply.

> "To maintain the bottom line, a company will have to achieve significant cost savings from the traditional supply chain in order to fund new delivery channels."

In addition to developing divergent product and delivery strategies, each company must also differentiate communications and sales strategies. Providers must offer to each consumer segment unique marketing messages, migration up-sell strategies and sales outreach plans. This will be crucial in moving all segments— at different rates and speeds—along the future path. Asymmetrical strategies will be required in service packaging, marketing reach and communication integration, among other things (see Figure10).

"One-size-fits-all" no longer works in our heterogeneous marketplace. Simply put, to segment is to succeed.

2. Innovate: Take risks today with business models, pricing, windows and packaging. To avoid losing market position in the long term, you must be willing to risk aspects of your business today in the name of future success. To optimize uptake and profitability, companies across the TV landscape should:

- Create new innovative content, delivery models, pricing and packages
- Go to market with a dynamic schedule
- Calibrate pricing across all new and old windows of opportunity.

Figure 10. Suppliers will need divergent strategies for divergent consumers.

	Lean back consumers	Lean forward consumers	
	Massive Passives	**Gadgetiers**	**Kool Kids**
Screens	• TV	• HDTV • TV on PC	• TV on cell phone, PSP
Content preferences	• BBC World News • Good Morning America • World Cup Soccer • Monday Night Football	• The Office preview episodes • Daily Show interactive • CNET news segments	• Ring tones of Alias • Lost video blog • GameTap
Content consumption	• Appointment TV • Prime-time	• On demand • On replay via DVR • On own time	• P2P download • On replay via DVR • On demand to mobile device
Advertising	• 30-second spots • Program-integrated messages	• Click-throughs • Long-form/short-form content • Program-integrated messages	• Social networking links • Instant Message (IM) advertisements • Short-form content
Communication applications	• Traditional applications for each device	• Multi-purpose devices • Cell phone programming of DVRs and other convenience-oriented services	• Constant social connection across devices • Instant messaging and communities on TV screen
Service packages	• Bundled TV channels • Bundled "triple plays"	• A la carte niche channels • On demand season's pass by program	• Bundled channels (parents) • A la carte mobile VOD
Marketing outlets	• Best Buy • Reitangruppen • Wal-Mart	• BitTorrent • Google • Del.icio.us • Bic-Camera Yurakucho	• My Space • Facebook • Hi5

Sources: IBM Institute for Business Value analysis.

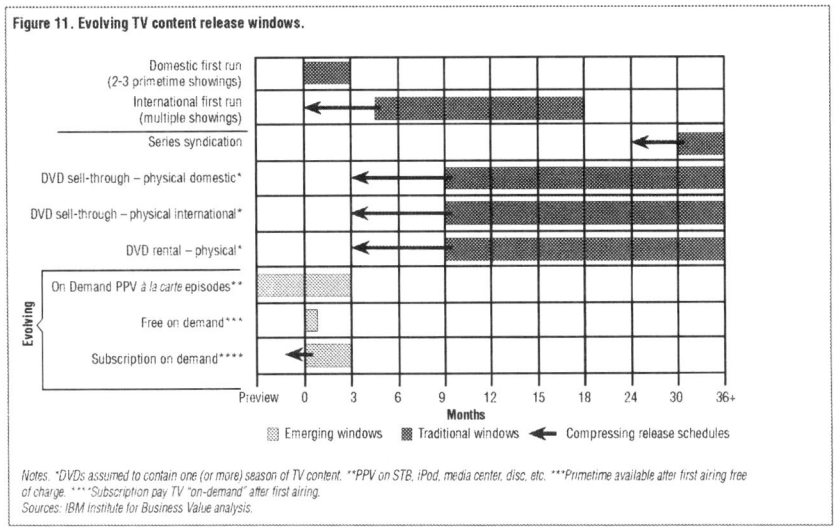

Figure 11. Evolving TV content release windows.

Notes: *DVDs assumed to contain one (or more) season of TV content. **PPV on STB, iPod, media center, disc, etc. ***Primetime available after first airing free of charge. ****"Subscription pay TV "on-demand" after first airing.
Sources: IBM Institute for Business Value analysis.

What does this mean? To start, companies will need a balanced, yet aggressive, stance toward new content bundles and packaging. For an executive upstream on the value chain, this will mean embracing new content form functions, as well as new delivery models such as subscription content on demand, free on demand, and *à la carte* pay-per-view (PPV); for an executive downstream, these necessary risks may span from *à la carte* channel rate cards to "quad play" mass bundling.

The economic pie will increase with more consumer choice. But, managing the right content (bundle, de-bundle or splice of content) *at the right time with the right price* will be critical for profits (see Figure 11).

Content will have to be divorced from its traditional platform or schedule in order to open new revenue sources. Illustrations include:

- Paid user content on demand (subscriptions or pay-per-view): Best suited for first-run shows or valuable branded archival programs with long commercial lifecycles. Includes "season passes," *à la carte* purchases and "long-tail."[42] niche acquisitions. Strategy capitalizes on user willingness to fund content directly; opens another revenue source.
- Free user content on demand: Best suited for content that is untethered to long commercial lifecycles. Includes perishable content (nightly news, weekly commentary, and late-night comedy), back-catalog, non-branded niche content or that funded by public license. Strategy extends loyalty, viewership and/or advertising reach.

At the same time, executives are charged with studying and reassessing pricing strategies. To optimize income, providers need to weight the price consumers will bear (with each package and offering, new and old) against all associated delivery and opportunity costs. For example, cost analysis for new digital downloads and on demand models will have to include physical transport, licensing costs and partner revenue-sharing, as well as lost revenues from traditional sources, like advertising. Further, strategists must face the ultimate question for the bottom line: "What pricing strategy forestalls the next illegal P2P forum, and keeps consumers in the fold?"

To fully leverage the complex demands from consumers, savvy providers need to commit to the ongoing innovation of business models, release windows and pricing strategy. Doing nothing is almost certainly the costliest option of all.

3. *Experiment: Develop, trial, refine, roll-out. Repeat.* Innovation only comes to life through experimentation and trial. In this age of complexity and uncertainty, ongoing experiments need to test uncharted territory. To win in the future, companies should:

- Conduct market trials *now* to gauge consumer behavior "in action"
- Constantly refine products
- Invest in underlining new metrics for new models.

At industry pivot points, user feedback arguably has its greatest impact. As such, companies must repeatedly test consumers on service options, product attributes, brand perception, pricing schemes and user-friendliness, to name only a few.

For illustration, consider next generation advertising models. With advertisers funding half the industry[43] and the DVR threatening revenue stability, it is paramount to surface and test models which augment (or replace) the 30-second spot. To invest most astutely in tomorrow, companies will need to be guided by demonstrated user acceptance, attention, retention, click-throughs and buy-rates associated with each new possible advertising model. In this case, options will range from short- or long-form advertising, interactive merchandising or time-sensitive overlays for archived on demand (see Figure 12). While advertising is the highlighted example, emerging content models and delivery channels all need to pass through similar rigorous trials and experimentation. And, experimentation cannot be a static exercise . . . it is a continual process with ongoing

Figure 12. The spectrum of possible future advertising models.

	Broadcast ads	Product placement and sponsorship	Operator driven ads	Localized ads/ targeted ads	Short- and long-form content	Customized video on demand	Interactive merchandise	Value added content	Time sensitive ad inserts
Potential revenue models	• Traditional cost per thousand (CPM)	• Fee-based model	• Premium CPM • Revenue-sharing • Cost per click-through (CPC)	• Premium CPM • CPC	• Premium CPM • CPC	• Video on demand (VOD) CPM • CPC	• Revenue-sharing on merchandise • CPC	• Premium CPM • CPC	• Premium CPM • CPC
	Low				Implementation complexity				High

Source: IBM Institute for Business Value analysis.

results which contribute to the dynamic refinement and distillation of the right end-user product.

To bolster new business models (advertising and far beyond), companies must invest in new metrics to monitor progress and success. Traditional metrics, like audience ratings, have not been based on realtime, individualized data. Instead, sampling methods were used to generalize consumer behavior.

In order to deliver segmented and tailored media experiences, it is imperative to capture more granular measurements and metrics. From individualized audience-tracking to click-stream analysis in the living room, companies will need new tracking systems to support more on demand and pseudo-individualized products, services and models.

As the industry transitions from a broadcast environment to its next manifesta-tion, companies must be dedicated not only to ongoing trials and experiments, but also to a culture and mantra of experimentation.

4. *Mobilize: Create seamless content mobility.* Companies have to strive to take content mobile for tech-forward users like Gadgetiers who want their entertainment and content "on the go." These users have steep requirements for portability of their devices, media and experiences, and keeping apace of user demand will require companies to:

- Deliver easy synchronization among devices
- Provide consumer-friendly services without required user modification.

Two early market examples illustrate an evolutionary trek for mobile content. TiVo ToGo, a service extension offered by U.S.-based TiVo, enables users to move recorded TV programs from their home TiVo DVR to PCs, MS Windows-based portable devices or DVD-Rs. As of September 2000, TiVoToGo had an install base of 1.1 million users with the requisite physical hardware.[44]

Another company, Porto Media, leverages retail space to introduce and assist in mobile experiences. This Irish service provider and technology developer has launched a flash memory module that enables fast, secure, digital content downloads via in-store kiosks to secure digital (SD) cards. With Porto Media technology, a DVD quality movie can be burned to an SD card in less than 20 seconds.[45]

Industry Perspectives:

"Customers want content across platforms. This is the three-screen future."

—*North American IPTV Telecom Executive*[46]

Industry players need to act or consumers will simply find low-cost solutions of their own. For example, two key components of do-it-yourself services—video streaming and video storage costs—are tumbling downward, *à la* Moore's Law. Total costs of 10,000 hours of video storage are projected to shrink from US$2205 in 2005 to US$56 by 2010, and significant cost declines are also forecasted for

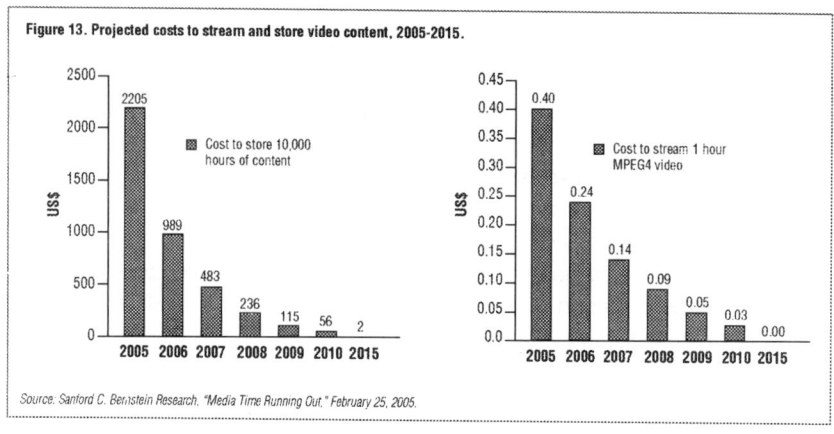

Figure 13. Projected costs to stream and store video content, 2005-2015.

Source: Sanford C. Bernstein Research, "Media Time Running Out," February 25, 2005.

streaming video (see Figure 13).[47] If providers do not act quickly, self-sufficient, high-value consumers (namely those of the Gadgetier ilk) will likely choose to create their own mobile services rather than pay TV value chain players to play.

5. *Open: Open and standards-based content delivery platforms.* Companies up and down the TV value chain need open and standards-based delivery networks to optimize content development and distribution—as well as to enable continuous improvements in business flexibility and network cost-efficiency. Forward-thinking companies can leverage these capabilities to bolster content protection (with enhanced consumer flexibility) and for essential plug-and-play upgrades necessary in the ever-changing marketplace. This includes standards-based or open:

- Interfaces
- Content ingestion/indexing
- Encryption/decryption
- Encoding/decoding
- Middleware
- Storage
- Home networking, and much more.

By moving to such optimized delivery platforms, companies have reported positive movement along performance metrics: faster time-to-market with new products, improved agility in reacting to production needs, reduced cost structure, improved asset use better integration of third-party content, improved procurement leverage, greater responsiveness to market demands, reallocation of resources to value-added activities and much more. Several companies have begun large-scale initiatives in this area:

- The National Football League (NFL), the body which oversees the most popular U.S. sport, as well as its NFL Films division, implemented an open digital workflow in order to optimize content collection, management and use. Its network is "architected" as the digital foundation for content creation and distribution. The NFL enables on demand access to its films division for every play from every game on a weekly basis, allowing editors, producers and analysts to access any game content for near-realtime repurposing and distribution in new programming.

- China Central Television or CCTV, China's largest national TV network with fifteen content channels and international coverage, launched an all-digital TV solution with centralized storage across the enterprise. The all-digital supply chain allows consumer services such as viewing archived video or live broadcasts over a standard IP network. On an open platform, CCTV is able to upgrade features and services as needed.

- Singapore telecommunications carrier MoblieOne Ltd. moved to an open delivery solution to manage, provision and bill for delivery of downloadable content services to a variety of mobile devices. With its open delivery solution, MobileOne Ltd. can deliver multiple content types to different devices using different protocols.

High Definition (HD) and Standards-Based Initiatives

Consumers go for it. HDTV is ready to take off around the world. HDTV sets boast four times as much picture information on the screen as "regular" TV, creating a higher resolution picture and richer viewing experience. With a widescreen aspect ratio (16:9), better sound quality (often Dolby 5.1 or better), and ready content for sports fans and cinephiles, consumers are trading up current TV sets as prices drop. Five years ago, an HDTV 32-inch set might have cost US$5000, but today average prices are dropping below US$1000 in major Asian, U.S. and U.K. retail outlets. As a result, by 2009, the HDTV market is expected to grow to US$65 billion in the U.S. alone.[48]

Industry promotes content management standards. As HDTV rolls out, content owners, technology and electronics companies are working together on next generation content management for HD optical media in Advanced Access Content System Licensing Administrator—(AACS LA). The major studios and consumer electronics firms have been enmeshed in a "format war" between Blu-ray and HD-DVD. Whichever format is chosen, the content owners and electronics companies are dedicated to using the HD technology inflection point to industry advantage by introducing more compelling entertainment experiences, with more secure formats and greater storage for additional value-added content, HD with robust content management technology will create opportunities for new business models for content owners, distributors, content aggregators and electronics companies.

6. *Reorganize: Assess assets and company "make up" against future requirements.* In planning for future competitiveness, forward-thinking executives must conduct inward and outward examinations of their business. To compete amid growing market complexity, companies must:

• Harness differentiated skills and competencies
• Leverage financial markets to buy, build or team to future success.

First, companies must turn the analytic microscope inwardly and identify the array of differentiated skills and competencies needed for future competitiveness and advantage. Concurrently, executives should also assess the aspects of business which are basic and, therefore ripe for consolidation, outsourcing or partnering. Through this process of "componentizing" the business, companies can focus on components—or groups of business activities—that move the enterprise toward greater future specialization in comparison to competitors. In doing so, a leaner, stronger company of tomorrow can be built by securing differentiated and competitive assets, while the rest are delivered most cost-efficiently and without disproportionate management attention.

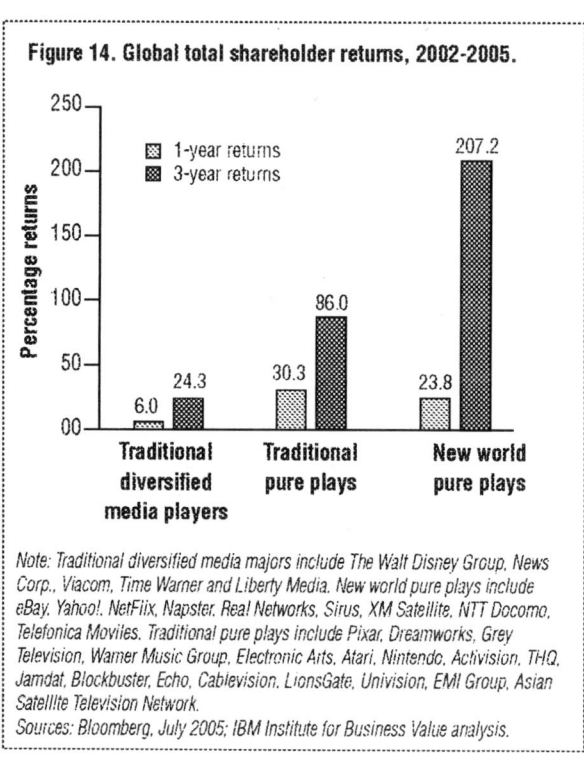

Figure 14. Global total shareholder returns, 2002-2005.

Note: Traditional diversified media majors include The Walt Disney Group, News Corp., Viacom, Time Warner and Liberty Media. New world pure plays include eBay, Yahoo!, NetFlix, Napster, Real Networks, Sirus, XM Satellite, NTT Docomo, Telefonica Moviles. Traditional pure plays include Pixar, Dreamworks, Grey Television, Warner Music Group, Electronic Arts, Atari, Nintendo, Activision, THQ, Jamdat, Blockbuster, Echo, Cablevision. LionsGate, Univision, EMI Group, Asian Satellite Television Network.
Sources: Bloomberg, July 2005; IBM Institute for Business Value analysis.

Companies also need to understand how best to optimize and leverage worldwide financial markets to buy, build or team to future competitiveness. The market itself has indicated favor for less diversified or pure-play media and entertainment companies. Financial markets have valued pure-play media organizations manifold over traditionally diversified companies (see Figure 14).

This recognition prompts another avenue for strategic analysis and decision-making. Within the next five to seven years, large TV/media companies should strategically capitalize on financial market trends with divestitures, vertical mergers and acquisitions, or company business unit spin-offs. We believe this period will be marked by concurrent disaggregation and reaggregation.

Reorganization is critical for market resilience and repositioning. Savvy executives must consider this lever—as well as those mentioned in the other recommendations—in the battle for future stronghold.

Conclusion: The Beginning of the End . . . Adapt or Succumb

"The end of TV as we know it" describes an industry facing changing consumer demand, misaligned traditional business models, converged competition and burgeoning IP services. Players within the TV industry sit on the precipice of an impending upheaval that promises to be no less dramatic than that experienced by the music industry.

Given the bimodal demand predicted through 2012, strategists must work amid fragmentation, divergence and opposition in the market to optimize across nascent and long-standing business models; across new and traditional release windows; with old and new content programmers and aggregators; and with both IP and traditional supply chains.

At a time of exquisite change in both demand and supply, immediate action is required. The six recommended priority actions offer a blueprint for proactive strategy. While each tenet is universal, it is incumbent upon each TV industry competitor to view the recommendations through the prism of its own particular business circumstances and uniquely prepare for the disruptiveness—and opportunity—ahead.

About the Authors

Dr. Saul J. Berman is a Partner, Global and Americas Business Strategy leader and Americas Media and Entertainment Strategy and Change Leader with IBM Business Consulting Services. In 2005, Saul was named one of the top 25 most influential consultants by *Consulting Magazine.* Saul has co-authored other titles including "Vying for Attention." "The Open Media Company" and "Beyond Access." Saul can be reached at *saulberman@us.ibm.com.*

Niall Duffy is an Associate Partner with IBM Business Consulting Services. Niall heads the Broadcast Solutions practice for Europe, the Middle East and Africa. Niall can be reached at *niall.dutty@uk.ibm.com.*

Louisa A. Shipnuck is the Global Media and Entertainment Industry Leader at the IBM Institute for Business Value and a Managing Consultant with IBM Business Consulting Services. Louisa can be reached at *louisa.a.shipnuck@us .ibm.com.*

Contributors

The authors wish to thank executive advisors Steven Abraham, Dick Anderson, William Battino, Steven Canepa, Jeanette Carlsson, Edward Hanapole, William Humphrey, Stephen Mannel, Neil Parker and Sony Suzuki. Further thanks are extended to contributing consultants Matthew Bakal. Hunter Gorog, Apur Parikh and the many IBM professionals who contributed expertise.

Acknowledgments

We would like to give a special thanks to those who participated in the study and interviews, but have chosen not to be named.

About IBM Business Consulting Services

With business experts in more than 160 countries. IBM Business Consulting Services provides clients with deep business, process and industry expertise across 17 industries, using innovation to identify, create and deliver value faster. We draw on the full breadth of IBM capabilities, standing behind our advice to help clients innovate and implement solutions designed to deliver business outcomes with far-reaching impact and sustainable results.

Notes

1. "Archives: Michael Faraday." The IEE. Institute of Electrical Engineers. http://www .iee.org/TheIEE/Research/Archives/Histories&Biographies/Faraday.cfm.
2. "Communications Industry Forecast and Report." Veronis Suhler Stevenson Media Merchant Bank. 2004.
3. Ibid.
4. Nielsen Media Research; U.S. Dept. of Labor; Sanford C. Bernstein, "Television: I'm Not Dead Yet." October 7, 2005.
5. "Communications Industry Forecast and Report." Veronis Suhler Stevenson Media Merchant Bank. 2004.
6. Rideout, Victoria, Donald F. Roberts, et al. "Generation M: Media in the Lives of 8–18 year olds." Kaiser Family Foundation Study. March 2005.
7. Ibid.
8. Nielsen Media Research; Sanford C. Bernstein, "Cable Networks: 2Q Data Affirms Slowing Ratings," June 26, 2005.
9. "Global Entertainment & Media Outlook: 2005–2009." PriceWaterhouseCoopers. June 2005.
10. Garrity, Brian. "Podcast at the Crossroads." Billboard. October 1, 2005.
11. International Federation of the Periodical Press Report. http://www.fipp.com/assets/downloads/05InternationalSummary.pdf
12. Internet Systems Consortium. http://isc.org/

13. "Communications Industry Forecast and Report." Veronis Suhler Stevenson Media Merchant Bank. 2004.

14. "Global Entertainment & Media Outlook: 2005–2009." PriceWaterhouseCoopers. June 2005.

15. Ibid.

16. Ibid.

17. IBM Institute for Business Value survey conducted by the Economist Intelligence Unit.

18. Wolzien, Tom and Mark Mackenzie. "Pipe Dreams: Media's Exploding Capacity" Sanford C. Bernstein. May 2004.

19. Hilton, Mike, Daniel Kerven, et al. "DVR—Broadcasters' Nemesis?" UBS Investment Research, Q-Series. October 8, 2004.

20. Executive interview conducted by the IBM Institute for Business Value.

21. "Global Entertainment & Media Outlook: 2005–2009." PriceWaterhouseCoopers. June 2005.

22. "2004 Year-End Industry Overview." National Cable and Telecommunications Association.

23. Ibid.

24. Bernoff, Josh. "The Advertising Model for Video On-Demand." Forrester Research. May 5, 2005.

25. Klasnik, Kathleen and Adrian Drozd. "IPTV: broadcasting over broadband: The emergence of a fourth platform for digital TV?" Datamonitor. April 2004.

26. "VOD Still Won't Grow in Europe." Forrester Research. December 2004.

27. Katz, Raymond Lee, Bryan Goldberg, et al. "Comcast Corporation: What's in a Share Price?" Bear Stearns Equity Research. June 8, 2005.

28. Ibid.

29. Executive interview conducted by the IBM Institute for Business Value.

30. Siklos, Richard and Geraldine Fabrikant. "For 'CSI', Press A1" *The New York Times.* November 12, 2005.

31. BBC Governors. "Annual Report and Accounts 2004/2005." Review of Objectives.

32. Wagner, Curt and Kris Karnopp. "Video on the go; Welcome to TV anytime you want it." *Los Angeles Times.* November 2, 2005.

33. "RIAA 1999 Year End Statistics." Recording Industry Association of America. 1999. http://www.riaa.com/news/marketingdata/pdf/md_riaa10yr.pdf

34. Grimes, Christopher. "Play it again—Napster proved there was a demand for online music." *The Financial Times.* August 29, 2001.

35. Bernoff, Josh. "Music Lessons: Is Your Industry At Risk?" Forrester Research. September 29, 2005.

36. "Clear Victory for Recording Industry in Napster Case." Recording Industry Association of America. February 13, 2001. http://www.riaa.com/news/newsletter/press2001/021301.asp.

37. Bernoff, Josh. "Music Lessons: Is Your Industry At Risk?" Forrester Research. September 29, 2005.

38. "Global Entertainment & Media Outlook: 2005–2009." PriceWaterhouseCoopers. June 2005.

39. Ibid.

40. Moffett, Craig and Michael Nathanson. "Turn Off Day is Coming but at What Cost and to Whom?" Sanford C. Bernstein. October 28, 2005.

41. Ibid.

42. The "long tail" concept: "our culture and economy is increasingly shifting away from a focus on a relatively small number of 'hits' (mainstream products and markets) at the head of the demand curve and toward a huge number of niches in the tail."

Anderson, Chris. "The Long Tail." *Wired.* October 2004. http://www.thelongtail.com/about.html.

43. "Global Entertainment & Media Outlook: 2005–2009." PriceWaterhouseCoopers. June 2005.

44. "TiVo tests video 'on-demand'." Online Reporter. August 1, 2005.

45. "Porto Media, IBM team up for new digital content delivery service." SelfServiceWorld September 9, 2005. http://www.selfserviceworld.com/article.php?id=3723&prc=299&page=75.

46. Executive interview conducted by the IBM Institute for Business Value.

47. Wolzein, Tom and Mark Mackenzie. "Media: Time Running Out to Protect Video; Rights Management Essential to Monetize Content." Sanford C. Bernstein, February 25, 2005.

48. Parks Associates. "HDTV Sales in the U.S. to Grow 71% by 2009." Market Wire. October 27, 2005. http://www.parksassociates.com/press/press_releases/2005/hdtv-1.html.

Additional Media and Entertainment Publications

• Berman, Dr. Saul J., Adam R. Steinberg and Louisa A. Shipnuck. "Beyond access: Raising the value of information in a cluttered environment." IBM Institute for Business Value. June 2005. http://www-1.ibm.com/services/us/indiex.wss/ibvstudy/imc/a1011966?cntxt=a1000062

• Berman, Dr. Saul J. "Media and entertainment 2010: Open on the inside, open on the outside: The open media company of the future." IBM Institute for Business Value. March 2004. http://www-1.ibm.com/services/us/index.wss/ibvstudy/imc/a1001755?cntxt=a1000062

• Parker, Neil. "The 30-hour day: On demand for media and entertainment." IBM Institute for Business Value. August 2003. http://www-1.ibm.com/services/us/index.wss/ibvstudy/imc/a1001309?cntxt=a1000062

• Berman, Dr. Saul J. "Vying for attention: The future of competing in media and entertainment. Our industry perspective 2001–2005." IBM Institute for Business Value. November 2002. http://www-03.ibm.com/industries/media/doc/isp/resource/thought/index.jsp

IBM.

Introduction: Where in the World Are We?

Samuel Weber

In May and June of 1992 I spent several weeks in Australia giving a series of lectures, seminars and interviews. Out of the intense and exhilarating exchanges that marked my visit came the idea of collecting the various talks and discussions into a volume. The result is *Mass Mediauras: Form, Technics, Media*. The book is a collective effort, if ever there was one. But it is a curious collection, in more ways than one. First of all, the persons involved in its production came from highly divergent backgrounds and, to some extent at least, were moving in equally divergent directions. What made the exchange of views fruitful and exciting was the fact that, despite, or rather, because of, such divergencies, everyone was willing and able to put themselves, their projects and their premises into question. This, however, is easier said than done. For questioning is never innocent. No question can ever be asked without some sort of answer being anticipated. One can, however, distinguish between questions asked primarily to reach an answer and a questioning that is after something else, something that can not be measured in strictly cognitive terms.

Such is the questioning that traverses this book. This might not be immediately evident. For the essays and discussions collected in it often take the form of statements, propositions, declarations. And yet such assertiveness knows better what it is challenging than where it is going. One of the beliefs being so challenged is nothing less than the touchstone upon which much of modernity has relied in defining itself: the notion of its radical distinctiveness from all that has come—or gone—before. Nothing is more modern than the idea of the radical break, separating the 'new' decisively from the 'old'. A classic articulation of this sentiment is the declaration with which Rousseau introduces his *Confessions*: 'I feel my heart and I know people. I am made like no one existing. If I am no better, then at least I am different'.

It is precisely the nature of this *difference* that is in question in this book. In place of the perspective that construes difference in terms of an interval or interstitial break—*either* something is different *or* it is the same—the essays gathered in this volume display difference more as a structuring fissure or fracture. In the sense of a Heideggerian *Riß*-potentially dividing and fracturing individual works, brushing them against the grain, as it were, deforming and dislocating them and in the process making way for a spaciousness in which the remote and the intimate uncannily converge.

This convergence is both a very old story and yet surprisingly new. It confounds the still prevalent conception of history as a more or less linear, if not developmental, process. Instead, the figure of history that emerges from the readings undertaken in this book is one of conflict, compromise and negotiation, resulting not so much in *breaks* as in *shifts,* that is, in a movement that is never simply irreversible.

The terrain upon which these shifts play themselves is demarcated on the one side by the aesthetically oriented notions of art and reality, form and work, and on the other by that of media. If the word 'media' is used here without a definite or defining article, it is because one of its singular characteristics is to undercut the ostensibly clear-cut oppositional relationship between singular and plural, general and particular, genre and work, and in so doing, to call attention to the irreducible significance of the space in-between—and outside of—such polar oppositions. To retrace mediatic articulation at work within the boundaries of the individual *work* is to call attention to the way in which what had hitherto been considered to be accessory and intermediary—the program, its transmission, reception, storage, recycling, retransmission, etc.—infiltrates the inner integrity of the work, revealing it to be inscribed in, and as, a *network.*[1]

It is not that the idea of a radical discontinuity—the break—thereby disappears or is invalidated. Far from it. Rather, such discontinuity is shown to be itself continually at work within the work itself. As network, the work reveals itself to be what it has probably always been: a relational process which depends as much upon what it is not as upon what it is.

Such dependency or relationality brings with it an important corollary, one that again goes against the idea of a radical break separating the old from the new, the other(s) from the Self. As the passage from Rousseau's *Confessions* indicates, the radicality of the New can ultimately be measured only in terms of the emergence of a unique and distinctive subject, and ultimately, of an *I*: 'I may be no better, but at least I am different (*au moins je suis autre)*'. What diverges from the past decisively and definitively is ultimately an *individual* (even if that individual can come to be identified with a *collective*). The 'break' becomes the setting for that which is supposedly *unbreakable:* in-dividual. One nation, indivisible . . . *E pluribus unum.*

By contrast with this scheme, the following essays tell the story not so much of the individual Self as of its highly divisible *Settings.* This is a book about *places* and *positioning* rather than about human beings. Or rather, it suggests that the *being* of human being has had more to do with *setups* and *sets* than with *subjects* and *objects,* unified in and through self-consciousness. By focusing upon an emerging crisis in the definition of space and place, the essays here collected retrace how the development of aesthetic theory can be understood as a (perhaps ultimate) effort to defend the notion of the indivisibility of place as a condition of the individuality of the subject. This effort to establish a concept of place as self-contained and unified, as well as the problems it encounters, can be traced back to the earliest stages of Western philosophy—to Plato's discussion of the *chora* in the *Timaeus*[2]—and there is every indication that the task has become one of the most powerful forces driving the modern period. For without the unity of place, the unity of the subject becomes difficult to conceive. It is the function of aesthetic theory, as it is developed by Kant, to help secure this ever more problematical unity of place by introducing the no less problematical notion of *form.* That Kant's effort, in the Third Critique, is more significant in coming undone than in succeeding 'sets' the scene for the following essays, which explore the unraveling of form as the 'setting' for the rise of the media.

The relation of form, place and media is, to be sure, highly complex, conflictual and dynamic. It is above all a relation of forces rather than of substances, subjects or entities. Two recent events can serve as indications of how this relation shapes the contemporary situation.

Shortly after the January 17, 1994 Northridge earthquake, a front page article appeared in the *Los Angeles Times* under the heading, 'Where in the World are We?'. It introduced its readers to the story of the emergence of a new technology: a worldwide satellite system developed by the Pentagon for purposes of military surveillance, and which now was being increasingly adapted to civilian uses. The system bore the acronym GPS, for *Global Positioning System.* Through its intervention, movement on the earth could now be located with a precision heretofore impossible. It was GPS that enabled geologists to determine the movements of the Los Angeles basin following the January earthquake with unprecedented accuracy and speed, just as the same technology had allowed the Allied military commanders to locate, and annihilate, units of the Iraqi Army in the so-called 'Gulf War'.

'Where in the World are We?' One answer is that we are in a world overseen, in its planetary totality, by GPS. Small black-box GPS-receivers are now showing up in taxies and trucks, permitting drivers to determine their location instantaneously and precisely. In that sense, at least, we—or others—can soon hope to know *just exactly where we are.* As mobile as we may be, or become, we are even more *localizable.* We are, as it were, on call—and from this call it is difficult to imagine any escape.

This brings me to the second incident. It was the televised spectacle of O.J. Simpson, invisible in a white 'Bronco', returning to his home after an unsuccessful attempt at escaping arrest for the brutal murder of his former wife and her friend. Sports and its practitioners have long been a cultural paradigm for American society, and the power of that paradigm is inseparable from the advent of the media. The one 'mirrors' the other, in complex and intricate ways. Certain aspects of that relationship are interpreted in this book, in particular at the end of the essay 'Television: Set and Screen'.

The prime-time spectacle of O.J.'s Homecoming brought to the fore another decisive element in the fascination sports exercises upon America in the Age of Media. O.J. Simpson made his athletic reputation above all as a running back. His most memorable sporting achievements involved precisely what the final cortege both recalled and mourned: the ability to *break out* of what seems to be—and what in reality generally is—an inextricable confinement and to *break through* what appear to be—and in reality generally are—insuperable obstacles. To *break out* and *break through*, however, one must first be enclosed, embedded, in a firm and fixed location (the sort of location that GPS appears at long last to offer and to confirm).

It is this ambivalence, between the desire to occupy a place of one's very own and the desire to break out of a place in which one is caught, that is raised to incalculable proportions in the modern period generally and in the Age of the Media more particularly. Hence, the pathos that *riveted*—the word is hardly fortuitous here—millions of viewers to their TV *sets* at dinnertime, as that 'white Bronco', escorted by a phalanx of LAPD vehicles, with countless television helicopters whirring overhead, made its slow, ceremonious way along the Los Angeles 'free-ways', past the cars slowed down on the opposite side of the road, past the throngs gathered on the overpasses, towards an uncertain but inevitable destination: 'home'.

The hero comes home, but the sport goes on. The essays in this volume recount the sport of homecoming and the homecoming of sport as a movement that is reducible neither to escape nor to return, to breaking out nor breaking through. A movement difficult to name, and surely impossible to name univocally, it nevertheless emerges, in the following pages, as having something to do with what an older form of discourse called: *coming-to-pass*.

In the age of the media, things, people and places *come to pass,* in an *event* more sportive than any sporting event, and more spectacular than any spectacle. It is the coming-to-pass of such an event that these essays seek to stage. Such a staging opens onto questions far richer than any imaginable answers: how do 'technics', film and television, the 'setup' and the 'set', change our relation to *places, positions* and *emplacements*? What is left over when *forms unravel* and *works* come undone? What happens to reality when our traditional access to it— sense-perception—is no longer restricted to the individual body? What comes *after deconstruction*? What is *coming to pass*?

So many questions, so few answers. If a book is measured by the answers it gives to the questions it raises, then this is not a book, or—what amounts to the same—not a very good one. But despite the need for reassurance that, understandably, has become increasingly insistent over the past years, questions do not go away simply because they seem to have been 'answered', any more than problems disappear when they seem to have been 'solved'.

We live in an age of increasing uncertainty, when the solutions and answers that were taken for granted until recently no longer seem viable. It is an age in which the technology and media that were supposed to bring about the 'global village' have contributed to the revival of 'ethnic cleansing' and religious fundamentalism. It is an age in which economic competitiveness goes hand in hand with mass unemployment, when 'prosperity' means growing economic inequalities and when the much heralded end of the Cold War coincides with spreading social and political disintegration.

One of the few advantages of this strange and dangerous age is the possibility not just of asking questions but of letting them make their way, without feeling obliged to provide definitive answers. This is a book of questions, then, and of curious conclusions, for readers who can confront problems without demanding recipes of salvation.

It is also a way of saying thanks to those participants and interlocutors in Australia whose hospitality demonstrated what seems to be increasingly overlooked in our age of identificatory constraint: that the encounter with the other need not be simply a threat to oneself.

A special word of thanks goes to Alan Cholodenko, Head of the Power Department of Fine Arts, whose initiative is responsible both for my visit to Australia and for this book. Without his tireless efforts and incisive editorial input none of this would have been possible.

Notes

1. See, in this context, the pioneering work of Friedrich Kittler, and in particular his *Discourse Networks 1800/1900, 1990*. Kittler's work, despite its unquestionable qualities, remains informed by the notion of the radical break alluded to above, which in turn reintroduces the traditional hermeneutics of the subject and of meaning by the back door of technological determinism.

2. See the remarkable text of Jacques Derrida, *Khora,* 1993. See also my discussion of the *chora* in 'The Parallax View', *assemblage* 20, 1993.

Television: Set and Screen

Samuel Weber

The following remarks seek to explore a phenomenon that is so close to us, so ubiquitous and so powerful, that it has proved particularly resistant to thought. Not that there has not been an enormous amount of literature written on the subject of television, much of which is extremely illuminating. But in reading through such work, one is struck by the fact that as soon as empirical description is forsaken and analysis or interpretation attempted, the results are generally quite disappointing. They are disappointing not because what they have to say is wrong or irrelevant but because the attempted analysis rarely seems to take sufficiently into account the *distinctive specificity of the medium.* What we most often find are content-analyses, which could just as well apply to other media, for example, to film or to literature. And where an effort is made to go beyond content-analysis to a discussion of formal elements, the latter in turn are generally borrowed from more traditional aesthetic genres—for instance, narrative fiction—thus leaving the question of the specificity of the televisual medium itself unaddressed.[1]

And yet, a simple *reaction* to this neglect or omission, one which would strive to articulate just what it is that makes television *different* and distinct from previous aesthetic media, almost inevitably finds itself confronted by another trap: that of ontologizing television.[2] The attempt to work out the *differential specificity* of the medium—to get at that which distinguishes it from other media—runs the risk of transforming, albeit unawares, a *differential determination* into a *positive* and *universal essence.* The apparently innocent fact that we use a singular noun, 'television', to designate an extremely complex and variegated phenomenon can all too easily encourage us to overlook the heterogeneity of the medium with which we are concerned.

This is why it seems advisable at the outset to emphasize that to attempt to uncover something of the specificity of television does not necessarily mean to suppose that the medium possesses an invariable and universally valid essence or structure. Rather, *specificity* here is used as a *differential category:* television is *different,* not just from *film,* as has often been observed and explored, but also from what we generally mean by the word *perception.* Television—despite its name—involves the transmission of sight *and sound;* and yet to take the *specificity* of it as a mode of transmission into account is to *distinguish* the way the sights and sounds it transmits are apprehended from the way sights and sounds have hitherto been perceived. Television entails artifice, technique and even technology; and yet here, too, its specificity is constituted by the way its technique *differs* from what we have previously called 'art' and 'aesthetics'.[3]

But the *constitutive heterogeneity* of television does not stop at such external contrasts and demarcations. What is perhaps most difficult, but also most important, to keep in mind are the ways in which what we call *television*—a singular noun—also *and above all differs from itself.* Television differs from itself in a number of ways. In the first place, the singular noun covers a complex process that can be divided into at least three distinct, albeit closely interrelated, operations. For the sake of convenience, those operations can be described by using terms that antedate the advent of television and that therefore may not be entirely apt to designate what is at stake in this medium. Nevertheless, in order not to complicate the matter excessively here at the outset, let us say that television consists primarily of three operations: *production, transmission* and *reception.* However unified one may take the medium of television to be, it should not be forgotten that the singular noun hides these interrelated but also very different operations, each of which raises a set of very distinct questions and issues.

However, this is not the only way in which 'television' can be said to differ from itself and, in so doing, to raise questions about its internal unity and self-identity. Other aspects of the diversity of the medium are related to differences that can be called 'cultural', 'national', 'linguistic' and 'socioeconomic'. By contrast, few discussions of television take this diversity sufficiently into account or even allow for its consideration. Most are restricted to the television of a single nation and, within that country, are generally limited to a single language. This is difficult to avoid, but it is possible to study and compare televisions of different countries and languages. What is far more difficult today, however, is to appreciate the differential specificity of socioeconomic factors, simply because a radical socioeconomic alternative to a capitalist market system has become almost impossible to find. Nevertheless, within that overall and increasingly global system, there remain sufficient differences to provide a kind of internal criterion for comparison. For instance, television in the United States and television in Europe remain even today sufficiently diverse to make any attempt at generalization based on only one national television extremely hazardous. To be sure, there is an undeniable tendency of American television to impose its laws, features and programming upon the other televisions of the world; and it also seems likely that this tendency towards homogenization is not unrelated to the global dynamics of the televisual medium itself. But the differences are still there, and they must be taken into account if one hopes to articulate the distinctive specificity of the medium.[4]

Let me therefore clarify, at the outset, that my own discussion of television is based on the experience I have had of it in the United States, in France and in Germany. Although they are diminishing, the differences among the televisions of these three countries remain striking enough to caution against any hasty attempt at generalizing about 'the medium'. And yet, although I hope it does not come across as hasty, I will still attempt precisely to uncover certain underlying features that I take to be characteristic of the medium in its specificity. I will be speaking of television as it is found in the countries I mention, but I strongly suspect that many of these traits will obtain in the television of countries that I know nothing about. The fact remains that, however general the traits I describe may be, they are formulated on the basis of television *as it exists today* in three countries and therefore cannot pretend to exhaust *all* the possibilities of the medium. Nevertheless, if television today has assumed the forms it has, nothing would be more naive than to suppose that its development has been the result of purely *external* forces, be these determined historically, socially, economically, politically, culturally, linguistically or technologically. Rather, it seems far more likely that a profound *complicity* obtains between the *medium of television* and the *world* composed by those forces; and one of the aims of this investigation is to move toward an understanding of this complicity. It is an aim that at best can only be adumbrated within the limited scope of the present essay. For in approaching the question of television, we must take as little for granted as possible. Television is very close to us, it is increasingly widespread; but it is not, for all of its ubiquitousness, very well understood.

In order to allow the medium of television to unfold as a question, then, I will begin by taking a detour that may seem unnecessary to many of you. I will approach television by a reflection on the way we speak about it in English, but I will also upon occasion compare the ways television is named and articulated in certain other languages with which I am familiar, above all, French and German.

Let us start, then, with the word used in English to designate the medium with which we are concerned. *Television*—and the words are essentially equivalent in French and German—means, of course, something like 'seeing at a distance'. What does 'seeing at a distance' entail? If we translate the Graeco-Latinate word into more familiar English roots, we come up with a curious, but suggestive, result—*farsightedness*. In English, this word has two interestingly divergent meanings, one general and more 'figurative', the other more specific and more literal. In the more general and perhaps more common use, the term signifies not so much a particular act of sense-perception as a *way of being*. Farsighted is something one *is*, not *does*. To be *farsighted* is to be ready for any eventuality. The spatial connotation suggested by *far* is transformed here into a primarily temporal one: to be *farsighted* is to anticipate what is likely to happen in the more or less distant future and to take appropriate actions in advance. Yet the second meaning of the word contrasts curiously with the first. Here the spatial dimension reasserts itself, but only at the cost of a strange trade-off, for 'seeing far' in its medical use does not, of course, simply mean seeing *better*. To be far-sighted is to see things that are distant more clearly than those that are close at hand. It is the opposite of being nearsighted, and what it suggests is that the ability to see at a distance is heightened only at the expense of the ability to see what is closest. Both notions of 'farsightedness', then, include a defensive, compensatory connotation. Were this to be limited to an isolated linguistic instance, it would hardly be worth retaining. But as we shall see, the paradoxical combination of increased power with increased vulnerability is something that will confront us again and again as we proceed in our discussion of television.

Let us for the moment continue to pursue certain of its linguistic aspects. If the notion of 'distance' and, in general, considerations of space have received less attention in English-language discussions of television than has the dimension of time, it is perhaps in part because in English the prefix *tele-* has tended to be absorbed into the set of nouns that it modifies and thus to lose its semantic independence. In nouns such as *telepathy, telephone, telescope* and *telegraph,* the notion of 'distance' is preserved only as an *obstacle* to be *surmounted,* either by an intangible 'sixth sense' (telepathy) or, more frequently, by some sort of mechanical device or electronic apparatus (telescope, telephone, television). Moreover, the overcoming of distance in all of these cases is linked to the ability to transcend the spatial limitations usually associated with the body. This technological triumph over distance reaches something of a linguistic high-point in American English, where the prefix tele- disappears practically without a trace in the abbreviation *TV.* Whether or not the notion of distance remains closer to consciousness in languages such as British English or French, in which the prefix *tele-* is retained to designate the medium, is a question I will not try to answer here.

More important, in any case, is that 'distance' figures in the designation of the medium as an obstacle to be overcome, a fact that is made quite explicit in the French designation for 'remote control': *télécommande.* The question that emerges here is whether this 'accessory' does not name one of the deepest phantasms provoked by the medium itself. The fascination and power of television as medium would derive, in great part, from its promise of providing a *remote control,* commanding not just *at a distance* but *over distance as such.*

Such a promise, however, has long been associated with technology in general. Ever since Plato, one of the most decisive purposes in the development of art, artifice and technology has been interpreted to be that of overcoming the shortcomings of nature, human or otherwise. This relationship has also been the source of a continuing suspicion that the reliance upon technique and technology could well turn out to be a cure worse than the disease. To resort to 'artificial' means of overcoming 'natural' deficiencies would thus be to confirm, and perhaps to aggravate, a relationship of dependency. The modern attitude toward television continues this tradition of ambivalence toward technology in general.

If we restrict this account to the specific case of television, the limitation that is to be overcome is tied to the individual body. The body as such has always been defined by a certain spatial limitation. A body is thus understood as something that occupies a determinate extent of space and occupies it exclusively. From this it follows that a body, as traditionally construed, can be defined in part as that which occupies a place, and more precisely, which occupies one place at a time. This means both that a body cannot take place in *more* than one place at a time and that the place it 'takes' is held to be off-limits to all other bodies: two bodies cannot take or share the same place at the same time. (The case of the *parasite* may be cited here as the exception that proves the rule.)[5]

If television thus names 'seeing-at-a-distance', what it appears to overcome thereby is the body, or more precisely, the spatial limitations placed by the body upon seeing and hearing. But the same, it could be remembered, was done some 400 years earlier by the telescope. The comparison between the telescope, at least in its original, mechanical form, and television allows us to elaborate just what is peculiar to the particular 'farsightedness' of the latter. First of all, it is significant that we speak of 'the' telescope, using the definite article to designate a particular kind of apparatus or instrument, whereas we speak of 'television' in general, without any article at all. This usage suggests that while our relation to the telescope is above all that to a particular kind of instrument, our relation to television confounds both apparatus and the medium in general. A second distinction, proceeding from the first, is that in contrast to the telescope, television does not merely allow the viewer to 'see at a distance' things that otherwise would be invisible. It *transports vision as such* and *sets* it immediately *before* the viewer. It entails not merely a heightening of the naturally limited powers of sight with respect to certain distant *objects;* it involves a transmission or transposition of vision itself. The televisual spectator can see things from places—and hence, from perspectives and points of view (and it is not trivial that these are often more than one)—where his or her body is not (and often never can be) situated.

Television can thus be considered the most detached type of vision and audition—and we should never forget that, despite its name, it entails both seeing *and hearing*—Insofar as it makes vision available to its viewers independently of the limitations of their physical situation. In this sense, television *overcomes* distance and separation; but It can do so only because it also *becomes* separation. Like radio, which in a certain manner it incorporates,[6] television is perhaps first and foremost a method of *transmission*[7]*;* and transmission, which is movement, involves separation.

One could say that this was already the case for film and photography, and indeed, for any form of inscription. But what distinguishes television from these other media is its power to combine such separation with the presentness associated with sense-perception. What television transmits is not so much *images,* as is almost always argued. It does not transmit *representations* but rather *the semblance of presentation as such,* understood as the power not just to see and to hear but *to place before us.* Television thus serves as a surrogate for the body in that it allows for a certain sense-perception to take place: but it does this in a way that no body can, for its perception takes place in more than one place at a time. Television takes place in taking the place of the body and at the same time in transforming both place and body. For, by definition, television takes place in *at least three places at once:* 1. In the place (or places) where the image and sound are 'recorded': 2. In the place (or places) where those images and sounds arc *received:* and 3. In the place (or places) *in between,* through which those images and sounds are transmitted.

The unity of television as a medium of presentation thus involves a *simultaneity* that is highly ambivalent. It overcomes spatial distance but only by *splitting the unity of place* and with it the unity of everything that defines its identity with respect to place: events, bodies, subjects.[8] The unity of place is split because the 'act' of viewing television does not 'take place' simply *in front* of the television set, as it might were it simply to involve the viewing of *images.* But, as I have already suggested, what one looks at in watching television is not first and foremost images. As the name of the medium says very precisely, one looks at *a certain kind of vision.* And that vision is taking place not simply on the screen but simultaneously—or rather, quasi-simultaneously, since there is always a time-lag—somewhere *else.*

Perhaps this is one reason why one does not usually speak, in English, of 'seeing' television but rather of 'watching' it. To 'see something' suggests a more or less direct contact of perceiver and perceived; and this in turn implies the givenness of an object to be *seen:* a *perceptum.* We do on the other hand speak of '*looking at* a television *program*'. To 'look at' entails a far more mediate, more distanced relationship. As the 'at' makes clear, we are dealing with an indirect object. But the verb that is most specific to television is not 'looking at' but rather 'watching'. For we still speak of 'looking at a painting' or a 'photograph'; but we would rarely dream of *watching* them. (Interestingly, we also do not speak of 'watching' a film.) Rather, *we watch* events whose outcome is in doubt, like sporting events. To *watch* carries with it the connotation of a scrutiny that suggests more and less than mere *seeing* or *looking at.* To watch is very close to *watching out for* or *looking out for,* that is, being sensorially alert for something that *may* happen. In the case of television, the primary 'object' of our watching is neither a particular image nor even a particular program: it is the medium itself, which includes its institutions—above all, stations and networks. We watch television—or CNN—just as we listen to *the radio.* The specificity of both of these media, radio and television, is that they confront their viewers and listeners primarily *as media,* and only secondarily as specific instantiations, that is, *as programs.*

This indicates that where television is concerned, one of the most fundamental categories of traditional aesthetics no longer retains its decisive status: the category of the individualized *work.* Art is inseparable from the *work of art:* a delimited, self-contained, significant unit, localizable in space and time. The language in which we speak of the media of tele-transmission—radio and television—

strongly suggests that with respect to these media such individuation is no longer a determining factor. This is one of the reasons why we do not speak of 'seeing' a 'work' of television but rather of watching television as such. The unity of the medium is no longer based upon the individuated unity of the work.

This also suggests a further reason why we 'watch' television. To 'watch' something that itself cannot simply be seen, because it is not composed primarily of *images,* is to *be on the alert,* to watch *out* for something that is precisely not perceptible or graspable as an image or a representation. To 'watch' is to look for something that is not immediately apparent. It implies an effort, a tension and a separation.

I have already outlined certain ways in which television sets a separation before us. And yet, again using as a guide the language in which we speak of this medium, we can also say that what television sets before us is first and foremost the television *set* itself. This set is defined by two factors: its situation and its screen.

Before we discuss either of these two determining factors, let us dwell for a moment on the word itself and what it implies. According to the *Oxford English Dictionary,* the use of the word *set* to describe a technical apparatus such as a radio or television receiver appeals to one of the traditional meanings of the term, namely, that of 'setting-together' or assembling. To be sure, the *OED* here seems to be referring to the assemblage of different parts that make up a complex apparatus. But not all such assemblages or apparatuses are designated as 'sets'. A further specification is thus required. Our previous discussion of the spatial dimension peculiar to television may help us further. As Mary Ann Doane, in one of the most thoughtful of recent essays on this medium, has observed. 'Television's greatest technological prowess is its ability to be there—both on the scene and in your living room',[9] to which one should add that this 'being-there and here' goes on *at the same time,* in that quasi-simultaneity to which I have referred. However, if television is both here *and* there *at the same time,* then, according to traditional notions of space, time and body, it can be *neither fully there nor entirely here.* What it sets before us, in and as the television *set,* is therefore split, of rather, it is a *split* or a *separation* that camouflages itself by taking the form of a visible *image.* That is the veritable significance of the term 'television *coverage':* it *covers* an invisible separation by giving it shape, contour and figure. The rendering visible of this coverage takes place before us, usually in our living room, not just on the screen but, even more, *as the screen.* What, however, is a screen generally, and what is peculiar to the television screen in particular?

A screen is first of all a surface upon which light and shadow can be projected. In film, this appears to take place in a relatively straightforward manner. Something that has already taken place is re-presented by being projected onto a screen. The temporal relation of past and present, the mimetic relation of a previously existent original and a subsequent copy, seems to remain essentially intact.[10] In television, however, as with radio before it, the hierarchy implied in this relationship is severely perturbed; and consequently, the logic and ontology that govern the traditional relationship of mimesis, reproduction and representation are unsettled. For what appears on the television screen is not a previously accomplished work but the quasi-simultaneity of *another vision* reproduced here and now. The minimal difference necessary to distinguish reproduced from reproduction, model from copy, repeated from repetition, is reduced, tendentially at least, to the imperceptible. One can no longer distinguish, visually or aurally, between that which is reproduced and its reproduction. Indeed, one cannot even discern *that* or *when* reproduction or repetition, in the manifest sense of recording or replaying, is taking place. We must be informed whether or not what we are seeing is 'live'. In short, we cannot distinguish through our senses alone between what we take to be simply 'alive' and what as reproduction, separated from its origin, is structurally posthumous. The television screen is the site of such an uncanny confusion and confounding. In the uncanniness of such confusion, what Derrida has called the irreducible 'iterability' of the mark[11]—that repeatability that both allows a trait to constitute its identity while splitting it at the same time—manifests itself in the only way open to it (since it is not of the order of manifestation), namely, as the *undecidable being of the televised images we see.*

Those images are undecidable not simply because they are separated from their previous context—and it is in this sense that I insist that what we see on the TV screen is not so much 'images' but *another kind of vision,* a vision of the other (to be understood as both an objective and subjective genitive). What we see on the screen is undecidably other for two reasons: first of all, because the power of vision that is transmitted is separated from its link to a situated individual body; and second, because whatever we see is no longer clearly distinguishable from the distant vision being transmitted. What we see, above and beyond the content of the images, is someone or something seeing. But that someone or something remains at an irreducible, indeterminable distance from the television viewer; and this distance splits the 'sameness' of the instant of perception as well as the identity of the place in which such viewing seems to occur. When we 'watch' television, we are watching out for this split, for this instant and place turned inside out.

The television transmission does not therefore, as is generally supposed, simply *overcome* distance and separation. (This is the illusion of a 'global village'.) It renders them invisible, paradoxically, by transposing them *into* the vision it transmits. Transmitted vision and audition 'contain', as it were, distance and separation while at the same time confounding the points of reference that allow us to determine what is near and what is far, what is connected and what is disconnected. For those points of reference involve precisely the unequivocal determination of place and of bodily situation that the television transmission tends to undermine. This is why the television set turns out to be something like a Trojan Horse introduced into the heart of the domestic fortress that we call 'home'. In front of it the family assembles as it once did before the Penates; but the space defined by the television set is already fractured by the undecidability of that which appears on the screen. Is it taking place here, or there, or anywhere? The development of video, and above all, of the digitalization of images, renders the question even less susceptible of an unequivocal answer.

In this sense, the television screen can be said to live up to its name in at least three distinct, contradictory and yet interrelated senses. First, it serves as a *screen* which allows distant vision to be *watched*. Second, it *screens,* in the sense of *selecting* or *filtering,* the vision that is watched. And finally, it serves as a screen in the sense of standing between the viewer and the viewed, since what is rendered visible covers the separation that distinguishes the *other vision* from that of the sight of the spectator sitting in front of the set.

Up to now, I have attempted to elaborate what I take to be certain of the distinctive traits specific to television as a medium. However, if the term 'uncanny' is at all appropriate to the undecidable effects I have tried to elaborate, then this would suggest that the specificity we are dealing with, although certainly 'new' in its particular configuration, is not simply *opposed* to the old but in a sense grows out of it. What I would like to argue is that the technological novelty of television must be understood both as the *consummation of a very old tradition* and at the same time as the *heightening of its internal ambivalences.* Perhaps the most comprehensive account we have of that tradition, insofar as it involves the process of thinking, is that of Heidegger. And interpreted in a Heideggerian perspective, television can be described as the culmination and consummation—the *Vollendung*—of the metaphysical tradition of representation. In German, the word that is translated as representation is *Vorstellung.* Curiously enough, however, in German it is primarily a spatial rather than temporal term. *Vorstellen* means, literally, to *place before.* It involves a determination of space and place such that a subject can take its place as the focal point of such 'placing-before'. To place before implies that there is a point that can be used to determine and distinguish *front* from *back,* 'before' from 'behind'. What is placed before, in and as the television set, is, as I have tried to emphasize, above all the very faculty itself of placing-before: the power of vision qua *Vorstellung.* In this placing-before, representation and presentation almost converge; but since the simultaneity of television transmission remains a *quasi*-simultaneity, the faculty of pre-senting sight and sound—that is, of bringing them *before* the *senses*—is itself re-pre-sented on and *as* the screen of the television set. This set remains a *re-ceiver,* which is to say, an apparatus that re-produces and re-peats. What television does, then, is to 'materialize', in a relatively immaterial manner, the irreducibility of that iterability, in the mode of presentation we call 'vision' and 'audition'.

In this sense, the television set can be said to consummate not just the metaphysical age of representation but, more specifically, that which, according to Heidegger, is its characteristically contemporaneous form: technology. The essence of modern technology for Heidegger is what he calls the *Gestell.* The word can be translated as 'framework', 'installation' or even 'skeleton'. I prefer *emplacement,* in order to retain the reference to place and to placing which is paramount in Heidegger's discussion of the phenomenon.[12] At the same time, the peculiar *reality* of television explains why the translation by 'skeleton' is also not inappropriate. For the more technology seeks to put things in their proper places, the less proper those places turn out to be, the more displaceable everything becomes and the more frenetic becomes the effort to reassert the propriety of the place as such. If the word 'television' in ordinary usage applies not just to the medium as a whole but, more precisely, to its materialization as the receiving *set,* this emphasizes just how determining the aspect of 'setting' and 'placing' is for a medium that deprives distance as well as proximity of their traditional stability and hence of their power to orient. What is distant is set right before us, close up; and yet what is thus brought close remains strangely *removed,* indeterminably *distant.* And what is traditionally proximate is *set apart,* set at a distance.

The reality of television thus no longer follows the traditional logic and criteria of reality. It is no longer a function of identity or of its derived form: opposition. Far and near are no longer mutually exclusive but rather converge and overlap. Such convergence brings a different aspect of reality to the fore—the reality of *ambivalence.* For what is ostensibly 'set in place' as the television set is also and above all *a movement of displacement,* of *transmission.* What results strongly resembles what Walter Benjamin, in his work on the German Baroque theatre of the 17th century, described as the 'court' that emanates from all allegory:

> Allegory [. . .] in its most developed form brings with it a court (*einen Hof*); around the figural center, which is never missing from genuine allegories, in opposition to conceptual circumlocutions, a host of emblems is grouped. They seem arbitrarily arranged: *The Confused 'Court'*—title of a Spanish mourning play [by Lope de Vega—SW]—could be cited as the schema of allegory. 'Dispersion' (*Zerstreuung*) and 'Collection' (*Sammlung*) name the law of this court. Things are brought together according to their meaning; indifference to their being-there (*Dasein*) disperses them once again. The disorder of the allegorical scenery stands in contrast to the gallant boudoir.[13]

Like the allegorical court, television brings the most remote things together only to disperse them again, out of 'indifference to their being-there', or rather, out of the undecidability of their being-there (*Dasein*). To be sure, in contradistinction to the allegorical court, television—in the sense of its reception—is generally situated in the private space of the home. But the uncanny undecidability of television—of the distant vision it transmits and renders visible—is probably as much a source of disorder today as the allegorical scenery was in the 17th century German principalities and duchies. Both then as now, the lack of a unifying, totalizing worldly instance—be it the Nation-State or the Universal Church—was keenly felt. What today in part claims to make up for that instance is television itself. The global network, CNN for instance, presents itself as a model for such totalization. But the all-encompassing unity that it proposes remains as ambivalent as the indefinitely repeated sets of television monitors that constitute its favorite backdrop. Thus, the question remains open as to how, out of indefinite repetition, anything like an integrated whole might emerge, or rather, whether such a whole is even thinkable any longer.

This, then, is one of the tendencies that renders television a set of the most ambiguous, most ambivalent kind: it sets only by unsettling. And yet, this unsettling tendency is also constantly being recuperated and reappropriated; and this allows television also to function as a bulwark of the established order. The more the medium tends to unsettle, the more powerfully it presents itself as the antidote to the disorder to which it contributes.

I want to conclude by briefly analyzing one such instance of recuperation. I have tried to describe how the primary setting of television, as a set, is the private space of the home. The major alternative to home viewing, in the United States at least, is the collective television watching usually situated in bars. The preferred program of such collective television watching is—once again, in the U.S.—almost exclusively the competitive sporting event. What does the viewing of a sporting event have to offer the television public? Precisely what television itself tends to undermine: the possibility of an unequivocal *decision*. In competitive sports, there is always a winner and a loser; and where there are more than one of each, there are unequivocal rankings to determine their *placement*. In professional competitive sports, which television does not merely transmit but also, through sponsoring, helps finance, the technological dream of planning and control is rendered visible. Whoever wins or loses, the outcome is clear and decisive. In watching such events, television viewers can forget, at least temporarily, just how ambivalent and undecidable the reality of their world has become, not least of all by virtue of television itself. In the world as we know it, seeing and hearing—understood as individual, self-contained acts of perception—are perhaps less than ever before reliable means of acceding to 'reality'.

Televised sports allows viewers to take comfort in the possibility of unequivocal decisions, of being able to distinguish winners and losers, as well as in the possibility of 'records' that are quantifiable and measurable. In so doing, televised sports reconfirms the individual body as focal point of a reality that television itself calls constantly into question. The body that appears in the televised sporting event is one that accepts its limitations only in order to surpass them, in an infinite progress of record-breaking and record-making performance. The shadows that such performances are meant to eclipse reappear on the margins, where, however, they often turn out to be quite determining for the field itself. For instance, the use of steroids to increase performance or the vulnerability of the superstar to AIDS serve as reminders of what the televisual sporting event— *media event* par excellence—simultaneously seeks to *cover*, to wit, the frailty and limitation of the individual body.

No wonder that the sporting event has emerged, in the United States at least, as one of the central discursive paradigms for representing reality, be it political, economic or social. Ever since the Vietnam War, conflicts of all kinds, even the most brutal and violent, have been described—and televised—as though they were sporting events. If this age turns out to be that of American television—a conjecture, not a hope—then the televisual sporting event will undoubtedly stand as its allegorical emblem, leaving everything as open and shut as the instant replay with which the medium demonstrates its control of the event, if not of its outcome.

Notes

1. I should mention a few of the more notable exceptions to this general tendency to ignore the question of the specificity of the medium: first. Stanley Cavell's 1982 essay. 'The Fact of Television'. In *Video Culture: A Critical Investigation*, 1986: second, Jane Feuer's 'The Concept of Live Television: Ontology as Ideology', in *Regarding Television: Critical Approaches—An Anthology*. 1983: and more recently, Mary Ann Doane's 'Information. Crisis and Catastrophe', in *Logics of Television: Essays in Cultural Criticism*, 1990. Finally, an as yet unpublished essay by Deborah Esch. 'No Time Like the Present', reflects, to my knowledge for the first time, on the 'allegorical' structure of the medium.

2. The essay by Jane Feuer mentioned in the previous note deals with this tendency.

3. The major shortcoming of Cavell's seminal essay, already mentioned, is that it does not sufficiently elaborate on this distinction. Television is defined in opposition to film but within a continuum of 'aesthetic' experience or perception, as Deborah Esch convincingly argues.

4. An example: according to a recent policy decision, the First German Television Channel, *ARD*, has decided to no longer broadcast operas since their viewer ratings are too low. If this indicates that the difference between 'public' and 'private' television programming is steadily diminishing in Europe. It also calls attention to the fact that such differences still are important enough to warrant attention. In France, a law prohibits more than one interruption for advertising during the broadcast of a film, on private as well as on state-owned stations.

5. In French, radio or television interference—'static'—is called *parasite*.

6. Without prejudicing the results of a more ample investigation than can be conducted here. It seems likely that the ambivalent character of the electronic media that we are elaborating with respect to television would be no less applicable to radio. By separating sound from sight, radio delocalizes and disembodies the relation to the world even more than does television. This *deprives* sound of its visual accompaniment, thereby impoverishing its 'reality', while at the same time *heightening* its power and scope by liberating it from the constraints of a visually determinate situation.

7. I wish to thank Professor Klaus Hofmann, of the University of Frankfurt, who read an earlier version of this paper, for having insisted on the importance of this elementary but essential aspect of television.

8. Stanley Cavell, in the essay mentioned (see note 1), uses the category of *simultaneity* to determine 'the material basis of television'. But his account of television 'as a current of simultaneous event reception' and his determination of 'monitoring' as the mode of perception peculiar to the medium leave little place for the ambivalent structure of television qua medium. Where ambivalence appears in his account. It is as a psychological after-effect, one which derives essentially from the *reality* the medium is felt to *represent*—'the growing uninhabitability of the world'—rather than from *the reality of the mode of representation itself* ('The Fact of Television', 217). The same observation holds for Cavell's discussion of 'monitoring', which describes it as a reaction to an inhospitable reality existing independently of television rather than as a function of the way in which the medium tends to redefine the relation to and the structure of 'reality'. If this is so, then the 'fact' of television, as Cavell conceives it, must be distinguished from Heidegger's notion of 'facticity'. which designates the

'thrownness' of being-there-and-then—*Dasein*—precisely insofar as it *resists* causal explanation.

9. Mary Ann Doane. 'Information, Crisis and Catastrophe'. 238.'
10. Needless to say, the importance of the cutting-table in the construction of the film indicates how tenuous such an ostensible linearity in fact is. The 'post-production' process of 'editing' has long been recognized as an essential dimension of film-making.
11. Derrida, 'Limited Inc a b c. . . '. *Limited Inc.* 1988, 53. Sec Weber, 'After Deconstruction'. In this volume.
12. See Weber, 'Upsetting the Setup', in this volume.
13. Benjamin, *Ursprung des deutschen Trauerspiels.* 1963. 210 [My translation—SW]. English as *The Origin of the German Tragic Drama*, 1977, 188.

Keywords for critical reading

At the end of this section, the student will be familiar with the significance and applicability of the following concepts:

- Componentizing
- Conversational content
- Constitutive heterogeneity of television
- Consumer bimodality
- Content access
- Digital incubators
- Dis-intermediation
- Farsightedness
- Follow Me TV
- Folksonomy
- 'Hot' vs. 'Cold' medium
- Gadgetier
- Globalization; Global village
- Media meshing; Media mashing
- Mobile platforms
- Online broadcasting
- Platform-agnostic content
- Peer, clip, blue, cell and mobcasting
- Radio's private experience
- Resonating dimension of radio
- Radio's natural bias
- Structural change
- Social networking
- Television set and screen
- User generated advertisements
- Webisodes and mobisodes

Key questions for critical learning

1. How does an apparently innocent media's technology, such as radio, lead us to rethink the idea of 'global village'? What we have today to accept the call of globalization?

2. Samuel Weber argues that television technology appears to allow human beings to overcome their perception of time and space. What does this mean?

3. What sort of future awaits the Canadian radio, television, and newspaper industries?

4. In an era where downloading is an unbridled and minimally controlled practice, who is going to pay for the content that we consume and share among our networks of friends?

5. What is the state of the 'old' media in this new social, cultural, and political contest?

6. Explain the ways in which television sets and screens could represent a different view of time and space.

7. What do you think about the future bimodality of television production and consumption as projected by Berman, Shipnuck, and Duff?

8. Explain to what extent the notion of "componentizing" advanced by Berman, Shipnuck, and Duff could lead mass media company to secure competitive assets and to deliver cost-efficiently programs.

9. Discuss the role of the CBC Radio in solidifying Canadian identity

10. Are there limits to 'freedom of expression' in broadcasting?

Part 2
Old/New Media

Section Editor: Boulou Ebanda de B'béri

Introduction

Though we use repeatedly the term "new media", as if this term is purely transparent, we do not easily recognize how complex this is. This section deals with three constitutive elements of mass media: science, technology, and the social and political implications of science and technology in our everyday life experience. The essays in this section begin with a review of the ways in which technology progressively creates new social environments, new communicational and cognitive habits, and certainly a new way to comprehend and analyze the relationship between mass media and society.

Building on McLuhan's idea of a newly-shaped social environment, George Grant's text illustrates the neutral values of technology, whose applications could only be determined by the 'paradigm of knowledge' that composes the technological apparatuses on the one hand, and the users on the other. Mike Gasher and Rowland Lorimer's text remind us how our Western society could hardly survive today without technology. Both authors produce a clear picture that outlines the nature of communications technology and the technological rationales and realities in our increased information world. Without reinforcing any specific position, this text is an excellent introduction to the conceptual struggle and to the questions related to regulatory matters of new media technology.

The next essays in this section deal with the political-economy of new media, the issues of intellectual property, and digital divide. Daniel Paré's text suggests an articulation between the rapid spread of the Internet infrastructure, the traditional and alternative types of the Internet governance, and the growing number of users. With examples showing numerous disputes among multiple actors, Paré demonstrates that the significance of the social dynamics must be embedded in technological innovations governing the architectural structure of Internet software, an element that most of the Internet-related governance literature has failed to address. The conjunction between the technological architecture of the Internet and the social dynamics must become part of the rules of the game for establishing new governing régime. Mark Warschauer explores the social and cultural governing-mentality of the Internet. The Internet technology, and any mass media indeed, contains positive aspects. Mark Warschauer first considers the state of global physical resources and the questions of accessibility before outlining major areas (e.g., economic, health, and education) in which the technological development serves as 'a vehicle for gathering and making available information'. Several other positive aspects could be found in specific content targeting people with disabilities. Beside these positive aspects, issues of dominant languages remain at the core of Internet development. Using the case of Hawaii's indigenous-language, Warschauer notes some efforts made to bridge a very special divide between many languages and cultures facing persecution or near elimination in a recent past. Today, some of these languages and cultures have entered the domain of new media, although the Indo-European and Chinese languages remain dominant.

Science, Technology, and the Human

Thinking about Technology

George Grant

A computer scientist recently made the following statement about the machines he helps to invent: 'The computer does not impose on us the ways it should be used.' Obviously the statement is made by someone who is aware that computers can be used for purposes of which be does not approve—for example, the tyrannous control of human beings. This is given in the word 'should'. He makes a statement in terms of his intimate knowledge of computers which transcends that intimacy, in that it is more than a description of any given computer or of what is technically common to all such machines. Because he wishes to state something about the possible good or evil purposes for which computers can be used, he expresses, albeit in negative form, what computers are, in a way which is more than their technical description. They are instruments, made by human skill for the purpose of achieving certain human goals. They are neutral instruments in the sense that the morality of the goals for which they are used is determined outside them.

Many people who have never seen a computer, and only slightly understand the capacity of computers, have the sense from their daily life that they are being managed by them, and have perhaps an undifferentiated fear about the potential extent of this management. This man, who knows about the invention and use of these machines, states what they are in order to put our sense of anxiety into a perspective freed from the terrors of such fantasies as the myth of Doctor Frankenstein. His perspective assumes that the machines are instruments, because their capacities have been built into them by human beings, and it is human beings who operate those machines for purposes they have determined. All instruments can obviously be used for bad purposes, and the more complex the capacities of the instrument, the more complex can be its possible bad uses.

But if we apprehend these machines for what they are, neutral instruments which we in our freedom are called upon to control, we are better able to come to terms rationally with their potential dangers. The first step in coping with these dangers is to see that they are related to the potential decisions of human beings about how to use computers, not to the inherent capacities of the machines themselves. Indeed the statement about the computer gives the prevalent 'liberal' view of the modern situation which is so rooted in us that it seems to be common sense itself, even rationality itself. We have certain technological capacities; it is up to us to use those capacities for decent human purposes.

Yet despite the seeming common sense of the statement, when we try to think the sentence 'the computer does not impose on us the ways it should be used,' it becomes clear that we are not allowing computers to appear before us for what they are. Indeed the statement (like many similar) obscures for us what computers are. To begin at the surface: the words 'the computer does not impose' are concerned with the capacities of these machines, and these capacities are brought before us as if they existed in abstraction from the events which have made possible their existence. Obviously the machines have been made from a vast variety of materials, consummately fashioned by a vast apparatus of fashioners. Their existence has required generations of sustained effort by chemists, metallurgists, and workers in mines and factories. Beyond these obvious facts, computers have been made within the new science and its mathematics. That science is a particular paradigm of knowledge and, as any paradigm of knowledge, is to be understood as the relation between an aspiration of human thought and the effective conditions for its realization.

It is not my purpose here to describe that paradigm in detail; nor would it be within my ability to show its interrelation with mathematics conceived as algebra. Suffice it to say that what is given in the modern use of the word 'science' is the project of reason to gain 'objective' knowledge. And modern 'reason' is the summoning of anything before a subject and putting it to the question, so that it gives us its reasons for being the way it is as an object. A paradigm of knowledge is not something reserved for scientists and scholars. Anybody who is awake in any part of our educational system knows that this paradigm of knowledge stamps the institutions of that system, their curricula, in their very heart, in what the young are required to know and to be able to do if they are to be called 'qualified'. That paradigm of knowledge is central to our civilizational destiny and has made possible the existence of computers. I mean by 'civilizational destiny' above all the fundamental presuppositions that the majority of human beings inherit in a civilization, and which are so taken for granted as the way things are that they are given an almost absolute status. To describe a destiny is not to judge it. It may indeed be, as many believe, that the development of that paradigm is a great step in the ascent of man, that it is the essence of human liberation, even that its development justifies the human experiment itself. Whatever the truth of these beliefs, the only point here is that without this destiny computers would not exist. And like all destinies, they 'impose'.

What has been said about the computer's existence depending upon the paradigm of knowledge is of course equally true of the earlier machines of industrialism. The Western paradigm of knowledge has not been static, but has been realized in a dynamic unfolding, and one aspect of that realization has been a great extension of what is given in the conception of 'machine'. We all know that computers are machines for the transmitting of information, not the transformation of energy. They require software as well as hardware. They have required the development of mathematics as algebra, and of algebra as almost identical with logic. Their existence has required a fuller realization of the Western paradigm of knowledge beyond its origins, in this context the extension of the conception of machine. It may well be said that where the steel press may be taken as the image of Newtonian physics and mathematics, the computer can be taken as the image of contemporary physics and mathematics. Yet in making that distinction, it must also be said that contemporary science and Newtonian science are equally moments in the realization of the same paradigm.

The phrase 'the computer does not impose' misleads, because it abstracts the computer from the destiny that was required for its making. Common sense may tell us that the computer is an instrument, but it is an instrument from within the destiny which *does* 'impose' itself upon us, and therefore the computer *does* impose.

To go further: How are we being asked to take the word 'ways' in the assertion that 'the computer does not impose the ways'? Even if the purposes for which the computer's capacities should be used are determined outside itself, do not these capacities limit the kind of ways for which it can be used? To take a simple example from the modern institutions of learning and training: in most jurisdictions there are cards on which children are assessed as to their 'skills' and 'behaviour', and this information is retained by computers. It may be granted that such information adds little to the homogenizing vision inculcated throughout society by such means as centrally controlled curricula or teacher training. It may also be granted that as computers and their programming become more sophisticated the information stored therein may be able to take more account of differences. Nevertheless, it is clear that the ways that computers can be used for storing and transmitting information can only be ways that increase the tempo of the homogenizing processes. Abstracting facts so that they can be stored as information is achieved by classification, and it is the very nature of any classifying to homogenize. Where classification rules, identities and differences can appear only in its terms. Indeed the word 'information' is itself perfectly attuned to the account of knowledge which is homogenizing in its very nature. 'Information' is about objects, and comes forth as part of that science which summons objects to give us their reasons.

It is not my purpose at this point to discuss the complex issues of good and evil involved in the modern movement towards homogeneity, nor to discuss the good of heterogeneity, which in its most profound past form was an expression of

autochthony. Some modern thinkers state that beyond the rootlessness characteristic of the present early stages of technological society, human beings are now
called to new ways of being rooted which will have passed through modern rootlessness, and will be able at one and the same time to accept the benefits of
modern homogenization while living out a new form of heterogeneity. These
statements are not at issue here. Rather my purpose is to point out that the sentence about computers hides the fact that their ways are always homogenizing.
Because this is hidden, questioning homogenization is closed down in the
sentence.

To illustrate the matter from another aspect of technological development:
Canadians wanted the most efficient car for geographic circumstances and social
purposes similar to those of the people who first developed the mass-produced
automobile. Our desire for and use of such cars has been a central cause of our
political and economic integration and our social homogenization with the people of the imperial heartland. This was not only because of the vast corporate
structures necessary for building and keeping in motion such automobiles, and
the direct and indirect political power of such corporations, but also because any
society with such vehicles tends to become like any other society with the same.
Seventy-five years ago somebody might have said 'The automobile does not
impose on us the ways it should be used,' and who would have quarrelled with
that? Yet this would have been a deluded representation of the automobile.

Obviously, human beings may still be able to control, by strict administrative
measures, the ways that cars are used. They may prevent the pollution of the
atmosphere or prevent freeways from destroying central city life. It is to be hoped
that cities such as Toronto will maintain themselves as communities by winning
popular victories over expressways and airports. Whatever efforts may be made,
they will not allow us to represent the automobile to ourselves as a neutral
instrument.

Obviously the 'ways' that automobiles and computers can be used are dependent on their being investment-heavy machines which require large institutions
for their production. The potential size of such corporations can be imagined in
the statement of a reliable economist: if the present growth of IBM is extrapo-
lated, that corporation will in the next thirty years be a larger unit than the economy of any presently constituted national state, including that of its homeland.
At the simplest factual level, computers can be built only in societies in which
there are large corporations. This will be the case whatever ways these institutions are related to the states in which they are incorporated, be that relation
some form of capitalism or some form of socialism. Also those machines have
been and will continue to be instruments with effect beyond the confines of
particular nation states. They will be the instruments of the imperialism of
certain communities towards other communities. They are instruments in the
struggle between competing empires, as the present desire of the Soviet Union
for American computers illustrates. It might be that 'in the long run of progress',

humanity will come to the universal and homogeneous state in which individual empires and nations have disappeared. That in itself would be an even larger corporation. To express the obvious: whatever conceivable political and economic alternatives there may be, computers can only exist in societies in which there are large corporate institutions. The ways they can be used are limited to those situations. In this sense computers are not neutral instruments, but instruments which exclude certain forms of community and permit others.

Communications Technology and Society: Theory and Practice

Mike Gasher and Rowland Lorimer

Introduction

There probably has been no better time since the Industrial Revolution to think about and reflect upon technology. The dot-com bubble notwithstanding, we are going through a major change in the nature and organization of society brought about by information and communications technology. Those who have been surrounded by computer/communications technology and who understand its logic and potential are working with others who understand information and communications needs and together they are creating new realities.

This chapter begins with a review of some well-established theories of technology. It provides an overview of the development of communications technology. It explores some recent technological developments in communications and reviews the categories of activity they are affecting. The chapter then concludes with some summary observations on communications technology and society.

Technology and Society

Even though some theorists have misgivings about the strength of the influence of technology on modern society (see, for example, Postman, 1993), we could hardly do without it. Indeed, some say that the distinguishing feature of Western society is its embrace of technology. From the first stick picked up and used by prehistoric human beings to the invention of the needle or even the sword, and much later the nuclear bomb and the robot, and from the printing press to the steam engine, telephone, television, computer, and satellite, technology has been inseparable from human activity. We depend on technology for the food we eat, for the homes we live in, for the work we do. The rank of nations in the world economy is profoundly affected by the great technological race. Indeed, the mental embrace of technological change is fundamental to the Western way of thinking. We simply cannot avoid thinking in a technological manner.

We depend on technology for our communications with others—whether they are just a house or two away or halfway around the world. In the second half of the twentieth century it became almost impossible to live without a television in our homes, much less without a telephone, and now we can hardly live without personal computers through which we gain Internet access and send and receive e-mail. The reality of new communications technology is that anyone is able to get in touch with anyone else, anywhere, at any time, for very little money—at least in the developed world.

As successive technologies have taken root in Western society and successive layers of infrastructure have been laid down, two highly significant developments have been occurring. First, our dependency on these systems has been growing. Second, the technological distance between developed and developing economies (and those that are not developing at all) has been increasing. This gap, which from time to time is brought forward for discussion, is often called the digital divide.

Yet another implication of the spread of technology deserves attention. The adoption and widespread use of any technology almost invariably create both negative and positive impacts on us and our environment.

Also, technology is not merely a spinoff of the pursuit of science but rather is an extension of our way of thinking. In fact, in most cases technology is a deliberate attempt to create material objects or interventions that, in changing or improving situations, can allow the developer to reap financial reward. In a sense, technological development is a business.

We are firmly in the clutches of the technological imperative, that is, we have convinced ourselves that we should continuously develop new technologies and apply them broadly. Therefore we must understand the fundamentals of technology—both the possible and the unavoidable consequences of its application. We must then invent laws to regulate and institutions to develop technology so that it is as generally and universally beneficial as possible. In communications, the keys to beneficial adoption of technology are patent and copyright laws, policy, regulations, and enabling legislation that cover information, education, libraries, the arts, broadcasting, and telecommunications.

Technology Defined

Technology is more than machinery. According to US communications scholar Langdon Winner (1977), technology encompasses at least three elements:

1. pieces of apparatus;
2. techniques of operation to make the apparatus work; and
3. social institutions within which technical activities take place.

Even if all these elements are present, however, the outcome is not predetermined. For instance, the same invention can lead to very different social impacts in different situations, as was the case with movable type in Europe and China. As Marshall McLuhan (1962), Elizabeth Eisenstein (1983), and others have pointed out, in Europe the introduction of movable type led to social change. In China, as David Ze (1995) has argued, it led to a reinforcement of social stability (see Chapter 1).

A substantial literature on the social impact of technology assumes Winner's broad definition. French philosopher Jacques Ellul, generally regarded as an insightful, if pessimistic, theorist of technology, discussed the nature and impact of technology in *The Technological Society* (1964). In that book Ellul's primary concern was to explore the past, present, and future impacts of technological change. Of the many conclusions and observations he drew, four, identified by technology scholar Wilson Dizard, stand out in particular:

1. All technical progress exacts a price; that is, while it adds something on the one hand, it subtracts something on the other.
2. All technical progress raises more problems than it solves, tempts us to see the consequent problems as technical in nature, and prods us to seek technical solutions to them.
3. The negative effects of technological innovation are inseparable from the positive. It is naive to say that technology is neutral, that it may be used for good or bad ends; the good and bad effects are, in fact, simultaneous and inseparable.
4. All technological innovations have unforeseen effects. (Dizard, 1985: 11)

In short, technology sets in motion powerful forces that rearrange the organizing attributes of any society. The challenge for a technological society is to invent social institutions to ensure that the technology in question is put to use for the greatest benefit for the greatest number.

A complementary viewpoint can be found in the writings of Canadian philosopher George Grant. In *Technology and Empire*, Grant argued that the foundation of all modern, liberal, industrial and post-industrial societies is to be found in technique and technology: 'the belief that human excellence is promoted by the homogenizing and universalizing power of technology is the dominant doctrine of modern liberalism, and—that doctrine must undermine all particularisms' (Grant, 1969: 69). In Grant's view, the powerful forces that Ellul identifies are homogenizing in their influence and hence are threatening the distinctive elements of societies that share the same technology.

Raymond Williams (1975) has argued that television technology is an extension of the Industrial Revolution and feeds the mass society that industrialization created. American Marxist scholar Herbert Schiller (1984) has turned this general perspective on technology around somewhat to expose a different angle. Schiller maintains that technological development and its application are an operating imperialist strategy on the part of the United States that is designed to maintain economic and political dominance, through technological prowess and technological gaps, between the US and other countries. Moreover, he sees this imperialism as steered by multinational corporations and stimulated by military research and development in communications hardware.

In contrast to these viewpoints, mainstream American scholars, like the mainstream of America and increasingly the world, have been inclined to see technology as benevolent and technological change as progressive. This optimism stems from an economic history in which the development and use of machines to create wealth has been regarded as of widespread benefit to American society over the past 200 years.

Technology and Technological Determinism

Technologically based societies affirm and embrace machinery, the social organization necessary to adopt that machinery, and the acquisition of the requisite skills needed for its operation. That embrace is so complete that both analysts (for example, George Gilder, 1991) and the general public (see media discussions of the Internet and the Web) accept projections about the future of society that are based on technological capacity. This is referred to as technological determinism—a belief that technological development equates to progress and that if technology (usually conceived of as some kind of apparatus) can do something, society will take full advantage of this technological capacity and will be shaped fundamentally by the apparatus.

For instance, technological determinism would argue that the moon landing changed society fundamentally: it was seen as the beginning of the colonization of space by humanity. Similarly, the Internet was supposed to democratize the world more completely than ever before. Of course, both technological developments have had profound impacts on society, but the extent to which they have met expectations is not borne out—mainly because this technological determinism does not account for all things.

Technological determinism fails to consider three fundamental variables. First, with reference to the idea that technology encompasses apparatus, technique, and social organization, devices that are developed emerge from a way of thinking and from the awareness of particular problems that appear in need of being solved. So it is not that the technology drops out of the clear blue sky or from the head of some unworldly genius; rather, it originates from specific efforts to address certain social realities. For example, the Internet was developed as a decentralized method of communication that could maintain itself even though parts of the network were destroyed (Leiss, 1990).

The second fundamental variable that technological determinism ignores is that the industrialized application of technology has social consequences. The Internet can as easily be a force for dictatorship or terrorism as for democracy, depending on how it is applied. In the end, at least in Western society, the matter is either or both political and/or economic. If politicians wish, they can erect policy so that a certain technology (e.g., the Internet) can only be used in certain ways (e.g., for Canadian content), and hence, with certain consequences (e.g., contributing to the cohesiveness of Canada or to massive rejection of such a policy by many Canadians). If policy is not enacted and matters are left to the marketplace or to the freedom of individuals to decide, and if a need can be created and affordable products and services developed, which, in turn, fit into existing patterns of life and are seen as beneficial, then, at least in a technological society, the particular technology will be developed and used, and society is left to adapt to the consequences.

The third fundamental variable that technological determinism ignores is that other powerful spheres of life affect the development of society. If a particular technology were to vastly distort the distribution of wealth, social action would intervene to destroy or render less powerful that technology. If a particular technology contradicted the basic values of a society then it would be ignored or, at least, not widely adopted. Stated slightly differently, technological determinism ignores the strength of the human spirit. While it is true that Soviet Communism undermined the human spirit for a period of almost 75 years, rarely can politicians prevail over the sense of survival, community, and justice that has asserted itself through history.

The Limitations of Technology

Implicit in technological determinism is the notion that technology can transform society. However, the consequences of the transformative dynamic of technology usually go unrealized in its initial application. And later, unanticipated problems can emerge that must then be counteracted. Take antibiotics, for example. While antibiotics have been a godsend in terms of public health, we now understand that resistant strains of bacteria have developed that the antibiotics cannot fight. Similarly, the development of monocultures, single varieties of plants that are most productive and produce the most valuable harvestable crop, makes vast food supplies extremely vulnerable to failure. The sinking of the *Titanic,* which was viewed as unsinkable because it was an example of the latest and greatest technology, was an example of technological arrogance. In communications, there are similar issues surrounding the limitations of technology. For instance, while a lot more people are able to access vast amounts of information, as economies of scale come to dominate in the preparation of information suddenly all kinds of information that has a limited audience goes missing. National, regional, and neighbourhood information ceases to reach us as we turn more and more to local and global broadcasting. Finally, elements so mundane as the number of hours one might spend sitting in front of a computer or the lack of socialization involved in working from home may have considerable negative consequences when multiplied throughout society. This is what Ellul meant by the inseparability of the good and bad effects of technology.

The Nature of Communications Technology

While Winner, Ellul, Grant, Williams, and Schiller provide some understanding of the nature of technology in general, it is in the literature on communications technology specifically that we find both a general definition of technology and a specific definition of communications technology. Shannon and Weaver, who put forward the mathematical model of communications we explored in Chapter 2, note that 'communications' includes 'all of the procedures by which one mind may affect another' (1949: 3–5). Technology theorist James Beniger (1986) maintains that information, which is the content of communications, derives from the organization of the material world, and technology is the manner in which that organization is brought about. Thus technology is 'any intentional extension of a natural process' (Beniger in Crowley and Heyer, 1991: 250), and communications technology is the intentional extension of the means to allow intelligence to move through time and/or space. For Beniger and others, the communications/information revolution (in both the evolutionary and turn-about sense of the word) is a revolution of who controls what information, generated by whom, over what geographical area. Communication and its technologies change the dynamics, the location, and the breadth of control.

The nature of control caused by communications technology has given rise to a greater separation between information about a phenomenon and the phenomenon itself. And this separation has resulted in the reorganization of space and power. Consider a few examples of the separation of a phenomenon and information. A thermostat exists in the middle of a house and a furnace in an out-of-the-way corner. The thermostat senses the pre-set temperature and turns the furnace off and on. A burglar alarm on a house sets off a signal at a police or security firm's dispatch office. A computer is programmed to monitor stock prices and alert a broker when certain stock prices rise or fall more than a set percentage. A computer monitors returning fish to a river mouth and determines how much should be caught, allocating quotas upriver.

In each case, local knowledge, sometimes of a higher quality, sometimes not, is replaced with knowledge further away from the phenomenon itself. This replacement of one kind of knowledge in the hands of one set of people with another kind of knowledge in the hands of another set of people (or machines) can have far-reaching consequences. Particular local knowledge, based on a vast storehouse of information coded in behaviour, feelings, superstitions, and understandings that are used to retrieve the past, explain the present, and foretell the future, is set aside. Relevant variables are identified, models created, monitoring programs set in place, laws passed, and authority anointed. Such is the power of formal knowledge, communications, and information-processing. Such also is its ability to eclipse a local culture, to shift control from a multiplicity of scattered points, each in close proximity to a phenomenon, to a central location that controls activities in a far-flung hinterland. Ideally, the centralization of control improves things for everyone. However, as illustrated by the federal government's setting of a cod fisheries quota after Newfoundland fishers were arguing for years that the fish were disappearing, centralization of control can also have its downside.

Once the central processing centre has gained appropriate levels of information, it can begin to replace the on-location decision-maker. The central processing centre can also introduce a further level of sophistication. It can bring in information about other locations—for instance, the state of world production, the state of markets, or even the state of government subsidies or restraints in other countries. It may even be able to predict events more accurately based on its knowledge of distant but related events.

The social and economic impact of the separation of information and entity is extensive. First, information itself becomes a separate product that can be bought and sold. Second, as noted, increased power accrues to the location of the information. Until recently, this was to be found in financial or manufacturing centres. Now, it can exist anyplace where there are sufficient technical and human resources. Third, distant homelands of indigenous peoples are turned into frontiers of industrial society, whether in the Arctic (now a source of both oil and diamonds) or the Amazon (increasingly a source of useful plant-based drugs).

Technology and the Communications Industries

Traditionally, communications industries have been differentiated on the basis of their technology. Thus, telephone systems were designed to facilitate point-to-point communications offering limited fidelity (an understandable voice) but sophisticated switching. On the other hand, broadcast technology was designed not only to carry signals from a single point to multiple points but also to have a satisfactory level of fidelity so that listening for a long time to voice and music would be an enjoyable experience. Recording technology was developed to carry the highest demands in terms of fidelity and the lowest in terms of universality of distribution, that is, available only by consumer purchase. And just as recording technology increased in its fidelity over the years from wax cylinders to 78s to LPs to tapes to CDs and now DVDs, so radio improved as stations migrated from AM (amplitude modulation) to FM (frequency modulation) and then to AM digital radio.

While no doubt many assumed that there was a technological base to this division of responsibilities, as Babe (1988, 1990) has pointed out, no such technological determinism existed. Telephones could easily have been turned into broadcast instruments as they were in the very first example of voice telephony by Reginald Fessenden (see Fessenden, 1974) and in early radio forms, and as they have been used in some Eastern European countries.

Technological Convergence

The separation of communications functions into separate industries and the development of technology that best suited the functions of telephony, broadcasting, and sound and video recording have served society well. This industrial and technological separation has prevented the overall control of communications by one set of companies by spreading ownership somewhat broadly. Imagine if the CBC or CTV were your telephone and cable company and one of five or so major recording labels.

With digitization, cameras, computers, musical instruments, radio, television, cable, and telephones are all information machines that essentially do the same job—collect, code, and thus transform information into digital form. They are merely specialized computerized transceivers. For instance, through sampling technology, an electronic keyboard can almost reproduce any sound. Electronic drums are digital encoding pads that are quite reasonable facsimiles of the real sound of drums. Each device is a specialized computer focusing on a particular sound and/or image and/or text format. The commonality—digitization—and hence the ability for one device to send output or receive input from another is what is meant by the term 'technological convergence'.

Technology and Policy

In the beginning years of the twenty-first century, we are once again facing many of the same choices that people confronted at the turn of the last century. Just as policy, not technology, determined that telephone and broadcasting would be separated into two industries (see Babe, 1988, 1990), so policy will encourage an industrial structure that, ideally, is of the greatest benefit to Canadians. The alternative, it appears, is a totally integrated communications system controlled by a very few mega-corporations that would dwarf the largest we see now.

The challenge here is twofold: (1) to ensure that the needs of the public and of business are met, and (2) to ensure that certain businesses do not become too powerful and thereby thwart the participation of others and prevent further social and technological development. The attempt of Microsoft to dominate in nearly every software market is a case in point. A myriad of other similar but less noticed situations also arise. In 1997, for example, the purchase of MCI Communications by WorldCom Inc. became an issue because the combined company would control up to 60 per cent of US Internet traffic and hence would have substantial power to control pricing of access both for consumers and for small access providers *(Globe and Mail,* 2 Oct. 1997, B15). In this case the fears were unnecessary. WorldCom filed for bankruptcy in 2002.

While allowing for convergence and competition sounds like a good idea, it is difficult for the CRTC to respond with appropriate policy. For example, the telephone and cable companies provide Internet access to consumers and are known as 'backbone providers'. They also provide connectivity to small Internet service providers (ISPs), who also sell access to the public. Similarly, the cable companies now own some of the specialty channels while also providing access to their competitors— clearly a conflict of interest that the cable companies exploit to the degree that they can get away with it. It is government policy that sets the rules of the game, determining whether, for instance, cable companies can own specialty channels.

When Convergence Works! and Not!

Some people call it convergence. Others call it concentration of ownership. Still others, such as *Globe and Mail* correspondent Simon Houpt, call it synergy. In the summer of 2002, AOL Time Warner released *Goldmember*. Here is a list of what the company did to ensure the movie was a hit.

- For weeks, AOL's on-line service had been promoting the movie to its 34-million-subscriber base.
- In the week of 27 July, the AOL-owned magazine, *Entertainment Weekly*, featured Austin Powers on the cover and carried several articles inside about the movie.
- The week before, a division of Warner music, also owned by AOL, released the film sound track.
- Also in the week of 27 July, AOL-owned cable station TBS aired the previous two Austin Powers movies to help the audience get ready for the new release.
- In the week of the release (Friday, 26 July) AOL-owned Moviefone.com was awash with Austin Powers ads.
- On Wednesday, 24 July, Mike Myers received a star in Hollywood's walk of fame, an event given ample coverage by AOL media properties, CNN, *People* magazine, and numerous Web sites.

And AOL didn't pull out all the stops. It could have scheduled an appearance of Myers at its baseball franchise, the Atlanta Braves. (Its other two sports franchises at the time, the Atlanta Thrashers [NHL] and Atlanta Hawks [NBA], were both in the off-season.)

According to Houpt (2002: R5), movies such as *Goldmember* are referred to as 'tent poles'. They are event movies (in that their release is a media event) that are strong enough in their earnings to carry a season's pictures, and when they are released on video they carry ads for the other movies the company has made or is making. But in a company that does US $169 billion in business each year, smaller pictures can get lost, even good pictures, and even pictures that cost $25 to $50 million to make. They just are not big enough.

There is also an international component to policy issues. For instance, while different countries have different laws on free speech, privacy, access to information, and so forth, the Internet breaks through those laws by being universally available. Were international bodies truly out to respect the laws and cultures of member nations, great effort would be expended to find a way of building 'metatags' on information so that its flow could be controlled. However, this is on no agenda of any international body with any power. Thus, what the national laws allow in the least restrictive countries will become the norm for the world. This is certainly the case with free speech: on 27 June 1997 the US Supreme Court ruled that a law making it a crime to put 'indecent' material on the Internet was unconstitutional. The ruling went as follows:

> Notwithstanding the legitimacy and importance of the congressional goal of protecting children from harmful materials, we agree . . . that the statute (the Communications Decency Act) abridges 'the freedom of speech' protected by the First Amendment. . . . 'Regardless of the strength of the government's interest' in protecting children, 'the level of discourse reaching the mailbox simply cannot be limited to that which would be suitable for a sandbox.' *(Globe and Mail,* 30 June 1997, A17)

Of course, once barriers are broken by the Internet then it will not seem unusual for other barriers to be broken in other media. Arguably, a good example of this occurred in February 1999 with the 'Canadian edition' of *Hustler* magazine. Faced with the occasionally tough-minded Sheila Copps and her leadership in bringing Bill C-55 towards passage in Parliament, *Hustler's* proprietor decided to run a fake naked picture of the minister, which readers were encouraged to match up to a choice of genitalia. Independent of what passes for pornography, it is doubtful that any Canadian magazine would ever think up such a scheme, let alone wish to undertake it. The Canadian media operate at a different level of decency.

It is precisely these sorts of situations that demand we create policy to address the increasingly complex issues surrounding communications technology, particularly technology that can ignore national borders.

Technological Development: Rationales and Realities

Technology has a way of propelling itself in technological societies by creating economic opportunity and by tapping into our natural curiosity with objects and the way things work. But for technology to be seized upon and heartily embraced by society requires the allocation of resources in the short term with the promise of long-term gain. The usual rationales used to encourage society's eager acceptance of technology are based on some idea that a particular technology will improve the lot of humankind. The specific areas in which that improvement is purported to arise for communications are customarily health, culture, and education. In health, the wide dissemination of preventive, diagnostic, curative, and emergency information is stressed. In culture, the inexpensive and more extensive dissemination of quality products is highlighted. In education, the availability of better information designed more effectively for the learner, with the possibility of interactivity and supplemented by motivational devices and workplace relevancy, is just a beginning. Other positive impacts are claimed in the areas of self-direction, social interaction, international and inter-ethnic tolerance, and even cognitive skills.

The realities of technological development are somewhat different, as most theorists would predict. As we all know, television and radio can open the world to people at its furthest reaches, especially now with satellite transmission and particularly to areas with low literacy rates. However, achieving the promise of universally available television—to educate, inform, empower, amuse, and enlighten—is another matter. Take, for instance, something as simple as the teaching of reading. In some societies reading is regarded as a selfish or an indulgent activity insulting to those around you because it shuts them out. Cultural barriers in the spread of technology are common. In some cultures television programs educating women on how to control their pregnancies are seen as an infringement on the male prerogative. In other cultures television programs on certain subjects break taboos on their discussion, or on their discussion in the company of certain others. This makes the possibilities for technological development more difficult to translate into a reality.

In addition to cultural barriers are economic ones. For example, education programs and educational television systems most often must be paid for by scarce public funds, which means their availability is limited. In contrast, entertainment programs that promote consumerism and are funded through advertisements are widely available. However, such commercial programs raise expectations often beyond the ability of the recipient society to fulfill.

This is not to discount developments in communications or to claim that they cannot serve the interests of culture, education, and health. However, neither satellites nor the Internet, nor computers or any other technology, is likely to bring about a new egalitarian world. These technologies have brought about extensive efforts at distance education both in the developed and developing world—for instance, in China, India, Mongolia, Indonesia, and Thailand. In some instances they have been successful in raising the levels of skills and knowledge of students. But the efforts of people ultimately make the difference. While distance education may use computers and digital communications, because such technology can cope so easily with distance, they are not necessary components of distance education programs. Satellites (and wireless communication in general) also have the major advantage that they can help serve large, sparsely populated developed countries or developing countries that lack a land-based communications infrastructure. But again, no amount of technology of any kind will make a bit of difference without knowledgeable teachers and without a nurturing recipient society.

The introduction of computers into the classroom and access to the Internet have become symbols of modernization. The most radical rationale for their introduction has been the projected positive effects on both cognitive processes and personality development. The individualization of the learning process has also been stressed. Most importantly, and obviously, these technologies change the nature of the classroom from a closed-off laboratory of learning to a window on the world of organized and spontaneously produced information, opinion, and analysis. Nevertheless, the correlation between the rationales for technological developments and how they are manifested in reality is not always true. Nowhere is this more obvious than in situations where technology is introduced from one part of the world to another, where the knowledge of the technology is either limited or non-existent.

Technology Transfer

The export of new technologies from one country to another, especially from developed economies to developing economies, is usually referred to as technology transfer. Research on technology transfer reveals a number of insights. Generally speaking, direct causal correlations between the introduction of a technology into developing economies and changes in social behaviour (for example, making greater use of birth control devices and procedures) cannot be identified. Combinations of technology with other changes *can* change behaviour. For example, economically speaking (and only economically), in many rural settings it is seen as a net asset for families to have more children whereas in a city they are a net expense. Hence, birth control information with a change of circumstances may have an effect as urban dwellers gradually change their orientation to size of family.

Relatedly, technically oriented approaches to the introduction of technology (skills training, explanation of the equipment) are limited in their effectiveness. The social element is missing. Nor does manufacture of equipment in developing economies necessarily remove barriers to its adoption and maintenance. Equipment can be assembled under direction and without any understanding of its operation or any conception of how such a machine might be used to advantage. The importation of turn-key operations—the importing country simply opens the box and turns the machine on—often proves of limited value for lack of prior study of needs and an emphasis on the package rather than the content and the technology itself. Finally, such transfers, if they do work, often create substantial long-term dependency relationships as the receivers of the technology continue to rely on those supplying it for instruction on its use and maintenance problems.

Negotiations of technology transfers designed to increase their effectiveness are well intentioned but often get bogged down in political and economic considerations. The value of transfers is also affected by limited exploration of the differing needs and dynamics of the society receiving the technology. For instance, at a most obvious level, blowing desert sand, high temperatures, and high humidity wreak havoc on almost any electronic equipment. Massive importation of equipment may be useless until software and technologists are there to instruct users. Even attempts to create teleports, that is, self-sufficient zones of advanced telecommunications and high-tech industries to serve as springboards for industrialization, have limitations as a consequence of the technology transfer itself (Jouët and Coudray, 1991: 37, 38).

The difference in the success of technology transfer from Europe and North America to countries such as Japan and now China can be explained in terms of the nature and organization of those societies in contrast to the societies of Africa and South America.

Regulating Communications Technology—The Fundamentals

By international covenant, countries currently have the right to participate in communications development and to protect themselves from it, a protection that has been set aside in free trade agreements such as those that apply in the European Union. For example, should an unwanted satellite signal spill over so that it is transmitting inside its boundaries, a country can object. Japan has adjusted some of its satellite footprints in response to such objections. Countries also have the power to forbid the importation or exportation of any other form of information, either, material or immaterial. These rights to protect groups, which are largely dependent on national status, are termed collective rights.

Existing in tension with these collective rights are individual rights. Building from the foundation of the United Nations' Universal Declaration of Human Rights, all individuals have the right to 'seek, receive and impart information'. The challenge is this: while the collectivity has the right to act in its own interests, individuals within the collectivity have the right to do so as well, and these interests may be contrary to those of the collectivity as a whole. Thus, while Canadians as a group might want regulation to ensure a predominance of Canadian broadcast signals, many individual Canadians might want the freedom to choose what broadcast signal to tune into. Once individual rights are extended to corporations on the basis that corporations have the status of persons (in most legal respects), not only is there the force of individuals that do not want the state to interfere with individual freedoms but also that of corporations, which have an interest in promoting 'individual freedom'. This pits the political, social, and cultural interests of the collectivity against the demands for a non-interfering state by individuals and business interests. What is called for is a balancing of rights such that both can exist.

Technological developments represent a continual challenge for legal systems and policy-makers. The foremost challenge is to respect both collective and individual rights and to ensure that the greatest number gain the maximum benefit. At times and in some countries, creating universal benefit means assisting dissemination. At other times in other countries it may mean denying people access to certain technologies and content in order to promote a more universal distribution of other content via alternative technology. For example, in Europe, cable TV has been a long time in coming. One reason it was not introduced earlier is that it would have undermined state monopolies (Collins, 1992).

Other rights enter into the picture in technological development. Personal privacy is one. The most obvious example of invasion of privacy is that which takes place when someone with a scanner intercepts a cell-phone conversation. Similarly, someone may intercept your credit card number as it is being transmitted along the Internet. But other aspects of privacy are equally important. Profiles of individual consumer behaviour gained by tracing a consumer's spending patterns potentially infringe on personal privacy. Indeed, a whole industry is developing because we have the technological capacity to monitor all sorts of information. It is commonly called data mining (data mining is discussed more fully later in this chapter). For now, we should note that determining the level of privacy to be protected and then protecting personal privacy are complex matters.

Protection of intellectual property has also become a salient issue in the context of the form in which intellectual property can exist and in the context of a vast increase in information products. The first question is: are patterns of electronic signals eligible for protection, and if so, over what period of time and under what regime? And what about trademarks, patents, copyright? Should vendors be allowed to sell products in which the vendor may confine the use and time period of ownership, as they now do? How should national laws be harmonized to allow international co-ordination if there are fundamentally different positions on these issues? What protection and compensation should creators receive from databases that organize information produced by them? How should financial gain be divided between the creators and the organizations or individuals that hire them? Should moral or personal rights be protected, that is, those rights having to do with who is acknowledged as the creator and who determines how the work can be used? Or should only economic rights be protected? Who has responsibility for libel in the chain of information producers, packagers, and transmitters?

Another significant issue involves piracy. Given the historical record, specifically of the American publishing industry, which was built on a foundation of piracy, what obligations should developing economies take on? Studies show that computer, sound, and video piracy are especially rampant. Lack of protection of intellectual property allows cheap consumption of products. However, it also stands in the way of legitimate business in intellectual property in piracy-condoning countries. In India, in the early 1990s, so many small theatres were screening pirated videos that the state introduced a licensing system to attempt to garner revenues. Although this was done, the videos shown continued to be illegal copies. However, as Urvashi Butalia (1994) notes, this should not lead to the conclusion that piracy is rampant in all media in India. On the contrary, at least in book publishing, countries such as India have come to realize that their interests are better served by enforcing copyright laws. The film industry of Egypt, for example, is severely crippled by the numerous bootleg copies made as soon as any film is finished. Nevertheless, the motivation for many countries to take decisive action is not strong—the effect of legislation would be primarily to protect the interests of US industries.

These are just some of the major issues coming forward as the information society develops. As McLuhan said: 'We shape our tools', and by inventiveness and through enacting policy, especially in the context of technological convergence and the current power of communications technology, we shape technology, its industrialization, and its impact, and 'thereafter our tools shape us.' Once in place, the logic of that technology begins to play itself out within the context of further policy. Historically, nations attempted to balance the social, cultural, economic, and technological for the benefit of the greatest number. As we move into an increasingly international arena, the technological design of our future communications system is being determined by international politics and economics. The specific institutions involved are the WTO (formerly GATT), NAFTA, the EU, and the Berne Convention on copyright. These international conventions set rules or regimes for international trade in communications products and address consumer freedoms and target audiences with shared viewing habits. However, they are weak or do not address the social and cultural needs of national and political communities and their cultures except as mediated by the marketplace.

Technology and the Special Case of the Internet

In an article on technology and the mass media written for a sociology textbook on the subject, Smith makes two points about the Internet and how different it is from most technological development (Lorimer and Smith, 2003). He calls attention to the open-source nature of the Internet, that is, how all of the elements of the Internet were developed in the public sphere by unpaid programmers, many of whom were students. Built into each new element was an RFC: a request for comment. The RFC was effectively an open peer review system where one person would have an idea for a system for exchanging messages. He would then write some lines of program and tentatively call it an electronic mail system. Another programmer might come along and build on that by grabbing the first person's idea, examining his code, and reconceiving it in a simpler and elegant fashion. Then another programmer might do that again. In such a way, various programmers, working as an electronic community, developed the basic functionality of the Internet. And that is how Eudora, the e-mail program developed at the University of Illinois, ended up as a product of a university. It was developed by students, professors, and technicians within the university. TCP/IP was a method of computers communicating with servers that developed from a doctoral dissertation. (See www.yale.edu/pclt/COMM/TCPIP.HTM for an explanation of the function of TCP and IP.)

In a way, the request for comment, the RFC, is a trivial yet profound element of the Internet that distinguishes it from most, but not all, technological development. It represents openness, a community of inquiry building a piece of technology, in this case a communication system in the public domain unencumbered by patents or other attempts to create, own, and protect intellectual property. The open Internet took the devices of Mr Gates and Mr Jobs and made them interconnectable and interoperable. This open development structure reflects the normal manner in which scientific inquiry is carried out, with no secrecy surrounding one's activities and with open publication of results. A good parallel would be the human genome project, which has scientists all over the world mapping the genes of various organisms, posting what they are doing, and posting the results for all to see. This form of open-source technological development is a dramatic contrast to the activities of Microsoft (and all commercial companies), which goes to great lengths to protect its code and make it impossible for others to access. Doing so has made Bill Gates the richest man in the world. None of the pioneers of the Internet got rich. Effectively, they gave their intellectual property to the world.

Smith (2003) points to a second significant element of this manner of technological development. Industrial interests are not placed first and foremost. In fact, Smith argues that the open structure led to a particular technological form in which the pioneers laid down some basic rules that are reflected in the manner in which the system still operates—the RFC, the decentralized system controlled by no one, the continued evolution of open-source alternatives such as Linux.

One such project involves a group of Canadian university libraries and a number of Canadian social science and humanities journals. It is called Synergies: The Canadian Scholarly Information Network. The project involves the development of an on-line journal publication system housed at a variety of university libraries across the country, the content of which, at the beginning of the project, is intended to be the vast majority of Canadian social science and humanities journals alongside some significant cultural periodicals.

Synergies is an open-source programming project that would allow the whole system to be replicated in any other country. It will be built so that other publications will be able to be added on—cultural magazines, journals from other countries, etc. Its beginnings are to be found in the on-line capability of several scholarly journals and on-line publishing initiatives, the activities of the University of New Brunswick library, the on-line Canadian scientific journals of the National Research Council, and Project Erudit at the Université de Montréal.

Technology at the Beginning of Millennium III

The history of the tools and techniques of humanity provides a certain insight into the preoccupations of the times when they were developed and thrived. Think, for example, of the mechanical age that was captured by Leonardo da Vinci in his notebooks and of the control of the physical world at which his inventions were directed. Building on a variety of techniques of the time, Leonardo intuited the basic principles of physics and mechanical advantage. Thus, just as a gigantic threaded shaft could be used to raise a dome to the top of a cathedral, so a whirling blade could be used to lift a machine into the air. Similarly, by dissecting cadavers, Leonardo gained a deeper knowledge of the architecture of the human body and was thereby able to present it visually with greater insight than his predecessors or contemporaries.

It is true that, at all times, understanding and control of various phenomena are being advanced on a variety of fronts—the physical, the biological, the social, the philosophical. But often one or two areas predominate in certain times—for example, philosophy and mathematics in ancient Greece. Humankind has sought to control, dominate, and transcend the physical through technology from the building of the pyramids, and perhaps before, through Leonardo's time and into the modern era, where we have broken the bonds of earth, floated around it in a balloon in the jet stream (21 March 1999), and looked into the heavens with the Hubble telescope back to the beginning of time. The conquering of the physical world has captured our attention and imagination even though we have made tremendous breakthroughs in other areas, such as in medicine, where we have learned to control a variety of diseases.

The predominance of our focus on physical technology is passing. It is being replaced with two types of technology vying for our allegiance—biotechnology and communications technology. On the biological side we are moving beyond the level of the quite impressive but nevertheless fancy band-aid solutions of the past. The human genome project, together with light-sensitive drugs and a host of other developments, is taking us closer to achieving a completely new level of control over the biological realm. At the same time, communications technology is reordering our lives, forging a new integration of activities around the world and creating one very large economic, and hence social and political, system.

Marshall McLuhan was the Leonardo of the information age. Building on the existence of a number of technologies, changing times, and the initial conceptions of Harold Innis, McLuhan was able to intuit the evolving shape and the organizing principles of the information society. In examining the current state of our information society, we ask what we can do, how things are changing, and the general shape of developments now arriving, as well as those on the horizon. As enthusiasts are fond of saying, radio reached 50 million listeners after 38 years. TV took 13 years to reach the same number of viewers. It has taken the Internet a mere four years to muster the same-sized audience of 50 million. True, in each case the population base had expanded, but not by enough to account for such a vast change.

Achievements in the Information World

Over the past three or four years many new devices, services, and capacities have emerged to enhance our ability to communicate and handle information. In categorizing them according to their purpose or focus, we can see the parts of our lives that are being changed as well as the patterns of change.

Increased Communication Capacity and Speed

While communications satellites are now commonplace, when they first went up in the 1960s they were very much a novelty. Newspapers provided information on what time they would pass over and where to look for them in the night sky. The idea that signals could be bounced off an orbiting satellite was stunning. Equally stunning, years later, was the technology surrounding the introduction of optical fibres. Consider this description from *The Economist* (6 July 1991: 87) of how optical fibres work:

> Some scientists are dissatisfied with electrons. This seems ungrateful. Electrons have served mankind well as carriers of energy; they have become adept as shufflers of information. Some of their attributes, however, offend purists. They have mass, which makes them a bit sluggish. They have electric charges, which means they interfere with one another. Fortunately, there is something better around, something with no mass, no charge, and no rival when it comes to speed: light.

Satellites and optical fibres have changed both capacity and speed of communication. And Canada has been quick to take advantage of such technology. Not only were we the first nation to launch a domestic communications satellite but the government of Canada has maintained a surprising commitment to both speed and capacity. As mentioned in Chapter 3, Canada boasts the world's fastest data network. CA*net 3 began operations in the summer of 1999. It can transfer 40 gigabytes of data per second—the entire two and a half hours of the movie *Titanic* in just half a second. This is 20 times faster than Abilene, the American Internet 2 network. The speed of CA*net 3 is 750,000 times as fast as CA*net, set up in 1993 (William Boei, *Vancouver Sun,* 16 Dec. 1998, D5). In the fall of 2002, CA*net 4 was announced. CA*net 4's initial capacity will be four to eight times that of CA*net 3.

The social meaning of these speeds is a greater and greater erasure of distance for an increasing data-rich array of digitized information. For example, since 1997 the Children's Telehealth Network has connected various centres in the Atlantic provinces to one of the regions best hospitals, the IWK Grace Hospital in Halifax. For the hospital, it was a way of extending itself to the rural communities that had provided it with support over the years. By 2002, software together with high-speed high bandwidth connectivity allowed a surgeon in Halifax to undertake an operation on a patient in St John's, Newfoundland. He controlled a robot in St John's by high-speed data networks.

Increased Flexibility in Personal Communications

When Alexander Graham Bell made the first phone call from Brantford, Ontario, to Paris, Ontario, on 10 March 1876, the notion that one could speak to a person in one location far distant from another inspired awe. Marconi's signalling by clicks and Fessenden's superimposing of music on radio signals anticipated Bell, but the idea of having a private conversation at a distance was some achievement. The drawbacks of the technology were never considered. First, the person you wished to reach had to be at a particular location, such as at home, at the office—anywhere there was a telephone. Second, you had to know where he or she was.

We have lived with that restriction for just over a hundred years. Only now are we moving beyond it. Pagers, cellphones, and satellite-based phones provide us with the ability to be reached anywhere and to initiate a call from anywhere to any other person, no matter their location. Whether on top of Everest, at the South Pole, sailing across the ocean, flying along in a plane, or merely eating in a restaurant, we need not lose touch with anyone—as long as we can all afford the technology.

Increased Flexibility in Producer Communications

Communications technology is helping develop a different kind of flexibility for the producers of information. Not only can information be sent to almost anyone anywhere, but all manner of content can be sent as well. As late as 1995, broadcasting stood apart from the Internet for its capacity to generate and carry audio and visual signals. The Internet appeared to best manage text, perhaps with a few graphics. All that has changed. With Real-Audio™ and Quicktime video™, sound and moving images have become so much a part of the Internet that the whole notion of broadcasting hangs on the gossamer threads of existing (outdated) distribution and receiving technology and the organization of production to allow for high-quality content.

For example, in 1997 a video conference involving several sites across Canada would have cost the producers more than $1,000 per one-hour session. In 1999 a course on the social implications of technology was conducted out of the University of Calgary by Professor David Mitchell. It involved students and professors from McGill University, York University, Ryerson University, University of Alberta, and Simon Fraser University. Using the M-bone technology and work stations of the Sun computer company, the course was undertaken on the Internet and was carried out within the normal communications carrying capacity of the universities involved—and there were no extra telecommunications costs. By 2002 Mitchell had moved on and was able to run a half-hour video conference from a hotel Internet café in Salvador, Brazil, for the $40 it cost to rent the room and gain access to an ordinary two-megabit cable modem.

The digital foundations of computer communications technology appear to be almost as powerful as the discovery of the atom. By breaking down information into binary digits, the simplest possible code (zeros and ones), scientists and scholars have been able to rebuild worlds of information and communications so that electrical communication of text, sound, and image at any distance has become commonplace.

The flexibility of the emerging system and its relative low cost have led to a number of developments. In October 1998 the House of Blues—a chain of night clubs co-founded by actor Dan Aykroyd—began Netcasting (broadcasting via the Internet) three live concerts and 10 album 'listening' parties each week. The chain has also installed full digital production studios at all its locations so that it can create broadcast-quality concert videos anywhere. Also in 1998, a few on-line businesses began to offer a *legal* service whereby they customize CDs to suit a consumer's taste.

Piracy—Historically and Today

The famous privateers of history were not unlike the pirates of intellectual property of today. Privateers were not outlaws. Rather, they were individuals with armed vessels authorized by a government to engage in hostile acts against enemies of the state, often to rob them of their property. Thus, Elizabeth I used Francis Drake and other pirates to raid Spanish galleons as they tried to bring back gold from the Americas to Spain. The history of privateers who operated on the Atlantic Ocean out of Canada stretches from 1613 to the Treaty of Ghent signed in 1815.

After the American Revolution, American printers, acting in a parallel fashion to the privateers and with the US government's full knowledge, began pirating English novelists in 1776. In fact, it was on this foundation that the US publishing industry was built. While pirating books differs from privateering in the sense that it was not the waging of physical combat to rob physical objects, it was clearly robbing English authors and publishers of their intellectual property. It was not until Canadians began to return the favour, pirating US authors and selling them back to the US, and Samuel Clemens, a.k.a. Mark Twain, started investing a great deal of time and effort to argue on behalf of his own copyright interests, that the US government considered respecting (and enforcing) copyright law.

Today, in China and other developing countries, even countries like Singapore, unauthorized copying of books, software, tapes, CDs, and videos—not to mention the production of fakes in the form of brand-name cameras, watches, and designer clothing—is common. No doubt a certain pirating in patented drugs also takes place. The US, more than any other country, makes a very large issue of this because American producers have the most to lose. Using US definitions of copyright and its own evaluation of the extent of illegal copying, losses are estimated to be in the billions of dollars. Of course, were those billions in royalties and licensing fees to be paid by the poor to the rich countries, it would only exacerbate the debt problems that already exist throughout the developing world.

With the expansion of intellectual property, and specifically the patenting of genetically modified life forms, piracy will increase. Whether this is a problem is all a matter of perspective. For instance, nations and cultures that have made plants and knowledge about the medicinal quality of plants available to Western drug and food companies have traditionally never been granted intellectual property rights for their contributions. However, the drug and food companies have benefited greatly from patenting medicines, and now foods, derived from these very same plants.

(Continued)

Given the inequities of such circumstances, you might ask: Why should drug companies be allowed to go to the Amazon to find out what plants are being used by Aboriginals and take them home and analyze them, identify their active ingredients, develop patented drugs, and under patent have a monopoly to sell them for a certain time span? Why is it acceptable for medical units to test African prostitutes who seem immune to the AIDS virus to identify that immunity and not promise them a share of the millions that the drug companies will make if they can turn the active ingredient into a vaccine? Similarly, why is it commonplace for book publishers to publish fine coffee-table editions featuring Aboriginal art with no recompense going to the group from which the art came? Part of the answer to these questions lies in what is defined as proprietary knowledge and intellectual property and what is not in the public domain. Increasingly, these issues are being examined and adjustments are being made to intellectual property laws so that some rough justice is created. Nevertheless, the developed world has been having a free ride on the common resources of the earth, mainly because we have made the laws.

MP3 computer audio format technology began to be used extensively in late 1998 to upload and download high-quality, highly compressed (up to 12 times) music files that can easily be stored or transferred over the Internet. At the time, hundreds of sites had large selections of illegal MP3 files and encouraged users to both upload the material and make it available to others. Users claimed that the technology allowed sampling and promoted purchases among those who really like a band or artist they have listened to. Such arguments are still put forward and they have some validity. The technology also allows users to download and listen to bands or artists that do not obtain heavy rotation or exposure on radio stations. Hence it is a threat to the market control of the music companies because it makes available music that is not under their control. In 1998, you could buy a portable player capable of downloading music from the Internet and playing it back from a memory card. In 2001, Apple purchased the rights to a whole variety of songs so that each new iMac and iBook came with a selection of songs. Users were encouraged to convert their own CDs to MP3 formats so they could have their music on their computer. Apple also introduced the iPod, a device with 5, 10, or 20 gigabytes of memory that could hold a whole library of music or equally serve as an external hard drive.

The development of MP3 and the availability of both legal and illegal material on the Internet energized SOCAN (the Society of Composers, Authors and Music Publishers of Canada) to seek to force Internet providers to pay a tariff for material distributed over their networks. In the US, the Recording Industry Association of America (RIAA) hired a company to use automated software to search the

Internet for sites offering illegal songs in an attempt to force providers to pay for the material they make available. At the same time, some bands were and still are giving their music away on the Internet. Other artists are selling their albums on the Internet.

Three arguments can be made in favour of the use of MP3 technology. First, the recording industry is forever crying wolf. Tape recorders, cassette tapes, DAT recorders were all supposed to spell the end of the industry—of course, they did not. Second, with rampant piracy, producers (read rich, large companies) are forced to bring down their prices. This happened with computer software in the early 1990s. For instance, in August 1993, Microsoft's CD-ROM encyclopedia, *Encarta*, was selling at between $495 and $529. In March of 1994 its price had dropped to $189. By December of 1994 it was on sale for $79. *The Canadian Encyclopedia*, which began selling in 1994 at $79, is now available on CD in gas stations for $9.95. Third, MP3 has developed into a legitimate and extremely useful audio compression technology that can be used to distribute any kind of audio material via the Internet.

Increased Flexibility in Sourcing Through Easy Communications

Increased flexibility has not been restricted to private communication and the production of information. The entire economic system is reorienting itself to take advantage of easy and cheap communication of all kinds of messages around the world. The best example of this is the sourcing of production off-shore, where labour is cheap and restrictions are few. Designer clothes are now made in Asia; sports equipment is manufactured almost any place where cheap labour is available; data processing is done in the Caribbean; and software production is pursued in India. Often, certain areas are designated as specifically available to facilitate sourcing for foreign companies.

The views people take on such matters can vary considerably. For example, designer clothing companies can be seen as intrepid explorers who have tamed the human labour pools of the developing world for world commodity production and consumption. Or, those same corporations can be seen as rip-off artists that exploit poor people and poor countries and take advantage of human resources unavailable to small business firms. As many have pointed out, it would take a single worker about 10,000 years to earn the same amount given to a single sports celebrity for endorsing a brand of shoe.

The case of Japan is interesting. After World War II (though it started earlier), Japan began building itself into an economic powerhouse by using cheap domestic labour and producing a whole range of low-priced utilitarian products for the North American and European markets, usually under licence to US and European technology developers and manufacturers. As an economic giant, Japan increasingly developed its own brands, moved up-scale in its product mix, and began outsourcing its own manufacture to other parts of Asia, where labour costs were lower. All this was made possible and eased by communications technology, which allowed the Japanese companies to follow the North American market and develop products to meet emerging demands.

Increased Ability to Perform Tasks

The number of tasks that have become less labour-intensive as well as easier continues to expand at a dizzying pace. For instance, arithmetic teaching programs are readily available for children to use along with typing programs to encourage touch typing. A scanning device that works like a magic marker is able to translate words on the fly. The translation is then displayed on the LCD (liquid crystal display) screen. The device is about the same size as a cellphone.

Wizards—small computerized programs that provide a set of predetermined alternatives for common tasks—are increasingly being made available to shorten the time required to perform certain tasks and to enhance the ability of the user to communicate effectively. Like their more powerful brethren, the software program, and indeed in parallel with many modern conveniences, wizards encourage the user to set his or her sights higher: dress up a letter to make it appear more professional; create personal stationery rather than using blank paper; keep track of one's own financial accounts meticulously rather than haphazardly; use a thesaurus, grammar checker, and dictionary rather than let mistakes slip by.

Web Ownership and Culture

Lawrence Lessig is a Stanford University professor who argues that intellectual property law is undermining fundamental freedoms of US and world citizens. Many references to his writing and speeches can be found on www.slashdot.com. He has also written two books on the subject, *The Future of Ideas: The Fate of the Commons in a Connected World* and *Code, and Other Laws of Cyberspace,* and was named one of *Scientific American's* top 50 visionaries. In a speech called 'Free Culture' he focused on four points.

1. Creativity and innovation always build on the past.
2. The past always tries to control the creativity that builds upon it.
3. Free societies enable the future by limiting this power of the past.
4. Ours is less and less a free society.

The Recording Industry Association of America (www.riaa.com) represents the other side of the argument, as does the Motion Picture Association of America (www.mpaa.org).

Source: cyberlaw.stanford.edu/lessig/

The manipulation of text by new communications technologies is only one area of possibility. Photos and movies can be retouched to make them more attractive or, indeed, to create false impressions. Such technology was used in the movies *Forrest Gump*, in which old and new footage were merged, and *What Dreams May Come*, in which Robin Williams apparently tromps through an oil-painting heaven. As well, satellites are sent into space, guided to their destinations by computer control; computer-controlled aircraft with no persons aboard and sometimes no fuel undertake weather reconnaissance; schedules are optimized and maps are drawn using Global Positioning System (GPS) units; goods, as well as people, can be tracked; robots can even be sent into poisoned environments to retrieve, neutralize, or dispose of hazards. The possibilities for new technology seem endless.

The mother of all technologies for increasing the ability to perform tasks and decreasing the effort is database technology, specifically relational databases. We have spoken in an earlier chapter of the ONIX (Online Information Exchange) standard used by book publishers. The standard calls for the creation of a bibliographic record of each title that a publisher publishes, which, when combined with other records, forms a bibliographic database. Its primary use is to allow publishers to send information to the computers of large bookstores such as Chapters/Indigo and Amazon.ca. But being a database, the information can be entered once and retrieved for many purposes. It can be used to provide title information for the publisher's Web site. It can also be used to flow the information into templates for the creation of catalogues. Or, it can be used to generate publicity materials. In addition, whenever any member of the company needs to obtain precise information on a title, she or he can do so simply by accessing the bibliographic record of the title in the database. In addition, by granting access to authorized persons, should data change, the book go out of print, the price change, etc., those authorized can change the information and, in certain cases, trigger a message to be sent to those who should have the information. All this may sound quite mundane to any person who is not a publisher. But when you realize that in many of the uses mentioned, the information must be re-created, and each time information is created it must be proofed, and in spite of this mistakes are still created, you can see how this fundamentally changes the nature of a publisher's operations.

New Services and Products

In 1999, new Web-based services and products were emerging at a fast and furious pace. For example, a Web site matched lawyers with motorists who have received speeding tickets in the lawyers' home territory. Other sites offered a selection of books to download—the first half of the book was free; for a fee you could download the second half of the book. And access to the Encyclopedia Britannica was available at www.eb.com. By 2002 the site had turned into a place where the owners attempt to sell users a package and the vast majority of products and services had disappeared.

In 1999, there also was much talk of the electronic book. In October 1998, Softbook Press offered its version of the electronic book (see www.softbook .com). It was followed by the Rocket e-book and others and then Microsoft itself came out with an electronic book plus e-book reader technology that could be downloaded onto one's computer. By late 2002, e-books had disappeared, perhaps to reappear when the technology is better, perhaps to be replaced by charged plastic sheets.

Capturing and Changing Behaviour

Above and beyond the new services and products that technology has introduced and that are supposed to improve our lives, communication technology allows organizations and people to capture, analyze, mimic, and even change human behaviour.

You might not remember how speedy it used to be at the checkout in the grocery store, or indeed in any other store. Items were rung in quickly, the total was immediately available, you handed your cash to the cashier, collected your change, and were done. Now things are much slower. The slowdown is caused both by credit cards and the computerized 'cash register'—these two technological developments require that credit cards be verified, transactions registered, and your name and purchases processed in the computer. This may eat up your time but it produces valuable information for the retailer. Such information includes inventory monitoring as well as patterns of purchasing by groups and by individual consumers. Your behaviour has been captured for the benefit of the seller at the cost of your time, though we tend to believe in the speed of technology.

Every electronic transaction is recorded and the sum total of transactions creates a body of data, which, in turn, can be mined for valuable information. This information can then be used by the person who collects it or it can be sold to another party. The direct recording of information also results in a net decrease in the costs of the transactions. No longer is paying for an item one function, assessing the store's stock levels another, counting cash yet another: with electronic transactions all this and more are rolled into one.

Speed may return. Just as ATMs (bank machines) lessen the need for tellers, the grocery store cashiers' days may be numbered. For between $150,000 and $400,000, Symbol Technologies has developed a system of scanners that it can install in stores for consumers to do their own checkout *(Globe and Mail,* 9 Dec. 1997, C10). To shop is to scan; to scan is to pay. Watch for the day when you own your scanner, which is programmed by a radio wave as you enter the store. You will hear a voice greeting that will provide you with information on specials in certain categories from which you frequently buy and will ask you, after you press 'no more items', whether you have forgotten the buttermilk. Such a scenario was played out in the movie *Minority Report.*

While the above is exciting in its own way, it is important to recall that all it does is mimic human behaviour. In a small business, a one-person or one-family operation, information is constantly being processed by the person in charge. The small business often knows its customers intimately: 'The usual, Mr Wodehouse?' With all this fancy computerization we merely approximate normal, human, interactive behaviour by members of a community.

In addition to introducing new ways of doing what we already do and in offering up new work procedures and leisure pursuits, information and communications technology is changing our daily behaviour. For instance, in terms of leisure, according to a study done for America Online *(Globe and Mail,* 1 Oct. 1998, C6), the average family with Internet access watches 15 per cent less TV than families without such access. Our work behaviour has also changed. Working at home

Windows as a Horseless Carriage

The idea of an e-book seems to exemplify Marshall McLuhan's idea that we look into the future with our eyes fixed on our rearview mirror. In other words, we desire the technologies we develop to perform tasks established technologies can already do. This rearview mirror idea recognizes the control the past exerts on the present and the future.

A similar idea can be found in McLuhan's discussion of the automobile as a horseless carriage. In that discussion, he explores the role of historically grounded metaphor for thinking about an ever-changing world. Thus, rather than seeing the automobile for what it was, people and society of the time compared the automobile to the most appropriate mode of transportation with which they were familiar, the horse-drawn carriage. Even the inventors saw it this way. For example, they put the steering at the front rather than at the rear and it took until the 1950 for Buckminster Fuller to demonstrate the greater efficiency of rear-wheel steering. In the early years of the automobile the controls society wanted to put on it were extensions of the ways in which people thought about horse-drawn carriages.

Windows, which is a not particularly high-quality adaptation of Mac OS technology, is based on horseless carriage features. It is a credit to Steve Jobs and his partner that they were able to see the value of historically grounded metaphors and so created icons of files and file folders and directories that computer users could understand. Even the trash gave people the comfort of a known environment.

Indeed, when you move a file from one folder to another, you are participating in that metaphor. What is actually going on is that you are changing the document identifiers so that when you go to a directory and a file folder you initiate a retrieval mechanism that identifies information tagged as belonging to the 'document' you wish to access. In fact, however, the information is probably stored in fragments on various parts of your hard drive. How long the metaphors of files, file folders, and trash or recycling bins will last is anyone's guess.

(telecommuting) has become much more common, with some people carrying on work for firms in other countries. As well, our information-seeking behaviour has changed. The *Vancouver Sun* (18 June 1998, D11) notes that 47 per cent of college graduates in the US go on-line to get news at least once a week (news is not defined).

Creating Virtual Reality

While the notion of a 'true' virtual reality is overhyped, the retail world is attempting to create a shopping 'virtual reality'—an environment that has all the desirable elements required for a person to shop with confidence and enjoyment. This challenge has become quite a preoccupation in today's marketplace. If any crucial element is missing or awkward—whether browsing, payment, trying out the product, returning the product, or getting a good price—the on-line retailer will suffer. And if the respected firm Forrester Research is correct in its prediction that by 2003 $108 billion in goods and services will be sold on the Net, attentive retailers will take over the market.

The American company Amazon.com and Amazon.ca appears to be a fairly successful model of on-line book retailing, and in Canada, Chapters/Indigo is attempting to compete. The Chapters/Indigo site provides many features:

- 2.9 million listed titles (this does not mean they are in stock, only that the company is prepared to search for the book for you);
- sourcing from Canadian publishers and distributors (this means that you are supporting the Canadian publishing industry and Canadian authors);
- biographies of 20,000 authors;
- a comprehensive literary awards listing;
- editorials on the book world and reviews dating back 20 years;
- audio clips of author interviews and readings;
- on-line discussions;
- a list of literary events.

Yet to date, financially, the site has not broken even.

Nuisances, Problems, Dangers

Though plenty has been achieved in the past few decades thanks to communications technology, a number of problems have also arisen. As stated earlier, with technology the good is always accompanied by the bad. Below we explore some of the not-so-helpful effects that new technologies are having, from the bothersome to the dangerous.

System Vulnerability

Moving to a computer- and communications-dominated world introduces certain vulnerabilities, some a result of human intervention, others a result of nature. For instance, it has yet to be seen whether a major cosmic event could wipe out the ever-more-delicate computer systems that are being developed. Major electronic discharges, perhaps major solar flares, could possibly interfere with computer communications. As well, gophers have been known to chew through the coatings on optical cables. Indeed, cable protection had to be developed to avoid such attacks.

In addition, satellites are vulnerable to the forces of the universe, as Canada learned when two of its communications satellites were hit with cosmic particles. This and other such events yielded extensive media coverage of the biggest non-event of 1998: scientists had predicted that the largest meteor storm in 32 years, with particles travelling as fast as 70 kilometres per second, could easily play havoc with the more than 500 communications satellites in orbit in November 1998. Called a Leonid shower because the particles came from the direction of the constellation Leo, more than $1 million was spent studying the shower and predicting its likely result. While the scientists expected the objects to vaporize on contact with the satellites—they were, after all, only about as large as a grain of sand—there was some chance that the result of the collision could be the release of an electrical charge that would disrupt or destroy service. Nothing happened. Chicken Little breathed a sigh of relief.

Beyond natural forces, human action can also expose how the technological system is vulnerable. For instance, one of the major features in Internet commerce is trust, the most obvious issue being whether or not your credit card number will be intercepted on its way to a legitimate vendor. But there are other issues as well. Will the quality of the items you purchase match what you expect? Will you be able to exchange an unsatisfactory item? Will there be prompt delivery? Will your privacy be respected and protected?

In 1997 Ian Goldberg, responding to a challenge made by RSA Data Security Inc., broke the code of its 40-bit encryption product. At the time, RSA was an industry leader. It appears that for every encryption code, an encryption breaker code can be written. This applies to viruses as well. According to Symantec's AntiVirus Research Centre there are 19,000 different viruses. So far SAM Intercept, Symantec's anti-virus program, has been able to neutralize most of the ones that have gained any real circulation.

In January 1999 Air Miles and its customers were shocked to find thousands of 'confidential' customer files open for viewing to passing Web browsers. While the problem was fixed quickly, the vulnerability of information collected by others is well illustrated by this unintentional breach of security—and this example did not even involve outside hackers breaking into the site. Even though the files do not contain credit card numbers, to make them publicly available is an invasion of privacy.

Or is it? Consider the issue this way. Why is it not an invasion of privacy when Air Miles compiles that information and puts it to use? Has Air Miles not invaded the privacy of the consumer in the same way in which that privacy obviously seems to have been violated through its public availability? That is, does the number of people who see the information determine if the privacy is invaded?

Or is there a fundamental principle involved that has no connection to the number of people who can access the information? When each magazine to which you subscribe, each charity to which you donate, each club to which you belong, or each government department with which you have dealt sells its data lists to others, is that not an invasion of privacy? These are issues that must be dealt with if we are going to address adequately the issue of system vulnerability.

On 21 October 2002 a massive denial-of-service attack was mounted on the domain-name root servers of the Internet. It pirated the use of 6,000 ordinary PCs and considerably slowed down eight of the 13 servers. The system was maintained and certain spokespeople were of the opinion that the perpetrators were attempting to demonstrate what was possible rather than bring about the collapse of the Internet (News.google.com, 23 Oct. 2002).

Hypes

Consider this statement made by Henry Blodget, analyst with CIBC Oppenheimer in New York: 'We continue to believe that Amazon.com is in the early stages of building an electronic retailing franchise that could generate $10 billion in revenue and earnings per share of $10 within five years' *(Globe and Mail,* 17 Dec. 1998, B15). Blodget could be right. Certainly the people at Amazon believe him and are determined to be a lead company in the age of on-line commerce. But Blodget could also be wrong. After all, he had only been covering the company for three months when he made the above statement. He began monitoring it when it was trading at $84. At the time of his pronouncement, the stock had reached $289. Who is to know? Who is to say that faith is all the company needs to achieve its goals? Hype seems to be a large part of the technology in the marketplace these days, often driving interest and investment. And it is becoming more difficult to assess or avoid hype.

In 2000, when the last edition of this book was written, it was reasonable to ask the question: 'Ever been spammed?' In 2003, to find an Internet user who has not been spammed would be a miracle. Anti-spam advisers recommend the following for avoiding the latest hype in advertising:

- Do not broadcast your e-mail address.
- Use filters that eliminate spams before they reach you.
- Use a code name for an on-line identity.
- Do not list yourself in directories.
- Complain to your Internet service provider if spammed.
- Do not respond.

Crime

Then there is crime, especially fraud. As if hacking was not enough, one group extracted information from the Web site of an investment dealer and superimposed a fictitious name, Turner Phillips, on the material. It was then able to sell stock in fictitious companies and refer investors to information contained on the Web site. Numbers of investors took the bait and lost significant amounts of money.

Phreakers, the telephone equivalent of hackers, cost Canadian businesses $40–$50 million in illegitimate long-distance calls. Most phreaker fraud is carried out through Direct Inward System Access (DISA), a system that allows employees to make work-related long-distance calls from home. The fraud artist dials the DISA number, enters a security code using a computerized speed dialer until the code is cracked, and is then able to dial anywhere at no cost.

Extreme fraud involves stealing the identity of another. According to the Ontario Privacy Commissioner, Ann Cavoukian, identity theft is 'an epidemic' in the US. Identity theft involves collecting enough information on someone that the fraud artist can begin to assume that person's identity. Having set up his or her own accounts, the thief then moves in on the victim and enters his or her financial life. Knowing this to be a possibility, people who make extensive use of the Internet routinely provide false information in response to Internet queries in order to protect themselves.

In January 1999 a Canadian hacker group called the 'Hong Kong blondes', led by 'Blondie Wong', claimed to have shut down a Chinese government satellite *(Vancouver Sun,* 15 Jan. 1999, A9). Obviously, this was not confirmed by the Chinese government. Given that such a feat is possible, intelligence agencies around the world are spending resources to develop such a capability and also to develop protective measures against it. In October 1997, the US government warned that neither government nor industry has the wherewithal to protect communications and power grids *(Vancouver Sun,* 8 Oct. 1997, D2).

Espionage

Spying on the Internet is undertaken by various individuals and groups who conform to different standards of behaviour. Those who spy include governments, persons paid to use any technique to perform their task, whether legal or illegal, persons paid to operate within the law, and curiosity seekers (who merge with hackers as a group). One former CSIS employee (not a bad place to have worked if you are seeking instant credibility in this business) runs a small business intelligence agency, Ibis Research Inc. (see www.ibisresearch.com) that can keep track of businesses by using such software as Highlights 2, which is programmed to look for changes in Web sites. Price changes, personnel changes, announcements—all are pieces of a puzzle that can provide information to competitors about changes about to take place in target firms. Patent applications, e-mail contributions to discussion groups, published papers by firm personnel are all grist for the mill. They also use other Internet tools, such as search engines, and try to refine their methods, such as by logging search terms and results in order to analyze success over time *(Globe and Mail,* 26 Nov. 1998, C3).

Though Ibis Research operates within the law, a seamier side of the business definitely exists. It is to be found in the environment surrounding high-tech companies and movie stars. All kinds of digital gumshoes will hack into telephone records (or pay off someone in the phone company) to obtain access to telephone records. They will look for unexplained calls and discover secrets that celebrities would rather keep hidden. By tracking purchasing, banking, in fact, any transactions done by particular persons, all sorts of information can be gained: where they shop, where they have been on a certain day, who they are in contact with, and so forth. Such techniques are just a different, more focused, version of the data mining undertaken by companies such as Air Miles.

Much different and more serious consequences can result from communications monitoring. For instance, in a speech he gave in Vancouver in early 1999, BBC news anchor Nik Gowing reported how the BBC was now using field television production units that could be carried in two medium-sized suitcases. These units are capable of recording sound and image and beaming back information to Britain using Iridium technology. The difficulty, he noted, was that while the plight of a refugee, for example, could be documented and the footage shown around the world, those desirous of causing harm to the individual could gain valuable information not only by monitoring the programs but also by monitoring the communications and the location of those communications. As a result, journalists, in order to protect the people they report on, are having to engage in a new kind of self-censorship.

Information Wars

On the war front, when the US and its NATO allies (including Canada) waged war on Yugoslav President Slobodan Milosevic, they also declared an infowar to supplement their bombing campaign. Infowar is defined by the US Air Force as 'any action to deny, exploit, corrupt or destroy the enemy's information and its functions; protecting ourselves against those actions; and exploiting our own military information functions' *(Globe and Mail,* 24 June 1999, T2). Buoyed by its assault on Iraq's information computer system by means of viruses, hackers were employed by the US government to attack the Serbian leader's foreign bank accounts. No doubt they also made use of the Global Hawk, an unmanned infowar drone airplane that flies over enemy territory to intercept messages and inject false data into computer networks.

In late 1998 the Pentagon declared cyberspace the fourth battleground, identifying human decision-making as its primary target. To provide a sense of its scope, the Information Warfare Research Centre contains a 22-page guide to US Department of Defense infowar organizations and on-line resources, including the Information Warfare Executive Board (ibid.).

One interesting element of the Iraq War of 2003 was that once the fighting started, there was very little discussion of an information war but a great deal about the inaccuracies and insipidness of US coverage (see Mitchell, 2003). In the lead-up to the war, a certain amount of attention was paid to leaflet dropping, and during the war commentators were surprised at how long the Iraqi state television remained functioning. Also, the spirited denials during the war of Iraq's Information Minister, Mohammed Saeed-al-Sahaf (dubbed 'Comical Ali') that flew in the face of televised reality were elements of an information war.

Of course, the whole pretext for the war was information-generated rather than action-generated. The US claimed that Iraq possessed or was assembling chemical, biological, and nuclear weapons of mass destruction. The US failed to convince the United Nations but went ahead anyway. In light of the lack of evidence of such weapons of mass destruction, well after the war ceased, on 22 May 2003, US intelligence agencies began an examination of information sources, not as an act of contrition but as an attempt to determine the quality of information-gathering (Lumpkin, 2003). Such a move completely sidesteps whether invasion was justified.

The 'So-What' of Technological Developments

From the beginnings of radio to 1990 the principal debate over communications was a cultural one. The central question asked was: What are the effects of the media on society? The next question was: How can society ensure that the media speak to the full range of citizens, with their broad range of tastes and desires for entertainment as well as information and enlightenment? The guiding question appears to have changed, however. Now it is: What economic benefit can we derive from developing and applying communications technology?

This transformation is no accident. Technology has combined with the search for profit to create a juggernaut of development that, from 1999 and to 2001, was seemingly unstoppable. With the burst of the dot-com bubble, development based on information technology has not stopped, however, it has just slowed to a more realistic pace. Added to the pressure of technology and business are the efforts of the large exporting countries—the US, the UK, the leading economic powers in Asia, and certain directorates within the EU bureaucracy. They have been pushing and continue to push economics and trade in every theatre, particularly the WTO (formerly GATT), the International Telecommunications Union (ITU), EU agreements, the OECD, the G-8, and the Asia-Pacific Economic Cooperation forum (APEC)—the Vancouver meeting of which got the Chrétien government into so much difficulty for effectively denying the rights of Canadians to free assembly and expression.

Countries such as Canada and France are also enthusiastic players, except that in the name of culture these countries are attempting to secure a lasting place for domestic cultural industries—publishing, broadcasting, film, video, and sound recording. Canada's concerns for distinctive voices and for speaking to all Canadians exist within this economic context of seeking to ensure a vibrant cultural production industry.

As art and culture become, more and more, areas of commodity production, artists and cultural producers are being more fairly rewarded for the use made of their work. However, they are also becoming more involved in the exploitation of their works, and hence more conscious of markets and exploitation strategies. Today's visual artists, for example, must address several important questions. Should they sell a hundred signed prints of their work, or sign a contract for unlimited reproduction with a royalty on sales of, say, 10 per cent? Which will enhance their reputation as an artist? Which will make them richer and allow them to paint more?

At the same time, and on the less pessimistic side of things, with new technologies come new industries and new players. For every business that fell victim to the march of rail and highways, vast new opportunities were created by the new transportation. Similarly, while lots of middlemen and women will find themselves displaced, job opportunities are opening in new industries. No doubt there is and will continue to be turmoil as people are forced to change jobs, and governments certainly should be looking for ways to assist in this transition. But with each new major technological development, there is an increase in wealth, and if governments do their job of ensuring that the benefits of technology are shared, there will be increased consumption and hence increased jobs.

Reflections on Our Technological Society

As McLuhan said: 'We shape our tools. . . .' Through inventiveness and the enactment of policy, especially in the context of the evolving power of communications technology, we shape technology, as well as its industrialization. And McLuhan added: '. . . thereafter our tools shape us.' Once in place, the logic of that technology begins to play itself out within the context of further policy.

At the most general level, the major implication of information technology is it is creating a separate sector of society, the information sector. It is separating information from whole sets of actions and making that information actionable. As a result of business firms collecting our shopping patterns, we can be targeted for relevant information rather than deluged with a lot of information that is rather irrelevant to our consumer behaviour. By creating a database of book title information we decrease the work required to generate different information packages that require that information. By the establishment of Internet commerce, the purchase of goods and financial transactions from the home are facilitated. However, each of these examples has a set of unintended consequences.

While companies knowing our shopping patterns may decrease our junk mail, independent of the feeling of our privacy being invaded, we may lose touch with the general information we gain by browsing through flyers of advertised products. True, we might never buy many of these products, but the flyers tell us that such products exist and inform us about consumer culture and how others in the world live. By decreasing the number of times title data must be entered and the number of people who must enter title data in a publishing house, independent of the loss of jobs, we may find that fewer people in a publishing firm have passing familiarity with exactly what titles are being published. This may decrease the identification employees feel with the firm's titles and authors and cause other types of unanticipated problems. By facilitating Internet commerce, independent of the opportunities for theft, we may affect socialization among various groups and thereby cause social instability.

Thus, policy is needed. Independent of the need for band-aid policy to ensure privacy and the need of severe disincentives for such non-violent crimes as identity theft, we need to understand in a very broad sense what the reorganizing consequences of a separate information sector are. We must return to Innis's notion of the bias of information. What biases will be introduced into society by the ability to collect information on just about everything or by the ability to copy easily every information package? These are difficult to imagine because most observers are either enthusiasts or resistors of new technology. The significance of commentators such as Lawrence Lessig (cyberlaw.stanford.edu/lessig/) is that they point out how, through intellectual property law, information owners are gaining an advantage to the detriment of the general social interest.

The development of new ways of doing things, new industries, and new opportunities will continue and so will the concomitant disruptions. The internationalization of markets and hence globalization, which we discuss in the next chapter, are also issues to observe. Internet-based companies will arise, but whether they will be worldwide or North American in scope, like Amazon.com, national, like Indigo.ca, or local, like your nearby independent bookseller, remains to be seen. What products will work on the Internet and how are also yet to be determined.

In terms of culture per se, as opposed to economics, it appears that in our wired world there will be increased trade and less centralized production, but only time can affirm this. In the social arena, we continue to hear about the bizarre, such as the women who create their own exhibitionist Web sites and are the inheritors of the centrally organized exploiters of the female body, such as *Playboy's* Hugh Hefner. Then there are the porn sites, the news sites, and so on. Unsung in our increasingly sensation-oriented media, specifically the Internet, are the wellness sites, the information sites, the medievalist sites, the research and scholarly journal sites, the social and professional organizations, and so on. Such Internet sites increase access to many for their material.

Technological Theft Protection

Weep no more for your lost computer. For less than $100 plus a monthly monitoring charge, you can buy software, for example, Computrace from Absolute Software Corp. or similar software from ADT Security Services Canada Inc., which causes your computer to periodically phone a central location and record the number from which it is calling (suppressing any indication of the activity). With the number in hand, the police can locate the computer and pick it up.

Equally as interesting as speculating on the future is looking at theories of technology. Given the rapid pace of change, are features in the interaction of technology and society emerging that are not accounted for in current theories? The theories stand up fairly well. The intended and unintended effects of technology are wrapped up together. A price is being exacted even as we 'advance'— there is, for instance, more information, but public access to information, especially on a percentage if not an absolute basis, may actually be diminishing. As well, problems are being both solved and created. For example, banking is faster and less vulnerable to human error, but banking systems are less personal and can crash or be hacked into. Many new, increasingly centralized businesses are being created—large, dynamic, national and international companies with sophisticated information systems, as well as Internet companies—while old, perfectly fine, friendly neighbourhood businesses are being destroyed. The locus of control is changing, as is the nature of control. And unforeseen consequences are constantly emerging. Who could have imagined computer viruses before they arrived (except, of course, for the hackers and companies that first created them)? Who, 20 years ago, when the largest looming problem seemed to be what we were all going to do with our leisure time, would have thought that the average professional would be working an increased number of hours per day, per week, per month, and per year? As apparatuses of technology evolve so do new professions—the best examples are the database builders and the Web site designers.

Perhaps changes in the dynamics of work have been the biggest surprise. Those who have work appear to have to work harder, even though technology seems to have facilitated our workplaces and jobs. And many are economically worse off rather than better off. Communications technology has not translated into a net increase of efficiency. Rather, it is just a new way of doing things that seems absolutely unstoppable. Along the same lines, the digital deficit is something to take very seriously as the developed world surges ahead and developing economies do not keep pace.

Summary

This chapter began with two definitions of technology. One defined technology as encompassing apparatus, techniques, and social institutions. The other saw technology as an intentional extension of a natural process. We reviewed several complementary theoretical perspectives of technology, which emphasized how the positive and negative consequences of technology are always intertwined and unpredictable. We examined technological determinism and the limitations of the influence of technology on society.

Communications technology is closely linked to control, and in the past century this technology has been governed by policy. Indeed, at the beginning of the twenty-first century, as a result of digitalization and technological convergence, we are facing many of the same policy problems that we faced at the beginning of the twentieth century—how to provide for the greatest social benefit given the technologies and industries that are currently emerging.

The social rationales most often used in favour of technological development highlight health and education. On the other hand, the realities of technological communications systems, once they are introduced, involve commercial exploitation. Communications technology, like all technology, does not immediately transfer to developing societies. Some basic concepts in the regulation of communications technology are individual rights, collective rights, privacy, and intellectual property.

The state of communications technology at the dawn of the third millennium is nothing short of astonishing. Optical fibres can be impregnated with rare earths, which serve as natural amplifiers; cable signals can ride free of electricity lines; and dolls can have more computing power than the desktop computer of a mere decade ago.

Computers have combined with communications to make location irrelevant to the efficacy of personal communication. Video, audio, data—any kind of information—can be transmitted with ease to any location in the world and into outer space. Production need no longer be highly centralized because high-quality hardware is relatively portable and inexpensive. Indeed, so inexpensive is it and so available are transmission technologies that protection of intellectual property has become increasingly problematic. Ease of communication is creating, if not a global village, then certainly a global marketplace of producers in which dominant economies can outsource production to inexpensive labour pools.

Previously complex tasks have been simplified and aided by portable translators and macro programs or wizards. Objects can be located and maps can be drawn with ease. Vast pools of information are readily available. Behaviour of all different kinds can be monitored and patterns identified that are even a surprise to those whose behavioural patterns are being monitored. And shopping is being transformed into a virtual experience.

These developments come at a cost, however. Communications systems can be shut down by natural forces and by sabotage. No information is entirely secure because, just as computers can build walls, other computers can knock them down. Active Internet users can become unwitting victims of spams and viruses. Their whole systems can be shut down. With copying being so difficult to control, corporations are vulnerable to piracy and sabotage. Individuals can have their identities stolen and any electronic transaction can be accessed by a determined hacker. But at the same time, homing devices can be attached to private property to prevent loss.

Although communications have a cultural component, the development of communication technologies is firmly within the political and economic domain. Canada, France, and certain other nations continue to attempt to preserve cultural communication against the ravages of information and entertainment exporters led by the US. What the final balancing of interests will be remains to be seen. Indeed, the evolving shape of society as the dynamics of digital communication technologies, play themselves out also remains a matter of speculation.

It is clear that the unintended consequences are rarely thought through, nor can they ever be entirely predicted. There has been very little consideration of the macro implications of the development of the information sector. This lack of prior consideration is part of the technological imperative, which assumes that any unforeseen problems can be solved in time by ever newer technological solutions. The blithe acceptance by society of technology because it means economic gain, at least for some, blinds us to considering the desirability of technological development, whether that development involves genetic or communications research and development.

Technology, Intellectual Property, and the End-of-Privacy?

Master of My Domain: The Politics of Internet Governance

Daniel Paré

Introduction

As we move into the first decade of a new century, the evolving capabilities asso-ciated with Internet working are becoming increasingly central to the way busi-ness and everyday life are organized. The rapid spread of the components of the Internet infrastructure and the enormous growth in the range of its applications mean that the manner in which it is governed and the outcomes of alternative types of governance regimes will have major consequences for a growing number of users. Controversies have erupted internationally over the appropriate forms of governance for the Internet and these have their counterparts within regional and national contexts. This chapter offers an in-depth examination of one such controversy and its resolution within a national context.

During the mid-1990s the Internet-addressing regime for the United Kingdom underwent a period of institutional reconfiguration. This process culminated in the establishment of Nominet UK, the domain name registry responsible for administering and managing the *.uk* top-level domain (ITU 1999b). Domain names are unique identifiers and their creation and registration are among the 'few centralized points of authority in the supposedly open, decentralized world of the Internet' (Mueller 1997). Domain name registries may be regarded as inter-mediary organizations. They coordinate and administer the linking of identities in the physical realm with a specific type of virtual identification—a domain name. The conflicts associated with the restructuring of the management and administration of the *.uk* name space were not restricted to the technical features of the UK registry system.[1] Instead, they encompassed a transformation and reor-ganization of the institutional framework of Internet governance in the United Kingdom.

The ongoing efforts to restructure the global Internet-addressing regime have given rise to numerous controversies, some of which are also visible in the con-flicts associated with the UK case. At both the international and domestic levels, conflict is often generated by the actors' perceptions of the goals of the Domain Name System (DNS) and how these goals might best be achieved.[2] The fundamental issue in these disputes is the management of value allocations and choice alternatives. The disputes that have coincided with attempts to reconfigure the manner in which the DNS is coordinated appear to be directly and/or indirectly related to the economic significance of the technology involved. Within the UK context the manner in which a diverse set of actors interacted to resolve these controversies has affected the perceived flexibility and efficacy of Nominet UK as an intermediary between those who manage and administer one dimension of the Internet architecture, and those who seek to use the Internetworking infrastructure.

The issues that have given rise to controversy over the restructuring of the DNS have provided a focal point for discussions about appropriate forms of governance for the Internet. However, the processes through which changes in governance are being negotiated and implemented have received relatively little attention. In fact, the bulk of Internet-related research on governance tends to treat Internetworking as a conceptual black box. Consequently, relatively little attention has been given to the role of power and politics in influencing the success or failure of organizational and administrative innovations with respect to Internet-addressing regimes. The analysis in this chapter is developed to illustrate how the collective and individual actions of industry players, Internet and non-Internet organizations, government authorities, and specific individuals have influenced the scope and direction of change for a key dimension of the architecture supporting internetworking.

The discussion presented in this chapter focuses on the events leading to the formation of Nominet UK. This is a story about the mediation of the contending interests of various organizations and individual actors. The features of the mediation process are examined by focusing on the organizational, commercial, and technical factors that appear to underpin the social dynamics of the governance process. A detailed analysis of these features reveals how the dynamic relationships between social actors led to the establishment of an intermediary organization that is now responsible for coordinating and administering the *.uk* name space. In the case of Nominet, informal processes of interest mediation appear to have coalesced in a manner that legitimated the outcome of a protracted period of institutional reconfiguration. Analysis of this process of institutional transformation offers considerable insight into the dynamics of organizational change in the context of 'cyberspace' or the 'virtual society'.[3]

The Reconfiguration of the UK Domain Name Registry System

Formation of the UK Naming Committee

This story begins at a time when UK domain registrations were handled by an organization composed primarily of a relatively small group of academics working in computer networking research, the Joint Network Team. From the late

1980s up to 1993, this team was responsible for overseeing the development of the Joint Academic Network (JANet), a major internetworking backbone in the UK.[4] With the growth of commercial internetworking in the UK, increasing numbers of organizations sought to register names in the *co.uk* sub-domain. EUnet GB Ltd, a private commercial Internet Service Provider (ISP) founded by a group of academics in 1993, assumed responsibility for maintaining the *.uk* root name server on a voluntary basis for the Joint Network Team.[5]

In early 1993 UnipalmPIPEX, at the time the only UK Internet Access Provider with its own international transmission capacity, approached the Joint Network Team to express its concern with this arrangement. PIPEX claimed that it was unfair that one of its competitors, EUnet GB, should control the domestic domain name registry.[6] Shortly thereafter, Demon Internet,[7] the first commercial Internet Access Provider to offer low-cost Internet dial-up access in the UK, also approached the Joint Network Team with similar concerns about the way the *co.uk* sub-domain was being managed. A series of informal discussions between representatives of these four organizations produced an agreement that domain name registrations 'should be handled in a more democratic way' (email interview, 2 Sept. 1998). Under the new arrangement, authority for coordinating and administering the *co.uk* sub-domain was delegated to a Naming Committee made up of three commercial and two non-commercial Internet Access Providers. However, the Joint Network Team, which subsequently evolved into the UK Education and Research Networking Association (UKERNA), maintained a right of veto over decisions reached by this committee.[8]

The five founding Naming Committee members were: The Joint Network Team (Network Registration Scheme) Administrator;[9] JANet; EUnet GB Ltd; Demon Internet Ltd; and UnipalmPIPEX Ltd. In late 1993, BT Internet Services became the sixth organization to join the Naming Committee.[10] Through the voluntary activities of representatives from these organizations, the Naming Committee operated as a self-governing body with no formal structure or chairperson. In essence, the 'committee' consisted of a group of closed electronic discussion lists, where domain name registration requests were processed and naming-related issues were discussed. Commenting on these events, one founding member noted that these operations were very 'amateurish' and that 'everything was happening so quickly, and no one had really thought it through. Basically the system was embryonic' (interview, 3 Sept. 1998).

In October 1994 the London Internet Exchange (LINX) was established to provide a point of physical interconnection for ISPs to exchange Internet traffic through cooperative peering agreements.[11] In order to ensure that member organizations were serious backbone providers, membership of this association was made contingent upon meeting two criteria.[12] First, applicants were required to own a permanent, independent, international connection to the Internet. Secondly, members had to sell Internet services, including at least one public service allowing customers to connect to the Internet. The five founding LINX members were the same five organizations that had founded the Naming Committee in October 1994.

Although the Naming Committee and LINX were completely separate organizational entities, representatives of the former decided that LINX membership requirements should also be used as the criterion for establishing full membership of the Naming Committee.[13] Consequently, each company that joined LINX simultaneously became a full member of the Naming Committee. This decision appears to have been taken primarily on the grounds that LINX membership was seen as the easiest and most efficient way of establishing the eligibility of prospective members of the Naming Committee. One former representative of the Committee pointed out, however, that the decision to establish joining criteria was made 'because it was to our [member organizations'] advantage, but from a long-term business point of view this was a definite weakness because it was an arbitrary action' (interview, 3 Sept. 1998). The consequences of this arbitrary action for the restructuring of the naming system are examined in the next section in order to highlight how informal processes of interest mediation between social actors gave rise to an administrative innovation that altered the way in which the *.uk* domain was managed.

The Dynamics of the UK Naming Committee

Two aspects of the Naming Committee's operations need to be singled out. First, the activities of Naming Committee members' representatives were subject to very little scrutiny by senior management in their respective organizations.[14] Secondly, in its early days the UK domain name registration system was regarded by members of the committee as being relatively flexible and reliant upon both interactions and mutual cooperation between Internet access providers. The registry system was believed to have benefited from an ethos that stressed the maintenance of technical continuity and integrity.[15] As a result, many individuals felt that, prior to 1995, this evolutionary process had the cumulative impact of forging 'good' relationships between competing organizations in the UK Internet industry.

By 1995 the rapid increase in demand for Internet-related services began to accentuate procedural and structural weaknesses in the Naming Committee's registration practices.[16] Structurally, there was a growing division between a rapidly evolving commercial Internet-working industry and a technical infrastructure that was operated and maintained on a volunteer basis. Procedurally, the Naming Committee's administrative processes were highly contentious, fuelling disputes between full members with voting rights and guest members, as well as between individuals within the voting member constituency. At the root of these controversies were questions about the registry's decision-making authority and its legitimacy. The next two subsections highlight some of the features of the power struggles between these social actors that were associated with the use of specific techniques to allocate domain names prior to the establishment of Nominet UK.

The Naming Committee Voting Structure

By late 1994 the technical, social, and political relationships that evolved around the management and administration of the *co.uk* name space achieved a form of closure. At the technical level, closure was reflected in the stabilization of the technology facilitating the registration of names in the *.uk* domain. Socially, the domain was managed by a relatively small homogenous group of technical engineers with shared perceptions about how to structure and administer addressing needs within the *.uk* name space. At the political level, power relationships within the Naming Committee had been structured in a manner that allowed representatives from a relatively small number of ISPs to determine the acceptability of name requests. Simply put, the closure reached reflected the fact that by late 1994 internetworking in the UK was characterized both by the presence of relatively few actors with a limited variety of needs, and by a relatively limited set of ideas about how best to meet these needs.

This closure manifested itself in two ways. The first was due to the fact that the ability to submit requests for domain names was restricted to members of the Naming Committee. Individual network-users and providers of Internet services were not permitted to apply directly to the registry for domain names. From the perspective of non-members, this was problematic because, although the registration of domain names was a service that was provided free, member registrars were levying fees for providing this service.[17]

The second manifestation of closure was attributable to the Naming Committee's bifurcated voting structure. In order to offer domain name registration services in the *co.uk* sub-domain, domain name registrars who were unable to meet the LINX/Naming Committee membership criteria (that is, a permanent, independent, international connection to the Internet and the sale of Internet connection services) had to be introduced electronically to other Committee members by a full/voting member. In most cases, the introduction to the Committee's discussion list was made by the full/voting member that provided bandwidth for the applicant organization. The applicant was granted guest status and permitted to apply for domain names on his or her own organization's behalf and that of its customers. Guest members were not permitted, however, to vote on domain name requests or policy-related matters.

Some of the founding Naming Committee members claimed that there was no reason for denying voting rights to guest members. Rather, the diversity of the organizations that might wish to offer clients domain name registration services had been underestimated and it had been assumed that, if an organization did not provide Internet access services, it would not require input into how the registry system was managed. Other full voting representatives, however, suggested that the reasons for denying voting rights for guest members were somewhat different. 'The rationale for not allowing guests to vote was that it would have involved too much administration. Counting up just a few votes was much easier to do. Besides if we allowed all the resellers/guests to vote, they could have theoretically voted to dismiss all the rules, and one has to ask where this would have left the system' (interview, 9 Sept. 1998). One consequence of this action was that the Naming Committee structure was perceived by most guest member representatives, and by some full/voting member representatives, as being elitist. One former voting member representative who was sympathetic to this view pointed out that the lack of congruence between LINX membership criteria and eligibility for voting membership in the committee meant that guest members were prevented from exercising the same powers as their access providers (interview, 5 June 1998). This state of affairs underpinned a popular consensus among guest member representatives that this exclusionary voting structure meant that they were being subjected to the tyranny of the larger providers of Internet services.

The fact that all domain name requests were made in a 'public' forum reinforced concerns about the arbitrary and subjective nature of the Naming Committee's decision-making processes. Discussion-list members were able to identify who was registering domain names for various companies simply by looking at the messages posted to the naming discussion list. The discussion list was described as 'a source of free intelligence' that allowed members to keep tabs on their rivals (interview, 9 Sept. 1998). The fact that full/voting members also registered domain names on behalf of their clients further bolstered the perception of the Naming Committee as an elitist organization because voting members had the authority to object to their competitor's requests for names. In the light of these circumstances, at least one company began recommending that its clients register domain names under the generic *.com* top-level domain, since registrations in this domain were not public knowledge and the process in *.com* was believed to be far less arbitrary than in the *co.uk* domain (interview, 29 Apr. 1998).

The Subjective Implementation of Arbitrary Rules

The absence of a comprehensive and unambiguous rule set indicating the criteria and policies for domain name registration in the *co.uk* domain perpetuated numerous disputes amongst the actors. The guidelines for suitable names were originally expected to function on the basis of the 'common-sense interpretations' that manifest themselves 'in a gentlemanly environment' (interview, 9 Sept. 1998). In essence, there were no formal rules for registering domain names. Instead, committee members used guidelines outlining what might be regarded as 'good' or 'bad' names. The voting members were supposed to base their decisions about the acceptability of requested names on these guidelines (see Box 10.1).

Examination of this box suggests that, although some of the guidelines were based on technical requirements (that is, two-character names may conflict with top-level and second-level domains), others focused on non-technical requirements that some voting representatives believed domain names should represent (for example, only one domain name per trading entity; no registration of

Summary of Naming Committee *co.uk* Registration Rules

Restriction	Rationale
1. No two- or three-character domain	Two-letter names may clash with two-letter country name designation[a] Not sufficiently informative
2. No abbreviations of company names	Not sufficiently informative
3. Only one domain name per company	Use of hierarchical structure of the DNS and sub-domains of common domain more appropriate
4. No registration of brand names	Domain names should not represent products. Facilitate the prevention of cyber-squatting.
5. No offensive names (i.e. *rudeword.co.uk*)	Such names convey the wrong image and are immoral

[a]Country code top-level domains are based on two character codes detailed in ISO-3166, an international standards agreement establishing two and three character abbreviation country codes for sovereign nations (see ITU 1999).

Source: Naming Committee Information Sheet 1999.

acronyms; and restrictions on registration of potentially offensive names). Efforts to enforce this highly subjective rule set led to a situation where requested names were often objected to, and/or rejected, on stylistic grounds. In numerous instances, voting representatives objected to requests for names and suggested alternative names that were in line with their personal interpretations of the registration guidelines. For instance, law firms often had their name requests rejected on the grounds that the *law.co.uk* sub-domain was more informative for people seeking to find law firms on the Internet than *co.uk*.

Initially, the Naming Committee approved registration requests in the *co.uk* sub-domain only for limited companies, as it was argued that this implied commercial legitimacy. This policy prevented organizations that were not registered with Company's House in the UK—for example, trading companies, partnerships, and sole traders—from registering domain names matching the character string under which they had established a commercial reputation. It also meant that companies trading under a name that was different from their registered name were prevented from registering the name(s) with which they were commonly identified in the physical realm. To overcome this, a decision was made by the voting representatives to register names for entities that could provide 'proof of existence'. However, the meaning of 'proof, was never clearly defined. As a result, the kind of information solicited upon submission of requests for names tended to be arbitrary and dependent upon the whims of representatives from voting member organizations.[18] In the face of difficulties in enforcing this ambiguous rule set, some representatives argued that the process of voting on domain name requests was an impediment to the commercial provision of registration services.

Between 1995 and 1996 the problem of subjective implementation of arbitrary rules and guidelines was aggravated by the rapid growth in the number of full/voting and guest members of the Naming Committee. By July 1995 the number of voting members had increased from five to eleven and the number of guest members had increased to thirty-seven. By August 1996 the number of voting members had more than doubled over the previous year to twenty-four organizations. Figures for the numbers of guest members are not available, but it is estimated that their ranks grew dramatically during this period to approximately 100 organizations. As the numbers of full/voting members with a major interest in the registration process decreased relative to guest members, the earlier goodwill and camaraderie that had characterized member interrelationships began to wane. An 'us-and-them' environment developed between those representatives seeking to exercise ill-defined control over the registry process and the advocates of a more open registry system.

Proponents of a 'closed' process tended to be technical engineers serving as representatives of voting members. Their primary concerns tended to focus on the technical and moral dimensions of the registry system.[19] Advocates of a more 'open' registry system sought the establishment of a neutral body that would process domain name registrations on the basis of a non-restrictive formal rule set that would operate on the principle of first come, first served. There was a consensus among advocates of this approach that proponents of a 'closed' process often lacked an understanding of the commercial realities and were concerned instead with how the Internet as a whole should evolve.

The Emergence of Nominet UK

A meeting convened to address the problems associated with the Naming Committee's operations was held in Cambridge in September 1995. This meeting was the product of a posting on the committee's discussion list soliciting interest in an informal gathering. The meeting was the first opportunity for the majority of member representatives to meet in person. It was agreed that the meeting would incorporate a discussion of procedural issues with respect to the .*uk* domain and its future management, and that votes should be taken on the issues raised. The meeting was attended by thirty-five people, including representatives from seven full/voting organizations and eighteen guest organizations.

The meeting achieved very little in terms of tangible outcomes. The attendees agreed that the registry system needed to be changed, but how it should be changed, remained elusive. Agreement was reached on the need to formalize rules for registration procedures and membership, but no immediate action was taken. It was decided that new full/voting members would be accorded guest status during their first three months on the committee. In addition, it was agreed that the ranks of the voting membership would be enlarged to include two members co-opted from, and elected by, guest members as representatives of their interests. And, finally, because of growing dissatisfaction with the operation and maintenance of the registry database, EUnet GB was required to commit to a service level agreement.[20]

In the light of the problems facing the Naming Committee, representatives from UnipalmPIPEX and BTnet submitted proposals reflecting their personal views about the establishment of alternative registry procedures to UKERNA in late 1995. Their documents closely paralleled one another.[21] Both called for the abolition of the committee structure and a shift of the registration process into the commercial realm. The creation of a more centralized registry structure incorporating other neutral sub-domains—that is, *ltd.uk, org.uk*—was also recommended. Both documents also called upon UKERNA to take a greater role in overseeing the registry to reduce the likelihood that committee members would exploit the registration process to their advantage. The proposal from the BTnet representative went further than that of his counterpart in this regard, suggesting that, if UKERNA was not prepared to perform registration services, the rights of administration and operation of the *co.uk* name space should be sold to an organization that would be willing to run the UK Internet Naming Service in a manner that would guarantee high-quality service.

In January 1996 a second meeting to remedy the problems facing naming administrators was held. It was attended by twenty representatives of full/voting and guest members of the Naming Committee. The meeting was chaired by Dr William Black, the then director of UKERNA and the person responsible for the *.uk* domain.[22] Building on the ideas in the BTnet and UnipalmPIPEX proposals, he called for the creation of a neutral legal body to run the name spaces under the *.uk* domain. By this time similar approaches to the management of national domains had been adopted in The Netherlands, Germany, and Japan. Three working groups charged with developing more detailed proposals were created. Dr Black took responsibility for developing a business plan for the proposed registry organization, a representative from BTnet volunteered to establish a financial working group to create a funding model, and a representative from UnipalmPIPEX volunteered to establish a working group to develop an operational model dealing with the technical requirements of the naming functions to be performed by the new entity.[23] These working groups were composed of several volunteer representatives from a range of UK-based providers of Internet services. A formal proposal for the development of a new registry organization was presented to the UK Internet service provider community at a public meeting in April 1996. The proposal consisted of three components:

- the establishment of a not-for-profit management company providing legal protection, limited liability, and a professional full-time organization to carry out the necessary tasks;
- the creation of a Steering Committee open to all organizations that were prepared to pay membership fees; and
- the establishment of a charging regime for sub-domains registered under the neutral domains.

This became the proposal for the establishment of Nominet UK.

Although being the 'responsible person' appears to have given Black considerable *de jure* power, his *de facto* power depended upon the support of the interested parties in the UK Internet industry. Consequently, views about this initiative were sought from a broad array of participants in the UK Internet industry. However, uncertainty about this proposal led to further disputes between actors, mainly regarding the extent to which a new organization would ameliorate the structural and administrative weaknesses of the Naming Committee.

According to the business plan, the new organization would operate on the basis of a Shared Registry System where all members would manage the registry. The proposed organization would have two executive directors, two non-executive directors, and a steering committee composed of all the organizations that were willing to pay nominal annual subscription fees. The function of members would be to decide on a naming policy for the *.uk* domain and on the appointment of non-executive directors. A particularly contentious issue was the voting structure of this new organization. Many smaller service providers were critical of this aspect of the proposal, suggesting that it would simply graft the elitist structure of the Naming Committee onto the new registry organization.

Subscription fees were initially to be based on the annual turnover of members and voting entitlements were to be proportional to the fees paid up to a maximum of £5,000. However, at the first annual general meeting of the new organization, Nominet UK, the number of votes for members was linked to their respective rates of name registration and provisions were made allowing all members to purchase votes up to a defined limit.[24] A voting structure where the number of votes was proportional to respective registration volumes was seen as a means of ensuring that the steering committee would be representative of the relative commercial strengths of its members, thus minimizing the risk of unrepresentative groups exerting undue influence on the registry.

The business plan for Nominet indicated that it would introduce a charge for each name registered in neutral sub-domains of *.uk*. Prior to the start of Nominet's operation in August 1996, the registration of domain names had been free to Naming Committee members. When Nominet began administering the *.uk* domain, the registration of names in the *.uk* sub-domains became subject to a fee of £100 per name for the first two years of registration, followed by a renewal fee of £50 for every subsequent year that the registration was maintained. However, member organizations were entitled to a 40 per cent discount on the cost of registering domain names. Despite this discounted rate, there was some initial concern that these charges would be levied before names had been entered into the registry database and that the prices might be beyond the expenditure capabilities of small entities. This might benefit large providers of Internet services, who would be able to afford larger capital expenditures up front. Such fears were allayed by an agreement to levy charges on domain name registrars on a monthly per registration basis for registrations during the preceding month.

Another key area of controversy focused on Dr Black and how best to limit the power he could exert personally over the registry process. He had offered to leave UKERNA to become the managing director of Nominet UK, and some feared that he might seek to take advantage of his position for personal gain.[25] The majority of actors regarded the new registry as being responsible for coordinating and administering a 'public good', and there was a consensus that this entity should not be run as a for-profit endeavour. This concern was circumvented by recommending the creation of a not-for-profit company limited by guarantee.[26]

There was also uncertainty regarding Dr Black's suitability for the position of managing director of Nominet. He had an academic background and some industry participants asserted that the new registry should be managed by an individual with a commercial background. Dr Black served as managing director in a voluntary capacity from Nominet's incorporation in May 1996 until it commenced operations in August 1996. At the first annual general meeting in August 1996, he was formally elected to the position.

By 1999 Nominet had come to be perceived within the UK Internet industry as having successfully remedied the structural and administrative weaknesses plaguing the old registry system. A survey of UK-based providers of Internet services in November 1998 indicates that Nominet's operations were regarded positively at that time.[27] Respondents were asked to indicate the strengths, weaknesses, and relevance of nine factors pertaining to Nominet's operations (see Fig. 1).

The results shown in Fig. 1 suggest that the technical features of the registry system were held in high regard by UK-based domain name registrars. Approximately three-quarters of the respondents indicated that the transparency of Nominet's rule set was one of its strengths. Nominet's open policy-making forum was seen by 73 per cent of respondents as another of its strengths. By establishing formal registration rules and practices Nominet appears to have succeeded in removing the ambiguities that had been associated previously with the registration of domain names in the UK. In other words, domain name registrars and registrants were no longer believed to be subject to the *tyranny* of any particular group of actors after the establishment of Nominet.

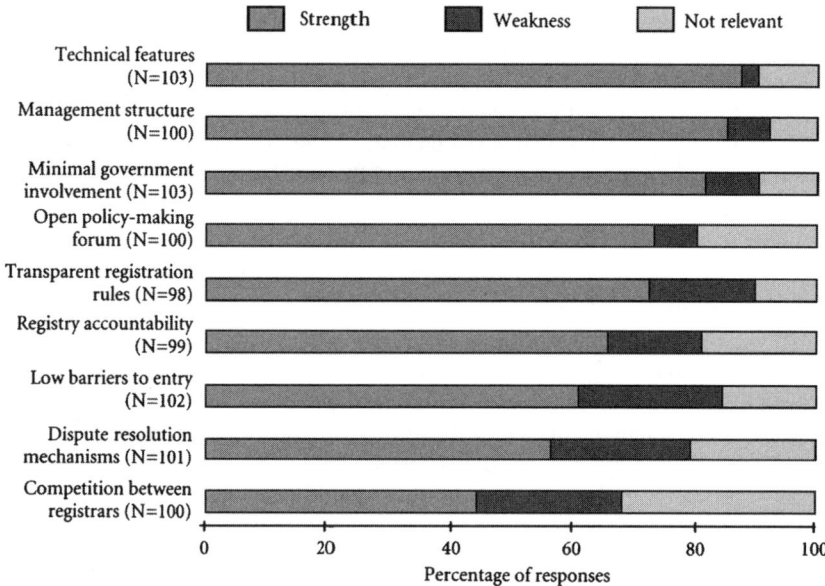

Figure 1 UK Internet industry perceptions of Nominet operations

The Politics of Internet Governance

There has been a dramatic surge of interest in Internet governance in recent years. Prescriptive accounts of developments in Internet governance reflect bipolar perceptions of how Internet working should evolve. Some authors argue that the Internet encompasses numerous technical and non-technical elements that, when taken together, constitute a conceptual whole. They tend to advocate the implementation of top-down governance frameworks to ensure the well-being of the conceptual whole (Foster 1996; Gould 1996a; Mathiason and Kuhlman 1998a,b). In contrast, others assert that there is no conceptual 'whole' and that the only policy required is one of *laissez-faire* (Gillett and Kapor 1996; Mueller 1997, 1998; Rutkowski 1998a,b). These authors do not account for emergent or changing structures of Internet-addressing regimes and they offer relatively little insight into the dynamic relationship between regulatory change and the technical characteristics of networks.

Another line of work on Internet governance has pursued a process-oriented approach. In this case, the focus is on procedures that give rise to various outcomes in the cyber-realm. Adopting a libertarian perspective, Johnson and Post (1996a,b) maintain that Internet working, including Internet addressing, can be governed by 'decentralized, emergent law',[28] where privately produced rules would be fashioned through decentralized collective action, leading to the emergence of common standards for mutual coordination. They suggest that these processes might lead to a redefinition of notions of civic virtue within online environments (Johnson and Post 1996a,b).[29] In contrast, Reidenberg

(1996, 1998) suggests that the hardware and software that constitute the virtual realm impose a set of default rules or *Lex Informatica* on communication networks. Reidenberg argues that, whereas political governance processes usually establish the substantive laws of nation states, in the cyber-realm the primary sources of default rule making are the technology developer(s) and the social processes through which customary uses of the technology evolve.[30] These default rules define possible behaviours and the values that are upheld within the cyber-realm.[31] Similarly, Lawrence Lessig argues that architecture is the most significant constraint on behaviour within physical and cyber domains.[32] It establishes conditions of entry and participation and reflects a distinct philosophy of social ordering (Lessig 1998*b*, 1999).[33] Because values underpin the architecture, there is the potential both for government encroachment into the virtual realm and for the private sector to embed its values within the code. Therefore, according to Lessig there is a need to ensure that the architectures of cyberspace protect values such as liberty, free speech, privacy, and access (Lessig 1998*a*, 1999).

Internet governance entails a mixture of regulations embedded within the architecture and other forms of regulation that apply to various aspects of the cyber-realm. Unfortunately, the perspectives outlined above are highly speculative and seem to underestimate the significance of the social dynamics of governance processes. They yield little insight into how regulatory initiatives establish social, political, and cognitive legitimacy within cyberspace. This highlights the need for empirical analysis of what social actors actually do rather than prescriptive, ideologically laden speculations about what they should do. In the context of implementing changes to the *.uk* domain and the global Internet addressing regime, the catalysts for change were embedded in the techniques employed by social actors to administer the DNS.

In so far as specific design features of a system establish the patterns and boundaries of interaction, the choices and decisions that are implemented by social actors may be regarded as a political phenomenon (Barley and Tolbert 1997; Easton 1965; Wendt and Duvall 1989; Wendt 1987). These interactive processes involve multifaceted power relations that give rise to the authoritative allocation of values. These relationships can be understood as reflecting the instrumental use of resources to attain specific goals such as motivating an organization, or group of organizations, to do something that they would not otherwise do (Dahl 1957; Lasswell and Kaplan 1950). However, the analysis of power relationships cannot focus solely upon overt conflict because power may also be exercised in a manner that limits the scope of, or even restricts, decision making (Bachrach and Baratz 1962, 1963). Power may also operate in a more sublime manner in the form of institutional norms and procedures that bind and constrain the arenas of conflict and its resolution (Lukes 1974). This multidimensional view of power offers a framework for examining how organizational politics influence innovation in the present case of changes in the Internet domain naming system.[34]

Recognizing that organizational politics consist of power in action as well as power in conception, this framework is premised upon a notion of dynamic interactions between 'surface-level' and 'deep-structure' politics. The former are the day-to-day contests and struggles for collaboration between actors—for example, 'attempts by one or more parties to exploit (bend, resist, implement) the rules of the situation that are to their own advantage' (Frost and Egri 1991: 236). Less easily observable deep-structure politics refer to power that influences, 'usually in hard to detect ways, not only the way the rules of a situation are played but the very way the rules are framed in the first place' (Frost and Egri 1991:236). Power relations in the deep structure covertly, and/or overtly, shape and influence actions at the surface level. Surface-level actions shape the articulation of power in the deep structure, thereby influencing future surface-level politics.

Frost and Egri postulate that conflict over the introduction of a proposed organizational innovation involves conflict between the status quo and the implementation of change. However, in the case of the restructuring of the Internet-addressing regime at both the *.uk* and international levels, there was agreement on the part of all the relevant actors that a change was required. Thus, conflicts, and their resolution by social actors, are likely to be manifest in the process leading to the definition of the appropriate parameters for change.

To understand the dynamics of innovation in cyberspace, the architectural issues that influence both the deep-structure and the surface-level politics need to be taken into account. The architecture defines the parameters of the deep-structure relationships through which actors seek to influence the outcomes of the value allocation process.[35] The architecture is not deterministic and perceptions about default rule sets may also be influenced by the history of internetworking and the value structures coinciding with that process. Given this interpretative diversity, we should expect that deep-structure power relations will be manifest in the relevant actors' perceptions about the Internet's architecture.[36] In negotiating new domain-naming regimes, efforts to establish social, political, and cognitive legitimacy are likely to manifest themselves in the form of conflicts between those who advocate governance regimes in accordance with the inclusive values traditionally associated with internetworking and those who advocate governance regimes that are more exclusive.[37] The concept of surface level politics that is used here is similar to that suggested by Frost and Egri (1991). It refers to the strategies and tactics employed by actors to manipulate and influence outcomes to benefit themselves or others.

In the following discussion a three-tier model of the interactions between surface-level and deep-structure politics and the Internet's architecture is used to understand the processes leading to the reconfiguration of the *.uk* addressing regime. The objective is to show how the actors involved in these processes sought to identify and establish a consensus on the attributes of intermediaries for managing Internet addressing.[38]

In the period preceding the reconfiguration of the *.uk* addressing regime, appeals for change were often presented as loose collections of ideas arising from a variety of ill-defined and frequently inconsistent individual preferences. Those actors who perceived the architecture—that is, the Naming Committee registry structure—as an impediment to commercial success emphasized the need to eliminate restrictions on the registration process. Those actors who viewed the architecture as a necessary extension of the hardware and software comprising the domain name system stressed the importance of maintaining technical continuity and integrity. These divergent perspectives can be understood as a reflection of differences in deep-structure interests. Some actors were able to prevent changes in the existing architecture by employing deep-structure tactics. Such tactics included treating the architecture as inviolate, presenting positions as being unbiased, and adopting higher values—for example, the need to convey a positive image of internetworking. In contrast, others employed surface-level tactics such as deliberate testing of the allocation process to highlight discrepancies and contradictions in the Naming Committee's operating procedures. These surface-level actions, combined with the rapid increase in both the volume of registration requests and the number of committee members, altered the power relationships within the deep structure. The interactions between the social agents, along with the technical shortcomings of the registry, undermined the Naming Committee's authority and legitimacy.

A significant aspect of this process of change in the power relationships was the interactions between two individuals who were perceived to be advocating diametrically opposed values. The interactions between these two individuals, and their outcomes, served as a catalyst for transforming the administration and management of the *.uk* domain. The notion of establishing a neutral legal body to manage the *.uk* name space emerged as a product of these exchanges and, ultimately, from their proposals for the establishment of alternative registry procedures.

The unanimous dissatisfaction with the existing registry system makes it unlikely that the proposal to establish a new registry architecture in line with principles of neutral service provision represented a threat to any deep-structure power interests. Therefore, most of the political activity occurred at the surface level. Much of the controversy focused on finding optimal strategies for ensuring the impartiality of a new organization. Although the legitimacy of Dr Black's authority over the *.uk* domain was broadly accepted, this did not hold for the proposed Nominet organization. Given the widely held perception of Nominet's predecessor as a closed structure, the social, political, and cognitive legitimacy of the new registry architecture hinged on its openness to participation by all interested actors and on its technical merit.[39]

A number of supportive political tactics were deployed to ensure the success of the Nominet proposal. No interested parties were restricted from participating in the development of a coherent proposal and participants were able to define the parameters of the features of the proposed architecture—that is, structure, technical base, and funding model. When concerns were raised that the voting arrangements might graft the elitist voting structure of the previous registry onto the new architecture, the allocation of votes was modified. Once this was implemented, membership in Nominet remained open to all, thus empowering all interested parties to contribute to domain name policy for the *.uk* name space. The initiative acquired legitimacy, in part, because its detractors were also incorporated in the planning processes and, later, within the company itself.[40] By the time Nominet commenced operation in August 1996 virtually all opposition had been diffused.

This initiative was entirely industry based with little or no government involvement. This was perceived by participants in the process as giving social, political, and cognitive legitimacy to the new organization. The UK government's interest had focused on the extent to which user interests, business and individual, would be adequately represented in the restructuring process. According to the former head of Infrastructure and Convergence Policy at the Department of Trade and Industry, 'the key issue is that the registry system be open, transparent, and objective; which Nominet is' (interview, 13 May 1998). The Nominet approach was regarded as a good model reflecting a pragmatic industry decision.

The perception of the parties concerned with Nominet was that it was inclusive; it prevented the interests of any entity from dominating the process; and it was independent and therefore not in competition with industry players. The perceived degree of openness of the process of change appears to have been the primary deep-structure consideration of the social actors involved. Consistent with historically embedded values of internetworking, the openness of the processes associated with the establishment of a new regulatory regime allowed interested parties to define the types of checks and balances that would be incorporated in the new architecture. The initiative acquired legitimacy because it was perceived as a bottom-up endeavour that permitted the actors to define the constraints that would be placed on their behaviour. Once established, the continuing legitimacy of Nominet was related to its technical efficacy and to the maintenance of its neutrality.

Conclusion

The Internet is comprised of the hardware and software that make internetworking possible, and of the formal and informal organizational structures that are evolving around the technical infrastructure. The structures responsible for coordinating and administering core functions, such as addressing, are important dimensions of the architecture. Because of its prescriptive overtones and its tendency to underestimate the significance of the social dynamics of the infrastructure, much of the Internet-related governance literature does not address the importance of social dynamics in the establishment of new architectural configurations.

The catalyst for establishing a new governance regime for the *.uk* domain was embedded in the power struggles over the techniques for domain name allocation and the Naming Committee's administrative procedures. Change did not occur as a result of a specific plan. Instead, it was shaped by dynamic processes of cooperation and competition between participating social actors. The analysis of the dynamics of Internet politics illustrates how the characteristics of internetworking influenced the actors responsible for managing one of the Internet's core functions. These dynamics have been revealed by examining the processes of interest mediation associated with the changes in the coordination structures for managing domain name registrations and allocations.

A focus on changing power relationships offers a means of interpreting the way that the social, political, and cognitive legitimacy of regulatory organizations is being established in the cyber-realm. Although the 'responsible person' for the *.uk* domain had authority over this segment of the Internet, maintenance of the legitimacy of this authority depended upon the extent to which interested parties perceived this individual as a neutral actor. The success of the Nominet initiative can be attributed to the inclusive strategies adopted to develop a proposal for change. The bottom-up manner in which collective decision making was conducted was congruent with the values of internetworking. The outcomes of these processes influenced the legitimacy bestowed on the new intermediary organization—that is, Nominet—by all interested parties.

This analysis of the particular case of the transformation of the governance regime for the *.uk* name space suggests that other features of the evolution of Internet governance can best be understood by examining the manner in which new configurations of power constellations are influencing the emergence of the structures responsible for managing and administering the Internet's core functions. The benefit of this approach is that it does not fall prey to ideologically motivated positions with respect to the appropriate roles of the private sector or governments in the evolution of governance regimes for the Internet. It also offers a means of coupling investigations of the determinants of the technical architecture of the Internet and the way the social and political interests of its designers and users become embedded in that architecture.

Notes

1. This chapter is based on a review of primary archive documents, including the UK Naming Committee discussion-list archives; personal interviews undertaken between April and October 1998, and email exchanges with members of the UK Internet industry, government policy-makers, and other individuals who are known specialists on the Internet between November 1997 and April 1999; and the results of a questionnaire distributed to members of the UK Internet industry in November 1998.

2. The Domain Name System is a distributed database within which each unit of data is indexed by a unique name. These names are paths that classify computers on the basis of an inverted 'tree' scheme. The term 'name space' refers to this treelike structure. See Albitz and Liu (1997: ch. 2) and Rony and Rony (1998: ch. 3).

3. Gould (1996*b*: 199) defines these terms as referring to 'human and computer interactions across open networks and without reference to geographical location (and therefore legal jurisdiction) or real-world social understanding'.

4. In hierarchical networks, the term 'backbone' refers to the top-level transmission paths that other transit networks feed into; see www.whatis.com/backbone.html (accessed 1 Apr. 1999). The Joint Network Team coordinated network addressing in accordance with its Name Registration Scheme (NRS). This was a centralized naming system for UK universities that operated as an equivalent to DNS. The primary difference between NRS and DNS was that, under the former, all entries into the registration database were made in UK domain order—e.g., *.uk.ac.sussex.* At that time, a gateway between the NRS and the DNS was maintained at University College London, which

translated names between the two addressing systems once in every twenty-four-hour period. This service allowed American network-users to see normal DNS names for UK hosts, while UK network-users were able to read DNS names in NRS format.

5. Name servers are programs that store information about the domain name space and are employed to perform name-to-address mapping (Albitz and Liu 1997:21–4). Before April 1993, EUnet GB, owned by the University of Kent at Canterbury, had been trading under the name UKnet and providing email, news, and full Internet access to more than 800 UK sites. It was also a founding member of the independently run EUnet Europe, serving as the UK backbone portion of that organization's network. In July 1995, EUnet GB was acquired by Performance Systems International Inc. (PSI).

6. PIPEX was founded in January 1992 with fifty-six employees by Unipalm, a UK-based company that produced computer networking products based on the Internet Protocol (IP) suite. In March 1994 it was floated on the London Stock Exchange and, in late 1995, it merged with UUNET, which subsequently merged with Microwave Communications Inc. (MCI) Worldcom in December 1996. See www.uk.uu.net, (accessed 1 Apr. 1999).

7. Demon Internet Ltd was founded in June 1992 by Demon Systems Ltd, a UK-based firm that specialized in software production. It sought to expand the market for Telnet, email, Gopher and File Transfer Protocol (ftp) services to the public, as these services were largely restricted to academic and research environments. Demon Internet grew from a subscriber base of 100 to in excess of 180,000 dial-up subscribers in May 1998. It was subsequently purchased by Scottish Telecom, the telecommunications division of Scottish Power, for £66 million. See www.demon.net (accessed 1 Apr. 1999).

8. In April 1994 the Joint Network Team became the JNT Association, which now trades as UKERNA. This organization's mandate focuses on the management of the UK's Higher Education and Research Community Network Program. It also manages the *.ac.uk* name space, and, with the UK Central Computer and Technology Agency, the *.gov.uk* name space. See www.ukerna.ac.uk (accessed 1 Apr. 1999).

9. The role of the NRS representative was to provide continuity between the segment of DNS under commercial control and those segments that remained under the direct control of the Joint Network Team.

10. BT Internet Services included all British Telecom Internet products before BTnet became a trademark name in January 1995. Prior to the launch of BTnet, BT Internet Services consisted of a team of six individuals responsible for most aspects of the provision of corporate Internet services. BT Internet Services joined the Naming Committee through an informal process. The technical services manager, who was well known throughout the UK Internet community, sent an email message to a representative of the Committee requesting information about how to register a name in the *co.uk* subdomain for a client. The individual who was contacted responded by informing him that he would add BT Internet Services to the Committee's discussion lists because it was a known Internet Access Provider (interview 5 June 1998 and 9 Sept. 1998).

11. LINX was incorporated as a non-profit association of ISPs in December 1995. A single network connection to LINX is sufficient to carry traffic generated by any LINX provider, thereby eliminating the need to have an extensive network of links to each provider. See www.linx.org (accessed 1 Apr. 1999).

12. For a detailed list of LINX membership requirements, see the LINX Memorandum of Understanding, www.linx.org/mou.html (accessed 1 Apr. 1999), and LINX Articles of Association, www.linx.org/ manda.html (accessed 1 Apr. 1999).

13. At this time the organizational representatives to the Naming Committee were primarily technical engineers, most of whom were directly involved to varying degrees in the establishment of LINX.

14. Former members of the committee generally suggested that the relatively high degree of autonomy they exercised was attributable to the newness of the Internet at the time.

15. This corresponds to the institutional ethos of consensual adoption of ethics and the propagation of voluntary technical standards, or *rough consensus and running code*

that characterized the early history of Internet working (Hafner and Lyon 1996; Rony and Rony 1998; see also Bradner 1996, Hanseth, Monteiro, and Hatling 1996, and Malkin 1994).

16. When the Naming Committee began processing requests for domain names in 1993, it was receiving, on average, two to three requests per week. By mid-1995 it was receiving in excess of 100 requests per day.

17. Most interviewees claimed that the registration process was very competitive because service registrars were competing on the basis of price.

18. The evidence demanded ranged from requests for company letterheads to demonstrating the existence of a bank account in a company's name.

19. 'Moral' refers here to concerns about possible misuses of the DNS that might cast a negative light on Internet working—for example, allowing the registration of names that might be seen as offensive, such as *rudeword.co.uk.*

20. A representative from UnipalmPIPEX proposed that his organization should assume control of the registry database because it was better equipped to meet the technical needs of the registry, but this motion was not passed.

21. This was somewhat ironic, because these two individuals were generally perceived by the other representatives as antagonists, and their exchanges on the discussion list were among the most heated debates concerning the registry's procedures and structure.

22. Dr Black's authority over the *.uk* domain was rooted in RFC-920 and was independent of his membership of UKERNA. RFCs are official Internet documents that provide information about Internet standards, specifications, protocols, organization notices, and individual points of view. RFC-920 outlined the norms for assigning responsibility for two-letter top-level domains. It was also in this document that the association of domains with specific organizations, and the concept of domain registration entailing a hierarchy of delegation among organizations, were initially outlined.

23. The BTnet and UnipalmPIPEX representatives who assumed responsibility for creating these working groups were the same two individuals who had submitted proposals to UKERNA for reforming the *.uk* registry structure.

24. The upper limit on the number of votes allowed per member was set at ten. Members with lower registration volumes were permitted to purchase additional voting entitlements for a fee of £500 per vote.

25. This would have been in contradiction with RFC-1591, a document focusing on the structure of top-level domain names and the administration of domains, which states that, for responsible persons, 'concerns about "rights" and "ownership" of domains are inappropriate. It is appropriate to be concerned about "responsibilities" and "service" to the community' (Postel 1994: 4).

26. In the UK, companies limited by guarantee have no shares or shareholders; and those who control the company have no financial interest in the company's assets.

27. The sample population for this survey encompassed the diverse UK-based companies that potential registrants could approach to register domain names in the autumn of 1998. The sample comprised service providers of various sizes, specializing in the provision of a variety of Internet working based services, targeted to an assortment of potential clients. Potential participants were selected on the basis of whether their respective organization offered domain name registration services. The questionnaire was sent to 408 potential respondents; or approximately one half of the organizations offering this service in the UK at the time. The majority of companies who participated in the survey viewed the provision of domain name registration services as an important aspect of their competitive strategies.

28. This is similar to the concept of polycentric or non-statist law (see T.W. Bell 1992, 1998).

29. For instance, the ability of network-users to enter or exit online spaces may increase the probability that the democratic tradition of rational debate among elected

representatives would be replaced by more dispersed and complex interactions at local levels.

30. See also Quintas (1996) on the role of software designers in default rule making.

31. Adopting a perspective based on Foucault's work, Boyle (1997: n.p.) expands on this theme to demonstrate how, rather than enabling users to circumvent state rules, certain information technologies may provide the state with 'a different arsenal of methods to regulate content materially rather than juridically, by everyday softwired routing practices, rather than threats of eventual sanction'.

32. He labels the architecture of cyberspace *code*. It refers to the 'software and hardware that constitutes cyberspace as it is—the set of protocols, the set of rules, implemented, or codified, in cyberspace itself, that determine how people interact, or exist in this space . . . It [code], like architecture, is not optional' (Lessig 1998*b*: 4).

33. Lessig's approach to Internet governance is based on an assumption that behaviour in the physical and virtual realms is regulated by four constraints. Law that regulates by the imposition of sanctions *ex post;* social norms that regulate by enforcing expectations within particular communities; markets that regulate through price and availability; and architecture, or the constraints imposed upon behaviour by the world as we find it. Regulation is the sum of the interactions of these constraints (see Lessig 1999). For an alternative view, see Post and Johnson (1997*a,b*).

34. This framework was developed by Frost and Egri (1991) and has been used in the industrial networks literature to interpret decision-making processes within asymmetrical exchange networks of interdependent firms (see Elg and Johansson 1997).

35. This perspective draws on two interpretations: (1) the manner in which specific design features or arrangements of artefacts and systems influence power relations and patterns of authority; (2) the linking of technological properties with institutionalized relations of power and authority. See Winner (1986: 3–58) for a comparative analysis of these interpretive traditions.

36. Although this level is embedded and implicit, it has been suggested that some actors can recognize and harness deep-structure power relations to their advantage (Frost and Egri 1991).

37. The degree of community dependence on new organizational forms correlates positively with legitimacy problems because stakeholders may not fully understand the nature of new ventures (Hunt and Aldrich 1998). Moreover, pioneering organizations cannot base trust-building strategies only on technological efficiency. Uncertainties must be framed in such a way that the proposed innovation becomes credible (Aldrich and Fiol 1994).

38. The intensity of participation in the Naming Committee's activities and interactions was fluid and occurred on a volunteer basis. Variations in participation levels may have influenced the constellations of power relations that emerged and some of the value allocation decisions that were made (Denis, Langley, and Cazale 1996; Wallis and Dollery 1997).

39. Suitable degrees of openness have become a focal point of debate about reconfiguring the technical management of Internet names and addresses at the global level.

40. For example, at Nominet's first annual general meeting, the members elected one of the most vehement opponents of this organization as a non-executive director. According to him, getting 'on board' offered a means of improving the system from within (interview, 1 May 1998).

Digital Resources: Content and Language

Mark Warschauer

Computers and the Internet are not much use without content and applications that serve people's needs. With the surge of material published in recent years on the World Wide Web—and millions of more Web pages added every month—it might seem that any shortage of online information and content has been long overcome. And from the point of view of a middle-class English-speaking American, that may well be the case. However, for those who live in different sociocultural environments or speak different languages, the situation is often very different. As this chapter argues, the massive amount of digital content being created on the Internet does not necessarily meet the needs of diverse communities around the world, and this has important consequences for issues of social inclusion. Fortunately, some excellent models exist of ways to develop relevant local content through active participation of diverse groups, and these models will be highlighted.

Global Web Content Production

It is impossible to determine the exact number of Web pages in the world, though current estimates top one billion.[1] It is somewhat easier, though still not exact, to count the number of Internet host domain names, such as www.harvard.edu, www.nytimes.com, or www.greenpeace.org, each of which, of course, can contain any number of pages within them. The number of Internet host domains rose nearly a hundredfold from 1993 to 2001 and now tops one hundred million.[2]

Matthew Zook of the University of California, Berkeley, has conducted extensive analyses of the concentration of domain names by city and country around the world (e.g., Zook 2001c). According to his latest figures, some 65% of the domains in the world are located in the United States, the United Kingdom, and Germany—a figure that remained fairly steady from 1998 to 2001 (Figure 1). This signals a great disparity in terms of number of domain names per person, even among the wealthy countries themselves (Figure 2), let alone between the

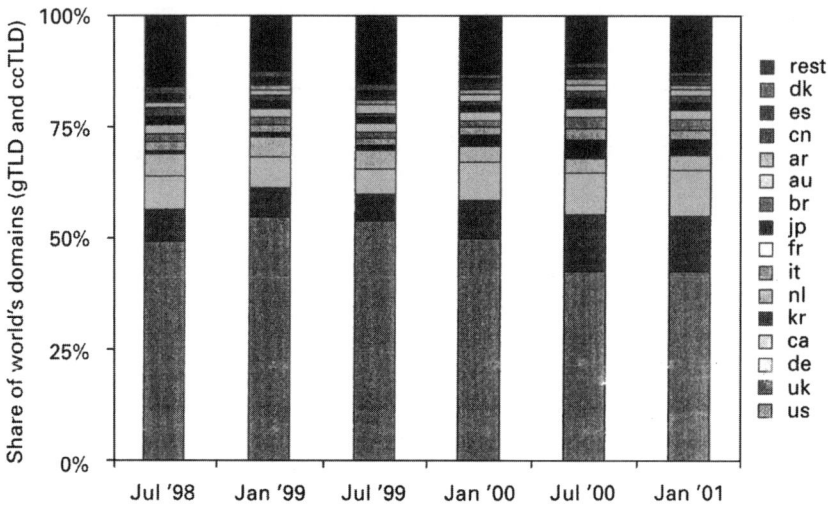

Figure 1 Share of world's Internet domains, by country, 1998–2001

Source: Zook (2001a). Copyright 2001 by Matthew Zook. Used with permission

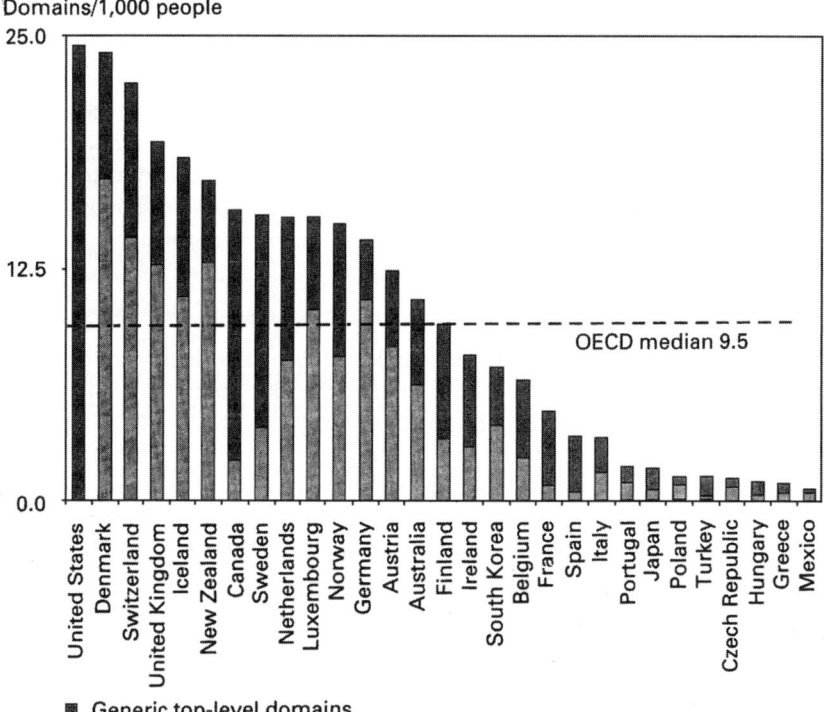

Figure 2 Internet domains per 1,000 people in OECD countries, January 2000

Source: Zook (2001b). Used with permission from Matthew Zook

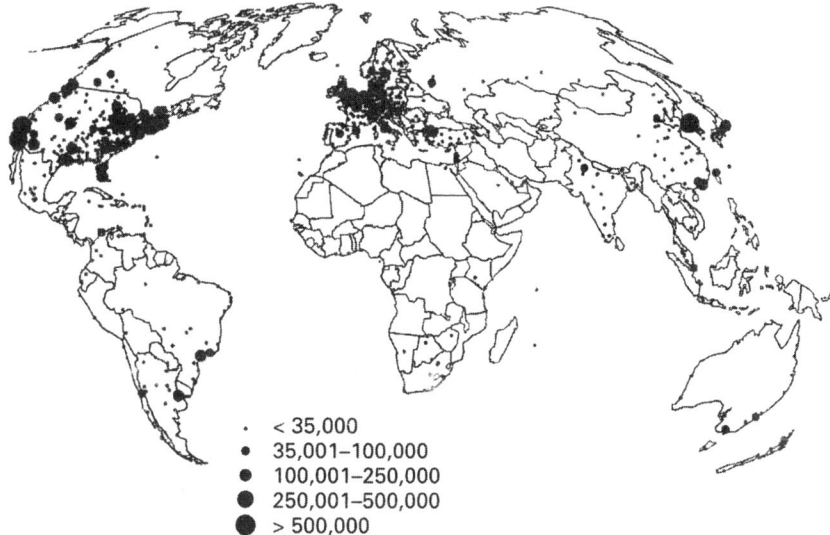

Figure 3 Total number of top-level domains (.com, .net, .org, country codes), by city,
July 2000

Source: Map based on methodology described in Zook (2001c). Used with permission from
Matthew Zook. See also Zook's Internet Geography Project, http://www.zooknic.com/

developed and developing countries. Within individual countries, the most
domain names are located on servers in major cities. Thus Internet content is
overwhelmingly concentrated in the major cities of the United States and Europe,
with only a few other key Internet server sites located in East Asia, the Middle
East, and Latin America, as illustrated by Zook's map of global domain names
(Figure 3). There is also great disparity in regard to representation of languages
online; this is a pressing issue and is the focus of the second half of this chapter.

Content and International Development

The geographic imbalance of Internet content production suggests that the content needs of diverse communities are not being met. For example, small-scale
farmers and agricultural laborers in rural areas of Africa, Latin America, and Asia
have little use for the types of material currently available on the Internet in their
languages, and these rural areas of developing countries are almost completely
univolved in production of Internet content. As a representative of M. S. Swaminathan Research Foundation told me, "The villagers in Kannivadi [in southern
India] are not interested in what's going on in the White House or even in Chennai
[the state capital]; they are interested in the price of rice in the local market."
Governments, nongovernmental organizations, and community groups seeking
to use the Internet for social development thus have to pay serious attention to
the question of creating new digital content.

Some of the content and application areas that have been targeted as important for international development include the following.

Economic Development Information

In countries such as India, the population is made up mostly of small farmers raising a few crops each year on tiny plots of land. These farmers can benefit greatly from greater access to key information. For example, small-scale farmers often suffer financially from not knowing current crop prices in various markets in nearby cities. In response to this dilemma, several Internet projects for rural development in India collect crop prices and post this information as part of their intranets. For example, in the Gyandoot Internet kiosks in the Dhar district of India, a farmer can come to a local kiosk and pay the equivalent of $0.10 USD to receive the market prices on that day for a particular crop at several local, regional, and national sales points. The farmer can then make a better-informed decision about whether to harvest the crop soon or let it continue growing and, when harvested, where to sell it for the best price.

Other types of information of value to small-scale farmers include data on soil testing, crop management, crop rotation, local crop varieties, and composting. Local projects in India, such as the M. S. Swaminathan Foundation's village knowledge centers, have taken the initiative togather this information, rewrite it in local languages, and make it available to small farmers through local and regional intranets. Farmers can drop into the village knowledge centers that are located in fourteen villages of Pondicherry and Tamil Nadu and request free information from the kiosk operators.

Health Care

Some of the most promising information and communication technology (ICT) applications for telecommunications development are in the area of health care. The village knowledge centers are also used in India to deliver health-related information to rural areas. This information includes topics such as prenatal care, postnatal care, child immunization, tropical diseases, and local and regional health care resources. Rural areas in India suffer from a lack of trained medical personnel. For this reason, community development groups are working to develop software applications that could assist health workers with early disease diagnosis and prevention efforts. For example, the George Foundation in Bangalore is developing a software application known as the Early Detections and Prevention System 2000 (EDPS2000). This application is designed to enable the early detection of diseases and nutritional deficiencies among the rural population. It is intended for use in primary health centers, which often are unable to deal with early detection of diseases because of a lack of multidisciplinary medical expertise and laboratory facilities. EDPS2000 consists of a database of disease characteristics and conditions and a symptom diagnosis program. The program prompts the user for a step-by-step description of symptoms, followed by subsequent diagnostic questions. The software is designed to identify whether blood, urine, stool, or other laboratory tests are required in response to the answers keyed in by a health care worker. The system also indicates whether further investigation by a physician is warranted. In addition, the software maintains an exhaustive database of patient medical history and treatment visits to the health clinic and allows gathering of statistics about diseases, deaths, vaccinations and inoculations, pregnancies, and contagious diseases, thus enabling improved rural health care management.

Internet-based applications services also serve rural health care needs. One of the largest and most important is HealthNet,[3] which is used by approximately 19,500 health care workers in more than 150 countries worldwide (Accenture et al. 2001). HealthNet offers e-mail connections through low-orbit satellites to medical personnel in various locations throughout Africa. Beyond that, it has created online content and applications that are of use to medical practitioners throughout the world. These include two weekly online newsletters that focus on health issues in developing countries (one newsletter deals with general health issues and the other reports on AIDS issues), links to disease-specific online information, discussion forums on topics related to medical and pharmaceutical issues in the developing world, and a GetWeb application that allows people to download this Internet-based information using basic e-mail functions. HealthNet has had its greatest impact in sub-Saharan Africa, where it has local affiliates in Eritria, Ethiopia, Ghana, Kenya, Sudan, Uganda, and Zimbabwe. HealthNet is used for long-distance consultation among doctors in different African countries, for the scheduling of medical appointments in rural areas, and for gathering medical data for clinical trials.

Education

Most people in rural areas need to travel outside their communities to further their education. Information about places to study and entrance requirements is often difficult to access in remote areas. The Internet offers a vehicle for gathering and making available information about schools, courses, fees, schedules, and sample examination questions.

One of the most popular uses of rural Internet telecenters in India has been to get information on examination results. This information is often lost or delayed in the mail, making it difficult for rural youth to make plans for following up on their education. The information is available on the Internet and can be downloaded free or for a small fee at village Internet centers.

In the long run, rural development organizations need to develop computer-based and online content and applications not just *about* educational opportunities but to be directly used in teaching and learning. The possibilities and limitations of online education are discussed in more detail in chapter 5.

Community Affairs and Culture

Low-income urban and rural groups in developing countries often lack resources to express and share their own community's culture. Since it is less expensive to produce on the Internet than via print, television, or radio, online publications can provide an excellent medium for sharing locally developed community content and can often contribute to minority language and culture preservation.

For example, São Paulo, Brazil, is one of the most socially, economically, and geographically divided cities in the world. The wealthy residents of the city, including many of Latin America's leading bankers, financiers, and media moguls, live a world apart from the working class residents of the city's infamous *favelas* (shantytowns). Newspaper reporters and television journalists also keep a distance from the *favelas* except to report on drug wars or murders. Slum dwellers thus lack cultural and news outlets that report on events directly concerning their own lives. A community coalition called Sampa.org has stepped into this gap and established a community news service that gathers and publishes online information about local affairs, community services, neighborhood news, and cultural events. Sampa.org has also established an MP3 (music file) server, so that local hip-hop bands can share their music with each other and with listeners. All of this, of course, involves the active participation of the community itself.

Online Content in the United States

Even the United States, which leads the world in Web site production, suffers from significant content gaps that affect underserved communities. An in-depth study of Internet content and diversity in the United States was carried out by the Children's Partnership (Lazarus and Mora 2000). The study combined discussions with user groups, interviews with community center directors, and the analysis of 1,000 Web sites linked to commercial and noncommercial portals to evaluate the extent to which currently available content meets the needs of diverse U.S. communities. They identified four main content-related barriers that affected large numbers of Americans.

Perhaps the greatest barrier was a lack of locally relevant information. According to the study, low-income users seek practical, relevant information that affects their daily lives, such as the following:

- *Education.* Adult high school degree programs, adult literacy programs, financial aid, homework assistance, telementoring
- *Family.* Low-cost child care, low-cost enrichment activities for children, public programs for families
- *Finances.* Public benefits news, consumer information, credit information
- *Government and advocacy.* Immigration assistance, legal services, tax filing support
- *Health.* Easy-to-understand health encyclopedias, local clinics, low-cost insurance resources

- *Housing*. Low-cost housing, low-cost utilities, neighborhood crime rates
- *Personal enrichment*. Foreign language newspapers and search engines, communities of interest for youth and adults
- *Vocational*. Low-cost career counseling programs, job training programs, job readiness programs; job listings

In some of these cases, the information may be located in print documents, but these documents are difficult to locate and obtain. In many other cases, general or partial information may exist online, but not information that is particularly suited to low-income communities. For example, online job services generally target the higher-end market rather than entry-level jobs. Similarly, most online housing services focus on the higher end of the rental market rather than on low-rent apartments.

A second need was for information at a basic literacy level. For example, there are a large number of tutorials online that cover different computer and Internet skills, such as the use of spreadsheets, Web page design, or photo editing, but these generally demand a high level of literacy. Materials tailored to limited-literacy populations are badly needed by community technology centers, which often present computer instruction for those with limited English-language or literacy skills.

A third need is for content for non-English speakers. While there is a large amount of information on the Web in languages such as Spanish, there is little public information in Spanish directed towards U.S. audiences. Users seek information related to governmental programs that affect them, for example, Medicare, taxes, voting.

Finally, more diverse cultural resources are desired. Although some local U.S. communities are starting to build a cultural presence online (e.g., HarlemLive), users still feel that far more needs to be done to develop Web sites that reflect diverse cultural heritages and practices (Lazarus and Mora 2000).

The Children's Partnership has recently developed a major new portal in an attempt to address the lack of online information for low-income Americans. The portal includes sections for planning personnel, such as administrators of community technology centers, and for the lay public on topics like health, housing, employment, education, and culture.[4]

Content for the Disabled

Both developed and developing countries require content that addresses the special needs of the disabled in format and subject matter. As to formatting, the best and most up-to-date source of information is the Web Accessibility Initiative, supported by governmental and non-governmental bodies in the United States, Canada, and Europe. These Web sites describe how online content should be developed so that it can be accessed by the disabled.[5] A principal requirement is to provide a redundancy of output mechanisms, that is to ensure that all graphical content has a text equivalent (for the blind, who can then convert the text to speech); that all audio content has a text equivalent (for the deaf); and that animated graphics can be frozen (for those with attention deficit disorder or learning disabilities). It is also recommended that sites allow users to input via both keyboarding or pointing (e.g., a "submit" button can be designed to also accept the input of the letter *s*) and that sites use a clear, consistent, well-labeled format (to benefit all users, and especially those with disabilities). Accessibility criteria exist on a continuum, so it is difficult to determine the exact percentage of existing Web sites that are or are not accessible, but by any measure there is still a long way to go. For example, one report found that the Web sites of all nine U.S. presidential candidates in 2000 failed to fully meet even the first level of accessibility requirements for the disabled (Báthory-Kitz 1999).

Beyond formatting, it is also important to develop online content for the disabled. Some of the best work in this regard has been carried out in Europe, where several countries have Internet portals for the disabled, with information on rehabilitation programs, assistive technology, special education, workplace adaptations, legislation, and training (European Commission 2001a; 2001b).

Community Mobilization and Content Development

The successful development of online content demands the active participation of the communities that will make use of the materials. There are three principal ways that community participation is achieved: through needs assessment, database development, and content production.

Needs Assessment

The approach of Participatory Rural Appraisal (PRA) provides a model of how a community can be engaged in helping define and determine its own needs (Mukherjee 1993). PRA has been used in development projects throughout the world over the last two decades, evolving from a prior, similar approach known as Rapid Rural Appraisal (RRA) (Chambers 1992). PRA uses focus groups, interviews, door-to-door surveys, community meetings, and special participatory exercises to maximize a community's involvement in defining its own needs. Rural Internet projects in India, such as Gyandoot and the M. S. Swaminathan village knowledge centers, were launched through intensive PRA in local villages. This appraisal of needs helped determine what resources villagers already had access to and what resources they needed.

Database Development

One important area of online content is listings, maps, and databases of local community resources. The community itself ought to be centrally involved in gathering and mapping those data. For example, the Camfield Estates project in

Massachusetts, which placed computers and Internet access in many apartments in a low-income housing area, brought together a team of community residents to survey residents' existing skills, capacities, and interests and to identify other local assets, such as businesses, churches, and child care facilities. This information became a key part of the Web portal that served the Camfield Estates community.[6]

Community members can also contribute to databases through online communication. The city of Muenster, Germany, for example, has published a database and interactive street map for mobility-impaired people, with detailed and easily accessible information on public institutions, recreation facilities, social services, doctors, and information bureaus with barrier-free or disability-compatible buildings and services (Neumann and Uhlenküken 2001). One interactive feature being developed will allow community members to contribute directly to the database so that they themselves can point out urban locations that need to be altered or physical barriers that need to be removed. This system of community contribution is designed to make the database more comprehensive and informative while actively involving the disabled as consultants and partners in the project.

Content Production

The third major area of community involvement is through specific content development. Teams of community residents can be trained to develop Web-based information about their community that focuses on news, current events, culture, or any other items of interest or concern. One example is São Paulo's Sampa.org project, discussed earlier, which involves teams of community residents in producing a local online news service. Another excellent example is HarlemLive in New York.[7] HarlemLive is an Internet-based youth publication launched in 1996. It has a close relationship with the Playing2 Win community technology center in Harlem, which hosts the publication on its Web site and provides office and production space for the publication's editorial team. Columbia University and a number of other local organizations provide additional support.

HarlemLive is a high-quality online publication, with general news reports, articles on community issues, arts and culture articles, photo galleries, a creative writing section, and a special women's section. The publication thus provides current, topical information by and for the Harlem community. Equally important, HarlemLive has trained several hundred Harlem young people as journalists, photographers, media administrators, Webmasters, and public speakers. The publication thus serves as a focal point for young people to develop and showcase their technical and communication skills while they address issues of concern to the community and create original content that helps give the community voice.

In summary, there are many types of online content of use to marginalized communities. Some of this content can be provided by outside agencies. But, for the most part, active involvement of the targeted populations—in defining their needs, collecting data, and authoring and publishing content—is usually required for success. This kind of approach, based on active community involvement, also helps guarantee the kinds of community training and mobilization necessary for long-term success.

Language

Language is one of the most complex and significant issues related to content and to broader issues of ICT and social inclusion. Language intersects with many other forms of social division related to nationality, economics, culture, education, and literacy. Language questions dramatically affect how diverse groups can access and publish information on the Web as well as the extent to which the Internet serves as a medium for expression of their cultural identities.

Language and Identity in the Age of Information

The critical role of language is situated in the broader social and economic transformation of recent decades. The information revolution, accompanied by the processes of international economic and media integration, has acted like a battering ram against traditional cornerstones of social authority and meaning. Throughout the world, shifts in economic and political power have weakened the role of the state, new forms of industrial organization have decreased the possibilities for long-term stable employment, and women's entry into the work force has shaken up the traditional patriarchal family (Castells 1997).

But every action brings a reaction. The last quarter-century has also witnessed a worldwide surge of movements of "collective identity" that "challenge globalization and cosmopolitanism" on behalf of people's control over their culture and their lives (Castells 1997, 2). These differ from earlier social movements, which in many parts of the world were based on struggles of organized workers. As Alain Touraine explains, "In a postindustrial society, in which cultural services have replaced material goods at the core of production, *it is the defense of the subject, in its personality and its culture, against the logic of apparatuses and markets, that replaces the idea of class struggle*" (quoted in Castells 2000b, 23, emphasis in original). Castells (1997) further explains the central role of identity in today's world:

> In a world of global flows of wealth, power, and images, the search for identity, collective or individual, ascribed or constructed, becomes the fundamental source of social meaning. This is not a new trend, since identity, and particularly religious and ethnic identity, have been at the roots of meaning since the dawn of human society. Yet identity is becoming the main, and sometimes the only, source of meaning in a historical period characterized by widespread destructuring of organizations,

delegitimation of institutions, fading away of major social movements, and ephemeral cultural expressions. People increasingly organize their meaning not around what they do but on the basis of what they are. (3)

Within this contradictory mix of global networks and local identities, language plays a critical role. With other cornerstones of social authority, such as nation, family, and career, battered by the processes of globalization, language can become "the trench of cultural resistance, the last bastion of self-control, the refuge of identifiable meaning" (Castells 1997, 52). The struggle over bilingual education in the United States; the Québécois, Basque, and Kosovar separatist movements; the battles over language and citizenship in post-Soviet countries; and language revitalization movements in Ireland (Gaelic), New Zealand (Maori), Morocco (Tamazight), and many other countries indicate the powerful role of language-based identity in today's world.

It is not surprising that language and dialect have assumed such a critical role in identity formation. The process of becoming a member of a community has always been realized in large measure by acquiring knowledge of the functions, social distribution, and interpretation of language (Ochs and Shieffelin 1984). In most of the world, the ability to speak two or more languages or dialects is a given, and language choice by minority groups becomes a symbol of ethnic relations as well as a means of communication (Heller 1982). In the current era, language signifies historical and social boundaries that are less arbitrary than territory and more discriminating (but less exclusive) than race or ethnicity. Language-as-identity also intersects well with the nature of subjectivity in today's world. Identity in the postmodern era has been found to be multiple, dynamic, and conflictual, based not on a permanent sense of self but rather on the choices that individuals make in different circumstances over time (Henriquez et al. 1984; Schecter, Sharken-Taboada, and Bayley 1996; Weedon 1987). Language, though deeply rooted in personal and social history, allows a greater flexibility than race and ethnicity, with people able to consciously or unconsciously express dual identities by the linguistic choices they make even in a single sentence (e.g., through switching or combining languages; see Blom and Gumperz 1972). By means of choices concerning language and dialect, people constantly make and remake who they are. For example, a Yugoslav becomes a Croatian, a Soviet becomes a Lithuanian, and a Canadian becomes a Québécois.

Yet, at the very time that linguistic diversity is becoming more critical than ever in people's lives and identities, a new communication medium has emerged that has been dominated by a single language: English. The dominance of English, not just on the Internet but also in many other international media and communications forums, has led to the rise of new concepts such as "global English." In order to fully appreciate the issues associated with ICT and social inclusion, it is necessary also to understand global English and how it has come to dominate digital telecommunications.

Global English

Although there have been many important international languages over time, including Latin, French, Russian, Chinese, Arabic, and Spanish, English is generally considered to be the first global language because of its current dominant role as a *lingua franca* in international communications. The rise of global English is the flip side of movements for local identity; it represents the need for an international medium of communication for global economic, political, and social exchange. According to information gathered by Crystal (1997), 85% of international organizations make use of English as at least one of their official languages, 85% of the world's film market is in English, and 90% of the published articles in leading journals of linguistics are in English.

Nevertheless, these statistics belie the fact that English is only spoken as a native language by a relatively small minority of people in the world. According to calculations, about 350 million people around the world speak English as a native language (Crystal 1997; Graddol 1997; 1999), representing some 6% of the world's population. This places English well behind Chinese in its number of native speakers, and not that far ahead of Spanish, Hindi, and Arabic, all of which may catch up or pass English in number of native speakers in the next sixty years (Graddol 1997). Another 350 million people are estimated to speak English as a second language, in countries such as India, Nigeria, the Philippines, and Singapore. There are also an estimated 700 million people who speak English as a foreign language, albeit with varying degrees of proficiency. Putting these numbers together, we see that three-quarters of the world's population knows almost no English, and even among the one-quarter who are said to speak it, the degree of competence varies markedly.

In many countries, unequal access to learning English overlaps with other social inequalities. Even though English is almost universally taught in secondary schools and universities, the majority of people in many developing countries never attend secondary school. Even those who do often face poorly trained teachers who do not speak English well themselves. Indeed, in many countries, the only reliable route to learning English is through expensive private education. With knowledge of English a requirement for access to many professions and university programs, English becomes one more barrier to equal opportunity for the poor. And even many people who speak English well may not be happy with the thought of its supplanting their own local language in as important a medium as the Internet.

English on the Internet

One of the first published studies of language on the Internet, and conducted in 1997, indicated that some 81% of international Web sites were in English ("Cyberspeech" 1997). At the time these results were made public, the dominance of English on the Internet caused great consternation around the world.

Anatoly Voronov, director of a Russian internet service provider, voiced the sentiments of many when he said:

> It is just incredible when I hear people talking about how open the Web is. It is the ultimate act of intellectual colonialism. The product comes from America so we either must adapt to English or stop using it. That is the right of any business. But if you are talking about a technology that is supposed to open the world to hundreds of millions of people you are joking. This just makes the world into new sorts of haves and have nots. (Cited in Crystal 1997, 68)

Within three years of this study, the percentage of English Web sites had fallen to 68% (Pastore 2000), still a sizable majority and well out of proportion to the number of English speakers in the world. A calculation of the ratio of Web pages to speakers of leading languages indicates that English speakers are still better represented and served on the Internet than speakers of other languages (Table 1).

The question remains as to whether this drop from 81% to 68% represents the beginning of the end of English dominance online, or whether it marks a continuation of that dominance at an unacceptably high level. To better understand and interpret these figures, and to predict the likely trend in international communication online, it is necessary to distinguish between the short-term and long-term advantages that English has in the computing and Internet realms.

The short-term advantages were principally two: the Internet first arose in the United States and speakers of English were its designers—they thus wrote programs that relied on an English-language interface; and the Internet, in its early iterations, functioned best in the ASCII code, which is very difficult to read and write with non-Roman alphabets.

These short-term reasons have already started to fade in significance and impact. As discussed earlier, Internet access is starting to reach saturation point in the United States but it is just taking off in many other countries around the world. As a critical mass of users gets online in a particular language, more people and businesses create Web sites in that language, and speakers of the language also have a greater number of potential partners for computer-mediated communication. This trend is also accelerated by the expansion of operating systems and Web page authoring software in non-Roman scripts, which allows people to communicate more easily in non-alphabetic languages such as Japanese, Chinese, and Hebrew. Because of these trends, the proportion of Web sites in English is expected to drop to 40% in the next decade (Graddol 1997).

However, even as English's short-term advantages decrease, it will still maintain a strong position over other languages on the Internet because of its long-term advantages. Principal among these is the historical fact that English was already the de facto global language at the time the Internet was created, and remains so today. The Internet, by enabling global communication, requires a global standard, and English's default advantage thus remains and is in fact strengthened. A mutually reinforcing cycle takes place, by which the existence

Table 1 Ratio of Speakers of a Language to Web Pages in That Language, 2001

Rank	Language	No. of Web Pages	No. of Speakers (thousands)	Speakers/ Web Page
1	English	214,250,996	322,000	1.5
2	Icelandic	136,788	250	1.8
3	Sweden	2,929,241	9,000	3.1
4	Danish	1,374,886	5,292	3.9
5	Norwegian	1,259,189	5,000	3.9
6	Finnish	1,198,956	6,000	5.0
7	German	18,069,744	98,000	5.4
8	Dutch	3,161,844	20,000	6.3
9	Estonian	173,265	1,100	6.4
10	Japanese	18,335,739	125,000	6.8
11	Italian	4,883,497	37,000	7.6
12	French	9,262,663	72,000	7.8
13	Catalan	443,301	4,353	9.8
14	Czech	991,075	12,000	12.1
15	Basque	36,321	588	16.2
16	Slovenian	134,454	2,218	16.5
17	Korean	4,046,530	75,000	18.5
18	Latvian	60,959	1,550	25.4
19	Russian	5,900,956	170,000	28.8
20	Hungarian	498,625	14,500	29.1
21	Portuguese	4,291,237	170,000	39.6
22	Greek	287,980	12,000	41.7
23	Spanish	7,573,064	332,000	43.8
24	Lithuanian	82,829	4,000	48.3
25	Polish	848,672	44,000	51.8
26	Hebrew	198,030	12,000	60.6
27	Chinese	12,113,803	885,000	73.1
28	Turkish	430,996	59,000	136.9
29	Bulgarian	51,336	9,000	175.3
30	Romanian	141,587	26,000	183.6
31	Arabic	127,565,000	202,000	1,583.5

Source: Adapted from Carvin (2001)

of English as a global language motivates (or forces) people to use it on the Internet, and the expansion of the Internet (and online English communication) thus reinforces English's role as a global language. This cycle can occur even when more and more people are using the Internet in their own languages. They may use the Internet in their own language for local or regional communication, but they will continue to use the Internet in English for global communication.

This trend is illustrated in a study conducted by the Organization for Economic Cooperation and Development ("The Default Language" 1999). The OECD study found that while only 78% of the regular Internet sites surveyed were in English, some 91% of the sites on what are called secure servers were in English and 96% of the sites on secure servers in the .com domain were in English. This is significant because secure servers, especially in the .com domain, are most frequently used for e-commerce. This means that even as people increasingly use languages other than English for local communication, they can be expected to use English for many international transactions. Of course, this latter trend may not be permanent as more companies may localize their e-commerce in the languages of the consumers.

Furthermore, long-term advantages do not necessarily mean permanent advantages. It is entirely possible that a century from now English will no longer be the dominant language on the Internet (or on whatever has replaced the Internet), either because of the weakening of English as a global language (because of demographic or economic changes) or because of the development of improved machine translation techniques (thus allowing everyone to communicate in the local language). Machine translation already exists online, but it is of such poor quality (based on word-by-word translation) that it does not now mitigate the need for a *lingua franca,* nor is it predicted to be of sufficient quality to mitigate such a need for a long time. For the foreseeable future, then, a disproportionate percentage of the world's Web sites, especially those necessary for international exchange, will be in English, and that is an important factor limiting access to Internet content.

The role of English vis-à-vis other languages online can be illustrated through analyses from Egypt (where English is spoken as a foreign language), India (where it is spoken as a second language), and Hawai'i (where it is spoken as a first language, though in a diverse multilingual setting).

Language Online in Egypt

Egypt is an excellent example of a highly stratified country in which English plays a dual role. On the one hand, English helps connect Egypt to the world by facilitating international commerce, tourism, and exchange. On the other hand, unequal access to English within the country serves to heighten the nation's already substantial social and economic disparities.

Arabic is the official language of Egypt and virtually the entire population speaks a dialect of this, referred to as Egyptian Arabic. Those that can read and write also know Classical Arabic, the main written variety of the language. Other languages in the country include ancient Coptic (used in Coptic Christian church services), a variety of African languages spoken by refugees, and European languages used in business and tourism. The use of European languages in Egypt has a long history dating back to periods of French and British colonialism, and at the time the Egyptian elite often preferred to be educated in French or English rather than Arabic (Haeri 1997). Most recently, though, the use of English has far surpassed that of French and other foreign languages by Egypt's elite. English is used not only in communication with foreigners—for example, in international commerce—but also for internal communications in a number of privileged occupations, especially in the fields of information technology, engineering, medicine, dentistry, and sciences. It is not unusual for Egyptian professionals in these areas to hold their conferences or produce their publications in English, even if the intended audience is other Egyptians.

English is essential for participation in elite professions, yet it is spoken by only a small minority of the population, estimated at some 3% (Warschauer 2001b). English is a mandatory foreign language taught in all schools beginning in the fourth year of elementary school, but it is learned very poorly, if at all, because of huge class sizes, poorly trained teachers (many of whom themselves barely know the language), and the country's high dropout rate (with half the adult population completing less than five years of schooling) (Fergany 1998). The elite, many of whom are bilingual in English and Arabic, usually learn English in private schools (a large number of which offer English medium instruction), private tutoring, English-medium private universities in Egypt, and study abroad in England or the United States (see discussion in Schaub 2000).

Even though English is spoken by just a small percentage of the population in Egypt, it is a dominant language of the Internet in that country (Warschauer, Refaat, and Zohry 2000). Many Egyptian Web sites, including those targeted exclusively for use inside the country, are only in English (see, for example, Figure 4, showing Otlob.com, a popular site for ordering food delivery from restaurants in Cairo and Alexandria). Some 70% of young professionals I surveyed use English exclusively in formal e-mail communication (Warschauer, Refaat, and Zohry 2000). Arabic, when added in e-mail, is most often written in Roman characters and used principally for religious or highly emotive expressions.

The reasons for English's dominant role in Egyptian online communications are multiple. First, no single standard of Arabic-language computing has emerged yet, so Web producers are often forced to convert Arabic-language content into slow-loading images if they want to guarantee that their content can be read in Arabic. This lack of a common standard also discourages Arabic-language e-mail. In addition, the Internet first arose in Egypt in the very sectors that operate in English, such as the information technology industry and international

Figure 4 Ordering food in Egypt

Source: http://otlob.com. Used with permission

businesses. Finally, the early adopters of the Internet in Egypt were mostly people who—owing to their schooling and work experience—write, compute, type, and keyboard better in English than they do in Arabic, and using English online thus comes naturally to them.

Some of these conditions are bound to change over time, especially with the emergence of common Arabic-language standards for computing. However, in the meantime, the 97% of the Egyptian people who do not know English are excluded from full access to Egyptian online content written in English, let alone international English-language Web sites.

Multilingual Computing in India

India is another country where English plays a stratifying, if also a unifying, role. People in India speak some 850 local and regional languages (Todd and Hancock 1987) of which 58 are taught in schools, 87 are used in newspapers, 71 in radio programs, and 15 in films ("Indian Languages" 2001). A total of 18 of these are considered official languages.

English is spoken by an elite throughout the country and is used in scientific, technological, and business communications. However, despite the national prominence of English in India and India's reputation as an English-speaking country, only about 5% of the people speak English (Crystal 1997). In contrast, nearly half the people of the country speak Hindi and almost another quarter speak dialects of Tamil, Bengali, Kannada, or Marathi ("India" 2001).

Indian-language computing thus is complicated by many factors, including the fact that each major Indian language has its own script. Not surprisingly, English has emerged as the dominant language of the information technology industry in India, which serves the industry's booming export business well. However, English is much less useful as a language of communication for national development purposes, especially for projects that target India's poor. In short, the potential of ICT for aiding rural development will not be reached without adequate Indian-language software and content.

For this reason, a number of Indian organizations are trying to develop software solutions to promote Indian language computing. One of the more promising is being produced by a group called Chennai Kavigal, which is collaborating with the Institute of Indian Technology in Madras to develop low-cost Indian-language software solutions for both Windows and Linux platforms. One of their products, a complete office suite with a word processor, spreadsheet, database, and presentation software, is being made available to development projects for only $6 USD. Other products include e-mail, paint, browser, and programming software. The products are being developed with special attention to the needs of Indian users. For example, all products have complete Indian-languages interfaces, including navigation menus. The e-mail software comes with separate password-protected folders, ideal for a situation in which many users share one machine. A compiler of the C and C++ computer languages enables programming to be done in English (essential for getting a job) but allows comments and error messages to be written in Indian languages, thus providing important support to limited-English speakers who are in the process of becoming software programmers. Finally, to encourage international communication between India's different regions, the word processing and communication software products are programmed to automatically convert from one language scrip to another. This is especially helpful for the many millions of people in India who can read and write one Indian language but speak others. For example, a writer of Tamil (but speaker of Hindi) can write a Hindi-language message in the Tamil script and have it automatically converted to Hindi script to be read by someone in a Hindi-speaking region of the country. These conversions can even be performed instantaneously using synchronous communication software so that one's own script appears on one's own screen while the other script appears instantly on the correspondent's screen.

These software solutions are helping rural development projects in India to develop Internet content in local languages. Much useful content in these projects is not necessarily original material but rather public information already available elsewhere on the Web that is carefully selected, translated into Indian languages, and presented in a simplified form in easy-to-navigate pages.

Language and Identity in Hawai'i

Multilingual software solutions are only the first step. To help promote technology for social inclusion, it is also necessary to use the software to develop and make available relevant content. This can be don by translating material and, more important, by developing original material in the minority language itself. One of the more interesting examples of minority language content development is from Hawai'i.

The situation in Hawai'i differs markedly from those in India and Egypt. In Hawai'i, almost everyone except some recent immigrants speaks English. Why then is Hawaiian-language computing and Internet content even necessary? To understand this, it is necessary to examine briefly from a sociopolitical angle the history of Hawaiian language use.

Hawaiian was the national language of the sovereign Hawaiian monarchy of the nineteenth century. At the end of that century, however, wealthy American landowners backed by the U.S. government overthrew the Hawaiian kingdom and forcefully incorporated Hawai'i as a U.S. territory. Laws forbidding the use of the Hawaiian language were passed and vigorously enforced through beating children who dared speak their native tongue in school (Wilson 1998). By the time Hawai'i became a U.S. state in 1959, Hawaiian was spoken by only a few thousand elders and the language was seriously endangered. The suppression of the Hawaiian language went hand-in-hand with the subjugation of the native Hawaiian people, whose numbers gradually diminished and who found themselves at the bottom of all social and economic indicators with little room to move in terms of rescuing their dying language.

Nonetheless, a strong Hawaiian resistance movement emerged in the 1970s to fight for Native Hawaiian rights, including revitalization of the Hawaiian language. As a result of this effort, the Hawaiian language was legalized and a number of Hawaiian immersion schools were established by the state government. New undergraduate and graduate programs in Hawaiian studies and Hawaiian language were launched in the state's public universities. Ever since, defense of the Hawaiian language has continued to be a central element for defense of the Hawaiian people. This is especially so because of the complex nature of Hawaiian identity. There are almost no "pure" Hawaiians left, although some 20% of the people in the islands have part-Hawaiian ancestry. In this context, many Hawaiians believe that revitalization of their language is critical to their survival as a people.

The Hawaiian language is no longer facing extermination; nevertheless, it still faces an uphill battle to be reestablished as a stable living language used regularly in daily life. There are no daily Hawaiian-language newspapers or full-time Hawaiian-language television stations. The handful of elders who learned to speak Hawaiian as a first language are dying. The Hawaiian immersion schools are trying to teach Hawaiian but are confronted by a lack of curricular content and a dispersion of its speakers in small pockets spread out over several islands.

It was within this context that Hawaiian educators from the University of Hawai'i launched Leokī (powerful voice), believed to be the first online bulletin board system that functioned completely in an indigenous language (Warschauer and Donaghy 1997). The provision of Hawaiian-language content and communication media was intended to boost the Hawaiian revitalization effort, and particularly the Hawaiian-language programs in the immersion schools. As Keiki Kawai'ae'a, the director of Hawaiian-language curriculum materials, explained,

> Without changing the language and having the programs in Hawaiian, they wouldn't be able to have computer education *through* Hawaiian, which is really a major hook for kids in our program. They get the traditional content like science and math, and now they are able to utilize this *'ono* (really delicious) media called computers! Computer education is just so exciting for our children. In order for Hawaiian to feel like a real living language, like English, it needs to be seen, heard and utilized everywhere, and that includes the use of computers. (Quoted in Warschauer 1998, 147–148)

All the interfaces, menus, and content for Leokī are written in Hawaiian. The board also contains an extensive array of features (Figure 5):

- *Leka Uila* (electronic mail). Each user has a private mailbox for sending and receiving mail to and from other users on Leokī as well as via the Internet.
- *Laina Kolekole* (chat line). An online chat area for real-time interaction. Users can also create their own private chat rooms.
- *Ha'ina Uluwale* (open forum). Public synchronous computer conferences for discussion, debate, and surveys.
- *Ku'i ka Lono* (newsline). Advertisements, announcements, and information about Hawaiian-language classes and important upcoming events.
- *Hale Kū'ai* (marketplace). Announcements and online order forms for the purchase of Hawaiian-language books and materials.
- *Papa Hua'ōlelo* (vocabulary list). Dissemination of Hawaiian words being coined by the Hawaiian-language lexical committee. Users can suggest new words and offer input on terms being considered or search vocabulary databases.
- *Nā Maka o Kana* (The Eyes of Kana). The current and all back issues of the *Nā Maka o Kana* newspaper, published by and for the Hawaiian immersion program.
- *Noi'i Nowelo* (Search for Knowledge). Shared resource area for old and new Hawaiian-language materials. Posting of stories, articles, and songs.
- *Nā Ke'ena 'Ōlelo Hawai'i* (Hawaiian language offices). An information section about the various agencies that provide educational support for Hawaiian studies coursework and Hawaiian-medium programs throughout the state.

Leokī has been installed on the computers in the Hawaiian immersion schools and preschools, Hawaiian-language departments of colleges and universities, and in Hawaiian-language support organizations. Most recently, a public version has been made available to any Hawaiian-language speaker.[8]

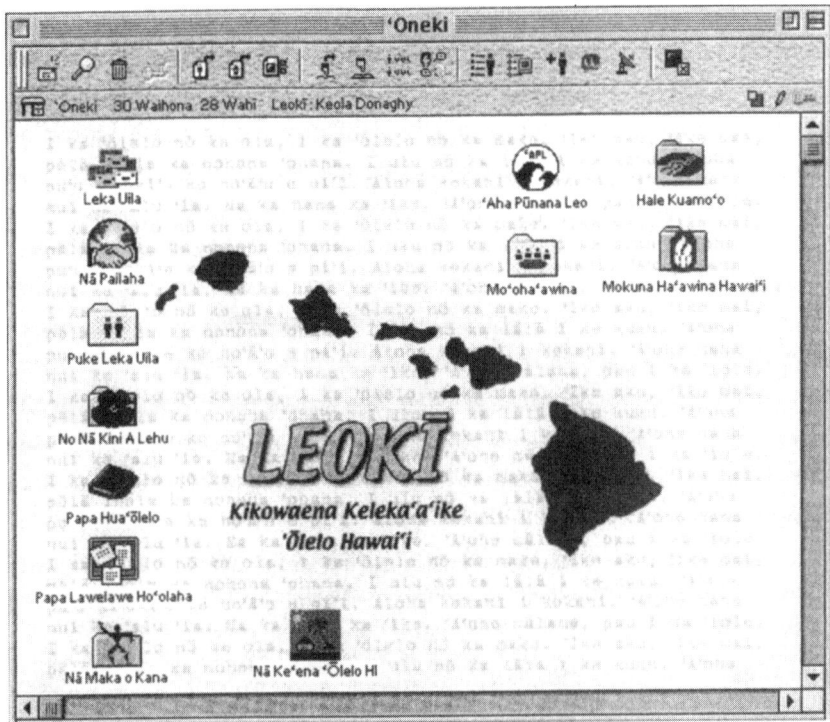

Figure 5 Hawaiian language bulletin board system

Source: Kualono (2001). Used with permission from Kualono

In addition, Hawaiian educators have actively mobilized the Hawaiian-language community to create content for Leokī and for the broader Internet. In 1997 I conducted an ethnographic study of a Hawaiian-language class at the University of Hawai'i that worked to develop a Web site in the Hawaiian language. The students in the course chose topics related to Hawaiian history and culture, including Hawaiian chanting and music, Hawaiian leaders, and the geography and nature of Hawai'i. The Web pages that they developed were highly sophisticated in language, content, and design, and the experience proved highly motivating for the students. As one of the students explained,

> It's like a double advantage for us, we're learning how to use new tools, like new technology and new tools, at the same time we're doing it in Hawaiian language, and so we get to learn two things at once. . . . It looks almost as if it's a thing of the future for Hawaiian, because if you think about it, maybe there's [only] a few Hawaiian-language papers. But instead of maybe having a Hawaiian-language newspaper, you have something that might be just a little bit better, like the World Wide Web, it's like building things for all the kids who are now in immersion and even for us, someplace to go and get information, and so that's kind of neat what

we're doing, we're doing research and then finding out all that we can about a topic and then actually putting it on the World Wide Web, and then having that be useful to somebody else in the future. (Warschauer 1999)

Nancy Hornberger (1997) once said that "Language revitalization is not about bringing a language back, it's about bringing it forward." For students in Hawai'i, indigenous-language content creation is bridging a very special divide, that between a recent past in which their language and culture faced persecution and near elimination, and a future in which their words, chants, songs, and stories will thrive with the assistance of new media.

Conclusion

Physical resources such as computers and connectivity mean little without sufficient digital content that is relevant to people and in the language of their communities. As many of these examples have shown, the most important content production is often done by people in the targeted communities themselves. This, in turn, demands literacy and education. It is to those issues that I turn now.

Keywords for critical reading

By the end of this section the student should be able to define and illustrate their understanding of each of the following key concepts and notions:

- Accessibility (physical access, physical connection)
- Authoritarian school system
- 'Civilizational' destiny
- Collective rights, vs. Individual rights.
- Content providers
- Data mining
- Digital divide (Ethnic divide; Gender divide; Global divide)
- Dynamics of differential access
- E-governance
- Information age
- Internet-based economy
- Service providers
- Knowledge gap; Knowledge generation capacity
- Learning to learning-to-learn
- Libertarian strand
- Modern dominant doctrine (imperialist strategy).
- Preferential clients
- Social learning; Social inequality
- Technological convergence
- Technological determinism; Technological pessimism
- Turn-key operations

Key questions for critical learning

1. How could the technological developments in Western countries allow us to understand the social divide between the haves and the have-nots?
2. What are the key elements of the structural economies of new-media technology?
3. Why do the notions of 'time' and 'space' continue to be two central concepts for the understanding of traditional and modern forms of communication?
4. Using specific examples, explain why our Western society could hardly achieve most simple task today without technology.
5. What does George Grant mean by the paradigm of knowledge?
6. Explain at least one dimension of the digital divide and its social repercussion in our school.
7. Why should the government create policies that place restrictions on data mining?
8. Is the Western concern with intellectual property rights a matter of ethics or economics?
9. Although new technologies enable us to access vast amounts of information from around the world, they can also cut us off from local information sources. Have you encountered this phenomenon in your own life? What sources of information have disappeared from your local community?

Part 3

Media Theories and Communication Research

Section Editor: Mahmoud Eid

Introduction

This section consists of three parts that introduce the reader to major approaches and theories in media studies and communication research. It demonstrates the basic concepts and themes of these theories, outlines the debates between the major schools of thought in the field, and then relates these discussions to Canadian trends in communication and media studies.

Stephen W. Littlejohn and Daya Kishan Thussu introduce the central ideas of some of the major theories of mass communication and international communication. Littlejohn, in his chapter 'Communication and Media', introduces the concepts of *macro* and *micro* in terms of mass communication theory. At the macro level, media scholars are interested in the media–society link, the ways media are embedded in society, and the mutual influence between larger social structures and the media. At the micro level, theorists are interested in the media–audience link and focus on group and individual effects and outcomes of media transactions. Littlejohn also explains the basic concepts of many of the major theories of media and mass communication including medium theory, semiotics of media, audience research, the diffusion of information and influence, public opinion and spiral of silence, cultivation analysis, the agenda-setting function, the effects tradition, and the uses-and-gratifications approach, and sheds light on their main critiques. Thussu, in his chapter 'Approaches to Theorizing International Communication', takes the discussion about theories of communication to a global level. He introduces historical backgrounds and basic concepts, and then critically analyzes major themes, approaches, and theories of international communication. These include free flow of information, modernization theory, dependency theory, structural imperialism, hegemony, critical theory, the public sphere, cultural studies perspectives on international communication, theories of information society, discourses of globalization, and a critical political-economy for the twenty-first century.

Mahmoud Eid and Hanno Hardt discuss two major schools of thought in the field of communication research, *administrative research* and critical theory. Eid, in his article 'Paul Lazarsfeld's Ideational Network and Contribution to the Field of Communication Research', introduces the work of Paul Lazarsfeld, one of the 'founding fathers' of communication research in the United States. Through his major publications, influential studies, and innovative social research methodologies and techniques, Lazarsfeld created the administrative approach to research on the processes and effects of mass communication media. Eid analyzes Lazarsfeld's career, demonstrating how he was committed to investigating individual behaviour in a social context for the betterment of social conditions. He also shows how Lazarsfeld's media effects studies and major works gave rise to a series of arguments from his critics, most notably theorists of the *critical theory*. Harzdt, in his chapter 'On Introducing Ideology: Critical Theory and the Critique of Culture', discusses the major concepts of *critical theory*. Hardt demonstrates the alternative visions of communication and society that followed the introduction of communication research by Lazarsfeld and others. These visions were expressed in the context of literature and sociology through a critique of mass culture that emerged from Marxism and from the contribution of critical theory to American social theory.

Sheryl Hamilton and John D.H. Downing bring debates about approaches, theories, and schools of thought in the field of communication research to Canada's ground. Hamilton, in her chapter 'Considering Critical Communication Studies in Canada', discusses the debate between administrative and critical communication research in a Canadian context. Hamilton questions the claim that Canadian communication studies are critical, and analyzes the term itself in terms of the shared characteristics of critical communication research. Downing, in his review essay 'New Communication Research from Canada', reviews a group of Canadian texts that address pivotal topics in communication. This essay is aimed at expanding United States and other communication researchers' awareness of what he calls 'the stimulating and varied research conducted in Anglo Canada and Québec'.

Theories of Media and Communication

Communication and Media

Stephen W. Littlejohn

We are living in what Marshall McLuhan calls the "global village." Modern communication media make it possible for millions of people throughout the world to be in touch with nearly any spot on the globe. George Gerbner points to the importance of the media in society:

> This broad "public-making" significance of mass media of communications—the ability to create publics, define issues, provide common terms of reference, and thus to allocate attention and power—has evoked a large number of theoretical contributions.[1]

Mass communication is the process whereby media organizations produce and transmit messages to large publics and the process by which those messages are sought, used, understood, and influenced by audiences.

Central to any study of mass communication are the media.[2] Media organizations distribute messages that affect and reflect the cultures of society, and they provide information simultaneously to large heterogeneous audiences, making media part of society's institutional forces.

"Media," of course, imply "mediation" because they come between the audience and the world. Denis McQuail suggests several metaphors to capture this idea: Media are *windows* that enable us to see beyond our immediate surroundings, *interpreters* that help us make sense of experience, *platforms* or *carriers* that convey information, *interactive communication* that includes audience feedback, *signposts* that provide us with instructions and directions, *filters* that screen out parts of experience and focus on others, *mirrors* that reflect ourselves back to us, and *barriers* that block the truth.[3] Joshua Meyrowitz adds three additional metaphors—media as *conduits,* media as *languages,* and media as *environments.*[4] What are media, then? There is no single or simple definition.

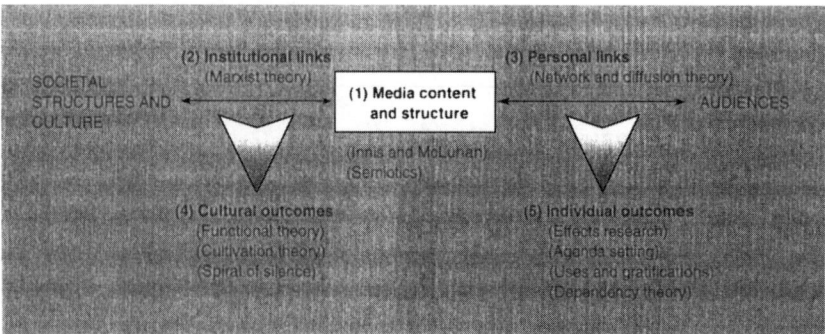

Figure 1 An organizing model

An Organizing Model

Media scholars recognize two faces of mass communication.[5] One face looks from the media to the larger society and its institutions. Theorists interested in the media–society link are concerned with the ways media are embedded in society and the mutual influence between larger social structures and the media. This is the *macro* side of mass communication theory.

The second face looks toward people, as groups and individuals. This face reflects the link between the media and audiences. Theorists interested in the media–audience link focus on group and individual effects and outcomes of the media transaction. This is the *micro* side of mass communication theory.[6]

Figure 1 illustrates the two faces of mass communication. The model may imply that these two sides are different things, but in truth they are the same thing looked at from different perspectives. The relationship between media and institutions is possible only through the media's transaction with audiences, and the audience–media relationship is impossible to separate from the institutions of the society in which those audiences reside. Thus, the model is not a map of the mass communication process but depicts the areas of media research and theory.

The chapter is divided into *five* sections corresponding to the parts of the model: (1) media content and structure, (2) the media–institution link, (3) the media–audience link, (4) cultural outcomes, and (5) individual outcomes.

Media Content and Structure

Certain theories have emphasized intrinsic structural properties of media and media messages. Of particular concern here is the "sending" side of the mass communication process, or what media producers actually produce. A useful term for this general process is *encoding*.[7] There are two aspects of production considered important. The first is the medium in which communication takes place, and the second is the content of mediated messages. In the following two sections, we look at each of these.

Medium Theory

Perhaps Marshall McLuhan is most responsible for calling our attention to the importance of media as media. He is a well-known figure in the study of popular culture, receiving attention because of his interesting and bizarre style and his startling and thought-provoking ideas.[8] Although the specifics of McLuhan's theory are often rejected today, his general thesis has received widespread acceptance: Media, apart from whatever content is transmitted, impact individuals and society. This idea in its various forms is what we mean by "medium theory."

McLuhan was not the first to write about this idea. Indeed, his ideas were profoundly affected by the work of his mentor Harold Adams Innis, who taught that communication media are the essence of civilization and that history is directed by the predominant media of each age.[9]

For McLuhan and Innis, media are extensions of the human mind, so that the primary interest of any historical period is biased by the predominant media in use. In other words, what happens and what seems significant in a historical period are determined by the media. Heavy media such as parchment, clay, or stone are lasting and therefore *time binding*. Because they facilitate communication from one generation to another, these media are biased toward tradition. In contrast, *space-binding* media such as paper are light and easy to transport, so they facilitate communication from one location to another, fostering empire building, large bureaucracy, and the military.

Speech as a medium, because it is produced one sound at a time, encourages people to organize their experience chronologically. Speech also requires knowledge and tradition and therefore supports community and relationship. Written media, which are spatially arranged, produce a different kind of culture. The space-binding effect of writing produces interests in political authority and the growth of empires across the land.

McLuhan's thesis is that people adapt to their environment through a certain balance or ratio of the senses, and the primary medium of the age brings out a particular sense ratio, thereby affecting perception.[10] McLuhan sees every medium as an extension of some human faculty, exaggerating the sense. "The wheel . . . is an extension of the foot. The book is an extension of the eye. . . . Clothing, an extension of the skin. . . . Electric circuitry, an extension of the central nervous system."[11]

Before printing was invented, tribal people were primarily hearing-oriented communicators, emotionally and interpersonally close. For the tribal person, "hearing was believing." But the invention of the printing press changed all that. The Gutenberg age brought a new sense ratio into being, in which sight predominated. The rise of print in Western culture forced people into a linear, logical, and categorical kind of perception.

Electronic technology has brought back an aural, or hearing, predominance. The Gutenberg technology of printing created an explosion in society, separating and segmenting individual from individual, but the electronic age has created an implosion, bringing the world back together in a "global village." As a result, "it is forcing us to reconsider and reevaluate practically every thought, every action, and every institution formerly taken for granted."[12] If McLuhan had lived long enough, what would he have said about the Internet?

McLuhan is perhaps best known for his saying "The medium is the message."[13] This curious and thought-provoking catchphrase highlights the general influence that a medium has apart from its content. Tom Wolfe puts the matter this way: "It doesn't matter if the networks show twenty hours a day of sadistic cowboys caving in people's teeth or twenty hours of Pablo Casals droning away on his cello in a pure-culture white Spanish drawing room. It doesn't matter about the content."[14] And here, of course, McLuhan parts company from most contemporary mass communication researchers, who believe that the content matters a great deal. Today, most media theorists would agree that both content and medium matter.

Donald Ellis summarized the literature on medium theory and presented a well-codified set of propositions representing a contemporary perspective on this subject.[15] Following Innis and McLuhan, Ellis notes that the predominant media at any given time will shape behavior and thought. As media change, so do the ways in which we think, manage information, and relate to one another. There are sharp differences among oral, written, and electronic media.

Oral communication is highly malleable and organic. Oral messages are immediate and ephemeral, so that individuals and groups must keep information in their minds and pass it on through speech. Because everyday experience cannot really be separated from the oral medium of transmission, life and knowledge cannot be separated. The telling and retelling of stories over time privilege narrative as a form of communication and require group memory as the "holder" of society's knowledge. This can lead to a collective consciousness in which little distinction is made between self and group. Group identification and cohesiveness are high when oral media predominate.

Writing, and especially the advent of printing, led to profound changes in society. When you can write something down, you can separate it from the moment. You can manipulate it, change it, edit, and recast. In other words, you can "act on" information and knowledge in a way that is not evident in the oral tradition. This leads to a separation of knowledge (what is known) from the knower (who knows it). Those who can read and write have special status, so that formal education takes on an important role. What can be known (that which is written down) can become known by reading. Knowledge, then, becomes objectified and can assume the status of truth, and individuals and groups can be divided among those who "have" the truth and those who do not. Further, information can be stored, or saved, which makes literacy a tool of conservation. Importance is assigned to that which is "stored" in written language.

The third major shift occurs when electronic media come to the fore. Electronic media are something like orality in that they can be immediate and ephemeral, but they are not tied down to a particular place because they can be broadcast. Electronic media extend your perception beyond where you are at any given moment, creating the "global village." At the same time, like print, electronic media allow information to be stored. Because they are more readily available than print, electronic media create an information explosion, and a great competition occurs among various media to be heard and seen. Information in electronic media is sold like a commodity, which creates pressure for information to be attractive. Knowledge in the electronic age changes rapidly, and we become aware of different versions of truth. The constant change created by electronic media can make us feel confused and perhaps unsettled.

If orality creates a culture of community and literacy creates a culture of class, then electronic communication creates a culture of "cells," or groups pitted against one another to promote their special interests. A new kind of public not bound to place is created. The politics of interest prevails, and democracy, along with its attendant value of civility, assumes importance as a way to manage differences. Yet, ironically the competition and commodity-based economy that accompanies electronic media fight against the very values most needed in this environment— civility and collegiality. So, electronic communication creates the paradox of separation through difference and the importance of participatory democracy.

If you were a member of a primarily oral culture, difference would be minimal, and decisions would be made collectively based on the wisdom of tradition as it has been passed down generation to generation. If you were a member of a primarily print-oriented culture, decisions would rely on "truth" stored in documents, and those who had access to information would have great influence as a class in society's decision making. But today, you are likely a member of a primarily electronic culture in which you identify with interest groups that vie against one another. You experience many voices, and societal decisions must be made by hearing all the voices, integrating these in some way, and creating forms that accommodate as many interests as possible.

Ellis' compilation of ideas about media give us a good sense of medium theory and how it places media qua media at the center of social structure and change. To continue this analysis, we turn now to the work of Jean Baudrillard.

Jean Baudrillard and the Semiotics of Media

Semiotics has provided a powerful tool for examining the impact of mass media. For the semiotician, content is important, but content is a product of the use of signs. This approach focuses on the ways producers create signs and the ways audiences understand them.

Semiotics has a long history of development in the twentieth century (see Chapter 4).[16] This field helps us see how signs are used to interpret events and can be an especially good tool for analyzing the content of media messages.[17] Most would agree that signs take on special significance in the media, and the media shape in many ways how signs function for us. To pursue this idea in greater detail, we will take a closer look at the work of the French social critic Jean Baudrillard.[18]

Baudrillard believes that signs have become increasingly separated from the objects they represent and that the media have propelled this process to the point where nothing is real. The media did not suddenly create this condition but exacerbated a tendency that has been going on throughout modern history.

Sign use has gone through an evolution in society. At first, a sign was a simple representation of an object or condition. The sign had a clear connection with the signified. This Baudrillard calls the stage of the *symbolic order,* common in feudal society. In the second stage, *counterfeits,* common from the Renaissance to the Industrial Revolution, signs assumed a less direct relationship to the things of life. Signs actually produced new meanings not necessarily a natural part of the experience of that which was signified. For example, status, wealth, and prestige were connected to things because of how they were signified. The next stage, that of the Industrial Revolution, is that of *production,* in which machines were invented to take the place of humans, making objects independent of any human use of signifiers.

Today we are in an era of *simulation,* in which signs no longer represent—but create—our reality. Simulation determines who we are and what we do. No longer tools to represent our experience, signs establish it. Disneyland epitomizes the era of simulation. Theme parks are fantasies constructed from signs. The real thing—pirates, frontier, fantasyland, and so on—can be reproduced any time anywhere. Because they dominate our lives, the new media bombard us with simulation, literally creating our worlds. Rather than have genuine communication involving interaction among people, the media dominate our lives with information that forms what we perceive to be genuine experience, but it is far removed from the natural order of things. This leads us to obscenely exaggerated forms of life. We feel that these are real experiences, but in fact they are experiences within the simulations created by the media.

Our commodity culture is one aspect of the simulation in which we live. The simulated environment tells us what we want. It forms our tastes, choices, preferences, and needs. Consumption takes on value in and of itself. Most important is that we are consuming, not that we desire real things that have actual functions. We think we are different, but in fact most people's values and behaviors are highly constrained by the "reality" simulated in the media. We think that our individual needs are being met, but those are homogenized needs shaped by the use of signs in the media.

Because objects are separated from their original natural state, they take on bizarre meanings for us. Possession is more important than use. Where once we needed farm animals to do work for us, we now value pets as a matter of ownership. Our lives are full of gizmos that have no real use, but sit on shelves for us to possess and look at and make a life of pure "symbolicity." We buy a watch, not really to tell time, but to wear as a form of apparel.

As a result of this process of simulation, we make fewer and fewer distinctions. Meanings collapse, or implode, into a huge mass, which Baudrillard refers to as *hypertelia*. This is a process of exaggeration in which we thrive on hype. Rather than distinguish between good and bad, beautiful and ugly, we mash everything together into the hyperreal, leading to a life of excess in which nuance is unimportant.

The line of thinking begun by Innis and continued today by scholars like Baudrillard may resonate with your experience. You probably have a sense that the ubiquitous media of mass communication do affect our lives in profound ways, but this approach may also feel overly simple and reductionistic. We begin this chapter with this line of work because it brings out the importance of media, but much more work has been done to isolate other factors and effects, as we will see below.

Media as Social Institution

Media are more than simple mechanisms for disseminating information: They are complex organizations and an important social institution of society. Perhaps the most important line of theory to address the institutional aspect of media is marxist critical theory. Because critical theory is discussed in Chapter 11, we will not cover it in great detail here.[19] Recall that critical theories are concerned with the distribution of power in society and the domination of certain interests over others. Clearly, the media are a major player in this ideological struggle. Dominant ideologies can be perpetuated by the media. Most critical communication theories are concerned with mass media primarily because of the media's potential for disseminating dominant ideologies and their potential for expressing alternative and oppositional ones. For some critical theorists, media are part of a culture industry that literally creates symbols and images that can oppress marginalized groups.

According to McQuail there are five major branches of marxist media theory.[20] The first is *classical Marxism*. Here, the media are seen as instruments of the dominant class and a means by which capitalists promote their profit-making interests. Media disseminate the ideology of the ruling classes in society and thereby oppress certain classes.

The second is *political-economic media theory*, which, like classical Marxism, blames media ownership for society's ills. In this school of thought, media content is a commodity to be sold in the marketplace, and the information disseminated is controlled by what the market will bear. This system leads to a conservative, non-risk-taking operation, making certain kinds of programming and certain media outlets dominant and others marginalized.

The third line of theory is the *Frankfurt School*. This school of thought, seeing media as a means of constructing culture, places more emphasis on ideas than on material goods. In this way of thinking, media lead to the domination of the ideology of the elite. This outcome is accomplished by media manipulation of images and symbols to benefit the interests of the dominant class.

The fourth school is the *hegemonic theory*. Hegemony is the domination of a false ideology or way of thinking over true conditions. Ideology is not caused by the economic system alone but is deeply embedded in all activities of society. Thus, ideology is not forced by one group on another but is pervasive and unconscious. The dominant ideology perpetuates the interests of certain classes over others, and the media obviously take a major role in this process.

The final approach to marxist media studies is the *sociocultural approach*, usually called simply "cultural studies." Relying largely on semiotics, this group of scholars is interested in the cultural meanings of media products, looking at the ways media content is interpreted, including both dominant and oppositional interpretations. Cultural studies sees society as a field of competing ideas in a struggle among meanings. What, for example, is the meaning of a music video? In cultural studies, various competing meanings are viewed as cultural productions. Cultural studies is becoming an increasingly popular and useful approach, and it can be used to integrate insights from a variety of schools of thought.[21]

Although critical communication theories have gained presence in North America, their real development and strength occurred in Europe and Latin America. European critical theory is perhaps more widely known, because of the larger number of sources translated into English and the greater attention paid to European traditions. In contrast, Latin American communication theory, which remains largely untranslated, has received relatively little attention in the United States. Robert Huesca and Brenda Dervin have written a good summary of this work.[22]

According to Huesca and Dervin, Latin American communication scholarship challenges the predominant North American approach on many fronts. In general, this work honors horizontal, artistic, democratic, and participatory communication over vertical, industrial, authoritarian, and elite forms. It tends to look more at grass-roots efforts rather than top-down ones, and self-managed communication systems rather than centralized systems. Latin American communication research also concentrates on human liberation rather than information transfer, conscience building rather than domination, unity rather than fragmentation, and antiauthoritarian rather than authoritarian content.

Although these trends tend to be as dualistic as is most North American scholarship, pitting one point against another, many Latin American scholars have attempted to overcome dualism altogether. They have done this in a number of ways. For example, they have refused to dichotomize the communication source from the audience and have shown that the audience itself participates in the creation of meaning. These scholars have also emphasized global over national trends and have called for coalitions, networks, and dialogue among groups and ideas.

Media and Audience

No area in media theory has presented such quandaries and debates as studies of the audience. Media theorists are far from consensus on how to conceptualize the audience and audience effects. Disputes on the nature of the audience seem to involve two related dialectics. The first is a tension between the idea that the audience is a mass public versus the idea that it is a small community. The second is a tension between the idea that the audience is passive versus the belief that it is active. Let us consider each of these debates in turn.

Mass Society Versus Community

This controversy involves different opinions about the audience. Some see the audience as an undifferentiated mass, and some see it as a variegated set of small groups or communities. In the case of the former, audiences are viewed as a large population that can be molded by the media. In the case of the latter, audiences are viewed as discriminating members of small groups who are influenced mostly by their peers.

The theory of mass society is a concept growing out of the large, complex, bureaucratic nature of the modern state.[23] The theory envisions a malleable mass of people in which small groupings, community life, and ethnic identity are replaced by societywide depersonalized relations. This conception of society has led to widespread criticism of modern life and of the media. We already got a taste of mass society theory in the work of Baudrillard above.

Critics of the mass society have suggested several propositions. First, rapid developments in transportation and communication have increased human contact, and economic considerations have made people more and more interdependent. Thus, like a giant system, imbalance in one part affects everybody. Ironically, we are all more interdependent while becoming increasingly estranged from one another. Community and family ties are broken, and old values are questioned.

Second, because society is no longer believed to be led by the elite, morals, tastes, and values decline.[24] Rapid changes in society hurl men and women into multiple-role situations, causing a loss of the sense of self.[25] People become more anxious, and a charismatic leader ultimately may be required to lift society out of the abyss.

The dismal view of the theory of mass society has several implications for the mass media of communication. Critics of mass society fear that minds will be pounded and altered by propaganda through the media. As Paul Lazarsfeld and Robert Merton state: "There is the danger that these technically advanced instruments of mass communication constitute a major avenue for deterioration of aesthetic tastes and popular cultural standards."[26]

Add to this the thesis that the media are blurring social boundaries and community divisions that previously gave stability and meaning to the lives of citizens. Joshua Meyrowitz writes in his book *No Sense of Place* that television has caused us to lose our sense of boundaries—between the private and public, between the physical and social, and between social groups. People are essentially losing their "place" in the world.[27]

The theory of mass society is still popular among the general population. Although this theory is not as prevalent among scholars today as it was a few decades ago, it still has an influence. McLuhan's theory is certainly a mass society theory, as are some of the marxist theories. Certain "powerful-effects" theories, including the well-known cultivation theory discussed later in the chapter, are strongly influenced by mass society thinking.

In contrast to mass society thinking is the position that the audience cannot be characterized as an amorphous mass, that it consists of numerous highly differentiated communities, each with its own values, ideas, and interests. Media content is interpreted within the community according to meanings that are worked out socially within the group, and individuals are influenced more by their peers than by the media.[28] We explored the idea of media-interpretive communities in Chapter 10, where we saw that the meanings of media messages are worked out interactively within groups of people who use a medium in a similar way.

Gerard Schoening and James Anderson call the community-based approach *social action media studies,* and they outline six premises of this work.[29] First, meaning is not in the message itself but is produced by an interpretive process in the audience. Different audiences will interpret or understand what they read and view in different ways. For example, talk radio programs may be taken to mean many things, depending on who is listening.

The second premise of social action media studies is that the meaning of media messages and programs is not determined passively, but produced actively. This means that audiences actually do something with what they view and read. They act as they view. Some listeners, for example, may turn on talk radio to combat boredom while driving, others may turn it on late in the evening as a sleep aid, and still others may listen to it actively during the day as a means of getting information about current events. What a particular talk radio program means, therefore, is a product of how listeners treat it, what they do with it.

The third premise is that the meanings of media shift constantly as the members approach the media in different ways. Sometimes the talk radio program may be strictly entertainment, sometimes serious information, and sometimes just background noise, depending on when and how it is listened to.

Fourth, the meaning of a program or message is never individually established, but communal. It is part of the tradition of a group, community, or culture. The implication of this is that when you join a community (by birth or membership), you accept the ongoing activities and meanings of that community or group. Your own behavior may influence the group or change the activities and meanings in some way, but the outcome at any given time is always sitting in the community or group.

Fifth, the actions that determine a group's meanings for media content are done in interaction among members of the group. In other words, how we act toward the media and what meanings emerge from those actions are social interactions. This does not mean that you never watch TV by yourself, but it does mean that how you watch TV and what you do with the television set are part of an ongoing interaction between yourself and others. If you listen to talk radio in the car while you commute to work, this pattern is part of a larger web of interactions with people at home and at work. It is a routine that is made possible by a huge network of interactions involving work, home, radio, boredom, cars, highways, and so on.

Finally, the sixth premise of social action media studies is that researchers join the communities they study, if only temporarily, and therefore have an ethical obligation to be open about what they are studying and share what they learn with those studied.

Active Audience Versus Passive Audience

Another controversy is the passive versus active audience. The passive-audience view suggests that people are easily influenced in a direct way by the media, whereas the active-audience view suggests that people make more active decisions about how to use the media. For the most part, mass society theories tend to subscribe to a passive conception of audience, although not all passive-audience theories can legitimately be called mass society theories. Similarly, most community theories subscribe to an active notion of audience.

These ideas about audiences are associated with various theories of media effects discussed later in the chapter. The "powerful-effects" theories tend to be based on the passive audience, whereas the "minimal-effects" theories are based more on an active one.

Frank Biocca discusses five characteristics of the active audience implied by the theories of this genre.[30] The first is *selectivity.* Active audiences are considered to be selective in the media they choose to use. The second characteristic is *utilitarianism.* Active audiences are said to use media to meet particular needs and goals. The third characteristic is *intentionality,* which implies the purposeful use of media content. The fourth characteristic is *involvement,* or effort. Here, audiences are actively attending, thinking about, and using the media. Finally, active audiences are believed to be *impervious to influence,* or not very easily persuaded by the media alone.

Many media scholars believe that the mass community and active-passive dichotomies are too simple, that they do not capture the true complexity of audiences. It may be that audiences have some elements of mass society and other elements of local communities. Audiences may be active in some ways and passive in others or active at some times and passive at other times. Rather than ask whether audiences are easily influenced by the media, it might be better to ask when and under what conditions they are influenced and when they are not. This view changes the debate from one over what the audience really is to its meaning for people at different times and in different places.[31]

Theories of Cultural Outcomes

We turn now to a study of the outcomes of media communication. Of all areas of mass communication research, outcome studies are the most prevalent, especially in the United States. An overriding question throughout the history of media theory has been the effects of media on society and individuals.[32]

Karl Erik Rosengren shows that media outcomes are complex and wide-ranging.[33] Various theories concentrate on different outcomes—short term and long term, narrow and individual, broad and cultural. He lists five examples of such differences:

- News diffusion research (hours and days)
- Agenda setting (weeks and months)
- Spiral of silence (months and years)
- Cultivation (years and decades)
- Research on public sphere (decades and centuries)

The theories included here are divided into two sections: those focusing on general cultural outcomes and those focusing on individual effects. This section deals with the former and the next section with the latter.

The Functions of Mass Communication

For many years, media theory concentrated on how media work and their effects on audiences. This was essentially a functionalist approach (see Chapter 1) that concentrated on the system of mass communication, how it works, and what it does.[34]

One of the earliest and best-known theorists in this tradition was Harold Lasswell. In his classic 1948 article, he presented the simple and often quoted model of communication:[35]

Who
Says what
In which channel
To whom
With what effect

This model outlines the basic elements of communication, the last element of which directs us to the entire outcome-research literature.

Lasswell identifies three functions of the media of communication. These are providing information about the environment, which he terms *surveillance;* presenting options for solving problems, or *correlation;* and socializing and education, referred to as *transmission.*[36]

The Lasswell model is a classic. Notice that it essentially lists the parts of the mass communication system and the things that mass communication accomplishes. Since this early work, many other functions have been explored. We will look at several in this chapter, beginning in the following section with the diffusion of information and influence.

The Diffusion of Information and Influence

The community view of audience discussed above was given impetus by a now-classic voting study in 1940 conducted by Lazarsfeld and his colleagues in Elmira, New York.[37] The researchers unexpectedly found that the effect of media was influenced by interpersonal communication. This effect, which came to be known as the *two-step flow hypothesis,* was startling, and it had a major impact on our understanding of the role of mass media.

This study was the beginning of a line of research on how information and influence are distributed in society. Lazarsfeld hypothesized that information flows from the mass media to certain opinion leaders in the community, who pass information on by talking to peers. He found that voters seem to be more influenced by their friends during a campaign than by the media. Since the original Elmira study, much additional data have come in, and this hypothesis has received substantial support.[38]

The two-step flow theory is best summarized in Elihu Katz and Paul Lazarsfeld's classic work *Personal Influence.*[39] These authors confirm that certain individuals known as *opinion leaders* receive information from the media and pass it to their peers.[40] Opinion leaders are in all groups: occupational, social, community, and others. These individuals are difficult to distinguish from other group members because opinion leadership is not a trait but a role taken by some individuals in certain circumstances. Opinion leadership changes from time to time and from issue to issue.

Opinion leaders may be of two kinds: those influential on one topic, or *monomorphism,* and those influential on a variety of topics, or *polymorphism.* Monomorphism becomes more predominant as systems become more modern.

Research more recent than the Lazarsfeld study has shown that the dissemination of ideas is not a simple two-step process. A *multiple-step model* is now more generally accepted.[41] This model is similar to the two-step hypothesis but admits to more possibilities. Research has shown that the ultimate number of relays between the media and final receivers is variable. In the adoption of an innovation, for example, certain individuals will hear about it directly from media sources, whereas others will be many steps removed.

The diffusion of information and innovations is now part of the interactional and network tradition discussed in some detail in Chapters 13 and 14. We saw in those chapters that interaction in networks plays an important role in relationships, small groups, and organizations. Here, we see that it plays an important role in mass communication too. The diffusion of information is one of the most significant outcomes of communication. Often distributed information promotes the adoption of innovations.

The diffusion of an innovation occurs when the adoption of an idea, practice, or object spreads by communication through a social system. Several prominent American and foreign researchers in fields such as agriculture and rural studies, national development, and organizational communication have been responsible for this line of research.

The broadest and most communication-oriented theory of diffusion is that of Everett Rogers and his colleagues.[42] Rogers relates dissemination to the process of social change, which consists of invention, diffusion (or communication), and consequences. Such change can occur internally from within a group or externally through contact with outside change agents. Contact may occur spontaneously or accidentally, or it may result from planning on the part of outside agencies.

In the diffusion of innovations, many years may be required for an idea to spread. Rogers states, in fact, that one purpose of diffusion research is to discover the means to shorten this lag. Once established, an innovation will have consequences—be they functional or dysfunctional, direct or indirect, manifest or latent. Change agents normally expect their impact to be functional, direct, and manifest, although this positive result does not always occur.

The diffusion of innovations is well illustrated by the family-planning program instituted in South Korea in 1968. Mothers' clubs were established in about 12,000 villages throughout Korea for the purpose of disseminating information about family planning. Overall, the program was successful, and Korea saw a major decline in birthrate during this period. This program was built on the idea that interpersonal channels of communication would be crucial to the adoption of birth control methods. In 1973 Rogers and his colleagues studied the Korean case by interviewing about a thousand women in twenty-four villages to gather information about the networks the women used for family planning.[43]

They found that the village leaders initially received their information about family planning from the mass media and family-planning worker visits, but interpersonal networks turned out to be most important in the dissemination-adoption process. Two network variables were especially important. The first was the degree to which the mothers' club leader was connected with others in the village network. The second variable was the amount of overlap between the family-planning network and the general village network. Birth control adoption was greatest in the villages in which the leader talked to many people personally, and the village women talked about it among themselves. Rogers has found that people do talk about ideas, and that is how change happens.

When innovations such as the cell phone, DSL lines, a new HIV therapy, or Internet shopping are introduced, it takes a while for them to catch on. Some innovations never catch on, but others spread with varying amounts of speed. Interpersonal influence is very important in this process. People raise awareness of the innovation as they talk with one another about it. They share opinions, discuss their experience with the innovation, sometimes advocate its use, and sometimes resist it. The rate of adoption is determined by perceptions of the innovation's relative advantage and its compatibility with existing values and experiences. The complexity of the innovation matters, and potential adopters will more readily accept an innovation with which they can experiment, or try out, without making a huge commitment. They may also want to observe others' adoption before taking the plunge.

People do vary in their levels of resistance and the social support needed to adopt the idea, practice, or object. There are always individuals who will adopt an innovation early, before most others consider doing so. These early adopters will set the stage, and they usually have an influence on others. As more and more people adopt, a critical mass of adoption occurs that gives rise to a rapid increase in general adoption.[44] A few people may be very slow to adopt and must see the innovation all around them before they will consider it. These are the late adopters. Of course, some may never adopt the new practice. In general, Rogers and his colleagues have found that adoption approximates an S-curve. On a time scale, the rise of adoption is slow at first, a critical mass is hit after which a sudden rise in adoption occurs, and then it levels out.

In some circumstances, however, people do not talk, and now we will look at a theory that explains why.

Public Opinion and the Spiral of Silence

As the research on Korean family planning discussed above illustrates, communication has much to do with public opinion. The topic of public opinion has been of great concern in political science, in which the concept represents opinions publicly expressed, opinions regarding public affairs, and opinions of the general public as a group rather than of smaller groups of individuals. Elisabeth Noelle-Neumann's theory of the "spiral of silence" continues this analysis by demonstrating how interpersonal communication and media operate together in the development of public opinion.[45]

As a political researcher in Germany, Noelle-Neumann observed that in elections certain views seem to get more play than others. Sometimes people mute their opinions rather than talk about them. Noelle-Neumann calls this the *spiral of silence*. The spiral of silence occurs when individuals who perceive that their opinion is popular express it, whereas those who do not think their opinion is popular remain quiet. This process occurs in a spiral, so that one side of an issue ends up with much publicity and the other side with little.

In everyday life we express our opinions in a variety of ways: We talk about them, we wear buttons, and we put bumper stickers on our cars. According to this theory, people are more apt to do these kinds of things when they perceive that others share their opinion and less apt to do so when they do not.

This thesis rests on two premises. The first is that people know which opinions are prevalent and which are not. This is called the *quasi-statistical sense* because people are not reluctant to make educated guesses about public opinion and have a sense of the percentages of the population for and against certain positions. The second assumption is that people adjust their expressions of opinion to these perceptions.

Noelle-Neumann presents much research evidence to support these assumptions. In political elections, for example, people usually perceive quite accurately the prevailing opinion about the candidates and issues, and they are likely to express their preferences when these are shared by others.

An interesting test of the tendency to remain silent on unpopular positions is the "train test."[46] Here, respondents are asked to imagine that they were in a train compartment with a stranger for five hours and to decide whether they would be willing to discuss certain topics with this person. Respondents were told that they were to imagine that the other person mentioned his or her opinion on the subject and were then asked whether they would prefer to talk to the other person about this topic or not. Topics ranged from spanking children to the government of Germany.

Interviewers presented this problem to 3,500 respondents covering numerous topics over several years. The overwhelming tendency was to freely discuss the topic when one agrees with the majority but to let it slide when one does not. People seem to not want to "make waves."

Of course, other factors enter into the decision to express one's opinion: Young people are more expressive than older people; educated individuals will speak up more than uneducated ones; men are generally more willing to disclose their opinions than women. However, the spiral of silence is also a factor, and according to this research, a powerful one.

The spiral of silence seems to be caused by the fear of isolation. The spiral of silence is not just a matter of wanting to be on the winning side but is an attempt to avoid being isolated from one's social group. Threats of criticism from others were found to be powerful forces in silencing individuals. For example, smokers who are repeatedly criticized for advocating smokers' rights were found to remain silent rather than state their views on this subject in the presence of vocal nonsmokers.

In some cases the threat of expressing an opinion is extreme:

> Slashed tires, defaced or torn posters, help refused to a lost stranger—questions of this kind demonstrate that people can be on uncomfortable or even dangerous ground when the climate of opinion runs counter to their views. When people attempt to avoid isolation, they are not responding hypersensitively to trivialities; these are existential issues that can involve real hazards.[47]

One can easily see how this process affects public opinion. There are, of course, exceptions to the spiral of silence. There are groups and individuals who do not fear isolation and who will express their opinions no matter what the consequences—a characteristic of innovators, change agents, and the avant-garde.

When polled, individuals usually state that they feel powerless in the face of media. Two kinds of experience accentuate this feeling of helplessness. The first is the difficulty of getting publicity for a cause or point of view. The second is being scapegoated by the media in what Noelle-Neumann calls the *pillory function* of media. In each case the individual feels powerless against the media, making the media an important part of the spiral of silence. The media publicize which opinions are prevalent and which are not.

Although public opinion is formed by both personal observation and media, individuals mix the two and confuse what is learned through the media with what is learned through interpersonal channels. This tendency is especially true for television, with which so many people have a personal relationship:

> The longer one has studied the question, the clearer it becomes that fathoming the effects of the mass media is very hard. These effects do not come into being as a result of a single stimulus; they are as a rule cumulative, following the principle that "water dripping constantly wears away stone." Further discussions among people spread the media's messages further, and before long no difference can be perceived between the point of media reception and points far removed from it. The media's effects are predominantly unconscious; people cannot provide an account of what has happened. Rather, they mix their own direct perceptions and the perceptions filtered through the eyes of the media into an indivisible whole that seems to derive from their own thoughts and experiences.[48]

It sometimes happens that journalists' opinions differ from those of the general public, so that media depictions contradict the prevailing expressions of individuals. When this occurs, a dual climate of opinion results. Here, two versions of reality operate: that of the media and that of the public. Noelle-Neumann likens this event to an unusual weather situation—interesting and seemingly bizarre.

The spiral of silence, then, is a phenomenon involving personal and media channels of communication. The media publicize public opinion, making evident which opinions predominate. Individuals express their opinions or not, depending on the predominant points of view; the media, in turn, attend to the expressed opinion, and the spiral continues.

Cultivation Analysis

Another theoretical program dealing with the sociocultural outcomes of mass communication is that of George Gerbner and his colleagues.[49] These researchers believe that because television is the great common experience of almost everyone, it has the effect of providing a shared way of viewing the world:

> Television is a centralized system of storytelling. It is part and parcel of our daily lives. Its drama, commercials, news, and other programs bring a relatively coherent world of common images and messages into every home. Television cultivates from infancy the very predispositions and preferences that used to be acquired from other

primary sources. Transcending historic barriers of literacy and mobility, television has become the primary common source of socialization and everyday information (mostly in the form of entertainment) of an otherwise heterogeneous population. The repetitive pattern of television's mass-produced messages and images forms the mainstream of a common symbolic environment.[50]

Gerbner calls this effect *cultivation,* since television is believed to be a homogenizing agent in culture. Cultivation analysis is concerned with the totality of the pattern communicated cumulatively by television over a long period of exposure rather than by any particular content or specific effect. In other words, this is not a theory of individual media "effects" but instead makes a statement about the culture as a whole. It is not concerned with what any strategy or campaign can do but with the total impact of numerous strategies and campaigns over time. Total immersion in television, not selective viewing, is important in cultivation of ways of knowing and images of reality. Indeed, subcultures may retain their separate values, but general overriding images depicted on television will cut across individual social groups and subcultures, affecting them all.

As you might imagine, the theory predicts a difference in the social reality of heavy television viewers as opposed to light viewers. Heavy viewers will believe in a reality that is consistent with that shown on television, even though television does not necessarily reflect the actual world. Gerbner's research on prime-time television, for example, has shown that there are three men to every woman on television, there are few Hispanics and those shown are typically minor characters, there are almost entirely middle-class characters, and there are three times as many law enforcement officers as blue-collar workers.

One of the most interesting aspects of cultivation is the "mean-world syndrome." Although less than 1 percent of the population are victims of violent crimes in any one-year period, heavy exposure can lead you to believe that no one can be trusted in what appears to be a violent world.

Nancy Signorielli reports a study of the mean-world syndrome, in which violent acts in children's television programming were analyzed.[51] Over 2,000 programs, including 6,000 main characters, during prime time and weekends from 1967 to 1985 were analyzed with interesting results. About 71 percent of prime-time and 94 percent of weekend programs included acts of violence. Prime-time programs averaged almost five acts of violence each, and weekend programs averaged six. That amounts to over five acts per hour during prime time and about twenty per hour on weekends.

As part of this study, people were surveyed on five occasions between 1980 and 1986 regarding their views of the state of the world. To measure feelings of alienation and gloom, they were asked whether they agreed with three statements: (1) "Despite what some people say, the lot of the average man is getting worse, not better." (2) "It's hardly fair to bring a child into the world with the way things look for the future." (3) "Most public officials are not interested in the problems of the average man."

In addition, they were asked three questions to measure feelings about a mean world: (1) "Would you say that most of the time people try to be helpful, or are they mostly just looking out for themselves?" (2) "Do you think that most people would try to take advantage of you if they got a chance, or would they try to be fair?" (3) "Generally speaking, would you say that most people can be trusted, or you can't be too careful in dealing with people?" The findings indicate that heavy viewers tend to see the world as gloomier and meaner than do light viewers, and heavy viewers tend to mistrust people more than light viewers do.

Cultivation analysis has also found that there is a general fallout effect from television to the entire culture so that culture becomes homogenized, or *mainstreamed,* through TV. Television is not a force for change as much as it is a force for stability.

Mainstreaming can be seen in the mean-world data reviewed above. Even though heavy viewers scored higher on the mean-world index than did light viewers, a substantial number of light viewers also scored high. In fact, if you remove people with a college education from the sample, heavy and light viewers scored about the same.

Although cultivation is a general outcome of television viewing, it is not a universal phenomenon, despite the mainstreaming effect. In fact, different groups are affected differently by cultivation. Your interaction with others affects your tendency to accept TV reality. For example, adolescents who interact with their parents about television viewing are less likely to be affected by television images than are adolescents who do not talk with their parents about television. Interestingly, people who watch more cable television tend to manifest more mainstreaming than do people who watch less.

The Agenda-Setting Function

Scholars have long known that media have the potential for structuring issues for the public.[52] One of the first writers to formalize this idea was Walter Lippmann, a prominent American journalist. Lippmann is known for his journalistic writing, speeches, and social commentary.[53] Lippman took the view that the public responds not to actual events in the environment but to "the pictures in our heads," which he calls the *pseudoenvironment:*

> For the real environment is altogether too big, too complex, and too fleeting for direct acquaintance. We are not equipped to deal with so much subtlety, so much variety, so many permutations and combinations. And altogether we have to act in that environment, we have to reconstruct it on a simpler model before we can manage with it.[54]

The agenda-setting function has been described best by Donald Shaw, Maxwell McCombs, and their colleagues.[55] These authors write:

> Considerable evidence has accumulated that editors and broadcasters play an important part in shaping our social reality as they go about their day-to-day task of choosing and displaying news. . . . This impact of the mass media—the ability

to effect cognitive change among individuals, to structure their thinking—has been labeled the agenda-setting function of mass communication. Here may lie the most important effect of mass communication, its ability to mentally order and organize our world for us. In short, the mass media may not be successful in telling us what to think, but they are stunningly successful in telling us what to think about.[56]

In other words, agenda setting establishes the salient issues or images in the minds of the public.

Agenda setting occurs because the press must be selective in reporting the news. The news outlets, as gatekeepers of information, make choices about what to report and how to report it. What the public knows about the state of affairs at any given time is largely a product of media gatekeeping.[57] Further, we know that how a person votes is determined mainly by what issues the individual believes to be important. For this reason some researchers have come to believe that the issues reported during a candidate's term in office may have more effect on the election than the campaign itself.

There are two levels of agenda setting. The first establishes the general issues that are important, and the second determines the parts or aspects of those issues that are important. In many ways the second level is as important as the first, because it gives us a way to frame the issues that constitute the public and media agendas. For example, the media may tell us that deregulation of the electric industry is an important issue (first level), but they may also focus on differences between the states, framing this issue as a question of *how* deregulation is accomplished (second level).[58]

The agenda-setting function is a three-part linear process.[59] First, the priority of issues to be discussed in the media, *or media agenda,* must be set. Second, the media agenda in some way affects or interacts with what the public thinks, or the *public agenda.* Finally, the public agenda affects or interacts in some way with what policymakers consider important, or the *policy agenda.* In the theory's simplest and most direct version, then, the media agenda affects the public agenda, and the public agenda affects the policy agenda.

Although a number of studies show that the media can be powerful in affecting the public agenda, it is still not clear whether the public agenda does not itself affect the media agenda. The relationship may be one of mutual causation rather than linear causation. Further, it appears that actual events have some impact on both the media agenda and the public agenda.

The prevailing opinion among media researchers seems to be that the media can have a powerful effect on the public agenda, but not always. The power of media depends on such factors as media credibility on particular issues at particular times, the extent of conflicting evidence as perceived by individual members of the public, the extent to which individuals share media values at certain times, and the public's need for guidance. Media most often will be powerful when media credibility is high, conflicting evidence is low, individuals share media values, and the audience has a high need for guidance.

Karen Siune and Ole Borre studied some of the complexities of agenda setting in a Danish election.[60] Because in Denmark the election campaigns last only three weeks and the number of political broadcasts are more limited than in the United States, the researchers had an excellent opportunity to study the agenda-setting process.

Three kinds of political broadcasts on radio and television were aired in this election. These included programs made by the political parties, programs in which the candidates were asked questions by a panel of journalists and citizens, and debates. All these programs were recorded and analyzed by counting the number of statements made about each issue in the campaign. In addition, about 1,300 voters were interviewed at various points in the campaign to establish the public agenda. From this data the researchers could determine the media agendas of the politicians, the press, and voters.

This study suggests three kinds of agenda-setting effects. The first is the degree to which the media reflect the public agenda, called *representation*. In a representational agenda, the public influences the media. The second is the maintenance of the same agenda by the public the entire time, which is called *persistence*. In a persistent public agenda, the media may have little effect. The third occurs when the media agenda influences the public agenda, referred to as *persuasion*. This third kind of effect—media influencing the public—is exactly what classic agenda-setting theory predicts.

If you determine agendas at three points in a campaign—at the beginning (time 1), at the middle (time 2), and at the end (time 3)—you can get a sense of these three effects. A correlation between the public agenda at time 1 and the media agenda at time 2 suggests representation, or audience influencing media. A correlation between the public agenda at time 1 and at time 3 suggests persistence, or stability of the public agenda. Finally, a correlation between the media agenda at time 2 and the public agenda at time 3 suggests persuasion, or media influencing the public agenda. It is possible for any combination of these three to occur at the same time.

In their Danish study, Siune and Borre found much persistence in the public agenda, but there was also some persuasion in the sense that the broadcasts seemed to affect the public agenda somewhat. The most persuasive effects seemed to come from programs in which citizens set the media agenda. There was also a fair agenda-setting effect from the reporters and from the politicians themselves. The researchers did not find a representation effect in which the public affected the media.

A natural question is, Who affects the media agenda in the first place? This is a complex and difficult question. It appears that media agendas result from pressures both within media organizations and from outside sources.[61] In other words, the media agenda is established by some combination of internal programming, editorial and managerial decisions, and external influences from nonmedia sources such as socially influential individuals, government officials, commercial sponsors, and the like.

The power of media in establishing a public agenda depends in part on their relations with power centers. If the media have close relationships with the elite class in society, that class will probably affect the media agenda and the public agenda in turn. Many critical theorists believe that media can be an instrument of the dominant ideology in society, and when this happens, that dominant ideology will permeate the public agenda.

Four types of power relations between the media and outside sources can be found. The first is a high-power source and high-power media. In this kind of arrangement, if the two see eye to eye, a positive symbiotic relationship will exert great power over the public agenda. This would be the case, for example, with a powerful public official who has especially good relations with the press. On the other hand, if the powerful media and the powerful sources do not agree, a struggle may take place between them.

The second kind of arrangement is a high-power source and low-power media. Here, the external source will probably co-opt the media and use them to accomplish its own ends. This is what happens, for example, when politicians buy airtime or when a popular president such as Ronald Reagan gives the press the "privilege" of interviewing him.

In the third type of relation, a lower-power source and high-power media, the media organizations themselves will be largely responsible for their own agenda. This happens when the media marginalize certain news sources such as the student radicals in the 1960s.

The fourth type of relation is where both media and external sources are low in power, and the public agenda will probably be established by the events themselves rather than the media or the leaders.

As you can see, agenda setting is no simple matter, and our understanding of its complexity has come a long way since the early days of simplistic agenda-setting theory.

Theories of Individual Outcomes

The theories summarized in the previous section emphasize societal and cultural outcomes of mass communication. Other research has dealt with the *individual effects* of mass communication. In this section we discuss several of the theories of this individual-effects tradition.

The Effects Tradition

The theory of mass communication effects has undergone a curious evolution in this century.[62] Early on, researchers believed in the "magic bullet" theory of communication effects. Individuals were believed to be directly and heavily influenced by media messages, since media were considered to be extremely powerful in shaping public opinion.[63] According to this model, if you heard on the radio that you should try Pepsodent, you would.

Then, during the 1950s when the two-step flow hypothesis was becoming popular, media effects were considered to be minimal. It was believed that a commercial for Pepsodent would not directly influence very many people to try it. Later, in the 1960s, we came to think that the media effects were mediated by other variables and were therefore only moderate in strength. A Pepsodent commercial might or might not influence you, depending on other variables.

Now, after research in the 1970s and the 1980s, many scholars have returned to the powerful-effects model, in which the public is considered to be heavily influenced by media. This later research centers on television as the powerful medium.

Limited or Powerful Effects?

Perhaps the best-known early work on limited effects was the reinforcement approach most notably articulated by Joseph Klapper.[64] Klapper, in surveying the literature on mass communication effects, developed the thesis that mass communication is not a necessary and sufficient cause of audience effects but that it is mediated by other variables. Thus, media are only a contributing cause.

Raymond Bauer observes that audiences are difficult to persuade, and he calls them *obstinate*.[65] Bauer denies the idea that a direct hypodermic-needle effect operates between communicator and audience. Instead, many variables involved in the audience interact to shape effects in various ways.[66] Audience effects are mediated by group and interpersonal factors and by selectivity, among others. Studies have shown that audience members are selective in their exposure to information.[67] In its simplest form, the hypothesis of selective exposure predicts that people in most circumstances will select information consistent with their attitudes.

The reinforcement approach was a definite step in the right direction at the time it was in vogue. Compared with the bullet theory, the reinforcement approach viewed mass communication as more complicated than had previously been imagined. It envisioned situations ripe with mediating variables that would inhibit media effects. The research in this tradition did identify some important mediating variables, completing a more elaborate puzzle than had previously been constructed.

The problem of the limited-effects model is that it maintained a linear, cause-to-effect pattern.[68] It failed to take into account the social forces on the media or the ways that individuals might affect the media. In addition, the limited-effects model concentrated almost exclusively on attitude and opinion effects, ignoring other kinds of effects and functions such as cultivation or diffusion. Finally, true to tradition, such research focused on short-term effects of mass communication without questioning whether repeated exposure or time might affect the audience.

The work of Klapper and others on limited effects resulted in two general types of response. The first was a rejection of limited effects in favor of powerful effects, and the second was an attempt to explain limited effects in terms of the powers of audience members rather than media.

Perhaps the most vocal contemporary spokesperson in favor of powerful effects is Noelle-Neumann.[69] She believes that limited-effects theory has "distorted the interpretation of research findings over the years," and "that the 'dogma of media powerlessness' is no longer tenable."[70] Noelle-Neumann claims that the pendulum, which began swinging in the other direction after Klapper's famous work, has now reached its full extension and that most researchers believe that the media indeed have powerful effects.

Noelle-Neumann says that most limited-effects researchers were either academic journalists or people who held the media in a free society in high regard. They were interested in painting a picture of the media as disseminators of information, but not of influence. If viewed as important but not controlling, the media would continue to have the freedom to investigate and report whatever they felt to be important at a particular time, and journalists liked that. This interest led to the tendency to "see" limited rather than powerful effects in media-research results, which Noelle-Neumann calls "the media's effect on media research."

In summarizing the research literature on the effects of media violence, James Potter reports several clear effects.[71] For example, viewing violent portrayals can lead to increased aggressiveness, fear, and desensitization in the short term. Long-term exposure to violence can create increased aggression, which in turn can lead to more viewing of violence. It can also lead to an increased feeling of being potentially victimized and to the greater acceptance of violence. Potter is careful to point out, however, that these results do not necessarily support a powerful-effects model because effects are mediated by individual, situational, institutional, and message variables, all of which complicate the effects picture. Indeed, Potter himself says that the powerful-effects model has been discredited for fifty years![72] He calls for a systemic approach that looks at a host of factors along with methods that admit to more complete definitions of violence and effects.

It is clear, then, that neither the limited-effects nor powerful-effects models have a great deal of credibility at this time. In the following sections, we review theories that paint a more moderate and complex picture than either the limited- or powerful-effects models portray.

Uses, Gratifications, and Dependency

One of the most popular theories of mass communication is the uses-and-gratifications approach.[73] Here, we examine the original idea of uses and gratifications and then look at some interesting extensions.

The Original Idea

The uses-and-gratifications approach focuses on the consumer—the audience member—rather than the message.[74] Unlike the powerful-effects tradition, this approach imagines the audience member to be a discriminating user of media. The basic stance is summarized as follows:

> Compared with classical effects studies, the uses and gratifications approach takes the media consumer rather than the media message as its starting point, and explores

his communication behavior in terms of his direct experience with the media. It views the members of the audience as actively utilizing media contents, rather than being passively acted upon by the media. Thus, it does not assume a direct relationship between messages and effects, but postulates instead that members of the audience put messages to use, and that such usages act as intervening variables in the process of effect.[75]

Here the audience is assumed to be active and goal-directed. The audience member is largely responsible for choosing media to meet needs and knows his or her own needs and how to meet them. Media are considered to be only one way of meeting personal needs, and individuals may meet their needs through the media or in some other way. In other words, out of the options that media present, the individual chooses ways to gratify needs.

As you can see, this is an interesting idea, but it really does not tell us very much. Let's look now at some extensions that add detail.

Expectancy-Value Theory

Acknowledging the lack of theoretical coherence in early uses-and-gratifications work, Philip Palmgreen created a theory based on his own work, that of Karl Rosengren, and others.[76] The theory is based on expectancy-value theory, which you read about in Chapter 7.

According to this theory, you orient yourself by your own attitudes. In Chapter 7 you learned that an attitude consists of a cluster of beliefs and evaluations, and this theory of media uses and gratifications is just an extension of this basic idea. Here your attitude toward some segment of the media is determined by your beliefs about and evaluations of it.

The gratifications you seek from media are determined by your attitudes toward the media—your beliefs about what a medium can give you and your evaluations of this material. For example, if you believe that sitcoms provide entertainment and you like to be entertained, you will seek gratification of your entertainment needs by watching sitcoms. If, on the other hand, you believe that sitcoms provide an unrealistic view of life and you don't like this kind of thing, you will avoid viewing them.

Of course, your opinion of sitcoms consists of several beliefs and evaluations, and whether you actually watch them will be determined by several things. Your orientation to any type of program will be determined by your entire cluster of beliefs and evaluations. Palmgreen's formula for this, which mirrors the general expectancy-value formula presented in Chapter 7, is as follows:

$$GS_i = \sum_i^n b_i e_i$$

where

GS = gratification sought
b_i = belief
e_i = evaluation

The extent to which you seek gratifications in any segment of the media (a program, a program type, a particular kind of content, or an entire medium) would be determined by the same formula. As you gain experience with a part of the media, the gratifications you obtain will in turn affect your beliefs, reinforcing the viewing pattern.

To test the connection between expectancy values and media gratifications, David Swanson and Austin Babrow conducted a study of the television news-viewing habits of students.[77] About three hundred students at the University of Illinois were asked to fill out a questionnaire on their news viewing. To find out whether they watched the news and how they felt about it, the students were asked how many times a week they viewed network and local news, how likely they were to view news in an average week, and whether other people thought they should watch the news. The questionnaire also tested the students' attitudes toward the news.

To find out the extent to which the news gratified various media needs, the questionnaire asked whether each of a number of gratifications were met by watching the news. These included such items as keeping up on current events, getting entertained, and giving them things to talk about. In all, fourteen possible gratifications were included. The researchers found that the students' expectancy values (their attitudes) toward the news did relate to how much they used the news to gratify certain media needs.

Dependency Theory

The uses-and-gratifications approach is a limited-effects theory. In other words, it grants individuals much control over how they employ media in their lives. Although media scholars are divided on just how powerful the media are, some scholars have argued that the limited-effects and powerful-effects models are not necessarily incompatible. Dependency theory takes a step toward showing how both may explain media effects.

Dependency theory was originally proposed by Sandra Ball-Rokeach and Melvin DeFleur.[78] Like uses-and-gratifications theory, this approach also rejects the causal assumptions of the early reinforcement hypothesis. To overcome this weakness, these authors take a broad system approach. In their model they propose an integral relationship among audiences, media, and the larger social system.

Consistent with uses-and-gratifications theory, this theory predicts that you depend on media information to meet certain needs and achieve certain goals. But you do not depend on all media equally. What determines how dependent you will become? There seem to be two factors.

First, you will become more dependent on media that meet a number of your needs than on media that provide just a few. Media can serve a number of functions such as monitoring government activities and providing entertainment. For any given group of people, some of these functions are more important than others, and your dependence on information from a medium increases when it supplies information that is more central to you. If you follow sports carefully, you will probably become dependent on ESPN or *Sports Illustrated. A* person who is not interested in sports will probably not even know where ESPN is on the dial, may never have looked at *Sports Illustrated,* and typically skips the entire sports section of the newspaper.

The second source of dependency is social stability. When social change and conflict are high, established institutions, beliefs, and practices are challenged, forcing you to reevaluate and make new choices. At such times your reliance on the media for information will increase. At other, more stable times your dependency on media may go way down. During times of war, for example, people become incredibly dependent on news programming.

This model shows that social institutions and media systems interact with audiences so as to create needs, interests, and motives. These in turn influence the audience to select various media and nonmedia sources that can subsequently lead to various dependencies. Individuals who grow dependent on a particular segment of the media will be affected cognitively, affectively, and behaviorally by that segment. Consequently, people are affected in different ways and to different degrees by the media.

Of course, one's needs are not always strictly personal but may be shaped by the culture or by various social conditions. In other words, individuals' needs, motives, and uses of media are contingent on outside factors that may not be in the individuals' control. These outside factors act as constraints on what and how media can be used and on the availability of other nonmedia alternatives.

For example, an elderly person who does not drive and has few friends may come to depend on television in a way that other individuals, whose life situations are different, will not. A commuter may come to rely on radio for information and news. A teenager may become dependent on music videos because of certain norms in the social group. In general, "the more readily available, the greater the perceived instrumentality, and the more socially and culturally acceptable the use of a medium is, the more probable that media use will be regarded as the most appropriate functional alternative."[79]

Furthermore, the more alternatives an individual has for gratifying needs, the less dependent he or she will become on any single medium. The number of functional alternatives, however, is not just a matter of individual choice or even of psychological traits but is limited also by factors such as availability of certain media.

Commentary and Critique

Mass communication involves the dissemination of information and influence in society through media and interpersonal channels. It is an integral part of culture and is inseparable from other large-scale social institutions. Media forms like television, film, and print—as well as media content—affect our ways of thinking and seeing the world. Indeed, media participate in the very creation of culture itself, and many believe that media are instrumental in the dissemination of power and domination in society and are thereby instruments of ideology and hegemony.

Early mass communication theories concentrated on the structure and function of media. For example, Harold Lasswell's models outlined such functions as information, entertainment, and interpretation. Other functionalist theories presented additional ones such as shaping public opinion, diffusing innovations, cultivating common values, perpetuating majority views, and setting the public agenda. By the 1980s at least, this functionalist tradition was challenged vigorously by other perspectives.[80]

The extent and power of media influence is a matter of dispute. Mass communication is believed by some to reinforce attitudes and opinions, but evidence suggests that sometimes media effects are more profound than simple reinforcement. At the same time, however, people make active use of media to gratify their own needs. In fact, as people become dependent on certain types of media and content, the impact of those outlets may increase.[81]

The controversies about media functions reflect a persistent conflict in the study of mass communication. How powerful are media in the control of culture? Some, like McLuhan, Meyrowitz, and Gerbner, argue that media are powerful forces in determining the character of culture and individual life. Other theorists claim that individuals have much control over the outcomes of media transactions in their lives. Yet a third group believes that mass media are important but that they are only part of a complex of factors involved in social domination and that individuals are influenced by the entire system of dominating forces.

The outcome of the media-influence process is complex. In the final analysis, the outcome of mass communication may be a product of the interaction among various societal structures and individual needs, desires, and dependencies, and it seems unlikely that this system will ever be reduced to an identifiable calculus. The theories in this chapter emphasize different aspects of this complex relationship.

McLuhan's theory is not much in favor anymore, but few would deny that his basic idea—that media forms in and of themselves do have an impact on culture—has had a major effect on our thinking about media. Media scholars today are just less glib about what those specific effects are than was McLuhan.

McLuhan's ideas are useful for stimulating a fresh look at the subject matter,/but they provide little guidance on how to understand the process of mass communication. They are valuable in that they point to the importance of media forms in society, but they do not give a realistic picture of the variables involved in the effects of media forms. In sum, Kenneth Boulding points out, "It is perhaps typical of very creative minds that they hit very large nails not quite on the head."[82]

More popular today is semiotics. This field has had a major impact throughout communication studies, and it has been especially popular in media scholarship. The reasons are obvious. Semiotics provides a clear idea of what to look at when analyzing the meaning of media messages. In semiotics you look at visual, auditory, and verbal signs. Semiotics has also been useful to help explain why the media have differential effects. It is valuable, too, because it enables the observer to analyze the structure of media messages without ignoring the interpretive processes of the audience.

One of the most important lines of research on the cultural impact of media is critical theory, which maintains that media are powerful forces for dominant interests in society. The so-called media hegemony thesis maintains that media are instruments of the dominant ideology and by representing the interests of those already in power subvert the interests of marginalized groups. This thesis is hotly debated, as Kevin Carragee points out in a review.[83] Scholars opposing media hegemony claim that the media actually represent a diversity of values and often speak out in opposition to the ideology of the powerful in society.

One of the obvious issues in media studies is the role of groups and interpersonal communication in the mass communication process. A whole line of research on diffusion of ideas and innovation supports the idea that interpersonal communication is a powerful part of this process. Beginning with the work of Paul Lazarsfeld, the research and theory of diffusion has been immensely successful. Dennis Davis and Stanley Baran remark of Lazarsfeld: "If one person deserves the title of founder of the field of mass communication research, that person is Paul Lazarsfeld. No one has done more to determine the way in which theory and research methods would be developed to aid our understanding of mass communication."[84]

The parsimony of diffusion theories has enabled observers to deal with a huge and complex phenomenon with relative ease. Additionally, these theories have been highly heuristic and have produced a large body of research. For many years the idea of the two-step flow (and later multiple-step flow) in the diffusion of information and innovation has been a mainstay of mass communication theory.

Traditional diffusion theory uses a linear pattern in which messages flow from person to person along a network. Some contemporary diffusion theorists now believe that this logic does not explain enough. Research has not consistently supported this notion of how diffusion occurs. At times the media appear to inform the public directly, with little interpersonal involvement; at other times different forms of diffusion are revealed. Further, the strict dichotomy between opinion leaders and followers is overly simple. In the give-and-take of everyday conversation, people exchange information, question it, argue about it, and come to a shared understanding.

Another problem with the linear model of diffusion is that it downplays context; the actual circumstances under which diffusion occurs may have a great deal to do with the pattern of dissemination used by individuals in sharing information and innovations. Dissemination is more a matter of convergence or the achievement of shared meaning than of strict linear influence.

One of the problems of diffusion theory is to explain why information sometimes does not flow in the network. An interesting explanation is the spiral of silence. The spiral of silence exemplifies careful theory development through research. Beginning with a simple hypothesis in the early 1970s, Noelle-Neumann undertook numerous studies designed to test the basic hypothesis, its assumptions, and ramifications.

At the same time, however, the spiral of silence does not seem to apply in all societies. Hernando González, for example, in a study of public opinion in the Philippine revolution, says that the Philippine experience is not consistent with the spiral of silence. Indeed, alternative media were heard, and no spiral of silence appeared to be in favor of a dominant opinion in this society.[85]

From another corner, cultural scholars and Marxists would point to this line of research as an example of the kind of work they most distrust. First, they believe that it is false to assume that one can find an underlying structure to public opinion through surveys. Social science methods cannot be trusted to reveal any kind of reality beyond the meanings assigned by observers. Second, the failure to acknowledge the ideological nature of the public opinion is a major oversight. Third, critical scholars would point out that the spiral of silence is one possible factor in a general hegemony, in which the interests of dominant groups in society are perpetuated. Fourth, these critics would object to the suggestion that the spiral of silence is a universal phenomenon. All social life must be viewed in the context of history, and the spiral of silence, like most traditional social science findings, abstracts beyond the material world. Finally, this kind of research is truly "administrative" in the sense that it becomes a tool in which the dominant ideology can be managed or promulgated.

Another theory of cultural media outcomes is cultivation analysis. Cultivation analysis, which is bolstered by two decades of research on cultural indicators, calls our attention to the power of television; however, the cultivation hypothesis has not been without critique.[86] In fact, television researcher Paul Hirsch has spoken out harshly against the cultivation effect. He reanalyzed Gerbner's data and failed to find evidence for cultivation. Hirsch concluded that "acceptance of the cultivation hypothesis as anything more than an interesting but unsupported speculation is premature and unwarranted at this time."[87] Gerbner and his colleagues have responded to this critique by reaffirming the validity of their findings and concluding that "Hirsch's analysis is flawed, incomplete, and tendentious."[88]

The more common tendency is to look on the cultivation effect as a possible and significant finding but to be suspicious of the authors' precise explanation.[89] Cultivation theory is based on a simple premise: Television viewing causes individuals to accept the TV view of reality, and the more one watches television, the greater that acceptance. Critics question several things about this prediction. First, the effect may not be constant over all groups and all levels of viewing. Second, the causation may not be in the direction predicted; people may use TV to reinforce previously held beliefs. Third, there is some question about the strength or power of the cultivation effect among all of the other factors, such as education, that may affect our cultural beliefs. There is probably a grain of truth in cultivation theory, perhaps a very large grain, but some observers suspect that it does not tell the whole story.

Another important cultural outcome of media communication is agenda setting. Agenda-setting theory is appealing for two reasons. It returns a degree of power to the media after an era in which media effects were thought to be minimal, and its focus on cognitive effects rather than attitude and opinion change adds a badly needed dimension to effects research. The idea of issue salience as a media effect is intriguing and important.

The basic problem with this line of work is that although the theory is clear in positing a causal link between media and issue salience, the research evidence on this point is not convincing.[90] Research has uncovered a strong correlation between audience and media views on the importance of issues, but it does not always demonstrate that media choices cause audience salience. In fact, as we saw previously, some theorists argue that the emphasis given to issues in the media can be a reflection, not a cause, of audience agendas. This is a chicken-egg issue. Sometimes there may be an interaction between media and public in terms of the issue agenda, and situational factors probably always enter into how powerful the media are at any time in establishing the public agenda.

That certain studies do not support a direct causal link between media activity and audience attention does not mean that a relationship is not there. It may simply be a more complicated one. For example, there may be intervening variables or a nonlinear relationship. For example, W. R. Neuman explores the possibility that public response to an issue is aroused rather quickly at first and then levels off as a saturation point is reached.[91]

The uses-and-gratifications approach was like a breath of fresh air in media research. For the first time scholars in this tradition focused on receivers as active participants in the communication process, rather than the traditional viewpoint of the passive, unthinking audience. This approach is certainly one of the most popular frameworks for the study of mass communication, but a good deal of criticism has been leveled against it.[92]

The criticism of the uses-and-gratifications approach can be divided into three major strands.[93] The first set of objections deals with the lack of coherence and theory in the tradition. Although this objection had merit until recently, we have seen that more unified versions in the form of value-expectancy and value-dependency theories are emerging.

The second line of criticism focuses on social and political objections, which come primarily from critical theory. The problem is that uses and gratifications is so functional in orientation that it ignores the dysfunctions of media in society and culture. It is conservative at heart and sees media primarily as positive ways in which individuals meet their needs, without any attention to the overall negative cultural effects of media in society.

Finally, some critics have objected to the instrumental philosophy of uses and gratifications. Uses and gratifications makes media consumption extremely rational, behavioristic, and individualistic. Individuals are believed to control their media-consuming behavior according to conscious goals. No attention is paid to the ways media may be consumed mindlessly or ritualistically. The theory does not study the ways media content forms and reflects cultural values or patterns of action. In other words, much of our consumption of mass media may not be easily traced to individual needs but rather to habits of the culture. Also, individuals may not be aware of many of the factors that enter into their consumption choices. Attribution theory, which was covered in greater detail in Chapter 7, suggests that people often misjudge the causes of their own behavior; some research indicates that this principle holds true for media consumption as well.[94]

McQuail, a noted researcher of uses and gratifications, takes this third point seriously and proposes that the traditional gratifications model is only part of what happens in media use.[95] He suggests that although individuals do use media for guidance, surveillance, and information, they also have a generalized arousal need that comes from and is informed by the culture.

Dependency theory makes an attempt to reconcile some of the problems of uses and gratifications with other powerful-effects models. This theory accounts for both individual differences in responses to media and general media effects. As a system theory, it shows the complexity of the interactions among the various aspects of the media transaction. The fusion of uses-and-gratifications and dependency theories provides an even more complete integration.

Like most of the theories in this chapter, however, both dependency theory and uses-and-gratifications theory clash with the critical theory school. This clash points out a number of stasis points in media theory: Are media powerful in influencing culture, or are effects and cultural realities the accomplishments of individuals and interpretive communities? Do individuals make real choices, and how extensive are the cultural limits on individual media choice? To what extent should theory describe and explain, and to what extent should it reform? There will always be answers to these questions, but consensus will probably never be achieved.

Notes

1. George Gerbner, "Mass Media and Human Communication Theory," in *Human Communication Theory,* ed. F. E. X. Dance (New York: Holt, Rinehart & Winston, 1967), p. 45.

2. For recent overviews and histories of mass communication theory, see Bradley S. Greenberg and Michael B. Salwen, "Mass Communication Theory and Research: Concepts and Models," in *An Integrated Approach to Communication Theory and Research,* eds. Michael B. Salwen and Don W. Stacks (Mahwah, NJ: Erlbaum, 1996), pp. 63–78; and Robert S. Fortner, "Mediated Communication Theory," in *Building Communication Theories: A Socio/Cultural Approach,* ed. Fred L. Casmir (Hillsdale, NJ: Erlbaum, 1994), pp. 209–240. Definitions of *mass communication* are discussed in Sandra J. Ball-Rokeach and Muriel G. Cantor, eds., *Media, Audience, and Social Structure* (Beverly Hills, CA: Sage, 1986), pp. 10–11; and Denis McQuail, *Mass Communication Theory: An Introduction* (London: Sage, 1987), pp. 29–47.

3. McQuail, *Mass Communication,* pp. 52–53.

4. Joshua Meyrowitz, "Images of Media: Hidden Ferment—and Harmony—in the Field," *Journal of Communication* 43 (1993): 55–67.

5. For an excellent exploration of the links between the media and larger sociocultural structures and smaller personal and individual effects, see Karl Erik Rosengren,

"Culture, Media, and Society: Agency and Structure, Continuity and Change," in *Media Effects and Beyond: Culture, Socializations, and Lifestyles,* ed. Karl Erik Rosengren (London: Routledge, 1994), pp. 3–28. See also Veikko Pietilä, "Perspectives on Our Past: Charting the Histories of Mass Communication Studies," *Critical Studies in Mass Communication* 11 (1994): 346–361.

6. This conceptualization is adapted from a discussion of mass communication theory by McQuail, *Mass Communication,* pp. 53–57.

7. An excellent summary of the vast amount of work in this area is provided by David Barker and Bernard M. Timberg, "Encounters with the Television Image: Thirty Years of Encoding Research," in *Communication Yearbook 15,* ed. Stanley Deetz (Newbury Park, CA: Sage, 1992), pp. 209–238.

8. McLuhan's best-known works are *The Gutenberg Galaxy: The Making of Typographic Man* (Toronto: University of Toronto Press, 1962); *The Mechanical Bride* (New York: Vanguard, 1951); *Understanding Media* (New York: McGraw-Hill, 1964); Marshall McLuhan and Quentin Fiore, *The Medium Is the Massage* (New York: Bantam, 1967). I have relied on the synthesis of Bruce Gronbeck, "McLuhan as Rhetorical Theorist," *Journal of Communication* 31 (1981): 117–128.

9. J. W. Carey, "Harold Adams Innis and Marshall McLuhan," *Antioch Review* 27 (1967): 5–39. Innis' works include *The Bias of Communication* (Toronto: University of Toronto Press, 1951); and *Empire and Communications,* 2nd ed. (Toronto: University of Toronto Press, 1972).

10. Good brief summaries of McLuhan's theory can be found in the following: Kenneth Boulding, "The Medium Is the Massage," in *McLuhan: Hot and Cool,* ed. G. E. Stearn (New York: Dial, 1967), pp. 56–64; Tom Wolfe, "The New Life Out There," in *McLuhan: Hot and Cool,* ed. G. E. Stearn (New York: Dial, 1967), pp. 34–56; Carey, "Innis and McLuhan."

11. McLuhan and Fiore, *Massage.*

12. McLuhan and Fiore, *Massage.*

13. McLuhan, *Understanding Media,* p. 7.

14. Wolfe, "New Life," p. 19.

15. Donald G. Ellis, *Crafting Society: Ethnicity, Class, and Communication Theory* (Mahwah, NJ: Erlbaum, 1999).

16. See, for example, Wendy Leeds-Hurwitz, *Semiotics and Communication: Signs, Codes, Cultures* (Hillsdale, NJ: Erlbaum, 1993).

17. Especially good summaries of this field are provided by Donald L. Fry and Virginia H. Fry, "A Semiotic Model for the Study of Mass Communication," in *Communication Yearbook 9,* ed. M. L. McLaughlin (Beverly Hills, CA: Sage, 1986), pp. 443–462; and Klaus Bruhn Jensen, "When Is Meaning? Communication Theory, Pragmatism, and Mass Media Reception," in *Communication Yearbook 14,* ed. James A. Anderson (Newbury Park, CA: Sage, 1991), pp. 3–32.

18. Among Baudrillard's many works are *Simulations,* trans. Paul Foss, Paul Patton, and Philip Beitchman (New York: Semiotext(e), 1983); *The Illusion of the End,* trans. Chris Turner (Cambridge: Polity, 1994); *Symbolic Exchange and Death,* trans. Iain Hamilton Grant (Thousand Oaks, CA: Sage, 1993). For a good summary of his work, see Sonja K. Foss, Karen A. Foss, and Robert Trapp, *Contemporary Perspectives on Rhetoric,* 3rd ed. (Prospect Heights, IL: Waveland), in press.

19. See the Chapter 11 section of the Selected Bibliography for readings in this area. McQuail's *Mass Communication* (1987) discusses marxist theories of media in some detail. See also Lawrence Grossberg, "Strategies of Marxist Cultural Interpretation," *Critical Studies in Mass Communication* 1 (1984): 392–421.

20. McQuail, *Mass Communication,* pp. 63–68.

21. Dennis K. Davis and Thomas F. N. Puckett, "Mass Entertainment and Community: Toward a Culture-Centered Paradigm for Mass Communication Research," in *Communication Yearbook 15,* ed. Stanley Deetz (Newbury Park, CA: Sage, 1992), pp. 3–34.

22   Robert Huesca and Brenda Dervin, "Theory and Practice in Latin American Alternative Communication Research," *journal of Communication* 44 (1994): 53–73.

23   The most prominent critics of mass society are Ortega y Gasset, Karl Mannheim, Karl Jaspers, Paul Tillich, Gabriel Marcel, and Emil Lederer. Syntheses can be found in a variety of sources. See, for example, Patrick Brantlinger, *Bread and Circuses: Theories of Mass Culture as Social Decay* (Ithaca, NY: Cornell University Press, 1983).

24   See, for example, E. D. Hirsch, *Cultural Literacy: What Every American Needs to Know* (Boston: Houghton Mifflin, 1987); Allan Bloom, *The Closing of the American Mind* (New York: Simon & Schuster, 1987).

25   See, for example, Kenneth J. Gergen, *The Saturated Self: Dilemmas of Identity in Contemporary Life* (New York: HarperCollins, 1991).

26   Paul Lazarsfeld and Robert K. Merton, "Mass Communication, Popular Taste, and Organized Social Action," in *The Process and Effects of Mass Communication*, eds. W. Schramm and D. Roberts (Urbana: University of Illinois Press, 1971), p. 557.

27   Joshua Meyrowitz, *No Sense of Place: The Impact of Electronic Media on Social Behavior* (New York: Oxford University Press, 1985).

28   For an excellent statement of this position, see Thomas R. Lindlof, "Media Audiences as Interpretive Communities," in *Communication Yearbook 11*, ed. J. A. Anderson (Newbury Park, CA: Sage, 1988), pp. 81–107. Supportive of this position, too, is reader reception theory, which is most notably developed by John Fiske, *Introduction to Communication Studies* (New York: Methuen, 1982); *Television Culture* (New York: Methuen, 1987); *Reading the Popular* (Winchester, MA: Unwin Hyman, 1989); and *Understanding Popular Culture* (Winchester, MA: Unwin Hyman, 1989).

29   Gerard T. Schoening and James A. Anderson, "Social Action Media Studies: Foundational Arguments and Common Premises," *Communication Theory* 5 (1995): 93–116.

30   Frank A. Biocca, "Opposing Conceptions of the Audience: The Active and Passive Hemispheres of Mass Communication Theory," in *Communication Yearbook 11*, ed. J. A. Anderson (Newbury Park, CA: Sage, 1988), pp. 51–80. This article is an excellent discussion of the active-passive distinction and provides a review of the various theories on each side.

31   This view is espoused by Martin Allor, "Relocating the Site of the Audience," *Critical Studies in Mass Communication* 5 (1988): 217–233.

32   See, for example, Pietilä, "Perspectives"; Jennings Bryant and Dolf Zillmann, eds., *Perspectives on Media Effects* (Hillsdale, NJ: Erlbaum, 1986).

33   Rosengren, "Culture, Media, and Society."

34   For a brief history of this tradition, see Carl Patrick Burowes, "From Functionalism to Cultural Studies: Manifest Ruptures and Latent Continuities," *Communication Theory* 6 (1996): 88–103.

35   Harold Lasswell "The Structure and Function of Communication in Society," in *The Communication of Ideas*, ed. L. Bryson (New York: Institute for Religious and Social Studies, 1948), p. 37. For information regarding Lasswell's contribution to communication, see Everett M. Rogers, *A History of Communication Study: A Biographical Approach* (New York: Free Press, 1994), pp. 203–243.

36   Lasswell, "Structure and Function."

37   Paul Lazarsfeld, Bernard Berelson, and H. Gaudet, *The People's Choice* (New York: Columbia University Press, 1948). See also Rogers, *A History,* pp. 244–315.

38   An excellent summary of this hypothesis is Elihu Katz, "The Two-Step Flow of Communication," *Public Opinion Quarterly* 21 (1957): 61–78.

39   Elihu Katz and Paul Lazarsfeld, *Personal Influence: The Part Played by People in the Flow of Mass Communications* (New York: Free Press, 1955).

40   Research on opinion leadership is summarized in Everett M. Rogers, *Diffusion of Innovations* (New York: Free Press, 1995), pp. 290–304.

41   Rogers, *Diffusion of Innovations,* pp. 281–334.

42 Rogers, *Diffusion of Innovations*. For a summary of this theory, see John F. Cragan and Donald C. Shields, *Understanding Communication Theory: The Communicative Forces for Human Action* (Boston: Allyn & Bacon, 1998), pp. 175–207.

43 Everett M. Rogers and D. Lawrence Kincaid, *Communication Networks: Toward a New Paradigm for Research* (New York: Free Press, 1981). The Korean case is discussed throughout the book. See especially pages 258–285.

44 The idea of critical mass is discussed in Alwin Mahler and Everett M. Rogers, "The Diffusion of interactive Communication Innovations and the Critical Mass: The Adoption of Telecommunications Services by German Banks," *Telecommunications Policy* 23 (1999): 719–740; and Everett M. Rogers, "Diffusion Theory: A Theoretical Approach to Promote Community-Level Change," in *Handbook of HIV Prevention*, eds. John L. Peterson and Ralph J. DiClemente (New York: Kluwer Academic, 2000), pp. 57–65.

45 Elisabeth Noelle-Neumann, *The Spiral of Silence: Public Opinion—Our Social Skin* (Chicago: University of Chicago Press, 1984). See also "The Theory of Public Opinion: The Concept of the Spiral of Silence," in *Communication Yearbook 14*, ed. J. A. Anderson (Newbury Park, CA: Sage, 1991), pp. 256–287. For a brief summary, see Charles T. Salmon and Carroll J. Glynn, "Spiral of Silence: Communication and Public Opinion as Social Control," in *An Integrated Approach to Communication Theory and Research*, eds. Michael B. Salwen and Don W. Stacks (Mahwah, NJ: Erlbaum, 1996), pp. 165–180.

46 Noelle-Neumann, *Spiral*, pp. 16–22.

47 Noelle-Neumann, *Spiral*, p. 56.

48 Noelle-Neumann, *Spiral*, p. 169.

49 George Gerbner, "Living with Television: The Dynamics of the Cultivation Process," in *Perspectives on Media Effects*, ed. Jennings Bryant and Dolf Zillmann (Hillsdale, NJ: Erlbaum, 1986), pp. 17–40; Michael Morgan and James Shanahan, "Two Decades of Cultivation Research: An Appraisal and Meta-Analysis," *Communication Yearbook 20*, ed. Brant R. Burleson (Thousand Oaks, CA: Sage, 1997), pp. 1–45; Nancy Signorielli and Michael Morgan, "Cultivation Analysis: Research and Practice," in *An Integrated Approach to Communication Theory and Research*, eds. Michael B. Salwen and Don W. Stacks (Mahwah, NJ: Erlbaum, 1996), pp. 111–126; Nancy Signorielli and Michael Morgan, eds., *Cultivation Analysis: New Directions in Media Effects Research* (Newbury Park, CA: Sage, 1990).

50 George Gerbner, Larry Gross, Michael Morgan, and Nancy Signorielli, "Living with Television," in *Perspectives on Media Effects*, eds. J. Bryant and D. Zillmann (Hillsdale, NJ: Erlbaum, 1986), p. 18.

51 Nancy Signorielli, "Television's Mean and Dangerous World: A Continuation of the Cultural Indicators Perspective," in *Cultivation Analysis: New Directions in Media Effects Research*, eds. N. Signorielli and M. Morgan (Newbury Park, CA: Sage, 1990), pp. 85–106.

52 For an overview, see Maxwell McCombs and Tamara Bell, "The Agenda Setting Role of Mass Communication," in *An Integrated Approach to Communication Theory and Research*, eds. Michael B. Salwen and Don W. Stacks (Mahwah, NJ: Erlbaum, 1996), pp. 93–110.

53 See, for example, M. Childs and J. Reston, eds., *Walter Lippmann and His Times* (New York: Harcourt Brace, 1959).

54 Walter Lippmann, *Public Opinion* (New York: Macmillan, 1921), p. 16.

55 Donald L. Shaw and Maxwell E. McCombs, *The Emergence of American Political Issues* (St. Paul, MN: West, 1977). For a very good summary of this whole line of work, see Jian-Hua Zhu and Deborah Blood, "Media Agenda-Setting Theory: Telling the Public What to Think About," in *Emerging Theories of Human Communication*, ed. Branislav Kovačić (Albany: SUNY Press, 1997): pp. 88–114. See also Maxwell McCombs, "New Frontiers in Agenda Setting: Agendas of Attributes and Frames," *Mass Communication Review* 24 (1997): 4–24; Everett M. Rogers and James W. Dearing, "Agenda-Setting Research: Where Has It Been, Where Is It Going?" in *Communication Yearbook 11*,

204   *Introduction to Media Studies*

ed. J. A. Anderson (Newbury Park, CA: Sage, 1988), pp. 555-593; Stephen D. Reese, "Setting the Media's Agenda: A Power Balance Perspective," in *Communication Yearbook 14,* ed. J. A. Anderson (Newbury Park, CA: Sage, 1991), pp. 309-340. See also David Protess and Maxwell McCombs, *Agenda Setting: Readings on Media, Public Opinion, and Policymaking* (Hillsdale, NJ: Erlbaum, 1991).

56 Shaw and McCombs, *Emergence*, p. 5.

57 Pamela J. Shoemaker, "Media Gatekeeping," in *An Integrated Approach to Communication Theory and Research,* eds. Michael B. Salwen and Don W. Stacks (Mahwah, NJ: Erlbaum, 1996), pp. 79-91.

58 The idea of framing as a media effect is explored by Dietram A. Scheufele, "Framing as a Theory of Media Effects," *Journal of Communication* 49 (1999): 103-122. See also McCombs, "New Frontiers."

59 This idea is developed by Rogers and Dearing, "Agenda-Setting Research."

60 Karen Siune and Ole Borre, "Setting the Agenda for a Danish Election," *Journal of Communication* 25 (1975): 65-73.

61 Reese, "Setting the Media's Agenda."

62 This chronology is discussed by McQuail, *Mass Communication*, 1987, pp. 252-256. For a recent survey of a portion of this literature, see Tara M. Emmers-Sommer and Mike Allen, "Surveying the Effect of Media Effects: A Meta-Analytic Summary of the Media Effects Research," *Human Communication Research* 25 (1999): 478-497. For an especially good overview of theories of media violence, see W. James Potter, *On Media Violence* (Thousand Oaks, CA: Sage, 1999), pp. 11-24.

63 For explorations of the history of the magic bullet or hypodermic needle theory, see J. Michael Sproule, "Progressive Propaganda Critics and the Magic Bullet Myth," *Critical Studies in Mass Communication* 6 (1989): 225-246; Jeffery L. Bineham, "A Historical Account of the Hypodermic Model in Mass Communication," *Communication Monographs* 55 (1988): 230-246.

64 Joseph T. Klapper, *The Effects of Mass Communication* (Glencoe, IL: Free Press, 1960).

65 Raymond Bauer, "The Obstinate Audience: The Influence Process from the Point of View of Social Communication," *American Psychologist* 19 (1964): 319-328.

66 Raymond Bauer, "The Audience," in *Handbook of Communication,* eds. I. de sola Pool and others (Chicago: Rand McNally, 1973), pp. 141-152.

67 Studies on selectivity are well summarized in David O. Sears and Jonathan I. Freedman, "Selective Exposure to Information: A Critical Review," in *The Process and Effects of Mass Communication,* eds. W. Schramm and D. F. Roberts (Urbana: University of Illinois Press, 1971), pp. 209-234.

68 Criticism of the limited-effects approach can be found in Werner J. Severin and James W. Tankard, *Communication Theories: Origins, Methods, Uses* (New York: Hastings House, 1979), p. 249.

69 Elisabeth Noelle-Neumann, "Return to the Concept of Powerful Mass Media," in *Studies of Broadcasting,* eds. H. Eguchi and K. Sata (Tokyo: Nippon Hoso Kyokii, 1973), pp. 67-112; "The Effect of Media on Media Effects Research," *Journal of Communication* 33 (1983): 157-165.

70 Noelle-Neumann, "Effect of Media," p. 157.

71 Potter, *On Media Violence*, pp. 25-42.

72 Potter, *On Media Violence*, p. 211.

73 For historical overviews, J. D. Rayburn, II, "Uses and Gratifications," in *An Integrated Approach to Communication Theory and Research,* eds. Michael B. Salwen and Don W. Stacks (Mahwah, NJ: Erlbaum, 1996), pp. 145-163; Alan M. Rubin, "Audience Activity and Media Use," *Communication Monographs* 60 (1993): 98-105.

74 Elihu Katz, Jay Blumler, and Michael Gurevitch, "Uses of Mass Communication by the Individual," in *Mass Communication Research: Major Issues and Future Directions,* eds. W. P. Davidson and F. Yu (New York: Praeger, 1974), pp. 11-35. See also Jay Blumler

and Elihu Katz, eds., *The Uses of Mass Communication* (Beverly Hills, CA: Sage, 1974). See also the entire issue of *Communication Research* 6 (January 1979).

75 Katz, Blumler, and Gurevitch, "Uses," p. 12.

76 Philip Palmgreen, "Uses and Gratifications: A Theoretical Perspective," in *Communication Yearbook 8,* ed. R. N. Bostrom (Beverly Hills, CA: Sage, 1984), pp. 20–55. See also K. Rosengren, L. Wenner, and P. Palmgreen, eds., *Media Gratifications Research: Current Perspectives* (Beverly Hills, CA: Sage, 1985).

77 David L. Swanson and Austin S. Babrow, "Uses and Gratifications: The Influence of Gratification-Seeking and Expectancy-Value Judgments on the Viewing of Television News," in *Rethinking Communication: Paradigm Exemplars,* eds. Brenda Dervin, Lawrence Grossberg, Barbara J. O'Keefe, and Ellen Wartella (Newbury Park, CA: Sage, 1989), pp. 361–375.

78 Sandra J. Ball-Rokeach and Melvin L. DeFleur, "A Dependency Model of Mass-Media Effects," *Communication Research* 3 (1976): 3–21. See also Melvin L. DeFleur and Sandra J. Ball-Rokeach, *Theories of Mass Communication* (New York: Longman, 1982), pp. 240–251.

79 Alan M. Rubin and Sven Windahl, "The Uses and Dependency Model of Mass Communication," *Critical Studies in Mass Communication* 3 (1986): 193.

80 Burrowes, "From Functionalism to Cultural Studies."

81 This issue is explored in some detail by Roger Desmond and Rod Carveth, "Illuminating the Black Box: The Psychological Tradition in Media Studies," in *Watershed Research Traditions in Human Communication Theory,* eds. Donald P. Cushman and Branislav Kovačić (Albany: SUNY Press, 1995), pp. 241–265.

82 Boulding, "The Medium," p. 68.

83 Kevin Carragee, "A Critical Evaluation of Debates Examining the Media Hegemony Thesis," *Western Journal of Communication* 57 (summer 1993): 330–348.

84 Dennis K. Davis and Stanley J. Baran, *Mass Communication and Everyday Life: A Perspective on Theory and Effects* (Belmont, CA: Wadsworth, 1981), p. 27.

85 Hernando González, "Mass Media and the Spiral of Silence: The Philippines from Marcos to Aquino," *Journal of Communication* 34 (1988): 33–48. For a summary of the failure of international research to confirm the theory, see Salmon and Glynn, "Spiral of Silence."

86 Morgan and Shanahan, "Two Decades of Cultivation Research."

87 Paul M. Hirsch, "The 'Scary World' of the Nonviewer and Other Anomalies: A Reanalysis of Gerbner et al.'s Findings on Cultivation Analysis," *Communication Research* 7 (1980): 404. See also Paul M. Hirsch, "On Not Learning from One's Own Mistakes: A Reanalysis of Gerbner et al.'s Findings on Cultivation Analysis, Part II," *Communication Research* 8 (1981): 3–38.

88 George Gerbner, Larry Gross, Michael Morgan, and Nancy Signorielli, "A Curious Journey into the Scary World of Paul Hirsch," *Communication Research* 8 (1981): 39.

89 A critique of this type is W. James Potter, "Cultivation Theory and Research: A Conceptual Critique," *Human Communication Research* 19 (1993): 564–601. See also John Tapper, "The Ecology of Cultivation: A Conceptual Model for Cultivation Research," *Communication Theory* 5 (1995): 36–57.

90 Criticism of this work can be found in Severin and Tankard, *Communication Theories,* pp. 253–254.

91 W. R. Neuman, "The Threshold of Public Opinion," *Public Opinion Quarterly* 54 (1990): 159–176.

92 See especially Philip Elliott, "Uses and Gratifications Research: A Critique and Sociological Alternative," in *The Uses of Mass Communication,* eds. J. Blumler and E. Katz (Beverly Hills, CA: Sage, 1974), pp. 249–268; and David L. Swanson, "Political Communication Research and the Uses and Gratifications Model: A Critique," *Communication Research* 6 (1979): 36–53.

93   Denis McQuail, "With the Benefits of Hindsight Reflections on Uses and Gratifications Research," *Critical Studies in Mass Communication* 1 (1984): 177–193.

94   See, for example, Dolf Zillmann, "Attribution and Misattribution of Excitatory Reactions," in *New Directions in Attribution Research*, vol. 2, eds. J. H. Harvey, W. Ickes, and R. F. Kidd (Hillsdale, NJ: Erlbaum, 1978), pp. 335–368.

95   McQuail, "Hindsight."

Approaches to Theorizing International Communication

Daya Kishan Thussu

Theories have their own history and reflect the concerns of the time in which they were developed. This chapter examines some that offer ways of approaching the subject of international communication and assesses how useful their explanations are in terms of an understanding of the processes involved. This is by no means a comprehensive account of theories of communication (see McQuail, 1994; Mattelart and Mattelart, 1998), nor does it set out an all-embracing theorization of the subject, but looks at the key theories and their proponents, which together with the preceding chapter on the history of international communication, should help to contextualize the analysis of contemporary global communication systems in subsequent chapters.

It is not surprising that theories of communication began to emerge in parallel with the rapid social and economic changes of the Industrial Revolution in Europe, reflecting the significance of the role of communications in the growth of capitalism and empire, and drawing also on advances in science and the understanding of the natural world. One of the first concepts of communication, developed by the French philosopher Claude Henri de Saint Simon (1760–1825), used the analogy of the living organism, proposing that the development of a system of communication routes (roads, canals and railways) and a credit system (banks) was vital for an industrializing society and that the circulation of money, for example, was equivalent to that of blood for the human heart (Mattelart and Mattelart, 1998).

The metaphor of the organism was also fundamental for British philosopher Herbert Spenser (1820–1903), who argued that industrial society was the embodiment of an 'organic society', an increasingly coherent, integrated system, in which functions became more and more specified and parts more interdependent. Communication was seen as a basic component in a system of distribution and regulation. Like the vascular system, the physical network of roads, canals and railways ensured the distribution of nutrition, while the channels of information (the press, telegraph and postal service) functioned as the equivalent of the nervous system, making it possible for the centre to 'propagate its influence' to its outermost parts. 'Dispatches are compared to nervous discharges that communicate movement from an inhabitant of one city to that of another' (Mattelart and Mattelart, 1998: 9). At the same time, contemporary commentators were anxious about the social and cultural impact of the speed and reach of the new means of communication and the rise of a mass society fuelled and sustained by them.

In the twentieth century, theories of international communication evolved into a discrete discipline within the new social sciences and in each era have reflected contemporary concerns about political, economic and technological changes and their impact on society and culture. In the early twentieth century, during and after the First World War, a debate arose about the role of communication in propagating the competitive economic and military objectives of the imperial powers, exemplified in the work of Walter Lippmann on 'public opinion' (1922) and Harold Lasswell on wartime propaganda (1927). Lippmann's concerns were mainly about the manipulation of public opinion by powerful state institutions, while Lasswell, a political scientist, did pioneering work on the systematic analysis of propaganda activities.

After the Second World War, theories of communication multiplied in response to new developments in technology and media, first radio and, then television, and the increasingly integrated international economic and political system. Two broad though often interrelated approaches to theorizing communication can be discerned: the political-economy approach concerned with the underlying structures of economic and political power relations, and the perspectives of cultural studies, focusing mainly on the role of communication and media in the process of the creation and maintaining of shared values and meanings (Golding and Murdoch, 1997; During, 1999).

The political-economy approach has its roots in the critique of capitalism produced by the German philosopher, Karl Marx (1818–83), but it has evolved over the years to incorporate a wide range of critical thinkers. Central to a Marxian interpretation of international communication is the question of power, which ultimately is seen as an instrument of control by the ruling classes. In his seminal text, *German Ideology*, Marx described the relationship between economic, political and cultural power thus:

> The class which has the means of material production has control at the same time over the means of mental production so that, thereby, generally speaking, the ideas of those who lack the means of mental production are subject to it . . . Insofar, therefore, as they rule as a class and determine the extent and compass of an epoch, it is self-evident that they . . . among other things . . . regulate the production and distribution of the ideas of their age: thus their ideas are the ruling ideas of the epoch.
>
> (cited in Murdoch and Golding, 1977: 12–13)

Much of the critical research on international communication has been an examination of the pattern of ownership and production in the media and communication industries, analysing these within the overall context of social and economic power relations, based on national and transnational class interests. Researchers working within the Marxist tradition were concerned, for example, with the commodification of communication hardware and software and its impact on inequalities of access to media technologies.

The influence on international communication of the growing literature of cultural studies, increasingly transnational in intent, if not yet in perspectives, grew significantly in the late twentieth century. Social-science analyses of mass communication have been enriched by concepts from the study of literature and the humanities. Cultural Studies, which started in Britain with the study of popular and mass culture and their role in the reproduction of social hegemony and inequality, is now more generally concerned with how media texts work to create meaning (on the basis of analysis of the texts themselves), and how culturally situated individuals work to gather meaning from texts (increasingly based on observation of media consumers). Cultural Studies' discovery of polysemic texts (the potential for readers to generate their own meanings) fitted well with a politically conservative era and the reinvigoration of liberal capitalism which accompanied it.

'Free Flow of Information'

After the Second World War and the establishment of a bi-polar world of free market capitalism and state socialism, theories of international communication became part of the new Cold War discourse. For the supporters of capitalism, the primary function of international communication was to promote democracy, freedom of expression and markets, while the Marxists argued for greater state regulation on communication and media outlets.

The concept of the 'free flow of information' reflected Western, and specifically US, antipathy to state regulation and censorship of the media and its use for propaganda by its communist opponents. The 'free flow' doctrine was essentially a part of the liberal, free market discourse that championed the rights of media proprietors to sell wherever and whatever they wished. As most of the world's media resources and media-related capital, then as now, were concentrated in the West, it was the media proprietors in Western countries, their governments and national business communities that had most to gain.

The concept of 'free flow' therefore served both economic and political purposes. Media organizations of the media-rich countries could hope to dissuade others from erecting trade barriers to their products or from making it difficult to gather news or make programmes on their territories. Their argument drew on premises of democracy, freedom of expression, the media's role as 'public watchdog' and their assumed global relevance. For their compatriot businessmen, 'free flow' assisted them in advertising and marketing their goods and services in foreign markets, through media vehicles whose information and entertainment products championed the Western way of life and its values of capitalism and individualism.

For Western governments, 'free flow' helped to ensure the continuing and unreciprocated influence of Western media on global markets, strengthening the West in its ideological battle with the Soviet Union. The doctrine also contributed to providing, in generally subtle rather than direct ways, vehicles for communication of US government points of view to international audience (UNESCO, 1982; Mosco, 1996; Mowlana, 1997).

Modernization Theory

Complementary to the doctrine of 'free flow' in the post-war years was the view that international communication was the key to the process of modernization and development for the so-called 'Third World'. Modernization theory arose from the notion that international mass communication could be used to spread the message of modernity and transfer the economic and political models of the West to the newly independent countries of the South. Communications research on what came to be known as 'modernization' or 'development theory' was based on the belief that the mass media would help transform traditional societies. This pro-media bias was very influential and received support from international organizations such as UNESCO and by the governments in developing countries.

One of the earliest exponents of this theory was Daniel Lerner, a political science professor at the Massachusetts Institute of Technology, whose classic work in the field, *The Passing of Traditional Society* (1958)—the product of research conducted in the early 1950s in Turkey, Lebanon, Egypt, Syria, Jordan and Iran— examined the degree to which people in the Middle East were exposed to national and international media, especially radio. In this first major comparative survey, Lerner proposed that contact with the media helped the process of transition from a 'traditional' to a 'modernized' state, characterizing the mass media as a 'mobility multiplier', which enables individuals to experience events in far-off places, forcing them to reassess their traditional way of life. Exposure to the media, Lerner argued, made traditional societies less bound by traditions and made them aspire to a new and modern way of life.

The Western path of 'development' was presented as the most effective way to shake off traditional 'backwardness': according to Lerner:

> [The] Western model of modernisation, exhibits certain components and sequences whose relevance is global. Everywhere for example increasing urbanisation has tended to raise literacy; rising literacy has tended to increase media exposure; increasing media exposure has 'gone with' wider economic participation (per capita income) and political participation.
>
> (Lerner, 1958: 46)

Western society, Lerner argued, provided 'the most developed model of societal attributes (power, wealth, skill, rationality)', and 'from the West came the stimuli which undermined traditional society that will operate efficiently in the world today, the West is still a useful model' (ibid.: 47).

Another key modernization theorist Wilbur Schramm, whose influential book, *Mass Media and National Development,* was published in 1964 in conjunction with UNESCO, saw the mass media as a 'bridge to a wider world', as the vehicle for transferring new ideas and models from the North to the South and, within the South, from urban to rural areas. Schramm, at the time Director of the Institute for Communication Research at Stanford University, California, noted:

> the task of the mass media of information and the 'new media' of education is to speed and ease the long, slow social transformation required for economic development, and, in particular, to speed and smooth the task of modernising human resources behind the national effort.
>
> (Schramm, 1964: 27)

Schramm endorsed Lerner's view that mass media can raise the aspirations of the peoples in developing countries. The mass media in the South, he wrote, 'face the need to rouse their people from fatalism and a fear of change. They need to encourage both personal and national aspirations. Individuals must come to desire a better life than they have and to be willing to work for it' (ibid. 1964:130).

The timing of Schramm's book was significant. The UN had proclaimed the 1960s as 'the Decade of Development' and UN agencies and Western governments, led by the USA, were generously funding research, often in conjunction with private companies, through universities and development bureaucracy, notably the newly established United States Agency for International Development (USAID), the United States Information Agency (USIA), and the Peace Corps, to harness the power of the mass media to 'modernize' the newly independent countries of the South.

In the 1970s, modernization theorists started to use the level of media development as an indicator of general societal development. Leading theorists of the 'development as modernization' school, such as Everett Rogers, saw a key role for the mass media in international communication and development (Rogers, 1962; Pye, 1963). Such research benefited from the surveys undertaken by various US-government-funded agencies and educational foundations, especially in Asia and Latin America for what Rogers (1962) called 'disseminating innovations'.

This top-down approach to communications, a one-way flow of information from government or international development agencies via the mass media to Southern peasantry at the bottom, was generally seen as a panacea for the development of the newly independent countries of Asia and Africa. But it was predicated on a definition of development that followed the model of Western industrialization and 'modernization', measured primarily by the rate of economic growth of output or Gross National Product (GNP). It failed to recognize that the creation of wealth on its own was insufficient: the improvement of life for the majority of the populations depended on the equitable distribution of that wealth and its use for the public good. It also failed to ask questions like development for whom and who would gain or lose, ignoring any discussion of the political, social, or cultural dimensions of development In many Southern countries, income disparities in fact increased over the succeeding thirty years—despite a growth in GNP.

Moreover, the mass media were assumed to be a neutral force in the process of development, ignoring how the media are themselves products of social, political, economic and cultural conditions. In many developing countries economic and political power was and remains restricted to a tiny, often unrepresentative, elite, and the mass media play a key role in legitimizing the political establishment. Since the media had, and continue to have, close proximity to the ruling elites, they tend to reflect this view of development in the news.

The international communication research inspired by the modernization thesis was very influential, shaping university communication programmes and research centres globally. Though such research provided huge amount of data on the behaviour, attitudes and values of the people in the South, it tended to work within the positivist tradition of what sociologist Paul Lazarsfeld (1941) had long identified as 'administrative' research, often failing to analyse the political and cultural context of international communication.

However, the outcomes of this type of research in international communication can be useful in analysing the relationship of media growth to economic development, measured in terms of such indicators as sales of communication hardware and gross national product. They are also useful in international promotion of advertising and marketing.

It is important to understand the Cold War context in which modernization theory emerged, a time when it was politically expedient for the West to use the notion of modernization to bring the newly independent nations of Asia, the Middle East and Africa into the sphere of capitalism. As Vincent Mosco comments: 'The theory of modernisation meant a reconstruction of the international division of labour amalgamating the non-Western world into the emerging international structural hierarchy' (1996: 121). It is now being accepted that some of modernization research was politically motivated. It has been pointed out that Lerner's seminal study was a spin-off from a large and clandestine government-funded audience research project, conducted for the Voice of America by the Bureau of Applied Social Research (Samarajiva, 1985).

Despite its enormous influence in the field of international communication, Lerner's research had more to do with the East–West ideological contest of those days of Cold War, when in the Middle East radical voices were demanding decolonization—Iran had nationalized its oil industry in 1951, leading to the CIA-backed coup, two years later, which removed the democratically elected Prime Minister Mohammed Musaddiq. Given the prominence of radio propaganda during the 1950s, this research could also be seen as an investigation of radio listening behaviour in a region bordering the Soviet Union. In this context it is interesting to note that Lerner had worked for the Psychological Warfare Division of the US Army during the Second World War.

One major shortcoming of the early modernization theorists was their assumption that the modern and the traditional lifestyles were mutually exclusive, and their dismissive view of the culture of the 'indigent natives' led them to believe in the desirability and inevitability of a shift from the traditional to the modern. The dominant cultural and religious force in the region—Islam—and a sense of collective pan-Islamic identity were seen as 'sentimental sorties into the symbolism of a majestic past'. The elites in the region had to choose between 'Mecca or mechanisation'. The crux of the matter, Lerner argued, was 'not whether, but how one should move from traditional ways toward modern life-styles. The symbols of race and ritual fade into irrelevance when they impede living desires for bread and enlightenment' (Lerner, 1958: 405).

What modernizers such as Lerner failed to comprehend was that the dichotomy of modern versus traditional was not inevitable. Despite all the West's efforts at media modernization, Islamic traditions continue to define the Muslim world, and indeed have become stronger in parts of the Middle East. In addition, these cultures can also use modern communication methods to put their case across. In the 1979 Islamic revolution in Iran, for example, radical groups produced printed material and audiocassettes and distributed them through informal networks to promote an anti-Western ideology based on a particular Islamic view of the world (Mohammadi and Sreberny-Mohammadi, 1994).

In Latin America most communication research, often funded by the US government, was led by proponents of the modernization thesis. However, since the gap between the rich and poor was growing, as elsewhere in the developing world, critics started to question the validity of the developmentalist project and raised questions about what it left out—the relationship between communication, power and knowledge and the ideological role of international organizational and institutional structures. This led to a critique of modernization in Latin America, most notably from Brazil's Paulo Freire, whose *Pedagogy of the Oppressed* (1970) had a major influence on international development discourse, though how far his views were adopted in devising international communication strategies remains an open question.

Southern scholars, especially those from Latin America, argued that the chief beneficiaries of modernization programmes were not the 'traditional' rural poor in the South but Western media and communication companies, which had expanded into the Third World, ostensibly in the name of modernization and development, but in fact in search of new consumers for their products. They argued that modernization programmes were exacerbating the already deep social and economic inequalities in the developing countries and making them dependent on Western models of communication development.

Partly as a result of the work of Latin American scholars, the proponents of modernization in the West acknowledged that the theory needed reformulation. Despite decades of 'modernization', the vast majority of the people in the South continued to live in poverty, and by the mid-1970s the talk was of the 'passing

of the dominant paradigm' (Rogers, 1976). In a revised version of modernization theory, a shift has been detectable from support for the mass media to an
almost blind faith in the potential of the new information and communication
technologies—in what has been called 'a neo-developmentalist view' (Mosco,
1996: 130). Also noticeable is the acceptance of a greater role for local elites in
the modernization process. However, the importance of Western technology
remains crucial in the revised version too. According to this view, modernization
requires advanced telecommunication and computer infrastructure, preferably
through the 'efficient' private corporations, thus integrating the South into a
globalized information economy.

Dependency Theory

Dependency theory emerged in Latin America in the late 1960s and 1970s, partly
as a consequence of the political situation in the continent, with increasing US
support for right-wing authoritarian governments, and partly with the realization
among the educated elite that the developmentalist approach to international
communication had failed to deliver. The establishment, in 1976, in Mexico City
of the Instituto Latinamericano de Estudios (ILET), whose principal research
interest was the study of transnational media business, gave an impetus to a critique of the 'modernization' thesis, documenting its negative consequences in
the continent. The impact of ILET was also evident in international policy
debates about NWICO, particularly through the work of Juan Somavia, a member
of the MacBride Commission.

Though grounded in the neo-Marxist political-economy approach (Baran,
1957; Gunder Frank, 1969; Amin 1976), dependency theorists aimed to provide
an alternative framework to analyse international communication. Central to
dependency theory was the view that transnational corporations (TNCs), most
based in the North, exercise control, with the support of their respective governments, over the developing countries by setting the terms for global trade—
dominating markets, resources, production, and labour. Development for these
countries was shaped in a way to strengthen the dominance of the developed
nations and to maintain the 'peripheral' nations in a position of dependence—in
other words, to make conditions suitable for 'dependent development'. In its
most extreme form the outcome of such relationship was 'the development of
underdevelopment' (Gunder Frank, 1969).

This neo-colonial relationship in which the TNCs controlled both the terms of
exchange and the structure of global markets, it was argued, had contributed to
the widening and deepening of inequality in the South while the TNCs had
strengthened their control over the world's natural and human resources (Baran,
1957; Mattelart, 1979).

The cultural aspects of dependency theory, examined by scholars interested
in the production, distribution and consumption of media and cultural products, were particularly relevant to the study of international communication.

The dependency theorists aimed to show the links between discourses of 'modernization' and the policies of transnational media and communication corporations and their backers among Western governments.

Dependency theorists both benefited from, and contributed to, research on cultural aspects of imperialism being undertaken at the time in the USA. The idea of cultural imperialism is most clearly identified with the work of Herbert Schiller, who was based at the University of California (1969/92). Working within the neo-Marxist critical tradition, Schiller analysed the global power structures in the international communication industries and the links between transnational business and the dominant states.

At the heart of Schiller's argument was the analysis of how, in pursuit of commercial interests, huge US-based transnational corporations, often in league with Western (predominantly US) military and political interests, were undermining the cultural autonomy of the countries of the South and creating a dependency on both the hardware and software of communication and media in the developing countries. Schiller defined cultural imperialism as:

> the sum of the processes by which a society is brought into the modern world system and how its dominating stratum is attracted, pressured, forced, and sometimes bribed into shaping social institutions to correspond to, or even to promote, the values and structures of the dominant centre of the system.
>
> (Schiller, 1976: 9)

Schiller argued that the declining European colonial empires—mainly British, French and Dutch—were being replaced by a new emergent American empire, based on US economic, military and informational power. According to Schiller, the US-based TNCs have continued to grow and dominate the global economy. This economic growth has been underpinned with communications know-how, enabling US business and military organizations to take leading roles in the development and control of new electronically-based global communication systems.

Such domination had both military and cultural implications. Schiller's seminal work, *Mass Communications and American Empire* (1969/1992), examined the role of the US government, a major user of communication services, in developing global electronic media systems, initially for military purposes to counter the perceived, and often exaggerated, Soviet security threat. By controlling global satellite communications, the USA had the most effective surveillance system in operation—a crucial element in the Cold War years. Such communication hardware could also be used to propagate the US model of commercial broadcasting, dominated by large networks and funded primarily by advertising revenue.

> Nothing less than the viability of the American industrial economy itself is involved in the movement toward international commercialisation of broadcasting. The private yet managed economy depends on advertising. Remove the excitation and the manipulation of consumer demand and industrial slowdown threatens.
>
> (Schiller, 1969: 95)

According to Schiller, dependence on US communications technology and investment, coupled with the new demand for media products, necessitated large-scale imports of US media products, notably television programmes. Since media exports are ultimately dependent on sponsors for advertising, they endeavour not only to advertise Western goods and services, but also promote, albeit indirectly, a capitalist 'American way of life', through mediated consumer lifestyles. The result was an 'electronic invasion', especially in the global South, which threatened to undermine traditional cultures and emphasize consumerism at the expense of community values.

US dominance of global communication increased during the 1990s with the end of the Cold War and the failure of the UNESCO-supported demands for NWICO, Schiller argued in the 1992 revised edition of the book. The economic basis of US dominance, however, had changed, with TNCs acquiring an increasingly important role in international relations, transforming US cultural imperialism into 'transnational corporate cultural domination' (Schiller, 1992: 39).

In a recent review of the US role in international communication during the past half-century, Schiller saw the US state still playing a decisive role in promoting the ever-expanding communication sector, a central pillar of the US economy. In US support for the promotion of electronic-based media and communication hardware and software in the new information age of the twenty-first century, Schiller found 'historical continuities in its quest for systemic power and control,' of global communication (1998: 23).

Other prominent works employing what has come to be known as 'the cultural imperialism thesis' have examined such diverse aspects of US cultural and media dominance as Hollywood's relationship with the European movie market (Guback, 1969); US television exports and influences in Latin America (Wells, 1972); the contribution of Disney comics in promoting capitalist values (Dorfman and Mattelart, 1975) and the role of the advertising industry as an ideological instrument (Ewen, 1976; Mattelart, 1991). Internationally, some of the most significant work has been the UNESCO-supported research on international flow in television programmes (Nordenstreng and Varis, 1974; Varis, 1985).

One prominent aspect of dependency in international communication was identified in the 1970s by Oliver Boyd-Barrett as 'media imperialism', examining information and media inequalities between nations and how these reflect broader issues of dependency, and analysing the hegemonic power of mainly US-dominated international media—notably news agencies, magazines, films, radio and television. Boyd-Barrett defined media imperialism as:

> The process whereby the ownership, structure, distribution or content of the media in any one country are singly or together subject to substantial external pressures from the media interests of any other country or countries, without proportionate reciprocation of influence by the country so affected.
>
> (1977: 117)

For its critics, dependency literature was 'notable for an absence of clear definitions of fundamental terms like imperialism and an almost total lack of empirical evidence to support the arguments' (Stevenson, 1988: 38). Others argued that it ignored the question of media form and content as well as the role of the audience. Those involved in a cultural studies approach to the analysis of international communication argued that, like other cultural artefacts, media 'texts' could be polysemic and were amenable to different interpretations by audiences who were not merely passive consumers but 'active' participants in the process of negotiating meaning (Fiske, 1987). It was also pointed out that the 'totalistic' cultural imperialism thesis did not adequately take on board such issues as how global media texts worked in national contexts, ignoring local patterns of media consumption.

Quantifying the volume of US cultural products distributed around the world was not a sufficient explanation, it was also important to examine its effects. There was also a view that cultural imperialism thesis assumed a 'hypodermic-needle model' of media effects and ignored the complexities of 'Third World' cultures (Sreberny-Mohammadi, 1991; 1997). It was argued that the Western scholars had a less than deep understanding of Third World cultures, seeing them as homogeneous and not being adequately aware of the regional and intra-national diversities of race, ethnicity, language, gender and class. However, there have yet been few systematic studies of the cultural and ideological effects of Western media products on audiences in the South, especially from Southern scholars.

Despite its share of criticism (Tomlinson, 1991; Thompson, 1995), the cultural imperialism thesis was very influential in international communication research in the 1970s and 1980s. It was particularly important during the heated NWICO debates in UNESCO and other international fora in the 1970s. However, even a critic such as John Thompson, while rejecting the main thesis, has conceded that such research is 'probably the only systematic and moderately plausible attempt to think about the globalisation of communications and its impact on the modern world' (Thompson, 1995: 173).

Defenders of the thesis found the 1990s' debates criticizing cultural imperialism 'lacking even the most elementary epistemological precaution and sometimes actually bordering on intellectual dishonesty', arguing that the critics of this theory have often 'taken the notion out of context, abstracting it from the concrete historical conditions that produced it: the political struggles and commitments of the 1960s and 1970s' (Mattelart and Mattelart, 1998: 137–8).

With changes in debates on international communication reflecting the rhetoric of privatization and liberalization in the 1990s, theories of media and cultural dependency have become less prominent. However, Boyd-Barrett has argued that while media imperialism theory, in its original formulation, did not take into account intra-national media relations, gender and ethnic issues, it is still a useful analytical tool to make sense of what he terms as the 'colonisation of communications space' (Boyd-Barrett, 1998: 157).

One of the limits of the cultural and media imperialism approach is that it did not fully take into account the role of the national elites, especially in the developing world. However, though its influence has dwindled, the theory of structural imperialism developed by the Norwegian sociologist Johan Galtung, also offers an explanation of the role of international communication in maintaining structures of economic and political power.

Structural Imperialism

Galtung argues that the world consists of developed 'centre' states and underdeveloped 'periphery' states. In turn, each centre and periphery state possesses a 'core'— a highly developed area—and a less developed 'periphery'. He defines structural imperialism as a 'sophisticated type of dominance relation which cuts across nations basing itself on a bridgehead which the centre of the centre nation establishes in the centre of the periphery nation for the joint benefit of both'. For Galtung, there is a harmony of interest between the core of the centre nation and the centre in the periphery nation; less harmony of interest within the periphery nation than within the centre nation and a disharmony of interest between the periphery of the centre nation and the periphery of the periphery nation (Galtung, 1971: 83).

In other words, there exists in the countries of the South a dominant elite whose interests coincide with the interests of the elite in the developed world. This 'core' thus not only provides a bridgehead by which the centre nation can maintain its economic and political domination over the periphery nation, but is also supported by the centre in maintaining its dominance over its own periphery. In terms of values and attitudes, the elite group is closer to other elites in the developed world than with groups in their own country.

Galtung defines five types of imperialism that depend upon the type of exchange between centre and periphery nations: economic, political, military, communication and cultural. The five types form a syndrome of imperialism, and interact, albeit through different channels, to reinforce the dominance relationship of centre over periphery. Communication imperialism is intimately related to cultural imperialism and news is a combination of cultural and communication exchange (Galtung, 1971: 93).

Periphery–centre relationships are maintained and reinforced by information flows and through the reproduction of economic activities. These create institutional links that serve the interests of the dominant groups, both in the centre and within the periphery. Institutions in the centre of the periphery often mirror those of the developed world and thus recreate and promote the latter's value systems.

According to Galtung, the basic mechanism of structural imperialism revolves around two forms of interaction, 'vertical' and 'feudal'. The 'vertical' interaction principle maintains that relationships are asymmetrical; that the flow of power is from the more developed state to the less developed state, while the benefits of the system flow upwards from the less developed states to the centre states.

The 'feudal' interaction principle states that there 'is interaction along the spokes, from the periphery to the centre hub; but not along the rim, from one periphery nation to another' (Galtung, 1971: 89).

The feudal interaction structure reinforces the inequalities produced by the vertical interaction structures. Communication and information flow from the centre to the periphery and back again: for example, Southern states receive information about the North but little information about fellow developing countries.

Galtung's theory maintains that communication imperialism is based on the feudal interaction structure in which the periphery states are tied to the centre in particular ways. Information flows from different core states in different proportions, determined by capital and trade flows, as well as historical, colonial ties.

According to Galtung, the pattern of news flow exhibits these vertical and feudal patterns: news flows from the core to the periphery via the transnational news agencies, while journalists gather information in Southern countries that is eventually retransmitted via the agencies. The effect of this feudal structure is that Southern nations know virtually nothing about events in neighbouring countries that has not been filtered through the lenses of the developed media systems.

The theory argues that if the core actors are defining news according to the criteria and demand for news in the developed world market, then the demand for and criteria of news will be similar in the centre of the peripheral nation. This has been called the 'agenda-setting function' of the international media. Information is transferred to the Southern elite in such a way that primary importance is attached to the same issues the developed world sees as important. The identity of interests between the centre of the centre and the centre of the periphery greatly influences the acceptance of an international agenda and thus Galtung's theory is particularly relevant in understanding global news flow.

A striking similarity can be found in Galtung's theory of structural imperialism with Schiller's definition of cultural imperialism. Both maintain that the structure of political and economic domination exercised by the centre over the periphery results in the re-creation of certain aspects of the centre's value system in the periphery.

There is also evidence of a dependency relationship in the field of media and communication research in Southern countries. As British media analyst James Halloran notes:

> Wherever we look in international communication research—exports and imports of textbooks, articles and journals; citations, references and footnotes; employment of experts (even in international agencies); and the funding, planning and execution of research—we are essentially looking at a dependency situation. This is a situation which is characterised by a one-way flow of values, ideas, models, methods and resources from North to South. It may even be more specifically as a flow from the Anglo-Saxon language fraternity to the rest of the world.
>
> (1997: 39)

Dependency theory has enjoyed widespread influence and equally widespread criticism. It was criticized for concentrating on the impact of transnational business and the role of other external forces on social and economic development to the neglect of internal class, gender, ethnic and power relations. Theorists such as Galtung responded by examining the roles of the often unrepresentative elites in the South in maintaining and indeed benefiting from the dependency syndrome. While the globalization of new information and communication technologies and the resultant wiring up of the 'globe, and the emphasis on cultural hybridization rather than cultural imperialism, have made dependency theories less fashionable, the structural inequalities in international communication continue to render them relevant.

Another concern for scholars working within the political economy approach has been to analyse the close relationship between media and foreign policy. The role of the mass media as an instrument of propaganda for corporate and state power has been an important area of inquiry among critical scholars (Herman and Chomsky, 1988/1994). In their 'propaganda model' US economist, Edward Herman, and the renowned linguist, Noam Chomsky, examine through a range of detailed case studies, how news in mainstream US media system passes through several 'filters', including the size, concentrated ownership and profit orientation of media firms; their heavy reliance on advertising and dependence on business and governmental sources for information; and the overall dominant ideology within which they operate. These elements, write Herman and Chomsky, 'interact with and reinforce one another and set the premises of discourse and interpretation, and the definition of what is newsworthy' (1994: 2).

For Herman and Chomsky, a propaganda approach to media coverage suggests:

> a systematic and highly political dichotomisation in news coverage based on serviceability to important domestic power interests. This should be observable in dichotomised choices of story and in the volume and quality of coverage . . . such dichotomisation in the mass media is massive and systematic: not only are choices for publicity and suppression comprehensible in terms of system advantage, but the modes of handling favoured and inconvenient materials (placement, tone, context, fullness of treatment) differ in ways that serve political interests'.
>
> (ibid.: 35)

Despite meticulously researched case studies—ranging from the US media's coverage of the war in Vietnam in the 1960s and 1970s, to its treatment of US involvement in subversive activities in Central America during the 1980s—the propaganda model has received more than its share of criticism, especially in the West. Internationally, however, *Manufacturing Consent,* a title borrowed from a phrase used by Lippmann in a 1922 publication, had a profound influence. Though criticized for its 'polemical' style, the book remains one of the few systematic and detailed studies of the politics of mass media.

Hegemony

By arguing that the propaganda model succeeds because there is no significant overt coercion from the state, Herman and Chomsky, in some ways, were following the European analyses of the role of ideology and state power in a capitalist society, articulated by, among others, the French Marxist Louis Althusser who called the media 'ideological state apparatus' (1971).

Another major influence on critical theorists as well as on cultural critics in the study of ideology is the writings of Italian Marxist Antonio Gramsci (1891–1937). The impact of the ideas of Gramsci, who died in prison under the Fascist regime, has been widespread in critical studies of international communication. However, it was not until the translation into English of his most famous work, *Selections from the Prison Notebooks,* in 1971, that Gramsci's ideas became a major influence in the Anglo-Saxon world.

Gramsci's conception of hegemony is rooted in the notion that the dominant social group in a society has the capacity to exercise intellectual and moral direction over society at large and to build a new system of social alliances to support its aims. Gramsci argued that military force was not necessarily the best instrument to retain power for the ruling classes, but that a more effective way of wielding power was to build a consent by ideological control of cultural production and distribution.

According to Gramsci, such a system exists when a dominant social class exerts moral and intellectual leadership—through its control of such institutions as schools, religious bodies and the mass media—over both allied and subordinate classes. Social and intellectual authority is exercised by the government 'with the consent of the governed—but with this consent organised, and not generic and vague' in such a fashion that its right to govern is rarely challenged seriously. The 'state does have and request consent but it also "educates" this consent' (Gramsci, 1971).

One of the most important functions of the state, Gramsci wrote in his *Prison Notebooks,* 'is to raise the great mass of the population to a particular cultural and moral level, a level (or type) which corresponds to the needs of the productive forces for development, and hence to the interests of the ruling classes'. Schools, courts and a multitude of 'initiatives and activities . . . form the apparatus of the political and cultural hegemony of the ruling classes' (Gramsci, 1971: 258–9). This, he argued, was in contrast with a situation in which the dominant class merely rules, that is, coercively imposes its will on subordinate classes. This consent thus manufactured, however, cannot simply be assumed or guaranteed and has to be renewed, indicating that hegemony is more of a process—which is to be continually reproduced, secured and lost—rather than an achieved state of affairs.

In international communication, the notion of hegemony is widely used to conceptualize political functions of the mass media, as a key player in propagating and maintaining the dominant ideology and also to explain the process of media and communication production, with dominant ideology shaping production of news and entertainment (Hallin, 1994). Thus, though the media are notionally free from direct government control, yet they act as agents of legitimization of the dominant ideology.

Critical Theory

Among the substantial body of research undertaken by the Frankfurt School theorists, the concept of the 'culture industry', first used by Adorno and Horkheimer in a book entitled *Dialectic of Enlightenment* written in 1944 and published in 1947, has received the widest international attention. Identified with the staff of the Institute for Social Research, founded in 1923 and affiliated with the University of Frankfurt, its key members included Max Horkheimer (1895–1973), Theodor Adorno (1903–69) and Herbert Marcuse (1898–1979).

Analysing the industrial production of cultural goods—films, radio programmes, music and magazines, etc.—as a global movement, they argued that in capitalist societies the trend was towards producing culture as a commodity (Adorno, 1991). Adorno and Horkheimer believed that cultural products manifested the same kind of management practices, technological rationality and organizational schemes as the mass-produced industrial goods such as cars. This 'assembly-line character', they argued, could be observed in 'the synthetic, planned method of turning out its products (factory-like not only in the studio but, more or less, in the compilation of cheap biographies, pseudo-documentary novels, and hit songs)' (Adorno and Horkheimer, 1979 [1947]: 163).

Such industrial production led to standardization, resulting in a mass culture made up of a series of objects bearing the stamp of the culture industry. This industrially produced and commodified culture, it was argued, led to a deterioration of the philosophical role of culture. Instead, this mediated culture contributed to the incorporation of the working classes into the structures of advanced capitalism and in limiting their horizons to political and economic goals that could be realized within the capitalist system without challenging it. The critical theorists argued that the development of the 'culture industry' and its ability to ideologically inoculate the masses against socialist ideas benefited the ruling classes.

Marrying the psychoanalytical theories of Sigmund Freud with Marxian economic analysis, the critical theorists borrowed the notion of commodification from Marx, who had argued that objects are commodified by acquiring an exchange value instead of their intrinsic value. In their analysis of cultural products, they argued that in a capitalist economy cultural products are produced and sold in media markets as commodities and the consumers buy them not just because of their intrinsic worth but in exchange for entertainment or to fulfil their psychological needs.

The concentration of ownership of cultural production in a few producers resulted in a standardized commercial commodity, contributing to what they called a 'mass culture'—influenced by the mass media and one which thrived on the market rules of supply and demand. In their view, such a process under-mined the critical engagement of masses with important socio-political issues and ensured a politically passive social behaviour and the subordination of the working classes to the ruling elite.

Marcuse, who migrated to the USA where he had a huge influence on the labour movement, argued that technological rationality or instrumental reason had reduced speech and thought to a single dimension, establishing what he called a 'one-dimensional society' which had abolished the distance required for critical thought. One of the most incisive chapters of Marcuse's book *One Dimensional Man* (1964), discusses 'one-dimensional language' and frequently refers to media discourse.

In an international context the idea of 'mass culture' and media and cultural industries has influenced debates about the flow of information between countries. The issue of the commodification of culture is present in many analyses of the operation of book publishing, film and popular music industries. One indication of this was the 1982 UNESCO report which argued that cultural industries in the world were greatly influenced by the major media and communication compa-nies and were being continually corporatized. The expansion of mainly Western-based cultural products globally had resulted, it argued, in the gradual 'marginalisation of cultural messages that do not take the form of goods, primar-ily of values as marketable commodities' (UNESCO, 1982: 10).

This emphasis on ownership and control of the means of cultural production and the argument that it directly shapes the activities of artists has been con-tested by several writers, arguing that creativity and cultural consumption can be independent of production cycles and that the production process itself is not as organised or rigidly standardized as stated by the Frankfurt School theorists.

The Public Sphere

A natural heir to the critical theorists, the German sociologist Jürgen Habermas (born 1929) also lamented the standardization, massification and atomization of the public. Habermas developed the concept of the public sphere in one of his earliest books, though it was 27 years before it appeared in English translation as *The Structural Transformation of the Public Sphere: An Inquiry into a Category of Bourgeois Society*, in 1989. He defined the public sphere as

> an arena, independent of government (even if in receipt of state funds) and also enjoying autonomy from partisan economic forces, which is dedicated to rational debate (i.e. to debate and discussion which is not 'interests', 'disguised' or 'manipu-lated') and which is both accessible to entry and open to inspection by the citizenry. It is here, in this public sphere, that public opinion is formed.
>
> (quoted in Holub, 1991: 2–8)

Habermas argued that the 'bourgeois public sphere' emerged in an expanding capitalist society exemplified by eighteenth-century Britain, where entrepreneurs were becoming powerful enough to achieve autonomy from state and church and increasingly demanding wider and more effective political representation to facilitate expansion of their businesses. In his formulation of a public sphere, Habermas gave prominence to the role of information, as, at this time, a greater freedom of the press was fought for and achieved with parliamentary reform. The wider availability of printing facilities and the resultant reduction in production costs of newspapers stimulated debate contributing to what Habermas calls 'rational-acceptable policies', which led by the mid-nineteenth century to the creation of a 'bourgeois public sphere'.

This idealized version of a public space was characterized by greater accessibility of information, a more open debate within the bourgeoisie, a space independent of both business interests and state apparatus. However, as capitalism expanded and attained dominance, the call for reform of the state was replaced by an effort to take it over to further business interests. As commercial interests became prominent in politics and started exerting their influence—for example, by lobbying parliament, funding political parties and cultural institutions—the autonomy of the public sphere was severely reduced.

In the twentieth century, the growing power of information management and manipulation through public relations and lobbying firms has contributed to making contemporary debates a 'faked version' of a genuine public sphere (Habermas, 1989: 195). In this 'refeudalization' of the public sphere, public affairs have become occasions for 'displays' of power in the style of medieval feudal courts rather than a space for debate on socioeconomic issues.

Habermas also detects refeudalization in the changes within the mass media systems, which have become monopoly capitalist organizations, promoting capitalist interests, and thus affecting their role as disseminators of information for the public sphere. In a market-driven environment, the overriding concern for media corporations is to produce an artefact which will appeal to the widest possible variety of audiences and thus generate maximum advertising revenue. It is essential, therefore, that the product is diluted in content to meet the lowest common denominator—sex, scandal, celebrity lifestyles, action adventure and sensationalism. Despite their negligible informational quality such media products reinforce the audience's acceptance of 'the soft compulsion of constant consumption training' (Habermas, 1989: 192).

Though the idealized version of the public sphere has been criticized for its very male, Eurocentric and bourgeois limitations, the public sphere provides a useful concept in understanding democratic potential for communication processes (Calhoun, 1992; Dahlgren, 1995). In recent years, with the globalization of the media and communication, there has been talk about the evolution of a 'global public sphere' where issues of international significance—environment, human rights, gender and ethnic equality—can be articulated through the mass media, though the validity of such a concept is also contested (Sparks, 1998).

Cultural Studies Perspectives on International Communication

While much of the debate on international communication post-1945 and during the Cold War emphasized a structural analysis of its role in political and economic power relationships, there has been a discernible shift in research emphasis in the 1990s in parallel with the 'depoliciticization' of politics towards the cultural dimensions of communication and media. The cultural analysis of communication also has a well established theoretical tradition to draw upon, from Gramsci's theory of hegemony to the works of the critical theorists of the Frankfurt School.

One group of scholars who adapted Gramsci's notions of hegemony were based at the Centre for Contemporary Cultural Studies at the University of Birmingham in Britain. Led by the Caribbean-born scholar Stuart Hall, 'the Birmingham School', as it came to be known in the 1970s did pioneering work on exploring the textual analysis of media, especially television, and ethnographic research. Particularly influential was Hall's model of 'encoding-decoding media discourse' which theorized about how media texts are given 'preferred readings' by producers and how they may be interpreted in different ways—from accepting the dominant meaning; negotiating with the encoded message, or taking an oppositional view (Hall, 1980).

The model was widely adopted by scholars interested in the study of the ideological role of the mass media. However, the research focus of the Birmingham School was largely British, and more often than not, its perceptions of the 'global' were based on the ethnographic studies of migrant populations—their television viewing habits, consumption of music and other leisure activities. The undue emphasis on ethnic and racial identity and 'multiculturalism', tended to limit their research perspectives, exposing them to the danger, for example, of confusing 'British Asian cultural identity' with the diverse cultures and subcultures of the South Asian region, with its multiplicity of languages, ancient religions and ethnicities.

The dominant Western view of the global South is profoundly influenced by Eurocentrism, defined by the Egyptian theorist Samir Amin as constituting 'one dimension of the culture and ideology of the modern capitalist world' (Amin, 1988: vii). Many other scholars from the developing world have argued that contemporary representations of the global South are affected by the way the Orient has been historically constructed in Western thinking, for example, through travel writing (Kabbani, 1986), literature (Said, 1978; 1993) and films (Shohat and Stam, 1994), contributing to a continuity of subordination of non-European peoples in Western imagination. The US-based Palestinian scholar Edward Said has explored how dominant culture participated in the expansion and consolidation of nineteenth-century imperialism. Taking the Gramscian view of culture, Said writes:

> Western cultural forms can be taken out of the autonomous enclosures in which they have been protected, and placed instead in the dynamic global environment created by imperialism, itself revised as an ongoing contest between North and South, metropolis and periphery, white and native.

(1993: 59)

Though the cultural studies approach professes to give voice to such issues—race, ethnicity, gender and sexuality remain its key concerns—it has generally rendered less importance to class-based analysis, despite the fact that championing the 'popular' has been a major achievement of this tradition. The cultural studies approach to communication has become increasingly important, especially in the USA and Australia and with its new-found interest in 'global popular', the trend is towards the internationalization of cultural studies.

Theories of The Information Society

Spectacular innovations in information and communication technologies, especially computing, and their rapid global expansion have led to claims that this is the age of the information society. Breakthroughs in the speed, volume and cost of information processing, storage and transmission have undoubtedly contributed to the power of information technology to shape many aspects of Western, and increasingly, global society. The convergence of telecommunications and computing technologies and the continued reductions in the costs of computing and international telephony have made the case for the existence of the information society even stronger.

According to its enthusiasts, an international information society is under construction which will digitally link all homes via the Internet—the network of networks. The information grid of networked computers is being compared with the electricity grid, linking every home, office and business, to create a networked society, based on what has been termed as the 'knowledge economy'. These networks have become the information superhighways, providing the infrastructure for a global information society (Negroponte, 1995; Kahin and Nesson, 1997). However, critics have objected to this version of society, arguing that these changes are technologically determined and ignore the social, economic and political dimensions of technological innovation (Webster, 1995).

The technologically-determinist view of communication was promoted by Canadian media theorist Marshall McLuhan (1911–80), one of the first thinkers to analyse the impact of media technology on society. Arguing that, 'the medium is the message', he maintained that viewed in a historical context, media technology had more social effect on different societies and cultures than media content (McLuhan, 1964). McLuhan, a Professor at the University of Toronto, was working within the tradition of what came to be known as 'the Toronto School' of thought, identified with the research of economic historian Harold Innis ([1950] 1972). McLuhan argued that printing technology, for example, contributed to nationalism, industrialism and universal literacy. Though at the time he was writing, electronic media, especially television, were confined to few Northern nations, McLuhan foresaw the impact of international television, suggesting that new communication and information technologies would help create, what he called a 'global village'. The rapid changes in international communications, spurred on by the expansion of direct satellite broadcasting in the 1980s and the Internet in the 1990s, seem to made the world shrink, generating renewed interest in McLuhan's concept of global village.

The term 'information society' originated in Japan (Ito, 1981), but it was the USA where the concept received its most ardent intellectual support. In the USA, even in the early 1960s the 'economics of information' was being considered as an important area of research activity. Fritz Machlup (1902–83), whose 1962 work, *The Production and Distribution of Knowledge in the United States,* was one of the first attempts to analyse information in economic terms. Changes in industrial production and their effect on Western societies informed the work of sociologist Daniel Bell, who became an internationally known exponent of the idea of a 'post-industrial' society—one in which the service industries employ more workers than manufacturing.

In his hugely influential book, *The Coming of Post Industrial Society,* published in 1973, Bell argued that US society had moved from an industrial to post-industrial one, a society characterized by the domination of information and information-related industries. Bell contended that not only was more information being used but a qualitatively different type of information was available. Bell's ideas were keenly adopted by the scholars who wanted to pronounce the arrival of 'the information age'. Another key figure, Alvin Toffler, though more populist than Bell, was very influential in propagating the idea of an information society, calling it the third wave—after the agricultural and industrial eras—of human civilization (Toffler, 1980).

The 'third wave' was characterized by increasing 'interconnectedness', contributing to the 'evolution of a universal interconnected network of audio, video and electronic text communication', which, some argue, will promote intellectual pluralism and personalized control over communication (Neuman, 1991: 21).

In this version of the information society, the democratic potential of new technologies is constantly stressed. However, critics such as Frank Webster emphasize 'historical antecedents', arguing that 'there is no novel, "post-industrial" society: the growth of service occupations and associated developments highlight the continuities of the present with the past' (Webster, 1995: 50). These continuities need to be underlined, especially in the global context, as the transnationalization of media and communication industries has been greatly facilitated by expansion of new international communication networks, for example, among non-governmental organizations (Frederick, 1992). The resultant 'time–space compression' is implicated in what has been called, taking up McLuhan's phrase, the phenomenon of 'global villagization' (Harasim, 1994).

With its growing commodification, information has come to occupy a central role as a 'key strategic resource' in the international economy, the distribution, regulation, marketing and management of which are becoming increasingly important. Real-time trading has become a part of contemporary corporate culture, through digital networking, which has made it possible to transmit information on stock markets, patent listings, currency fluctuations, commodity prices, futures, portfolios, at unprecedented speed and volume across the globe.

The growing 'informatization' of the economy is facilitating the integration of national and regional economies and creating a global economy, which continues to be dominated by a few megacorporations, increasingly global in the production, distribution and consumption of their goods and services. The growth of Internet-based trading, the so-called E-commerce (electronic commerce) has given a boost to what has been called 'digital' capitalism (Schiller, 1999).

In the analysis of the emerging global information society, the most significant input has come from the Spanish theorist Manuel Castells. In his trilogy *The Information Age,* Castells gives an extensively researched and detailed analysis of the emerging trends in global condition. The first volume focuses on the new social structures at work in what Castells calls the 'network society'; the second volume examines social and political processes within the context of such a society, while the third volume includes integration and information-based polarization in the international 'informational economy' in which communication becomes both global and customized.

Informational capitalism, Castells argues, is increasingly operating on a global basis, through exchanges between electronic circuits linking up international information systems. This bypasses the power of the state and creates regional and supranational units. In this 'networked' globe, he contends, flows of electronic images are fundamental to social processes and political activity, which has been progressively affected by mediated reality (Castells, 1996, 1997, 1998). Though he rejects technological determinism, his ideas are fundamentally shaped by the new technological paradigm.

It has also been claimed that new technologies have contributed to the decline of ideology. For example, a visually based medium such as television has shifted ideology from 'conceptual to iconic symbolism' (Gouldner, 1976). The growing use of computer-mediated communication could further reduce the impact of ideology in daily life, though the empowering potential of Internet could, on the other hand, create new forms of transnational ideological alliances. However, the possibilities of the Internet creating new communicative space (Poster, 1995), have been opposed with questions about access to the new technologies, within and between nations (Golding, 1998).

Some critics have been concerned with the growing commodification of personal information, from database marketing to individually targeted personalized advertising and consumer sales (Gandy, 1993). With the growing use of the Internet, companies can exploit commercially valuable data on their users, for example, by so-called Cookies (Client-Side Persistent Information). Others have raised questions about the use of new technologies for personal and political surveillance (Lyon, 1994). US dominance of global military surveillance and intelligence data gathering through spy satellites and advanced computer networks, for political, and increasingly trade-related espionage, must also be considered an integral part of the push towards creation of a global information society. The 'control revolution' (Beniger, 1986), though more pronounced in all modern organizations in 'networked societies', is in the process of going global (see Chapter 7, pp. 246–47).

Discourses of Globalization

Despite the disputed nature of the utility of globalization as a concept in understanding international communication, there is little doubt that new information and communication technologies have made global interconnectivity a reality. It has been argued that 'globalisation may be the concept of the 1990s, a key idea by which we understand the transition of human society into the third millennium' (Waters, 1995: 1). The term has also been used more generally to describe contemporary developments in communication and culture.

Wallerstein (1974; 1980) sees globalization as a world system, a theory rejected by others on the grounds that his 'mechanisms of geosystematic integration are exclusively economic' (Waters, 1995: 25), while Robertson argues that 'globalisation analysis and world-systems analysis are rival perspectives' (Robertson, 1992: 15).

In its most liberal interpretation, globalization is seen as fostering international economic integration and as a mechanism for promoting global liberal capitalism. For those who see capitalism as the 'end' of history (Fukuyama, 1992), globalization is to be welcomed for the effect that it has in promoting global markets and liberal democracy. The triumph of democracy is celebrated through increasing emphasis on global governance (UN, 1995), 'cosmopolitan democracy' (Archibugi and Held, 1995) and even 'cosmopolitics' (Cheah and Robbins, 1998). In this dominant view of globalization, the expansion of information and communication technologies coupled with market-led liberal democracies are contributing to the creation of what has been called a global civil society, though others have identified tensions between globalization and fragmentation (Clark, 1997).

The economic conception of globalization views it as denoting a qualitative shift from a largely national to a globalized economy, in which although national economies continue to predominate within nations, they are often subordinate to transnational processes and transactions (Hirst and Thompson, 1996). The arguments for economic globalization focus on the increasingly internationalized system of manufacture and production, on growing world trade, on the extent of international capital flows and, crucially, on the role of the transnational corporations. Liberal interpretations of globalization see markets playing the key role at the expense of the states. Japanese business strategist Kenichi Ohmae, who has been included in the category of 'extreme globalization theorists', claims that, in the globalized economy the nation–state has become irrelevant and market capitalism is producing a 'cross-border civilisation' (Ohmae, 1995).

Both Marxists and world-system theorists stress the importance of the rise of global dominance of a capitalist market economy that is penetrating the entire globe–pan-capitalism is how one commentator described the phenomenon (Tehranian, 1999). With the collapse of communism, the disintegration of the Soviet Union and the eastern bloc, seen by many as alternative to capitalism, the shift within Western democracies from a public to a private sector capitalism, and the international trend towards liberalization and privatization have contributed to the acceptance of the capitalist market as a global system.

However, questions remain about the extent of globalization (Ferguson, 1992). It is argued that many of the indices of globalization are concentrated within the OECD countries, especially between the USA–EU–Japan triad, prompting scholars to talk of 'triadization' rather than the globalization of the world economy. It is beyond dispute, however, that in the post-Cold War world, transnational corporations have become extremely powerful actors, dominating the globalized economy. They must compete internationally and will, if necessary, sever the links to the nations where they originally operated, a trend which has been described as reflection of the 'global footlooseness of corporate capitalism' (Sassen, 1996: 6).

In sociological interpretations of globalization, the notion of culture is of primary importance. British sociologist Anthony Giddens (1990) sees globalization as the spread of modernity, which he defines as the extension of the nation–state system, the world capitalist economy, the world military order and the international division of labour. Waters argues that globalization is 'the direct consequence of the expansion of European culture across the planet via settlement, colonisation and cultural mimesis' (1995: 3–4).

Enthusiasts talk of a new 'global consciousness' as well as physical compression of the world, in which cultures become 'relativized' to each other, not unified or centralized, asserting that globalization involves 'the development of something like a global culture' (Robertson, 1992). Others have been more cautious, arguing that globalizing cultural forces, such as international media and communication networks, produce more complex interactions between different cultures (Appadurai, 1990; 1996). Some have made the case for considering cultural practices as central to the phenomenon of globalization (Tomlinson, 1999).

Global homogenizing forces such as standardized communication networks—both hardware and software, media forms and formats—influence cultural consciousness across the world. However, as the US-based anthropologist Arjun Appadurai argues (1990), these globalizing cultural forces in their encounters with different ideologies and traditions of the world produce 'heterogeneous dialogues'. Appadurai specifies five 'scapes'—ethnoscapes, technoscapes, finanscapes, mediascapes and ideoscapes—to describe the dynamics of contemporary global diversity.

'Ethnoscape' denotes the flow of people—such as tourists, refugees, immigrants, students and professional—from one part of the globe to another. 'Technoscape' includes the transfer of technology across national borders while 'finanscape' deals with international flow of investment. 'Mediascape' refers to global media, especially its electronic version—both its hardware and the images that it produces while 'ideoscape' suggests ideological contours of culture. Appadurai argues that the five 'scapes' influence culture not by their hegemonic interaction, global diffusion and uniform effects, but by their differences, contradictions and counter-tendencies—their 'disjunctures' (Appadurai, 1990).

Some critics see globalization as a new version of Western cultural imperialism, given the concentration of international communication hardware and software power among a few dominant actors in the global arena who want an 'open' international order, created by their own national power and by the power of transnational media and communication corporations (Latouche, 1996; Amin, 1997; Herman and McChesney, 1997). A fear of what the US sociologist George Ritzer called the McDonaldization of society, is also expressed by scholars. Ritzer says he prefers the term 'Americanization' to globalization, since the latter implies more of a 'multidimensional relationship among many nations' (Ritzer, 1999: 44).

While conceding the pre-eminence of Western media and cultural products in international communication, scholars influenced by post-structuralism dispute whether the global flow of media and cultural products is necessarily a form of domination or even a strictly one-way traffic, arguing that there is a contra-flow from the periphery to the centre and between the 'geo-cultural markets', especially in the area of television and films (Jacka *et al.*, 1996). Ulf Hannerz contests the notion that globalization reinforces cultural movement from the 'centre' (the modern industrial West) to the peripheral 'traditional' world in a largely one-way flow, arguing that centre–periphery interactions are more complex with cultural flows moving in multiple directions, and thus the outcomes are opposite tendencies, both towards what he calls saturation and maturation, for homogenization and heterogenization (Hannerz, 1997).

Scholars broadly following this line of argument also question the assumptions about the process of homogenization as a result of the diffusion of the Western media and cultural products globally, arguing that the forces of fragmentation and hybridity are equally strong and they affect all societies. Tomlinson argues that 'the effects of globalisation are to weaken cultural coherence in all individual nation-states, including the economically powerful ones—the imperial powers of a previous era (1991: 175). Others such as Mexican anthropologist Nestor Garcia Canclini (1995 [1989]) see possibilities offered by migration and modernity to broaden cultural territory beyond the nation—state. The so-called 'deterritorialization' and the relocation of 'Third World' cultures in the metropolitan centres is considered an enriching experience for the receiving as well as the migratory cultures.

The apparent growth of alternative media and the possibilities opened up by the Internet are also seen to be a trend towards the disruption of the oneway flow of information. Robertson adopts the concept of 'glocalization', a term whose origins are in the discipline of marketing, to express the global production of the local and the localization of the global, while Nederveen Pieterse (1995) maps out how hegemony is not merely reproduced but 'refigures' in the process of hybridization.

The increased level of transnational information flows, made possible by the new technologies of communication and shifts in the institutional organization—economic, political and legal—on the means of communication, have profoundly affected global media industries. Increasingly, the emphasis is shifting from the traditional approach of considering the role of media in the vertical integration of national societies, to studying information flows which show patterns of transnational horizontal integration of media and communication structures, processes and audiences. This has become necessary because of the harmonization of international regulatory and legal frameworks and the globalization of ownership and control in the telecommunication and media sectors—including television, films and on-line media.

This horizontal communication is facilitating transnational patterns of marketing and political communication, where people are increasingly being addressed across national boundaries on the basis of their purchasing power. Transnational communication is also used by international non-governmental organizations (INGOs) whose politics and actions are being affected by the use of the Internet. The increasingly complex relations between local, national, regional and international production, distribution and consumption of media texts in a global context further complicate the globalization discourse.

Accompanying the dramatic expansion of capitalism and new transnational political organisation is a new global culture, emerging as a result of computer and communication technology, a consumer society with a wide range of products and services consumed internationally. Global culture includes the proliferation of media technologies, especially satellite and cable television, that veritably create McLuhan's dream of a global village in which people all over the world watch spectacles like the Gulf War, major sports events, entertainment programmes and advertisements which relentlessly promote free market capitalism.

With the expansion of Internet access, more and more people are entering into the global computer networks that instantaneously circulate ideas, information and images throughout the world, overcoming boundaries of space and time. What kind of international communication this is generating remains a hotly disputed subject, given that culture is an especially complex and contested terrain as 'modern' culture permeates traditional ones and new configurations emerge.

The debates about global culture have been largely ignored by many previous forms of modernization theories that tended towards economic, technological and political determinism. In classical Marxism, culture was sometimes reduced to a crass economic commodity, with scarce importance given to local forms of associations—whether based on ethnicity, religion, race or gender. It also did not take on board the issue of cultural diversity, aesthetics and spirituality, being preoccupied with the study of the production and consumption of material culture. For traditional liberalism, the advancement of the modern economy and technology was necessary for creating world markets and consumers.

Both classical Marxists and liberals predicated a borderless world—in the idealized Marxian version the proletariat across the world were to lead international communism that would eliminate nationalism, class exploitation and war, while liberal interpretations saw the market as eroding cultural differences and national and regional particularities, to produce a global consumer culture. Missing from both models has been an understanding of the complexity of the interaction of class with nationalism, religion, race, ethnicity and feminism to produce local political struggles. Despite claims for the end of ideology and history and the 'peace dividend' since the end of the Cold War, the world has witnessed a rise in ethnic and religious conflict.

The intellectual uncertainty that the end of the Cold War produced in the West and the dismantling of the last vestiges of progressive ideology in the former socialist camp, are reflected in an increasing blurring of boundaries between various strands of international communication theory. In this postmodern landscape, there appears to be a fragmentation of theories, with an emphasis on the personal and the local while macro issues affecting international communication are often ignored. Postmodernists argue that developments in transnational capitalism are producing a new global historical configuration of post-Fordism, or postmodernism as a new 'cultural logic' of capitalism (Harvey, 1989; Jameson, 1991). Yet the proliferation of difference and the shift to more local discourses and practices define the contemporary scene, and theory, postmodernists argue, should shift from the level of globalization and its often totalizing macrotheories to focus on the micro, the specific and the heterogeneous. A wide range of theories associated with postculturalism, postmodernism, feminism and multiculturalism and post-colonial studies tend to focus on difference and specificity rather than more global conditions (Lyotard, 1984; Baudrillard, 1994; Bhabha, 1994, Sreberny-Mohammadi, 1994; Garcia Canclini, 1995; Ang, 1996).

A Critical Political-economy for the Twenty-first Century

One of the significant contemporary themes in international communication research within the critical political economic tradition is the transition from America's post-war hegemony to a world communication order led by transnational businesses and supported by their respective national states increasingly linked in continental and global structures. Researchers working within this area have focused on transnational corporate and state power, with a particular stress on ownership concentration in media and communication industries world-wide—and the growing trends towards vertical integration—companies controlling production in a specific sector—and horizontal integration—across sectors within and outside media and the communication industry (Garnham, 1990; Tunstall and Palmer, 1991; Herman and McChesney, 1997; Bagdikian, 1997; McChesney, 1999).

Other scholars have supported movements for greater international information and communication equality, with concerns about incorporating human rights into international communication debates (Hamelink, 1983). Sceptical of the dominant market-based approach, many scholars have defended the public-service view of state-regulated media and telecommunication organizations and advanced public interest concerns before government regulatory and policy bodies both at national (Garnham, 1990), regional (Collins, 1998) and international levels (Mattelart, 1994).

In the twenty-first century, the focus of critical scholars is likely to be the analysis of the characteristics of the transnational media and communication corporations and locating them within the changes in international organizations such as the World Trade Organization or the International Telecommunication Union, which have played a crucial role in managing the transition to a market-driven international communication environment. The role of new technologies, especially the Internet, in international communication has also informed the critical research agenda.

The dismemberment of the Soviet Union and the advent of 'market socialism' in China and the rightward shift of the left in Europe and across the developing world, have posed a challenge to the political economic theoretical framework. However, a critical understanding of the political economy of international communication is essential if one wants to make sense of the expansion, acceleration and consolidation of the US-managed global electronic economy.

Schools of Communication Research

Paul Lazarsfeld's Ideational Network and Contribution to the Field of Communication Research

Mahmoud Eid

Abstract

Paul Lazarsfeld began his career as a European mathematician and later became a prominent American sociologist with a passion for social, psychological, and political research. Working at the center of a wide intellectual network, this innovative methodologist, creative intellectual, and eminent philosopher opened new research fields, including the study of voting behavior, mass media and communications, political sociology, applied sociology and mathematical sociology, market research, modern empirical sociology, and four significant research institutes. He is considered a 'founding father' of communication research in the United States through his major publications, influential studies and innovative social research methodologies and techniques. His particular approach to research on the processes and effects of mass communication media, that is, 'administrative research', and his media effects studies and major works gave rise to a series of arguments from his critics, which, rather than deter him, instead helped him to refine the articulation of his methods and goals. Analysis of Lazarsfeld's career shows that throughout his life he was committed to investigating individual behavior in a social context for the betterment of social conditions.

Keywords: Paul Lazarsfeld, communication research, administrative research, Critical School, media effects, research methods

Introduction

How often does a young scholar rise from research institutes that he had to support during the depths of a depression on no income other than market research—rise from that to become head of the best-known communication research institute in the world, director of the Bureau of Applied Social Research, Quételet Professor and Chairman of Sociology at Columbia University, and the only American sociologist on whom the University of Paris has ever conferred an honorary degree? (Chaffee and Rogers, 1997: 45)

Paul Felix Lazarsfeld (1901–1976) began his distinguished career in Europe as a mathematician; later he studied psychology, and eventually he became a prominent American sociologist. An original thinker with a passion for research, he is known as the founder of market research, and, for his innovative quantitative and qualitative empirical social research, the founder of modern empirical sociology.

He was "hearty, humorous, warm, energetic, vital . . . [and] a great entrepreneur" (Chaffee and Rogers, 1997: 43). Although he was "not especially good at handling the details of administration," he was "remarkably capable at getting money to support an ongoing institute or department and even more remarkable at stimulating its members" (Ibid.). He founded four research institutes: Vienna's Research Center for Business Psychology, the Newark University Research Center, the Princeton Office of Radio Research, and the Bureau of Applied Social Research at Columbia University in New York. Additionally, he made key contributions to research in many other areas: unemployment, public opinion, the study of voting behavior, mass media and communications, methodology, political sociology, applied sociology, and mathematical sociology.

From 1949 until 1971, Lazarsfeld taught at Columbia University: "[He] was a brilliant teacher. He trained generations of social scientists to think analytically . . . His major effect was on his apprentices, those who worked on projects he initiated, including writing their dissertations" (Donsbach et al., 2001: 227). According to Rogers (1994: 274), Lazarsfeld[2] was a toolmaker, "generally more interested in the methods of research than in the substantive content that was being studied", and his enthusiasm for tool-making "fit with [his] role in establishing and directing research institutes like the Office of Radio Research and, later, the Bureau of Applied Social Research at Columbia University". As an innovator, Lazarsfeld introduced, in the institutions he founded, distinctive methodological innovations in social science, of which the most important were elaboration formula, program analyzer, mathematical sociology, reason analysis, panel analysis, survey analysis, latent structure analysis, and contextual analysis.

Lazarsfeld was born on February 13, 1901, in Vienna into a politically active, intellectual Jewish family. He was fortunate to grow up in an enlightened and coherent environment. His father, a lawyer, and his mother, a psychologist and writer, enthusiastically embraced the socialist movement. His active participation in political affairs, which spurred him to help organize a League of Socialist Gymnasium Students, was the result of the influence of leaders of the Social Democratic Party in Austria, such as Victor and Friedrich Adler and Paul Renner, who were regular visitors to the Lazarsfeld home.

The path of Lazarsfeld's education was the normal one taken by the upper-middle-class at that time in Europe: grammar school, gymnasium, and university. His outstanding ability in many fields of study made him uncertain about which university subjects to specialize in, until he received a letter from Friedrich Adler advising him to study mathematics. Adler was a strong influence on Lazarsfeld both politically and academically. He was not only a scholar—a mathematician and physicist—who worked on relativity theory even while he was in prison, but also the organizer of the Karl Marx Association in Vienna.

Lazarsfeld, with his mother, Sophie, made frequent visits to Adler while he was imprisoned in Fortress Stein. Lazarsfeld was very excited about these meetings because, at that time, Adler was considered a revolutionary hero. Later he spoke of Adler's effect on him:

> Well, here you know you have a rather glorious hero. Adler corresponded with me. I have a letter . . . I reported to Adler my progress in school and I have a letter from Adler in 1916. I was 15 . . . "Dear Paul, I'm glad to hear that you are doing well in mathematics. Whatever you will do later mathematics will always be useful to you." You see that undoubtedly is of considerable interest if a glorious murderer wrote it to you from jail, to stick at doing mathematics.   (Cited in Morrison, 1998: 37)

Lazarsfeld studied mathematics at the University of Vienna. After graduating, he worked as a mathematics teacher in a gymnasium in Vienna. Around this time, as a result of his superior knowledge of mathematics and statistics, he became the assistant of Charlotte Bühler after attending lectures in psychology given by her and her husband, Karl Bühler.

Many important books and collections of papers have been written on the life and work of Paul F. Lazarsfeld. His best-known biographers are Allen H. Barton, Paul Neurath and David L. Sills. As a testament to Lazarsfeld's intellectual legacy, Paul Neurath[3] assembled a large collection of his written works, along with many other related materials, and organized them into the Paul Lazarsfeld Archive in Vienna, which contains the most complete collection anywhere of Lazarsfeld's books, articles, unpublished manuscripts, letters, records, etc.

Lazarsfeld as Founding Father and Leader

One might be surprised to learn that such an American discipline as market research, a by-product of capitalism, was invented in Europe, specifically in Austria, on the initiative of an eager socialist: Paul Lazarsfeld.

In 1928, due to the University of Vienna's inability to support an institute for research purposes, Lazarsfeld established a research center related to the university with the support of grants from various businesses and associations and the help of the Austrian government, where psychology students and graduates from the University of Vienna worked under his leadership. That group was made up of Marie Jahoda, Hans Zeisel, Gertruda Wagner, Herta Herzog, Lotte Rademacher, and many others. The president of the center was Karl Bühler, professor of psychology at the University of Vienna, and Lazarsfeld himself was the director. In 1931, he officially named the center *Wirtschaftspsychologische Forschungsstelle* ('Research Center for Business Psychology' (Jeřábek, 2001: 231) or 'Research Center for Economic Psychology' (Barton, 2001: 246)). He started with small research projects in the field of market research, a completely new field at that time. This was the major area of specialization for the center. When the center obtained funds from the labor movement for a major study, *The unemployed workers of Marienthal,* conducted by Marie Jahoda, Paul Lazarsfeld, and Hans Zeisel, many field workers and various methods were employed on a large scale. He presented the results of the Marienthal research at a psychology congress in Hamburg in 1932. Also in Vienna, immediately after World War I, Lazarsfeld founded, along with several others, the *Vereinigung Sozialistischer Mittelschüler* (League of Socialist Gymnasium students) (Neurath, 2001: 308).

While Lazarsfeld was engaged in his leading research, Austria saw the rise of the fascists, who initiated a purge of the Austrian Social Democrats. Most of Lazarsfeld's relatives were arrested during the first months of this regime, but in 1933 Lazarsfeld was rescued by the Rockefeller Foundation, which awarded him a fellowship in the U.S. as a result of his work on unemployment and his great experience with market research in Vienna. After taking up residence in the U.S. he would never again return to Austria to live there as a citizen. In 1935 he briefly went back to take his family and some colleagues with him to America.

As an immigrant in the United States, Lazarsfeld looked for a job and an institution in which to pursue his goal of creating methods for understanding the problems of society. Not only did he succeed in that, but also he multiplied his success. As Allen Barton (2001: 248) puts it, "A typically Lazarsfeldian pattern of multiple-role, multiple-location activities ensued". In 1935, Robert Lynd, chair of Columbia University's Department of Sociology, recommended Lazarsfeld to Frank Kingdom, the President of the University of Newark, "for the job of analyzing 10,000 questionnaires collected from unemployed young people by the National Youth Administration" (Barton, 2001: 247). It led Lazarsfeld to create the Newark University Research Center in New Jersey. Subsequently, in 1937 at Princeton University, he became the director of a project studying the impact of radio on American society, on the strength of a similar pioneering study he had carried out in Austria and his expertise in data analysis. At the same time, the Office of Radio Research was established at Princeton, headed by Professor Hadley Cantril. Lazarsfeld was involved as research associate. The radio research project used several of Lazarsfeld's methods as well as a group of his clever assistants. The project applied Lazarsfeld's techniques of cross-tabulation; developed qualitative interview techniques to investigate the listeners' gratification in soap operas and quiz programs; and used content analysis to characterize the programs. Robert Lynd further supported Lazarsfeld for two important positions; first as a lecturer and later as a professor, in the Department of Sociology at Princeton. As a result, the Office of Radio Research was attached to the Department as a research laboratory. In the following years, Lazarsfeld expanded the activities of the research center to include more topics and consequently renamed it in 1944 as the Bureau of Applied Social Research

(BASR), often simply referred to as "The Bureau" (Jeřábek, 2001: 235). Barton (2001: 249) relates that the center started with mainly business-supported studies, and that funding—in the form of grants, mostly from government and partly from foundations and non-profit associations—exceeded $1 million a year by the mid-1960s. Lazarsfeld's influence during the 1950s and 1960s on the institutions of social research, according to Boudon (1993: 1), was significant; without him, institutes of applied social research throughout Eastern and Western Europe, Asia and America would neither work the way they do today nor be as numerous.

Lazarsfeld's expertise in a wide range of fields and many specialized lines of work contributed to his becoming an influential leader to a remarkable group of clever, creative and active intellectuals. The fact that Lazarsfeld's achievements are attributed to groups, not individuals, reflects his team-oriented style of work. He never hid that reality, but instead considered it an ideal way to achieve reliable, objective scientific results that would be useful in the particular area of studies. "Intellectual conflict is always limited by focus on certain topics, and by the search for allies" (Collins, 1998: 1). Lazarsfeld's group consisted of a variety of his colleagues, co-workers, correspondents, co-authors, students, and his eventual successors, hundreds of whom he had educated, trained, and supported, and thousands of whom he had influenced. If his name will be forever connected to his four research institutes or his research workshops, it will also be allied with his colleagues, co-workers and co-authors, either in Vienna or America[4], and his outstanding students and followers[5]. For all of them, Lazarsfeld provided a challenge and an example; with all of them, he shared his knowledge. His best-known biographer, Paul Neurath, said of him:

> If a mighty censor for some reason decided to wipe out that man's work by destroying every single line he had ever written, this censor's work would be in vain. Because there would still be the dozens of books and hundreds of articles by his students and the students of his students, all of which still breathe the spirit of this man's work and from which, if not word for word, nevertheless idea for idea it could all be reconstructed again.   (Cited in Jeřábek, 2001: 230)

In Vienna, in the earlier days of his life, Lazarsfeld, with his first wife Marie Jahoda, launched a group of socialist scholars dedicated to developing research methodology towards the goal of social development, a goal which would enhance their progress in social research. Later in America, Lazarsfeld influenced his colleagues and students, in the Columbia Bureau of Applied Social Research for example, in many ways. According to Chaffee and Rogers (1997: 63), Lazarsfeld influenced Katz as a teacher and research supervisor; Merton by helping to provide money and a staff for field research, and a stimulating atmosphere in which to work; and Coleman, Klapper, and Herzog by providing a place to work where they could exercise their creativity and interact with others.

The fruitful cooperation between Lazarsfeld and his colleagues can be evidenced by a number of examples, of which four will suffice here. First, according to Glander

(2000: 83), the relationship between Stanton, the CBS mass communications researcher and subsequent network executive, and Lazarsfeld, the university-based mass communications researcher, was a long, important, and contingent one[6], and it facilitated many personal as well as institutional collaborations. Second, Robert Smith (2001: 286) gives an account of how Lazarsfeld and Katz in their *Personal influence* (1955), among their many collaborations, established that some people were opinion leaders and others were not, and tested the idea of the two-step flow of influence. Third, Grunig (1996: 460) describes how, in 1969, Lazarsfeld and Menzel established a framework for research in the social sciences that offered special promise for studying public relations by adding a new level of analysis: the structural or relational. Fourth, Lazarsfeld was, according to David Sills (1996: 113), the co-author of both of Merton's major papers on mass communication—a wartime study of propaganda in 1943 and a study of conflicts between advocates of popular culture and high culture in 1948[7].

The fear of propaganda in the years surrounding World War I, which was increased by the sophistication of advertising and public relations, resulted in the emergence of mass communication research. Wilbur Schramm, the founder of the field of communication, identified Paul Lazarsfeld, among others (Kurt Lewin, Harold Lasswell, and Carl Hovland), as a 'founding father' of communication research in the United States. Though they came from different disciplines—sociology, psychology, political science, and experimental psychology, respectively—Schramm (1996: 125) asserted that they were united in their determination to explore the causes and effects of communication. Given that Schramm's view of communication research, according to Hardt (1992: 86), was "quantitative, rather than speculative" and that he saw "practitioners [as being] deeply interested in theory, but in the theory they can test", he considered the four founding fathers as behavioral researchers who "are trying to find out something about why humans behave as they do, and how communication can make it possible for them to live together more happily and productively". Hardt (1992: 101–102) argues that Schramm's admiration of Lazarsfeld's work at Columbia University, especially his approach to a systematic, efficient and practical analysis of the media, led him to establish a similar research bureau at the University of Iowa, before he moved to the University of Illinois and founded the Institute of Communication Research. Schramm's conviction of the importance of Lazarsfeld's notion of communication research, which led him to apply the same concept during his career at the University of Illinois and Stanford University, was expressed in the dedication in his book *Mass Communications* (1949) to Lazarsfeld, "who has done perhaps more than any other man toward bringing the social sciences to bear on the problems of communications".

Lazarsfeld's contribution to the field of communication research became more concentrated in 1937 when he launched the Princeton Radio Project to examine the influence of radio broadcasting on listeners[8]. This project had three important results, as Barton (2001: 251–252) explains. First, it established the field of mass communications research; second, it discovered psychological and social mecha-nisms theoretically general-izable beyond the field of radio-listening behavior; and third, it disclosed the inadequacy of simple cross-sectional surveys to answer questions on the effects of media exposure. Lazarsfeld used the data of commer-cial consumer studies, public opinion polling, and radio audience surveys as "the raw material for the new field of communication and opinion research" (Chaffee and Rogers, 1997: 54). In fact, his contribution to the field of mass media studies helped to accelerate the analysis of media effects on society. Many researchers and theorists of that period believed that it was increasingly necessary to investigate and explain social processes in order to find solutions for social, political and eco-nomic problems. Hardt (1992: 100), who considers Lazarsfeld a major force in the definition of modern communication research, argues that while Schramm defined the parameters of the field through the continuous publication of text-books, Lazarsfeld delivered the social-scientific expertise and new insights into the role of communication in American society and helped establish the credibil-ity of the field as a social-scientific endeavor in the university environment.

Lazarsfeld's enormous contribution to the field of mass communications research, which has been widely recognized and acknowledged by his former stu-dents and colleagues[9], differed in certain key respects from Dewey's intellectual contribution to the field of American mass communication theory. John Durham Peters (1989: 200) considers the social thought of John Dewey and the social research conducted by Paul Lazarsfeld and his associates as two major move-ments in the development of American mass communication theory. For Peters, Dewey stands for the social thought of the American Progressive Era (the 1890s through the 1920s) and Lazarsfeld for the early days of American mass communi-cation research (the 1940s and 1950s). Peters (1986: 533–534) believes that social science became increasingly technical and less concerned with the moral ques-tions, and, that after Dewey, it was simply the precise codification of his prophetic visions. Peters claims that Lazarsfeld was the symbol of this transformation from prophet to priest, both in forms of social science and conceptions of communica-tion, because he was instrumental in inventing both new kinds of research and new research institutions. Peters argues that due to Lazarsfeld's being an immi-grant, he was unaware of the tradition of American social thought that had been in the making for nearly half a century, and thus his research on communication had little to do with the speculations on democracy and the great community so important in previous American social thought. Moreover, Lazarsfeld's arrival in the United States coincided with the transformation of the meaning and domain of communication in American life, CBS radio and the FCC being the telling symbols. At that time, Peters argues, the previously key part of a theory of democratic social organization, communication, came to refer to a collection of institutions and tech-nologies, the mass media. On the other hand, "communication in Dewey's sense is participation in the creation of a collective world, which is why communication for Dewey always raises the political problem of democracy" (Peters, 1999: 19).

Dewey doubted that democracy could survive in an urbanized mass society unless certain of the essentials of the rural community could be restored (Rogers, 1994: 163). Dewey's main agreement with critics of U.S. life, Glander (2000: 18) explains, was that he regarded the U.S. movement toward quantification, mechanization, and standardization as a pervasive money culture that subordinated human values to pecuniary interests, in the service of which technology and the notion of individualism had been put. Nevertheless, Dewey hoped that the media of communication might re-create public life, might bring a great community of rational public discourse into existence (Carey, 1996: 36).

Lazarsfeld's Mathematical Background and the Originality of Social Research

Randall Collins (1998: 697) explains that, although the widespread belief among leading mathematicians in the 1780s was that "mathematics had exhausted itself, that there was little left to discover," the following century "was the most flamboyant in the history of the field, proliferating new areas and opening the realms of abstract higher mathematics. The sudden expansion of creativity arose from shifts in the social bases of mathematics." Collins (1998: 536) puts mathematics as one of the two alternative routes to rapid-discovery science, the other is laboratory technology. He calls the invention of the techniques of rapid discovery "scientific revolution," which, he argues (1998: 559), came later than the mathematical revolution[10]. He situates (Ibid.) the mathematical revolution as a fourth link in the chain of successive innovations that began with astronomy, followed by medical physiology and chemistry.

Collins (1998: 538) argues that the chief dynamic of scientific discovery is new technology or equipment rather than theory; for example, he says, the great scientific advances of the 1600s began with Galileo's use of the telescope to discover new phenomena in astronomy. Meanwhile, mathematics as an alternative route to rapid-discovery science is another key to the scientific revolution. While Collins (1998: 538) accepts that the two routes may coincide—"many aspects of the scientific revolution of the 1600s and 1700s were carried out not only by experiment but also by formulating quantitative principles for the results"—he also argues that they were not identical: "Traditional mathematical science, such as astronomy among the Greeks, Chinese, or Indians, does not have the characteristics of consensus and rapid discovery which are central to modern science". He claims, therefore, that mathematics in general are not sufficient to bring about consensus-making, fast-moving science, but can accomplish only a specific aspect of it, mathematics as a research technology. In this way the mathematical revolution spreads, since technology is a set of embodied practices which lead to reliable and repeatable results. Collins (1998: 557) asserts that the increasing interest in mathematics came from practical interests: "The take-off of math occurred when it became an intellectual game as well as a matter of practical application".

If Collins' two claims that "innovative mathematicians emerged in the philosophical networks" (1998: 557) and that "all of the important philosophers were at least connected to one or more circles" (1998: 531) are true, then Lazarsfeld can be considered both an innovative mathematician and an important philosopher. Lazarsfeld, in relation to other European philosophers and social scientists, called himself "a 'European positivist' who had been influenced by Ernest Mach, Henri Poincaré and Albert Einstein, and who felt intellectually close to members of the Vienna Circle"[11] (Hardt, 1992: 99). In addition to Lazarsfeld's studying mathematics at the university, which led to his dissertation *"The movement of the perihelion of Mercury in the light of Einstein's theory of relativity"* (Barton, 2001: 246), he also studied psychology and was influenced by his professors Charlotte Bühler and Karl Bühler. Henceforth, Lazarsfeld perceived that social psychology would be a useful scientific method for understanding human behavior. At this point, his mathematical knowledge effectively helped him to analyze the behavioral data gathered in human action studies.

Lazarsfeld (1954b: 3) asserted the increased interest in the role of mathematical thinking in the social sciences. He saw two sources of that increased interest: "The success of mathematics in the natural sciences is a lure for the younger social sciences, and the prestige and charm of mathematical work a temptation for many of its practitioners . . .[12] In addition, sociologists and social psychologists have increasingly felt the need for a more rigid and precise language". In his 1966 study with Neil Henry, Lazarsfeld gave two examples of where that increased interest in mathematics was being applied to the social sciences: economics and psychology. Economists have worked with mathematical formulations of their theories for a long time, and psychologists have used mathematical tools in certain aspects of their work, especially in the development of tests and in psychophysics. For Lazarsfeld, the increasing development of mathematical models in disciplines that were known behavioral sciences, especially social psychology, sociology, and political science, was something new. Functions of those models were sometimes used to provide a language to clarify the assumptions behind, and the consequences of, ideas that were vague when expressed in conventional verbal terms; and, in other cases, to represent real theories of their own that could be tested against empirical data. Lazarsfeld saw an additional reason for some social scientists' interest in mathematical formulations: mathematics had played a crucial role in the growth of the physical sciences and was becoming increasingly important in biological work.

In his paper "A conceptual introduction to latent structure analysis" (1954a: 349–350), for example, Lazarsfeld dealt with the application of a mathematical model to one problem of measurement in the social sciences. He used a measurement, which he called 'the procedure of itemized tests', that consists of making a number of qualitative observations on a person, and then attributing to him/her a 'measure' of some kind by which s/he can be compared with other persons who have also undergone the test. He assumed that all items of observation are of a dichotomous nature. He focused on answering the question of how such sets of qualitative observations are translated into measurement. For him, the purpose of latent structure analysis is to provide mathematical models by which the various uses of itemized tests can be related to each other, mainly to bring out the assumptions which are implicit in that type of measurement. Lazarsfeld's main claim in that study (1954a: 350) was that "latent structure analysis puts practices and discussions in the measurement field into reasonable axiomatic form, and that its axioms permit algebraic operations which lead to hitherto unobserved relationships and suggest more precise meanings of the notion of measurement in the social sciences".

> Empirical knowledge which is applicable to man . . . [which] we may still term 'human sciences' . . . has a relation to mathematics: like any other domain of knowledge, these sciences may, in certain conditions, make use of mathematics as a tool; some of their procedures and a certain number of their results can be formalized. It is undoubtedly of the greatest importance to know those tools, to be able to practise those formalizations and to define the levels upon which they can be performed.
> (Foucault, 1994: 349)

Michel Foucault (1994: 246) discusses two fields of sciences; *a priori* sciences and *a posteriori* sciences. He explains that the field of *a priori* sciences is "pure formal sciences, deductive sciences based on logic and mathematics", while the domain of *a posteriori* sciences is "empirical sciences, which employ the deductive forms only in fragments and in strictly localized regions". He gives (1994: 349) historical examples of the use of mathematics as a tool in human sciences; in politics, Condorcet was able to apply the calculation of probabilities to politics; in psychology, contemporary psychologists make use of information theory in order to understand the phenomena of learning.

> Modern philosophies are heavily influenced by the expansion of science . . . Mathematics had become the intellectual network which had achieved the highest degree of self-consciousness on its structures of argument . . . Mathematical logic was a tangential interest among mathematicians as among philosophers, and it is a good question how this obscure area became the defining identity of a large movement of twentieth-century philosophers.
> (Collins, 1998: 695–696)

For Collins (1998: 533–535), European rapid-discovery science was the reason for the sharpening of the difference between science and philosophy. He sees the crucial difference as the heightened degree of consensus in science. He argues that philosophical controversies tend to remain unresolved while science arrives at agreement and social consensus. He calls science before and after the scientific revolution 'traditional science' and 'rapid-discovery science,' respectively. The social conditions that Collins suggests as possibilities that lead to the combination of rapid research and consensus on older results are *empiricism*, *research technology*, and *mathematics*. Collins (1998: 382) argues that there were two main networks that together produced a current stream of new phenomena for scientific research: the scientific and mathematical research network associated with the network of genealogies of machines and techniques. In sum, "rapid-discovery science is not just a network of persons or of ideas; it is the connection between the human network and a genealogy of research technologies" (Collins 1998: 535).

On the basis of his pioneering work in the field, Lazarsfeld, according to Jeřábek (2001: 236–239), is considered "the co-founder of mathematical sociology". In the early 1950s, Lazarsfeld produced three major works on mathematical sociology. Excerpts from his mathematically oriented lectures on methodology were brought together in the first work, *Mathematical thinking in the social sciences* (1954). In 1966, Lazarsfeld and Neil Henry edited the second, *Readings in mathematical social science.* The third, in Italian with Vittorio Capecchi, *Metodologia e ricerca sociologica,* was published in 1967. During the 1960s and 1970s Lazarsfeld concentrated his work on the applications of sociology to many different aspects of social life and co-authored two influential books, *The uses of sociology* (1967) and *An introduction to applied sociology* (1975). In 1973 he published *Main trends in sociology.*

Lazarsfeld participated in the history of sociological research in various ways. In 1962 he published *Notes on the history of quantification in sociology: Trends, sources and problems.* Then, in cooperation with his students, he wrote two important studies. One in 1965, with Anthony Oberschall, on Max Weber and his significance in the field of empirical sociological research; and the other in 1968 with David Landau about Adolphe Quételet, who was important for the beginnings of sociology. The persistence of Lazarsfeld's efforts in the field of empirical sociological research are described in books by his younger colleagues A. Oberschall, Susan Schad, S. Cole, and T N. Clark.

[Paul Lazarsfeld is] the founder of modern empirical sociology . . . Without him, sociology today would not know terms and concepts such as panel study, opinion leader, latent structure analysis, program analyzer, elaboration formula, reason analysis, and many others. Lazarsfeld's influence on empirical sociological research, market and public opinion research, and communication research has been much stronger than most of us realize. He belongs to the small set of scholars whose work led to results that in time became so well-accepted that today we consider them to be self-evident.   (Jeřábek, 2001: 229)

Lazarsfeld did much to codify empirical research methods to create a professional school of social research: "Lazarsfeld's prime concern with methodology was embodied in a series of projects for *codification* of social research methods, by which he meant the documentation of examples accompanied by logical analysis" (Barton, 2001: 260). One of the major consequences of his thorough understanding of social research was a systematic social-scientific study of a new medium, the radio, and its social and political impact on society.

Lazarsfeld's Creative Energy, Cultural Capital, and Fundamental Ideas

For the purpose of this discussion, it is useful here to clarify the distinction between the concepts of creation and innovation. Creation, or invention, on the one hand, according to Margret Boden (1994: 75), is mysterious for two reasons. First, inventors rarely know how their original ideas arise, nor can psychologists tell us much about it; and second, the very concept is seemingly paradoxical. To 'create,' according to the dictionary definition, means "to bring into being or form out of nothing". Thus, for Boden, creation seems not only to be beyond any scientific understanding, but even impossible. So, she is not surprised that some people explain it in terms of divine inspiration and others in terms of some kind of romantic intuition or insight. Hans Eysenck (1994: 200), on the other hand, claims that there is a good deal of agreement on what we mean by creation. Creativity, he says, denotes "a person's capacity to produce new or original ideas, insights, inventions, or artistic products, which are accepted by experts as being of scientific, aesthetic, social, or technical value".

Innovation is defined by Lawrence Mohr (1969: 112) as "the successful introduction into an applied situation of means or ends that are new to that situation". For Mohr, the major distinction between creation or invention and innovation is that creation implies bringing something new into being, while innovation implies bringing something new into use. Collins (1998: 31) brings together these two distinct aspects of 'newness' in his analysis of how an intellectual succeeds in the struggle for ritual centrality: 'My ideas are new' and 'My ideas are important'. For him, the judgment of one generation upon another is an indication of the interest of other people in these ideas, and speaks to their creativity.

Given Lazarsfeld's multifarious achievements as a founder of new research fields and creator of new methodologies and techniques for use in social, psychological, and political research, this research study argues that Lazarsfeld was both a creative scholar and an innovative methodologist. Merton (1979: 19) describes him as "one of the most innovative social scientists of our time". This section of the study investigates Lazarsfeld's cultural capital combined with the creative and emotional energy he shared with his colleagues by shedding light on some of Lazarsfeld's work; major publications, influential studies and innovative methodologies.

Collins (1998: 14, 22–23, 29, 32–33, 45, 379) explains that intellectual creativity occurs at the center of networks where members of chains of personal contacts pass emotional energy and cultural capital from generation to generation. He considers the most successful intellectuals those who tend to be linked together across periods of time in such a way that the cultural capital of each one is built on the accomplishment of his or her predecessors. These people, charged up with emotional energy and cultural capital, occupy a small number of centers of attention (ritual centrality). By emotional energy (EE), Collins means the result (a kind of strength) of a successful interaction ritual (IR). This interaction ritual consists of six components: 1) a physical assembly of a group of at least two people, 2) who focus attention on the same object, 3) share a common mood or emotion, 4) intensify both focus of attention and common mood, 5) consequently feel as members of a group, and 6) are filled with emotional energy for the intensity of the interaction. For Collins, emotional energy is a continuum ranging from a high level of confidence or enthusiasm (positive self-feelings), through a lesser emotional intensity in the middle level, to a low level of depression or lack of initiative (negative self-feelings). He considers emotional energy as a feature of creativity by assuming that its social distribution through eminent intellectuals, which means having access to a large amount of cultural capital and recombining it into new ideas and discoveries, would make creativity a matter of emotional energy in using cultural capital. This means, for him, that individuals who have high access to cultural capital through their previous experience, their teachers, and their participation in social networks have high emotional energy. Cultural capital, for Collins, is constituted of a "symbolic repertoire" of "abstraction and reification"—the result of intellectuals' exposure to cosmopolitan or social situations—of different generalized and particularized contents. Figure 1, Ideational Network of Paul Felix Lazarsfeld, illustrates the complex network of intellectual chains of contact which linked Lazarsfeld, in the center, with his predecessors, his colleagues, and his successors.

Lazarsfeld's major publications and influential studies dealt with market research, unemployment, research methodology, and communications research. During the 52 years, beginning with his first book with Wagner in 1924 until his death in 1976, Lazarsfeld wrote two dozen scholarly monographs, which have been translated into English, German, French, Italian, Japanese and Korean; authored and co-authored more than twelve symposia and anthologies; and published over 600 scholarly articles and studies (Jeřábek, 2001: 230, 237). In 1929, to meet the needs of his students at the university and in the research center, Lazarsfeld wrote what was probably the first textbook in Europe on the practical elements of mathematical statistics aimed at social scientists, entitled *Statistisches Praktikum für Psychotogen und Lehrer* (A Handbook of Statistical Methods for Psychologists and Teachers) (Jeřábek, 2001: 231). In his first research monograph, *Jugend und Beruf,* in 1931, he presented a picture of the proletarian consumers. Later, Lazarsfeld published three anthologies which were particularly significant for the teaching of the methodology of sociological research: *The language of social research* with Morris Rosenberg in 1955; a three-volume publication entitled *Méthodes de la sociologie* with Raymond Boudon between 1965 and 1970; and *Continuities in the language of social research* with Ann Pasanella and Morris Rosenberg in 1972. In these texts, Lazarsfeld put everything he considered fundamental for supporting the Columbia strategy of social research and thus for his concept of the analytical research paradigm in sociology. Lazarsfeld's work on general methodology, the history of empirical sociological research, and other qualitative issues was published in many articles and in two major books: *Philosophie des Sciences Sociales* by

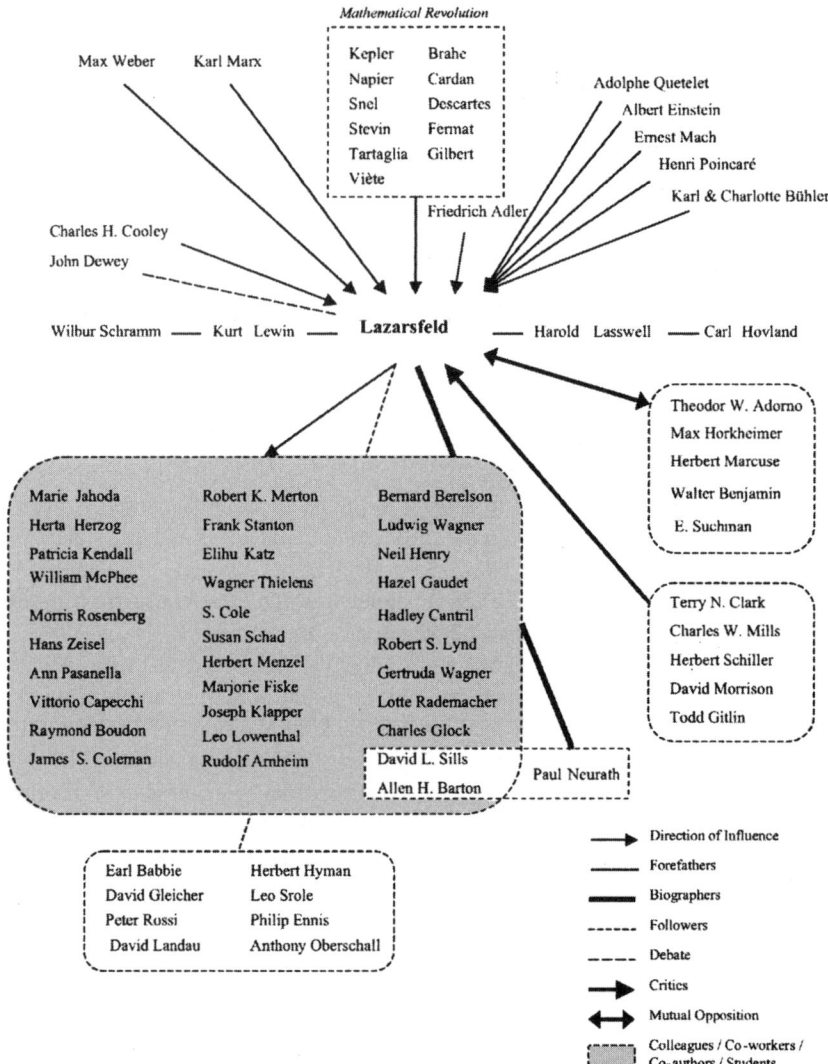

Figure 1 Ideational Network of Paul Felix Lazarsfeld

Raymond Boudon in 1970, which focused on Lazarsfeld's philosophical and methodological studies; and *Qualitative analysis: Historical and critical essays* in 1972, which emphasized Lazarsfeld's interests in sociological knowledge as a whole. Also, Lazarsfeld and his colleagues, such as Berelson, Gaudet, and Katz, focused their studies on the role of the media in influencing voters' decisions, the bias of the press in political campaign coverage, the influence of political advertising, the importance of the media in setting the agenda for public policy deliberation or political decision-making, and many other areas.

With Merton at Columbia, Lazarsfeld co-authored two major papers on mass communication. The first, in 1943, a wartime study of propaganda, summarized and re-conceptualized many studies of the impact of radio broadcasts and propaganda films on listeners (Sills, 1996: 113). The second, in 1948, *Mass communication, popular taste and organized social action,* offered an analysis[13] of 'culture wars'; its core theme dealt with the main functions of mass media in society. Lazarsfeld and Merton examined the social role of the press and then asked: "What role can be assigned to the mass media by virtue of the fact that they exist?" (Peterson, 1996: 91). They found that mass media perform three highly significant social functions for the society: status conferral, enforcement of social norms, and narcotizing dysfunction (Sills, 1996: 113; Schiller, 1996: 57; Peterson, 1996: 91). Mass media, they observed, first confer status on individuals, issues, organizations, and social movements whether deserved or not; second, help enforce social norms by forcing each individual to take a stand, because the publicity that the media give to deviant social behavior closes the gap between private attitudes and public morality; and third, degrade listeners and viewers into passivity instead of energizing them. As to the structure of ownership and operation, according to Schiller, Lazarsfeld, and Merton explained that because in the United States the mass media are supported by large business concerns geared to the current social and economic system, it was only to be expected that the media would contribute to the maintenance of that system, specifically by restraining the development of a genuinely critical outlook or by cultivating conformism.

Lazarsfeld conducted three key studies using theoretical models to guide his studies of voting and social influence and the cumulative empirical findings: *The people's choice: How the voter makes up his mind in a presidential campaign* in 1944; *Personal influence* in 1955; and *Voting* in 1954. *The people's choice,* written in collaboration with Bernard Berelson and Hazel Gaudet, measured the influence of the media on 600 voters in Erie County, Ohio, during the presidential campaign of 1940. The survey used a seven-wave panel of 600 respondents and three control groups.

> Public opinion research is frequently misunderstood at the present time . . . Social scientists want to know the process by which the various sectors of public opinion influence legislative action and other decision-making in government. Furthermore, we are eager to discover in what ways attitudes themselves are formed. *The people's choice* focused its attention on this latter problem, the formation, change and development of public opinion.   (Lazarsfeld, Berelson, and Gaudet, 1964b: 231)

The authors were mainly interested in exploring mediators in the communication process and evaluating their influence on the media effects, and in ascertaining how the electorate made their voting decisions in presidential elections. "We are interested here in all those conditions which determine the political behavior of people. Briefly, our problem is this: to discover how and why people decided to vote as they did. What were the major influences upon them during the campaign of 1940?" (Lazarsfeld, Berelson, and Gaudet, 1968: 1). This work was instrumental in guiding academic interest toward the mechanisms of personal influence[14]. According to Smith (2001: 281, 285), Lazarsfeld in this study tested his presumptive stimulus-response psychological model, which he had derived[15] from his early research with Stanton in 1944 on the effects of radio, which suggests that people choose candidates the way they choose what products to buy. The authors realized that the "campaign activated the indifferent, reinforced the partisan, and converted the doubtful". By the end of their study, they had hypothesized that there was a two-step flow of communications; ideas flowed from the mass media to opinion leaders, and then from them to the less-interested populace.

Adopting the conclusions of *The people's choice*, Lazarsfeld and Elihu Katz co-authored *Personal influence*, which examined voting behavior as well as the behavior of consumers in choosing consumer goods, fashion, and leisure activities, especially films. They studied[16] individual decision processes using reason analysis of a socio-metric survey of a target group of 800 women living in Decatur, Illinois, a city of 60,000. As in the previous study, they discovered the importance of 'primary groups'—a concept originated by Charles H. Cooley (Mattelart, 1999: 91; Schiller, 1996: 60)—and they understood the flow of communication as a two-stage process where the role of 'opinion leaders' was essential. The hypothesis of two-step flow suggested that "ideas often flow *from* radio and print *to* the opinion leaders and *from* them *to* the less active sections of the population" (Katz and Lazarsfeld, 1955: 309). On the first level of the model are those who are relatively well-informed, because they are exposed directly to the media; on the second are those who have less contact with the media and depend on others to obtain information. 'Opinion leaders,' who are recruited from the first level, retransmit information to the second group via interpersonal channels. The authors criticized their precursors for relying on a concept of society inscribed as amorphous social organization having a scarcity of interpersonal relations.

Lazarsfeld came back to the topic of voting behavior, which had interested him in Austria with its socialist versus conservative politics, in the context of the politics of America's New Deal liberalism versus Republican conservatism. Berelson, Lazarsfeld, and McPhee's *Voting: A study of opinion formation in a presidential campaign* (1954) contained the most fruitful results in research on voting behavior. Using a four-wave panel design of a thousand respondents, they studied how citizens in Elmira, New York, voted in the 1948 election. With this work, they refined the results of the two previous studies, *The people's choice* and *Personal influence*. Smith (2001: 286–287) explains that *Voting* focused on the formation of intentions and their implementation, that is, how social influence processes transformed the voting intentions into final electoral choices. In *Voting*, Lazarsfeld refined his psychological model of the voter as one of stimulus-predisposition-organism-response. The stimuli are the issues and propaganda of the campaign. The citizens selectively perceive and evaluate these issues in terms of their predispositions, which they had previously learned through a process of political socialization. Given that the political parties represent the interests of different social strata, and alliances with different social strata influence political pre-dispositions, partisan pre-dispositions tend to be aligned with one party or the other. Then the political campaign combines the political stimuli with these pre-dispositions to create an activated state in the citizen, who may have an intention to vote for one party or the other, or not to vote at all. In a later study, these authors confirmed the importance of group membership, in contrast to rational judgment, in voter decision.

> Many voters vote not for principle in the usual sense but 'for' a group to which they are attached—their group . . . The democratic citizen is expected to exercise rational judgment in coming to his voting decision. He is expected to have arrived at his principles by reason and to have considered rationally the implications and alleged consequences of the alternative proposals of the contending parties.
>
> (Berelson, Lazarsfeld, and McPhee, 1971: 32)

During the period of McCarthyism when the Ford Foundation wanted to discover the effects of McCarthyism and other political pressures on professors in the social sciences, Lazarsfeld organized a survey in universities and colleges. For his last major empirical study, *The academic mind: Social scientists in a time of crisis* (1958), Lazarsfeld, in cooperation with Thielens, conducted a study of the attitudes and behavior of university professors when academic freedom was threatened. Lazarsfeld considered this work a chance to draw cluster samples of professors from a large number of colleges and universities (Barton, 2001: 259). He found it possible to measure the attitude climate of each institution and the formal institutional characteristics. In the study, each college's social science faculty was treated as a small community which could be characterized by aggregating the responses of its members; their own attitudes and behavior, their reports of local incidents threatening academic freedom, and the response of the college administration. The data of this study later contributed to a methodological paper presented by Lazarsfeld and Menzel in 1961 entitled *On the relationship between individual and collective properties.* The authors of *Academic mind* in a later study explained that they wished in that work to classify social scientists according to a concept which might be called their "eminence" (Lazarsfeld and Thielens, 1972: 62). They believed that such a concept, which they said they had "taken over from everyday language", could be translated into a research instrument in many ways.

Lazarsfeld's Innovative Methodologies: An Overview

Lazarsfeld's concern with reference group theory led him to the methodological idea of contextual sampling and analysis. This methodological approach, according to Jeřábek (2001: 238–239), emphasizes a combined analysis of data gathered from the responses of individuals and of global characteristics describing a collective (group) as a whole. Before developing contextual analysis, Lazarsfeld's first original contribution to the research procedures of the empirical sociologist was *reason analysis.* Lazarsfeld first described this method in his now famous article of 1935, *The art of asking why* (Jeřábek, 2001: 233). Reason analysis uses an individual strategy to ascertain the reasons and motives that lead somebody to a particular type of behavior, decision, or deed. This analysis had been applied to market research and was later applied to voting preferences.

The panel technique is another development in social research introduced by Lazarsfeld to overcome the ambiguity of time-order in surveys whose purpose is to relate communications exposure to attitudes and behavior. Lazarsfeld's methodological contributions to panel analysis were numerous. He explained its essentials as "[consisting] of repeated interviews made with the same group of persons. The people participating as subjects in such studies are commonly known as panel members and the whole procedure has become widely known under the name of panel technique" (Lazarsfeld, 1972b: 330). This technique is mainly used in two types of research problems or situations; firstly, when the effect of some specific event or series of events is to be studied; and secondly, in a situation that results from cross-pressures in a complex society as our own, where the individual must harmonize the different elements of his experience. Lazarsfeld realized that re-interviewing a sample of people could provide time-ordered measurements of variables, thus creating quasi-experiments in natural settings (Barton, 2001: 253). This panel method uncovered certain social processes that fed into a middle-range theory of influence on decisions: the effects of cross-pressures on decision-making; opinion leadership and the two-step flow of communication; and the effects of interpersonal environments.

Lazarsfeld and Frank Stanton, the psychologist who created the research department of the Columbia Broadcasting System (CBS) in the late 1930s and early 1940s, invented the Program Analyzer. This was an electronic device that permitted researchers to measure audience reactions to various media stimulation by recording second-by-second the likes and dislikes of captive audiences, who were then asked to explain their reactions in group interviews (Barton, 2001: 248; Glander, 2000: 83). Thus the Program Analyzer provided a means by which the success or failure of planned programming could be predicted. It was a useful device for conducting formative evaluation of radio broadcasts so that the effectiveness of the radio message could be improved by revision.

Snowball sampling was developed by Lazarsfeld and his colleagues in the Bureau as a way to overcome the limitations of random sampling; specifically, as Sills (1996: 110) explains, in order to trace patterns of influence from person to person. Sample members are asked to identify persons who had influenced them in the formation of an opinion. Afterwards, these persons are interviewed about the discussion reported by the first respondent. The method makes possible the identification and analysis of interpersonal networks. Again, the need to overcome the difficulties of snowball sampling of interaction partners led Lazarsfeld and his students to find situations in which one could reliably identify' who interacts with whom: the 'dense sampling' method[17].

Survey analysis, the methodology of multivariate statistical analysis of survey samples, according to Jeřábek (2001: 235), was clearly Lazarsfeld's masterpiece. It is quite frequently referred to as the *elaboration formula*, a detailed analysis or elaboration of parallel active influences. Lazarsfeld's 1955 article *The interpretation of statistical relations as a research operation* explained the essence of the approach[18], which lies in the gradual search for deeper and deeper bases in the social reality under observation. Hypotheses on causal links between observed phenomena are submitted to empirical tests, while the influence of other observed variables is controlled. Lazarsfeld published, with his third wife Patricia Kendall, an article entitled *Problems of survey analysis,* in which the principles of the approach are presented in detail.

Latent structure analysis was another of Lazarsfeld's famous contributions to the methodology of multi-dimensional analysis of data. Lazarsfeld saw the essence of this method as the search for response patterns to dichotomized questions (Jeřábek, 2001: 236–237). The concluding phase in the application of this method involves determining the latent classes, within which basic variables are not correlated. These classes are then ordered according to trace lines. In *Voting,* Lazarsfeld developed an empirical measure of class-consciousness in Americans, of which he commented, "Such a measure could lead to some intriguing comparisons among different regions and occupational groups" (1972a: 41). In addition to latent structure analysis, Lazarsfeld's model of the *dichotomical cube* is also of great significance. With the aid of this design, the mutual relationships[19] of three dichotomous variables are examined.

Criticism of Lazarsfeld's Work

Intellectual life is first of all conflict and disagreement . . . Conflict is the energy source of intellectual life, and conflict is limited by itself . . . Conflicts are the lifeblood of the intellectual world . . . [Intellectuals'] focus is on truth, and they attack their predecessors and compatriots for failing to arrive at it. (Collins, 1998: 1, 80)

Lazarsfeld described (1972c: 155–159) his particular approach to research on the processes and effects of mass communication media as 'administrative research':

During the last two decades the media of mass communication . . . have become some of the best-known . . . spheres of modern society. Careful studies have revealed the size of the audiences of all major radio programs and the composition of this audience . . . The circulations of newspapers and magazines are recorded by specially organized research outfits . . . A number of important new techniques have been developed . . . Modern sampling techniques . . . have made great progress . . . Interviewing techniques have been greatly refined . . . Behind the idea of such research is the notion that modern media of communication are tools handled by people or agencies for given purposes . . . Research of the kind described so far could well be called *administrative research.* It is carried through in the service of some kind of administrative agency of public or private character.

By introducing the notion and practice of administrative research, Lazarsfeld came head to head with members of the Frankfurt School, particularly the significant critical scholars Theodor Adorno, Max Horkheimer, Walter Benjamin, and Herbert Marcuse, who had developed the idea of critical research. Peters (1999: 223) considers the debate which ensued between Lazarsfeld and the Frankfurt scholars as "the key conflict in the history of mass communication theory in this century". While Lazarsfeld credited Horkheimer with the idea of critical research, he did not pursue its theoretical implications for media research. At the same time, Lazarsfeld respected Adorno intellectually, writing to his co-directors of the Radio Research Project, Hadley Cantril and Frank Stanton, that it was "a great relief to me to have someone around whose problem is that he has too many ideas and not too few" (cited in Morrison, 1998: 109). For his part, Adorno was not willing to take Lazarsfeld's administrative research seriously, referring to the Lazarsfeld-Stanton program analyzer as 'that machine', and expressing his great reluctance to study the empirical audience, certainly not by 'that machine'. His concentration was on the text, and not the audience.

Hardt (2001: 13) argues that the division between critical-intellectual and administrative-bureaucratic views of communication and media resulted from the emerging antithesis of utopia and reality. One of the debates played out between the Frankfurt and Vienna Schools concerned the appropriate method for communication research after the war. While the critical view seeks to make practice conform to theory, it is more interested in general principles, and is based on specific human values. The administrative view, on the other hand, is characterized by its empirical basis and the fact that practice or action is more important than theoretical propositions. From the administrative point of view, there are strong ties between existing economic and political powers in society and, generally, between them and the social forces that support the established order. According to Stevenson (1996: 184) and Fortner (1994: 217), Lazarsfeld's administrative research was probing the crucial links between the mass media and the power structure of society. On the critical research side, the focus was on the use of communication to maintain political and economic power systems at the national or global level and was disdainful of empirical data and the scholar's traditional aloofness from political activism. Meanwhile, the administrative side relied on sophisticated data analysis to generate fragments of middle-range theories, unconcerned with the broader issues of distribution of wealth and power. Lazarsfeld (1972c: 160) defined how critical theory was distinguished from administrative research in two respects: critical theory "develops a theory of the prevailing social trends of our times, general trends which yet require consideration in any concrete research problem; and it seems to imply ideas of basic human values according to which all actual or desired effects should be appraised"[20]. Although it is generally agreed that critical theory and administrative research should be different views, Rosengren (1989: 35) argues that they are similar in that both are instrumental; administrative research is carried out in the interest of those in power; critical research is carried out in the interest of those without power.

Here this study begins a discussion of the major criticisms of Lazarsfeld's work and ideas on two levels. The first level covers critiques by Theodor W. Adorno of Lazarsfeld's *Administrative research,* by Charles W. Mills of *Abstract empiricism,* and by Terry N. Clark of the *Columbia sociology machine.* The second level explores the critique of Lazarsfeld's media effects studies and his major works, *The people's choice, Personal influence, Two-Step-Flow,* etc., by several scholars, but mainly by Todd Gitlin.

The criticism of Lazarsfeld's notion of administrative research by Adorno, an important representative of the Frankfurt school, goes back to 1941 when Lazarsfeld first formulated the dilemma of administrative versus critical research. Mattelart (1999: 202) explains that administrative research had long masked the theoretical poverty of empiricist sociology, a sociology that Adorno had considered to be incapable of epistemological distance as a result of having reduced the notion of methodology to technical practices of research. Hardt (1992: 109) argues that Lazarsfeld's definition of critical research ignored the historical nature of critical research in the tradition of the Frankfurt School and failed to consider the role of culture in the positioning of the media, opting instead for his own ideological position. However, Donsbach et al. (2001: 227) defend Lazarsfeld against Adorno in that Lazarsfeld concentrated particularly on the relationship between concepts and empirical indicators: "How do we construct scales of different concepts?"

Mills, in his famous 1959 work *Sociological imagination,* criticized Lazarsfeld's 'abstract empiricism.' Rogers (1994: 312) explains that the source of hostility against Lazarsfeld's felt by some sociologists, particularly those engaged in scholarly, non-empirical, social philosophy in the European tradition, was that they saw a discipline being captured, taken away from them, moving in directions they neither liked nor had the skills to pursue. Though Lazarsfeld was deeply devoted to empirical social science research, Mills, his younger colleague in sociology at Columbia University, had harsh words for what he called 'abstracted empiricism': "As a style of social science, abstracted empiricism is not characterized by any substantive propositions or theories". Mills elaborated, "From [*The people's choice*] we learn that rich, rural, and Protestant persons tend to vote Republican; people of opposite type incline toward the Democrats; and so on. But we learn little about the dynamics of American politics". Mills also criticized Lazarsfeld for the bureaucratization of social research.

Another major criticism aimed at Lazarsfeld's work was Terry N. Clark's 1998 study, *Paul Lazarsfeld and the Columbia sociology machine.* Jeřábek (2001: 240) explains that Clark perceived, in Lazarsfeld's research, a style of work in which everything was subordinate to the result, and in which the individuality of the researchers involved was lost, while only the director's ideas of which research was important counted.

David Morrison, one of the first individuals to examine Lazarsfeld's contributions to mass communication research, according to Glander (2000: 106), argued that Lazarsfeld "had no interest in mass communication-as-such", but instead had gravitated to the discipline to pursue methodological interests. Herbert Schiller, one of the most widely recognized critics of mass communications in the United States, maintained that the 'Lazarsfeld contingent' at Columbia's Bureau of Applied Social Research had paid little or no attention to either the work of those who were concerned with the global arena or to the role of mass communication in securing the political attachment of people outside the United States. Glander's analysis of both Morrison's and Schiller's views is that there is some truth in both claims. Lazarsfeld was interested in methodology, and the 'Lazarsfeld contingent' did perhaps pay less attention to the development of international propaganda techniques than did some other mass communication research groups. However, Glander notes, it is equally true that Lazarsfeld possessed very early interests in propaganda and mass communications, and it is also equally true that Lazarsfeld and the bureau he directed engaged in extensive analysis of the role of mass communications in shaping political allegiances in foreign countries during the Cold War.

Peters (1989: 213) criticizes *The people's choice* on the grounds that although it is striking in that it takes on an obvious problem of public and political life, it fails to theorize it adequately or explicitly. For him, *The people's choice* is an extended footnote to Lippmann's demolition of faith in the rational citizen's existence, in that a chief finding of the study is that the reasoning, independent voter who carefully ponders all the issues and votes accordingly is a fiction. Peters' view (1989: 214) of the hypothesis of two-step-flow in *Personal influence* is that it is an enduring contribution to the understanding of mass media processes and effects, but can also be read as a tactical maneuver in the heated war about mass culture and mass society that was going on in American intellectual life in the 1950s. Peters holds that *Personal influence,* like much mass communication research conducted after it, assumes an image of democracy but does not argue it. However, he does see that the genius of *Personal influence* could rescue the public sphere from the media. *Personal influence* is more than a solution to a conundrum in social science; it is a solution to a major crisis of its age; the possibility of participatory democracy in an age of mass media. Also, he considered the two-step flow model to be profoundly satisfying to the democratic imagination.

Severin and Tankard (1988: 202–203) summarized the numerous criticisms that have been made of Lazarsfeld's two-step flow model as follows: 1) many studies have indicated that major news stories are spread directly by the mass media to a far greater extent than by personal sources; 2) the definition of the opinion leader versus non-opinion leader dichotomy is unclear and varying operationalizing methods further confound the problem; 3) opinion leaders can be either active or passive, whereas the two-step flow model implies a dichotomy between active information-seeking opinion leaders and a mass audience of passive individuals who then rely on the opinion leaders for guidance; 4) empirical definitions of *mass media* vary, and in some instances specialized media have been used, but in other instances they have not been part of the definition of the mass media; 5) the original model is limited to two steps, whereas the process may involve more or even fewer.

One of the sharpest critics of Lazarsfeld is sociologist Todd Gitlin, a cultural critic of media performance. Gitlin was mainly concerned with the received knowledge of Lazarsfeld's *Personal influence* and limited effects models (Robinson, 1989: 205). In 1978, Gitlin published his *Media sociology: The dominant paradigm,* a critique of *Personal influence,* denouncing the Bureau tradition as masking the true power of the media (Katz, 1987: 530). Gitlin complains that Lazarsfeld's study highlights the recalcitrance of the audience, not its acquiescence and gullibility. As Gitlin sees it, the opinion leader is constructed as an influential figure because administrative researchers study proximate causes, which are accessible to their patrons, even if it is obvious that the opinion leaders are mere conduits for the media, in the way that city streets carry the waters of a flood. Schiller (1996: 82–83) assesses Gitlin's major criticisms—that *Personal influence* invalidly truncated and downplayed the reality of media power over consciousness and experience, and that its authors chose to chart 'influence' almost exclusively in terms of people's activity as consumers—as both elegantly expressed and perfectly well justified. Gitlin stated that "the dominant paradigm in the field [of media sociology] since World War II has been, clearly, the cluster of ideas, methods, and findings associated with Paul F. Lazarsfeld and his school; the search for specific, measurable, short-term, individual, attitudinal and behavioral 'effects' of media content, and the conclusion that media are not very important in the formation of public opinion" (Rogers, 1994: 289). According to Glander (2000: 117), Gitlin argued that the theory of effects was first developed for the direct, explicit use of broadcasters and advertisers. However, Lazarsfeld saw no problem in his close association with commercial agencies, nor was he apparently concerned about the way in which these commercial sponsors were shaping the research agenda for the Office of Radio Research, despite widespread opposition in academia during that time to attempts by industry to dictate the focus of social and educational research. Gitlin wrote:

> Effects of mass media lay on the surface; they were to be sought as short term effects on precisely measurable changes in attitude or in discrete behavior. Whether in Lazarsfeld's surveys or the laboratory experiments of Carl Hovland and associates, the purpose was to generate predictive theories of audience response, which are necessarily-intentionally or not-consonant with an administrative point of view, with which centrally located administrators who possess adequate information can make decisions that affect their entire domain with a good idea of the consequences of their choices.   (Cited in Wartella, 1996: 174)

Conclusion: The Search for Explanations

This research study draws on both Lazarsfeld's academic work, which was influenced by his education, his origins, his political and social concerns, and critiques of his work seeking explanations or better understandings of his ideas and concerns.

Although Lazarsfeld was undoubtedly the most important intellectual influence in shaping modern communication research, he never considered himself a communication scholar. In fact it is difficult to define him as affiliated with any specific field since he was a multidisciplinary scholar. However, being named as the Quételet Professor of Social Science at Columbia University in 1962 pleased him, because of his admiration of both Quételet and the discipline of social science. Adolphe Quételet was a Belgian statistician-anthropologist-sociologist, whom Lazarsfeld considered the founder of empirical social research, and social science was a field that was wide enough to include most of the disciplines to which Lazarsfeld contributed. Analyzing his career, one sees that Lazarsfeld throughout his life was devoted to investigating individual behavior in a social context, and that although he worked in many fields, it can be said to his credit that he never worked outside his original area of interest. Lazarsfeld's articles, collected in his book *Qualitative analysis: Historical and critical essays* (1972c), emphasize how his interests had always lain in sociological knowledge as a whole, and that he was motivated by the obvious fact that "in all periods of history, it has been important for administrators and intellectuals to obtain information on social matters" (Lazarsfeld, 1973: 10). Thus, Lazarsfeld, it is argued here, never gave up the specific field of knowledge in which he began his career, nor did he renounce his early commitment to Socialism; rather he adopted what he saw as effective methods or strategies to continue working towards the goal of better social conditions for all.

Lazarsfeld asserted that the investigation of radio could also lead to understanding social and cultural values in society. Certainly, with his innovations in research, he started something that continues, and will continue, to be relevant, that is, models and methods that help us to better understand social phenomena. Commenting on the work of sociologists, Lazarsfeld said that he saw them as the methodologists of social science. He explains that the first function of the sociologist is to be

> the *pathfinder* of the advancing army of social scientists, when a new sector of human affairs is about to become an object of empirical scientific investigations. It is the sociologist who takes the first steps. He is the bridge between the social philosopher, the individual observer and commentator on the one hand, and the organized team work of the empirical investigators and analyzers on the other.
>
> (Lazarsfeld, cited in Hardt, 2001: 11)

David Morrison (1998: 34) argues that Lazarsfeld's Jewishness made for difficulties at the university and also produced a sensitivity and awareness of his marginality, and further, that this experience of marginality existed beyond the psychological level. Morrison (1998: 64) assumes that Lazarsfeld was aware that anti-Semitism in America could restrict the advancement of his career, but that his Marxism presented no barrier to acceptance. Lazarsfeld had not been long in America when he described himself at one lecture as a Marxist on leave. Bernard Berelson's comment on that was, "Well, it was certainly a long leave"

(Morrison, 1998: 64). Lazarsfeld's Jewishness was, in fact, less of a concern to him than his delicate position as an 'outsider':

> You know, when I first came here there was still a certain amount of genteel anti-Semitism . . . As a matter of fact, I was less affected because my being a foreigner over-shadowed my being Jewish. No one thought of me as Jew because of my foreignness—[my] accent saved my life.   (Lazarsfeld, cited in Morrison, 1998: 65)

Morrison, relying on Marie Jahoda's description of Lazarsfeld, that he was "always sensitive about his Jewishness—he had the most idiotic, but persistent inferiority feeling", argues (Ibid.) that Lazarsfeld fooled himself about his escape and that his apparent acceptance of his 'foreignness' fed a basic insecurity.

Lazarsfeld, who was accused by critics such as Gitlin in 1978 for selling out to industry when he obtained substantial industry funding, was very aware of such dangers and warned: "We academic people always have a certain sense of tightrope walking: at what point will the commercial partners find some necessary conclusion too hard to take and at what point will they shut us off from the indispensable sources of funding and data?" (Lazarsfeld, cited in Greenberg and Salwen, 1996: 66). It is argued here that, for Lazarsfeld, many factors, including the nature of his innovations, social dreams, and funding for research were important justifications for his work, and his awareness of the dangers of 'tightrope' walking was his protection against making the mistakes that his critics warned about. It is also argued that the idea that Lazarsfeld made the transition from an 'outsider' who came to America with activist idea, to an 'insider' who was complicit in the capitalist agenda, is not accurate. Rather, Lazarsfeld maintained his 'continuous self-interest' in his original main principles, and used various different methods to achieve his final social goals. Indeed, the most scathing criticism that might have given him pause instead helped him to refine the articulation of his methods and goals.

Katz (2001: 270–271), looking for an explanation of what happened to communication research, has often asked his fellow sociologists why sociology abandoned communications research after its auspicious American beginnings at the University of Chicago in the 1930s. The most telling answer, he reports, was "It's your fault". This response means, he explains, that the Columbia University tradition initiated by Paul Lazarsfeld and his Bureau of Applied Social Research mistakenly spent itself on questioning the ability of mass-mediated messages to change opinions, attitudes, and actions in the short-run.

Although often attacked by critical thinkers, Lazarsfeld recommended that critical theory be included in American communication studies along with his own style of research. When Lazarsfeld sparred with the Frankfurt School, he discovered a mutual interest in the problems of mass culture. Lazarsfeld's social and political concerns, as well as the nature of his methodological innovations and the scarce sources of available funding, moved him in the direction of research areas where he could find funds. However, his main interest in developing his understanding of mass society was to improve the standards of people living under the conditions of industrialization. Towards this end he was deeply into developing innovative methodologies in sociological research.

Acknowledgement

I would like to truthfully thank Professor Michael Dorland, of the School of Journalism and Communication at Carleton University, Canada, for his comments, suggestions, and evaluations of this work.

Notes

1. By "empirical social research" Lazarsfeld (1993: 283) means "studies of a contemporary situation using various techniques, such as questionnaires, field observations, existing records, and generally giving priority to. quantitative data, though without excluding case studies and other qualitative material".

2. *Appreciation of Lazarsfeld*: in a brief collection documenting awards and appreciations honoring Lazarsfeld, Hynek Jeřábek (2001: 241) records that Lazarsfeld, who worked at Columbia University until his retirement in 1971, continued teaching as a Distinguished Professor at the University of Pittsburgh during the 1970s after his retirement. Lazarsfeld was honored several times for his contribution to the development of sociology. He was elected as President of the American Association for Public Opinion Research (AAPOR) in 1950, four years before being the first person ever to be honored with the AAPOR Woodward Prize. In 1962, Lazarsfeld was granted the honorary title of Quételet Professor of Social Sciences in remembrance of Adolph Quételet, a famous Belgian natural and social scientist, statistician, astronomer, and, for Lazarsfeld, the founder of sociology. In the same year he became President of the American Sociological Association (ASA). He was awarded honorary degrees at many universities (Yeshiva, Chicago and Columbia, University of Vienna). He was the first American to receive an honorary degree at the Sorbonne in Paris. In addition, he was given the Golden Cross of Merit, a national decoration, in Austria. In 1997, Columbia University re-named his former research center the Paul Lazarsfeld Center of the Social Sciences to honor his pioneer work in social research methods.

3. In his 2001 paper *The Paul F. Lazarsfeld archive at the University of Vienna: Its history and its contents,* Neurath narrates that he had been Lazarsfeld's student at Columbia University in the early 1940s and one of his research assistants at the Office of Radio Research. For the archive Neurath assembled material written or, edited by Lazarsfeld covering many fields: mass communication, market research, mathematical statistics, public opinion, etc., along with works written about Lazarsfeld, and many others influenced by him or his work. On March 11, 1983, the Paul F, Lazarsfeld Archive at the University of Vienna was opened for users with a one-day symposium where several papers were presented about Lazarsfeld's life and work and about his importance for the development of modern empirical social research and its various sub fields. Neurath summarizes the material held by the Archive under 12 categories: books that Lazarsfeld wrote as sole author or as co-author (24 volumes); books (anthologies) with Lazarsfeld as either sole editor or as co-editor (17 volumes); Lazarsfeld's published articles in journals, or as contributions to books, etc. (300 published pieces); Lazarsfeld's unpublished but completed writings (300 pieces of so-called 'grey' publications); materials towards Lazarsfeld's own biography and the history of his institutes; parts of Lazarsfeld's scientific correspondence; large quantities of Lazarsfeld's own work files; project reports that Lazarsfeld's institutes produced between 1937 and 1977; 780 articles published by staff members or students of the Bureau; 80 books written by staff members on the basis of Bureau research projects; 3,000 volumes of Lazarsfeld's own working library; and books relevant to Lazarsfeld's work.

4. Such as Robert K. Merton, Hans Zeisel, Ann Pasanella, Marie Jahoda, Charles Glock, David Sills, Allen H. Barton, Patricia Kendall, Frank Stanton, Bernard Berelson, Elihu Katz, Joseph Klapper, Leo Lowenthal, Rudolf Arnheim, Herta Herzog, Herbert Menzel, William McPhee, Morris Rosenberg, Vittorio Capecchi, S. Cole, Susan Schad, Marjorie

Fiske, Hadley Cantril, Robert S. Lynd, Gertruda Wagner, Lotte Rademacher, Ludwig Wagner, Wagner Thiclens, Neil Henry, and Hazel Gaudet.

5. Such as James S. Coleman, Peter Rossi, Raymond Boudon, Earl Babbie, David Gleicher, David Landau, Herbert Hyman, Leo Srole, Philip Ennis, and Anthony Oberschall.

6. David Sills (1996: 232) said of their relationship that it endured for "approximately 30 years" and was a "truly rewarding symbiotic relationship. Stanton, through CBS, provided both funds and data for much of Lazarsfeld's research program at Columbia University's Bureau . . . [and] he provided his share of ideas for research as well. Lazarsfeld directed research that often proved to be beneficial to them both. The Lazarsfeld-Stanton Program Analyzer was jointly developed and used; in fact, at CBS it was called the Stanton-Lazarsfeld Program Analyzer. Three of the major collections of papers resulting from the research at the Columbia bureau are jointly edited books [published in 1941, 1944, and 1949]. There seem never to have been any significant misunderstandings between them".

7. Looking back on his relationship with Lazarsfeld, Merton (1979: 19) said that he was able to express only "a very little of what Paul meant to me, these past thirty five years, as colleague, friend, collaborator, teacher and, I realize now, as brother".

8. According to Hynek Jeřábek (2001: 232), Lazarsfeld, together with various other authors, published, from 1940 to 1949, seven monographs devoted to research on the mass media and on interpersonal communication.

9. Timothy Glander (2000: 105–106) details how James Coleman, one of these former students, credited Lazarsfeld with nine significant contributions on various subjects: initiating the use of survey panel methods in public opinion polling; creating the prototype for conducting large-scale, university-based social research; and becoming the chief proponent of the 'two-step flow of mass communications, which was to become the dominant paradigm in mass communication research. Lazarsfeld's Office of Radio Research at Princeton University was the very first academic unit in the United States to be devoted solely to the study of mass communications research; Lazarsfeld's published work dominated the mass communications research field during its early years so much that he had to often use the pseudonym 'Elias Smith' in order to avoid the embarrassment of having his own name appear on published communication research too frequently; and Lazarsfeld greatly influenced the thinking of many graduate students who assisted him and took their degrees under him.

10. For Collins (1998: 571), the men who affected the mathematical revolution were Cardan, Tartaglia, Viète, Descartes, Fermat, Brahe, Kepler, Napier, Gilbert, Stevin, and Snel.

11. This was one of approximately fifteen circles that organized European thought during the eleven generations from 1600 to 1965 that Collins talks about (1998: 531). He explains that "the Vienna Circle . . . was the personal seminar conducted by Schlick from 1924 to 1936; as the movement grew, it became formalized through the leadership of Neurath with its manifesto in 1929 and its own journal. *Erkenntnis,* in 1930" (1998: 1016).

12. Collins (1998: 558) commented that "mathematics was becoming a matter of public prestige".

13. Their formulation of the basic issues was as follows: "Industrial organizations no longer compel eight year old children to attend the machine for fourteen hours a day; they engage in elaborate programs of 'public relations'; they place large and impressive advertisements in the newspapers of the nation; they sponsor numerous radio programs; on the advice of public relations counselors they organize prize contests, establish welfare foundations, and support worthy causes. Economic power seems to have reduced direct exploitation and turned to a subtler type of psychological exploitation, achieved largely by disseminating propaganda through the mass media of communication" (Schiller, 1996: 57).

14. Lazarsfeld, Berelson, and Gaudet (1964b: 237–240) summarize, in a series of major interrelated points, their conclusions about the social processes through which

attitude changes occur. The stability of attitudes helps people to avoid or to minimize conflicts and disagreements with the persons in their social environments who share these attitudes. "Thus attitude stability is instrumental in preserving feelings of individual security". While individuals preserve their security, they find those attitudes reinforced in their contacts with other members of their group, then they tend to share similar attitudes and exhibit similar selective tendencies. It is important, therefore, to determine the conditions under which attitudes lose their stability, and the processes through which the change takes place. One process depends on the activation of previous experiences and ideas. Such predispositions to change are more typical for individuals in whom cross-pressures operate. In our complex society, individuals do not belong to one group only. One of the functions of opinion leaders is to mediate between the mass media and other people in their groups. Opinion leadership, however, is only one of the mechanisms through which the attitudes of a group are formed. Another is what has been called the 'emergence' or 'crystallization' of opinion. Opinions seem to be organized in a hierarchy of stability.

15. Collins' (1998: 31) theory: "Intellectual creativity comes from combining elements from previous products of the field."

16. Smith (2001: 286) explains results of this study as follows. Opinion leaders in public affairs, compared to the women in the sample, tended to have higher education and social status, to have more information, and to be more gregarious. For married women, the husband was the most influential male; while friends, neighbors, and co-workers were the most influential females. For single women, the father was the most influential male; while friends, neighbors, and co-workers were the most influential females. Gregariousness had an important direct effect on opinion leadership. Lazarsfeld and Katz showed that opinion leaders were more exposed to the mass media—they read more magazines and books than non-leaders. Opinion leaders were more cosmopolitan—they read out-of-town newspapers and news in national magazines rather than only local journals. In sum, people who were gregarious and those with higher social status were more likely to be opinion leaders in public affairs.

17. When a pharmaceutical firm wanted to study how doctors come to adopt one of their new drugs, three of Lazarsfeld's collaborators—Coleman, Katz, and Menzel—in 1966 designed a survey of all the doctors in certain specialties in four towns, asking each doctor who were their advisors and social contacts within the medical community. By this method of *dense sampling* most of the interaction partners are caught in the sample (Barton, 2001: 256).

18. In another study, Kendall and Lazarsfeld (1964: 291–296) explain how survey analysis works. "In order to have a uniform and neutral terminology, we shall use the following expressions. A *personal datum* is a fact predicated about a single individual. If several personal data about the same person are combined in some way, we shall talk of a *personal index*. Any kind of aggregate of persons will be called a *unit* . . . A *unit datum* is any fact predicated about a unit. If a number of unit data are combined to characterize a single unit we shall talk of a *unit index*. Units as well as persons can form the elements of a statistical analysis . . . just as we can classify people by demographic variables or by their attitudes, we can also classify them by the kind of environment in which they live. The appropriate variables for such a classification are likely to be unit data. A survey analysis would then cover both personal and unit data simultaneously."

19. Lazarsfeld (1964: 115) explains that "whenever an investigator finds himself faced with the relationship between two variables he immediately starts to 'cross-tabulate,' that is, to consider the role of further variables."

20. Babe (2000) argues that the Canadian discourse is more *critical* in Lazarsfeld's sense of the term explained in these two distinctions: "Indeed it is from this notion of *appraisal* that the very name, *critical*, derives. Critical research, then, being evaluative, presumes *enduring values* (an ontological presupposition) whereby policies, activities, events, modes of human interaction, institutions, and so forth may be appraised, and which serve also as goals to which one may aspire."

References

Babe, R. (2000). Foundations of Canadian communication thought. *Canadian Journal of Communication, 25*(1).

Barton, A. H. (2001). Paul Lazarsfeld as institutional inventor. *International Journal of Public Opinion Research, 13(3)*, 245–269.

Berelson, B., Lazarsfeld, P., and McPhee, W. (1971). Democratic practice and democratic theory. In P. Bachrach (Ed.), *Political elites in a democracy* (pp. 27–48). New York: Atherton Press.

Boden, M. A. (1994). What is creativity? In M. A. Boden (Ed.), *Dimensions of creativity* (pp. 75–117). Cambridge, MA: Massachusetts Institute of Technology.

Boudon, R. (1993). Introduction. In R. Boudon (Ed.), *On social research and its language* (pp. 1–29). Chicago, IL: The University of Chicago Press.

Carey, J. W. (1996). The Chicago School and mass communication research. In E. E. Dennis and E. Wartella (Eds.), *American communication research: The remembered history* (pp. 21–38). Mahwah, NJ: Lawrence Erlbaum.

Chaffee, S. H. and Rogers, E. M. (1997). *The beginnings of communication study in America: A personal memoir by Wilbur Schramm.* Thousand Oaks, CA: Sage.

Collins, R. (1998). *The sociology of philosophies: A global theory of intellectual change.* Cambridge, MA: The Belknap Press of Harvard University Press.

Craig, R. T. (1989). Communication as a practical discipline. In B. Dervin, L. Grossberg, B. J, O'Keefe, and E. Wartella (Eds.), *Rethinking communication: Paradigm issues* (pp. 97–122). Thousand Oaks, CA: Sage.

Donsbach, W. et al. (2001). Editorial: Paul Lazarsfeld (1901–1976). *International Journal of Public Opinion Research, 13*(3), 225–228.

Dubin, R. (1959). Deviant behavior and social structure: Continuities in social theory. *American Sociological Review, 24*(2), 147–164.

Eysenck, H. J. (1994). The measurement of creativity. In M. A. Boden (Ed.), *Dimensions of creativity* (pp. 199–242). Cambridge, MA: Massachusetts Institute of Technology.

Fortner, R. S. (1994). Mediated communication theory. In F. L. Casmir, (Ed.), *Building communication theories: A sociolcultural approach* (pp. 209–240). Hillsdale, NJ: Lawrence Erlbaum.

Foucault, M. (1994). *The order of things: An archaeology of the human sciences.* New York: Vintage.

Glander, T. (2000). *Origins of mass communications research during the American cold war: Educational effects and contemporary implications.* Hillsdale, NJ: Lawrence Erlbaum.

Greenberg, B. S. and Salwen, M. B. (1996). Mass communication theory and research: Concepts and models. In M. B. Salwen and D. W. Stacks (Eds.), *An integrated approach to communication theory and research* (pp. 63–78). Hillsdale, NJ: Lawrence Erlbaum.

Grunig, L. A. (1996). Public Relations. In M. B. Salwen and D. W. Stacks (Eds.), *An integrated approach to communication theory and research* (pp. 459–477). Hillsdale, NJ: Lawrence Erlbaum.

Hardt, H. (1992). *Critical communication studies: Communication, history and theory in America.* New York: Routledge.

Hardt, H. (2001). *Social theories of the press: Constituents of communication research, 1840s to 1920s.* Lanham, MD: Rowman and Littlefield.

Jeřábek, H. (2001). Paul Lazarsfeld—The founder of modern empirical sociology: A research biography. *International Journal of Public Opinion Research, 13*(3), 229–244.

Katz, E. and Lazarsfeld, P. F. (1955). *Personal influence: The part played by people in the flow of mass communications.* New York: The Free Press of Glencoe.

Katz, E. (1987). Communications research since Lazarsfeld. *Public Opinion Quarterly, 51*(2), 25–45.

Katz, E. (1996). Diffusion research at Columbia. In E. E. Dennis and E. Wartella (Eds.), *American communication research: The remembered history* (pp. 61–69). Hillsdale, NJ: Lawrence Erlbaum.

Katz, E. (2001). Lazarsfeld's map of media effects. *International Journal of Public Opinion Research, 13*(3), 270–279.

Kendall, P. L. and Lazarsfeld, P. F. (1964). The relation between individual and group characteristics in 'the American soldier.' In P. F. Lazarsfeld and M. Rosenberg (Eds.), *The language of social research: A reader in the methodology of social research* (pp. 290–296). New York: The Free Press of Glencoe.

Lazarsfeld, P. F. and Henry, N. W. (1966). Mathematics and the social sciences. In P. F. Lazarsfeld and N. W. Henry (Eds.), *Readings in the mathematical social science* (pp. 3–18). Chicago, IL: Science Research Associates, Inc.

Lazarsfeld, P. F. and Thielens, W. (1972). Comments on the nature of classification in social research. In P. F. Lazarsfeld, A. K. Pasanella, and M. Rosenberg (Eds.), *Continuities in the language of social research* (pp. 62–65). New York; The Free Press.

Lazarsfeld, P. F. (1954a). A conceptual introduction to latent structure analysis. In P. F. Lazarsfeld (Ed), *Mathematical thinking in the social sciences* (pp. 349–387). New York: Russell and Russell.

Lazarsfeld, P. F. (1954b). Introduction: Mathematical thinking in the social sciences. In P. F. Lazarsfeld (Ed.), *Mathematical thinking in the social sciences* (pp. 3–16). New York: Russell and Russell.

Lazarsfeld, P. F. (1964). Interpretation of statistical relations as a research operation. In P. F. Lazarsfeld and M. Rosenberg (Eds.), *The language of social research: A reader in the methodology of social research* (pp. 115–125). New York: The Free Press of Glencoe.

Lazarsfeld, P. F. (1972a). Development of a test for class-consciousness. In P. F. Lazarsfeld, A. K. Pasanella, and M. Rosenberg (Eds.), *Continuities in the language of social research* (pp. 41–43). New York: The Free Press.

Lazarsfeld, P. F. (1972b). The use of panels in social research. In P. F. Lazarsfeld, A. K. Pasanella, and M. Rosenberg (Eds.), *Continuities in the language of social research* (pp, 330–331). New York: The Free Press.

Lazarsfeld, P. F. (1972c). *Qualitative analysis: Historical and critical essays.* Boston, MA: Allen and Bacon.

Lazarsfeld, P. F. (1973). *Main trends in sociology.* London: George Allen and Unwin.

Lazarsfeld, P. F. (1993). History of social research. In R. Boudon (Ed.), *On social research and its language* (pp. 275–298). Chicago, IL: The University of Chicago Press.

Lazarsfeld, P. F., Berelson, B., and Gaudet, H. (1964a). Political interest and voting behavior. In P. F Lazarsfeld and M. Rosenberg (Eds.), *The language of social research: A reader in the methodology of social research* (pp. 155–158). New York: The Free Press of Glencoe.

Lazarsfeld, P. F., Berelson, B., and Gaudet, H. (1964b). The process of opinion and attitude formation. In P. F. Lazarsfeld and M. Rosenberg (Eds.), *The language of social research: A reader in the methodology of social research* (pp. 231 –242). New York: The Free Press of Glencoe.

Lazarsfeld, P. F., Berelson, B., and Gaudet, H. (1968). *The people's choice: How the voter makes up his mind in a presidential campaign.* New York: Columbia University Press.

Mattelart, A. (1999). *Mapping world communication: War, progress, culture* (S. Emanuel and J. A. Cohen, Trans.). Minneapolis, MN: University of Minnesota Press.

Merton, R. K. (1979). Remembering Paul Lazarsfeld. In R. K. Merton, J. S. Coleman, and P. H. Rossi (Eds.), *Qualitative and quantitative social research: Papers in honor of Paul F. Lazarsfeld (pp. 19–22).* New York: The Free Press.

Mohr, L. B. (1969). Determinants of innovation in organizations. *The American Political Science Review, 63*(1), 111–126.

Morrison, D. E. (1998). *The search for a method: Focus groups and the development of mass communication research.* Luton: University of Luton Press.

Neurath, P. (2001). Collections and recollections—The Paul F. Lazarsfeld archive at the University of Vienna: Its history and its contents. *International Journal of Public Opinion Research, 13*(3), 299–314.

Peters, J. D. (1986). Institutional sources of intellectual poverty in communication research. *Communication research, 13*(4), 527–559.

Peters, J. D. (1989). Democracy and American mass communication theory: Dewey, Lippmann, Lazarsfeld. *Communication, 11,* 199–220.

Peters, J. D. (1999). *Speaking into the air: A history of the idea of Communication.* Chicago, IL: The University of Chicago Press.

Peterson, T. (1996). The press as a social institution. In E. E. Dennis and E. Wartella (Eds.), *American communication research: The remembered history* (pp. 85–93). Hillsdale, NJ: Lawrence Erlbaum.

Robinson, G. J. (1989). Communication paradigm dialogues: Their place in the history of science debate. In B. Dervin, L. Grossberg, B. J. O'Keefe, and E. Wartella (Eds.), *Rethinking communication: Paradigm Issues* (pp. 204–208). Thousand Oaks, CA: Sage.

Rogers, E. M. (1994). *A history of communication study: A biographical approach.* New York: The Free Press.

Rosengren, K. E. (1989). Paradigms lost and regained. In B. Dervin, L. Grossberg, B. J. O'Keefe, and E. Wartella (Eds.), *Rethinking communication: Paradigm Issues* (pp. 21–39). Thousand Oaks, CA: Sage.

Schiller, D. (1996). *Theorizing communication: A history.* New York: Oxford University Press.

Schramm, W. (1996). The master teachers. In E. E. Dennis and E. Wartella (Eds.), *American communication research: The remembered history* (pp. 123–133). Hillsdale, NJ: Lawrence Erlbaum.

Severin, W. J. and Tankard, J. W. (1988). *Communication theories: Origins, methods, uses.* New York: Longman.

Sills, D. L. (1996). Stanton, Lazarsfeld, and Merton: Pioneers in communication research. In E. E. Dennis and E. Wartella (Eds.), *American communication research: The remembered history* (pp. 105–116). Hillsdale, NJ: Lawrence Erlbaum.

Smith, R. B. (2001). A legacy of Lazarsfeld: Cumulative social research on voting. *International Journal of Public Opinion Research, 13*(3), 280–298.

Stevenson, R. L. (1996). International communication. In M. B. Salwen and D. W. Stacks (Eds.), *An integrated approach to communication theory and research* (pp. 181–193). Hillsdale, NJ: Lawrence Erlbaum.

Wartella, E. (1996). The history reconsidered. In E. E. Dennis and E. Wartella (Eds.), *American communication research: The remembered history* (pp. 169–180). Mahwah, NJ: Lawrence Erlbaum.

On Introducing Ideology: Critical Theory and the Critique of Culture

Hanno Hardt

> *Pragmatism reflects a society that has no time to remember and meditate.*
>
> Max Horkheimer

The prevalence of a social-scientific vision of the world with its own positivistic claims on truth and reality remained a major issue following the introduction of communication research by Lazarsfeld and others. However, there were alternative visions of communication and society, although marginal at the time, which had always existed outside the social science establishment. They were expressed in the context of literature and sociology through a holistic approach to the study of society by those working with an understanding of culture as a dramaturgy of symbolic expression, and by others through a critique of mass culture which emerged from Marxism and, more specifically, from the contribution of Critical Theory to American social theory. Both traditions shared an abiding belief in the importance of exposing the destructive power of progress and the deprivation of the individual caught in an increasingly barbaric world, and working toward a more humane society. Thus, a critique of culture evolved from the writings of Kenneth Burke and sociologists like Hugh Dalziel Duncan, or the sociological work of David Riesman or C. Wright Mills next to intensely theoretical contributions by Horkheimer, Adorno, Marcuse and Lowenthal, in particular. Their ideas emerged during a period of political and social upheaval in the United States which provided the context for a significant critique of modern society.

The dilemma of a cultural approach to the study of society, which had been contested successfully by mainstream sociology, was reflected in Duncan's call for "a return to humanism, but a humanism conceived in a passion for understanding contemporary America." He added, "We must return to the belief that, while man has a nature and a history, he also has a community" (1953: ix).

Duncan proposed to overcome the fixed belief in specific positivistic methods by offering a symbolic analysis of literature for the benefit of understanding contemporary society, fully "aware that many American social scientists consider inquiry into the structure and function of symbolic expression hardly a reputable preoccupation for a 'scientific' social scientist" (1953: ix). He saw himself surrounded by opponents and spoke in an indirect reference to Harvard sociology, and Talcott Parsons in particular, of the "mechanists, and particularly those whose signatures appear at the end of the 'General statement' of *Toward a General Theory of Action.*" Duncan did not believe that "roles should be studied as 'mechanisms,' nor that symbolic systems 'gear' or 'mesh',", and he thought that "Many sociologists (certainly many American sociologists) are mechanists" (1968: vii).

Although American sociology since Cooley, Dewey, Mead and Park, for example, had acknowledged the symbolic dimension of social relations with its extensive writings about the role of communication in society, it had failed to produce a social theory. Duncan insisted that communication theory as social theory had to be based on an analysis of symbolic forms and their effect on the social order. His reason was that traditional studies of communication had been "modeled after the study of material objects, as symbols were reduced to things in space" (1967b: 241), resulting in the emergence of techniques, like Bernard Berelson's influential *Content Analysis in Communication Research* (1952), which concentrated on the collection and processing of data "for the objective, systematic, and quantitative description of the manifest content of communication" (1952: 18). Duncan suggested that those who practice content analysis "are apt to confuse what they are doing as technicians with what should be done in theory and methodology. What can be quantified is studied, what cannot is neglected, and, among parochial behaviorists, is even described as 'beyond' science" (1967b: 260).

At the same time, he dismissed negative criticism of sociology, and, implicitly, empiricism in communication studies, as long as technicians dominate theoreticians, or, as long as theorists fail to produce theories "that can be reduced to hypotheses useful to technicians" (1967b: 260).

Duncan declared an end to the era of "American sociologists who have mortgaged the future of sociology to the methods of the physical sciences." It had become obvious to him that "such methods are not useful in discovering what we need to know, namely, the how and why of consensus as it arises in the most basic of all human experience—communication" (1962: ix). A few years later he proposed that a "break-through in communication theory that will advance social theory cannot come so long as we reduce communication to an event which must be studied by existing methods of research," and he warned against the appropriation of a physical science methodology that reveals answers about "motion in time and space, not about man in society. Questions about communication must be about communication as a social, not a physical event" (1968: 15).

Ultimately, his critique of sociology was a critique of mechanistic models which reduce communication to processes or states without providing knowledge about how words, or forms of communication, determine an individual's action in social relationships. Indeed, he felt that modern American sociology had produced theoretical monsters which "almost rival the chimeras of antiquity; firebreathing monsters, with a lion's head, a goat's body, and a serpent's tail, have been matched by grotesques with mechanical heads and symbolic bodies" (1968: 17).

Duncan attributed the change of perspective among those interested in communication theory, from sociology to anthropology and literature, to the lack of theory and the failure of sociology to come to terms with the need for symbolic analysis. In his words, "If communication was social, and the social was the communicative, something must be said about how communication determined social relationships, and, at the same time, something equally pertinent must be said about how social relations affected communication" (1967b: 241).

Duncan thought that the search for a theory of communication grounded in a theory of society could somehow reunite mainstream sociology with the tradition of Dewey, Mead, Cooley or Burke and form a coherent view of the symbolic nature of the world. He maintained that, despite their differing emphases, communication scholars could agree that social reality is constituted by symbolic forms. In fact, they shared the belief that *"how we communicate determines how we relate,* just as how we relate determines how we communicate" (1967b: 261).

Kenneth Burke represented this tradition which inquired about communication in terms of symbolic action, grammar, rhetoric and dialectic with sophistication and foresight. His discussion of "dramatism" in *A Grammar of Motives* (1945) "is full-blown structuralism well in advance, of course, of the French structuralist movement," according to Frank Lentricchia (1982: 130).

The publication of *Attitudes toward History* (1937), in particular, helped establish Burke's reputation as a social critic and theorist. It was received critically by a number of academic fields, including sociology and history, as a language-centered study of reality. Burke addressed the destruction of traditional values and the emergence of technical-political forces that resulted in the existential dilemma of modern individuals: the replacement of a faith in individuality by a submission to the rule of state or economic authority.

Burke, whose analyses frequently contained a sociological dimension, based his own contributions as a critic on an integration of technical criticism and social criticism "by taking the allegiance to the symbol of authority as our subject." He found that "Since the symbols of authority are radically linked with property relationships, this point of departure automatically involves us in socioeconomic criticism" (1937: 234). Burke offered views of the individual as a symbol-using animal and insisted throughout his work on the values of knowing the symbol systems that surround and affect the lives of people. His discussions of the historical process of maintaining authority and the desire for change, as well as his own role as an intellectual and participant in society, were based on understanding and expanding on the centrality of language. In fact, he demonstrated long before others had grasped the importance of language for the study of human relations, that the study of words and symbolic action was the most revealing, and therefore effective, exercise of helping expose and explain the problems of contemporary society, among them alienation and hegemonic struggle. People are connected by language, and the individual, "by reason of his 'property in' the public grammar, the 'collective' property of speech, becomes concerned with processes of socialization" (1937: 252). Burke argued that these needs "are implicit in the nature of language that gets its shape by reference to such economic foundations" as the "productive and distributive patterns" of human relations (1937: 252).

Burke identified the processes of history and the strategies of those in authority (and in possession of the authoritative symbols), by addressing the forces of alienation and suppression. He observed that although "the dispossessed struggle hard and long to remain loyal . . . the bureaucratic order tends simply 'to move in on' such patience and obedience." Moreover, authority will "drive the opposition into a corner by owning the priests (publicists, educators) who will rebuke the opposition for its disobedience to the reigning symbols" (1937: 68). When Burke elaborated on social relationships, he characterized the struggle between dominating forces in society and their efforts to survive in terms of a "stealing back and forth of symbols" (1937: 229), and he described the hopes of the "dispossessed" to regain possession as resting in an "allegiance to the structure that has dispossessed him" (1937: 232).

Burke developed a rationale of history as an organizing principle for recapturing or repossessing a sense of place, and the need to "own a 'myth' to take up the slack between what is desired and what is got" (1937: 212). In his *Attitudes toward History* (1937)—as well as in *Permanence and Change* (1935), *A Grammar of Motives* (1945), or *A Rhetoric of Motives* (1950)—Burke continued to offer not only an original, American perspective on authoritative strategies of domination in a manner that has now become known as a Gramscian approach to the struggle for hegemony, but, equally important, he advanced a theory and methodology for integrating questions of communication and media into an analysis of culture.

As early as 1951 Duncan had suggested the importance of Burke's intellectual contribution to the study of communication in his review of *A Rhetoric of Motives*. He said that it would be "unwise to talk about communication without some understanding of Burke, for he has assumed the burden of constructing hypotheses on the social effects of communication in terms of the process of identification as this takes place through the use of symbols" (1951: 594). Although he urged that "particularistic studies in the field of communication research" should be continued, Duncan emphasized the need for theoretical contributions and concluded that "Burke is asking the important question which is not only who reads what but how those who read are affected by what they read" (1951: 594).

But even Duncan's own project to involve contemporary sociology in a meaningful dialogue with existing theoretical premises and his propositions toward a sociological theory of communication remained a partial success at best, despite a conciliatory attempt with assurances that the occasional sharpness or teasing in his disagreement with behaviorists was merely argumentative and not intended to insult or ridicule (1968: viii).

Nevertheless, Burke and Duncan raised the level of skepticism about the state of communication research not only by questioning the theoretical consequences of working with reified concepts and of being preoccupied with the processing of data, but also, and more importantly, by introducing a dialogic model of social-scientific inquiry. In addition, their work directed other disciplines or fields, such as literature, literary criticism, or social theory, to the exploration of language and the potential of communication as a theoretical framework for an analysis of social relations and processes, for instance, between artists and audiences, writers and readers, or leaders and followers of social and intellectual movements within a cultural context.

Duncan developed a dramatic model of social relations to explain the social use of symbols and to raise questions about how communication determines social order. He insisted that *"how* we communicate determines *what* we communicate" and reminded his readers that communication occurs in public and private forms and "if there are no common symbols there can be no common meanings, and hence no community" (1968: 32). His scholarly work also reflected the political conditions of a country in turmoil, and he observed decisive changes of the community in the presence of the Viet Nam War, which darkened his sense of the future. Duncan did not share the earlier faith of Dewey or Mead in the survival of democracy, or the blind confidence of his contemporaries in the success of modern society. Progress for Duncan meant becoming humane first, and he articulated a need for making future generations understand that "we cannot become humane until we understand our need to visit suffering and death on others—and ourselves" (1968: 39).

Consequently, Duncan urged the undertaking of "vast and profound changes . . . in the way we study society," beginning in "anguished awareness that victimage is the means by which people purge themselves of fear and guilt in their relations with each other" (1968: 39). This awesome perspective held a hope, however, for understanding what communication is by insisting on the dislocation of traditional communication research in favor of a cultural approach which would be invested by knowledge about the forms of social interaction and a profound interest in being.

Earlier, Burke suggested the importance of recognizing the essence of being in the study of culture. He reminded his readers that science is involved with processes and not concerned with substance or being, and that "any attempt to deal with human relationships after the analogy of naturalistic correlations becomes necessarily the reduction of some higher or more complex realm of being to the terms of a less complex realm of being" (1945: 506). Consequently, social scientists must realize that to engage in the study of human communication, that is, to preserve and build on complexity which characterizes the substance of being, means taking into account the whole from all perspectives. The result is the creation of an environment in which a "dialectic of participation" produces certainty based on the requirement "that all the sub-certainties be considered as neither true nor false, but *contributory*" (1945: 513).

Thus, the conventional certainty of scientific knowledge gives way to the possibility of many insights or interpretations. In this spirit, for example, history appears as a "dialectic of characters," changing expectations, not "to see 'feudalism' overthrown by 'capitalism' and 'capitalism' succeeded by some manner of national or international or non-national or neo-national or post-national socialism," and emphasizing the permanent existence of elements of these positions "attaining greater clarity of expression or imperiousness of proportion of one period than another" (1945: 513).

This is not only a critique of the social sciences, but also encouragement to promote different ways of thinking about culture and communication. It breaks with scientific models of development and change, or with the flow or process of communication, by introducing the notion that final answers are unobtainable and that solutions are the interplay of positions or voices. In Joseph Gusfield's interpretation of Burke, the sociologist is "the critic whose task is to point to the multiple understandings, the alternative possibilities inhering in situations, to bring new meanings and metaphors to bear on taken-for-granted assumptions" (1989: 27). A sociology of communication, in this view, becomes a form of criticism and a creative activity that builds on knowledge without the constraints of a positivistic vision of communication and human behavior.

Burke contributed significantly to making rhetorical analysis available to communication and media research by suggesting its usefulness to the study of human interaction. According to Gusfield there are

> three ways in which Burke's rhetorical perspective has been productive for sociologists. The first is found in the enormously insightful approach to human interaction as persuasional. The second is in the understanding of social science research as affected by rhetorical elements.

And the last one is the "common framework, which literature and literary analysis, as rhetoric, share with sociology," providing "basic categories for seeing and interpreting social action" (1989: 19). It is especially this latter area of legitimate common concerns and scholarly interests that constituted the most fruitful environment for the development of a critique of culture and communication.

Burke may have anticipated modern ideas concerning the uses of language or symbolic analysis, but he received only marginal attention by (mass) communication scholarship between the 1940s and 1960s. In fact, Lentricchia's remark that "the ambitious studies of contemporary critical theory, with few exceptions, continue to ignore Burke almost totally" (1982: 119) can also be extended to include past and present activities of (mass) communication research. Similarly, Frederic Jameson has observed that Burke's "immense critical corpus" of work had "been utterly without influence in its fundamental lessons," namely, "as an interpretative model to be studied and a method to be emulated" (1982: 70). He proceeded to determine whether Burke's work "can be reread or rewritten as model for contemporary ideological analysis" (1982: 71) and concluded that since "Burke's system has no place for an unconscious," his "symbolic act is thus always serenely transparent to itself, in lucid blindness to the dark underside of language, to the ruses of history or desire" (1982: 88).

There is no evidence of Kenneth Burke in the major writings on communication and media in American culture and no significant impact of his scholarly contributions, which reflect the social and political engagements of an intellectual life in the 1930s and 1940s. At the same time, there is also no rediscovery of the potential of Burke's dramatistic paradigm in the contemporary pursuit of understanding the world of symbols. His work has simply failed to engage the imagination of social theorists and those who have been eager to analyze the symbolic environment in the guise of communication research or media studies.

Similarly, the work of Erving Goffman, who had continued the Burkean tradition with his specific interest in social reality and the development of a dramaturgy of human interaction, promised to advance the understanding of social communication and, therefore, the definition of social action. His contribution to a microanalysis of communication within the cultural contexts of individuals, consisting of image management and the staging of appearances before others, concentrated on the structure of individual experience and took role theory to its logical conclusions. Goffman described the individual actor operating in a social space that seemed out of institutional control, thus elevating the creation of social roles to a central concern in social thought and replacing the idea of society.

More recently, Richard Lanigan has argued that Goffman's claim that method alone is a sufficient theory was an example of "a-historical sophism by which much of positive science also justifies its claims to objectivity," and he called on phenomenological theorists "to improve on the legacy of Erving Goffman" (1988: 343). On the other hand, Goffman's ideas had a marginal impact on the field as a theory or method of critical communication research.

In discussing the contributions of Burke, Duncan and Goffman to the study of life as drama, Taline Voskeritchian has noted a "gradual tightening of the parameters of social life with a parallel diminution of the *philosophical* idea of man." Thus, "for Burke the problems of man are timeless, inborn, incurable," while "for Duncan and Goffman, man is a social problematic, a problematic formulated against the background of an increasingly ominous world which generates in its inhabitants a sense of marginality and exile" (1981: 279).

Together, their scholarship offered an opportunity to rethink the study of society; their works stand as a persuasive critique of modern life, and as a challenge to old ways of studying society. Dramaturgical analysis posed individuals in the context of a secularized, urban environment. It identified communication as a central problematic and proceeded to develop strategies of inquiry that focused on form instead of content. In so doing it turned from a mechanistic view of human conduct to offer an alternative, humanistic context for the study of communication in which the dialectic becomes the method of analysis. Voskeritchian talked about "skepticism and pluralism as the foundations of their methodology" (1981: 296).

Throughout their writings there is a recurring faith in the workings of democratic principles, that is, in the individual's power of self-regulation or correction, reflecting a continuation of the "optimistic mood" of Pragmatism. It permeates Burke's discussion of the dialectic as a source of reason that will prevail over dogmatism and Duncan's discussion of the power of the dramatic dialogue to sustain egalitarian conditions for participation in communication; it even surfaces in Goffman's view of individuals, who seem trapped in the modern world, but able to maintain continuity in their encounters.

Hugh Dalziel Duncan emerged during the 1960s as a major critic of traditional sociological approaches to the study of communication and society. Like Goffman, Duncan had been educated at Chicago and informed by the theoretical contributions of Pragmatism in the tradition of James, Dewey, Mead and Cooley. He had been encouraged by the work of Burke to refine his ideas about the importance of the symbolic environment. His theoretical position may also have grown out of his own biographical circumstances. For instance, Voskeritchian has noted that both Duncan and Goffman were non-Americans who displayed "an intellectual and methodological attitude which combines a European (in this case Anglo-Saxon) cosmopolitan sensibility with the empathetic, essentially optimistic mood of American Pragmatism and symbolic interactionism" (1981: 277).

However, when Duncan, in particular, insisted on the possibility of a theory of society that was grounded in the symbolic nature of the individual, his criticism of the dominant perspective was largely ignored. Indeed, the original efforts to establish a dramaturgical analysis of communication were replaced by a critique of mass culture which also questioned, albeit implicitly, the state of communication and media research in the United States.

Such a critique emerged from a tradition of Marxist scholarship in the United States, which was joined by the contributions of the Frankfurt School in the 1940s. Both formed a nucleus of alternative theories of society based on an intensive treatment of questions related to mass culture and mass society. In fact, they added a new perspective to an ongoing debate and examples of their work began to appear in the standard communication literature, perhaps as an implicit acknowledgment of theoretical strengths in an era that lacked a sense of theory.

In particular, the paucity of theoretical contributions to the study of communication and society was a well-recognized dilemma of the American social sciences. Duncan recalled its history and the position of *émigré* scholarship by saying that

> Up to the thirties, we were producing an indigenous school of social theory in America that we had every reason to have hope for. We certainly were proud of it, and

then we got fat and lazy. We began to rely far too much on the brains of refugee scholars, as we once did on European theorists. In our generation (with the notable exception of Talcott Parsons), few American social scientists have made many contributions to social theory. We have been pilfering foreign brains so long now that it's getting to be downright embarrassing.

He ended by urging the development of the American tradition of theory (1967a: 226).

At the same time, the prevailing pressures of positivism and an intellectually confining and dogmatic approach to communication research hardly left room for the type of critical research proposed by Max Horkheimer and Theodor Adorno with their introduction of Critical Theory to an American environment that was not particularly receptive to Marxist theorists, especially foreign ones. Sproule has reported that the "idea that critical social analysis was somehow unpatriotic" was even taken up by Congress and its House Un-American Activities Committee (1987: 72). Carey's impression that "the term 'critical' did not so much describe a position as a cover under which Marxism might hide during a hostile period in exile" (1982: 22) alludes to the problems of Marxist scholarship as an alien phenomenon in the United States. But he totally disregards the history of Critical Theory, including the significance of its earlier phase in Germany, the specificity of the concept itself, and the relationship of Critical Theory to Marxism. The result was the emergence of distinct philosophical perspectives by a number of German *émigrés* who were also critics of contemporary bourgeois societies, including the practice of the social sciences.

For instance, Adorno had always felt rather pessimistic about his work with Lazarsfeld. When stipulations concerning the Princeton radio project insisted that the limits of analyses be defined by the American commercial radio system, he concluded that "it was thereby implied that the system itself, its cultural and sociological consequences and its social and economic presuppositions were not to be analyzed" (1969: 343). More important perhaps was Lazarsfeld's insistence on the quantification of culture, which struck Adorno as a "demand to 'measure culture'," and as quite inappropriate for someone who had come to the conclusion that "culture might be precisely that condition that excludes a mentality capable of measuring it" (1969: 347).

Lazarsfeld, on the other hand, reported that he had drawn upon Adorno's studies for his version of critical research, but his own discussion of Critical Theory was limited to acknowledging its stimulating effects upon administrative research. There was no attempt to deal with the theoretical (and ideological) consequences of integrating Critical Theory into mainstream communication research. Lazarsfeld's conclusion—that "if it were included in the general stream of communications research, [Critical Theory] could contribute much in terms of challenging problems and new concepts useful in the interpretation of known, and in the search for new data" (1941: 16)—remained a vague and noncommittal statement. It also implied that Critical Theory would not determine the type of (mass) communication research, but would function as a source of ideas for the execution of administrative research. And finally, these remarks also help demonstrate Lazarsfeld's shotgun approach to rendering ideas capable of supporting his own research interests.

There were other, basic differences between German *Sozial-forschung* and American social science research methodology, most importantly, perhaps, the question of empirical verification, which preoccupied American social scientists. Horkheimer had explained the methodological viewpoint of critical social research in the issue of *Studies in Philosophy and Social Science* that carried Lazarsfeld's article on administrative and critical communication research. His comments were concise and to the point; he explained that the formation of categories for critical research must consider "the historical character of the subject matter to which they pertain, and in such a way that the categories are made to include the actual genesis of that subject matter." Subsequently,

> the general concept is thus not dissolved into a multitude of empirical facts but is concretized in a theoretical analysis of a given social configuration and related to the whole of the historical process of which it is an indissoluble part.
>
> (1941b: 122)

Horkheimer developed a critical rationale for the formation of social theory by describing one of the major issues in the relationship between individuals and media, and therefore in the realm of communication research. He observed that public media

> constantly profess their adherence to the individual's ultimate value and his inalienable freedom, but they operate in such a way that they tend to forswear such values by fettering the individual to prescribed attitudes, thoughts, and buying habits. The ambivalent relation between prevailing values and the social context forces the categories of social theory to become critical and thus to reflect the actual rift between the social reality and the values it posits.
>
> (1941b: 122)

This was a clear challenge to traditional theories of communication and a source of inspiration for new contributions to the field, but it is difficult to imagine that Lazarsfeld or Schramm, for that matter, would have joined forces with Horkheimer's critical position.

In fact, Horkheimer argued that the "real social function of philosophy lies in its criticism of what is prevalent" (1989: 264). What was prevalent was the replacement of philosophy by sociology and the domination of the study of society by a social-scientific perspective, which continued to excel in the production of information about communication, media and people and their social, political or economic relations. Horkheimer recognized the American preoccupation with the

> assiduous collecting of facts in all the disciplines dealing with social life, the gathering of great masses of detail in connection with problems, the empirical enquiries, through careful questionnaires and other means, which are a major part of scholarly activity,

and he suggested that all are adding up "to a pattern which is much like the rest of life in a society dominated by industrial production techniques" (1972: 190–1). A Critical Theory of society, however,

> has for its objects men as producers of their own historical way of life in its totality. The real situations which are the starting point of science are not regarded simply as data to be verified and to be predicted according to the laws of probability. Every datum depends not on nature alone but also on the power man has over it. Objects, the kind of perception, the questions asked, and the meaning of the answers all bear witness to human activity and the degree of man's power.
>
> (1972: 244)

Horkheimer insisted that the "chief aim of such criticism is to prevent mankind from losing itself in those ideas and activities which the existing organization of society instills in its members" (1972: 265). Therefore, it must be one of the goals of Critical Theory to make individuals realize their relationship to society and the differences between their everyday activities and the guiding ideas of society which they acknowledge.

Horkheimer's positioning of Critical Theory coincided with a period in the history of Western thought when fascism and communism threatened the existence of democracy, and when a critical attitude toward the social and economic consequences of late-industrial capitalism was needed to help redefine the nature of a democratic society. Indeed, it became a moral obligation to expose and learn from the failures and weaknesses of a capitalist system that provided the only alternative for creating desirable changes. In their 1972 preface to *Dialectic of Enlightenment*, Horkheimer and Adorno reflected on the continuing threat of totalitarianism and restated that "critical thought (which does not abandon its commitment even in the face of progress) demands support for the residues of freedom, and for tendencies toward true humanism, even if these seem powerless in regard to the main course of history" (1972: ix–x).

A critical analysis of society meant to engage in criticism which was an

> intellectual, and eventually practical, effort which is not satisfied to accept the prevailing ideas, actions, and social conditions unthinkingly and from mere habit; effort which aims to coordinate the individual sides of social life with each other and with the general ideas and aims of the epoch, to deduce them genetically, to distinguish the appearance from the essence, to examine the foundations of things, in short, really to know them.
>
> (1972: 270)

But the recognition of a critical position, based on a notion that the substance of truth is historical, was rare in sociological analyses of communication and particularly absent from Lazarsfeld's discussion of critical research. It reflected fundamental differences between two intellectual traditions and their approach to culture, society and media phenomena. Pragmatism—with its suggestion that ideas or theories are plans of action and that truth is nothing but the success of an idea—had promoted the view that, in an atmosphere of competing statements or ideas, significance is defined in terms of consequences. According to Horkheimer, "Pragmatism has from its beginnings implicitly justified the current substitution of the logic of probability for that of truth, which has since become widely prevalent" (1947: 43). In such an atmosphere prediction becomes the mechanism of social thought, while practice replaces thought, like Dewey's idea that knowing is doing, Horkheimer charged that

> pragmatism tries to retranslate any understanding into mere conduct. Its ambition is to be itself nothing else but practical activity, as distinct from theoretical insight, which, according to pragmatistic teachings, is either only a name for physical events or just meaningless.
>
> (1947: 48)

He saw that the rise of Pragmatism coincided with the development of industrial power and technological superiority in the United States. It was the philosophy of an age of science in which experimentation succeeded over meditation and challenged a philosophical tradition which accepted the primacy of thought and theoretical insight. Horkheimer exposed the dangers of Pragmatism, which attempted "to model all spheres of intellectual life after the techniques of the laboratory," becoming the "counterpart of modern industrialism, for which the factory is the prototype of human existence, and which models all branches of culture after production on the conveyor belt, or after the rationalized front office." Accordingly,

> Thought must be gauged by something that is not thought, by its effect on production or its impact of social conduct, as art today is being ultimately gauged in every detail by something that is not art, be it box-office or propaganda value.
>
> (1947: 50–1)

The location of communication research in the scientific culture of society, its self-defined role of providing insights into the position and function of communication and media in American life, and its narrow understanding of the nature of communication in compliance with the needs of industry and politics, are evidence of its allegiance to a Pragmatic world view, and perhaps an explanation for the different nature of theoretical work in the field. Indeed, ideas about communication and media can be conceived as providing mechanisms to promote series of events toward specific practical goals; for instance, a conceptualization of models to serve experimentation and the verification of facts also helps determine the discourse about communication and media effects. The result is the production of "the knowledge of domination, not the knowledge of cultivation" (Frankfurt, 1972: 125). Under such conditions, there was no place for a historical process which provided knowledge about the relationship between individuals and technology and the processes of communication that locate and identify the individual in the age-old struggle for survival against domination or oppression. In fact, there was no time for history, or reflection in general.

The differences between the theoretical requirements of a critical analysis of contemporary society offered by Critical Theorists and the premises for observations of social phenomena occupied by American social scientists were significant and obviously unacceptable to those controlling communication research. Robert Merton once referred to these differences in the study of society in terms of knowledge and information. He suggested that knowledge

> implies a body of facts or ideas, whereas information carries no such implication of *systematically connected* facts or ideas. The American variant accordingly studies the isolated fragments of information available to masses of people; the European variant typically *thinks about a total structure of knowledge* available to a few.
>
> (1957: 441)

American communication research in the 1960s provided an example of information-gathering practices with a decidedly future-oriented frame of reference, which determined the nature of data collection concerning socially or economically relevant communication behavior. Specifically, public opinion research occurs as an information-gathering activity that has little potential for contributing to the knowledge about people and society. It reveals the commodification of information as the product of a mass culture industry which sells people a way of life that they may recognize as their own, while it remains ahistorical and divorced from the culture which it purports to understand and insists on interpreting.

Consequently, the approach to the study of culture by members of the Frankfurt School (and their development of an aesthetic theory that had originated during the early days of the Institute of Social Research) would be significantly different from American concerns with communication, mass society and mass culture. Horkheimer and Adorno presented their theory of mass culture as early as 1944 in *Die Dialektik der Aufklärung,* which was issued as *Dialectic of Enlightenment* in 1972 when it began to have an impact on the American mass society debate.

An understanding of a theory of culture by Horkheimer and Adorno, equally shared by Marcuse, Lowenthal and Benjamin, is based in the rise of civil society and, more specifically, the development of capitalism. The early work of Georg Lukács, particularly his *Theory of the Novel* (1916) and *History and Class Consciousness* (1923), addressed the contemporary crisis of culture, that is, the disintegration of community and the decline of the subject, and provided a Marxist perspective on the fate of the individual in modern society. Extrapolating from Marx, Lukács used the notion of commodity fetishism to introduce reification as a "deadening" of social and intellectual processes which extended beyond the economic to characterize bourgeois life and to confirm atomization and fragmentation under advanced capitalism.

Dialectic of Enlightenment introduced the specter of reification and its consequences for contemporary society, that is, the destruction of the Enlightenment and the dilemma of criticism. But while Horkheimer and Adorno revealed a profound pessimism in face of the aftermath of the Second World War, the obscenity of fascism, the failure of socialism under Stalinist rule, and the increasingly authoritarian nature of American society, their work is also an expression of a need for the Enlightenment to *"consider itself"* and to redeem the "hopes of the past" (1972: xv). They acknowledged the paradox of human suffering and social progress and confronted conditions under which the "flood of detailed information and candy-floss entertainment simultaneously instructs and stultifies mankind" (1972: xv). *Dialectic of Enlightenment* contained a critique of mass culture, albeit truncated, that was revealing and instructive for those searching for a theory and method of dealing with communication and media.

The problematic of communication in the modern world emerges through an examination of the history of language and thought, the growth of civil society and the rise of capitalism, when the commodification of ideas resulted in the development of the culture industry. It is located in the social, political and economic conditions of contemporary mass culture and its understanding rests on the ability to trace the relationship between individuals and the alienating environment of modern institutions. Thus, the study of communication is also the study of alienation and desertion, while the history of the media is also the story of separation and isolation of individuals.

According to Horkheimer and Adorno, the formalized production of goods, including culture, aiming at uniformity and efficiency, is based on the "predominance of the effect" (1972: 125), which replaces the work or idea. Consequently, consumers choose technique over content, and perfection of the production over distraction of the arts. The culture industry embraces the ideology of business in its creation of needs; it obtains power from "its identification with a manufactured need" (1972: 137) and the promise of escape from the work process through its production of amusement. Escape, however, is nothing but an approximation or "prolongation" of work (1972: 137), since it makes no new demands and requires no independent thought from the audience.

Horkheimer and Adorno described the reduction of individuals to customers and therefore to elements or objects in the processing of information that serves to maintain the status quo, based on the vague and noncommittal nature of communication, which becomes the *modus vivendi* of the culture industry. They concluded that "Anyone who doubts the power of monotony is a fool" and reminded the reader that "the bread which the culture industry offers man is the stone of stereotype" (1972: 148).

Attacking the perpetuation of political values by the media, the authors suggested that the culture industry treats individuals as illusions and will tolerate them as long as they maintain an unquestioned identification with the public. In effect, "The peculiarity of the self is a monopoly commodity determined by society; it is falsely represented as natural" (1972: 154). In such a society, individuals, culture and advertising merge to produce a seamless stream of communication and images, strengthening the bonds between industry and consumers, between the media and audiences, and ultimately, serve to maintain the economic and political power structure. Consequently, "freedom to choose an ideology—since ideology always reflects economic coercion—everywhere proves to be freedom to choose what is always the same" (1972: 166–7).

Horkheimer and Adorno questioned not only the contemporary manifestations of the media industry; they also raised doubts about the values perpetuated in defense of the prevailing ideology and scrutinized the mechanisms of social criticism. In fact, Adorno proposed elsewhere that the

> task of criticism must be not so much to search for the particular interest-groups to which cultural phenomena are to be assigned, but rather to decipher the general social tendencies which are expressed in these phenomena and through which the most powerful interests realize themselves. Cultural criticism must become social physiognomy.
>
> (1981: 30)

Under such a redefinition of cultural criticism, Adorno suggested that Critical Theory could not accept alternatives or choices between transcendent or immanent criticism of culture, that is, "either calling culture as a whole into question from outside under the general notion of ideology, or confronting it with its norms which it itself has crystallized" (1981: 31).

As a contributor to US communication research literature, Adorno outlined the manner and methodology with which Critical Theory would attack the problems of media in contemporary society (1954). He suggested that historical insights into the development of media in American culture were absolutely necessary to "do justice to all such complexities" that existed in the rise of mass culture (1954: 214). But the quest for knowledge about the nature of modern media also needed a "depth-psychological approach," since the "media are not simply the sum total of the actions they portray or of the messages that radiate from these actions," but have a "heritage of polymorphic meaning" which has been "taken over by the culture industry inasmuch as what it conveys becomes itself organized in order to enthrall the spectators on various psychological levels simultaneously" (1954: 221). Adorno provided a wide-ranging discussion of ways in which to address the cultural problems of television and suggested that the "effort here required is of a moral nature itself: knowingly to face psychological mechanisms operating on various levels in order not to become blind and passive victims" (1954: 235).

Critical research in the tradition of Critical Theory, with its speculative approach to contemporary culture and society, sought to challenge the theoretical basis of traditional social research. Critical-administrative research, on the other hand, in the tradition of a progressive American sociology, was driven by methodological considerations and the immediacy and potential threat of mass culture phenomena to the social or political status quo.

At this time American communication research had begun to expand upon the pioneering work of Lazarsfeld, Hovland, Lasswell and others, and was drifting into what Lazarsfeld had labeled "administrative" research with an increasing sophistication of its empirical methodology. Members of the Frankfurt School identified this trend as market research, and Leo Lowenthal suggested that it could only reflect "reified unmediated reactions rather than the underlying social and psychological function of the cultural phenomena under scrutiny" (Jay, 1985: 50).

The problems of mass society, with its feared cultural and political consequences, particularly in the face of fascist and communist threats from Europe, had encouraged an American response, when earlier research into questions of collective behavior (Blumer), media and diffusion (Lazarsfeld), persuasion (Hovland), and propaganda (Lasswell), sought empirical evidence to demonstrate the workings of a pluralist society in the United States. Among these contributors, Lasswell represented the most knowledgeable theorist, whose appreciation of Marx and Freud as major intellectual sources for the interpretation of cultures, and whose familiarity with the structure of Marxist ideology offered a comparative perspective for the study of political behavior long before many of his American colleagues acknowledged its relevance.

Lasswell had to overcome the fact that political science theory and academic research in the 1920s had not considered the importance of Marxist thought, because "America was protected by geographic distance and its own affluence and provincialism from a realization of the significance of the class struggles in Europe, and in part by the 'red scares' of the early 1920s" (Smith, 1969: 64–5). He appreciated the importance of a cultural approach to the study of communication; and his writings, since the publication of *Propaganda Technique in the World War* in 1927, reflected the need to sensitize communication researchers to the uses of language. He had pondered these issues in the wake of a number of important publications, particularly Lippmann's *Public Opinion* (1922) and *The Phantom Public* (1925), on the question of the public and its role in the political system.

Lasswell also represented a long-standing interest in the study of culture and symbols in the context of political communication. He had raised significant possibilities for the analysis of politics in cultural settings, that is, for "the study of changes in the shape and composition of the value patterns of society" (1935: 3). He had recognized the proximity between political and social practices and the significance of the symbolic environment and began to formulate communication research strategies that would systematically embrace "patterns of personality and culture" (1935: 208). Lasswell was convinced of a relationship between subjective and objective aspects of existence, and concluded that "in the culture that we know best the rearrangement of inner experience has become intimately connected with overt materializations" (1935: 268). His approach consisted of historical analyses and the use of empirical data to compose pictures of political reality, as in "News Channels and Attention Areas: The Role of Secondary Contact," which also described a variety of creative procedures to assess public communication (1935: 185–206). Cartier has called Lasswell "a humanistic behaviorist" in the tradition of the scientific naturalism of the Chicago School (1988: 187), while Lerner has observed that "Lasswell always stressed the importance of normative functions in human enterprises. Although a behaviorist, he never became an addict of behaviorism (or any other ideological 'ism')" (1979: 406).

In fact, Lasswell provided communication research with ideas about effects, content analysis and an approach to communication which overcame the simplicity of (his own) earlier stimulus—response models, and by doing so, probably contributed more to the field than most of his contemporaries in communication and media research. But he could not prevail theoretically in the sociological circles that dominated the developing stages of the field. Leo Rosten has called him "the most fertile catalyst and theorist of his generation," adding that Lasswell's "pioneering contributions to propaganda analysis, the pyramid of power, content analysis, political symbols, and political psychology are indisputable and historic" (1969: 9).

Nevertheless, while Lasswell's scholarship was impressive in its scope, its criticism was confined to the study of political behavior and the uses of symbolic analysis, and therefore removed from the most active realm of communication research. His position also highlights the consequences of segmentation when research interests divided political communication from mass communication. The result was a predictable but unfortunate power struggle among expert groupings seeking recognition of their narrow specializations from within and reinforcement through financial rewards from outside the academy. Such a development was certainly not in the interest of an interdisciplinary approach toward a social theory of communication.

After the Second World War, however, American society came under renewed scrutiny from a number of disciplines, emanating from postwar changes, like the rapid expansion of a peacetime economy and the widespread prosperity of a growing white middle class. David Potter's *People of Plenty* (1954), Vance Packard's *The Hidden Persuaders* (1957), and William Whyte's *The Organization Man* (1957) were examples of popular and critical accounts of this period when mass culture became the target of an attack on the American public. There were others, like David Riesman and C. Wright Mills, whose critical characterizations of American society caught the imagination of social critics and caused a considerable debate among social scientists.

Riesman had been influenced by Erich Fromm and psychoanalytic analyses of culture. His book, *The Lonely Crowd,* co-authored by Nathan Glazer and Reuel Denney, and first published in 1950, dealt with the problem of historical change in industrial Middle America. The book became a basic document for the discussion of American culture during the 1950s; according to Hartshorne, "It was one of those rare books which, though intended primarily for a scholarly audience, enjoyed an enormous popular success" (1968: 173). It was an account of the American dream turned into a nightmare, according to Paul and Percival Goodman, demonstrating that "our beautiful American classlessness is degenerating into a static bureaucracy; our mass arts are beneath contempt; our prosperity breeds insecurity; our system of distribution has become huckstering and our system of production discourages enterprise and sabotages invention" (1960: 5).

Riesman and his colleagues were most interested in the problems of a changing society and pursued the discovery of social history by utilizing "previously neglected and underprivileged data" (1961: xiv), based on the insights of neo-Freudian analysis of cultural and historical change. They revealed a decisive shift of American society from "inner-direction" to "other-direction" in a study of culture and history that was mindful of a traditional, holistic approach, while taking advantage of newer research techniques. Thus, they relied on Lazarsfeld's findings about the two-step flow of information, while concentrating on questions about the long-run effects of communication and media on the emotional and private lives of Americans, since the exercise of control over the individual by peer groups was a characteristic of the "other-directed" individual. The authors suggested that since the media seem to be less effective than "the controllers of the media and their critics like to think," they are "much freer than they realize, to attend to the medium itself, rather than to the message it purveys or is believed to purvey" (1961: 205). In an atmosphere of conformity, they advocated allowing for more genuine escape, so that "Americans would become stronger psychically and more ready to undertake an awakening of political imagination and commitment" (1961: 204). Their concerns and criticisms remained differentiated and concentrated on the potential of the media as agents of human liberation from the delusion of self-determination, exploring the possibilities of moving between high and popular culture, to make a difference in the lives of people.

A few years later, in a new preface to the edition, however, Riesman voiced "gravest" concerns about the ethnocentricity of the media and the slanting of news in a misleading and self-serving manner (1961: xliii). He had produced a study that suggested to communication research the complexity of formulating meaningful research agendas and the need to supplement the range of social-psychological methodologies with historical considerations of individuals in communication.

The sociology of C. Wright Mills was enriched by his refusal to accept a social-scientific study of society that lacked a historical perspective and that refused to take a moral stand on the subject of its analysis. He railed against the "abstract empiricism" of the social sciences and the dogma of methodology and provided a scathing critique of advanced urban society in a series of books, from *The New Men of Power* (1948) and *White Collar* (1951) to *The Power Elite* (1956). His belief in the significance of an intellectual tradition of social thought became the rallying point of a "new" sociology which called for the consciousness of "basic premises and principles," suggesting that the sociology of "Pareto, Durkheim, Weber, Znaniecki, Simmel, and Marx" was important, because "it is to them that we owe the firm distinction between science as clarification and information as manipulation" (Horowitz, 1964: 18).

One of the goals was the reclamation of social history and its relationship to sociology; Mills demonstrated how the intellectual tradition of social thought could provide methodological guidance to questions of time and specificity. He has also been called an "American conscience" at a time when imperialism and nuclear war threatened total destruction, struggling "against the liberal rhetoric, Marxist dogma, and sociological dehumanization" (Casanova, 1964: 71). His sociological imagination called for the acquisition of a quality of mind which would enable individuals to "grasp history and biography and the relations between the two within society" (1959: 12).

Mills issued a pessimistic view of the media in *The Power Elite*, revealing a market orientation that facilitates "psychological illiteracy" rather than public discourse and enlightenment (1956: 311). Accordingly, he saw the media as presiding over a "pseudo-world," having provided external realities and internal experiences and destroying privacy by destroying "the chance for the reasonable and leisurely and human interchange of opinion" (1956: 314). But the media were not only a major cause of the emergence of a mass society in the United States, they were also a means of power elites. Because media play an important role in the execution of authority, they help create one of the major problems of contemporary society, namely the denial of authority to the people. Mills argued that "the power of initiation is in fact held by small circles of men" whose "strategy of manipulation is to make it appear that the people, or at least a large group of them, 'really made the decision'" (1956: 317). The media represent an aspect of this strategy, and *The Power Elite* was an indictment of the American power structure. Its moral judgment and intellectual integrity challenged liberal-pluralist arguments and pointed the way toward a radical critique of society. It was also the contribution of an intellectual whose moral obligation to oppose the conditions of mass society resulted in an attack on the denial of rationality and freedom.

Riesman and Mills recognized the importance of analyzing power in society and sought to locate the basis for criticism in the socioeconomic distribution of property or influence. They were concerned with the structure of power and its consequences for American society; although positioned quite differently—Mills referred to Riesman's "romantic pluralism" (1956: 244), and Riesman saw Mills searching for a "ruling class" (1961: 225)—both observed a decline of political participation and the failure of public opinion. These issues involved social communication and the role of the media, and were central to communication research. But their contributions seemed to have been of only peripheral interest to the field, which had managed to retain a singularly narrow theoretical and historical base in its endeavor as a social-scientific enterprise.

Indeed, academic journals like *Journalism Quarterly, Public Opinion Quarterly, Journal of Broadcasting* or *Journal of Communication*, in particular, did not seek theoretical controversy or politicized participation in a critical assessment of

American media research, or question the premises of an implicit operating theory of communication and society.

Since the late 1960s, the field of communication research reflected the conditions of a society embroiled in controversies over a war in Viet Nam and experienced the emergence of a brand of social criticism strongly related to an earlier critique of American society. This tradition has spanned the socialist writings of political economists and sociologists during the turn of the century, the populist criticism of political and economic authority by publicists and muckraking journalists in the late 1920s, and the social criticism of social scientists since the 1950s.

Among the first contributors to a critical literature of media and communication was Herbert Schiller, whose *Mass Communications and American Empire* (1969) supplied readers with a critical approach to the political and economic functions of American mass communication structures and policies. According to Dallas Smythe's introduction, the book supplanted the tangential and often outdated work of Mills, Robert A. Brady, Thurman Arnold, or Robert S. Lynd (Schiller, 1969: viii), and was an effort that critically addressed communication issues. The book helped establish Schiller's reputation as a social critic and humanist who challenged the desirability of an industrialization of communication, calling "ownership, control, financial support, national sovereignty and the character of programming" the "unsettled agenda" of society (1969: 149). In a series of small books *(The Mind Managers,* 1973; *Communication and Cultural Domination,* 1976; *Who Knows: Information in the Age of the Fortune 500,* 1981; *Information and the Crisis Economy,* 1984; and *Culture Inc.: The Corporate Takeover of Public Expression,* 1989) Schiller continued to expose the manipulation of information and the problems of cultural domination from a political economy perspective of communication and media. His analyses of power, however, were not without hope for the betterment of society, since they were based upon a belief in the ability of individuals to participate in the life of society, despite the increasing controls of the communication system. His work has been the crusade of a humanist who always seemed to feel that a "heightened consciousness" may eventually "develop its own means to force the social changes so desperately needed in this country today" (1973: 191). In this sense, Schiller has been an interventionist, helping to provide a critical balance in a debate that celebrated information societies and dehumanizing technological progress in the name of freedom and democracy.

His ideas were enhanced and supported by the work of Dallas Smythe, whose critical historical materialism offered a political-economic perspective on the control of information, the invention of the media by monopoly capitalism to produce an audience commodity, and the consequences of a "mass communication theory [that] begins and ends with audiences, prospective and produced [and consumed]" (1981: xv). Together with Schiller he offered probably the most radical and steadfast economic critique in the field; but more importantly, both demonstrated through their work the possibility and the potential for Marxist criticism beyond the 1960s.

The introduction of Critical Theory since the 1940s as a competing social (and political) theory of society constituted a significant development in American social thought. It rekindled a Marxist debate, promoted radical criticism, and signaled the beginning of substantial Marxist scholarship which continued after the war and into the 1970s. The ensuing critique of contemporary American social theory and research practice also established the intellectual leadership of British, French and German social theorists, when the center of theoretical innovations and reconsiderations shifted to the intellectual milieu of postwar Europe.

Thus, the encounter with critical theorists provided a solid opportunity to examine form and substance of an ideological critique of society. Specifically, the cultural pessimism of Adorno and Horkheimer, together with the political critique of Herbert Marcuse, the popular culture critique of Leo Lowenthal and, later, the theoretical inquiries of Jürgen Habermas concerning the role of communication in the struggle against bureaucracies and authority, provided American social theorists with alternatives to questions of power, change, and the future of society.

In his response to the influence of the Frankfurt School on intellectual life in the United States, Shils attributed its critique of mass society to the conditions of exile rather than to the European experience. He suggested that "their anti-capitalistic and by multiplication, anti-American attitude found a traumatic and seemingly ineluctable confirmation in the popular culture of the United States" (1972: 263). In fact, their critical writings exemplified an abiding commitment to the study of culture—including the complicity of the media industry in the ideological struggle—and to an analysis of the cultural process. They were also the result of recognizing attempts throughout this century to merge the interests of science and industry under the auspices of various institutions, including universities.

According to Schroyer, the Marxist cultural critique of contemporary society stressed the "sociocultural consequences of stimulated economic growth." Consequently, it "transforms the human milieu into a technologically determined system, and systematically blocks symbolic communication by the superimposition of more and more technical rules and constraints deriving from rationalizing processes" (1975a: 223). These were continuing concerns among cultural critics, and Alvin Gouldner, in particular, has traced similarities and differences between the Pragmatism of the Chicago School and Critical Theory in their analysis of the "cultural apparatus" and the "consciousness industry," respectively (1976:167–78). He proposed that the common interest in public discourse manifested in the role of news in everyday life and the conditions of the public sphere were treated in a "taxonomic and positivistic" way by the Chicago School, while such interest received a historically specific treatment particularly by Habermas, who linked the deterioration of the public sphere with the development of a bourgeois economy (1976: 138–40).

When the debates over Critical Theory reached mainstream (mass) communication research in the 1970s, it had been a major theoretical event for over four decades, constituting a considerable body of theoretical literature which reflected the extent and quality of the modernist debate in a number of disciplines. Beginning with Martin Jay's *The Dialectical Imagination: A History of the Frankfurt School and the Institute of Social Research, 1923-1950* (1973), the volume of original works by Adorno, Horkheimer, Marcuse and Habermas, together with translations of German contemporaries and other secondary sources about the Frankfurt School increased dramatically,[1] although the subsequent readings and interpretations of Critical Theory by (mass) communication research remained a peripheral intellectual enterprise.

For instance, the marginal role of Critical Theory, or any other radical challenge of traditional social theories, had been revealed in the frequently cited 1959 *Public Opinion Quarterly* review of communication research. Berelson's pessimistic statement included no reference to Critical Theory as a potential source of theoretical stimulation (1959: 4), although in the same issue Riesman referred to a critique of society with the publication of *The Authoritarian Personality* (Adorno *et al.*) in 1950 and raised some questions concerning needed research on broader cultural and societal issues. He also mentioned the creative work of Leo Lowenthal, who had established himself as an early member of the Frankfurt School with his interest in the sociology of literature (Hardt, 1991).

Lowenthal was the most visible representative of Critical Theory in American communication research circles, having collaborated with Joseph Klapper (opinion research and psychological warfare) and Marjorie Fiske (popular culture), and having been included in a number of collected works edited by Lazarsfeld and Stanton, Schramm, and Jacobs.

He had understood better than some of his German colleagues how to bridge the differences between the methodological demands of a social-scientific analysis of media and society in the United States and the necessity of a historical dimension for inquiries into the nature of culture or cultural productions. He had gained acceptance (and respectability as a social scientist) with his widely quoted "Biographies in Popular Magazines" (1944) that was based on his earlier work in Germany and had appeared with Lazarsfeld's encouragement. In his recollections, Lowenthal remembered Robert Merton's favorable response as well as Lazarsfeld's complete misunderstanding of the "political and analytical meaning" of this study (1989: 234).

Underlying Lowenthal's contributions to the field was a deep-seated, European concern with the humanistic aspects of social theory and an active involvement in the promotion of theoretical and methodological traditions that had their origins in classic conceptualizations of culture. He became a mediator between the social and behavioral sciences and the humanities in their struggle for dominating the debate concerning the definition of fields of knowledge. In particular, his work on popular culture was influenced by a shared critical understanding of a pervasive attitude in society toward entertainment. According to Jay, members of the Frankfurt School argued that the notion of popular culture was ideological; in fact, "the culture industry administered a non-spontaneous reified, phony culture rather than the real thing" (1973: 216).

In a series of essays that he more recently combined under the title "Contributions to the Philosophy of Communication," Lowenthal produced a vision of the field through a discussion of the sociology of literature, the critique of mass culture and popular culture, and their proximity to communication research (1984).

He had established his own interest in the historical and sociological dimensions of literature early during his career and thought it essential in his approach to a sociology of literature and proceeded to argue for a materialistic explanation of literary history, but refused to place literature within a strictly economic explanation of culture. Instead, literature as a means of making culture transparent becomes also a reflection of ideology, while literary studies are "largely an investigation of ideologies" (1984: 248). His understanding of social theory as tentative and open to changes provided the necessary flexibility for incorporating new insights and meeting methodological demands in light of sociological criticism.

Lowenthal had recognized that the products of mass literature as increasingly popular objects of communication research had been neglected by literary studies. Academic disciplines which saw themselves in charge of accounting for literature had been "caught unaware by the impact of mass literature, the best seller, the popular magazine, the comics and the like, and they have maintained an attitude of haughty indifference to the lower depths of imagination in print" (1984: 257). He outlined a course of sociological action which included a number of suggestions related to communication research in an essay which reflected his unpublished remarks during the 1947 opening of the Institute for Communication Research at the University of Illinois, where he specifically addressed the requirements of critical communication research (1948).

Thus, it is necessary to place literature—and one could also include journalism as popular culture—within a "functional frame" within society, suggesting the location of literary material within a culture and its specific class stratifications, to gain an understanding of its social relevance. Such a positioning of literature or journalism in terms of their escapist or ideological functions would be supplemented with an analysis of specific forms. Lowenthal singled out his own work on popular biographies in mass circulation magazines to provide an example of how media succeed in constructing a topical environment in which the reader

> can experience the gratification of being confirmed in his own pleasures and discomforts by participating in the pleasures and discomforts of the great. The large confusing issues in the political and economic realm and the antagonisms and controversies in the social realm are submerged in the experience of being at one with the powerful and great in the sphere of consumption.
>
> (1984: 258–9)

Lowenthal would argue that the analysis of society from a literary (or journalistic) perspective must also include a discussion of the position of writers or journalists as intellectuals within the cultural milieu. Thus, the study of their political and economic standing and their own view of their function, including their treatment of social or political problems, is as important as seeking insights into conditions of production.

More significantly, Lowenthal felt that scholarly investigations should relate to the impact of the media. This had been a major area of traditional communication research, but Lowenthal argued that the question of effects involved more than the empirical analysis of consumption, but was destined to provoke theoretical explorations that would help define its "social determinants," including specific knowledge about the influence of "all-embracing social constellations on writing and the reading public," an understanding of "the influence of formal [and informal] controls of production and reading," and an assessment of "technological change and its economic and social consequences" (1984: 264–5).

Lowenthal urged sociologists of literature to join in the experiences of communication research, and he proposed a series of research projects that would enhance the standing of the discipline and add to its knowledge about culture and communication. He also offered a number of appropriate examples of critical research, including references to Walter Benjamin's "The Work of Art in the Age of Reproduction," Siegfried Kracauer's "From Caligari to Hitler," Adorno's "On Popular Music," and Horkheimer's "Art and Mass Culture."

His essay remains a remarkable, albeit incomplete, statement about critical communication research that has been virtually ignored since its publication in 1948. In fact, Lowenthal's analytical scheme, his themes and methodological suggestions, could be considered the beginning of a theoretical foundation of critical communication research in the United States.

The social and political movements of the time had been captured in Lowenthal's exposure of questionable communication practices, revealing the sensitivity of the foreign observer to the potential of aggression in society. Together with Norbert Guterman, he published *Prophets of Deceit: A Study of the Techniques of the American Agitator* in 1949, which appeared in the series on *Studies in Prejudice.* It became a significant contribution to the study of mass society, concentrating on the meaning of demagogy, its techniques and appeals, and served as a popular resource in the field of mass communication research. The volume also confirmed Lowenthal's own position among Critical Theorists; it remains a remarkable document of participation in the surveillance of the political and social environment of the United States. Lowenthal engaged in an analysis of the techniques of agitation, "turning psychoanalysis on its head," by suggesting that public agitation would result in neurotic and psychotic behavior and create a dependency on leadership. His purpose was the unmasking of "aggressive and destructive impulses hidden behind that rhetoric" on the basis of textual analyses which would reveal unconscious mechanisms of agitation (1989: 234).

The serious political engagement of Horkheimer, Lowenthal and others and the potential role of their work in the enlightenment process of American society were perhaps best illustrated by Lowenthal's revelation that Horkheimer intended to reproduce each book in the *Studies in Prejudice* series as a pamphlet for distribution to "so-called multiplicators," that is, journalists and opinion leaders, in a "given situation of anti-Semitic political outbreaks." He added that in the spirit of Critical Theory they wanted "to accomplish scientifically meaningful work in a manner that would allow its application to political praxis" (1989: 235). The series offered insightful analyses of power and authority in modern society, and *The Authoritarian Personality* (Adorno *et al.*, 1950) remains one of the seminal contributions from this era.

During the early 1960s Lowenthal continued to argue for a critical approach to (popular) culture and insisted on the recognition of the historical process in the definition of the cultural stimulus, since the relationship between stimulus and response has been "pre-formed and pre-structured" by their "historical and social fate" (1961: 13). In this context, he recognized the contributions of Park and Wirth who had "kept alive the conscience of a historical civilization" (1961: 8), and he concluded his assessment of American sociology with the observation that "expediency and the lack of a historical or philosophical frame of reference make a sorry marriage of convenience" (1961: 10).

Lowenthal's commitment to the exploration of mass culture was also confirmed in his reaction to Riesman's work about American mass culture with the publication of *The Lonely Crowd*. He praised the humanistic orientation of the book and used the opportunity to engage the field in a debate about the position of what he called "the scientific and the intellectual universe" (1984: 276). He credited the authors with helping reverse the dominant pattern of the social sciences, which had consisted of "a preeminent concern with methodology and with the construction of theoretical models" (1984: 279). Lowenthal acknowledged the difficulty of "interpreting within one conceptual framework the uniqueness of a historical period and the general features of human behavior prevailing in it" as a dilemma that must be faced "if one wants to understand *uno actu* individuals both in their social roles and in their personal imagery" (1984: 280). In addressing this dualism, Lowenthal also pointed to the failures of communication research which had usually remained closed to creative, intellectual risk-taking by relying solely on the promises of empiricism as an established social-scientific practice.

Lowenthal criticized this one-sidedness of communication research and suggested that, because the discussion of communication had deteriorated into discussion of the media, it had "seriously jeopardized productive discourse between social scientists and humanists" (1967: 335). He recounted how communication "has been almost completely divested of its human content" and projected the dehumanization of communication in a media culture that relied "on the ideological sanction of individual autonomy in the very process of exploiting individuality to serve mass culture" (1967: 336).

Earlier he had criticized the "splendid isolation" of social research and proposed that such a position may reinforce the suspicion that social research is "nothing but market research, an instrument of expedient manipulation, a tool with which to prepare reluctant customers for enthusiastic spending" (1961: 9).

In particular, Lowenthal accused social scientists of having evaded their moral commitment "by pretending to engage in value-free research—something that exists neither in logic nor in history." And he insisted, in the spirit of an applied and active Critical Theory, that in "an era of increasing positivistic infatuation . . . the inalienable birthright of the intellectual as a critic, trivial as it may sound, must be energetically asserted" (1967: 337).

Lowenthal turned to the experience of literature, philosophy and art to promote a humanistic meaning of communication that referred to genuinely productive imagination, free from instrumental concepts of language and communication as information technologies, and requiring intellectual effort and participation.

He reminded his readers of the human dimension of communication by citing Dewey's definition at a time when communication was becoming part of a culture which hardly distinguished between consumers and producers "because they are both the serfs of a life style of conformity and regulation" (1967: 344). And he reproached communication research for its failure to acknowledge the potential of a humanistic vision of culture and communication, based on his assessment of modern society and the problems of a displaced sense of participation.

From the beginning, Lowenthal's interest in popular culture and his recognition of media content demonstrated the effectiveness of historical analyses in a series of differentiated and time-bound observations about the role of escapism, ideology and information in the production of mass culture. Furthermore, he recognized the importance of levels of social stratification and, therefore, different bourgeois interests concerning media form and content, and suggested the need for investigating the relationship between class and media use. Thus, problems of consumption of mass culture are tied into the history of a dominant technological bureaucracy and the deteriorating psychological condition of individuals, like the loss of self-confidence and trust. Similarly, inquiries into the production of media content, in the form of a sociology of writers or news workers for instance, were bound to include questions about the impact of the cultural and political environment, economic decision-making, and the effects of role consciousness on the performances of these producers of mass culture.

Throughout his writings, but especially in his contributions to the sociology of literature, Lowenthal proposed a genuine interdisciplinary approach to critical communication research from a perspective of Critical Theory, which he defined as a "perspective, based on a shared critical fundamental attitude, that applies to all cultural phenomena without ever claiming to be a system" (1989: 112). This was a positioning of a critique of society in the tradition of Hegel's form of negation, on the periphery of the establishment and as an expression of marginality. For Lowenthal this meant a "critique of the production of commodities and words for a manipulated and manipulable mass market" (1989: 112).

Lowenthal's approach rested on the recognition of the separate roles of art and popular culture and incorporated the intellectual interests of a classic European tradition of social thought and the insights of a new American social science. Thus, an explanation of the uses of art and mass culture were dependent on the history of social and psychological conditions of society and individuals, respectively. His early work indicates the formulation of ideas toward a theory of reception and effects that were immersed in a critique of ideology. He rejected the behavioristic sociology of literature in the United States as ahistorical and limited in its scope to commercial and political propaganda and disapproved of a narrow Marxist inter-pretation of art as an ideological manifestation. According to Lowenthal,

> art teaches, and mass culture is learned; therefore, a sociological analysis of art must be cautious, supplementary, and selective, whereas a sociological analysis of mass culture must be all-inclusive, for its products are nothing more than the phenomena and symptoms of the process of the individual's self-resignation in a wholly admin-istered society.

(1989: 113)

Lowenthal's work was about the suppression of the imagination and the results of a mass culture that "reinforces and signals the instruction in the late-capitalist world that promotes a false collective" (1989: 119). Although his contri-butions turned out to be politically relevant and culturally instructive, they failed to impress the institutional forces of communication research enough to become a major theoretical and methodological resource. Nevertheless, in his analyses of literature and mass culture, Lowenthal demonstrated the richness of the material as a source of insights about the social and political conditions of a culture. His work also reminded the reader of his intellectual proximity to Walter Benjamin, whose work influenced the later period of cultural studies in the United States and elsewhere.

Lowenthal's self-defined position at the margins of an intellectual enterprise that dealt with questions of literature, culture and communication made him aware of the proximity of Burke and Duncan, for instance, but he was particularly attracted to the communication research of Paul Lazarsfeld. This may have been an indi-cation that Lowenthal saw real possibilities for his work in the area of communica-tion studies; it may also reflect the specific social and political conditions of the time, when Lowenthal, like other *émigrés,* depended on the influence and generos-ity of established individuals and their organizations. But more importantly, Lowenthal came to appreciate the concerns of interactionism with mediation as an aspect that was missing in Marxist theory, namely "the mediation between the fun-damental economic and social forces and actual human needs," as well as the materialistic character of functionalism (1987: 142), although he distanced himself from both theoretical trends. In his autobiographical reflections he concluded that he had been most disturbed about "the so-called empirical research enterprise, where one had the feeling that the research was actually being done only for the sake of the method and not for the sake of the objects of research" (1987: 143).

The discussion of mass society and the effects of technocratic rule as an underlying theme of Critical Theory of these years also characterized the work of Herbert Marcuse, who emerged as the most popular (e.g. most frequently cited) member of the Frankfurt School in the United States. In fact, Clecak has suggested that

> Marcuse made especially good copy because his association with New Left figures suggested such easy and satisfying interpretations. Journalists and critics accounted for the unlikely alliance in pop Freudian terms characterizing Marcuse as a surrogate father who encouraged and sanctioned political and sexual rebellion.
>
> (1973: 212)

He responded to his popularity with an assertion that affirmative culture means "a world brought about not through the overthrow of the material order of life but through events in the individual's soul. Humanity becomes an inner state" (1968: 103).

His position against the empirical sociology of communication emerged from a number of contributions to the critique of mass society. Marcuse felt that contemporary sociology, "freed from all theoretical guidance except a methodological one, succumbs to the fallacies of misplaced concreteness, thus performing an ideological service while proclaiming the elimination of value judgments," and demanded the intervention of Critical Theory (1964: 254).

His particular interests in the mass culture phenomenon were the result of two major themes in his understanding of the history of modern culture: the transition from a period of affirmation, when distinctions between the spiritual and the material world emerged, to a period of resignation; and the relationship between happiness and freedom under the conditions of a bourgeois society.

The developing tensions between the needs of the inner world and the conditions of the outer world could no longer be reconciled and individual desires had to give in to the demands of a dominant society. As a result, the preservation of the economic and political order threatened the spiritual or cultural repositories of the individual. Likewise, the notion of happiness had become defined as freedom from work and remained attached to the idea of leisure. For Marcuse, happiness was more than a feeling of satisfaction; it was found in "the reality of freedom and satisfaction." He added, "Happiness involves knowledge: it is the prerogative of the *animal rationale.* With the decline in consciousness, with the control of information, with the absorption of individual into mass communication, knowledge is administered and confined" (1955: 94).

The result of mass society is an atmosphere of collective anaesthesia, in which the repressed individual shares a reality shaped by the alienation of labor and his reduction to an exchangeable object. Marcuse followed Freud's explanation of the history of culture and argued from a socio-historical perspective that the differences between freedom and happiness and between sexuality and culture were the result of institutional domination and not the outcome of human nature.

He based his argument on the workings of "surplus repression" as a restrictive means of maintaining social domination and the "performance principle" under which individuals "do not live their own lives, but perform pre-established functions," working in alienation (1955: 41).

For Marcuse, the history of Western civilization was the development of the performance principle, which was perfected in the process of industrialization, and achieved when society gained total control of the individual by working conditions of alienated labor. Most recently, the concomitant reduction of leisure time to phases of passivity and "re-creation of energy for work" was redefined when "the technique of mass manipulation developed an entertainment industry which directly controls leisure time" (1955: 43).

Marcuse confirmed his understanding of the task of Critical Theory "to analyze society in the light of its used and unused or abused capabilities for improving the human condition" (1964: x) with the publication of *One-Dimensional Man* (1964).

Accordingly, such critical analysis must be based on value judgments, and Marcuse proceeded from a position of affirmation, suggesting that the foundation of social theory is based on "the judgment that human life is worth living, or rather can be and ought to be made worth living," and on a belief in the existence of specific possibilities "for the amelioration of human life" and the availability of "specific means and ways of realizing these possibilities" (1964: x–xi). For Marcuse, social theory is historical theory and since it is concerned with alternatives, it must "haunt the established society as subversive tendencies and forces" (1964: xii). Although his book is about these counterforces in modern society, which must act to realize the possibilities of a better life, Marcuse's efforts were devoted to showing that

> Technical progress, extended to a whole system of domination and coordination, creates forms of life [and of power] which appear to reconcile the forces opposing the system and to defeat or refute all protest in the name of the historical prospects of freedom from toil and domination.
>
> (1964: xii)

He envisioned a totalitarian society, that is, one in which forms of social control and social cohesion erase the differences between the private and public existence, while incorporating technology into systems of domination.

The role of mass culture and the use of media are crucial aspects of this vision of modern society in which consumption becomes a strategy of power. Rejecting charges that he possibly overrated the potential of the media as instruments of indoctrination, Marcuse suggested that individuals encounter media as "preconditioned receptacles of long standing," long before the impact of mass media technologies and their control. In fact, "the decisive difference is in the flattening out of the contrast [or conflict] between the given and the possible, between the satisfied and the unsatisfied needs" (1964: 8). Accordingly, media use by individuals regardless of their class differences does not indicate the dissolution of classes but "the extent to which the needs and satisfactions that serve the preservation of the Establishment are shared by the underlying population" (1964: 8). This is the emergence of the one-dimensional society, in which "Domination has its own aesthetics, and democratic domination has its democratic aesthetics." Marcuse recognized the benefits of a society in which people have instant access to culture, but he warned that "In this diffusion, however, they become cogs in a culture-machine which remakes their content" (1964: 65).

In *The Aesthetic Dimension* (1978) Marcuse placed art and aesthetics in a pivotal role within Critical Theory by developing dialectical aesthetics in which literature, in particular, functions as the conscience of society. He pronounced that "The truth of art lies in this: that the world really is as it appears in the work of art," and "the political potential of art lies only in its own aesthetic dimension. Its relation to praxis is inexorably indirect, mediated, and frustrating" (1978: xii).

His suggestions could have helped redirect (mass) communication research to explore alternative ways of social communication. One of them was the focus on the role of art in the process of revealing its own truth about reality and, therefore, sharing the experience of autonomy and freedom and providing a measure of the role of media in society.

Many issues pertaining to the consequences of mass society had been presented earlier by Lowenthal, Mills, Riesman and others; they now found support and one kind of theoretical unity in Marcuse's critique of contemporary society. It was characterized by a deeply pessimistic vision, painfully without solutions, except a commitment to remain firm under what seemed to be the hopeless condition of the One-Dimensional Man. Marcuse concluded that "the critical theory of society possesses no concepts which could bridge the gap between the present and its future; holding no promise and showing no success, it remains negative" (1964: 257).

Yet it is equally clear that the theorizing of Marcuse and his *émigré* colleagues did not replace praxis; instead, it was the beginning of a project that would liberate the individual from the abstraction of contemporary social sciences. Jay has concluded that "the Frankfurt School preserved the hope of a more truly humane society inhabited by concrete men rather than by the abstract subjects of the humanists, with whom they have so often been confused" (1972: 305).

Marcuse also produced a different kind of Marxism, according to Kolakowski, who has charged that Marcuse offered a

> Marxism without the proletariat [irrevocably corrupted by the welfare state], without history (as the vision of the future is not derived from a study of historical changes but from an intuition of true human nature), and without the cult of science, a Marxism furthermore in which the value of liberated society resides in pleasure and not creative work.
>
> (1978: 413)

Nevertheless, in the context of leveling dimensions of thought and action, Marcuse raised the problem of functional and manipulated communication in which the use of language of government public relations, advertising, or journalism becomes an agency of domination, linking individuals to the functions they perform in society. In fact, throughout most of his writings Marcuse posed the picture of individuals trapped by a consumer economy and the politics of corporate capitalism that have resulted in material dependency and need fulfillment and served to stabilize the system.

Communication research, stuck in the fallibility of empirical concreteness and constrained by the institutional demands in support of the market, failed to respond to a critique of society. It was caught in the demands for services by those who created the public and also controlled its needs. Communication research expressed itself in the creation of methodological instruments and asserted itself in the application of such methodologies to series of problems defined by organized capitalism. Thus, it participated in the defense of entrenched institutional interests and their media system, affirming the power of communication in the reproduction of capitalism, that is, in the improvement of its means of manipulation. But communication research, like other academic pursuits, also suffered under the consequences of a repressive society, when intellectual autonomy remained buried under authority relationships that fail to provide mental and social space for reflection and negation.

The writings of first-generation critical theorists, like Horkheimer, Adorno, Lowenthal and Marcuse, offered the basis for an intensive examination of the critique of modern society, including a discussion of its philosophical (and political) consequences for (mass) communication research. They were enriched by the work of Jürgen Habermas (1981), who offered an epistemological justification for human emancipation. Indeed, taken as a critical position rather than as a theory, Critical Theory embarked upon a critique of the present and pointed to the potential of the future. For Habermas it involved an emancipatory interest, with the potentiality of the human being at its center.

Specifically, communication is a central idea in Habermas' theoretical project. It surfaced with *Knowledge and Human Interest* (1971), in which he presented his approach to language in the context of the development of a critical social science, and culminated with the publication of *The Theory of Communicative Action* (1984a), which contains the normative basis of his social theory. In it he asserted,

> If we assume that the human species maintains itself through the socially coordinated activities of its members and that this coordination has to be established through communication—and in certain central spheres through communication aimed at reaching agreement—then the reproduction of the species *also* requires satisfying the conditions of a rationality that is inherent in communicative action.
>
> (1984a: 397)

Specifically, Habermas constructed the concept of communicative action from three "intertwined topic complexes": a communicative rationality freed from the limitations of individualistic approaches of social theory, a two-level concept that "connects the lifeworld and systems" paradigms, and a theory of modernity which accounts for "social pathologies." He added that "the theory of communicative action is intended to make possible a conceptualization of the social-life context that is tailored to the paradoxes of modernity" (1984a: xl).

The route toward such a theoretical position leads through the application of a reconstructive science. In *Communication and the Evolution of Society* (1979) Habermas already stressed the importance of understanding and asserted that the "task of universal pragmatics is to identify and reconstruct universal conditions of possible understanding [*Verständigung*]," arriving at "general presuppositions of communicative action" because he considered "the type of action aimed at reaching understanding to be fundamental" (1979: 1). Indeed, for Habermas, understanding meant to achieve an agreement that ends in mutuality and intersubjectivity, "shared knowledge, mutual trust, and accord with each other." Such an agreement rests on "recognition of the corresponding validity claims of comprehensibility, truth, truthfulness, and rightness" (1979: 3). The conditions underlying such a communicative practice are based upon a rationality which is determined by whether the participants "could, *under suitable circumstances*, provide reasons for their expressions." Habermas explained that "the rationality proper to the communicative practice of everyday life points to the practice of argumentation as a court of appeal" which will enable the continuation of communicative action under circumstances that would not allow for the "repair" of disagreements by "everyday routines," or the "use of force" (1984a: 17–18).

Since communicative practice occurs in the context of social and cultural structures, Habermas directed attention to the importance of the "lifeworld" as the context for symbolic reproduction. He identified and described three structural components that assist in creating favorable conditions for understanding. Individuals define themselves in terms of acting within their cultural tradition; they rely on their membership in social groups for the coordination of their actions "via intersubjective recognition of criticizable validity claims"; and they participate with younger generations which internalize "the value orientations of their social groups and acquire generalized capabilities for action" (1984a: xxxv). Thus, under these conditions communicative action serves to facilitate transmission and renewal of cultural knowledge, social integration and group solidarity, and personal identification.

The cultural context of the participants in communication, according to Habermas, consists of the objective, social and subjective worlds of the actors, which represent the totalities "of all entities about which true statements are possible," "of all legitimately regulated interpersonal relations," and "of the experiences of the speaker to which he has privileged access," respectively (1984a: 100).

Under these circumstances communication becomes a process of negotiation against the background of a shared culture, or a "lifeworld" which offers the presuppositional condition for any meaningful participation. Indeed, culture, society, and the individual are structural components of the "lifeworld" in which communicative action serves to reproduce cultural knowledge, to integrate individuals, and to shape personalities. Habermas sees *culture* as the reservoir of knowledge, from which participants in communication about the world take their interpretations; *society* represents the legitimate order, through which participants secure their membership in social groups and affirm their solidarity; and *personality* refers to the competencies which enable a subject to participate in the processes of understanding while maintaining its own identity. The semantic field of symbolic contents, the social space and historical time, form the *dimensions* in which communicative actions take place (1984b: 594–5).

The media as part of the everyday activities of the "lifeworld" function as generalized forms of communication. Thus the press, radio and television, for instance, have an enabling function. They free participants from their spatial–temporal limitations, provide availability of multiple contexts, and become instrumental in the creation of public spheres capable of serving authoritarian or emancipatory interests (1984a: 406).

Such perspective on communication and media suggests that (mass) communication theory and research are invariably tied to the analysis of communicative practices, that is, to issues of communicative competence, understanding, and participation of individuals in their lifeworld. In fact, Daniel Hallin has observed, that for Habermas, "all forms of human communication, even under conditions of mass dissemination, are essentially relationships between human subjects, derived ultimately from the elementary structure of dialogue" (1985: 142).

Habermas proposed that the study of the media must be a study of culture, the conditions of the lifeworld, and, indeed, the prospects of a public sphere that serves the emancipatory interests. For this purpose it must be based on a perspective of knowledge that is committed to openness (truth) and to the process of self-reflection. Richard Bernstein has argued that "an emancipatory interest is basic in the sense that the interest of reason is in furthering the conditions for its full development; the demand for non-distorted communication becomes fully explicit" since it "cannot exist unless we realize and institute the material social conditions that are required for mutual communication" (1985: 11).

With his latest work, Habermas has outlined a broad theoretical framework and provided a formidable agenda for communication research. The complexity of his work and the encyclopedic range of his intellectual effort offer a major challenge to the practitioners of communication theory and research in the United States. Indeed, problems of theoretical complexity and intellectual accessibility may have contributed to the failure of the field to participate actively in the critical assessment of Habermas' work. More likely, however, is the (intuitive) rejection of a theory of communicative action that seemed to interfere with the business of getting results. Such a practice is supported by Richard Rorty's conclusion that, desire for communication, harmony, interchange, conversation, social solidarity, and the merely beautiful wants to bring the philosophical tradition to an end because it sees the attempt to provide metanarratives, even metanarratives of emancipation, as an unhelpful distraction from what Dewey calls "the meaning of the daily detail."

(1985: 175)

In fact, the field of communication theory and research is most likely to follow Rorty, whose criticism of Habermas reveals a strong commitment to the writings of Pragmatism. His argument is based on the notion that the "progressive changes" in society may tell the story, "without much reference to the kinds of theoretical backup which philosophers have provided for such politics." Rorty claimed that

things like the formation of trade unions, the meritocratization of education, the expansion of the franchise, and cheap newspapers . . . have figured most largely in the willingness of the citizens of the democracies to see themselves as part of a "communicative community"—their continued willingness to say "us" rather than "them" when they speak of their respective countries.

(1985: 169)

Such perspective reflects not only the compelling influence of the Pragmatist tradition, but also reveals its continuing theoretical appeal. Habermas has concluded that Rorty "wants to destroy the tradition of the philosophy of consciousness, from its Cartesian beginnings, with the aim of showing the pointlessness of the entire discussion of the foundations and limits of knowledge." He also suggested that the

stubbornness with which philosophy clings to the role of the "guardian of reason" can hardly be dismissed as an idiosyncrasy of self-absorbed intellectuals, especially in a period in which basic irrationalist undercurrents are transmuted once again into a dubious form of politics,

and he charged that "it is precisely the neoconservatives who articulate, intensify and spread this mood via the mass media" (1985: 193, 195).

For Alvin Gouldner, however, the work of the Chicago School and the earlier work of Habermas revealed both "continuity and basic discontinuity," especially since "The Chicago School view of the 'public' had been largely taxonomic and positivistic, liberal in its political assumptions and therefore both optimistic and lacking in historical perspective." Gouldner claimed that "It manifested an almost total inability to analyze the public in relation to the emergence and transformation of bourgeois society" (1976: 138).

His work also reflects a belief in the centrality of critical interaction as a source of societal unity and the essence of public rationality. He stressed that "people's talk" was the most powerful mechanism in social change (1976: 149) and acknowledged the role of the media operating as major agencies in the public sphere. For this reason they were primary targets of a critique of modern society. Gouldner suggested that Habermas "used analysis of the public sphere as a

300 Introduction to Media Studies

decisive occasion to explore the prospects of a politics based upon critical and reflective discourse. His central aim was to begin clarifying the possibility and requisites of rational discourse in modern society" (1976: 138). In this context, the study of interpersonal communication, as well as media freedom, become crucial tasks for Critical Theory. Gouldner asked "how can persons *speak* to one another so as to strengthen their capacity for rational judgment and free them from the control of external or built-in censors, *without* the prior institution of an already ideal speech situation?" (1976: 150). He also suggested that Critical Theory address the issue of media freedom, because only media offer the possibility of mass enlightenment "that might go beyond what universities may elicit" (1976: 160).

For these reasons Gouldner concluded that

> the path from critical theory to the long march through the institutions must go over the bridge of the mass media, and undertake the struggle for and critique of these media for what they are: a complex system of property interests, technologies, professional skills, strivings for domination and for autonomy, all swarming with the most profound inner contradictions.
>
> (1976: 160)

In recent years communication research in the United States has acknowledged the existence of alternative explanations of society and embarked on a debate of Critical Theory as the foundation of a theory of communication, although quite late and less consistent or vigorous than the reaction to Critical Theory in the literature of social theory.

Until the 1980s, however, theoretical concerns of the field had remained within the narrow, administrative research tradition of earlier years. For instance, in their assessment of theoretical influences during the last decades Davison and Yu regretted the general "lack of broad theorizing," wondered about the "elder statesmen, the philosophers of the communication field" and asked why no names besides "Innis, McLuhan, Lasswell and a few others" had been added to the roster (1974: 200-1).

A few years later, Lerner and Nelson in their half-century appraisal of the field proposed that the "story of communication research begins with the 1927 publication of Lasswell's *Propaganda Technique in the World War*" and proceeded with a series of contributions by communication researchers who represent a traditional approach to the field (1977: 1). They failed to provide a wider social theoretical context or to offer a historical account of the place of theory.

A rather abbreviated and incomplete acknowledgment of Critical Theory by Rogers only obscured the differences between Lazarsfeld's use of critical research (with which he seemed to sympathize) and the concept of critical research in the spirit of the Frankfurt School and other Marxist positions (Rogers and Balle, 1985). Indeed, his assertion that the "Critical School" had Marxist beginnings in 1930s Germany and that "critical scholars" were those who "set themselves off from empirical scholars by objecting to the effects-oriented, empirically minded nature of most communication research" (1986: 115), also failed to distinguish between Marxist and non-Marxist critiques of positivism.

But at issue is not a dangerous polarization of "schools," but the ability to engage in a necessary, critical reexamination of communication research. The emergence of critical scholarship is the result of such self-reflection about the conditions of a theoretical premise that does not reflect the social and political tensions of everyday life. The problem of empirical research, at least in this context, remains a secondary issue. Indeed, George Gerbner asked in 1958 that mass communication research respond to the challenge of combining "empirical methods with the critical aims of social science" and to "join rigorous practice with value-conscious theory" (1958: 106); Kurt Lang (1979) has also addressed the compatibility of empirical research and critical scholarship, and years ago Siegfried Kracauer also suggested that "qualitative analysis proper often requires quantification in the interest of exhaustive treatment. Far from being strict alternatives the two approaches actually overlap, and have in fact complemented and interpenetrated each other in several investigations" (1952–3: 637).

In fact, the reaction to quantitative analyses can be traced to an epistemological issue of Pragmatism which understood the importance of measurement but indicated a reluctance to have "things qualitative unlike and individual to be treated as if they were members of a comprehensive, homogeneous, or non-qualitative system" (Dewey, 1960: 241). According to Shalin, such a position is the reflection of an epistemology which "diverged from the traditional one in its deliberate blurring of the borderline between scientific and common sense knowledge" (1986: 18); or as William James once proposed, there is "theoretic knowledge about things, as distinguished from living or sympathetic acquaintance with them" (1967: 249–50).

The issue of critical research emerged more substantively with the most recent debates concerning Critical Theory and other Marxist approaches to communication research in "Ferment in the Field," a special issue of the *Journal of Communication* (1983). However, despite its ambitious goals, the publication barely moved beyond an acknowledgment of Critical Theory or neo-Marxist perspectives on communication to engage the field in an epistemological debate of any significance. Instead, it became a statement of positions and intentions with rare insights into an understanding of the epistemological forces that had surrounded communication research for several decades. Nevertheless, Jennifer Daryl Slack and Martin Allor acknowledged "a range of developing alternative approaches to the study of communication," and they provided a description of the "critical" as an "appropriation of the term" from the Frankfurt School (1983: 208–9). Other authors were vague in their use of the term "critical research" or "European-style" research (Haight, 1983: 232; Schiller, 1983: 255; Mosco, 1983: 237; Stevenson, 1983: 262), although the implications were that such research activities involve questions of power and control. Slack and Allor offered the explanation that the "central concern of all critical positions is the effectivity of communication in the exercise of social power" (1983: 215). Dallas Smythe and Tran Van Dinh, while commenting upon the conditions of Marxist scholarship in communication studies, advanced a definition of Critical Theory which "requires that there be criticism of the contradictory aspects of the phenomena in their systems context" (1983: 123).

The range of Marxist and non-Marxist views on communication research was ultimately collapsed by George Gerbner into an extended notion of "critical scholar" which included those "who search and struggle" in order "to address the terms of discourse and the structure of knowledge and power in its domain and thus to make its contribution to human and social development" (1983: 362).

The presentation of critical alternatives to the traditional approach to communication research revealed that the choice is not between ideology and social science, but that social science practice remains imbedded in an ideological context. Although the language of orthodox Marxism, Critical Theory, or Cultural Studies is reflected throughout the discussion of the "ferment in the field," providing a vocabulary and a focus for a critique of contemporary societal practices, it was reproduced by many authors without further discussion of the consequences for the ideological perspective of mainstream American mass communication research.

It reveals a practice of collecting and adapting theoretical propositions and practical applications for the betterment of society which disregards cultural or political origins and ideological foundations. Such a practice also reflects an intellectual tradition of Americanizing foreign ideas. It occurred in the social sciences with the influence of European knowledge on American scholarship and is most clearly visible since Pragmatism, which seemed to acquire and apply suitable theoretical propositions according to the interests they served at the time. In this context, Novack's confrontation of Dewey's liberal position *vis-à-vis* the political reality of his days is an appropriate example of a Marxist critique of Pragmatism as a philosophical and political power in American society (1975).

Thus, to realize the potential contribution of Critical Theory to a critique of contemporary society, (mass) communication research needed to explore the rise of Critical Theory in the cultural and political context of Weimar Germany and its criticism of mass society in the United States. The decisive elements for this analysis were the attempts of Critical Theory to replace the preoccupation of traditional philosophy with science and nature by shifting to an emphasis on history and culture, and its acute awareness of the relationship between epistemology and politics.

The encounter with Critical Theory during the 1940s also came at the time when American (mass) communication research could have acted upon the fundamental difference between the ideas of culture and cultural critique offered by Critical Theory and traditional studies of culture and media, respectively. Critical Theory (and particularly Horkheimer and Adorno) insisted upon a holistic treatment of culture based upon the realization of the irreducible contradiction between elitist notions of culture and culture as a way of life. Indeed, Adorno felt that

> the greatest fetish of cultural criticism is the notion of culture as such. For no authentic work of art and no true philosophy, according to their very meaning, has ever exhausted itself in itself alone, in its being-in-itself. They have always stood in relation to the actual life-process of society from which they distinguished themselves.
>
> (1981: 23)

The media represent a major aspect of modern culture. They were identified by Horkheimer and his colleagues as part of the culture industry, and remained suspect when they became the "irrefutable prophet of the prevailing order" (1972: 147). On the other hand, the analysis of culture in the context of American (mass) communication research tried to resolve the operating contradictions between elitist and anthropological notions of culture; as a result, such critique of culture tended to be reduced to technological aspects of the media, for instance, the production and reproduction of messages, the size and demographic characteristics of audiences, and the transmission of symbols. These were irreducible differences, and, as Jay has observed, "Adorno was determined to preserve a critical vantage point towards cultural issues, which he felt was severely jeopardized by the empirical approach of mainstream sociologists of culture." He noted that Adorno "always contended that 'Culture is the condition that excludes the attempt to measure it'" (1984: 118).

The problematic of mass culture had been one of the major intellectual issues of the 1960s and 1970s. Fueled by the contributions of progressive Marxist and non-Marxist scholarship, including Critical Theory, American concerns over the cultural climate in society, caused by the uses of technology and reinforced by educational and cultural institutions, emerged from the social science literature and became a significant intellectual endeavor inside and outside of the academy. In these discussions it had become clear that the partisan nature of knowledge must lead to explorations and challenges of the dominant views of society and connect with visions of a different social environment. In this context social theorists must find appropriate links to the demands of their own times. Gouldner has expressed such a sentiment when he urged that "social scientists need to find a place for themselves beyond academic purism and cynical opportunism. With the understanding and the cooperation of informed laymen, they must edge out across the gap between what they know and what the times need" (1981: 82).

In addition, Critical Theory supported the possibilities of negation and introduced a political dimension to the discussion of mass culture and the prospects of mass society. It raised the specter of totalitarian rule and insisted on the investigation of authoritarianism as a way of learning about the psychological conditions of American society. Critical Theory enriched the theoretical discourse and demonstrated the need to question the vocabulary of political and social realities in the pursuit of exposing the suppression of history. The major thrust of Critical Theory against the undemocratic spirit of popular culture offered American communication research an opportunity to search for its own failures in the service of the dominant political and economic system, and to participate in a radical critique of society.

Instead, the field of communication theory and research maintained its posture of a traditional social science until the 1980s, when individual contributions to the literature revealed the presence of resistance and the possibilities of alternative perspectives on communication research with the emergence of Cultural Studies and a renewed effort to assess the conditions of society. They involved new journals, like *Critical Studies in Mass Communication,* discussions of paradigm changes, an increasing rate of "critical" research published in a variety of journals, and curriculum development in the area of critical media studies at a number of universities.

At the same time, however, the cultural pessimism of Horkheimer and his colleagues in the United States had been rejected, while the Habermasian struggle to forge a path for the position of an emancipatory social science in a world in which the problems of cultural reproduction create tensions and social conflicts, remained a solitary effort. By the end of this period communication research encountered a new challenge when the American exponents of British Cultural Studies popularized and revitalized the idea of culture as a necessary context for the study of communication and society.

Media Studies and Communication Research in Canada

Considering Critical Communication Studies in Canada

Sheryl N. Hamilton[1]

The claim is often made that Canadian communication studies is *critical* whereas American studies is merely *administrative*. Canadians apparently question what exists; Americans seek merely to profit from it. Therefore, we look with patronizing bemusement on American studies and the way it seems to promote corporate media interests and advertisers. We chuckle knowingly at the repeated folly of seeking to understand the effects of media messages on individuals. In contrast, we look fondly on Harold Innis, George Grant, Northrop Frye, and Marshall McLuhan, noting that they were politically committed and interested in exploring answers to "the big questions" for the greater social good.

The claim that Canadian communication studies is unique because it is critical may contain a kernel of truth, but it also produces blind spots. It might even assume more than it explains. If we want to argue that Canadian communication studies is critical, we must first define the term. In Canada, the claim to being critical is usually advanced as a good and desirable thing. However, the meanings associated with the word "critical" are frequently as unfavourable as favourable. As Halloran (1983) notes, "critical" when used to describe research has variously functioned as a synonym for "unscientific," "philosophical," "qualitative," and "politically motivated" (p. 270). Carey (1982) would add that "critical" has served to distinguish humanities from the sciences, interpretation from analysis, subjective from objective, and romanticism from rationalism.

Critical Versus Administrative: Two Communications Events

The notion of critical communication research forms an assumed perspective in much Canadian scholarship but is rarely defined. Any attempt to define it inherits the initial troubled distinction between administrative and critical communication research from the United States. Although there is no agreed-on definition of critical communication studies, it remains nonetheless possible to recognize a set of ontological, epistemological, and methodological commitments shared by scholars who identify themselves as critical communication researchers—commitments that can inform discussions in both the United States and Canada.

The distinction between critical and administrative research has functioned as one of communication's "principal fault lines" (Mosco, 1996, p. 247). Despite its inaccuracy and oversimplicity, the distinction continues to be one of the central underlying frames through which scholars have aligned, organizations have developed, and the history of the field is taught and understood. How did we come to divide the field into these two camps? There are two American communications events that establish the distinction between critical and administrative. The first is Paul Lazarsfeld's 1941 article, "Remarks on Administrative and Critical Communication Research," which first named the distinction and, while calling for a rapprochement, ensured the primacy of administrative over critical research approaches. The second event is the special issue of the *Journal of Communication,* published in 1983, that exposed tensions within the field, created the frames in which subsequent debate would take place, and demonstrated—counter to its stated purpose—that there could be no coming together of administrative and critical communication studies. These two events worked together to map the terrain on which all subsequent discussions of critical research have taken place.

Naming the Distinction

Paul Lazarsfeld is considered to be one of the "founding fathers" of communication studies. His research, along with that of such researchers as Harold Lasswell, Elihu Katz, Kurt Lewin, and Wilbur Schramm, produced some of the first communication theories in the United States. The research of these early scholars was generally funded through alliances between philanthropic foundations, universities, and interested corporations. Their primary concern was to explore the effects of different media on behaviour with the ultimate goal of using media more effectively.

In pursuing their research, the early scholars used quantitative research, focusing on large-scale surveys and statistical analysis. In the late 1930s, this approach was challenged by a group of émigré Jewish scholars who fled Nazi Germany to settle in the United States and came to be known as the Frankfurt School. Trained in European schools of thought, heavily influenced by Marxism, and. deeply concerned about what they saw as the industrialization of culture, scholars such as Max Horkheimer, Theodor Adorno, and Herbert Marcuse both enriched and came into conflict with the quantitative and industry-driven approach to communication being taken up in the United States at that time.

The impetus for Lazarsfeld's article came out of a particular set of circumstances involving himself and Theodor Adorno, perhaps the leading figure of the Frankfurt School. In 1937, the Rockefeller Foundation provided funds to establish the Office of Radio Research at Columbia University. The directors of the Office, Hadley Cantril (Princeton) and Frank Stanton (CBS), hired Lazarsfeld as its research director. The following year, Lazarsfeld, with the collaboration of Max Horkheimer, invited Adorno to the United States to direct the music component of the Office of Radio Research. What followed was a very difficult year for both Lazarsfeld and Adorno as their very different research agendas and epistemological approaches came into conflict. That clash is what produced the distinction between administrative (Lazarsfeld) and critical (Adorno) research or, more broadly, American scholarship and the Frankfurt School. Lazarsfeld tried to persuade Adorno, whose ideas and prose style were strongly influenced by classical philosophy, to express his theoretical ideas in a manner that could be measured using quantitative methods. As it happened, "The actual course of events was quite different from those expectations (Lazarsfeld, 1969, p. 323).

In 1939, the Rockefeller Foundation refused to renew the music project because it was not producing useful results. Much discussion of these events has subsequently taken place (Fleming and Bailyn, 1969; Gitlin, 1981; Slack and Allor, 1983), but it was Lazarsfeld's 1941 article that created a distinction that would organize professional and intellectual practice in North American communication studies for at least the next 50 years. In the article, which was published in the Frankfurt School's journal, *Studies in Philosophy and Social Science,* Lazarsfeld grapples with the different approaches he (and his American colleagues) and the Frankfurt scholars brought to research. He characterizes the two styles of research as *administrative* and *critical.*

Administrative research is "carried through in the service of some kind of administrative agency of public or private character" (Lazarsfeld, 1941, p. 8). Viewing media as useful tools, administrative researchers pose such questions as "Who are the people exposed to the different media? What are their specific preferences? What are the effects of different methods of presentation?" (Lazarsfeld, 1941, p. 3). Lazarsfeld (1941) recognizes the limitations of administrative research approaches, noting that they may not take full account of history and that "they solve little problems, generally of a basic character, when the same methods could be used to improve the life of the community if only they were applied to forward-looking projects related to the pressing economic and social problems of our time" (p. 8).

In contrast, critical research assumes that "prior and in addition to whatever special purpose is to be served, the general role of our media of communication in the present social system should be studied" (Lazarsfeld, 1941, p. 9). It therefore differs from administrative research in two respects: "it develops a theory of the prevailing social trends in our times, general trends which yet require consideration in any concrete research problem; and it seems to imply ideas of basic human values according to which all actual or desired effects should be appraised" (Lazarsfeld, 1941, p. 9). Thus, critical research begins with social theory, contains normative values, and places communication in the larger social context.

Lazarsfeld (1941) suggests that critical scholars are always conscious that "what we need most is to do and think what we consider true and not to adjust ourselves to the seemingly inescapable" (p. 10). The concern of critical research with threats to human dignity and values is evident in the research questions it raises: "How are these media organized and controlled? How, in their institutional set-up, is the trend toward centralization, standardization and promotional pressure expressed? In what form, however disguised, are they threatening human values?" (Lazarsfeld, 1941, p. 10).

Lazarsfeld is suggesting that the purpose and methodologies of the research, the moral commitment of the scholar, the relationship between theory and empirical reality, and the place of values in research are crucial lines of distinction between critical and administrative research. In his view, critical research assumes the task of revealing how media function in order to reproduce dominant ideology in their given social context. Furthermore, he recognizes that such an approach is essentially theoretical because it makes certain assumptions (e.g., about the power of media, the susceptibility of audiences, the nature of the media–audience contact) that are not always empirically verifiable. It is this embrace of theory without concern as to its "prove-ability" that Lazarsfeld sees as the primary weakness of critical approaches (Lazarsfeld, 1941, pp. 12–13).

Lazarsfeld's short article has had a lasting impact in three ways. First, it named a distinction—between critical and administrative research—that has organized the discipline ever since. Second, it brought to the attention of communication studies the work of the Frankfurt School scholars. Third, it articulated the conditions for the ongoing domination of the administrative approach within the American context. Lazarsfeld concluded the article by expressing a desire for a convergence of European theory and American empiricism. Ultimately, his goal was not to challenge or change the underlying characteristics of research; rather, he sought to enhance administrative research by incorporating into it some of the theoretical richness of critical approaches. The debate did not end there, however.

Framing the Debate

Although the "dominant paradigm" in American communication studies continued to be administrative research until at least the 1980s, tensions between critical and administrative approaches also continued to simmer. They were spurred on by the translation of the work of European Marxist thinkers such as Antonio Gramsci and Louis Althusser, the development of cultural studies, and radical shifts in the social, economic, and cultural context of the mass media and their study in the United States.

The 1983 publication of a special issue of *Journal of Communication,* titled *Ferment in the Field,* marked another watershed event in the dialogue—and potential rapprochement—between critical and administrative research. The editor, George Gerbner, gathered together 35 original articles from 41 international scholars from both traditions to reflect on the distinction that Lazarsfeld had advanced 42 years earlier. As Gerbner (1983a) wrote in his introduction, "This volume represents the first time that so many internationally prominent scholars have examined and commented upon communications as a field of study in one publication" (p. 4).

Ferment in the Field remains one of the most significant reflections on the state of the field in the history of communication studies—in Gerbner's words, a "coming of age." Throughout the volume, the distinction between critical and administrative is accepted rather than challenged and the result is a much more detailed exposition of its parameters and implications than had been offered by Lazarsfeld. *Ferment in the Field* further entrenches the distinction between critical and administrative research and recognizes the conflicts and tensions at work in professional circles throughout the United States.

Defining Critical Communication Studies

In the late 1980s, Sholle (1988) noted that "[a] number of attempts to define the field of critical communication research have been [undertaken], but there is no widely accepted definition of the field" (p. 38). The same holds true today. What can be said about critical communication studies is that it is not a single entity. It includes approaches from political economy, cultural studies, Marxist sociology, semiotic analysis, institution studies, dependency theory, international communications, and more. What it offers is a range of different ways to study communication—all of which are in opposition to administrative research (Slack and Allor, 1983, p. 208).

Discussions of the distinction between critical and administrative research have been hindered by a number of trends present in both sides of the debate. First, there is a tendency to reduce the other position to a homogeneous straw man, rendering administrative research as simple-minded empiricism and critical research as ideological polemic. Second, there has been a lack of self-reflexivity, which shows up in the inability to recognize that one's own position may have weaknesses as well as strengths. Third, and especially within the critical tradition, debates sometimes serve not as a means of achieving genuine understanding, but rather as a forum for theoretical posturing. (The best example of such posturing may be the ongoing war between political economy and cultural studies.[2]) Finally, the very fact that the tension between the two approaches has been framed as a debate has led to an either/or attitude that hardly does justice to the range of research and analysis within communication studies.

A number of scholars have attempted to step outside of these limits. Schiller (1983) suggests that the *shared characteristics* of critical research include a focus on production rather than individual consumption; an examination of the sources and exercise of power; and an assumption of continuous change in social processes and institutions. According to Smythe and Van Dinh (1983), critical research sets as its problem how to reshape or create institutions to better serve the needs of a greater number of people; uses historical, materialist research techniques; and is ideological in the sense that it links critical problems and tools "with interpretations that involve radical changes in the established order" (p. 118) (see also Rogers, 1982; Slack and Allor, 1983). Commonalities identified by Carey (1983) include a less positivist approach to research; diverse methods; a sceptical view of the media; the occasional influence of pragmatism or symbolic interactionism; the inevitable influence of Marxism; and an interest in questions of culture and politics as they relate to communications and mass media.

The following sections examine the shared characteristics of critical communication research in the following categories: research problem, understanding of social power, methodology, researcher orientation, theoretical influences, and knowledge claims. These categories reflect beliefs about the nature of reality and the way we can know that reality. They set the limits as to what a critical approach to communication can offer.

The Research Problem

How does critical communication studies define its research problem? Critical communications scholars have generally focused on the relations between communication and social power. This focus has been variously framed as a question of (1) social control and power (Halloran, 1983); (2) concern with structures of power (Gerbner, 1983b); or (3) an investigation into domination, contradiction, and struggle (Mosco, 1983). The central unit of knowledge is society rather than the individual, and communication practices are considered within their various social contexts.

Simply stated, critical communication research takes on the larger questions. As Rogers (1982) notes, "Critical scholars believe that a theory of communication is impossible without a theory of society, so their scope of analysis is much wider than that of empirical scholars" (p. 125). Therefore, critical researchers ask such questions as: Who controls the media? How can media be used by a greater diversity of people? How do we negotiate our roles within and between social groups through practices of communication? How do communication structures work with other social, economic, and cultural structures to order society?

Generally, this focus has meant a shift in emphasis from the effects of media on individuals to analyses that are more historically grounded and socially situated. Critical work has concentrated on ownership and control of media systems, the linking of media structures to other larger social structures, and analyses of the institutional aspects of communication. When considering individuals, critical scholars view them as members of groups—groups already partly determined by social power arrangements—and explore their resistance and domination. As Slack and Allor (1983) note,

> The communication process . . . is no longer defined in terms of the effects of messages on individuals but on the effectivity (or social role) of communication (as both

institutional structures and symbolic constructions) in maintaining, enhancing, or disrupting the social formation (the existing interrelationship of politics, economics, and culture). (p. 214)

Understanding Social Power

Clearly, critical researchers ask the questions they do because they hold a different understanding of the relationship between communication and power. Bailie (1997) suggests that "[c]ritical communication scholarship is rooted in the assumption that social institutions and human relations are relations of history, power and struggle" (p. 33). Critical scholars therefore view social power as unequally distributed and generally subscribe to a conflict-based model of social relations that focuses on struggle and difference rather than on agreement and consensus. Indeed, critical communication studies rejects the *linear model of causality* at work in administrative research and replaces it with more *complex forms of social determination*. Consequently, whereas administrative research is content to study, for example, the impact that radio advertising might have on listeners, critical research wants to investigate the historical origin of radio advertising, the type of interest that tends to use radio advertising, the ways in which the advertising binds listeners to the capitalist system, and so on. Furthermore, it is precisely because the study of complex forms of social determination can lead in so many directions that distinctions— between cultural and economic determinism, for example—among critical scholars have emerged. Notwithstanding the specific areas to which critical scholars may direct their interest, all share an opposition to the *liberal pluralist notion* of social power, which sees power as potentially equally shared and as neutral.

In advancing a more diverse and less idealistic understanding of social power and how it intersects with communication structures and practices in society, critical scholars have been criticized for assuming rather than demonstrating that social power really works as they claim. The theory is powerful and seductive but not always easy to demonstrate. Furthermore, *postmodernist* and *poststructuralist* conceptions of power pose a challenge to the critical understanding. This is important because assumptions about the nature of social power and its organization—Does it always operate from the top down (i.e., from an elite to a mass)? Is it always coercive or can it also be productive? Axe there opportunities for resistance?—are at the heart of the often unstated norms and values that critical communication research espouses. Indeed, depending on one's definition of power, one will also draw different conclusions about what types of actions to take, what types of outcomes are appropriate, how power should be wielded, and who should wield it.

Methodology and Methods

As a result of the two preceding assumptions—(1) the appropriate object of study is the relation between power and communication, and (2) social power is unequally distributed—critical communication scholars use different methodologies and methods than administrative researchers. Indeed, it is because critical research defines its object of study differently and because it views social power as being unequally distributed that it *logically* uses methods that will reveal those facts.

Much of the debate between the critical and administrative approaches is concerned with distinctions in methodology. In fact, the administrative approach is sometimes called the *empirical* approach because it studies immediately observable phenomena using "scientific" methods. In contrast, critical research is often seen as methodologically unrigorous because it rejects empirical approaches to knowledge and is not concerned with demonstrating its theoretical claims through scientifically verifiable data. As a result, critical research is sometimes accused of producing ideological claims rather than scientific knowledge: "We can recognize that data without adequate theory are intellectually sterile, but we must also acknowledge that theory, unless subjected to rigorous and wide-ranging empirical test, is polemic" (Stevenson, 1983, p. 269).

Critical researchers have pointed out, however, that critical research frequently uses empirical methods (Mosco, 1983). As well, a number of scholars have observed that critical research is compatible with empirical methods (Allen, 1999; Elasmar, 1999; Gerbner, 1964; Halloran, 1983; Rogers, 1982). Whether or not critical scholars deploy empirical research methods, their epistemology—that is, their explanation of the process of knowing or knowledge construction—is very different from that of administrative or empirical scholars. Critical scholarship is not primarily interested in making scientifically verifiable knowledge claims.

The framing of the debate between critical and administrative approaches, as between qualitative and quantitative research methods or between science and the humanities, has resulted in three unproductive lines of discussion. First, it has led to claims of moral superiority by both sides of the debate. For critical scholars, the moral superiority derives from a sense of the importance of the work being done; according to Halloran (1983), "[W]e have to accept that it is more important to be important than to be impeccable" (p. 278). For administrative scholars, claims to moral superiority are grounded in science and "pure" knowledge untainted by ideology.

The second unproductive debate results from the fact that no distinction is being made between *empirical* and *positivist.* Empirical methods seek to describe, through the application of established procedures, an aspect of material reality; positivist methods emerge out of a belief that objective truth can be rendered through the scientific method. Although the methods employed by critical researchers can certainly produce empirical results, critical researchers make no claim to produce positivist (i.e., objective) results. On the contrary, they would argue that the claim to objectivity or *value neutrality* is itself a thoroughly ideological claim.

Third, debates about methodology have led to attempts to find a "middle ground," a strategy that often favours the empirical perspective. According to

Rosengren (1983), "Those who ask the most provocative questions often cannot provide sound empirical answers; those who can, often fail to ask the right questions" (p. 185). The search for a compromise and the ultimate favouring of the empirical approach are tendencies that are doomed to fail because the debate is not about *methods* (everyone can use the same methods), but about differing ontologies and epistemologies (what does the world consist of and how can we know it?). When the middle-ground strategy is applied, larger questions, debates, and positions are ultimately reduced to a debate about methods.

This reduction has imposed certain limitations on critical communication studies. Because issues of methodology have been aligned with positivism, questions of methodology and method often stop there. Interrogations of how nonpositivist methods can usefully inform and develop critical communication questions is an issue that requires more attention. Administrative researchers have been correct in pointing out that critical communication researchers have tended to devote insufficient attention to methodology and methods; however, the solution is not to be found in a turn to positivist or quantitative methods, but rather in a more sustained exploration of the relationship between theory and our ability to describe lived social reality.

Researcher Orientation

The first three assumptions of critical research are: (1) the appropriate object of study is the relationship between communication and power; (2) social power is unequally distributed; and (3) theory is more important than methods. Following from these is the fourth assumption advanced by critical researchers, which addresses the relationship between researcher and researched—in other words, the orientation of the researcher to his or her work. This debate has taken place on the field of ideology and interrogates what it means to do ideological research. Interestingly, both proponents and critics of the critical approach to communication research have labelled critical approaches "ideological." For critics, this label means that critical research is unscientific, polemical, and simply reflective of the beliefs of the researcher. One scholar offers a classic formulation of the criticism when he suggests that critical scholars often "mistake ideology for sociology" (Lang, 1979, p. 92).

For its proponents, however, the term "ideological" is a way to show that research not only *analyzes* ideology as an object (i.e., it demonstrates the symbolic traces of social power) (Sholle, 1988), but it is *also* political in itself because it is committed to the disruption of the status quo (Blumler, 1983; Mosco, 1983, 1996; Smythe and Van Dinh, 1983). Both sides of the debate therefore agree that critical communication research is not value-free (i.e., it is guided by its values in its selection and treatment of research questions). Critical researchers feel that applying values is an inevitable part—and, indeed, a positive aspect—of doing research. Administrative scholars, on the other hand, feel that values corrupt the objectivity of research. A critical approach argues, of course, that even if the administrative/empirical school of thought does not acknowledges its values (objectivity, truth, science, utility, pluralism), those values are still reflected in the choice of research questions and methods.

While critical scholars have been willing to acknowledge the existence of values in their research, they have become increasingly circumspect about what those values are. It is often assumed that critical researchers are on the "left" in political terms, but this orientation is not often defined (see, for example, Slack and Semati, 1997). Hence, critical research can affirm certain ideological and political norms even without intentionally articulating, considering, and discussing them.

Theoretical Influences

A fifth basis on which to understand critical communication research is to ask what are its theoretical influences. The theoretical legacies of critical communication research that are acknowledged within the field include European critical theory, American pragmatism and the Chicago School, and Marxist thought.

One of the distinguishing aspects of critical approaches is their recognition of the influence of European critical theory—specifically, the Frankfurt School (Hardt, 1992; Grosswiler, 1996; Jansen, 1983; Schramm, 1983; Sholle, 1988; Stevenson, 1983). European critical theory includes the work of first-generation Frankfurt School members such as Adorno, Horkheimer, and Marcuse, as well as second-generation thinkers such as Jürgen Habermas. The influence of European critical theory has been to frame critical communication research in relation to larger critiques of modernism, to explore the specificity of commodity culture, and to offer a stinging critique of the industrialization of the cultural domain, with hope for greater democratization of the means of communication and their divorce from industrial production.

The theoretical influence of American pragmatism and Chicago School symbolic interactionism comes from the work of John Dewey, Kenneth Burke, George Herbert Mead, and Herbert Blumer (Hardt, 1992; Carey, 1982, 1983). Emerging from this work is a concern with the practice of communication in relation to progressive social change and a shift from one-way models of communication to interactive models of meaning-making and identity formation.

The third major theoretical influence is Marxist theory. The development of this influence can be mapped through the shifting theorization of ideology and culture from more simple deterministic models to approaches from Althusser and Gramsci. As a result, critical communication attaches great importance to ideology, to debates about questions of determination and the related question of where to locate culture, and to a shared recognition that one cannot consider communication messages and practices outside of their socioeconomic contexts.

All three theoretical influences have obviously enriched the field of communication studies, particularly in relation to more administrative or liberal pluralist approaches. However, critical communication scholars have been slow to recognize the value of other critical approaches not growing out of a Marxist, class-based analysis or narrowly political economic analysis. For example, both feminism and postcolonialism have produced deeply interesting theory that could enrich the field of critical communication studies as a whole. While this work has been accepted within the field, its applicability has tended to be seen as specific to gender, race, and ethnicity, as opposed to offering rich resources for critical communication studies more broadly.

Knowledge Claims

The sixth shared assumption answers the question, What kinds of knowledge claims can—and do—critical communication researchers make? Critical communication seeks both to engage critically with existing social relations and to change those relations. Critical communication scholars work to produce "research that both advances criticism of the existing world system and promotes the 'critical state' that would transform it" (Mosco, 1983, pp. 245–246). Research should therefore offer resources to effect positive social change (Halloran, 1983). Slack and Allor (1983) suggest that

> [i]t is not possible to characterize approaches as "critical" based solely on their conceptions of causality. The epistemological consideration of the question of causality must necessarily be linked to the political consideration of the exercise of social power before discriminatory judgement is possible. (pp. 213–214)

Whether seen as creating conditions for free (or freer) communication, social democracy, or unfettered expressions of self, critical research sets as one of its central objectives the production of intellectual and political resources for social transformation and individual and collective emancipation (Bailie, 1997; Gerbner, 1964; Haight, 1983; Halloran, 1983; Jansen, 1983). Consequently, not only must communication be thought about more critically, but so too must the place of the researcher and his or her work in society. However, it must be underlined again that the normative standard that is implicitly at work in these claims is rarely articulated expressly. Who is to determine what counts as *positive change* and whose vision of emancipation is at work are questions that merit further reflection by critical communication scholars.

From the foregoing discussion of critical communication studies arising out of debates primarily within the American context, a set of elements emerges, shared ontological and epistemological assumptions through which we can begin to distinguish what constitutes a critical approach to communication studies. Critical communication studies (1) takes as its primary question the relationship between communication and social power; (2) understands social power as a dynamic structuring force and recognizes that power is unequally distributed within society; (3) privileges theory over method and is more concerned to produce social critique than objective knowledge; (4) embraces the role that values play in producing knowledge; (5) has its theoretical roots in American and European radical thought; and (6) seeks to produce knowledge that will effect positive social change.

Canadian Critical Communication Studies

The story of what constitutes critical communication studies in North America has primarily been defined as an American encounter with European theory, framed as an ongoing conflict between critical and administrative approaches. This section considers where Canada fits into this narrative. In a sense, Canada has functioned as a structuring absence in the debates, in part because of its instrumental marginality to American communication scholarship (as argued by Carey, 1975), but more significantly because Canadian communication studies sees itself as always, already critical. It sees itself as beginning where the American debates end.

The status of Canadian communication studies as critical does not arise from "ferment in the field," but from its very history. In this sense, "critical" is an underlying and often uninterrogated *assumption* in Canadian communication studies. In Canada, the question has not been whether or not Canadian communication studies is critical, but rather in what ways communication studies in Canada is distinctly Canadian.

The Ghost of Innis: Critical-ness Assumed

Babe (2000a), who has written that "Canada has a rich heritage of communication thought" (p. 19), traces the foundations of Canadian communication thought through the work of ten scholars: Graham Spry, Harold Innis, John Grierson, Dallas Smythe, C.B. Macpherson, Irene Spry, George Grant, Gertrude Robinson, Northrop Frye, and Marshall McLuhan. At its very foundations, Babe argues, Canadian communication thought is dialectical, holistic, ontological, oriented to political economy, and concerned with mediation; most significantly for our purposes, it is critical.

Babe sees Canadian communication thought as operating fundamentally within the critical tradition, in opposition to administrative or pluralist approaches. More specifically, by critical research he means "evaluative research, presuming enduring criteria for enduring goals towards which we should strive judging policies, activities, events, human relations, institutions and so forth" (Babe, 2000a, p. 16). It is this ability to evaluate critically that marks Canadian scholars as critical in the American sense of the term. Indeed, there is general agreement that, in its historical origins, Canadian communication thought is critical (Acland and Buxton, 1999; Carey, 1975; Kroker, 1984; Robinson and Theall, 1975). Theall (1975) suggests that Innis, through the "process of criticizing North American history by rewriting it, developed a 'critical' approach to communication studies" (p. 21). American scholars such as Carey (1975, 1983), Hardt (1992), and Grosswiler (1996) have lent American authority to the claims that

Canadian communication thought is a priori critical. Carey (in Salter, 1981a) suggests that "[Innis's] work was critical in the contemporary sense that he was not proposing some natural value free study, but a standpoint from which to critique society and theories of it in light of humane and civilized values" (p. 80).

What has been the legacy of these foundational thinkers in terms of understanding what critical communication studies means in Canada? According to the few scholars considering it, the question, like its American counterpart, takes as its central concern larger questions about the ways in which power and communication intersect. As Babe (2000a) notes, "Power considerations figure prominently in Canadian communication thought" (p. 310). Power in this context is understood with an attention to history and the interplay of historical forces (Kroker, 1984, Theall, 1975; Tremblay, 1981). It shares assumptions with other critical communication approaches about the nonlinear nature of social power, but theorizes that power in a specifically dialectical model (Babe, 2000a; Kroker, 1984; Theall, 1975). In other words, history is produced through the encounter of contradictory social forces. Furthermore, the historical legacy of foundational communication thought has offered some significant attempts to think through the place of technologies of communication (rather than only mass media) in processes of modernization (Carey, 1983; Kroker, 1984). As well, it has placed at the forefront values having to do with human emancipation and exploring the conditions of a better life (Babe, 2000a; Kroker, 1984).

Interestingly, a majority of the foundational thinkers identified as pivotal to Canadian communication thought were developing their communication ideas before the institutionalization of the field of communication studies in Canada. While most observers would agree that they were critical thinkers who contributed to the foundation of Canadian communication thought, it is less clear how their ideas have played out in communication studies as a discipline in Canada since the 1960s. According to Robinson (2000), "While the general outlines of Innis' and McLuhan's work are known, whether they have inspired a unique kind of Canadian scholarship is much more difficult to determine" (p. 122). In examining what critical communication studies might mean in Canada, can we escape the ghost of Harold Innis? Is die discipline of communication studies still critical?

Hurdles to Delimiting the Field

Any appraisal of Canadian communication scholarship as a discipline, or at least as a field with certain shared problematics, is hindered by the striking lack of a well-detailed and readily apparent map of the field. Robinson (1987) lamented that "[m]uch remains to be done in providing a detailed account of communication studies in Canada" (p. 4). Unfortunately, the need continues.

When and how did communication studies become institutionalized in Canada within the university? When were the first professional associations established and with what effect? What journals serve this academic community?

How can one characterize the work done in the field? Can we identify generational patterns? Is there a canon that emerges after Innis, McLuhan, et al.?

The first hurdle in answering these questions is the diffuse nature of Canadian communication scholarship. In the early 1980s, Salter (1981b) noted that much work in communication studies was appearing in the journals of other disciplines or was being published in communication journals in the United States or Europe. More than two decades later, and notwithstanding the 25-year history of the *Canadian Journal of Communication (CJC)*—the only English-language academic journal in Canada devoted to communication studies—Salter's claim remains true. The editor of the *CJC* himself regrets that we cannot look to *CJC* to map the history, development, and trends of communication studies in Canada; Canadian communication scholars, Lorimer (2000a) recognizes, continue to publish in international journals or in contexts outside of the discipline altogether, and many do not identify strongly with Canadian communication studies.

In addition to the diffuse nature of Canadian communication scholarship, another hurdle in delimiting the field is the lack of a comprehensive and accepted historical account of its development. Such an account might be found in a single work, and yet none exists. Lorimer had hoped the special issue of *CJC* published in 2000 might accomplish this. Instead, individual scholars offered reflections on the institutionalization of the discipline in their particular university (Tate, Osler, Fouts, and Segal, 2000). As well, one might look to undergraduate communication textbooks in Canada for such an overarching narrative. Yet a review of current undergraduate texts (e.g., Biagi and McKie, 1999; Holmes and Taras, 1992; Lorimer and Gasher, 2001; Lorimer and McNulty, 1996; McKie and Singer, 2001; Szuchewycz and Sloniowski, 1999; Vivian and Maurin, 2000) comes up empty, a fact recognized by others (Tate et al., 2000).

In terms of addressing these gaps in Canadian communication scholarship, the present collection is a welcome and significant contribution to the field. In the chapters by Michael Dorland, Roger de la Garde and François Yelle, Anne-Marie Kinahan, and others, students will gain a familiarity with the institutional, professional, and intellectual history of the field in English Canada and Quebec. Yet, without a recorded history, myths of origin are weak. Perhaps it has been this lack of well-established, historical myths and narratives that has structured the attempts to define Canadian communication studies into the predictable identity crisis of whether or not it is uniquely Canadian. It is in and through this issue that the critical elements of Canadian communication studies have been negotiated, articulated, and ultimately limited.

Uniquely Canadian

The debate about Canadian national identity, which is at the heart of so much substantive Canadian communication research, also plays itself out in the consideration of the discipline as a whole. In some ways, this is not surprising. The third goal of Babe's (2000a) book is "to discern whether there exists a mode of communication inquiry that might be termed 'quintessentially Canadian'" (p. 4). He has not been alone in this pursuit. Kroker (1984) attempts to map a distinctly "Canadian mind," while Robinson and Theall (1975) suggest that Canada can claim a "unique communications philosophy" (p. 1).

Claims to a specific Canadian approach to communication studies rest on two central arguments. First, Canadian communication studies is unique because it is critical. Critical functions as a largely undefined marker of distinction from the American administrative approach. It also casts Canadian communication studies research as morally superior to its American counterpart. Second, Canadian communication studies is framed as unique because of its distinctive epistemological position—one of in-betweenness or marginality—and it is this epistemological position that produces the specifically Canadian critical stance.

On his return to Simon Fraser University in the mid-1970s, Dallas Smythe, disheartened by his experience in communication studies in the United States, called for Canadian communication thought to distinguish itself from American approaches through its critical stance. He clearly hoped that Canadian communication research would not reproduce what he considered to be the errors of many American scholars. This notion of defining Canadian uniqueness through criticalness took hold in the field. Babe (2000a) argues that it is the values of Canadian scholarship that make it critical: "the fact that most of these theorists are able to contemplate a superior human nature, that is, to compare things as they should be with things as they are, qualifies them as critical theorists in the tradition acknowledged by Lazarsfeld" (p. 316). He recognizes the role of religion in foundational Canadian communication thought and suggests that it may be responsible for the "high moral standard" of these thinkers (Babe, 2000a, p. 308). The overtones of moral superiority or a location outside of ideology are also present in Kroker's (1984) claims that "the Canadian discipline . . . represents a courageous, and creative struggle to think outside of and against the closed horizons of technological society" (p. 13).

In these kinds of claims, which abound in Canadian communication conferences, analyses, and classrooms, the chain of reasoning proceeds as follows. Canadian communication thought is unique (i.e., non-American) because it is critical. It is critical now (in the present) because it was critical then (when Innis was writing). And because it is critical, ultimately it is better than communication studies in the United States.

Unfortunately, these assumptions can have unanticipated consequences for knowledge. First, there is a lack of considered attention to what critical might mean now, as opposed to when Innis was writing. The claim is simply made rather than demonstrated. Second, it sets as the standard the distinction between critical and administrative research articulated by Lazarsfeld, rather than the longer history of debates within American communication studies. Therefore, it does not engage with a more sophisticated understanding of what critical communication studies might be. Finally, it reduces the important question of what critical might mean to the less interesting question of how we are different from our American counterparts. A notable example of this third consequence appears in Babe (2000a); after offering what, despite its shortcomings, is an arguably seminal treatment of the foundations of Canadian communication thought, he concludes his book with the following paragraph:

> [I]t is worth remarking that a quite different field of questions is raised by the seminal and foundational Canadian communication theorists than by those often taken to be the founders of American communication thought (Lazarsfeld, Lasswell, Lewin, Hovland, Schramm). It is likely more than merely coincidental that raising important ontological questions, adopting a critical stance, and employing holistic modes of analysis detract from the lustre both of technological achievement and of the free flow of information—mainstays of American thought and policy. (p. 319)

There is a sense of superiority operating here that discourages ongoing self-scrutiny. Canadian communication studies research is assumed to be *already* within a critical paradigm, and the paradigm itself is assumed to be necessarily and essentially political economic. Unfortunately, such assumptions do not do justice to the diversity of work being produced under the name "critical," including policy studies, institutional analyses, feminist research, industry analysis, and technology studies. Indeed, an examination of the graduate communication theses deposited in Canadian universities quickly shows that the field is both broader and more vital than is imagined or promoted even by its proponents.

The second major defining characteristic of Canadian communication studies that has been identified is in its in-betweenness and marginality. Canadian political, social, geographic, and economic marginality (mostly in relation to the United States) is seen as producing an epistemology of the margins. A number of scholars identify Canadian communication scholarship as unique in that it draws on both European and American traditions. Hence, while it is concerned with social rather than individual effects and is theoretical like European approaches, it is also more grounded like American approaches (Salter, 1981a). Kroker (1984) sees Canadian communication thought as an oppositional mode between European and American perspectives; he feels it is characterized by its location "in-between," which he defines as "a restless oscillation between the pragmatic will to live at all costs of the American and a searing lament for that which has been suppressed by the modern, technical order" (p. 7). From this position of in-between, Canadians offer a unique, critical perspective.

Some scholars go further than in-betweenness and claim that a defining characteristic of Canadian communication thought—and, indeed, of all Canadian intellectual and cultural development—is its marginality (Babe, 2000a, 2000b; Carey, 1975; Robinson and Theall, 1975; Theall, 1975). The belief that a critical stance emerges from a sense of marginality is echoed in claims made by American and British critical scholars (Carey, 1982; Garnham, 1983; Hardt, 1992; Smythe and Van Dinh, 1983).

According to Robinson and Theall (1975), "Canada's geopolitical marginality on the fringe of the North American continent seems to have given rise to two distinct outlooks: a particular perception of this country's cultural mission and a unique communication studies philosophy" (p. 3). Babe (2000a) argues that "[p]eople at the margins can see things differently, that is, dialectically: unable to escape exposure to dominant discourses, they nonetheless understand that these discourses are not their own" (p. 23).

Yet what are the limits of this epistemological positioning on the margins? The claim to criticality through marginality rests on the examples of the canonical Canadian communication thinkers: Harold Innis, Marshall McLuhan, George Grant, and Northrop Frye. But how pertinent is the sense of geographical marginality expressed by a few great thinkers to our definition of "the margins" today? How does marginality play itself out in relation to the globalizing context of the early 21st century? Furthermore, how can marginality function as a self-conscious characteristic? Theall (1975) claims that "[t]his phenomenon of marginality provides a natural negative perspective" (p. 20), but how can a phenomenon that has been thus articulated be considered natural? He goes on to suggest that marginality must be explicitly recognized as a strength in intellectual criticism (Theall, 1975, p. 23). Perhaps, as Canadian musician Bruce Cockburn suggests, the trouble with normal is it always gets worse.

The Trouble with Normal

What can be seen from the foregoing discussion is that the critical-ness of Canadian communication studies has been mapped onto discourses of the ongoing search for a unique Canadian national identity. Indeed, the search for Canadian uniqueness has derailed a sustained interrogation of what a critical approach to communication might entail and whether or not it is even present in the Canadian field. In short, the criticism is that the field has not been critical enough. Lorimer (2000b) criticizes generations of communication scholars in Canada for not moving past Smythe's limited "political economy" understanding of critical communications; he suggests, as have others, that as the discipline has matured, its critical edge has dulled (see also Salter, 1987). De la Garde (1987) asks:

> [H]ave we embarked on a sea of intellectual calm following the rise of the Innis empire within the scientific community and are we falling prey to the "commodification of knowledge" with its monopolistic discourse or are we on the eve of renewing our problematic, even if it means living through a period of "disturbances," of vigorous debates—and of democracy? (p. 20)

In short, de la Garde is asking, has there been enough ferment in our field?

The mapping of a critical disciplinary identity onto a national identity has also produced certain blind spots. As Meisel (1987) notes, "[T]he questions asked by researchers—and the questions not asked—are greatly conditioned by their societal and national setting" (p. 57). The cultural nationalist position, for example, has always accepted a strong, legitimate state presence. Yet is approval of an interventionist state consistent with an approach that defines itself as critical and therefore as being in opposition to the normalizing power of any state? Although communication studies in Canada did not become institutionalized in the university system as a result of a close relationship with media industries (as in the United Sates), it might be that it has done so in a close relationship with government. In fact, a significant number of scholars attribute the rise of communication studies in Canada to the needs of royal commissions studying media (Robinson, 2000; Salter, 1987; Tate et al., 2000). Tate et al. (2000) regard this as a positive development:

> What tends to be invisible in the equation is precisely the important role which royal commissions and other government-created study groups and task forces have tended to play in our scholarly life. Focused stimulus, funding, and collegiality are generated that tend to give structure to new and emerging areas of organized scholarship. Arguably, it is not coincidental that the CCA [Canadian Communication Association] and the *CJC* (in its evolved form as a peer-reviewed scholarly journal) were established in the wake of the LaMarsh Commission. (p. 86)

Lorimer (2000b) calls for more such research: "We . . . must maintain the role of collecting information and providing analyses of those industries so that government has a sound foundation on which to act" (p. 14).

Yet one of the hallmarks of critical research, even as Lazarsfeld framed it, was its intellectual independence. Gerbner (1983b) reminds us that "[c]ritical inquiry is the distinguishing feature of a discipline and the hallmark of independent scholarship (p. 355). Others have urged more caution regarding this close relationship with the government's research agenda (de la Garde, 1987). Salter (1987) suggests that "[t]he influence of government funding on the research programs of a discipline should never be underestimated" (p. 35); she goes on to remark that "there are some dangers in relying upon the needs of government to create the research foci within a discipline" (p. 41). If we are to follow Gerbner's call for critical inquiry, it would seem that this relationship with the interests and agenda of the Canadian state requires more scrutiny—a scrutiny that will not take place if we do not recognize our institutional history and if we do not abandon the assumption that we are *already* critical.

Not Enough Ferment in the Field

Critical communication studies in Canada situates itself in relation to debates within American communication studies, and specifically the distinction between critical and administrative approaches. Critical communication studies in the United States can be described through a series of commitments to the question of the intersection of communication and power in society, to a nonlinear understanding of social power, to nonquantitative methods, to an epistemological position that recognizes the place of values in research, to theoretical roots in radical thought, and to the production of knowledge that contributes to a broader project of human emancipation.

When Canadian scholars have directed their minds to their own discipline, they have tended to focus on questions of national identity, assuming that Canadian communication studies is critical (as defined above) and mobilizing as their evidence the work of foundational thinkers such as Harold Innis, Marshall McLuhan, and Northrop Frye. Insufficient attention has been paid to writing, understanding, and engaging critically with the history of the field since the foundational thinkers. Current claims about critical-ness rest on the relationship of many scholars to political economy or critical cultural studies approaches, or generally to a leftist/humanist/cultural nationalist orientation. If a critical approach is going to mean something, and not be just a normal—and normalizing—label, then we need to think about the ways in which our work is truly critical. One way to do this would be to map out a broader critical approach to communication studies—an approach that draws on, rather than smugly ignores, the American experience and at the same time incorporates the specific Canadian contributions of a focus on history, a dialectical approach to power, a concern with technology and culture, an awareness of nondominant epistemological positions, and the inclusion of specific values. Arguably, in an era of attacks on universities, the erasure of the political left, a general anti-intellectual malaise, and economic and social globalization, critical communication research is as necessary as it has ever been.

Bailie (1997) suggests that "critical communication studies are intricately linked to a project that promotes a critical imaginary: the ability to think beyond present social, political, and economic conditions to participate in the construction of alternative futures" (p. 33). Carey, too, uses the language of imagination when he argues that "a critical theory of communication must affirm what is before our eyes and transcend it by imagining, at the very least, a world more desirable" (1982, p. 33). To echo and paraphrase C. Wright Mills, who was addressing the discipline of sociology in the 1950s, perhaps what we need in Canada is a more active critical communications imagination—the kind that might be sparked through both honouring our ghosts and encouraging more ferment in the field.

Questions

1. What are the major differences between administrative and critical research as defined by American communication studies?
2. What are the six shared assumptions of critical communication research?
3. Why is it difficult to determine if Canadian communication studies is critical?
4. How does Canadian communication studies define itself as unique (i.e., distinct from U.S. communication studies)?
5. Discuss the ways in which Canadian communication studies is and is not critical.
6. Select a current communications phenomenon. How would you analyze it as a critical communication scholar? What kinds of questions would you ask?

Web Sites

Journal of Communication: **http://joc.oupjournals.org/**
Journal of Communication Inquiry: **http://www.sagepub.co.uk/frame.html**
  http://www.sagepub.co.uk/journals/details/j0239.html
University of Iowa Department of Communication Studies, Links to Resources:
  http://www.uiowa.edu/ ~ commstud/resources/

Notes

1. The author wishes to thank Jessica Wurster for her invaluable research assistance and McGill University for its support of this research.
2. See the *Colloquium in Critical Studies in Mass Communication,* 1995 (special issue of the journal *Critical Studies in Mass Communication).*

References

Acland, Charles R., and William J. Buxton. (1999). *Harold Innis in the new century: Reflections and refractions.* Montreal and Kingston: McGill-Queen's University Press.

Allen, Mike. (1999). The role of meta-analysis for connecting critical and scientific approaches: The need to develop a sense of collaboration. *Critical Studies in Mass Communication, 16,* 373–379.

Babe, Robert E. (2000a). *Canadian communication thought: Ten foundational writers.* Toronto: University of Toronto Press.

———. (2000b). Foundations of Canadian communication thought. *Canadian Journal of Communication, 26,* 19–37.

Bailie, Mashoed. (1997). Critical communication pedagogy: Teaching and learning for democratic life in democratizing communication? In M. Bailie and D. Winseck (Eds.), *Democratizing communication? Comparative perspectives on information and power* (pp. 33–56). Creskill, NJ: Hampton Press.

Biagi, Shirley, and Craig McKie. (1999). *Media impact: An introduction to mass media.* Toronto: ITP Nelson.

Blumler, Jay G. (1983). Communication and democracy: The crisis beyond and the ferment within. *Journal of Communication, 33*(3), 166–173.

Carey, James. (1975). Canadian communication theory: Extensions and interpretations of Harold Innis. In G.J. Robinson and D. F. Theall (Eds.), *Studies in Canadian communications* (pp. 27–60). Montreal: Graduate Program in Communications.

———. (1982). The mass media and critical theory: An American view. In Michael Burgoon (Ed.), *Communication Yearbook 6* (pp. 18–34). Beverly Hills: Sage.

———. (1983). The origins of the radical discourse on cultural studies in the United States. *Journal of Communication, 33*(3), 311–313.

de la Garde, Roger. (1987, Winter). The 1987 Southam lecture: Mr. Innis, is mere life after the 'American Empire'? *Canadian Journal of Communication,* 7–21.

Elasmar, Michael G. (1999). Opportunities and challenges of using meta-analysis in the field of international communication in critical studies. *Mass Communication, 16,* 379–384.

Fleming, D., and B. Bailyn (Eds.). (1969). *The Intellectual migration: Europe and America, 1930–1960.* Cambridge, MA: Harvard University Press.

Garnham, Nicholas. (1983). Toward a theory of cultural materialism. *Journal of Communication, 33*(3), 314–329.

Gerbner, George. (1964). On content analysis and critical research in mass communication. In Lewis Anthony Dexter and David Manning White (Eds.), *People, society and mass communication* (pp. 476–500). New York: Free Press.

———. (1983a). Introduction. *Journal of Communication 33*(3), 1–4.

———. (1983b). The importance of being critical—In one's own fashion. *Journal of Communication, 33*(3), 355–362.

Gitlin, Todd. (1981). Media sociology: The dominant paradigm. In G. Cleveland Wilhoit and Harold E. Bock (Eds.), *Mass communication review yearbook, 12* (pp. 73–121). Beverly Hills: Sage.

Grosswiler, Paul. (1996). The dialectical methods of Marshall McLuhan, Marxism, and critical theory. *Canadian Journal of Communication, 21*(1), 95–124.

Haight, Timothy R. (1983). The critical researcher's dilemma. *Journal of Communication, 33*(3), 226–236.

Halloran, James D. (1983). A case for critical eclecticism. *Journal of Communication, 33*(3), 270–278.

Hardt, Hanno. (1992). *Critical communication studies: Communication, history & theory in America.* London and New York: Routledge.

Holmes, Helen, and David Taras (Eds.). (1992). *Seeing ourselves: Media power and policy in Canada.* Toronto: Harcourt Brace Jovanovich Canada.

Jansen, Sue Curry. (1983). Power and knowledge: Toward a new critical synthesis. *Journal of Communication, 33*(3), 342–354.

Kroker, Arthur. (1984). *Technology and the Canadian mind: Innis/McLuhan/Grant.* Montreal: New World Perspectives.

Lang, Kurt. (1979). The critical functions of empirical communication research: Observations on German-American influences. *Media, Culture and Society, 1*, 83–96.

Lazarsfeld, Paul Felix. (1941). Remarks on administrative and critical communication research. *Studies in Philosophy and Social Science, 9*(1), 2–16.

———. (1969). An episode in the history of social research: A memoir. In D. Fleming and B. Bailyn (Eds.), *The intellectual migration: Europe and America, 1930–1960* (pp. 270–337). Cambridge, MA: Harvard University Press.

Lorimer, Rowland. (2000a). Editorial: The genesis of this issue—Twenty-five years of the *CJC. Canadian Journal of Communication, 25*, 3–7.

———. (2000b). Introduction: Communications teaching and research—Looking forward from 2000. *Canadian Journal of Communication, 25*, 9–17.

Lorimer, Rowland, and Mike Gasher. (2001). *Mass communication in Canada.* Don Mills, ON: Oxford University Press.

Lorimer, Rowland, and Jean McNulty. (1996). *Mass communication in Canada.* Toronto: Oxford University Press.

McKie, Craig, and Benjamin D. Singer. (2001). Communications in Canadian society (5th ed.). Toronto: Thompson Educational Pubbishing.

Meisel, John. (1987, Winter). Some Canadian perspectives on communication research. *Canadian Journal of Communication*, 55–63.

Mosco, Vincent. (1983). Critical research and the role of labour. *Journal of Communication, 33*(3), 237–248.

———. (1996). *The political economy of communication.* Thousand Oaks, GA: Sage.

Robinson, Gertrude J. (1987, Winter). Prologue: Canadian communication studies: A discipline in transition? *Canadian Journal of Communication*, 1–5.

———. (2000). Remembering our past: Reconstructing the field of Canadian communication studies. *Canadian Journal of Communication, 25*, 105–125.

Robinson, Gertrude Joch, and Donald F. Theall (Eds.). (1975). *Introduction in studies in Canadian communications* (pp. 1–6). Montreal: Graduate Program in Communications.

Rogers, Everett M. (1982). The empirical and critical schools of communication research. In M. Burgoon (Ed.), *Communication Yearbook 5* (pp. 125–144). New Brunswick, NJ: Transaction Books.

Rosengren, Karl Erik. (1983). Communication research: One paradigm or four? *Journal of Communication, 33*(3), 185–207.

Salter, Liora (Ed.). (1981a). *Communication studies in Canada/Études Canadiennes en communication*. Toronto: Butterworths.

_____. (1981b). Editor's introduction. In L. Salter (Ed.), *Communication studies in Canada/Etudes Canadiennes en communication* (pp. xi–xxii). Toronto: Butterworths.

_____. (1987, Winter). Taking stock: Communication studies in 1987. *Canadian Journal of Communication*, 23–45.

Schiller, Herbert I. (1983). Critical research in the information age. *Journal of Communication, 33*(3), 249–257.

Schramm, Wilbur. (1983). The unique perspective of communication: A retrospective view. *Journal of Communication, 33*(3), 6–17.

Sholle, David J. (1988). Critical studies: From the theory of ideology to power/knowledge. *Critical Studies in Mass Communication, 5*, 16–41.

Slack, Jennifer Daryl, and Martin Allor. (1983). The political and epistemological constituents of critical communication research. *Journal of Communication, 33*(3), 208–218.

Slack, Jennifer Daryl, and M. Mehdi Semati. (1997). Intellectual and political hygiene: The 'Sokal' affair. *Critical Studies in Mass Communication, 14*(3), 201–227.

Smythe, Dallas W., and Tran Van Dinh. (1983). On critical and administrative research: A new critical analysis. *Journal of Communication, 33*(3), 117–127.

Stevenson, Robert L. (1983). A critical look at critical analysis. *Journal of Communication, 33*(3), 262–267.

Szuchewycz, Bohdan, and Jeannette Sloniowski (Eds.). (1999). *Canadian communications: Issues in contemporary media and culture*. Scarborough, ON: Prentice Hall/Allyn and Bacon Canada.

Tate, Eugene D., Andrew Osler, Gregory Fouts, and Arthur Segal. (2000). The beginnings of communication studies in Canada: Remembering and narrating the Past. *Canadian Journal of Communication, 25*, 61–103.

Theall, Donald F. (1975). Communication theory and the marginal culture: The socio-aesthetic dimensions of communication study. In G.J. Robinson and D.F. Theall (Eds.), *Studies in Canadian communications* (pp. 7–26). Montreal: Graduate Program in Communications.

Tremblay, Gaétan. (1981). Préface. In L. Salter (Ed.), *Communication studies in Canada/Études Canadiennes en communication* (pp. vii–x). Toronto: Butterworths.

Vivian, John, and Peter J. Maurin. (2000). *The media of mass communication* (2nd ed.). Scarborough, ON: Allyn and Bacon Canada.

New Communication Research from Canada

John D. H. Downing

A review essay by John D. H. Downing, University of Texas at Austin

> *Canadian Communication Thought: Ten Foundational Writers.* By Robert E. Babe. Toronto, Canada: Toronto University Press, 2000. x + 448 pp. $75.00 (hard), $29.95 (soft).

> *Citizens and Nation: An Essay on History, Communication and Canada.* By Gerald Friesen. Toronto, Canada: University of Toronto Press, 2000. x + 307 pp. $55.00 (hard), $22.95 (soft).

> *Human Rights and the Internet.* Edited by Steven Hick, Edward F. Halpin, & Eric Hoskins. New York: St. Martin's Press, 2000. xviii + 257 pp. $55.00 (hard).

> *Islamic Peril: Media and Global Violence.* By Karim H. Karim. Montréal, Canada: Black Rose Books, 2000. x + 204 pp. $24.99 (soft).

> *Les Médias Québécois: Presse, Radio, Télévision, Inforoute* (2nd ed.). By Marc Raboy, with the assistance of Geneviève Grimard. Boucherville, Québec: Gaëtan Morin Éditeur, 2000. xviii + 409 pp. (soft)

> *The Missing News: Filters and Blind Spots in Canada's Press.* By Robert A. Hackett & Richard Gruneau, with Donald Gutstein, Timothy A. Gibson, & NewsWatch Canada. Aurora, Ontario: Garamond Press, 2000. 258 pp. $21.95 (soft).

> *Variations sur l'Influence Culturelle Américaine.* Edited by Florian Sauvageau. Sainte Foy, Québec: Les Presses de l'Université Laval, 1999. xxviii + 262 pp. (soft)

For communication researchers, Canada presents a perplexing, and intriguing, puzzle. There is nothing straightforwardly unitary about this vast country with its colossal wilderness. Anyone who follows the news knows there is a Québec/Anglo Canada division, yet that is but a single rift, however salient. There are divisions of "race" and ethnicity among Anglophones and Francophones as a result both of labor migration and of capitalists' migration (especially the Hong Kong Chinese on the West Coast). There are also notable divisions between Aboriginal peoples and the settlers, whether Francophone or Anglophone, although federal policy toward First Nations's territorial rights has recently been much more constructive than in the U.S. There are quite vocal conflicts among the four giant Western provinces and both Ontario and Québec, and also more muted ones among the four marginalized Maritime provinces in the East and the rest of the country. There has been a federal multicultural policy for 3 decades, placing Canada with Australia as the only two nations that have adopted such policies (however ambivalently), and yet, for many Québécois, that policy was instituted to marginalize their particular historical position and reduce them to one of many competing "minorities." Yet, despite all these rifts, Canada has remained a remarkably peaceful nation, somehow hewing to a culture of often bitter verbal debate that practically never spills over into violence. Lastly, there is the ever-present and often resented cultural and economic influence of Canada's geographically smaller neighbor, the U.S., whose citizens may know less of Canada than of Mexico, their other NAFTA partner.

These books do not address every issue noted above; however, neither is Canada simply an overlooked laboratory for communication researchers. The texts reviewed here address pivotal topics in communication. Some smaller Canadian presses represented here (Black Rose, Broadview, Garamond) are too little known outside Canada, but have lists well worth checking. Finally, there are many significant Canadian scholars whose recent work is not addressed here.

Canadian Communication Thought by Robert Babe surveys 10 influential writers, some nationally so (the Sprys, Grant), others internationally (Innis, McLuhan, Smythe), though none from Québec.[1] Only one is of a living author (G. J. Robinson).[2] Babe defines communication very broadly, effectively to cover cultural commentary and public advocacy at least as much as media theory, and often effectively embracing analyses of Anglo-Canadian cultural identity as well. The writers range widely in primary discipline, from political philosopher C. B. Macpherson to literary critic Northrop Frye to documentarian John Grierson.

In general the book presents an absorbing account of these thinkers. Sometimes the breadth of their concerns means the focus becomes a little unsteady, and in the conclusion, Babe's endeavor to draw out common themes in their work appears a little labored. Nonetheless, issues of space and transportation, political economy, communication technology, art and media, media and democracy are well to the fore in this volume and, although the writers' positions on these themes at times clash with each other, they are still often rather distinct from typical U.S. approaches to the same themes. This is most evident in their tendency toward macroanalytic, nonempiricist perspectives and also in their tendency to operate from a certain level of humanistic, non-market-driven concern for the public good, one that never evinces the virtual terror of government protections so dear to official U.S. culture. Because their period of activity mostly predated the free market orientation and pro-U.S. stances of the Mulroney era, whether these characteristics mark them as a unique generation will be an interesting question to explore when a newer generation of Canadian communication theorists comes to be evaluated. In general, however, from the evidence of the recent books reviewed below, the stamp of these scholars appears still evident.

Gerald Friesen's *Citizens and Nation* is a communication-based exploration of the phases in the historical construction of Anglo Canadian and, to a small extent, Québécois identity. His methodology is imaginative and interesting, taking a select handful of autobiographies drawn from throughout the 20th century and weaving them together with much broader analyses of Canadian political, economic, and cultural development. The life stories on which he draws are mostly those of women and include those of two aboriginal women, one from the Northwest Territories and the other an urban white-collar employee, a village woman from Labrador, a German immigrant worker in Vancouver, and a political activist member of the French Canadian elite. He suggests by these means the interconnectedness of their lives and their everyday culture, notwithstanding its variations. Friesen defines Canada at one point (p. 225) as "one of the world's great national experiments in pluralism."

Friesen traces four cultural periods in the definition of time and space in Canadian history: the oral traditional, the textual settler, the print capitalist, and the screen capitalist. He acknowledges that the fourth category might be subdivided into the film and television era, and the computer era, or alternatively that it could be fused with the third category. He sees these periods as cumulative, as each having left distinctive imprints on contemporary Canadian culture. The book offers a very richly detailed interpretation of Canadian-ness precisely because of its primary focus on the roles of communication in the narrative and because of its deliberate selection of the stories of everyday Canadians with which to illustrate its themes.

Marc Raboy's *Les Médias Québécois* offers an excellent compendium of up-to-date material on the specifics of Québec media and telecommunications. In chapters 2–5 he covers their political economy, regulatory framework, media professionals, and both the production and reception of media content. There are many facets of the Québec situation that spark interest, not least (a) the history of continual strife with the federal authorities in Ottawa over communication policy, especially during the 1970s, and (b) the strength, though sharply diminished during the past decade or so, of community media, both print and radio. Raboy discusses, too, the popularity of Québécois TV soaps, sharply contrasted with the popularity of U.S. soaps in Anglo Canada; the relative weakness of computer use among Francophones compared with Anglophones; and the patterns of concentrated media ownership in Québec.[3]

Raboy's book brings together detailed empirical description—five lengthy appendixes cover his sources, profiles of leading media firms, media mergers and acquisitions during 1996–1999, the text of key legislation governing media, and selected readership and viewing statistics—and a critical perspective on the problems of gigantism and monopoly in media ownership.

The Missing News is a Canadian version of U.S. journalism Professor Carl Jensen's Project Censored.[4] The authors and sources are multiple, with James Winter[5] of the University of Windsor flagged in the acknowledgments as a key contributor. Canada, whose Charter of Rights and Freedoms (chap. 2) establishes protection of media freedom analogously to the U.S. First Amendment, is a nation whose less reflective citizens are equally prone as their U.S. counterparts to pronounce censorship a "foreign country" issue. Hackett[6] and Gruneau provide some very telling and carefully documented case studies pointing to the reality of censorship in Canadian media. In chapters 3 and 4 they report on the views of a number of journalists interviewed, and then on the views of 145 establishment interest groups and 155 public advocacy groups. Predictably, each group felt its own particular concern was inadequately represented, but interestingly, they discovered a degree of homogeneity between both sets on the absence in news media of coverage of the social implications of economic policy and international relations, as well as of "positive" news. Perhaps the most unanticipated finding was the degree of agreement between both groups on the influence of media megacorporations on the framing of news. For the public advocacy groups, the discrepancies were more foreseeable on issues of ethnicity and race, human rights, and religion, and for the more conservative groups, on defense and "objectivity" (the latter was typically the view of those who subscribed to the thesis that Canadian journalists were nearly all former leftist 1960s students).

Chapter 5 summarizes research done by Newswatch Canada in the years 1993–1995, focusing on Anglo Canadian and mostly on print media, and on content analysis studies conducted from 1996 onward. The stories nominated as seriously undercovered were submitted to a ranking panel of 31 "distinguished Canadians in . . . public service, academe and journalism, selected with an eye to regional, gender and political diversity" (p. 125). Chapter 6 summarizes content analyses from pilot studies conducted from 1996 (though the text does not make clear how long these continued, which is a weakness), and chapter 7 focuses on the weak coverage of labor, poverty, neoliberal policy agendas, and the power of media corporations themselves. The authors stress that their concern is heuristic and argumentative, to promote further exploration and discussion of problems their studies have raised, not to present their research as a totally finished product. They do stress, though (pp. 221–222), that the record of Canadian media sins of omission is "modestly favorable" when compared to evidence from the U.S.

The essay collection, *Human Rights and the Internet,* edited by Hick, Halpin, and Hoskins, is based upon a Canadian government-sponsored conference on the subject in 1998. Its mostly descriptive essays are on regions and nations (e.g., Africa, Latin America, Europe, East Timor, women's cross-national internet use in post-Yugoslavia), on specific issues (e.g., racist hate sites, child porn sites, Canadian free speech and privacy law under the Charter of Rights and Freedoms, commercial and political surveillance), and on activist projects (e.g., Derechos Human Rights/Equipo Nizkor and the Web's potential for human rights education). The book is a very useful compendium on a critically important topic, here and there inevitably a little dated by now, occasionally repetitive (some extra editing would have been useful), but a project that would serve as a valuable course text in this understudied zone in communication research.

The two final texts also address international themes. Sauvageau's collection, *Variations sur l'influence culturelle américaine,* contains 14 essays on the question of Americanization of Canadian and Québécois culture; Karim's *Islamic Peril,* winner of the 2001 Robinson Prize for communication scholarship, updates and substantially extends Edward Said's *Covering Islam.*[7]

The essays in Sauvageau explore a number of dimensions of U.S. cultural influence, a hot topic, needless to say, in many nations around the world, but from a variety of angles. Some of the chapters focus on historical themes, such as American "new journalism" and the Québec press at the close of the 19th century (de Bonville), or the political and economic backdrop of U.S. cultural influence on both Canada and Québec from Canada's foundation in 1967 through 1988 (Lemelin). Some essayists are media producers; most are academics.

Some are more critical, others more sanguine—Lelièvre (p. 128), a media producer, insists that all cultural production is in some sense mimetic and concludes, "I prefer the risk game to the resentment game." A topic taken up by several is the question of format, that is to say, U.S. cultural influence expressed not so much in importation of U.S. media products, but rather the hegemony of U.S. media formats in soaps (Nguyên-Duy) and computer software (Proulx). Bertrand (pp. 183–194) distinguishes three types of format. One he judges fairly malleable and pragmatic, such as the TV news magazine or sport reporting, and a second specific to a particular nation (e.g., the Western movie). The third is the one he critiques (p. 186), the format with a defined ideological viewpoint ("the simplistic manicheanism of some U.S. police series; the materialism of certain game shows, founded on the acquisitive instinct; puritanism, the fear (and exclusion) of sexuality, but also, naturally, the pathological obsession with sexual topics, as in the flock of talk shows; violence as . . . the solution to conflicts, or as spice"). The collection provides a very wide-ranging set of perspectives, none chauvinistic.

Karim, formerly a journalist and subsequently a Canadian civil servant, now a professor at Carleton University, suggests (chap. 7), as have others, that the frequent mainstream media characterization in the West of Islam and Muslims as enemies of peace, order, and Western countries' global rights has a great deal to do with two sets of circumstances: (a) the blows dealt to Western influence in the oil-producing heartland by the 1979 emergence of the Khomeini regime in Iran and the assassination of Egyptian President Sadat in 1981 on the part of those opposed to his accommodation with Israel; and (b) the 1989–1991 collapse of the Soviet bloc, which among other consequences removed a standard source of political threat that had been milked politically for decades to justify huge arms budgets and many Western interventions around the globe. The world's one billion Muslims, he argues, have all too often been harnessed over the past decade in the service of generating a political paranoia that fulfills the same ends.

In other chapters, Karim explores coverage of Muslims in the "Middle East," in Chechnya, in the civil wars that followed the breakup of Yugoslavia, and within the West itself. Images of terrorism and of the perpetually cited term *jihad* are subjected to detailed scrutiny. Karim is careful (pp. 189ff.) to note that there is no homogeneity of coverage, and that particular journalists and media have at times represented the Muslim world as being as complex, differentiated, and often positive a force as it is. It is paradoxical, though, how often the violently aggressive actions of a very small number of terrorists have been inflated by predominant media coverage into the universal lifestyle of a billion believers—perhaps U.S. citizens who are upset that a number of people in the rest of the world assume Americans are all as violent as their military interventions suggest should learn to reflect more deeply on how such discourses may be generated and how serious their consequences can be.

I have written this review article to try to expand U.S. and other communication researchers' awareness of the stimulating and varied research conducted in Anglo Canada and Québec. As we move, all too gradually, out of the era when British and U.S. scholarship dominated the field, alertness to other national traditions of scholarship and the media processes of other nations will become ever more important.

Notes

1. Babe notes (pp. 36–37) that some Québécois scholars' acknowledge that Québec has not generated a distinctive body of communication thought.
2. Robinson's 1999 Southam Lecture, "Remembering Our Past: Reconstructing the Field of Canadian Communication Studies," *Canadian Journal of Communication,* 25(2000), pp. 105–125, offers a stimulating counterpoint to Babe's book.
3. In their research study, *Les Journalistes Canadiens: Un Portrait de Fin de Siècle* (St. Nicolas, Québec: Les Presses de l'Université Laval, 1999, pp. 87–111), David Pritchard and Florian Sauvageau explore the much-debated question of whether journalists have a different professional ethos in the two nations of Canada. Their conclusion is that the notion that only Anglo journalists subscribe to professional codes of objectivity, but Québécois journalists to a journalism of opinion is a myth unsupported by the evidence. The focus is often different, owing to national priorities, and both sets of journalists tend to read U.S. news magazines more than news magazines from the other part of Canada, but the ethos is no different.
4. Carl Jensen and Project Censored, *20 Years of Censored News,* New York: Seven Stories Press, 1997.
5. Winter is author of a series of books and articles that effectively produce a Herman-Chomsky "propaganda model" of Canadian and U.S. media.
6. See also one of the most penetrating analyses available of the philosophy and practice of journalistic objectivity, written in a rather less *engagé* style, in Robert Hackett and Yuezhi Zhau's *Sustaining Democracy? Journalism and the Politics of Objectivity,* Toronto, Canada: Garamond Press, 1998.
7. Edward Said, *Covering Islam* (New York: Pantheon Books, 1981, 1997).

Keywords for critical reading

This section explains two sides of mass communication theory—*macro* and *micro*. It discusses the central ideas of some of major theories of the media and mass communication and sheds light on their main critique. It also introduces historical backgrounds and basic concepts of, and critically analyzes major themes, approaches, and theories of international communication. The debate between two major schools of thought in the field of communication research—*administrative research* and *critical theory*—has been presented showing how Lazarsfeld's media effects studies gave rise to a series of arguments from theorists of the critical theory. This debate has been discussed in the context of Canadian trends in media studies and communication research. By now, you should be to understand, selectively discriminate against, and apply each of the following key concepts:

- Administrative research; Audience research; Communication research
- Communication approaches (Agenda-setting; Media effects; Uses-and-gratifications; Political-economy)
- Canadian communication studies
- Cultural studies
- Diffusion of innovations
- Hegemony
- International communication
- Free flow of information (Discourses of globalization)
- Public opinion; Public sphere
- Semiotics of media
- Spiral of silence
- Structural imperialism
- Theories of communication (Critical theory; Cultivation theory; Dependency theory; Medium theory; Modernization theory; Theories of information society)

Key questions for critical learning

1. Discuss the main concepts of both *administrative research* and *critical theory* in relation to Stephen Littlejohn's organizing model of theories of mass communication.
2. Comment on the debate between administrative research and critical theory, explaining their distinct understandings of conducting communication research that can lead to the social good.

3. Explain media studies and communication research in Canada in terms of theories and approaches of international communication.
4. State the main criticisms raised in discussing (1) some of the major theories of mass communication; (2) different communication research schools of though; and (3) the Canadian claims in communication studies.
5. What are the 6 shared assumptions of critical communication research?

Part 4
From Theory to Practice

Section Editor: Mark Lowes

Introduction

The purpose of this section is to introduce students to the process by which researchers take an idea from theory to practice. Our primary concern is with research design and methods for the study of media, culture and society—the familiar but largely invisible ideas and social structures that help shape who you are, what you do, when, why, and how.

In other words, we are primarily concerned with issues in *applied media analysis*—which explores the theory, methods, and techniques that underpin contemporary research on the often complex relations between media and society.

What binds the articles in this section together is a concern with challenging students to not only understand a wide range of issues related to media research, but also to *apply* that understanding to specific research problems. To this end the articles chosen for this section highlight exemplar cases, which will supplement the course lectures. These lectures, in combination with the articles, will portray the scope of the field of media research in specific cultural, contemporary, and historical contexts in terms of the key debates about the ways in which researchers wrestle with the challenges of integrating theory and the practice of research in their studies.

Manufacturing the Agenda

Sports Page: A Case Study in the Manufacture of Sports News for the Daily Press

Mark Douglas Lowes

This case study seeks to develop an understanding of why the sports pages of metropolitan daily newspapers are so regularly saturated with news of the major commercial spectator sports world, while noncommercial sports receive only a modicum of coverage at best. Using data gathered from fieldwork in the sports department of a large Canadian daily, this inquiry reveals that sportswriters depend on routine sources for the bulk of their raw news material. Almost invariably, these sources are athletes, spokespersons, and organizations with roots deep in the commercial sports world. This is a practical necessity, enabling sportswriters to cope with the pressures and constraints of their work. Consequently, work routines employed in the daily manufacture of sports news tend to privilege the major commercial spectator sports, thus "reading" noncommercial sports out of the news by omission.

Cette étude de cas tente de développer une compréhension du fait que les pages sportives des quotidiens métropolitains sont si régulièrement saturées de nouvelles du monde du sport commercial, alors que les sports noncommerciaux ne reçoivent qu'une minime couverture. À partir de données recueillies auprès du département des sports d'un quotidien canadien majeur, cette étude révèle que les journalistes sportifs dépendent de sources régulières pour la plus grosse part de leurs matériaux. Presqu' invariablement, ces sources sont des athlètes, des porte-paroles et des organisations profondèment ancrés dans le monde du sport commmercial. Ceci est une nécessité pratique permettant aux journalistes de faire face aux pressions et contraintes de leur travail. En conséquence, les routines de travail utilisées dans la fabrication journalière des nouvelles sportives tendent à privilégier les sports commerciaux majeurs et exclure les sports noncommerciaux.

This paper is a study of the work routines employed by newsworkers in the manufacture of sports news for the metropolitan daily press. More generally, I

Mark Douglas Lowes is a doctoral candidate in the School of Communication, Simon Fraser University, Burnaby, BC V5L 3B4.

offer an account of the lived work space of newspaper sport reporters and editors at one large Canadian daily, in an effort to explain why the sports pages are so regularly saturated with news of the major North American commercial spectator sports world while noncommercial sports receive only minimal coverage at best[1].

As we shall see, the sports newswork environment of a metropolitan daily is rife with pressures and constraints; and newsworkers have responded by institutionalizing various work routines to cope with these demands. Just to clarify my terms, by "institutionalized" work routines, I mean a distinctive set of patterns and rules of conduct that (a) persist in recognizably similar form across long spans of time and space; and (b) represent well-recognized and widely accepted ways of doing things in society (Giddens, 1982, p. 10; cf. Gruneau & Whitson, 1993, p. 34). In other words, today's patterns of action tend to reiterate past patterns. "Repeated time after time, these actions become standard operating procedures," they "take on a life of their own," simply becoming "the way things are done" (Sigal, 1973, p. 101). In this way, sports newswork becomes routinized, which has the effect of standardizing sports news content—it is mostly about major commercial spectator sports.

In this paper I argue if we want to understand why it is that some sports enjoy regular and voluminous press coverage and others virtually none, then we have to examine how and why newsworkers choose what will become sports news in the first place.

Method

Data were gathered during four months of field research conducted primarily in the newsroom of an eastern Ontario metropolitan daily newspaper, the *Bytown Examiner*[2]. This field research consisted of both nonparticipant observation of activities at the paper's sports desk and extensive interviews with the paper's sports editors and reporters. Essentially, the day-to-day routine activities of these people constitute the basic data of this study. In addition, several hours were spent interviewing and observing five media relations staffers from two major commercial sports organizations: the Hornets of the National Hockey League and the Flames of the Canadian Football League.

The *Examiner* has a staff of 10 sports newsworkers. There is one editor and one assistant editor, three beat reporters, and two columnists. In addition, there are two "deskers" who split their time between reporting and preparing the sports section for publication every day; this latter task involves such things as copy-editing, photo selection, and page layout. Finally, the *Examiner* has one freelance reporter generally responsible for covering Bytown's university and college sports scene; he also regularly writes on harness racing. Based on biographical data obtained during interviews, the typical *Examiner* sports newsworker is a 33 year-old White male with about 10 years experience doing sports journalism, and he holds a diploma in journalism from community college. At the time of study, there was one female working as a desker.

Initially, I was concerned that I might run into the same problems as Cavanagh (1989, pp. 218–221) in his study of sports production for CBC Television (Canada's public broadcaster). Cavanagh reports that he was initially treated with a certain amount of suspicion by producers and production staff because of his route into the CBC from the "top down;" that is, through the Deputy Head of TV Sports. Staffers believed Cavanagh was from CBC Headquarters in Ottawa, performing some sort of efficiency rating or audit on the department, and it was a while before their misconceptions were allayed and their cooperation attained.

My experience in the field was quite the contrary. Despite the fact I was introduced by the sports editor, I felt no sense of suspicion or the like from any of the sports staff. Indeed, it became clear within a few hours of my first visit to the *Examiner* that the sports newsworkers were genuinely interested in my project, as they all willingly took time out of their hectic schedules to speak with me whenever I had a question. Not once did I feel I was talked down to, or questioned about a possible hidden agenda in studying sports newswork at the paper. Furthermore, all those interviewed were quite open about their thoughts, philosophies, and criticisms of commercial sports generally, and sports newswork specifically.

Sports newswork at the *Examiner* is carried out at a very hectic pace. Indeed, at first glance to an outsider, activity in the newsroom seems completely incoherent, a senseless ball of confusion akin to the organized chaos that marks activity on the floor of the Toronto or New York Stock Exchanges. Sports newsworkers typically work a 3 p.m. to 11 p.m. shift, and as the evening wears on and deadline approaches the pace picks up. As reporters scramble to finish their stories, and editors and deskers await these news items so they can layout the sports pages, a constant barrage of questions and orders pounds the ears—"Who pitched for the Jays last night? What's his ERA?" "Do you know if Barrett is starting tonight or is he still benched?" "Hey Colvin! What's going on with Turlotte? Can you get confirmation from the Hornets that he's on the trading block or not?" "Who's covering the diving competition?"

This cacophony made it necessary to conduct most of my interviews "on the fly," as the organized chaos of the newsroom generally did not allow for long protracted interviews. However, I was fortunate that all of sports newsworkers made an effort to escape the newsroom to allow me to conduct more formally structured and lengthy interviews. To this end, I carried a series of questions—an interview schedule—in the back of my field diary that I would use as a loose guide.

To initiate an interview, I approached newsworkers in a conversational manner, trying to relate to them on a level of shared affection for sports and sports journalism rather than as a detached social scientist. I found it particularly useful to tell them I had been a varsity football player at one of the local universities for five years; this was a great "icebreaker" and led to many interesting conversations, especially with a few of the reporters who had, at various times, covered university football in the city. This approach worked well and, after a short while, I was on a first name basis with all of the sports newsworkers at the paper.

Each interview began with my explaining that I was interested in how the sports section of a metropolitan daily newspaper is put together each day and, in particular, what their role in this process is, either as a reporter or editor. I discussed anonymity and confidentiality, explaining how I would blend their views and opinions in with their colleagues, both in the analysis and in the writing. I told them I would illustrate and highlight certain points by using anecdotes from individual interviews and explained that I would identify individuals with either pseudonyms or by their occupational title (e.g., editor, desker, or beat reporter).

I then asked them to tell me about their work, beginning with a general overview of what their job is all about. As these discussions unfolded, I interjected questions along the way, loosely following the interview schedule, trying to focus the interview. In fact, the interview schedule was used only as a guide and no attempt was made to restrict the interview subject too much to any one topic. This allowed for probing and following leads provided by the subject. In fact, exploring the channels opened up by respondents offered a wealth of information that likely would not have come to the surface had I strictly adhered to an interview schedule. People were very candid in their responses to sometimes difficult and possibly uncomfortable questions. For example, when asked point-blank why commercial sports receive so much coverage in the paper and noncommercial sports so little— a potentially threatening question—not one respondent avoided making a direct and forthright response. Indeed, they did not hesitate in pointing to the economic logic of such biased coverage; "Because that's what people want to read about" and "[That's] what gets you readers" were typical responses.

I believe this frankness was, in large part, a reflection of voluntary participation. From the outset, the *Examiner's* sports newsworkers demonstrated a great deal of enthusiasm for this study, with many going out of their way to ensure I captured as much data as possible—"You should talk to Barnes about that," and "I really want to read this when you're done" are typical of the support I received. One reporter even gave me his home phone number so I could call him "any time" I had a question. This enthusiasm and support greatly contributed to the depth of analysis this study was able to achieve.

Scheduled interviews lasted from 40 to 60 minutes on average, depending on how busy the newsworker was; spontaneous interviews generally ranged from several minutes to 20. All interviews were tape-recorded without objection. Indeed, several seemed amused that they were now the ones being interviewed, sitting on the other side of the fence so-to-speak; one respondent commented that he "felt like a jock under the microscope after a big game." In addition to the interview data, a lot of empirical material was obtained by making an observation and then approaching a newsworker to ask about it. For example, when I observed a reporter casually stroll over to the fax machine and begin to sift through the faxes that had arrived in the last 15 minutes or so I asked him, "What are they? Get a lot of them?" These two simple questions led to a 20 minute discussion of press releases and their importance to sports newswork.

Sports Newswork at the *Examiner*

Although the primary focus of this paper is on newswork routines, the economics of the news business and its influence on content of the sports section cannot be ignored. Indeed, as we shall see, market forces play a big part in shaping the framework within which sports newswork is carried out.

Metropolitan daily newspapers, like any other free market enterprise, sell a product to buyers. Their market is advertisers; the "product" is readers. In effect, readers are a commodity generated by the news industry—an "audience commodity"—and access to them is sold as advertising space. Further, newspaper organizations are fully attuned to the crucial importance of audience "quality;" advertisers are interested in purchasing clearly defined and highly concentrated audiences, comprised of people inclined to purchase whatever product the advertiser is selling. This is what Ben Bagdikian (1992) calls "the iron rule" of advertising-supported media; it is less important that people buy your product than they be the right people.

For a metropolitan daily selling its sports readers, the "right people" are 18 to 49-year-old males with disposable income. This demographic is considered to have the most buying power and can be swayed by effective advertising (Sparks, 1992; Jhally, 1984; Parente, 1977). What's more, several studies show that the levels of knowledge and interest in sport are greater among men than women (Gantz & Wenner, 1991, 1995; Gantz, 1985). Thus, the prevailing philosophy in the news industry is that the most effective way to attract male readers is to provide extensive coverage of commercial spectator sports; that is, cater to perceived male tastes. Accordingly, the sports pages of metropolitan dailies are saturated with commercial sports news, as revealed by content analyses of several North American dailies (Gelinas & Theberge, 1986; Lever & Wheeler, 1984; Rintala & Birrell, 1984; Scanlon, 1970). Commercial sports are cash cows and metropolitan dailies depend on them to "deliver the male" (Sparks, 1992).

The *Examiner* is an advertising-supported daily, dependent on advertising sales to generate most of its revenue. As such, the paper must produce a "quality" audience commodity to sell to advertisers—one which is highly concentrated and identifiable. Accordingly, the paper openly courts male readers with its sports coverage—it covers primarily commercial spectator sports, widely considered most appealing to male readers. Wenner (1989, p. 15) has an interesting take on this. He suggests that in many ways the sports pages function as socially sanctioned gossip sheets for men; a place where "a great deal of conjecture is placed upon 'heroes' and events of little worldly import." The sports section is primarily the domain of men.

This philosophy—that the *Examiner* should cover the major sports events and issues that have the widest interest primarily to male readers—rarely embraces noncommercial sports, which are generally considered an afterthought at best. The paper's approach to covering sports is neatly summed up by one of its sports reporters:

> People want to read about professional sports, the big leagues. . . . A lot of people don't watch little Billy go play ball at Trillium Park on a Friday night. I mean, how much interest is there in amateur sports like that? Not enough to warrant a lot of coverage.

Commercial sports thus consumes the majority of available column space in the *Examiner's* sports section each day by default—it's what readers want.

Developing this last point further, the first concern at the *Examiner* when planning its sports section each day is with the commercial sports scene—reporting what's happening in "the big leagues." The standard fare of the paper's sports news is game results from the previous day, player movement through trades and outright releases, injury reports on athletes, and the current status of any labor unrest. Indeed, reporting this news seems to be the raison d'être of any metropolitan daily's sports section: "This is the stuff people want to read about . . . big time sports gets you readers," remarked the *Examiner's* sports editor. The paper's sports section is thus saturated with commercial spectator sports news, primarily as a matter of economics—this is how a quality audience is attracted and subsequently sold to advertisers. A commercial spectator sports bias is simply a matter of financial survival for the *Examiner.*

As we've seen thus far, the present logic of news industry economics lead metropolitan dailies like the *Examiner* to emphasize commercial sports coverage. Given this, the problem facing these organizations is how to cover such a vast expanse? After all, metropolitan dailies, like any news organization, have finite resources; they are not able to post reporters everywhere there is a major sports event happening. So, newspapers employ a coverage strategy that is an industry standard—the "beat" system of reporting. Beats are a way of "providing predictably available information to reporters and, as such, are an important means of reducing the variability of the news and bringing some order to the news world" (Theberge & Cronk, 1986, p. 199).

Briefly, beat coverage entails assigning a reporter to a particular organization in order to provide regular coverage of a subject. In regard to sports, it is exclusively major sports organizations that are assigned beat reporters. For example, a reporter is assigned to cover the Toronto Blue Jays beat. Day in and day out, he or she reports on the team's activities; that is, anything that happens involving the team's ownership, its management, and its players and coaches. The reporter is expected to know the beat intimately and write regular news items about its activities. In this manner, the newspaper gets regular coverage not only of the Blue Jays, but of Major League Baseball itself. How? Simply because the team does not exist in a vacuum. When the reporter writes about the Blue Jays, invariably this means covering the activities of all the other teams in the major leagues, or at least those the Jays come in contact with. The Blue Jays beat, therefore, generates a regular flow of baseball news not only about the team, but Major League baseball as a whole.

The beat system is used extensively by the *Examiner* to cover sports—major commercial spectator sports that is. The paper has reporters assigned to three beats; namely, the Hornets of the National Hockey League; the Flames of the Canadian Football League; and the Badgers, a Triple "A" baseball club. As for noncommercial sports, coverage for them is a patchwork at best; certainly none can claim the same privileged coverage enjoyed by "big time" sports. These sports are usually covered by a freelance reporter or one of the paper's two deskers. Beat reporters only cover sports of such marginal interest when they're not too busy with their regular duties (cf. Theberge & Cronk, 1986).

There's an important point to consider in all this: Establishing and maintaining a series of sports beats constitutes a significant investment of organizational resources. Quite simply, beat coverage does not come cheap; as the Examiner's sports editor remarked, "It costs us a hell of a lot of money" to establish and maintain these beats. For example, it costs the paper in excess of $10,000 per year to provide beat coverage of the Flames, the local CFL franchise, and "several times that" to cover the Hornets of the NHL. Over and above reporter salary, the paper has to pay for reporter transportation on road trips, their hotels, and provide per diem money to cover meals and incidentals.

Not only are there significant financial costs to consider, but human resources costs as well. When a reporter is assigned to cover a sports beat, the Flames beat for instance, that reporter is the *Examiner's* full-time Flames reporter; it is their job to generate regular news of the Flames' activities. As a result, he or she is mostly unavailable to write other sports news items. The impact of this on sports news content is significant. Essentially, the beat system limits the number of sports reporters available to cover noncommercial sports events—they're committed to major commercial sports teams. So, if the *Examiner's* three beat reporters are all occupied with their regular responsibilities (covering their respective teams), then that leaves only two deskers and one part-timer to cover Bytown's noncommercial sports scene. Obviously, under these conditions, the opportunity for noncommercial sports to wrestle some news space from commercial spectator sports is minimal because most staff are preoccupied with the latter. Moreover, because only the paper's best reporters are assigned to these beats, it's arguable that the quality of noncommercial sports coverage is significantly less than that afforded to commercial sports. After all, it is unlikely the paper will assign a cub reporter, a part-timer, or a reporter with marginal or average skills to cover a major sports beat; the newspaper has far too much invested in these beats to assign anyone but its best reporters to them.

The point I'm driving at is this: The costs of employing a beat system of sports reporting—demanded by the need for a steady supply of commercial sports news material—are restrictive. The range of coverage in the newspaper sports section is constrained by limitations of space and staff. It follows that beat subjects will be featured in the paper; that is, they will receive regular and extensive coverage in the most prominent pages of the sports section. It is not surprising then that the *Examiner* fills its sports "news hole" each day with news generated from its sports beats. Accordingly, noncommercial sports often find themselves buried in the back pages. The rationale behind this is straightforward: Why would a newspaper make this substantial investment of organizational resources to establish and maintain beats if not to use them to generate the bulk of the news it intends to fill the sports section with?

One consequence of the beat system, then, is that the paper's sports news content has a marked commercial sports bias. Indeed, the paper's assignment of beat reporters only to these sports is strong evidence of its commitment to providing extensive coverage of commercial spectator sports as a means of generating a quality audience commodity. In effect, the beat is an institutionalized barrier to the coverage of noncommercial sports (Theberge & Cronk, 1986).

In return for the enormous investment of human and financial capital in these beats, the *Examiner* expects its reporters to generate a vast and regular supply of news to be generated from them daily—this is not negotiable. As the sports editor explained, "Oh yeah, you bet they'd better produce! We spend a lot of money to have these guys know what's going on with their team and to write about it."

I asked a desker what would happen to a sports reporter who wasn't producing enough news from their beat. His reply is telling: "He won't have his job for very long."

Responsibility for covering a sports beat entails an obligation to write something every day about its activities. Indeed, the obligation to generate news from the *Examiner's* sports beats is so strong that reporters are expected to do so even if they don't think there is anything newsworthy to report (see Fishman, 1980). One reporter explained:

> There's always something to write about, whether it's the previous night's game, a trade rumor, maybe someone isn't playing well and they've been benched. . . . In the off-season it's not as bad [the pressure to produce news items every day] because there isn't as much happening day in and day out. But that doesn't mean a beat guy can let up because we don't want to get beat on a story, ever!

Another reporter complained that what this leads to, this need to generate sports news no matter what, is "bullshit stories"—stories that lack any real insight or importance. "There's a lot of pressure to write stories, even if nothing is really going on. To me, that's bullshit."

Lack of activity on a sports beat is thus insufficient grounds for a reporter not to generate any news. As Fishman (1980, p. 35) notes, "The sense of how little or how much is happening is largely irrelevant to the normative requirement for reporters to produce these stories." In short, the journalistic axiom "no news is news" appears to be a convention at the *Examiner.* There is always something on the beat to write about, even if it's just "bullshit." Thus, covering a sports beat for the *Examiner* entails a normative obligation to generate news from it daily.

Not only must sports reporters generate expectable quantities of fresh news from their beats, but they must do so under the constraints of fixed deadlines not of their choosing and beyond their control (Ericson et al., 1989, 1987; Fishman,

1980; Tuchman, 1978; Sigal, 1973). At the *Examiner,* sports stories must be submitted no later than the paper's 11 p.m. deadline. This poses a problem for beat reporters because Bytown's commercial sports teams almost invariably play their games in the late evening, often concluding only 45 minutes or so before deadline. The pressure is significant, as reporters have to complete their interviews with players and coaches after the game, and then write the story; all typically within 30 minutes or so[3].

Clearly, the *Examiner's* sports newswork environment is shot through with pressures and constraints. To cope, *Examiner* reporters need sources who can provide them with a steady flow of commercial sports news material. Indeed, reporters depend on routine sources—they're "lifeblood" as one reporter put it. There are two major routine source types: (a) commercial sports organizations, and (b) a network of personal contacts on the beat. Both are routine sources because they facilitate sports newswork—they satisfy reporters' need for fresh news material every day.

Routine News Sources
Commercial Sports Organizations

Commercial sports organizations routinely supply reporters with news material through the judicious use of press releases and a more selective use of news conferences. Both are channels through which these organizations pass on potentially newsworthy information to reporters, in effect offering reporters story ideas and the raw materials they need to write them.

The *press release* is a simple device whereby sources issue statements of current or upcoming events to reporters. Ericson et al., (1989, p. 229) refer to these as "knowledge packages," as they typically contain a detailed account of an event, including background information, primary facts and perhaps "quotable quotes" from source representatives. Press releases, in effect, offer story material to reporters. As one sportswriter noted, "Press releases give you pretty much all you need in terms of the background you need to write a story."

The Hornets' Director of Media Relations explains that his job is to offer story ideas to sports reporters and to provide them with the raw materials they need to write a news item. He does this primarily with news releases:

> I'm here to help [reporters] do their jobs. It's simply having to know what they want to know. For example, today we signed [names player]. First thing I did was prepare a complete news release on everything he's done and as soon as that was done, we sent it out to the media. Now it's up to them to decide if they want to cover that story; I just made sure they've got the information they need.

This is particularly helpful to a reporter who encounters a slow news day on their beat. Recall that reporters are obligated to generate fresh sports news from their beats every day, regardless of whether they feel anything newsworthy has really happened. They depend on media relations people to regularly supply them with story material.

> I'll send out a press release to [sports reporters] and it's their decision to cover it. *All I can do is let them know about something.* . . . I let them know about something and they'll decide, 'Is there a story in there.' If yes, they determine if there's space to run it. So they go through a checklist: Is this worth it? Do we have the space? What else is going on? Is it worth my [reporter's] time, can I physically get there in time, come back, and write the story before deadline? So this checklist, it comes from the media and they go through it and they will make their decision. *I'm just basically pitching ideas and stories at them.*

The press release is clearly an important device through which media relations people offer news material to reporters—in effect helping sports reporters do their work. This is particularly useful on slow news days when a reporter may be scrambling to come up with story ideas; whether reporters choose to follow up on the potential news item is a different matter. Nonetheless, they've had a potentially newsworthy event brought to their attention, with all a raft of necessary background materials to write it.

Press releases also are important vehicles that enable noncommercial sports to get some much-needed attention from the press. During my fieldwork at the *Examiner*, the paper was routinely swamped with news releases, its fax machine constantly spitting them out. I asked the paper's editor about this and he said laughing, "Oh it never stops, that thing is always going. It's mostly junk, but sometimes you get something worth sending someone to cover, or maybe make a couple of phone calls to get the results. We get a lot of our local news that way." One reporter commented:

> Press releases help with some things we don't cover that often . . . say, the Canadian Broomball Association gives us a release saying that some guy has been named to the North American All-Star team and he's from the local area. Well, no one's gonna be covering that as part of any beat, so it's good to know that kind of thing, you know, it's good to get a press release on it. It's the kind of story that might provide for an interesting little sidebar or a small feature or something like that.

Not so long ago, fax technology and the like was a luxury enjoyed almost exclusively by the major commercial sports organizations with ample resources at their disposal. This no longer appears to be the case. Fax machines can be found almost anywhere now, from printing and photocopy shops, schools, even corner stores and shopping malls to most businesses and homes; thus even the most resource-poor sports clubs and organizations can afford to fax reporters.

> Oh, we get faxes from everywhere you can imagine; big league teams of course, but we also get tons of them from local sports teams. . . . People pretty much know it's the best way to let us know if something's going on so they can get some coverage . . . a lot of the amateur stuff, we'd have no idea was happening if we didn't get a fax or a phone call.

Ultimately, press releases are used extensively by commercial and noncommercial sports alike in their quest to obtain press coverage. Of course, releases are by no means a panacea for attention-starved noncommercial sports; it is still commercial spectator sports that are privileged in terms of the amount of coverage they enjoy on a daily basis.

News conferences are prescheduled news events that have a function similar to press releases; they provide reporters with a wealth of sports news material. Unlike releases, which one reporter explained, "Maybe 10 percent of the press releases we get are followed up on," conferences more often constitute a significant news event—sure to garner lots of media attention.

The main reason for the prima facie news value of conferences lies in the fact that they're held only to announce a significant event, such as a major player trade or signing. Simply put, if sources can't make a big deal out of an event, they will rarely call a conference. This underscores the special nature of the conference as a channel through which reporters can expect especially newsworthy material to flow. Indeed, by tapping into this rich news source, sports reporters often access enough information to generate one and sometimes several news items from a single conference. News conferences organized by major commercial sports organizations thus provide reporters with a wealth of easily accessible and newsworthy material that moves them one step closer to fulfilling their daily obligation to generate sports news.

Besides news releases and conferences, Bytown's commercial sports organizations also facilitate newswork by providing reporters with various *facilities and services* at event venues and their corporate offices. The Badgers, Hornets, and Flames all subsidize sports newswork in this manner. Their corporate offices, for instance, have furnished meeting rooms where news conferences are held; these are equipped with all the amenities necessary to accommodate the various media (print, radio, and television), such as electrical outlets, telephones, and so on. Event venues have press boxes fully equipped with video equipment for instant video replays; television monitors that enable reporters to stay on top of other major sports events occurring at the same time as the event they're covering; electrical outlets and telephone jacks, enabling reporters to hook up lap top computers, faxes, and modems—"the tools of the trade," as one reporter put it.

One interesting service provided by both the Flames and Hornets to reporters in the press box is "runners," who are similar to parliamentary pages or newspaper copy chasers. Runners distribute information to the press box, mostly game statistics, but also scores and details from the other games around the league that night. For example, reporters covering the Flames' home football games regularly receive updated game statistics, delivered to them in the press box at the end of each quarter. This service provides reporters with the statistical details and such they need to write their news items as the game progresses; a great time-savings given the limited time they usually have after the game to do their interviews, complete the story, and submit it to the *Examiner* under the 11 p.m. deadline.

Yet another service provided by commercial sports organizations is pregame meals for reporters. The two commercial sports organizations that I closely studied provide reporters with catered meals prior to each home game for a minimal fee ($5 charge by the Hornets) or no fee at all (Flames). This is an especially useful service because, without having to stop for a meal, reporters can drive directly to the event venue, arriving well before the scheduled start of the game. This is important because the extra time enables reporters to do some of the legwork necessary to cover a major league sports event (things like doing pregame interviews, going over the teams' statistics, identifying player match-ups to follow during the game). Moreover, it is important for reporters to have plenty of time before a major sports event to roam about. As one beat reporter explained, it's important for sports reporters to arrive early to cover a commercial sports event because

> You get some really good stuff this way. Things happen during warm-ups all the time, like a fight might break out among the players . . . And there's a lot of scuttle-butt in the hallways before a big game, you know, there's player agents, league officials, and general managers all over the place and you'd be amazed at the sort of things you overhear them talking about. Really, it's astounding the number of great stories that have been uncovered simply because a reporter overhears a conversation in a hallway before a game . . . You also get some good [information] at the meal because all these same executive types [player agents and team and league officials] are usually there too, talking business or whatever. It's also a good opportunity to corner them for an interview or at least for some comments on that night's game.

Not only are sports reporters assured of a full stomach when covering a Flames or Hornets game but, more importantly, catered meals afford them an opportunity to go about their news gathering virtually from the moment they arrive at the venue, collecting information and rumors while they eat with colleagues and team officials. Once again, major league sports organizations facilitate sports newswork, making it easier for reporters to do their job.

With this last point in mind, it's important to briefly consider *why* commercial sports organizations go to all this trouble and expense to facilitate newswork. They do so to secure for themselves regular media coverage of their activities. Essentially, a new item in the paper is akin to publicity—"publicity-as-news"— and the continued existence of sport as a commodified form of entertainment and spectacle depends on media publicity.

In this vein, Koppett (1981) posits that when sport is participant-oriented, when it is played simply for fun, there is no urgent need to advertise events, publicize game results, and interpret what happened—the raison d'être of the newspaper sports section. However, commercial spectator sport is a unique form of entertainment that draws its very life's blood from media coverage. Mass media are necessary vehicles for providing the information that generates the public interest which makes commercial sports such a profitable business:

> No commercial sport could be economically self-supporting without some coverage from the media. . . . when a game or match is over, there are numerous things yet to

be discussed: Statistics, important plays, records, standings, the overall performances of the players and teams, upcoming games and matches, the rest of the season, next season, and so on. . . . After games or matches have been played, the scores [and event highlights] become sources of entertainment for fans, regardless of whether they were able to attend the event in person. (Koppett, 1981, p. 101)

As Leonard Schecter puts it:

No press, no [public] interest, no baseball, no 22-year-old shit-kicker making 35 grand a year at an animal occupation. (in Smith & Valeriote, 1986, p. 322)

While this "shit-kicker" now earns something more in the area of "35 grand" a week, the point underscores the need major commercial spectator sports have for publicity-as-news, and the lengths they will go to obtain lots of it. In a nutshell, reporters' need for a steady flow of accessible commercial sports news material is well-served by commercial sports organizations' need for publicity-as-news.

Personal Contacts on the Beat

The second routine source type reporters depend on for news material is an extensive network of personal contacts (or "inside sources"). "The best reporters have the best sources," remarked one beat reporter. Another commented, "These guys [beat reporters] have a lot of sources, you know, that's why they're so good, they get a lot of good information from their sources." Athletes and coaches, team trainers and equipment managers, front office staff, player agents, league and individual team executives—all are vital contacts for *Examiner* sports reporters.

These sources provide the "inside information" on the world of commercial spectator sport. Arguably, this is the sort of sports news most appealing to readers—it's titillating and sensational. In-fighting among management and players, star athletes who are demanding they receive exorbitant pay increases or be traded, secret negotiations among owners to impose salary caps, owners threatening to move their franchise to more lucrative markets in the face of poor attendance; this news is so desirable because it's exciting. Indeed a metropolitan daily with a reputation for providing this sort of coverage is likely to have a devoted following of predominantly male readers, clearly making it a prime candidate for businesses looking for a publication to invest their advertising dollars in (Wenner, 1989).

To get a better idea of why it is so important for beat reporters to have routine sources, especially personal contacts, I followed *Examiner* sports reporter Buck Colvin, who works the Hornets beat, through a typical work day. As Fishman (1981, pp. 37–44) has demonstrated, studying a beat reporter's routine round of activities—what he calls a "beat round"— reveals a great deal about the routine nature of news construction. Colvin follows this routine of activities on an almost daily basis throughout the Hornets' season, making highly regular, carefully scheduled rounds of the same people at the same locations.

Colvin begins a typical day around 9 a.m. The first thing he does is call his sources to "see if anything's going on," hoping to get some story ideas from them. As he puts it,

> I'm always looking to see if they've heard any *rumors* because that's how you get your best stories—someone on your beat hears something, they tell you and then you follow it up, see if there's anything to it.

Once he has completed this initial round of telephone calls, he calls the Hornets' media relations director, Gaston Rouge, to see if he has any information. Again, he is looking to find out if anything important has happened with the team since his contact the day before,

> Like, they may have been talking trade with another team the night before, or maybe someone isn't going on the road trip . . . anything that'll make a good story, you know. This is the sort of stuff I'll get from Rouge.

Ideally, Colvin is looking for information to generate two types of news item: Stories and briefs. *Sports stories* tend to be longer items, such as feature-length stories on star athletes, and are usually located in the first couple of pages of the sports section. *Sports briefs*, on the other hand, are very short items, "you know, small items, tidbits, like Joe Blow hurt his toe in practice last night and is a doubtful starter for tonight's game."

After completing this initial coverage work, that is, getting in touch with his sources to familiarize himself with the beat—" I get an idea of what kind of a news day it's going to be"—Colvin heads off to the Hornets practice facility at around 11 a.m. Typically, on-ice practice ends at 12:30 p.m., at which time the players head to the gym to continue their workout; "that's when I start to really dig for something." Colvin meets with the Hornets' coaches while the players are in the gym, following up on any rumors he's heard or hunches he may have.

> I'll be talking to [names the head coach] and tell him, 'Look, I heard Williams was on the trading block, what's going on with that?' Or maybe [names player] didn't get much playing time in last night's game, I'll ask Adams or one of his assistants [assistant coaches] if he's been benched or what. . . . I'm basically trying to get some stories from them, you know.

After meeting with the coaching staff, Colvin waits in the locker room for the players to return, usually at around 1 p.m. For the next hour or so, he "hangs out" with the players, talking to different guys, always looking for a potential news item.

> If I'm working on a feature that day, I do my interview for that feature; so if I'm doing a feature on, say, [names player], from 1 'til 2 o'clock I'll talk to him. But on most days I'll try to talk to at least four or five players.
>
> [What sort of information are you looking for from the players?]
>
> I'm always asking them about rumors. You always gotta go to the players because the players always know what's going on. They always act like they don't know what's going on, but they always know what's happening.

Having completed his daily round of activities with the Hornets, Colvin goes to lunch and then arrives at the *Examiner's* newsroom at around 3 p.m., when he begins to make more phone calls to his sources. Throughout the day, Colvin is constantly in contact with people who may be able to supply him with potentially newsworthy information about his beat. Typically, this is information he is not able to gather on his own because, as I noted earlier, it is financially impossible to do so. Colvin explains:

> The *Examiner* obviously can't afford to fly me all over the continent, you know, to every NHL city to write stories about the Hornets. . . . So I always stay in contact with sportswriters in other cities because they've always got something I can use. Like, if the Pittsburgh Penguins are coming into town for a game tomorrow, I may phone Pittsburgh just to, uh, say if a guy is listed as day-to-day, I'll ask the Penguins' beat writer what the guy's injury status is, you know, that's good information because I can work it into a story. Or, I'll ask what's going on with Mario Lemieux and how he's been doing. . . .
>
> I always, always, ask whether they've [other sportswriters] heard any good rumors, you know? I mean, we love rumors, so the big thing here is to get the rumors; they make for good stories.

Obviously, Colvin spends a great deal of his work day on the telephone; in a sense, it's a lifeline to his beat. Colvin indicated that in a typical day he'll easily make upwards of 20 to 30 phone calls. I asked him why he makes so many phone calls, if it is really necessary to spend that much of his work day on the phone.

> Oh yeah! I have to do this to know what's happening on my beat, you know, to stay on top of things. If I don't, then I'll get beat on a story, and like I told you, that's my greatest fear. . . . For me, meeting deadlines isn't the biggest pressure of my job. The biggest pressure is beating the competition, making sure that you're first. . . . I mean, I can meet deadlines. To me, it's bigger to have the story first and the only way you're gonna do that consistently is to have good sources and stay in touch with them.

Colvin usually wraps up this news gathering component of his day around 5:30 p.m. or 6 p.m. with yet another telephone call to the Hornets' media relations people, "just to see if there's anything else up." Then he'll set to work on writing his news items, or complete those he has been working on over the course of the day. Otherwise, if he has to cover a Hornets game that night, Colvin will head down to the arena an hour or two before game time and spend the rest of the evening there, covering the game and writing at least one news item for the 11 p.m. deadline.

The most important thing to note about Colvin's beat round is that it enables him to complete a lot of his basic coverage work, his news gathering, in one centralized location. On this particular day, the Hornets' practice facility was the source of much of Colvin's news material. Having accessible sports news material centralized in one or two locations makes it much easier for reporters to meet their deadlines. Notice Colvin only had to physically be at only one place to accomplish much of his basic coverage of the beat; the rest of his news gathering was accomplished over the telephone from his home in the morning and from his desk at the *Examiner* in the late afternoon.

This "idealization" (Fishman, 1980) of Colvin's beat round shows how vital it is for reporters to have a network of sources and to constantly stay in touch with them. As Colvin suggests, without sources, sports reporters wouldn't be able to do their work:

> Oh yeah, absolutely I need my sources. There's one guy on the Hornets that I talk to every day during the season; there's a couple I talk to at least three times a week; there's others I talk to once every two weeks. . . . I'm looking to see if they've heard any rumors, you know, who the Hornets might be signing, whether they've heard if the Hornets are after a player from another team. You see, I get this kind of information from players because players talk to agents and agents talk to scouts, uh, there's three or four NHL scouts I talk to every clay. I also talk to some other people in the [Hornets] organization every day to find out what's going on. . . . Good sources are invaluable! You can't do this job unless you've got good sources.

Without the wealth of news information provided by their sources, *Examiner* sports reporters would not be able to generate the quantities of fresh news demanded of them.

Moreover, having these sources centralized in some fashion—such as in a practice facility or accessible by telephone, as we saw with Colvin's beat round—goes a long way toward helping reporters cope with the pressures under which sports newswork is performed, namely, having to produce expectable quantities of fresh news under impending deadlines. Quite simply, sports newswork is more manageable when information sources are centralized, largely because centralization cuts down on travel time, leaving more time for news gathering and writing; therefore making it easier to cover a beat and ultimately to satisfy the expectations of the reporter's news organization.

Concluding Remarks

Because it is difficult to convincingly extrapolate general trends from only one case study, I suggest that more institutional studies of the sort I present in this paper are necessary to develop a more comprehensive theoretical understanding of the production of sports news for the daily press and its broader social implications. In particular, I should note one important comment made by an anonymous reviewer of an earlier draft of this paper: "There is no sense of multiplicity of points of view in this study: The sports department sounds like a terribly monolithic place." This is no quibble.

It has not been my intention to offer a unidimensional theory of economic rationality to account for the *Examiner's* profound commercial sports bias—market forces do not solely determine newswork routines and ultimately news content in the sports pages. Using this study as a springboard, future research should focus on the "representational politics" of newspaper work; that is, analyses of how gender, racial, and employment status hierarchies within the sports journalism subculture impact on sports news content.

References

Bagdikian, B. (1992). *The media monopoly* (4th ed.) Boston: Beacon Press.

Beamish, R. (1984). Materialism and the comprehension of gender-related issues in sport. In N. Theberge & P. Donnelly (Eds.), *Sport and the sociological imagination.* Fort Worth, TX: Texas Christian University Press.

Beddoes, D. (1970). Brief submitted to the special senate committee on the mass media, 28th Parliament, 2nd Session, Vol. 24 (pp. 64–75).

Bryant, J. (1980). A two-year selective investigation of the female in sport as reported in the paper media. *Arena Review, 4*(2).

Canadian Advertising Rates and Data. (1994, June). **67**(6), Toronto, ON: Maclean Hunter Publishing.

Cavanagh, R. P. (1989). *Cultural production and the reproduction of power: Political economy, public television, and high performance sport in Canada.* Unpublished doctoral dissertation, Carleton University, Ottawa, ON.

Chomsky, N., & Herman, E. (1988). *Manufacturing consent.* New York: Pantheon Books.

Ericson, R., Baranek, P., & Chan, B.L. (1987). *Visualizing deviance: A study of news organization.* Toronto, ON: University of Toronto Press.

Ericson, R., Baranek, P., & Chan, B.L. (1989). *Negotiating control: A study of news sources.* Toronto, ON: University of Toronto Press.

Fishman, M. (1980). *Manufacturing the news.* Austin, TX: University of Texas Press.

Gantz, W. (1985). Exploring the role of television in married life. *Journal of Broadcasting and Electronic Media,* **29,** 263–275.

Gantz, W., & Wenner, L. (1995). Fanship and the television sports viewing experience. *Sociology of Sport Journal,* **12,** 56–73.

Gantz, W., & Wenner, L. (1991). Men, women, and sports: Audience experiences and effects. *Journal of Broadcasting and Electronic Media,* **35,** 233–243.

Giddens, A. (1982). *Sociology: A brief but critical introduction.* New York: Harcourt, Brace, and Jovanovich.

Gelinas, M., & Theberge, N. (1986). A content analysis of the coverage of physical activity in two Canadian newspapers. *International Review for the Sociology of Sport,* **21,** 141–151.

Gruneau, R. (1989). Making spectacle: A case study in television sports production. In L. Wenner (Ed.), *Media, sports, and society.* Thousand Oaks, CA: Sage.

Gruneau, R., & Whitson D. (1993). *Hockey night in Canada.* Toronto, ON: Garamond Press.

Jhally, S. (1984). The spectacle of accumulation: Material and cultural factors in the evolution of the sports/media complex. *Insurgent Sociologist,* **12**(33), 41–57.

Koppett, L. (1981). *Sports illusion, sports reality.* Boston: Houghton Mifflin Co.

Leiss, W., Kline S., & Jhally, S. (1990). *Social communication in advertising* (2nd ed.) Scarborough, ON: Nelson.

Lever, J., & Wheeler, S. (1984). The Chicago Tribune Sports Page, 1900–1975. *Sociology of Sport Journal,* **1,** 299–313.

Lowes, M. (1995). *Sports page: Newswork routines and the social construction of sports news in the daily press.* Unpublished master's thesis, Carleton University, Ottawa, ON.

Parente, D. (1977). The interdependence of sports and television. *Journal of Communication,* **27**(3), 131–135.

McFarlane, B. (1955). *The sociology of sports promotion.* Unpublished master's thesis, McGill University, Montreal, PQ.

Rintala, J., & Birrell, S. (1984). Fair treatment for the active female: A content analysis of young athlete magazine. *Sociology of Sport Journal,* **1**(3), 231–250.

Scanlon, T.J. (1970). *Sports in the daily press in Canada.* Unpublished report prepared for the Directorate of Fitness and Amateur Sport, Department of National Health and Welfare.

Sigal, L. (1973). *Reporters and officials.* Lexington, MA: Heath.

Smith, G., & Valeriote, T. (1986). Ethics in sports journalism. In E. Lapchick (Ed.), *Fractured focus*. Lexington, MA: D.C. Heath and Co.

Sparks, R. (1992). Delivering the male: Sports, Canadian television, and the making of TSN. *Canadian Journal of Communication, 17,* 319–342.

Telander, R. (1984). The written word: Player-press relationships in American sports. *Sociology of Sport Journal, 1,* 3–14.

Theberge, N., & Cronk, A. (1986). Work routines in newspaper sports departments and the coverage of women's sports. *Sociology of Sport Journal, 3,* 195–203.

Tuchman, G. (1978). *Making news.* New York: The Free Press.

Wenner, L. (Ed.)(1989). *Media, sports, and society.* Thousand Oaks, CA: Sage.

Notes

1. By "major commercial spectator sports," I'm referring not only to professional sports, like the National Hockey League, National Basketball Association, National Football League, and so on, but also "amateur" sports spectacles such as the Olympic Games and high-profile university sports. Sporting practices that do not fall into this category I lump together as "noncommercial" sports.

2. To protect anonymity, "Bytown" and all individuals and organizations in it have been given pseudonyms. The *Examiner* has a weekly (Monday to Friday) circulation of approximately 52,290 readers in a market area of approximately 710,000 adults older than the age of 18 years (*Canadian Advertising Rates and Data,* June 1994).

3. To alleviate some of this pressure, a couple of reporters explained to me that they often write their stories "on the fly." As the game progresses, the reporter writes as much of the story as possible, concentrating on big plays, etc., and after the game reworks the story to correspond to a general theme.

Acknowledgments

As this article is drawn from my master's thesis, I want to acknowledge the tremendous personal and intellectual debt I owe Bruce McFarlane and George Pollard, my supervisors on that project. Robert Stebbins has become a welcomed long-distance mentor, and I want to thank him for his comments on earlier versions of this article and, most importantly, for his continuing interest in my work. Thanks are also due to Noam Chomsky, Richard Gruneau, and Cynthia Hasbrook who graciously read earlier versions of this article.

Differential Accounts of Race in Broadcast Commentary of the 2000 NCAA Men's and Women's Final Four Basketball Tournaments

Bryan E. Denham, Andrew C. Billings and Kelby K. Halone

A consistent finding in studies surrounding sports commentary on white and black athletes is that (a) white athletes are frequently praised for their perceived "intellect" and "leadership capacity," while (b) black athletes are often praised for being "naturally talented" (Davis & Harris, 1998). A mediated conclusion that one could derive from such findings is that black athletes are expected to succeed athletically; conversely, white athletes are expected to have an innate ability to overcome seemingly insurmountable odds to accomplish their athletic stature. This study examined the broadcast commentary surrounding white and black athletes at the 2000 NCAA Men's and Women's Final Four College Basketball Tournaments. The content analysis of 1,118 descriptors embedded in commentator discourse revealed that, while black athletes continue to be praised for their athleticism and physicality, they also are receiving a greater number of comments about their intelligence and ability to lead.

Un résultat commun aux études sur les commentaires sportifs au sujet des athlètes blancs et noirs est que: (a) les athlètes blancs sont fréquemment louangés pour ce qu'on perçoit être leur « intellect » et leurs « capacités de leadership », alors que (b) les athlètes noirs sont souvent louangés pour leurs « talents naturels » (Davis et Harris, 1998). Une conclusion possible de ce résultat est que l'on s'attend à ce que les athlètes noirs aient du succès sur la scène sportive et, en contraste, l' on s'attend à ce que les athlètes blancs possèdent une habileté innée à contourner des obstacles apparemment insurmontables pour en arriver au succès sportif. Cette étude porte sur les commentaires sportifs entourant les athlètes blancs et noirs lors des tournois nationaux 2000 de demi-finale et de finale en basketball universitaire masculin et féminin aux États-Unis. Une analyse de contenu des 1,118 termes descriptifs au sein du discours des commentateurs et commentatrices permet de conclure que si les athlètes noirs continuent à être louangés pour leurs qualités physiques et athlétiques, ils et elles sont l'objet d'un nombre plus grand de commentaires concernant leur intelligence et leurs habiletés de leader.

In the past four decades, scholars in the domain of sport have accumulated a knowledge base regarding the intersection of (a) broadcast commentary, (b) athletic performance (c) athlete race, and (d) performance stereotypes (e.g., Davis & Harris, 1998; Edwards, 1969; Eitzen, 1984; Hallinan, 1991; Williams & Youseff, 1971). This study builds on existing scholarship by examining the broadcast commentary surrounding white and black athletes at the 2000 NCAA Men's and Women's Final Four College Basketball Tournaments. The article is grounded theoretically in agenda setting theory (McCombs & Shaw, 1972), which suggests that while mass media may not tell us what to think, they do tell us what to think about, when the issues at hand do not otherwise obtrude into our lives (see also, McCombs, 1994). Thus, while media personnel need not tell us to think about the economy or the threat of terrorism, they may very well tell us in subtle and not-so-subtle ways to think about differences in athletic ability based on the race of an athlete.

The study makes several important advancements with respect to the knowledge base on stereotyping by race in sports. First, the work of Eastman and Billings (2001) is furthered as their previous study pinpointed racial characterizations within regular season games; this study addresses whether these same trends hold true at the highest level of college basketball. Second, this study implements the taxonomy first employed in the Eastman and Billings study to uncover the usefulness of the 15-category scheme as a viable method for analyzing sportcaster dialogue. Third, the study bridges the work of the past decades to pinpoint whether racial biases found in past generations are still true today. In sum, this study provides a valuable heuristic to studies that intersect the connotations of race within the realm of sport broadcasting.

Athleticism and the "Black Athlete": Differential Assumptions Throughout Sport Research

Differential assumptions surrounding athletes, and their subsequent performance, employed on the basis of racial differences has been readily implicated throughout contemporary accounts in sports journalism (for example, Davis & Harris, 1998). Interestingly, these assumptions surrounding the black athlete actually run counter to the performance of several black athletes in American society. For example, Michael Jordan led the Chicago Bulls in building a basketball dynasty in the 1990s. Tiger Woods has likewise become an icon of golf. Venus and Serena Williams have clearly established themselves as elite athletes in the realm of tennis. Thus, a paradox exists. While black athletes have made contributions of meritorious worth in their respective sports, there appears to be an implicitly communicated "climate of differentiation" that continues to exist. The primary focus of this article is to investigate such a premise.

An interdisciplinary body of research surrounding the genre of sports broadcasting would verify the contention that differential assumptions surrounding the intersection of (a) broadcast commentary, (b) athletic performance (c) athlete race, and (d) performance stereotypes readily exist. Studies have found that the nature of broadcast commentary has paradoxically described black athletes as "naturally gifted" (Harris, 1993; Jackson, 1989; Staples & Jones, 1985; Whannel, 1992) while concurrently calling attention to white athletes' perceived "intelligence," "work ethic," and "grace under pressure" (Birrell, 1989; McCarthy & Jones, 1997; Sage, 1990). The black athlete has been characterized by sportscasters as having "innate talent," while the white athlete has had to subsequently "overcome the odds" in order to achieve athletic stature. In other words, black athletes are expected to "make it," whereas white athletes must "pursue their dreams" with what-would-appear-to-be "limited ability" but endeavor to do so with tremendous heart and leadership skills (Wonsek, 1992). Dewar (1993) observed that, in effect, these differential assumptions are a covert way of explaining the lack of success many white athletes have experienced while concurrently minimizing the achievements of black athletes. Dewar's (1993) contention echoes that of Edwards (1969)—made more than 30 years ago—suggesting that white broadcasters did not sufficiently credit black athletes for their accomplishments, due in part to perceptions of race. Additionally, Rainville and McCormick (1977) found disproportionate praise for white football players in the NFL and disproportionate criticism for black players. Not surprisingly, white players received a disproportionately low amount criticism, just as black athletes received a disproportionately low amount of praise.[1] Davis and Harris (1998) offer additional insight:

> Media often reinforce the stereotype that African-Americans are 'natural athletes.' This stereotype poses white athletes as clearly disadvantaged relative to black athletes, who are seen as having superior physiology (cites removed). . . . Media treatment is more likely to give European-American athletes credit for being mentally astute, whereas African-American athletes are seldom credited for their intellect.
>
> (pp. 158–159)

Davis and Harris (1998) also made reference to a study conducted by Messner, Duncan, and Jensen (1993); the study addressed media efforts to suppress stereotyping by race. While the researchers did note a conscious effort on the part of broadcasters to avoid stereotyping, they nevertheless concluded that the effort seemed to be more of an "afterthought."[2] In terms of this "sensitivity training" initiated by the networks in the nineties, Davis & Harris (1998) note:

> While these recent changes offer some hope, the bulk of research findings show evidence of racism in sports coverage. Although overt racism has largely disappeared, covert racism, while perhaps less malignant than in earlier periods, can still be seen. New forms of racism may be evolving with the times.
>
> (p. 165)

Given that this article examines both the Men's and Women's Final Four Basketball Tournaments, the intersection between race and gender must be addressed. As argued by Duncan & Messner (1998), issues of power are present in broadcast commentary. Duncan and Messner (1998) use the term "hierarchy of naming" in describing their analyses of 1989 NCAA basketball data. They note that women were "infantilized" by being called by their first name at a rate much greater than men were, the last name being considered the more serious representation of the athlete.

Their work also provides some background for studying the *amount* of commentary offered about male and female athletes in sports broadcasting. Certainly if one examines web sites such as espn.com or cbs.sportsline.com, it becomes apparent that men's basketball takes precedence over the women's game, the latter of which can be located if one scrolls down the left margin far enough on "NCAA Hoops" to find the link. Duncan and Messner (1998) argue with respect to their analysis of the 1989 NCAA basketball commentary:

> Although some of the more overt media stereotyping has decreased since the 1990 study, we still discern gender differences in the media accounting of successes and failures, in the media descriptions of female and male athletes, in the quantities of media coverage, in the technical production of sporting events, and in the gender marking and naming of athletes. . . . We argue that these differences may have significant consequences in the ways audiences interpret mediated sporting events.
>
> (p. 184)

In addition, black athletes have been called by their first name at a greater rate than white athletes, a practice that conceivably portrays them as childlike or "clown-like" (Davis & Harris, 1998). So while broadcasters in the elite ranks may have been taught that they need to treat black athletes with the same respect that they would offer white athletes, their use of language actually may undercut the respect they attempt to extend.

In terms of the present study, mediated portrayals and hegemonic concerns provide a fundamental justification for examining differences across race and gender in terms of the descriptors used to identify the athletes, as the dominant hegemony can influence public perceptions of athletes by race. For instance, if policies and commentary stem primarily from white males of a certain age, the mediated reality of their comments may take a certain form, such that white athletes are portrayed to have a superior work ethic, or greater "heart" than black athletes have, or that female athletes are "humored" by broadcasters.

Eastman and Billings (2001) examined race as it related to on-air coverage of athletes in 66 American college basketball games, finding that commentators applied stereotypes consistently within both men's and women's games. The researchers found that while the amount of commentary was equal within both men's and women's games, commentators varied their descriptions depending on the race and gender of the athlete. For instance, white women athletes received a disproportionate amount of commentary (42%) when considering the percentage of white women athletes playing the game (32%). Additionally, the authors found that commentary about women players contained increased attributions of slower speed and team rather than individual effort. Messner, Dunbar and Hunt (2000) also offered discussion on the issue, addressing what they termed the "Televised

Sports Manhood Formula," which contains assumptions such as white males having the voices of authority, sports being considered part of a "man's world," and men being "foregrounded" in commercials. Their work provides an excellent review of gender issues within the realm of sports broadcasting.

Setting the Agenda

As indicated earlier, this study is grounded in the agenda setting theory of mass media (McCombs & Shaw, 1972), which suggests that while mass media may not tell us what to think, they often tell us what to think about, when the issues at hand do not otherwise obtrude into our lives.[3] Thus, we do not need the media to remind us to pay attention to our investments in the stock market, but they might tell us to think about issues less salient, such as black athletes having great "natural ability" and white athletes having great "work ethic" and "leadership" skills. It should be noted that broadcasters have a choice in their commentary, yet the prevailing commentary has focused on the "natural ability" of the black athlete and the "hard working" white athlete, who seems to have beaten the odds to achieve success. Such commentary can take on "a life of its own" and reinforce broadcaster perceptions and comments about athletes based on their perceived race. Clearly, the media have the power to shape a reality regarding racial assumptions of athletic performance. However, one might endeavor to examine if, and to what degree, such descriptive assumptions might continue to prevail in the context of a pinnacle athletic achievement of collegiate basketball; specifically, the 2000 Men's and Women's NCAA Final Four.

The Final Four as Dynamic Spectacle

Because the Men's and Women's Final Fours were telecast on major networks (CBS and ESPN, respectively) and occurred on the same extended weekend (March 31–April 3, 2000), conducting a comparative analysis of announcer commentary within both Final Fours provided an appropriate heuristic for the study of race descriptors within both men's and women's college basketball. Additionally, couple some of the best players in the game with the best broadcasters on television—broadcasters who have been coached very specifically on what to avoid saying on the air—and the Final Four becomes important to study. One then could examine local and regional broadcasting and compare comments. Presumably, local and regional broadcasters have not received the extent of communication coaching that those who report for national television have received.[4] CBS and ESPN also spend over $250 million each year to cover the NCAA tournaments ("At Home," 2001) because of the large audiences the telecasts garner: the men's final drew a 14.1 rating (Wicker & Zulgad, 2000), and the women's final drew a 3.0 rating (Eagan, 2001), both five times that of a regular-season game. Consequently, the Final Four telecasts are not merely seen as typical basketball games but instead serve as exemplar of basketball (as well as sports pageantry) in its highest, most visible form—qualifying the telecasts as what Procter (1990) terms the "Dynamic Spectacle." Procter argues that because "we do not experience most events personally, but rather learn of them through the spoken, written, or visual constructions of others . . . spectacles are constructions; they are transformations of some event" (p. 119). Ultimately, most individuals gain their understanding of things not through the mundane, but instead through the spectacles. For instance, while there are thousands of horse races each year, most Americans derive their understand of the sport from horse racings' dynamic spectacle: the Kentucky Derby. Thus, the Final Four offers a unique opportunity to study the agenda setting theory and the dynamic spectacle simultaneously. The former theory tells us what to think about when a viewer watches the games, while the latter ensures that these broadcaster evaluations appear particularly salient because they are occurring in a high-profile athletic event.

Thus, the following research questions and hypotheses were advanced to frame the study:

RQ1: What descriptors do broadcast commentators employ to account for athletic performance in the Men's and Women's NCAA Final Four basketball championships?

RQ2: To what degree do broadcast commentators differentially account for athletic performance on the basis of athlete race?

RQ3: To what degree do broadcast commentators differentially account for athletic performance on the basis of athlete sex?

H1a: Collectively, descriptors employed to address athleticism will be directed toward black athletes significantly more frequently than toward white athletes.

H1b: Collectively, descriptors employed to address intelligence will be directed toward white athletes significantly more frequently than toward black athletes.

H2a: Collectively, descriptors employed to address athleticism will be directed toward male athletes significantly more frequently than toward female athletes.

H2b: Collectively, descriptors employed to address intelligence will be directed toward female athletes significantly more frequently than toward male athletes.

Method

Content analytic methods (Kaid & Wadsworth, 1989) were employed to analyze broadcast commentary surrounding the Men's and Women's NCAA Final Four Basketball games.

Universe of Investigation

All Men's and Women's 2000 NCAA Final Four basketball games ($n = 6$) were subject to analysis. The NCAA men's games ($n = 3$) consisted of two semi-final games (Michigan State University vs. University of Wisconsin; University of Florida vs. University of North Carolina) and its championship game (Michigan State University vs. University of Florida). The women's games ($n = 3$) likewise entailed two semi-final games (University of Connecticut vs. Penn State University; University of Tennessee vs. Rutgers University) and its championship game (University of Connecticut vs. University of Tennessee).[5]

Unit of Analysis

As explained in the previous note, a line of broadcast commentary served as the unit of measurement here. The men's games generated 185 pages of broadcast commentary respectively among the two semi-final games ($n = 60$; 65 pages) and its championship game ($n = 60$ pages), with four different commentators/floor reporters contributing to the database. The women's games generated 87 pages of broadcast commentary respectively among the two semi-final games ($n = 35$; 24) and its championship game ($n = 28$ pages) with three different commentators/floor reporters contributing to the database. This initially resulted in 272 transcribed pages of broadcast commentary.

Following the work of Eastman and Billings (2001), broadcast commentary was analyzed from the beginning of the game (i.e., starting tip off) to the end of the game (i.e., where the second half clock strikes 00:00). This subsequently resulted in 160.5 pages ($n = 1,488$ lines) of broadcast commentary for the men's games, and 76.25 pages ($n = 879$ lines) of broadcast commentary for the women's games; a total of 236.75 pages ($n = 2,367$ lines) of broadcast commentary suitable for analysis.

Category Construction

Broadcast commentary was analyzed on eight ($n = 8$) criteria: (a) game status (semi-final; final), (b) game time (before half; after half), (c) broadcast announcer sex (male; female), (d) athlete sex (male; female), (e) athlete race (white; black), (f) commentary type (color; play-by-play; floor); (g) whether the athlete was accounted for in broadcast commentary line (yes/no; note descriptor); and (h) whether multiple descriptors were employed to account for an athlete in a broadcast category line (yes/no; if "yes," note additional descriptor).

Following the work of Eastman and Billings (2001), broadcast commentary accounts were initially categorized, and subsequently analyzed, according to (a) physicality/athleticism (e.g., "can physically dominate the lane"), (b) intelligence/mental skill (e.g., "can read defenses easily"), (c) hard work/effort (e.g., "going the extra mile tonight"), (d) determination/motivation (e.g., "he simply won't let them lose"), (e) speed (e.g., "blows past everyone"), (f) positive consonance (e.g., "he's feeling it"), (g) negative consonance (e.g., "her entire game is completely off"), (h) leadership (e.g., "everyone follows from her example"), (i) versatility (e.g., "he does it all out there"), (j) team-orientation (e.g., "always does what is best for the team"), (k) physical power (e.g. "knocks him over on the way to the hoop"), (l) mental power ("her smarts are the top reason she dominates"), (m) personality (e.g., "if you've ever met her, you'd know she's a good kid"), (n) looks/appearance (e.g., "sleek body"), (o) background (e.g., "grew up in Compton").

Coding Procedures

Four individuals (two white males and two white females) served as coders for the initial phase of the study. While not a bona fide delphi panel, two of the four individuals had been/was currently a student athlete, while two of the four were familiar with the culture of collegiate athletics. A training session was conducted, providing coders with a code book and procedural instructions to clarify subsequent coding responsibilities. With regard to the coding of race, the researchers chose to code an athlete based on whether they appeared to be white or black, regardless of actual racial background. This choice was made because (a) commentators were more likely commenting on the apparent race of an athlete rather than their genealogical biography, (b) all four coders were able to code all athletes into these two broad categories with 100% agreement by watching videotape of the telecasts, (c) no commentary within any of the telecasts specifically mentioned any other racial backgrounds, and (d) the choice is consistent with previous work on athlete race (see Eastman & Billings, 2001). Upon completion of the training session, a trial coding process was conducted. Broadcast commentary selected for inclusion in this trial process consisted of 10% of transcribed pages representing one men's final four game ($n = 6$ transcribed pages). This resulted in a sample of 101 lines of broadcast commentary. Selected transcript pages were generated as a result of employing systematic random sampling with a random start.

Each member of the coding team independently analyzed all 101 lines of broadcast commentary in light of the aforementioned categories ($n = 8$). Upon completion of this trial coding phase, intercoder reliability was assessed (Holsti, 1969). "Game status" achieved a reliability of 1.00. "Game time" achieved a reliability of 1.00. "Announcer sex" achieved a reliability of 1.00. "Athlete sex" achieved a reliability of 1.00. "Athlete race" achieved a reliability of 0.99. "Commentary type" achieved a reliability of 0.88.[6]

Overall, descriptor codes collectively achieved a reliability of 0.79. Individual reliabilities for each descriptor code were subsequently assessed, whereby (a) physicality/athleticism (.84), (b) intelligence/mental skill (.82), (c) hard work/effort (.79) (d) determination/motivation (.77), (e) speed (.83), (f) physical power (.72), (g) mental power (.70), (h) positive consonance (.80), (i) negative consonance (.77), (j) leadership (.81), (k) versatility (.79), (l) team-orientation (.82), (m) personality = .79, (n) looks/appearance (.84), and (o) background = .82. However, because of inconsistent coding among the four coders, the inconsistent reliabilities for (a) physical power and (b) mental power were collapsed with descriptor categories for (a) physicality/athleticism and (b) intelligence/ mental skill, resulting in new reliabilities of .85 for physicality/athleticism and .83 for intelligence/mental skill.

Overall reliability achieved from all categories in the coding process achieved a reliability of 0.96. Two members of the coding team subsequently continued to independently code the remaining lines of broadcast commentary. This phase of the coding process was conducted to address research questions 1, 2, and 3.

After all descriptors ($n = 1,118$) were coded, they were aggregated and considered across the race of athletes in a 2×2 cross-tabulation. This was done on an exploratory basis, to examine whether collapsing categories that seemingly relate would provide a more general, overall view of commentary. Prior to aggregation— and at a later point in the study—three coders who did not participate in the original coding of data inductively classified descriptors into three categories. These researchers placed the 15 forms of classification within three larger groups independently, with their classifications matching (1.00). As a result, three broader categories were included for exploratory purposes: (a) athleticism, (b) intelligence and (c) neither athleticism nor intelligence. The athleticism category contained descriptors of (a) physicality/athleticism, (b) speed, (c) positive consonance, (d) negative consonance, and (e) versatility. The intelligence category contained descriptors of (a) intelligence, (b) hard work/effort, (c) determination/ motivation, (d) leadership, (e) team orientation and (f) personality. The neither category contained descriptors of (a) looks/appearance, (b) background, and (c) other. This phase of the coding process was conducted in order to address the hypotheses.

After aggregating all descriptors, each was examined by race and the results are reported in tabular form, both for a grand total and for totals with gender controlled. Since white and black athletes constituted more than 99 percent of the participants in the respective Final Fours, race was contained in these two large groups. Differences between groups were determined using Chi Square, with the .05 level determining significant findings. In terms of computing Chi Square values, the total percentage of descriptors classified in each of the 15 categories was used to compute expected frequencies for both white and black athletes. Thus, if 52 percent of all descriptors were of physicality/athleticism, it was expected that 52.1 percent of all descriptors of white and black athletes would be of physicality/athleticism as well. Chi Square analysis revealed any deviation from this expected frequency.

Results

Research Question One

RQ1 sought to examine what descriptors broadcast commentators employed to account for athletic performance in the Final Four. Table 1 displays how the descriptors were differentially accounted for by broadcast commentary and provides examples of the commentary examined.

Table 1 Athlete descriptors

	Total/%
Physicality/Athleticism	582/52%
"That's how strong Mateen Cleaves is"	
Intelligence/Mental Skill	105/9%
"she keeps her head up and sees the whole floor"	
Other	89/8%
"Mateen's talked about the dream—now it's time to live it"	
Background	81/7%
"starting guard, and Philadelphia native, Kristen Ace Clement	
suffered a lateral right ankle sprain"	
Speed	42/4%
"she's like a train—fast, smooth, and quick"	
Positive Consonance	41/4%
"Really in-sinc tonight"	
Determination/Motivation	39/3%
"it's a game that she has wanted since she was a little	
girl playing football in D.C"	
Leadership	28/3%
"he steps up and tries to take charge"	
Negative Consonance	24/2%
"Dupay struggling shooting in the zone tonight"	
Looks/Appearance	24/2%
"and they're gonna need Tennessee, another good game like	
that from Pillow because of her size, she's got a big body"	
Versatility	20/2%
"nice move—Vershaw the other way"	
Hard Work/Effort	17/2%
"Catchings is right there plugging things up"	
Personality	14/1%
"she's got Philadelphia attitude for a Chicagoland kid"	
Team-Orientation	12/1%
"you have to love that every player is challenging each other"	
Total	1,118/100%

Research Question Two

RQ2 queried to what degree sportscaster dialogue differed based on athlete race. Table 2 displays these overall totals for descriptor type by race. Here, a significant difference across white and black athletes was achieved with respect to the category

Table 2 Descriptor codes across race

Descriptor	Race		Total	Prob. Chi square
	White	Black		
Physicality/Athleticism	221 (37.9) (56.0)	361 (62.1) (49.9)	582 (52.1)	
Intelligence/Mental Skill	29 (27.6) (7.3)	76 (72.4) (10.5)	105 (9.4)	
Hard Work/Effort	4 (23.5) (1.0)	13 (76.5) (3.3)	17 (2.0)	
Determination/Motivation	14 (35.9) (3.6)	25 (64.1) (3.5)	39 (3.5)	
Speed	13 (31.0) (3.3)	29 (69.0) (4.0)	42 (4.0)	
Positive Consonance	25 (61.0) (6.3)	16(39.0) (2.2)	41 (4.0)	0.001
Negative Consonance	11 (45.8) (2.8)	13(54.2) (1.8)	24 (2.1)	
Leadership	6 (21.4) (1.5)	22 (78.6) (3.0)	28 (3.0)	
Versatility	8 (40.0) (2.0)	12 (60.0) (1.7)	20 (2.0)	
Team-Orientation	3 (25.0) (0.1)	9 (7.5) (1.2)	12 (1.1)	
Personality	4 (28.6) (1.0)	10 (71.4) (1.4)	14 (1.3)	
Looks/Appearance	8 (33.3) (2.0)	16 (66.6) (2.2)	24 (2.1)	
Background	17 (22.0) (4.3)	64 (78.0) (8.8)	81 (7.3)	0.01
Other	31 (34.8) (7.9)	58 (65.2) (8.0)	89 (8.0)	
Total	394 (35.2) (100.0)	724 (64.8) (100.0)	1,118 (100.0)	

of positive consonance ($X^2 = 11.22$, $n = 41$, $df = 1$, P $<$ .001). White athletes received significantly more positive consonance (e.g., "she's on fire") than did black athletes, and black athletes received significantly more description with respect to the background (e.g., "Philadelphia native") category ($X^2 = 7.15$, $n = 81$, $df = 1$, $p < .01$).

Research Question Three

RQ3 pertained to whether sportscaster dialogue differs based on athlete sex. Table 3 displays those descriptor frequencies for male athletes only. Table 3

Table 3 Descriptor codes across race for males

| Descriptor | Race | | Total | Prob. |
	White	Black		Chi square
Physicality/Athleticism	197 (37.5)	329 (62.5)	526	
	(66.8)	(58.2)	(61.2)	
Intelligence/Mental Skill	26 (28.3)	66 (71.7)	92	
	(8.8)	(11.7)	(10.7)	
Hard Work/Effort	3 (20.0)	12 (80.0)	15	
	(1.0)	(2.1)	(1.7)	
Determination/Motivation	11 (39.3)	17 (60.7)	28	
	(3.7)	(3.0)	(3.3)	
Speed	6 (22.2)	21 (77.8)	27	
	(2.0)	(3.7)	(3.1)	
Positive Consonance	3 (23.0)	10 (77.0)	13	
	(1.0)	(1.8)	(1.5)	
Negative Consonance	10 (52.6)	9 (47.4)	19	
	(3.4)	(1.6)	(2.2)	
Leadership	3 (15.0)	17 (85.0)	20	0.1
	(1.0)	(3.0)	(2.3)	
Versatility	6 (37.5)	10 (62.5)	16	
	(2.0)	(1.8)	(1.9)	
Team-Orientation	1 (12.5)	7 (87.5)	8	
	(0.3)	(1.2)	(1.0)	
Personality	3 (60.0)	2 (40.0)	5	
	(1.0)	(0.3)	(1.0)	
Looks/Appearance	1 (50.0)	1 (50.0)	2	
	(0.3)	(0.2)	(1.0)	
Background	9 (17.0)	39 (83.0)	48	0.05
	(3.3)	(6.9)	(5.6)	
Other	16 (39.0)	25 (61.0)	41	
	(5.4)	(4.4)	(4.8)	
Total	295 (34.3)	565 (65.7)	860	
	(100.0)	(100.0)		

reveals that black athletes were represented, marginally, with a larger frequency of descriptors with regard to the category of leadership capacity ($X^2 = 3.3$, $n = 20$, $df = 1$, $P < .10$); Black athletes also received significantly more references to the background category ($X^2 = 5.11$, $n = 48$, $df = 1$, $P < .05$)

Table 4 displays descriptor frequencies for female athletes only. The findings reported in this table show that white athletes received 78.6 percent of the 28 descriptors regarding positive consonance ($X^2 = 19.5$, $n = 28$, $df = 1$, $p < .001$). While the negative consonance category did not contain enough observations for Chi Square analysis, 80 percent of the descriptors (e.g., "nothing's going right for her tonight") were directed toward black athletes.

Table 4 Descriptor codes across race for feales

Descriptor	Race		Total	Prob. Chi square
	White	Black		
Physicality/Athleticism	24 (42.9) (24.5)	32 (57.1) (20.0)	56 (21.7)	
Intelligence/Mental Skill	3 (23.0) (3.1)	10 (77.0) (6.3)	13 (5.0)	
Hard Work/Effort	0 (0.0) 0.0	2 (100.0) (0.7)	2 (0.7)	
Determination/Motivation	3 (27.3) (3.1)	8 (72.7) (5.0)	11 (4.3)	
Speed	7 (46.7) (7.1)	8 (53.3) (5.0)	15 (5.8)	
Positive Consonance	22 (78.6) (22.5)	6 (21.4) (3.8)	28 (10.9)	0.001
Negative Consonance	1 (20.0) (.1.0)	4 (80.0) (2.5)	5 (1.9)	
Leadership	3 (37.5) (3.1)	5 (62.5) (3.1)	8 (3.1)	
Versatility	2 (50.0) (2.0)	2 (50.0) (1.3)	4 (1.6)	
Team-Orientation	2 (50.0) (50.0)	2 (50.0) (50.0)	4 (1.6)	
Personality	1 (11.0) (1.0)	8 (89.0) (5.0)	9 (3.5)	
Looks/Appearance	7 (32.0) (7.1)	15(68.0) (9.8)	22 (8.6)	
Background	8 (24.2) (8.1)	25 (75.8) (15.6)	33 (12.8)	
Other	15 (31.3) (15.3)	33 (68.7) (20.6)	48 (18.6)	
Total	98 (38.0) (100.0)	160 (62.0) (100.0)	258 (100.0)	

Hypotheses la and lb

Table 5 characterizes a 2×2 cross-tabulation, examining aggregated totals involving collective descriptors representing the dimensions of athleticism and intelligence across athlete race. The table shows a statistically significant relationship ($X^2 = 9.19$, $n = 924$, $df = 1$, $p < .005$), although the results offer support for just one (H1a) of the two hypotheses. Specifically, descriptors representing the dimension of athleticism were directed toward black athletes 60.8 percent of the time. However, a greater disparity occurred with respect to perceived intelligence, whereby black athletes received 72.1 percent of all descriptors.

Table 5 Cross-tabulation of aggregated descriptors across race

Observed Row percent

Descriptor	Race White	Black	Total
Athleticism	278 39.20%	431 60.80%	709
Intelligence	60 27.90%	155 72.10%	215
Total	338	586	924

Note: X² = 9.19; df = 1; p < .005

Hypotheses 2a and 2b

Hypotheses 2a and 2b referred to increased references of men's athleticism and women's intelligence. Table 6 demonstrates that male athletes received a disproportionate number of descriptors. In each of the four Chi square tests, male athletes received significantly more descriptors with regard to athleticism/ physicality and intelligence, regardless of race. This finding lends support for Hypothesis 2a, as males did yield higher frequencies of comments regarding athleticism; yet, it does not support Hypothesis 2b, as there was a significant difference regarding comments about intelligence, however it was the males who received more comments about intelligence—not the women. This was true regardless of race, especially since black player Mateen Cleaves was referrred to as "smart" and a "table setter," the type of praise given to white athletes.

Table 6 Chi square statistics for gender comparisons

Observed Row percent

Descriptor	White (1) Male	Female	Black (2) Male	Female
Athleticism	222 80%	56 20%	379 88%	52 12%

Descriptor	White (3) Male	Female	Black (4) Male	Female
Intelligence	47 80%	12 20%	121 77.5%	35 22.5%
Total				

Note: (1) X² = 26.97, df = 1, p < .001, n = 278; (2) X² = 99.66, df = 1, p < .001, n = 431; (3) X² = 5.57, df = 1, p < .025, n = 59; (4) X² = 10.83, df = 1, p < .001, n = 156.

Discussion

With the racial biases now explicated within the study of the Final Four, conclusions can be drawn on theoretical and methodological levels. As a commentary on male hegemony in sports in general, the study revealed that more than three-fourths of all descriptors concerned male athletes. Less commentary was generated overall from both men and women commentators of the women's Final Four. However, larger factors could explain such a large difference in the amount of commentary, including the possibility that commentators announcing the women's games were not as familiar with the women athletes, which made them speak less. Additionally, the fact that comments concerning the appearance of female athletes outnumbered similar comments about male athletes by a 12:1 ratio reflects quite clearly the findings and sentiments of many sport researchers. Kinkema and Harris (1998) note:

> The media trivialize female athletes by devoting a disproportionately smaller amount of time to their performances as well as by highlighting physical attractiveness or their domestic roles such as wife, mother, or supportive girlfriend of a male. Female athletes are evaluated partially in terms of the extent to which their physical characteristics or domestic roles correspond to dominant notions of femininity.
>
> (p. 38)

The current study certainly lends support to the contentions of Kinkema and Harris (1998), at least with respect to gender; however, some noticeable changes appear to have taken place in terms of differential accounts of race. Consistent with previous scholarship, the study showed that black athletes are commonly praised for their "natural" athleticism, which includes attributes such as speed, strength and versatility. Unlike earlier research, the present study did not reveal dominant commentary about the perceived intelligence and leadership capacity of white athletes; it revealed the opposite (e.g., "And if you're talking about leadership, Cleaves is the best that come along in a long, long time"). This finding may be explained, in part, by the "coaching" that network executives do in order to teach commentators how to avoid racial imbalances—namely, how to avoid being viewed as treating the races differently when doing national broadcasts to thousands, if not millions, of fans (see Sabo et al., 1996). A logical extension of the present study would be to address local and regional broadcasts, examining whether commentators who are less prominent than seasoned national broadcasters stereotype athletes by race more often. One would intuit that they would, if marginally, as often they have not received as much training and are not quite as polished as those in the elite ranks.

In addition, it must be noted that Mateen Cleaves, then a point guard for Michigan State, received almost constant praise for leading the Spartans through the season and into the Final Four. Since Michigan State won the national championship, Cleaves appeared twice in the Final Four, first against Wisconsin and next against Florida. As veterans of televised sports can appreciate, announcers, and/or their producers, often choose a select few players on which to focus, as evidence by the number of background descriptors, for any number of reasons (e.g. exceptional talent, overcoming adversity, superb leadership qualities). Announcers have always done background stories of people from tough neighborhoods, for instance, overcoming the odds to make it all the way to the national championship. Some examples of background information include "Tom Izzo and the kids from Flint" as well as "The things you love about that basketball team. . . . It's the Flint connection." In this case, it may be that Cleaves' stellar leadership qualities—not to mention the fact that in the final game he went down with a severe ankle injury and managed to return—may have contributed to the patterns observed in this study, as they did feature human-interest information about him and his background.

Still, Table 2 reveals that less than a tenth of all descriptors focused on intelligence and mental skill, whereas there were over five times as many comments pertaining to physicality and athleticism. If one looks at additional figures in Table 2, the differences become even more pronounced. To an extent, the overall pattern could be expected; it was, after all, a sporting event. But the size of the disparity across descriptors lends a degree of support to scholars who have suggested and empirically documented the assumption, or stereotype, that black athletes are simply gifted. Again, most of the participants in the tournaments were black athletes.

In terms of research methodology, analysis of the Final Four telecasts justified the taxonomy employed by Eastman and Billings (2001). While physical power and mental power proved difficult to operationalize and were consequently collapsed, the remaining fourteen categories were found to contain at least 1% of all descriptors used by sportscasters. However, the significant percentage of comments labeled as "other" could lead one to argue that more classification categories within the taxonomy are warranted. Additionally, future studies should continue to explore the relationships between and among taxonomy categories. For instance, the potential relationship between comments about intelligence, positive consonance, and determination is quite different than the potential relationship between leadership and background. In subsequent studies, correlations between variables would be valuable to understanding potential dimensions of the taxonomy.

One clear limitation of the study is the use of the crudely defined categories of "white," "black," and "other" when coding for the race of a given athlete. While further research would ideally be able to construct more exact definitions of each athletes' race, it should also be noted that most studies—as well as stereotypes—are based on this broad construction of what constitutes a person's race.[7] Thus, it is important for preliminary investigations (such as this analysis) to use categorization structures that are most often applied to athletic evaluations. For instance, while Tiger Woods argues that he is "Cablinasian" because his ethnicity consists of a mix of Caucasian, Black, Indian, and Asian backgrounds (Eagan, 2001). Still, most broadcasters, fellow golfers, and fans refer to him exclusively as the general label of "black."

Ultimately, the stereotypes scholars have identified in previous studies did appear in this analysis of the 2000 Men's and Women's Final Four College Basketball Tournaments. But with respect to commentary about intelligence, mental skill and leadership capacity, the study did reveal findings that suggest more positive comments about black athletes, at least among black *male* athletes. To truly understand the impact of such descriptions on the overall scheme of NCAA basketball, one must look at the raw percentages of who is participating. The majority of NCAA college basketball players remains at 75% (Eastman & Billings, 2001), but the true inroads that have been made have been within the coaching ranks, as 21.6% of all Division I coaches are now Black (Center for the Study of Sport, 2001). Black coaches are finding positions at high-profile programs, such as Mike Davis at Indiana, Tubby Smith at Kentucky, and Tommy Amaker at Michigan. Still, while the percentage of coaches in Division I has steadily improved, the percentage of Blacks in upper management positions remains abominably low as only 2.4% of all Division I athletic directors are Black (Center for the Study of Sport, 2001). While one cannot argue the direct correlation between differential evaluations of Men and Women athletes by sportscasters and overall hiring practices, one can certainly claim implications do exist. While some of the traditional stereotypes were not pervasive within this current study, White and Black athletes continued to be described in different ways. Until such evaluations change, researchers must continue to study the roots and implications of such depictions.

References

At home in domes? Finalists lose shooting eye. (2001). *The Cleveland Plain Dealer,* p. 7-D.

Birrell, S. (1989). Racial relations theories and sport: Suggestions for a more critical analysis. *Sociology of Sport Journal, 6*(3), 212–227.

Davis, L.R., & Harris, O. (1998). Race and ethnicity in US Sports Media. In L.A. Wenner (Ed.), *MediaSport* (pp. 154–169). New York: Routledge.

Dewar, A. (1993). Sexual oppression in sport: Past, present and future alternatives. In A.G. Ingram & J.W. Loy (Eds.), *Sport in Social Development* (pp. 147–165). Champaign, IL: Human Kinetics.

Duncan, M., & Messner, M. (1998). The media image of sport and gender. In L. Wenner (Ed.), *MediaSport*. New York: Routledge.

Eagan, M. (2001, July 1). Pro golf remains over par on race. *The Hartford Courant,* p. A-l.

Eastman, S.I., & Billings, A.C. (2001). Biased voices of sports: Racial and gender stereotyping in college basketball announcing. *Howard Journal of Communication, 12*(4), 183–202.

Edwards, H. (1969). *Revolt of the Black athlete.* New York: Free Press.

Eitzen, D.S. (1984). *Sport in contemporary society: An anthology.* New York: St. Martin's Press.

Hallinan, C. (1991). Aborigines and positional segregation in Australian rugby league. *International Review for the Sociology of Sport, 26*(2), 69–81.

Harris, O. (1993). African-American predominance in collegiate sport. In D.D. Brooks & R.C. Althouse (Eds.), *Racism in college athletics: The African-American athlete's experience* (pp. 51–74). Morgantown, WV: Fitness Information Technology.

Holsti, O.R. (1969). *Content analysis for the social sciences and the humanities.* Menlo Park, CA: Addison-Wesley.

Jackson, D.Z. (1989, January 22). Calling the plays in Black and White. *Boston Globe,* pp. A30, 33.

Kaid, L.L., & Wadsworth, A.J. (1989). Content analysis. In P. Emmert & L. Barker (Eds.), *Measurement of communication behavior* (pp. 197–217). New York: Longman.

Kinkema, K.M., & Harris, J.C., (1992). MediaSport Studies: Key research and emerging issues. In J. Wenner (Ed.), *MediaSport* (pp. 27–54). New York: Routledge.

McCarthy, D., & Jones, R.L. (1997). Speed, aggression, strength, and tactical naivete. *Journal of Sport & Social Issues,* **21**(4), 348–362.

McCombs, M. (1994). News influence on our pictures of the world. In J. Bryant & D. Zillman (Eds.), *Media effects: Advances in theory and research.* Hillsdale, New Jersey: Lawrence Erlbaum Associates, Publishers.

McCombs, M.E., & Shaw, D.L. (1972). The agenda-setting function of mass media. *Public Opinion Quarterly,* **36**, 176–18.

Messner, M., Dunbar, M., & Hunt, D. (2000). The television sports manhood formula. *Journal of Sport & Social Issues,* **24**(4), 380–394.

Messner, M.A., Duncan, M.C., & Jensen, K. (1993). Separating the men from the girls: The gendered language of televised sports. *Gender and Society,* **7**(1), 121–137.

Procter, D.E. (1990). The dynamic spectacle: transforming experience into social forms of community. *Quarterly Journal of Speech,* **76**(2), 117–134.

Center for the Study of Sport. (2001). *Racial Report Card from the Center for Sport in Society* Northeastern University: Author.

Rainville, R.E., & McCormick, E. (1977). Extent of covert racial prejudice in pro football announcers' speech. *Journalism Quarterly,* **54**, 20–26.

Sabo, D., Jansen, S.C., Tate, D., Duncan, M.C., & Leggett, S. (1996). Televising international sport: Race, ethnicity, and nationalistic bias. *Journal of Sport & Social Issues,* **20**(1), 7–21.

Sage, G.H. (1990). *Power and ideology in American sport.* Champaign, IL: Human Kinetics.

Staples, R., & Jones, T. (1985). Culture, ideology and Black television images. *The Black Scholar,* **16**(3), 10–20.

Whannel, G. (1992). *Fields in vision: Television sport and cultural transformation.* London: Routledge.

Wicker, B., & Zulgad, J. (2000, Apr. 5). Next Final Four already coming into focus. *Minneapolis Star-Tribune,* p. 1-C.

Williams, R.L., & Youseff, Z.I. (1971) Stereotypes of football players as functions of positions. *Journal of Sports Medicine,* **3**(1), 7–11.

Wonsek, P.L. (1992). College basketball on television: A study of racism in the media. *Media, Culture and Society,* **14**, 449–461.

Notes

1. For "naturally talented/overcoming the odds" articles in the popular press, see Hendrick, 1995; Myers, 1991. For more on perceptions of Black athletes, see Sailes (1993); Lombardo, 1978; Wiggins, 1988.

2. Specifically, Messner, Duncan and Jensen (1993) examined men's and women's basketball games and tennis matches in terms of the language commentators used to describe the athletes, as well as the way the athletes were filmed. Their "hierarchy of naming" by gender and race is consistent with the study completed by Messner, Dunbar and Hunt (2000), which looked at how white males form the dominant sources of authority in the sports world. With regard to gender, Messner, Duncan and Jensen (1993) found camera angles to suggest a sexual orientation toward the female athletes.

3. Specifically, McCombs and Shaw (1972) studied the 1968 presidential campaign in Chapel Hill, North Carolina, sampling a group of 100 undecided voters, who they

deemed most likely to be affected by the agenda setting function of mass media. They found strong correlations between the issues the media reported and what respondents considered to be the most important issues of the day. Their study has been cited frequently, and to date, more than 100 studies have addressed agenda setting theory (see also, McCombs, 1994).

4. When we speak of "communication coaching," we suggest that network broadcasters receive training on what *not* say during a broadcast sporting event, but not necessarily on *how much* to say.

5. Each game was videotaped from pre-game commentary to post-game commentary. Word-for-word transcripts of broadcast commentary were typed from the videotape of each respective game. The sportscasting booths for both semifinal and final games consisted of Billy Packer (color), Jim Nantz (play-by-play), and Armen Keteyian (floor) for the men's games on CBS and Anne Meyers (color), Mike Patrick (play-by-play), and Michelle Tafoya (floor) for the women's games on ESPN. Transcription of broadcast commentary first consisted of literal transcription of the discourse employed between commentators (e.g., distinguishing broadcast commentary between CBS commentator Jim Nantz and CBS commentator Billy Packer). Commentary of each respective commentator was further divided into distinct lines (i.e., sentence by sentence).

6. Kaid and Wadsworth (1989) explain that in content analytic research, it is appropriate to gauge intercoder reliability for variables that are both objective and subjective to interpretation. Overall reliability rates can then be reported in addition to more specific coding choices.

7. Birrell (1989) has argued also that studies also need to move past examining black males almost exclusively and devote some focus to Native-Americans, Latino/a-Americans and Asian-Americans. As noted in the present article, however, more than 99 percent of the athletes in the respective Final Fours could be identified as white or black.

Acknowledgment

The authors would like to acknowledge the assistance of Amy L. Bruce, Michele M. Emlet and Aimee L. Hamburger, all students at Clemson at the time of this research, in addition to the helpful comments of the manuscript referees.

Manufacturing the 'Others'

Opinion Discourse and Canadian Newspapers: The Case of the Chinese "Boat People"

Joshua Greenberg

Abstract

"Opinion" discourse—editorials, op-ed articles, and guest columns—assumes an important communicative function by offering newsreaders a distinctive and authoritative voice that will speak to them directly, in the face of troubling or problematic circumstances. Opinion discourse addresses newsreaders embraced in a consensual relationship by taking a particular stance in relation to the persons and topics referred. Nevertheless, despite its communicative importance, opinion discourse has received less sustained theoretical and empirical attention from scholars than "hard" news. Where "hard" news purports to be balanced and fair, "opinion" discourse problematizes the world by taking up the normative dimension of issues and events as the justification and rationale for taking sides. Taking the arrivals to Canada of four boatloads of "illegal" Chinese migrants in 1999 as a case study, this article aims to contribute theoretical understanding about the import of opinion discourse to the critical study of news, whilst offering a contribution to scholarship on the social construction of the Other.

Résumé

Le discours d' « opinion »—éditoriaux, chroniques, et rubriques d'invités—remplit une fonction importante dans la communication en offrant aux lecteurs une voix distincte et fiable qui leur parle directement, lors de circonstances troublantes ou problématiques. Le discours d'opinion adresse les lecteurs en les accueillant dans une relation consensuelle où l'on prend une position spécifique par rapport aux personnes et aux sujets discutés. Néanmoins, malgré son importance dans la communication, les chercheurs ont porté une attention théorique et empirique moins

Joshua Greenberg is a doctoral candidate in the Department of Sociology, McMaster University, 1280 Main Street, Hamilton, ON L8S 4M2. E-mail: greenbjl@mcmaster.ca

Canadian Journal of Communication, Vol 25 (2000) 517–537

soutenue sur le discours d'opinion que sur les actualités. Alors que les actualités prétendent être justes et équilibrées, le discours d' « opinion » discute du monde en adhérant à la dimension normative de questions et d'événements, adhésion qui justifie et explique une prise de position particulière. En se rapportant comme étude de cas à l'arrivée au Canada de quatre bateaux transportant des émigrés chinois « illégaux » en 1999, cet article vise à contribuer une compréhension théorique de l'importance du discours d'opinion dans l'étude critique des nouvelles, tout en offrant une contribution au savoir relatif à la construction sociale de l'Autre.

Introduction

On July 20, 1999, an unmarked ship transporting 123 passengers from Fujian province in China was tracked and intercepted by Canadian citizenship and immigration authorities off the coast of British Columbia. The conditions aboard the ship ("abysmal" and "horrendous") and the physical state of its passengers ("filthy") became the primary focus of coverage in much of Canada's mainstream daily press. Amid speculation that several other such boats had illegally evaded federal border authorities, three more ships in similar condition arrived at numerous points along the B.C. coastline over the next couple of months (August 12, August 31, and September 9 respectively). In total, 599 migrants arrived without proper legal identification and many subsequently declared refugee status; this was a series of events which precipitated among political elites, media observers, and some Canadian citizens a general consensus that the immigration and refugee systems were in a "state of crisis" (see Clarkson, 2000; Greenberg & Hier, forthcoming).

Despite evidence that upwards of 30,000 refugees attempt entry to Canada each year (Beiser, 1999), the general feeling conveyed by news coverage of these events was that the immigration and refugee systems were being flooded by an influx of Asian "gatecrashers" (Francis, 1999a), whose presence posed numerous harms to the public. Almost immediately after the arrival of the first boat, the Victoria *Times-Colonist*, in a poll of its readership, reported that approximately 97% of respondents felt the migrants should be sent back to China immediately (July 30, 1999).[1] Although claiming to be "sympathetic" to the migrants' life-situations overseas, respondents expressed concern that the new arrivals constituted a threat to law and order and an insult to the integrity of Canadian citizenship. Furthermore, respondents overwhelmingly articulated a shared concern that the migrants' arrivals threatened the capacity of the Canadian and British Columbia welfare systems to respond to additional demands without putting the ability of the state to meet the needs of "legitimate" Canadians at risk (Greenberg & Hier, forthcoming).

News coverage assumed an increasingly critical and hyperbolic tone after the arrival of the second boat. With immigration and security officials warning that many more ships were on the way, groups of Canadian citizens began mobilizing at various B.C. ports, some in support of the migrants and many others shouting slurs and waving placards stating unequivocally that the migrants should "GO

HOME." The usual slowness of newsworthy events during the summer months, the spectacle-like coverage of each boat arrival, and the divisive public sentiments triggered by these events, gave rise to a veritable explosion of public records: numerous town-hall style debates, radio call-in shows, and an array of press reports. And the unanticipated, dramatic appeal of these events, a general right-ward shift in the national political spectrum, and a highly competitive news media environment thus made the migrants' arrivals especially attractive to news coverage. Indeed, as one reporter put it: "You've got hundreds of people standing on a ship out in the middle of nowhere—on a ship that looks like if you touch it too hard, it's going to sink. For lack of a better way of putting it, it's eye candy" (quoted in Clarkson, 2000, p. 6).

In developing understanding of these events and the role of the mainstream news media in constructing an ideology of consensus in the face of seemingly unusual or problematic circumstances, this study examines the content and rhetorical expressions of "opinion" discourses, that is, editorials, op-ed articles, and guest columns, in five mainstream Canadian daily newspapers. Opinion discourses assume an important communicative function by contributing to the media's role of formulating certain, "preferred" viewpoints about the world. The function of opinion discourse within the larger context of newspaper coverage is to offer newsreaders a distinctive and authoritative "voice" that will speak to them directly about matters of public importance. Opinion discourses "address newsreaders embraced in a consensual ('us') relationship, by taking a particular stance in relation to the persons ('them') and topics referred to" (Fowler, 1991, p. 221). Yet, despite this communicative importance, the study of "opinion" discourse has received less sustained theoretical and empirical attention by communications scholars and media sociologists than "hard" news, where conventional journalistic standards of balance, fairness, and objectivity can be scrutinized and challenged.[2] Therefore, this paper aims to contribute theoretical understanding of the import of "opinion" discourse to the critical study of news, in addition to offering a contribution to scholarship on the construction of the "Other" in press discourse.

Analytical Framework

This paper commences with the notion that at any given moment, certain, perhaps unexpected, events may come to be seen as fundamentally problematic to the identity of the state and the stability of its relations with its citizens. In Gramsci's (1971) original formulation, these "conjunctural moments" are to be seen as crucial to the ongoing, developmental character of modernity, insofar as they appear as if by accident, and in a way that is perceived to be immediate and threatening to the status quo (p. 177). According to t'Hart (1993), the most important instrument in the management of such moments is language, that is, those who are able to define what the problem is about "also hold the key to defining the appropriate strategies for its resolution" (p. 41; see also Edelman,

1977, 1988). For Hall, Critcher, Jefferson, Clarke, & Roberts (1978), discourses of crisis management that arise during such conjunctural moments bring about the construction of an "Other" (or several "Others")—an outsider(s) whose presence is seen to threaten the norm of consensus and whose identity, moreover, may serve as the basis of their eventual expurgation (see Cohen, 1972).[3] Such conjunctural moments, then, are not purely objective phenomena that define the contours for subsequent ideological contestation among elite and non-elite actors about institutional problems; rather, they are subjectively perceived and hence brought into existence through and by discourse (Hay, 1996).

Opinion Discourse: Some General Theoretical Remarks

Editorials are public, mass communicated types of opinion discourse that normally appear in the front section of a newspaper and are the "official" voice of a media outlet on matters of public importance. Op-ed articles are normally placed on the page opposite the conventional editorial and usually represent the expressed opinion of a single individual employed by the newspaper, or by an individual associated with an affiliate news outlet. While op-ed articles are subjective accounts, they are often perceived to carry an *objective-like* status; that is, they are generally, *though not necessarily,* associated with the opinions of the newspaper as an elite institution, since the author is normally a recognized and regular contributor.[4] Guest columns, on the other hand, appear in close proximity to the editorial page and are normally the expressed opinion of an accredited expert or recognized stakeholder outside the media industry, but who nevertheless possesses specialized, "insider" status, for example, a lawyer, physician, NGO, labour leader, or leading academic researcher.

After primetime television talk shows, newspaper editorials are probably the widest circulating forms of opinion discourse (van Dijk, 1996). Their influence upon political opinion-formation is formidable, extending not just to the ordinary, everyday reader but also, crucially, to institutional and/or elite actors, for example, Members of Parliament (MPs), corporate executives, and police. Moreover, editorial opinions are generally institutional, not personal, insofar as they are rarely perceived by newsreaders to be representative of purely subjective viewpoints. Rather, these opinions are often *perceived* by readers to be consistent with the viewpoints of the newspaper as an organizational entity equipped with the facts and information required for informed opinion formation, which are generally unavailable to the average newsreader (van Dijk, 1996).

The viewpoints expressed in opinion discourses are an important feature of news because, unlike conventional "hard" news reporting, they often blend what van Dijk (1998) calls "evaluative propositions" (normative prescriptions) and "factual beliefs" (social facts) (p. 29). The distinction is important because opinion discourses obfuscate the fundamental or basic problems of cognition, such as the basis of knowledge and belief, and truth and falsity. The crucial factor in determining whether or not an editorial viewpoint is normative or factual is whether the grounds or criteria of judgment are based merely on cultural or group norms or are socially-shared criteria of "truth" or other knowledge, based on valid inference, scholarly research, or expert observation. When facts are blended with values, notions of truth and falsity, knowledge and ideas, and, by extension, the very concept of "public opinion" itself, become analytically problematic.

Whereas "hard" news coverage purports to be fair, balanced, and objectively grounded in such "uniform technical criteria" as the prevention of personal bias, fact-opinion separation, and the inclusion of opposing viewpoints (Ericson, Baranek, & Chan, 1987, p. 105),[5] critical news analysis has shown "hard" news to be structured ideologically and inflected with "preferred" readings that frequently, though not necessarily, serve dominant interests, whilst containing and displacing contradiction (Fowler, 1991; Goldman & Rajagopal, 1991; Hall, 1977; Hall, Critcher, Jefferson, Clarke, & Roberts, 1978; Knight, 1998, forthcoming). Opinion discourses, on the other hand, are *not* bound by such claims to objectivity and balance, that is, they are overtly biased viewpoints that are not intended to be objective, fair, or balanced. Opinion discourses not only take sides by evaluating events, but they also explain these events in ways that have to do first and foremost with the attribution of responsibility.[6] They are primarily, but not exclusively, blame-oriented and, as such, they attempt to mobilize and enrol newsreaders around particular ideological positions by resonating in ways that will connect with their ethics and emotions.

While this blame-centredness is a crucial, indeed defining, feature of opinion discourse, it is also part of the critical nature of "hard" news texts. Both modes of news discourse are seen to problematize the world in terms of different issues and events.[7] However, what opinion discourses do differently than conventional "hard" news coverage is to take up the socio-emotional, that is, normative, dimension of this problematization as the *justification* and *rationale* for being opinionated and taking one side versus an/other(s). The implication of this rhetorical distinction is that, like "hard" news texts, opinion discourses are subject to their own limit points or spatial boundaries insofar as they have their own normative standards to uphold, in the sense that there are certain, contextually grounded, limits to what can or cannot be said, even in the form of opinions and judgments. Secondarily, and consequently, editorials, op-ed articles, and guest columns generally proffer solutions that (presumably) are not being followed by those with the authority and/or responsibility to act, and these discourses have the ability to *persuade* newsreaders to formulate (and act upon) their own opinions.

Framing and Narrativization

Underpinning these largely socio-cognitive assumptions about opinion discourse is an understanding of the ways in which news media construct mental representations, or *frames,* of everyday life in order to comprehend and respond to social situations. As principles of partiality and selectivity—that is, codes of emphasis, interpretation, and presentation—media frames are routinely used by newsmakers to organize verbal and visual discourses into formats that will be accessible to the everyday reader, viewer, or listener. In rendering opinions, laying blame, and presenting solutions about problematic issues, actors, and events, opinion writers inevitably accentuate some points of view while downplaying others, thus limiting the range of interpretable meanings available to the public (Entman, 1993; Gamson & Modigliani, 1989; Gitlin, 1980; Pan & Kosicki, 1993). It is in this sense that the concept of framing can be said to capture the numerous ways in which the media set the discursive context within which individuals may come to "locate, perceive, identify and label" the events and happenings going on around them (Goffman, 1974, p. 21). Regarded this way, the role of news media is to organize the "field of social intelligibility" (Knight, forthcoming) within which news comes to "make sense," not by telling people what to think, but telling them what to think about and how to think about it.

In addition to functioning paradigmatically, news discourse generally, and opinion discourse in particular, operates syntagmatically to account for the ongoing, shifting character of news. The temporal aspect of representation is best captured by the discursive technique of "narrativization" *(inter alia* Ricoeur, 1984). Narrative is a feature of news broadcasting and opinion-formation, where professional codes help to determine certain structures, orders, and components of a given story *(inter alia* Hartley, 1982). As Knight (forthcoming) argues, "narrative complements framing in that it deals with the movement of representation across time, and with the coordination of differentiated signs into a more or less coherent discourse" (n.p.) In the case of print news, narratives help to choreograph into a whole and complete story a series of complexly related events, and their articulations, in a way that will be meaningful to the reader(s). In the case of news that is "problematic," real world actions and events are extracted from their actual manner of occurrence in order that their *effects* can then be "recruited" to the discourse as symptomatic of other, broader, problems and anxieties (Hay, 1996). Such "reality effects" (Knight, 1989) are then re-embedded into a more generic discourse where they may be subjected to a further process of narration. It is in such configurations and re-configurations that "notions of responsibility, causality and agency may be deleted and replaced by an abstracted reference to causes of a more simplified degree of generality" (Trew, 1979, p. 108).

Data and Sampling Procedures

Conventional techniques of content and discourse analysis have been used to examine the spatial and temporal features of all editorials, op-ed articles, and guest columns (n = 57) appearing in five mainstream, English-language only print media: *The National Post, The Vancouver Sun,* the Victoria *Times-Colonist, The Toronto Star,* and *The Toronto Sun.* The frames identified in the coverage are represented in the data analysis below as frequency counts of the number of times each frame was referred to in a single paragraph.[8] In instances when more than one frame was mentioned together (this was rare), each frame was counted separately. The period of analysis extends from July 21 to October 1, 1999.

The media sampled can be said to comprise four different genres of news reporting—the logic of the sample, then, is governed principally by idiomatic consideration, and secondarily by geographic location and circulation.[9] *The National Post* is a right-wing, highbrow broadsheet that caters generally to the political and corporate elite, and at the time of the coverage was the flagship news outlet of Conrad Black's Hollinger Inc. media empire *(The Vancouver Sun* and the Victoria *Times-Colonist* were also Hollinger papers).[10] *The Vancouver Sun* and *The Toronto Star* are middlebrow newspapers insofar as they cater generally to a more socially and economically diverse readership. Despite this commonality, however, *The Toronto Star* is clearly more oriented to a social-liberal editorial stance than *The Vancouver Sun*. *The Toronto Sun* is a right-wing, tabloid daily. Its ethos represents what Fairclough (1998) has called "lifeworld discourse": the narrative logic is binary and underlined by a rhetorical current of conflict and confrontation, with emphasis normally placed upon common-sense interpretations of complex phenomenon. The *Times-Colonist,* finally, is a hybrid newspaper that is moderately populist in its idiomatic flavour. For analytic purposes it is therefore situated someplace in between the middlebrow and tabloid spectra.

Data Analysis

Each of the sampled media perceived and reported the migrants' arrivals as problematic, a focus which, after all, is precisely what defines as "newsworthy" unusual or out-of-the-ordinary events. When abstracted into a single, generalized issue, the four boat arrivals were a classic example of "bad" news in that the events were principally framed around the generic themes of public *disorder* and *conflict,* the *transgression* of norms and values, and *confrontation* (Glasgow University Media Group, 1976).

This negative coverage began with the media's characterizing the migrants in ways that highlighted a general ambiguity about their identity. On the one hand, the migrants were portrayed as "illegal," that is, they were treated as "economic migrants" whose motivation was not asylum from political persecution but upward socioeconomic mobility. This kind of lexical selectivity is noteworthy because it takes for granted the implications of these different terms of representation, insofar as "persecution" generally implies a definitive, identifiable subjective agency, in ways that economic negatives such as poverty, deprivation, and mass unemployment do not. On the other hand, the migrants were portrayed as pitiful dupes of unscrupulous human smugglers (so-called "snakeheads"). The "snakeheads," of course, had no concrete presence in the real events insofar as they were not known to be aboard the ships and were never arrested, but they still acquired a central presence in the media's representation, as an invisible, but causally blame-worthy, agent. While the migrants' agency occupied the centre of attention in "hard" news reports (Greenberg & Hier, forthcoming)—a predictable observation, given the emphasis on concrete events, identifiable and personalizable actors, immediacy, and the presence of official social control authorities—it was displaced from the centre in the "opinion" formats because the migrants are not discursively and normatively sustainable as blameworthy actors. They are poor ideological targets for the attribution of responsibility and blame because representation of their identity depended upon other representation of identities for other actors (i.e., government and the "snakeheads"). This general ambiguity where the migrants' identity is concerned was a central feature of the coverage and, not surprisingly, has played and continues to play an integral role in the present state of refugee debates in Canada and elsewhere in the West.

The media's portrayal of the migrants' identity blended discursively with the themes of the opinion discourse. Table 1 identifies and provides frequency counts of the general frames that organized the narrative structure of the coverage in these five newspapers. These data show generally how the migrants' arrivals served for the construction of a series of editorial "master frames" (Carroll & Ratner, 1996, p. 411). In terms of news coverage, master frames operate as central interpretive frameworks from which public opinion may be said to derive about people, events, and/or issues which the media have deemed "newsworthy." In the present case, five master frames are identified: (1) the problematization of government; (2) race relations; (3) moral health and national security; (4) identity and the integrity of national citizenship; and (5) migrants' welfare and safety. In regard to this final frame, when genuine concern for the migrants' welfare and safety was addressed as a primary frame, it was done so almost exclusively by guest columnists, whose opinions arguably carry less persuasive weight than the official opinion of the newspaper, as is featured in the main editorials.

The principal conclusion to be drawn from these data is that in all but one of

Table 1 Themes of editorial concern (%)

Theme	NP*	VS	STAR	SUN	TC
Problematization of gov't	41.8	36.5	43.4	45.7	29.4
Race relations	11.5	16.2	24.7	12.0	30.4
Health & security	25.7	24.8	13.5	23.7	14.7
Citizenship	15.1	11.4	8.1	11.3	5.9
Migrants' well being	2.2	5.3	9.3	4.1	16.7
Mixed/Other	3.7	5.7	2.3	3.3	2.9
Total	100.0	99.9	100.0	100.0	100.0

* NP = *The National Post;* VS = *The Vancouver Sun;* STAR = *The Toronto Star,* SUN; = *The Toronto Sun;* TC = Victoria *Times-Colonist*

the newspapers "problematization of government" was the overall dominant frame of concern.[11] This master frame denotes a range of references to the federal Liberal government's inability to stem the influx of undocumented and uninvited human population groups to Canada. First, it refers to the notion that the immigration and refugee system is inherently flawed, by virtue of its being based on a socially liberal ideology, an ideology popularized by the policy decisions of numerous postwar federal Liberal governments. Take, for example, the following two passages from *The National Post:*

> Liberals were not always this cavalier about foreign ships sailing into Canadian waters. In 1985, when the U.S. coast guard icebreaker Polar Sea dared to patrol the Northwest Passage without Ottawa's permission, the Liberals' fevered calls for territorial sovereignty, and even a naval build-up, were matched only by their anti-American bigotry. Unlike the current Chinese flotilla, however, the Polar Sea sailed to protect Canada from an invasion, not to facilitate one.
>
> (Levant, 1999, p. A18)

> Those Chinese women who find themselves paying off their passage in the whore-houses of Vancouver and Toronto will, I'm sure, be gratified to know that the federal government regards them as the moral corrective to the dark stain of Canada's history.
>
> (Steyn, 1999, p. A18)

Second, this frame included references, although these were far less frequent, to the opinion that the immigration and refugee systems were actually working smoothly and in the manner in which they were supposed to. As *The Toronto Star* argued, "Each time one of these smuggling dramas takes place, there are accusations that our immigration system is broken, our rules too lax and our authorities are too timid. In fact, the system worked quite well in the latest incident" ("Caplan Sends the Right Message," 1999, p. A22).

Third, this frame comprised references to criticisms of centralized state federalism more generally, such as bureaucratic inefficiency, over-bureaucratization, the mismanagement of tax dollars, regional political pandering, and patronage appointments that result, firstly, in the immigration and refugee systems working poorly, and secondly, in the accentuation of regional cleavages across the country:

> What angry British Columbians must now see is that where Ms. Caplan comes from, the system *is* working. It works to nurture a huge immigration industry of tax-paid lawyers, bureaucrats and social-service providers—all of whom have a keen sense of political loyalty. It also works as an easy sop to the immigration industry's cousin, the multiculturalism industry, based similarly on taxpayers' largesse. This is spoils-based politics: Ethnic vote-brokers in Ms. Caplan's Toronto are pleased, immigration and legal-aid lawyers are pleased, and Reform-voting British Columbians can pay the bill.
>
> (Levant, 1999, p. A18)

The point to be made is that when problematic or challenging circumstances arise, news discourse not only identifies those who are involved, but it also forces us to question and interrogate what we expect and understand to be the proper role of government in our lives.

The exception to the trend of privileging "problematization of government" as the dominant theme was the *Times-Colonist,* where the theme received roughly the same frequency of attention as that of "race relations." That the Victoria newspaper was as concerned about addressing the state of race relations as it was with the "problem of government" might be explained, first, by the legacy of racism toward ethnic minority groups, especially where people of Asian descent are concerned, in the province of British Columbia in particular (see Henry & Tator, 2000; Li, 1994, 1998; Li & Bolaria, 1988). Second, the political and ideological influence in British Columbia of the Reform Party, the official political opposition to the Liberals and the most outspoken critic of official multicultural and immigration policy, might also help to explain the frequency of this theme of concern in the Victoria newspaper, as compared with the other media. Nevertheless, given these more demographic considerations, one would have also expected *The Vancouver Sun* to address "race relations" more frequently than was actually the case.[12] In this newspaper, "race relations" figured only a distant third in terms of the total frequency of attention. Lastly, the *Times-Colonist* accentuated the more troublesome features of racism—conflict, anger, and a general disruption of the social order—more than *The Vancouver Sun,* an observation that might be attributed to the *Times-Colonist's* idiomatic shift to the tabloid spectrum in recent years. For example, one article in the *Times-Colonist* included the following passage:

> Groups like the Canada First Immigration Reform Committee are taking valid questions and concerns about immigration policy and dragging them across the line, using them to legitimize weak-minded xenophobia, pandering to our basest emotions and fears . . . . "Immigration is changing Canada to what more resembles a Third World country," it screams and splashes a picture of Asian drug dealers being taken down by police in Vancouver. At the foot of the site is a portion of Michelangelo's hand of God touching that of a man, accompanied by the slogan: "Made with European Culture—Accept no Substitute." It's nauseating; after five minutes of this, we feel we need a shower. But that isn't the real issue, is it? There are people exploiting our concerns about people-smuggling and twisting them into a campaign against non-white immigration. It's repugnant, and presents a much greater threat to our country than any 11-year-old girl from China.
>
> ("Far-right Stokes Refugee Fears," 1999, p. A14)

Since the *Times-Colonist* attended to the theme of "race relations," and that it did so in a negative way, it is also important to question why it paid considerably more attention than the other newspapers to addressing the general "safety and welfare" of the migrants, and to interrogate the rhetorical expressions that this frame elicited. As Greenberg & Hier (forthcoming) have shown, "hard" news coverage in the *Times-Colonist* propagated, far more than other Canadian media, the idea that B.C. was experiencing a protracted "flood of illegal migrants" whose presence would pose serious political, social, and economic problems for the province. In part, this concern for the migrants' safety and welfare might be seen as a discursive strategy for balancing these largely negative "hard" news representations, thereby suggesting how opinion formats are subject to their own kinds of normative limit points. Alternatively, or in addition, the ongoing public education and media relations work by NGOs working with new immigrants and refugees in Victoria might also account for this observation,[13] and may explain the proportionately greater number of guest columns provided in the *Times-Colonist,* as compared to the other newspapers.[14]

The theme of "race relations" was the second most frequent master frame in *The Toronto Star*'s editorials, op-ed articles, and guest columns. As the only nominally social-liberal newspaper in the sample, *The Toronto Star* often challenges the kinds of social conventions or standards that precipitate discriminatory practice among the general population (sexual, racial, socioeconomic, etc.). Whereas other newspapers took up this theme as well, *The Toronto Star* was unique in that it went beyond merely identifying the issue of institutional and systemic racism as just one factor in the migrants' treatment by the public and government.[15] It also used this social problem as a basis for political critique, ruminating sarcastically how

> pundits proclaimed [Prime Minister] Chrétien guilty of caving in to ethnic voters and immigration lawyers. In the media hierarchy of rights and wrongs, it is all right for a prime minister to bow to big business, to Quebec and other regions, and to this or that lobby, but not to "the ethnics," who remain undefined.
>
> (Siddiqui, 1999a, p. A11)

> "There's a flavour that all those coming in are all bad," reports lawyer Howard Greenberg. NGOs say the officers' starting assumption seems to be that everyone coming to them is a crook. The perception takes on racial overtones considering that an overwhelming majority of officers are white and two-thirds of their clients are not.
>
> (Siddiqui, 1999b, p. A13)

What is interesting about *The Toronto Star*'s coverage, moreover, is that while it expressed criticisms about the treatment of the migrants by federal authorities it also used these as a basis for re-problematizing the activities of government in a way that is generally consistent with the neo-liberal editorial tone of the more right wing news media. For example, *The Toronto Star* sees the problem of racism as linked to *bureaucratic inefficiency* within the immigration and refugee systems:

> But the same department that can't get the illegals out can't get the legal immigrants in, in an orderly, timely fashion either. The department has thus managed to miff both anti-immigrant and pro-immigrant advocates. But it wears its inefficiency as a badge of honour, akin to the media's perverse posture that they must be doing something right if they have maligned people on both sides of an issue. Outside Ottawa, the prevailing view is that the immigration department has become anti-immigrant.
>
> (Siddiqui, 1999b, p. A13)

This is significant insofar as *The Toronto Star* could still operate from a nominally altruistic editorial position as public defender of the weak and downtrodden, while at the same time directing firm criticism at the ruling Liberal Party. Although the government also expressed "concern" for the well being of the migrants and dismissed much of the criticism levied against it as either racist or racially motivated. *The Toronto Star* still positioned itself against the ruling Liberals in a manner consistent with its normally critical editorial role.[16]

Cross Articulation as Narrative Strategy in Opinion Discourse

Particularly noteworthy about these editorial master frames is the degree to which they were cross-articulated to one another. In instances when a variety of angles or themes are incorporated into the overall narrativization of a newsworthy event(s), a discursive blurring or hybridization among categories is not an uncommon occurrence. The themes identified in these opinion discourses were significant insofar as they were often expressed as partial units in an overarching meta-narrative of crisis regarding the federal Liberal government's immigration and refugee systems. Given that each of these frames becomes a mode of problematizing the situation at hand, each theme becomes, as it were, a vantage point from which to view, and pronounce upon, the others. In this sense, each theme becomes a point in a chain of articulation. In the case at hand, the problematic role of government clearly exercises a privileged role in the motivating and articulation of the other themes. It becomes, therefore, the driving force or hub of the chain, the nodal point that operates as a kind of "universal equivalent" which allows for the circulation and exchange of sign values between each of the themes. The problematization of government thus acts rhetorically as a discursive medium through which all the other themes can be transformed or translated into one another.

Immediately following the arrival of the first boat of 123 migrants, *The National Post* and *The Vancouver Sun* stressed that if the federal government allowed the migrants to stay in Canada, the country's sovereignty would be placed at significant risk. The *Times-Colonist* questioned the "absurdity" of an immigration law that allows "illegal aliens" to "bypass the immigration queue" and claim legal entitlement to refugee status ("Tightening Our Refugee Process," 1999, p. A9). Each of these three print media outlets believes that a firm precedent must be set by the federal government to protect the integrity of "our" borders against those "others" who use smugglers to get into the country.[17]

That the events were localized along the British Columbia coast would attest to the reasons for why *The Toronto Sun* and *The Toronto Star* took longer to address these events in their editorials and other opinion pieces than the other newspapers. This delay may also help to explain, if at least only in part, the difference in the kinds of concerns about the migrants of the Ontario media. While *The Toronto Star* focused largely upon the broader issues of systemic racism, on the one hand, and bureaucratic mismanagement and low morale in the immigration and refugee departments, on the other, *The Toronto Sun* juxtaposed the federal government's stance to the more local concerns of the city's municipal councils over the costs of immigrant and refugee transition and the threat to the physical safety and well being of "true" Canadians by those in the refugee and immigrant communities.[18]

As the summer proceeded and more boats arrived, the opinions of the news media about the migrants' arrivals also changed. In particular, *The Toronto Sun*'s coverage grew more vitriolic where the ability of the federal government to safeguard Canada's borders was concerned. The problem for *The Toronto Sun* was no longer that the federal Liberals were making decisions on refugee and immigration matters without consideration for how new arrivals will be dealt with financially by the nation's largest municipality, but rather that the government was to blame for making Canada "an easy mark for human smugglers" ("Save Our System," 1999, p. 14). Although in the main, the migrants were portrayed by *The Toronto Sun* as "desperate people" and "it is not the Canadian way to abandon them to their fates on the ocean" ("No Refuge," 1999, p. 14), a "real immigration system would deny refugee status to anyone who used blatantly illegal means to get to Canada" ("Save Our System," 1999, p. 14).

Following the arrival of the second boat (August 12), and amid speculation that many more "migrant ships" would soon be arriving to Canada, *The National Post* believes it is not only the integrity of the immigration and refugee systems that is at risk, but also, and more crucially, the health and welfare of Canadians that is being compromised by the migrants' arrivals, and the Liberal government's inadequate response:

> Through sheer incompetence, Ottawa is ruining lives, exposing Canadians to grave risks and financing the creation of a criminal class that will hurt this country for years to come. If these boatloads are not deported . . . the government of Canada should be sued by the provinces, municipalities, taxpayer organizations and other victims of refugee crimes.
>
> (Francis, 1999b, p. A8)

The Vancouver Sun editor shares the same concern for the well being of "real" Canadians. This concern emerged much earlier than it did in *The National Post;* the emphasis, however, was similar in terms of overdramatizing the conditions of the boat and the physical state of the migrants: "slop buckets overflowed on to the deck of the hold where the cargo slept, on wooden slats, and ate. The passengers had lice, scabies and the sundry ills that blossom wherever people are crowded together in their own filth" ("Ship's Passengers Must Be Sent Home," 1999, p. A10). Moreover, "once absorbed, those beholden to criminals for their passage will work it off, slowly, either in criminal activities such as operating brothels or dealing drugs, or as virtual slave labour" ("Humanitarian Nation Faces Moral Questions," 1999, p. A14). Thus, for *The National Post* and *The Vancouver Sun*, the issue of health and welfare was not just a matter of physical well being (both the migrants' and Canadians'), but also, and more crucially, it was one of economic safety and "moral" security. As *The National Post's* Tom Grimmer put it just after the third boat arrival (August 31, 1999), the response of the federal government to the arrivals of the migrants was neither simple nor efficient, but rather "characterized by a moral agony that is uniquely Canadian" (1999, p. A14).

The media's opinions about the migrants' arrivals and the weak responses of the federal government are suggestive of the subtle and overt basis of temporality within the context of power relations in advanced democratic, capitalist societies. In response to the decisions of governing authorities, media consistently seek to legitimize their interests and/or viewpoints by identifying the past performance of their subject(s) and objects(s) of criticism—normally those individuals and groups who occupy positions of authority—and then use the appraisals of those performances to frame their present opinion. Claims of (symbolically reconstructed) past successes, such as references to days past when Canadian governments could act without being overshadowed by clouds of political correctness and special interest, are gambits that force authorities to respond to partisan viewpoints in preferable ways. Once news media outlets can symbolically establish a legitimate past, they are in a much stronger position of making claims concerning how future public policies will be defined. In occupying such a position, media effectively use this social structural past to define the parameters for present and future relations. The media's ability to control the passage of time through narrative constructions of the present operates as the crux of its ability to define social-political reality and set the agenda upon which the public will base its own opinions.

Conclusion

Opinion discourses play an integral role in public opinion formation and assume a particularly critical role during periods when the social and political consensus gets called into question. Unlike "hard" news texts, opinion discourses (editorials, op-ed articles, or guest columns) possess a unique idiomatic character that "speaks" directly to the readership in a way that is familiar, habitual, and reliable. As Fowler (1991) argues, "the language employed will thus be the *newspaper's own version of the language of the public to whom it is principally addressed: its* version of the rhetoric, imagery and underlying common stock of knowledge which it assumes its audience shares and which thus forms the basis of the reciprocity of producer/reader" (p. 48, emphasis in original). Establishing a reliable style of discourse is fundamental to the building of consensus and is central to the ideological practice of news coverage (Chibnall, 1977; Hall, 1973; Hartley, 1982).

In general, each of these five media was critical of the federal government's handling of the four boat arrivals of Chinese migrants. Yet what became so problematic was the manner in which this "problem of government" was linked discursively to other issues of editorial concern. Opinion discourses in these mainstream media established a cause and effect relationship among a variety of themes: a poor government constructs weak or poor laws; these laws are believed to create the environment which makes possible the influx of several hundred unwanted and undocumented foreigners; a "weak" response in turn by the federal authorities is perceived to be an offer of admission to criminal elements in the future; the uncontrolled wave of migrants likely to precede such inaction is felt to place the integrity of the immigration and refugee systems at risk; such inaction is seen to put the lives of "real" Canadians at risk, as unscreened refugees will *ipso facto* bring with them disease, crime, and other unfavourable scourge. In this instance, anger and frustration were articulated against the government whilst also channelling resentment in the direction of the refugee-seekers. Unwaveringly, the "public" which consisted of these five newspapers was unified on this issue.

Upon closer analysis, differences could be identified among the opinions in each of the sampled news outlets. *The Toronto Star*'s editorials were unquestioningly more sympathetic to the migrants' agency than the other newspapers; at the same time, however, its op-ed articles and guest columns were harshly critical of the government's handling of the situation. The effect of this was the presentation of an ideologically disjointed point of view. Criticism of the government would lead to calls for tightening the refugee determination process, a policy recommendation that falls far too short of critically addressing the reality of increasing poverty in the peripheral economies of the world system, the crucial factor motivating the migrants' exodus to Canada in the first place. The *Times-Colonist* was also sympathetic, although in a different way than *The Toronto Star*—guest columns provided a balance to the more critical conventional editorials. The *Times-Colonist* also published far more opinion pieces of NGOs in the Vancouver area, as well as the opinion of the B.C. director of the Canadian Centre for Policy Alternatives (CCPA), who raised the issue of questioning the impact of globalization and the gross income gaps between wealthy and impoverished nations on transnational population movements.[19]

Editorials, op-ed articles, and guest columns in *The National Post* and *The Vancouver Sun* were unambiguously critical of the federal government's actions and official position. In comparison, like the Victoria newspaper, *The Vancouver Sun* provided greater discursive space for individuals working within the 'immigration industry" to express their opinions, notably NGOs and immigration lawyers. *The National Post*, on the other hand, was consistently and overwhelmingly insensitive to the lived realities motivating the migrants' exodus from China. As a result of this insensitivity, this newspaper went as far in its editorials, op-ed articles, and guest columns as the official opposition (Reform Party), in terms of negatively stereotyping the migrants as a disease-carrying embodiment of danger whose presence posed a significant threat to the moral, physical, and economic well being of "legitimate" Canadians. According to Leon Benoit. Reform MP and co-chair of the House of Commons Standing Committee on Citizenship and Immigration: "The consequences [of the migrants' arrivals] are Canadians facing increased health risks through diseases like tuberculosis and AIDS, which are coming to our country increasingly through various types of immigration" (quoted in Danard, 1999, p. A3).

The Toronto Sun, finally, began its editorial coverage cautiously, though still in a manner consistent with its tabloid format: polarizing the actions and positions of the federal with the municipal governments and the needs and wants of the migrants with "real" Canadians. Like *The National Post*, it also accentuated negative stereotypes, so that the migrants would be seen not as possible contributors to the overall prosperity of the country, but rather as a hindrance to continuing economic, social, and political growth and development.

The ideological and hegemonic effects of these kinds of media coverage are significant and numerous. The pretext, of course, consists of newsmakers' choices of words or labels for making sense of the migrants' arrivals: terms such as "invasion," "flood," or "wave" were used as "designators" (Pan & Kosicki, 1993, p. 62) for interpreting the events as just another form of "catastrophe." Such factual disproportionality and journalistic hyperbole has the effect of substituting what is real with a variety of symptoms or "reality effects" (Knight, 1989). The specificity and complexity of events around the arrival of each boat was consequently denied and replaced by a more simplified narrative which could account for every symptom or outcome, whilst unambiguously attributing responsibility for the immigration and refugee crisis.

In addition, the migrants were objectified as greedy, selfish, and economically driven individuals whose disdain for the proper channels of entry to Canada was simplified by the media's use of such terms as "illegal migrant" or "economic migrant" (see Hier & Greenberg. 2000). As van Dijk (1988) notes, these types of lexical terms are common in countries where tolerance of diversity is a socially recognized norm. The effect, however, is that language such as this mitigates and disguises a speaker or writer's tendency to discriminate by appearing to be more temperate, less severe and cruel, than the opinions they may actually hold.[20] They were seen to take advantage of a generous, albeit flawed, refugee system; hence, their presence was represented as a threat not just to the image of those who have already arrived as immigrants to Canada and made a positive contribution to society but, more crucially, to those who might wish to come to Canada in the future. The state, on the other hand, was discursively constructed as a kind of "worthy victim" in its own right, a subject whose harm or loss was made ideologically sympathetic to the citizenry on terms that would establish a consensus about the undesirability of illegal migration (as phenomenon) and the undesirability of illegal migrants (as people). An underlying discourse of state victimization was thus constructed in these media in such a way that displaced the migrants' political-economic hardship—that is. as losers of global neo-liberalism—onto the state, in a manner that mobilized Canadians to inhabit the states narrativized subject position as its own (Greenberg & Hier, forthcoming).

The opinions expressed in these mainstream media, whether in the form of an editorial, op-ed article, or guest column, unambiguously represented the viewpoint that the immediate and future costs associated with allowing the Chinese migrants to remain in the country would have an indelibly harmful impact on an already overburdened and overextended state. While the impact of refugees on the state's social welfare and humanitarian-aid programs is a valid and realistic concern that is worthy of public debate, what demands punctuation, and this is precisely where this discourse was incomplete, is that the public must have access to *all* of the correct and proper information if it is to make informed decisions about who is entitled to belong and who is not. The opinion discourses propagated by the mainstream news media has the potential to go a long way in terms of constructing the kind of empathetic and humanitarian community Canada proclaims itself to be.

Acknowledgments

The author wishes to thank Graham Knight, Sean Hier, and two anonymous reviewers for their helpful comments and suggestions.

Notes

1. The poll was unscientific and its findings are clearly dubious, at best. What is so problematic, however, is that the results of the poll were subsequently reproduced in other mainstream news media in the form of a "hard" news item distributed by Canadian Press. See "B.C. Residents Tell Newspaper . . ." (1999) and "Send Chinese Illegals Packing . . ." (1999).

2. There are some exceptions to this general pattern of less sustained attention. See Fowler (1991) and van Dijk (1998) for useful discussions of the rhetorical and stylistic character of editorials. The Canadian literature consists primarily of Hackett (1991), the collection of papers in Grenier (1992), and, most recently, Bright, Coburn, Faye, Gafijczuk, Hollander, Jung, & Symbros (1999). Not all of these studies, however, have sufficiently developed a theoretical model for the analysis of opinion discourse.

3. Using a different theoretical tradition, the notion of the "Other" may be recast using Simmel's (1950) concept of "the stranger." Alternative interpretations of this study might fruitfully draw on such a concept by analyzing the position of the migrant (as abjectly poor Chinese newcomer; *contra* the wealthy or middle-class Chinese migrant Canada is used to and comfortable with) as "a person fixed within a particular group (e.g. Chinese race), but whose position in the group is determined, essentially, by the fact that he *[sic]* has not belonged to it from the beginning . . . he *[sic]* imports qualities into it, which do not and cannot stem from the group itself, (p. 402). That many within the Chinese-Canadian community rejected the migrants, identifying and labelling them as criminals ("not like us"), that is, as the "Other" within, is instructive here. On the opinions of the Chinese-Canadian community, see Chong (1999). The Chinese Consolidated Benevolent Association of Victoria was also "against" the migrants' arrivals. According to Thomas Ho of the Chinese-Canadian Friendship Association, the migrants' arrivals "makes me feel embarrassed" (see McCulloch, 1999).

4. Having suggested that not all columnist opinions will be consistent with the viewpoint of the newspaper, Rick Salutin, media critic for *The Globe and Mail,* is a good example of a columnist paid by the newspaper to provide commentary that generally deviates from the "official" view of the newspaper.

5. For Saint-Jean (1998), the question of media professionalism is also one which acknowledges such "journalistic ethics" as "notions of duty, of individual conscience, and of social morality . . . constrained by prevailing legal frameworks" (p. 37). The implication of a normatively grounded approach to newsmaking is the same.

6. Opinion discourses also play an important symbolic function. The various headings ("editorial," "opinion," "comment," "we say," etc.) partition off the "opinion" component of the paper, implicitly supporting the claim that the other sections are, by contrast, a purely "factual report" of reality (Fowler, 1991, p. 208).

7. In this sense, therefore, the ideological effect of opinion discourse and patterns of "hard" news should be seen as complementary. Where opinion discourses are felt to be of a more persuasive (and effective) character than "hard" news is in news coverage of local phenomenon, when people turn to the regional/local paper for orientation. Although the migrants' arrivals were portrayed as events of "national importance" their impact—both symbolically and materially—was principally felt locally. The author acknowledges Reviewer A for supplying this observation.

8. Although an inter-coder reliability test was not formally conducted, the author wishes to acknowledge Sean Hier for reading and providing commentary on the data. Moreover, in order to ensure that the themes identified are not merely arbitrary or intuitive, I have used as a sensitizing framework the thematic findings in Greenberg & Hier's (forthcoming) examination of patterns of "hard" news coverage of these events, where an inter-coder reliability test was done.

9. Average circulation figures, as provided by each newspaper's advertising department in September 2000, are as follows: *The National Post*—360,000 (Mon.–Fri.) and 428,000 (Sat.); *The Vancouver Sun*—202,000 (Mon.-Sat.); *Times-Colonist*—84,000 (Daily); *The Toronto Star*—500,000 (Daily); *The Toronto Sun*—244,000 (Mon.–Fri.), 192,000 (Sat.) and 413,500 (Sun.). A more reliable measure of receptivity would be the audience-reach statistic; however, each newspaper uses a different methodology which makes cross-comparison problematic.

10. In the period since these events, Hollinger liquidated 200 of its newspapers, including its controlling shares in the Vancouver and Victoria newspapers, as well as half of its shares in *The National Post,* to the Can-West media conglomerate.

11. The term "problematization" derives from Foucault's (1984) work on modern forms of government. It refers to the development of a domain of thoughts that seem to pose problems for politics. For example, it suggests that in regard to the phenomenon of "illegal" migration or the performance of government vis-à-vis illegal migration, there is not any "politics" that provides a definitive or just solution. Rather, in addressing social or political problems of any kind, there are reasons for questioning the politics behind it. Hence, "problematization of government" operates as a fluid category that accommodates numerous ways of posing questions about and interrogating the role of government (i.e., as institution, as practice).

12. When *The Vancouver Sun* did address the theme of race relations, it tended to frame the issue in terms of the kinds of negative effects that these events would have on the Asian community in British Columbia. This approach was also detected in the coverage of this theme in *The National Post.* The opinion discourses in both newspapers frequently referred to prominent members of Victoria and Vancouver's Chinese community as criticizing the migrants for giving honest, hard-working Asian migrants a "bad name."

13. This point is anecdotal only and stems from discussion with NGO members and anti-racist activists working in the Victoria area.

14. The following are figures for the numbers of guest columns published by individuals working or living in the refugee or new immigrant communities: *Times-Colonist* (n = 4); *The Vancouver Sun* (n = 2); *The National Post* (n = 0)*; The Toronto Star* (n = 0); *The Toronto Sun* (n = 0).

15. Whereas *The Toronto Star* used journalists and other individuals employed by the newspaper to articulate this concern about systemic racism, the *Times-Colonist's* expressions were articulated by NGOs and others with a stake in the country's immigration industry. The difference is that while the *Times-Colonist's* op-ed and guest columnists' opinions can be attributed to, and critiqued for, a level of self-interestedness, *The Toronto Star,* on the other hand, would likely be seen to be still more objective and distanced from the emotional aspects of the situation.

16. This suggests how opinion discourse within the same publication may vary significantly over time on the same theme depending, among other variables, on the author.

17. *Times-Colonist* (Victoria): "How we handle these people will determine how many others try to use smugglers to get into this country illegally. If we let them stay, others will surely come" ("Tightening Our Refugee Process," 1999, p. A9). *The National Post:* "To accept these arrivals without questions would send three powerful messages. First, it would condone and reward illegal people smuggling. Second, it would send a message to would-be immigrants that our rules and processes for immigration are meaningless. It would confirm that a quicker and more certain way to live in Canada is to deliberately avoid the legal process and attempt to sneak in. Finally, and, most importantly, it would admit that our borders are unguarded, and that the hospitality of our citizens can be commanded, not earned" (Francis, 1999a, p. A19*). The Vancouver Sun:* "If Canada gives safe haven to the 122 people aboard a decrepit ship, it will give the green light to the criminals who traffick in people. Bypassing immigration channels cannot be sanctioned. . . . These people should get food, medical treatment, clean clothing— and a safe passage home" ("Ship's Passengers Must be Sent Home," 1999, p. A10).

18. *The Toronto Star:* "Robillard's successor, Elinor Caplan, will soon see that she is presiding over a largely dysfunctioning [sic] department choking on red tape, inefficiency, low morale and inconsistent application of law. Its reputation is bad, abroad and at home, among foreigners wanting to come to Canada—as visitors or as immigrants, and, more important, among Canadian citizens forced to deal with it" (Siddiqui, 1999a, p. A11). *The Toronto Sun:* "Ottawa has to start helping Toronto cope with the costs of treating immigrants and refugees for serious diseases. . . . Fact is, Ottawa always sets immigration and refugee policy with little regard for the ability of Toronto—where almost half of new arrivals end up—to cope, whether it's in health care, English as a second language programs or the ability to provide jobs" ("Healthy City," 1999, p. 14). *The Toronto Sun:* "Also very worrisome is the health of many of these people who have gone through no formal health examination before they left their homelands. Some have already been found to be carrying dangerous communicable diseases" (Crispo, 1999, p. 15).

19. The point of the CCPA's argument was that economic globalization—through which Canada has become one of the world's most prosperous nations—is a primary structural factor influencing patterns of transnational population flow; therefore, the negative side-effects of globalization (e.g., "illegal" migration) ought to be examined and questioned critically but only within a broader critical examination of the impact of globalization. This opinion, however, was not picked up by any of the other media in any kind of comprehensive way. And although the *Times-Colonist* did allow for the problem of globalization to be addressed, it was raised in a marginal sense and did not achieve any significant expression elsewhere in this newspaper's definition of the situation.

20. To conclude that news coverage in this case was racist or, worse yet, that the Canadian news media is a racist institution (see Henry & Tator, 2000) requires due attention be paid to the debate over the actual pervasiveness of "racism" in Canada (see, for example, Fleras & Elliott, 1992; Levitt, 1997; Guppy & Davies, 1998; Henry, Tator, Mattis, & Rees, 2000; Hier, 2000; Reitz & Breton, 1994; Satzewich, 1991, 1998). This represents an important discussion in its own right and goes beyond the scope of this paper. Moreover, the sociological meaning of the term "racism" is itself hotly contested between those who treat racism as a "social fact" (e.g., Banton, 1967; Rex, 1970) and those who treat it primarily as an ideological construct (Hall, Critcher, Jefferson, Clarke, & Roberts, 1978; Miles 1989). My point is that it is reasonable to draw conclusions about the social construction of the "other" from this analysis. To draw conclusions about the propagation of racist ideology is an entirely different matter and *should* be the focus of another paper.

References

B.C. residents tell newspaper poll they want 250 migrants returned to China. (1999, August 16). *The National Post*, p. A6.

Banton, M. (1967). *Race relations*. London: Tavistock.

Beiser, M. (1999). *Strangers at the gate: The 'boat peoples' first ten years*. Toronto: University of Toronto Press.

Bright, R., Coburn, E., Faye, J., Gafijczuk, D., Hollander, K., Jung, J., & Symbros, H. (1999). Mainstream and marginal newspaper coverage of the 1995 Quebec referendum: An inquiry into the functioning of the Canadian public sphere. *Canadian Review of Sociology and Anthropology, 36(3)*, 313–330.

Caplan sends the right message. (1999, August 13). *The Toronto Star*, p. A22.

Carroll, W., & Ratner, R. (1996). Master frames and counter-hegemony: Political sensibilities in contemporary social movements. *Canadian Review of Sociology and Anthropology, 33(4)*, 407–436.

Chibnall, S. (1977). *Law-and-order news*. London: Tavistock.

Chong, G. (1999, September 4). Refugee loophole must be plugged. *The Toronto Sun*, p. 15.

Clarkson, B. (2000, Spring). 600 is too many. *Ryerson Review of Journalism,* pp. 6–10.

Cohen, S. (1972). *Folk devils and moral panics.* London: MacGibbon & Kee.

Crispo, J. (1999, September 25). What to do with illegal immigrants. *The Toronto Sun,* p. 15.

Danard, S. (1999, September 3). Reform sees AIDS risk. *Times-Colonist* (Victoria), pp. A1, A3.

Edelman, M. (1977). *Political language: Words that succeed and policies that fail.* New York: Academic Press.

Edelman, M. (1988). *Constructing the political spectacle.* Chicago: University of Chicago Press.

Entman, R. M. (1993). Framing: Toward a clarification of a fractured paradigm. *Journal of Communication, 43(A),* 51–58.

Ericson, R., Baranek, P., & Chan, J. (1987). *Visualizing deviance: A study of news organization.* Toronto: University of Toronto Press.

Fairclough, N. (1998). Political discourse in the media. In A. Bell & P. Garrett (Eds.), *Approaches to media discourse* (pp. 142–162). Oxford: Blackwell.

Far-right stokes refugee fears. (1999, September 1). *Times-Colonist* (Victoria), p. A14.

Fleras, A., & Elliott, J. (1992). *Multiculturalism in Canada: The challenge of diversity.* Scarborough, ON: Nelson.

Foucault, M. (1984). Polemics, politics, and problemizations: An interview with Michel Foucault In P. Rabinow (Ed.), *The Foucault reader* (pp. 381–390). New York: Pantheon.

Fowler, R. (1991). *Language in the news: Discourse and ideology in the press.* London: Routledge.

Francis, D. (1999a, July 22). Gatecrashers are not welcome. *The National Post,* p. A19.

Francis, D. (1999b, August 13). Refugee process in this country needs makeover. Boat incidents an example of Ottawa's mismanagement. *The National Post,* p. A8.

Gamson, W A., & Modigliani, A. (1989). Media discourse and public opinion on nuclear power: A constructionist approach. *American Journal of Sociology, 95(1),* 1–37.

Gitlin, T. (1980). *The whole world is watching.* Berkeley: University of California Press.

Glasgow University Media Group. (1976). *Bad news.* London: Routledge & Kegan Paul.

Goffman, E. (1974). *Frame analysis: An essay in the organization of experience.* New York: Harper and Row.

Goldman, R., & Rajagopal, A. (1991). *Mapping hegemony: Television news coverage of industrial conflict.* Norwood, NJ: Ablex.

Gramsci, A. (1971). *Selections from the prison notebooks.* (Q. Hoare & G. Smith, Trans.). New York: International Publishers.

Greenberg, J., & Hier, S. (forthcoming). Crisis, mobilization and collective problematization: Illegal migrants and the Canadian news media. *Journalism Studies.*

Grenier, M. (Ed.). (1992). *Critical studies of Canadian mass media.* Toronto: Butterworths.

Grimmer, T. (1999, September 7). Send them right back. *The National Post,* p. A14.

Guppy, N., & Davies, S. (1998). Race and Canadian education. In V. Satzewich (Ed.), *Racism and social inequality in Canada: Controversies, concepts and strategies of resistance* (pp. 131–156). Toronto: Thompson Educational Publishing.

Hackett, R. (1991). *News and dissent: The press and the politics of peace in Canada.* Norwood, NJ: Ablex.

Hall, S. (1973). A world at one with itself. In S. Cohen & J. Young (Eds.), *The manufacture of news: Social problems, deviance and the mass media* (pp. 85–94). London: Constable.

Hall, S. (1977). Culture, the media and the 'ideological effect.' In J. Curran, M. Gurevitch, & J. Woollacott (Eds.), *Mass communication and society* (pp. 315–348). London: Edward Arnold.

Hall, S., Critcher, C., Jefferson, T., Clarke, J., & Roberts, B. (1978). *Policing the. crisis: Mugging, the state and law and order.* London: MacMillan.

Hartley, J. (1982). *Understanding news* London: Methuen.

Hay, C. (1996). Narrating crisis: The discursive construction of the 'winter of discontent *Sociology, 30(2),* 253–277.

Healthy city. (1999, September 2). *The Toronto Sun,* p. 14.

Henry, F., & Tator, C. (2000). *Racist discourse in Canada's English print media.* Toronto: Canadian Race Relations Foundation.

Henry, F., Tator, C., Mattis, W., & Rees, T. (2000). *The colour of democracy* (2nd ed.). Toronto: Harcourt Brace.

Hier, F. (2000). The contemporary structure of Canadian racial supremacism: Networks, strategies and new technologies. *Canadian Journal of Sociology, 25*(4), 1–24.

Hier, S., & Greenberg, J. (2000). *News discourse and the problematization of Chinese migration to Canada.* Unpublished manuscript. Hamilton, ON: McMaster University, Department of Sociology.

Humanitarian nation faces moral questions. (1999, July 29). *The Vancouver Sun,* p. A14.

Knight, G. (1989). Reality effects: Tabloid television news. *Queen's Quarterly, 96*(1), 94–108.

Knight, G. (1998, Spring). Hegemony, the press and business discourse: News coverage of strike-breaker reform in Quebec and Ontario. *Studies in Political Economy, 55,* 93–125.

Knight, G. (forthcoming). Prospective news: Press pre-framing of the 1996 Ontario public service strike. *Journalism Studies.*

Levant, E. (1999, September 15). To the Liberals go the immigration spoils. *The National Post,* p. A18.

Levitt, C. (1997, September-October). The morality of race in Canada. *Society,* pp. 40–47.

Li, P. (1994). Unneighbourly houses or unwelcome Chinese: The social construction of race in the battle over 'monster homes' in Vancouver, Canada. *International Journal of Comparative Race and Ethnic Studies, 1*(1), 14–33.

Li, P. (1998). *The Chinese in Canada.* Toronto: Oxford University Press.

Li, P., & Bolaria, S. (1988). *Racial oppression in Canada* (2nd ed.). Toronto: Garamond Press.

McCulloch, S. (1999, August 7). Victoria Chinese want migrants out. *Times-Colonist* (Victoria), pp. A1, A2.

Miles, R. (1989). *Racism.* London: Routledge.

No refuge. (1999, September 23). *The Toronto Sum,* p. 14.

Pan, Z., & Kosicki, G. M. (1993). Framing analysis: An approach to news discourse. *Political Communication, 10*(1), 55–73.

Reitz, J., & Breton, R. (1994). *The illusion of difference.* Toronto: CD Howell Institute.

Rex, J. (1970). *Race relations in sociological theory.* London: Weidenfeld & Nicolson.

Ricoeur, P. (1984). *Time and narrative* (Vol. 1). Chicago: University of Chicago Press.

Saint-Jean, A. (1998). Journalistic ethics and referendum coverage in Montreal. In G. Robinson, *Constructing the Quebec referendum: French and English media voices* (pp. 37–54). Toronto: University of Toronto Press.

Satzewich, V. (1991). *Racism and the incorporation of foreign labour: Farm labour migration to Canada since 1945.* New York: Routledge.

Satzewich, V. (1998). Race, racism and racialization. In V. Satzewich (Ed.), *Racism and social inequality in Canada* (pp. 25–45). Toronto: Thompson.

Save our system. (1999, August 14). *The Toronto Sun,* p. 14.

Send Chinese illegals packing: B.C. poll. (1999, August 16). *The Toronto Sun,* p. 21,

Ship's passengers must be sent home. (1999, July 23). *The Vancouver Sun,* p. A10.

Siddiqui, H. (1999a, August 8). Close eye is needed at immigration. *The Toronto Star,* p. A11.

Siddiqui, H. (1999b, August 15). Immigration needs to put house in order. *The Toronto Star,* p. A13.

Simmel, G. (1950). *The sociology of Georg Simmel.* (K. Wolff, Trans. & Ed.). New York: Free Press.

Steyn, M. (1999, September 23). We're in the same boat now. *The National Post,* p. A18.

t'Hart, P. (1993). Symbols, rituals and power: The lost dimensions of crisis management. *Journal of Contingencies and Crisis Management, 1*(1), 36–50.

Tightening our refugee process. (1999, July 30). *Times-Colonist* (Victoria), p. A9.

Trew, T. (1979). Theory and ideology at work. In R. Fowler, B. Hodge, G. Kress, & T. Trew (Eds.), *Language and control* (pp. 94–116). London: Routledge.

van Dijk, T. (1988). *Racism and the press.* London: Routledge.

van Dijk, T. (1996). *Opinions and ideologies in editorials.* Paper presented to 4th International Symposium of Critical Discourse Analysis, Language, Social Life and Critical Thought, Athens, 1995. 2nd draft.

van Dijk, T. (1998). Opinions and ideologies in the press. In A. Bell & P. Garrett (Eds.), *Approaches to media discourse* (pp. 21–63). Oxford: Blackwell.

A Hazardous Profession: War, Journalists, and Psychopathology

Anthony Feinstein, John Owen, and Nancy Blair

Objective: *War journalists often confront situations of extreme danger in their work. Despite this, information on their psychological well-being is lacking.*

Method: *The authors used self-report questionnaires to assess 140 war journalists, who recorded symptoms of posttraumatic stress disorder (PTSD) (with the Impact of Event Scale—Revised), depression (with the Beck Depression Inventory-II), and psychological distress (with the 28-item General Health Questionnaire). To control for stresses generic to all journalism, the authors used the same instruments to assess 107 journalists who had never covered war. A second phase of the study involved interviews with one in five journalists from both groups, using the Structured Clinical Interview for Axis I DSM-IV Disorders.*

Results: *The rates of response to the self-report questionnaires were approximately 80% for both groups. There were no demographic differences between groups. Both male and female war journalists had significantly higher weekly alcohol consumption. The war journalists had higher scores on the Impact of Event Scale and the Beck Depression Inventory. Their lifetime prevalence of PTSD was 28.6%, and the rates were 21.4% for major depression and 14.3% for substance abuse. War journalists were not, however, more likely to receive treatment for these disorders.*

Conclusions: *War journalists have significantly more psychiatric difficulties than journalists who do not report on war. In particular, the lifetime prevalence of PTSD is similar to rates reported for combat veterans, while the rate of major depression exceeds that of the general population. These results, which need replicating, should alert news organizations that significant psychological distress may occur in many war journalists and often goes untreated.*

Journalism can be a hazardous profession. During 2001 alone, 100 journalists were killed and many hundreds imprisoned and maltreated (1). While the majority were local journalists, targeted for exposing corruption or expressing political dissent, the names of foreign war correspondents feature prominently among those killed or detained. It should be self-evident that war is dangerous and that those who report on it run the risk of becoming casualties themselves, a point poignantly made by a collection of photographs of the Vietnam war assembled from the work of photographers killed in the conflict (2). What is new, however, is a perception in the profession that the number of war journalists killed may be on the increase (3). The recent ambush and murder in Sierra Leone of two of the most respected war journalists shocked the industry and demonstrated that experience, knowledge, and common sense are not guarantees of survival.

It is therefore notable that despite the risks inherent in reporting war, we could find no research on the psychological health of war reporters. In the absence of empirical data, eloquent anecdotal evidence remains the only source offering clues as to the mental well-being of war journalists. Ranging from Robert Capa's memoir of World War II (4), through Michael Herr's account of Vietnam (5), to Anthony Loyd's self-revelatory telling of the Balkans tragedy (6), war journalists' accounts have spelled out not only the horrors of conflict, but also the journalists' reactions to the considerable dangers they confront in getting news to the public.

The lack of research in this area contrasts with a burgeoning trauma literature on the emotional effects of combat on soldiers (7, 8) and civilians (9, 10). The psychological consequences of being subjected to life-threatening events include posttraumatic stress disorder (PTSD), major depression, substance abuse, and dissociative disorder, four of the most common and disabling conditions. Similar responses have been documented after both man-made (11, 12) and natural (13, 14) disasters. What all these reports have in common is the conclusion that individuals will develop an array of psychopathology in response to situations of great personal danger.

Given the dearth of data in relation to war journalists, coupled with concerns that reporting war may be becoming increasingly dangerous, we investigated the extent and nature of psychopathology among those who bring us the news from the world's conflict zones.

Method

We approached six major news organizations—CNN, BBC, Reuters, CBC, Associated Press, ITN (Independent Television News)—and an organization representing freelance journalists (the Rory Peck Trust) and explained the purposes of the study. All of the organizations agreed to participate and provided 170 names, together with work and e-mail addresses. Only journalists fluent in English and currently covering war were assessed.

First Phase

The first phase of the study involved asking the journalists to complete a series of self-report questionnaires. The itinerant nature of war journalism, the far-flung geographic locations involved, and the fact that postal services frequently stop during periods of conflict made contacting the journalists problematic. To overcome this difficulty, we developed an interactive web site. Each journalist was assigned an individual, confidential identification number that had to be entered to access the web site. The contents of the paper and Internet versions were identical and covered 1) basic demographic data, 2) details of alcohol and illicit drug use, and 3) assessment of PTSD, depression, psychological distress, and personality traits by four self-report questionnaires.

The basic demographic data included the number of years the respondent had worked as a war journalist, the list of wars covered, and past psychiatric history. Attempts at tallying all traumatic events were abandoned given the impracticality of the task. The average duration of time spent in zones of conflict by the war journalists (approximately 15 years) meant that the hazardous events experienced were too numerous to accurately recall. For example, the one war that attracted the greatest number of war journalists was the Bosnian conflict, which lasted many years. Journalists took to living in cities under siege, such as Sarajevo, where their attempts at reporting or filming the news often exposed them daily to life-threatening situations.

A unit of alcohol was defined as a regular-size bottle of beer, a glass of wine, or a shot of spirits. Fourteen units of alcohol per week for men and 9 units for women were considered the upper limits of acceptable weekly intake (15).

The Impact of Event Scale—Revised (16) contains 22 questions that closely follow the DSM-IV criteria for PTSD. Thus, the questionnaire contains three subscales for intrusive (reexperiencing), avoidance, and hyperarousal phenomena. We followed the rating scale instructions by asking subjects to indicate symptoms that occurred during the past 7 days only and were related to traumatic, dangerous, or disturbing life experiences. Given the many wars covered by the group, we did not specify any particular conflict or event but allowed the journalists to chose single, multiple, or no events, as they deemed suitable. We did, however, ask the journalists to specify what events had been most troubling to them. For all the war journalists, the events chosen related to their war exposure.

The Beck Depression Inventory-II (17). which contains 21 mood-related questions, was used to assess depression. It provides a choice of four responses per question and is scored in a Likert fashion (the possible scores are 0, 1, 2, 3).

The 28-item General Health Questionnaire (18) contains four subscales, each with seven questions, describing symptoms of somatic complaints, anxiety, social dysfunction, and depression, respectively. A choice of four responses is provided for each question. The subscale scores are summed to give an overall index of psychological distress. A simple Likert scoring method (possible scores of 0, 1, 2, 3) was used as this is preferred for detecting between-group differences in subscale scores.

Second Phase

The second phase of the study involved direct interviews. The difficulties in contacting the group were magnified when it came to direct interviews, and because of time and cost restraints, it was not possible to interview the entire study group. Therefore, a random sample of 20% of the responding journalists were approached for interview. None refused. The interviews took place in New York, London, Paris, Madrid, Barcelona, and Johannesburg. The 28 journalists were interviewed with the Structured Clinical Interview for Axis I DSM-IV Disorders (SCID) (19), and the prevalences of PTSD, mood disorders, and substance use disorders (lifetime, current, and before war exposure) were ascertained. The interviewer was blind to the results of the self-report questionnaires.

Comparison Group

Irrespective of setting, there are stressors generic to journalism (e.g., deadlines, "scooping" the competition). To control for these in symptom expression, we assessed a comparison group of non-war journalists. A group of 107 domestic journalists who did not report on war were approached to undergo the same assessment procedure used with the war journalists. While some in this group also occasionally reported on distressing events (e.g., plane crashes), care was taken to exclude those who had traveled to report on war. Similarly, a random sample of 19 of these journalists (18%) were selected for interview with the SCID. None refused. The interviews were conducted face-to-face or by telephone.

Statistical Analysis

We compared the two groups by using t tests and chi-square analyses. All two-by-two chi-square analyses were two-sided and Yates corrected. If any one cell in a two-by-two analysis had a count of less than 5, a two-sided Fisher's exact test was used. With respect to between-group t test analyses, the Levene test for equality of variance was applied, and where appropriate, the unequal-variance t values and significance levels were reported. All t tests were two-tailed. To control for multiple comparisons, we applied a Bonferroni correction (0.05/22, setting the significance level at 0.002). Transmitting data from a web site relied on the variable quality of the Internet connection. In a few cases, this resulted in lost data. Since the number of subjects varied slightly between tests, the results are presented with the relevant numbers of subjects.

Consent

Both the paper and Internet versions of the study received ethical approval. After complete description of the study to the subjects, written informed consent was obtained. On the web site, subjects gave consent by clicking on the "I agree" box after reading the descriptive preamble.

Results

Self-Report Questionnaires

One journalist was murdered before the questionnaire reached him, thereby reducing the number of subjects to 169. Of these, 82.8% (N = 140) gave their consent. The response rate in the comparison group was similar, i.e., 79.9% (107 of 134). The war group had spent, on average, 15 years reporting on wars; the list of conflicts covered included every major conflagration during this period, i.e., Bosnia, Rwanda, Chechnya, the Gulf war and Middle East, Congo, Sierra Leone, Indonesia, Somalia, Ethiopia, Afghanistan, and others. The two groups of journalists were well matched with respect to age, gender, and years of work as a journalist (Table 1). An analysis of marital status revealed similar proportions of divorced journalists in the two groups but more unmarried journalists in the war group (Table 1). A reanalysis of marital status with divorced journalists excluded did not reveal a significant group difference ($x^2 = 9.0$, df = 1, p = 0.003) after Bonferroni correction.

When it came to psychiatric comparisons, the war group performed significantly worse on a number of variables (Table 2). The mean weekly alcohol consumption levels, 14.7 units for men and 10.8 units for women, were two and

Table 1 Demographic characteristics of war journalists and comparison
journalists reporting on other subjects

Characteristic	War journalists (N = 140)		Comparison journalists (N = 107)		Analysis		
	Mean	SD	Mean	SD	t	df	p
Age (years)	39.2	6.3	39.0	8.2	0.2	192.5	0.84
Length of career as a journalist (years)	15.6	6.8	15.5	8.5	0.1	186.2	0.94
	N	%	N	%	Yates-Corrected x^2(two-sided)	df	p
Gender					1.9	1	0.18
Male	110	78.6	76	71.0			
Female	30	21.4	31	29.0			
Marital status					9.2	2	0.01
Single	61	43.6	28	26.2			
Married	64	45.7	69	64.5			
Divorced	15	10.7	10	9.3			

Table 2 Psychiatric measures for war journalists and comparison journalists reporting on other subjects

Measure	War journalists (N = 140)				Comparison journalists (N = 107)				Analysis			
	N	%	Mean	SD	N	%	Mean	SD	t	df	Fisher's exact test, two-sided (p) / p	95% CI of difference
Cannabis use	34	24.3			20	18.7					0.29	
Use of other substances[a]	9	6.4			2	1.9					0.12	
Weekly units of alcohol[b]												
Men			14.7	12.3			7.6	7.1	5.0	178.9	0.0001	4.3 to 10.1
Women			10.8	9.4			3.9	3.7	3.8	37.7	0.001	3.2 to 10.7
Scores on impact of Event Scale—Revised[c]												
Intrusion			9.2	7.1			4.3	4.4	6.5	226.6	0.0001	3.4 to 6.4
Avoidance			6.7	6.2			3.1	4.0	5.4	229.1	0.0001	2.3 to 4.9
Arousal			4.7	4.9			2.0	2.8	5.2	215.1	0.0001	1.6 to 3.6
Total			20.2	16.0			9.1	9.5	6.5	210.1	0.0001	7.7 to 14.4
Score on Beck Depression Inventory-II[d]			10.1	7.8			6.4	6.1	4.1	235.8	0.0001	1.9 to 5.4
Scores on General Health Questionnaire[e]												
Somatic			4.4	3.4			4.2	2.9	0.6	243	0.54	-0.6 to 1.1
Anxiety			5.9	4.0			4.7	3.5	2.3	243	0.02	0.2 to 2.1
Social dysfunction			7.3	3.0			6.7	2.2	1.9	243.5	0.05	-0.0 to 1.3
Depression			2.2	3.4			1.0	2.3	3.4	239.5	0.001	0.5 to 1.9
Total			19.8	10.6			16.6	7.8	2.7	243.6	0.008	0.9 to 5.5

[a] Amphetamines, cocaine, barbiturates, heroin.

[b] A unit of alcohol was defined as a regular-size bottle of beer, a glass of wine, or a shot of spirits. Fourteen units of alcohol per week for men and 9 units for women were considered the upper limits of acceptable weekly intake (15).

[c] Number of war journalists: intrusion, N = 135; avoidance, N = 134; arousal, N = 133; total N = 127.

[d] For war journalists, N = 132.

[e] Number of war journalists: somatic, N = 138; anxiety, N = 138; social dysfunction, N = 139; depression, N = 139; total, N = 138.

401

three times those of the nonwar group, respectively. With 14 units of alcohol per week considered the upper limit of acceptable drinking for men (15), 45 war journalists as opposed to 13 nonwar journalists were drinking excessively ($X^2 = 11.9$, df = 1, p = 0.001). The comparable numbers of women, at a weekly limit of 9 units, were 15 and two, respectively (p=0.0001, Fisher's exact test, two-sided). There were no differences between groups in use of cannabis or hard drugs.

Psychometric comparisons based on the three rating scales are also displayed in Table 2. Regarding symptoms of PTSD, the war journalists endorsed more symptoms of intrusive thoughts and images of trauma events (all war related in the case of war journalists) while displaying greater avoidance and hyperarousal phenomena. The war journalists had significantly higher scores on the Beck Depression Inventory, and this difference was confirmed by the scores on the depression subscale of the General Health Questionnaire (Table 2).

The war journalists were not significantly more likely to have received psychiatric help; 24.6% (34 of 138) had received psychotropic medication, psychotherapy, or a combination of the two treatments, compared with 16.2% (17 of 105) of the comparison journalists ($X^2 = 2.6$, df = 1, p = 0.11).

Subject Interviews

Every fifth journalist from the war (N=28) and nonwar (N=19) groups was interviewed. For the war group, lifetime, current, and prewar diagnoses of PTSD were made for eight (28.6%), three (10.7%), and one (3.6%) subject, respectively. For major depression the numbers were six (21.4%), two (7.1%), and one (3.6%), respectively. For substance abuse the numbers were four (14.3%), two (7.1%), and one (3.6%), respectively. No journalist in the comparison group had had PTSD, while one (5.3%) had a lifetime diagnosis of major depression and one (5.3%) a lifetime diagnosis of substance abuse; in both cases the disorders had begun before the individuals began working as journalists.

Discussion

In this study of 140 war journalists, drawn from the world's major news organizations, we found higher rates of psychopathology than in a demographically matched comparison group of 107 nonwar journalists. Specifically, the war journalists drank more heavily and showed higher rates of PTSD and major depression. They were not more likely to receive treatment for these conditions. Before discussing these results in greater detail, we would like to address the composition of the study group.

Experienced war journalists are relatively few in number. The 170 names forwarded by organizations such as the BBC and CNN represent a sizable segment of those who travel to areas of conflict. Our response rate of greater than 80% therefore suggests our subjects are representative of war journalists in general.

The fact they have been reporting wars for, on average, 15 years highlights not only their experience but also our success in capturing the central core of bona fide war journalists, as opposed to those who cover a conflict or two before moving on to less hazardous news work. It is also important to note that while war journalists are never openly forced into covering a particular conflict by their news bosses, it is generally recognized that a pattern of refusing dangerous assignments may have adverse career consequences. Thus, when starting out in their career there is a tendency to accept every war story. Only as established war journalists can they be more selective in choosing when and where they are sent.

A significant number of war correspondents, particularly women, drink excessively, with a weekly alcohol consumption well above that of their nonwar colleagues. However, heavy drinking did not necessarily translate into a diagnosis of alcohol abuse or dependence as defined by DSM-IV. The lifetime prevalence of alcohol abuse did not differ from that in the general population (20). While heavy drinking may not have rendered the majority dysfunctional with respect to their work, it does leave the individual at risk for a host of long-term medical problems (15).

Results from all self-report measures of PTSD and depression revealed higher scores in the war group. While useful as screening instruments, self-report questionnaires cannot by themselves generate psychiatric diagnoses. Furthermore, the Impact of Event Scale—Revised, Beck Depression Inventory-II, and General Health Questionnaire provided indices of current symptoms only. These two limitations do not, however, apply to a structured clinical interview, such as the SCID. The fact that only one in five war journalists could be interviewed was due solely to logistical difficulties. The 28 journalists selected at random were scattered over three continents during the course of the study, and it often took months to finally connect and complete the process. Nevertheless, the clinical interviews corroborated the finding of significant psychopathology in approximately one-quarter of the group.

Of the 28 war journalists interviewed, all had been shot at numerous times, three had been wounded (of whom one had been shot on four separate occasions), three had had close colleagues who were killed while they were working together on assignments, two had been subject to mock executions, two had had bounties placed on their heads, one had survived a plane crash (the pilots were killed) only to be subsequently robbed by soldiers who looted the wreckage, and two had had close colleagues who committed suicide. Given these descriptive details, higher scores on the Impact of Event Scale, an index of PTSD, were not unexpected in the war group. While symptoms from all three subscales were frequently endorsed, intrusive and hyperarousal symptoms, i.e., unwanted recollections of specific events accompanied by hypervigilance and autonomic arousal, were more common than avoidance phenomena. Of note was the fact that the avoidance item "I stayed away from reminders of the trauma" was endorsed least often. Rather, the avoidance pattern incorporated such maladaptive strategies as

"My feelings about it were kind of numb" and "I felt as if it hadn't happened." Thus, despite deeply troubling recollections of events witnessed, the war journalists returned constantly to the scenes of old or new traumas, a pattern of behavior sustained over many years. This could contribute to their high lifetime prevalence of PTSD, i.e., 28.6%. In addition, the fact that PTSD, in all but one case, developed after the journalists began working in war zones suggests a strong connection between the dangers confronted in war and the development of psychopathology.

It is noteworthy that the lifetime prevalence of PTSD in war journalists exceeds the 7%–13% reported for traumatized police officers (21, 22) but is equivalent to (23) or less than (24) figures for combat veterans, depending on the source cited. Such comparisons, while placing the result within a comparative frame of reference, are nevertheless misleading. Soldiers and policemen receive extensive training to deal with violence. War journalists do not. In recognition of this deficiency, innovative trauma education programs for journalists in training have begun to be offered by some universities (25).

The high PTSD figures are matched by the rates for major depression. Once again, the figures for the war group are substantially higher than those for the comparison group. With the structured interview, the lifetime prevalence of major depression in the war group was 21.4%, which exceeds the 17.1% rate reported for the general population in the United States (20). If one removes the one subject whose major depression predated work in war zones, the prevalence drops to 14.3%. However, it is important to note that the U.S. data are made up of equal numbers of male and female subjects, and the latter have a lifetime prevalence of 21.3%, almost double the approximately 12% in males. In our predominantly male study group, even after we controlled for the cases predating war exposure, the result still translates into a lifetime prevalence of major depression above that in the U.S. National Comorbidity Study (20). The high comorbidity of major depression and PTSD in this study is in keeping with figures from trauma studies of other population groups (26, 27).

With the stringent Bonferroni correction factor applied to the data, the results from the 28-item General Health Questionnaire essentially confirmed the preceding finding with respect to depression. This instrument was used previously as an index of psychological distress in trauma settings (28, 29). The higher total scores in the war journalists were driven mostly by elevated depression scores and, to a lesser extent, symptoms of anxiety and social dysfunction.

The interviews with 20% of the group revealed that war journalists are profoundly affected by their symptoms of PTSD. While we had no clear way of judging the effects of the syndrome on the quality of their work, every war journalist with PTSD spoke of considerable social difficulties, such as an inability to adjust to life back in a civil society, a reluctance to mix with friends, troubled relationships, the use of alcohol as a hypnotic, and embarrassing startle responses that led to social avoidance. With such difficulties, they fulfilled the DSM-IV criterion that specifies that the symptoms must cause "significant distress or impairment in social, occupational or other important areas of functioning."

Perhaps our most telling observation was that despite greater levels of psychopathology than in the comparison group, the war journalists were not more likely to have received help, be it pharmacotherapy or psychotherapy. The clear implication is that many war journalists are not receiving treatment for their PTSD, depression, and alcohol abuse. The reasons for this are many and varied and not the subject of the present study. However, this observation together with the fact that we have found no previous research on this topic speak to a culture of silence on the part of the news bosses and the journalists themselves.

This last point touches on an intriguing question: What motivates war journalists to return to situations of extreme peril, particularly when almost one in four have suffered from PTSD at some point in their careers? While we plan to report this separately, a few comments are called for here. The first salient observation is that, until recently, discussing psychological distress within the profession was discouraged. A prevalent view was that to be a war journalist you had to have the "right stuff." An admission of emotional distress in a macho world was feared as a sign of weakness and a career liability. Ambition, coupled with a belief that war reporting enhances a career by giving a high media profile, left journalists reluctant to speak out about their fears and insecurities. Many chose to suffer in silence. The recent death of two celebrated war journalists on assignment in Sierra Leone (mentioned earlier) was, in part, the catalyst for a reappraisal of these views. Another, lesser factor that could have contributed to repeated exposure to trauma despite adverse consequences is the psychological naiveté inherent in some members of the profession. A number of journalists interviewed were deeply unhappy, prey to symptoms of PTSD and depression, but surprisingly unaware of what afflicted them. Thus, while giving articulate voice to subjective distress, a diagnosis such as PTSD was for the most part unknown. Such naiveté is also consonant with a belief that as a profession they can go off to war and emerge psychologically unscathed. This denial may be a necessary, albeit distorted prerequisite allowing war journalists to venture repeatedly into situations of grave physical danger.

We believe that our study is the first to explore the psychological status of war correspondents. As such, the results need replicating, more so as we were able to interview only one in five journalists. While we did not find strong evidence that psychopathology in the war group predated their exposure to war, the limited number of subjects suggests this question may not be definitively answered here. However, our findings that PTSD may affect a quarter of war journalists and that they have a high lifetime prevalence of major depression deserve serious consideration. These disorders adversely affect quality of life (30) and may tend toward chronicity if left untreated (31). The data should therefore come as a wake-up call to the news organizations that all is not necessarily well with the men and women who, at considerable risk, bring us news of the world's conflicts.

Received Aug. 6. 2001; revision received Jan. 30, 2002. accepted April 18, 2002. From the Department of Psychiatry, University of Toronto and Sunnybrook and Women's College Health Sciences Centre: and the Freedom Forum European Centre, London. Address reprint requests to Dr. Feinstein, Department of Psychiatry, University of Toronto and Sunnybrook and Women's College Health Sciences Centre, 2075 Bayview Ave., Toronto, Ont., Canada M4N 3M5; ant.feinstein@utoronto.ca (e-mail).

Supported by grants to Dr. Feinstein from the Freedom Forum and the Guggenheim Foundation.

The authors thank Vin Ray and Jackie Owen (BBC), Chris Cramer (CNN), Stephen Jukes (Reuters), Dave Modrowski (Associated Press Television News), Richard Tait (ITN), Dan Halton, George Hoff and Tony Burman (Canadian Broadcast Corporation), and Tina Carr (Rory Peck Trust).

References

1. Journalists and Media Staff Killed in 2001: An IFJ Report on Media Casualties in the Field of Journalism and Newsgathering. Brussels, International Federation of Journalists, 2001

2. Faas H, Page T: Requiem: By the Photographers Who Died in Vietnam and Indochina. New York, Random House, 1997

3. Corera G: Trends in violence and intimidation against journalists: British Broadcasting Company memo. London, BBC, 2000

4. Capa R: Slightly Out of Focus. New York, Random House (Modern Library), 1999

5. Herr M: Dispatches. New York, Vintage Books, 1991

6. Loyd A: My War Gone By, I Miss It So. New York. Atlantic Monthly Press, 1999

7. Lee KA, Vaillant GE. Torrey WC, Elder GH: A 50-year prospective study of the psychological sequelae of World War 11 combat. Am J Psychiatry 1995; 152:516–522

8. Wolfe J, Erickson DJ, Sharkansky EJ, King DW, King LA: Course and predictors of posttraumatic stress disorder among Gulf War veterans: a prospective analysis. J Consult Clin Psychol 1999; 67:520–528

9. Sack WH, Seeley JR, Clarke GN: Does PTSD transcend cultural barriers? a study from the Khmer Adolescent Refugee Project. J Am Acad Child Adolesc Psychiatry 1997; 36:49–54

10. Michultka D, Blanchard EB, Kalous T: Responses to civilian war experiences: predictors of psychological functioning and coping. J Trauma Stress 1998; 11:571–577

11. Epstein RS, Fullerton CS, Ursano RJ: Posttraumatic stress disorder following an air disaster: a prospective study. Am J Psychiatry 1998; 155:934–938

12. Eriksson NG, Lundin T: Early traumatic stress reactions among Swedish survivors of the Estonia disaster. Br J Psychiatry 1996; 169:713–716

13. Wang X, Gao L, Shinfuku N, Zhang H, Zhao C, Shen Y: Longitudinal study of earthquake-related PTSD in a randomly selected community sample in North China. Am J Psychiatry 2000; 157: 1260–1266

14. Najarian LM, Goenjian AK, Pelcovitz D. Mandel F, Najarian B: Relocation after a disaster: posttraumatic stress disorder in Armenia after the earthquake. J Am Acad Child Adolesc Psychiatry 1996; 35:374–383

15. Bondy S, Ashley MJ, Rehm JT, Walsh G: Low risk drinking guidelines: the scientific evidence. Can J Public Health 1999; 90:272-276

16. Weiss D, Marmar CR: The Impact of Event Scale—Revised, in Assessing Psychological Trauma and PTSD: A Practitioner's Handbook. Edited by Wilson JP. Keane TM. New York, Guilford, 1996, pp 399–411

17. Steer RA, Ball R, Ranieri WF, Beck AT: Dimensions of the Beck Depression Inventory-ll in clinically depressed outpatients. J Clin Psychol 1999; 55:117–128

18. Goldberg DP, Hillier VF: A scaled version of the General Health Questionnaire. Psychol Med 1979; 9:139–145

19. First MB, Spitzer RL, Gibbon M, Williams JBW: Structured Clinical Interview for DSM-IV Axis I Disorders, Patient Edition (SCID-P), version 2. New York, New York State Psychiatric Institute. Biometrics Research, 1994

20. Kessler RC, McGonagle KA, Zhao S, Nelson CB, Hughes M, Eshleman S, Wittchen H-U, Kendler KS: Lifetime and 12-month prevalence of DSM-III-R psychiatric disorders in the United States, results from the National Comorbidity Survey. Arch Gen Psychiatry 1994; 51:8-19

21. Carlier IV, Lamberts RD, Gersons BP: Risk factors for posttraumatic stress symptomatology in police officers: a prospective analysis. J Nerv Ment Dis 1997; 185:498–506

22. Robinson HM, Sigman MR, Wilson JP: Duty related stressors and PTSD in suburban police officers. Psychol Rep 1997; 81: 835–845

23. Centers for Disease Control: Health status of Vietnam veterans, psychosocial characteristics. JAMA 1988; 259:2701–2707

24. Kulka RA, Schlenger WE, Fairbank JA. Hough RL, Jordan BK, Marmar CR, Weiss DS: Trauma and the Vietnam War Generation: Report of Findings From the National Vietnam Veterans Readjustment Study. New York, Brunner/Mazel, 1990

25. Coté W, Simpson R: Covering Violence: A Guide to Ethical Reporting About Victims of Trauma. New York, Columbia University Press, 2000

26. Bleich A, Koslowsky M, Dolev A, Lerer B: Posttraumatic stress disorder and depression: an analysis of comorbidity. Br J Psychiatry 1997; 170:479–482

27. Brady KT: Posttraumatic stress disorder and comorbidity: recognizing the many faces of PTSD. J Clin Psychiatry 1997; 58(suppl 9):12–15

28. McFarlane AC, Papay P: Multiple diagnoses in posttraumatic stress disorder in the victims of a natural disaster. J Nerv Ment Dis 1992; 180:498–504

29. Turner SW, Thompson J, Rosser RM: The Kings Cross fire: psychological reactions. J Trauma Stress 1995; 8:419–427

30. Zatzick DF, Marmar CR, Weiss DS, Browner WS, Metzler TJ, Golding JM, Stewart A, Schlenger WE, Wells KB: Posttraumatic stress disorder and functioning and quality of life outcomes in a nationally representative sample of male Vietnam veterans. Am J Psychiatry 1997; 154:1690–1695

31. Hierhollzer R, Munson J, Peabody C, Rosenberg J: Clinical presentation of PTSD in World War II combat veterans. Hosp Community Psychiatry 1992; 43:816–820

The 'Others' as Commodities

"I Don't Want Them Living Around Here": Ideologies of Race and Neighborhood Decay
Timothy A. Gibson

In a brief but vivid passage in his Prison Notebooks, Italian Marxist Antonio Gramsci makes an intriguing claim. "Everyone," he writes, "is a philosopher" (in Bennett 1981, 205). What Gramsci's famous statement highlights is that despite the fact that some of us are formally designated "doctors" of philosophy, we all must come to grips with our place, time, and position within society. By using whatever resources and discourses we have at hand, we all try to impose some sense of order and coherence on the flow of events we encounter during our everyday lives. It is this process of "sense-making" that highlights the crucial importance of ideology for Marxist scholars. Ideologies are these sense-making resources or, as Stuart Hall writes, the "frameworks of thinking and calculation about the world—the 'ideas' which people use to figure out how the social world works, what their place is in it, and what they ought to do" (1985, 99). There-fore, if Marxist scholars wish to understand the process by which individuals come to understand their society, their place within it, and how they should act within this social position, then a close investigation into the ideological dimen-sions of sense-making is clearly in order.

But before we make the practice of squeezing sense out of experience sound too heroic, it must be said that the process is thoroughly social; we inevitably come to terms with experience as part of a society, a collective, a community. As Gramsci writes, "we are all conformists of some conformism or other, always man-in-the-mass or collective man." The crucial question therefore is, "of what historical type is the conformism . . . to which one belongs?" (Bennett 1981, 201). In other words, Gramsci's question encourages us to ask: What ideological resources do we have available to us, from within our particular social milieu, in order to make sense of the conditions of our existence? And what are the political implications of the *kind* of sense we make of reality (i.e., the historical type of conformism to which we belong)? In the end, the kinds of ideological resources we use to make sense of daily events and experiences will go a long way in determining whether we actively work to change or to reproduce existing social relations.

This paper, therefore, offers an investigation structured by these questions. Taking a white, working-class neighborhood in Philadelphia (as depicted on *ABC News Nightline*) as a case study, this paper will begin with a discussion of the nature of ideology and its most powerful cousin, common sense, analyze the ideological resources used by white residents to make sense of the events surrounding an attempt by a young African American family to move into their neighborhood, and discuss the political implications of the kind of "sense" made by some white residents in their linkage of discourses of race and stories of postwar urban decay. As will be shown, this unfortunate articulation of race and neighborhood decay has serious political consequences, not the least of which involves the displacement of blame for economic insecurity away from wider social and historical forces. In the end, it is hoped that a better understanding of how individuals make sense of their own conditions of existence can lead to the elaboration of a more progressive and complex "common sense" about economic restructuring and neighborhood instability.

Ideology and Common Sense

The concept of ideology dies hard. During its almost two-hundred-year history, it has been declared dead on any number of occasions but, like Lazarus, each time ideology somehow manages to return from the beyond. The source of its longevity, I believe, is that "ideology" expresses something important: the sense that the dominant ideas of the day do not reflect our interests, whoever "we" are and whatever "our interests" might be. Moreover, ideology implies that that dominance over the realm of meaning is not accidental; it is made and sustained somehow through concrete practices and actions. It is the realization that dominance extends into the meanings that animate our lives that provokes the "aha!" response common to many first-year students of political economy and the media.

However, this initial realization only serves to plunge us into the daunting complexity that has characterized the last two hundred years of thought on the concept. One historically important and influential version of ideology during this time dates back to Marx and Engels's *The German Ideology* and treats ideological formations (for example, the conservative meanings associated with God, country, and family) as primarily superstructural apologia for a more basic material class rule. In Marx and Engels's early writings, ideology has primarily a mystifying function; it masks and distorts the real conditions of existence and the reality of class-based domination in the economic realm. For the early Marx, then, the effects of ideology would seem to be entirely *negative*. In this perspective, bourgeois ideologies do not *produce* sensibilities or subjectivities; rather, they *prevent* already constituted individuals from correctly perceiving the reality of their own lives.

As Terry Eagleton writes, treating ideology as a "mist" or "screen" between individuals and reality transforms it into "merely a set of chimeras which perpetuate [a class-based social] order by *distracting* its citizens from otherwise palpable inequality and injustice" (1991, 77; emphasis added). Given this definition, it is difficult to see how

> ideology can be in any sense an active social force, organizing the experience of human subjects in accordance with the requirements of a specific social order . . . It is as though ideology has no particular interest in, say, inculcating the virtues of thrift, honesty, and industriousness in the working class by a range of disciplinary techniques, but simply denies that the sphere of work has much significance at all in contrast with the Kingdom of Heaven or the Absolute Idea. (77)

Eagleton concludes by questioning whether any society could reproduce itself "by dint of an ideology as generalized and negative as this" (77). In the end, Marx and Engels's early definition of ideology forgets that "what distinguishes the human animal is that it moves in a world of meaning, and these meanings are constitutive of its activities, not secondary to them" (73). If meaning is at least partly constitutive of human action, then ideologies cannot be viewed as mere distractions but rather, as a *necessary* part of human existence, "as much a part of our biological make-up as the need to eat" (82). Therefore, if ideologies are to be viewed as more than mystifications of real social relations, then implicit in this move toward a more positive definition is a sense that ideologies provide individuals with the symbolic resources from which their subjectivity and consciousness can be built.

In this way, "ideology" as a concept covers the same general terrain as "meaning"; ideology somehow plays a role in linking purpose or significance to action. As Hall writes, this overlap with meaning moves the search for a more useful definition of ideology into the heady realm of signification and, therefore, into semiology: "Things and events in the real world do not contain or propose their own, integral, single and intrinsic meaning, which is then merely transferred through language. Meaning is a social production, a practice. The world must be *made to mean*" (1982, 67). Since the world must be "made to mean," semiology tells us, the social practice of signification will always be a part of human activity. As Hall writes, it is not possible to bring ideology to an end and simply to live in the real: "We always need systems through which we represent what the real is to ourselves and to others" (1985, 104). These systems of representation provide the resources with which men and women "make sense of the conditions of their existence" (104). Moreover, they give a sense that the world is "objective" and patterned in particular ways, allowing us to "go on" with at least some confidence from one moment to the next (Shearing and Ericson 1991, 485).

Therefore, ideologies—defined now as systems of representation which link significance and action—can be *positive* forces, actively constructing and generating ways of seeing and being, as opposed to merely blinding already constituted subjects to the so-called real conditions of existence. Given this, the next question is: if such structures of meaning have the power to constitute individuals as particular subjects, then *whose* systems of representation are to prevail at any one historical moment? According to Hall, certain ideologies can gain purchase within the social formation through a long process of historical struggle over how persons, events, and policies are to be signified and understood (1982, 77).[1] For Hall, then, the links between "ruling classes" and "ruling ideologies" are never guaranteed; rather, they must be created and sustained through the ongoing articulation between social or economic forces and those forms of political and ideological practice that help dominant groups to establish and sustain hegemony over the social body (1985, 95).[2]

In the most cursory review of the daily newspaper, we can discern in the social formation a range of struggles concerning *whose* articulations between ideological discourses and economic and political interests are dominant within a particular social domain. Typically, such struggles involve the attempt of certain social interests, dominant or otherwise, to define the meaning of crucial symbols (for example, symbols of nationalism, law and order, family, and education) in such a way that certain interests or perspectives are privileged over others. For example, consider the potent symbol of "choice" in U.S. political discourse. In the last presidential election, the Republican party attempted to appropriate this symbol to promote its plan to privatize the U.S. educational system. Couched in the language of "school choice," the Republicans sought to link this aggressively American symbol to their proposal to enact a voucher program through which private schools could be subsidized with public money. This was a quintessential ideological struggle: what does "choice" mean, and whose political program will be able to appropriate this powerful symbol?

Such ideological struggles over the sociopolitical meaning of symbols and images are, for the most part, fairly easy to recognize. However, if particular ways of interpreting the world, if particular ways of seeing and being (that have been articulated with the interests of particular social groups) can be privileged to the extent that they seem *natural* and beyond everyday political controversy, *then relations steeped in domination can be reproduced with a minimum of effort from dominant groups.* It is at this point—the point where meanings that emanate from particular interests become generalized and therefore seem "natural"—that we enter the realm of what Gramsci calls "common sense" (Bennett 1981). It is when particular ideologies become disguised as common sense and therefore as non problematic statements of reality that they are at their most powerful. Therefore, what at first appears to be nonideological and even invisible—the *common-sense* practical knowledge of a given historical moment—now begins to look more like a powerful means of reproducing consent to domination.

Roland Barthes, in particular, locates the ideological power of common-sense knowledge in its ability to present historically based (i.e., politically charged) meanings as natural and inevitable (1972, 122). In short, ideology disguised as common sense allows chains of constructed associations and connotations to be consumed and reproduced innocently: "after all," as we usually say when referring to the commonsensical, "it's just the way things are." The translation of particular systems of meaning into general common sense in this way is heady territory for ideological struggle. As Hall writes, the naturalization of ideology into common sense is a moment of extreme ideological closure: "Here we are under the sway of the most highly ideological structures of all—'common sense,' the regime of the 'taken for granted.' The point at which we lose sight of the fact that sense is a product of our systems of representation is the point at which we fall not into Nature, but into the naturalistic illusion: the height (or depth) of ideology" (1985, 105). Common sense, therefore, is ideology at its most powerful and productive. It is the point at which *particular* systems of meaning (ways of seeing and being) are taken to be *universally* true. It is the point at which knowledge that is *historically* constructed and tied to particular interests and social groups is instead widely viewed as *natural* and *nonpolitical*—as just "the way things are."

If common sense is such a powerful form of ideological discourse, then it behooves us to understand more accurately how common sense is created and reproduced within everyday social relations.[3] We should, in short, begin to search for common-sense ideologies in the most humble of places (for example, the everyday chatter of human beings in specific social contexts) for it is within this context of everyday life that we tell each other, quite innocently, the ideological stories that serve to construct our political and social sensibilities. By locating the practices and contexts wherein common sense is most often articulated, we can discover and denaturalize the dominant structures of meaning at work within any particular ideological domain. It is toward such an analysis that we turn next.

A Case Study: Race, Crime, and Neighborhood Decay in Philadelphia

To illustrate how this sort of research might work, I will conduct a brief analysis of the cultural discourses—specifically discourses of race, crime, and neighborhood decay—which some white Americans employ in order to come to grips with the recent history of economic and social instability within U.S. cities. For the purpose of this analysis, I will use as my primary data source the transcript of one ABC News *Nightline* program entitled "America in Black and White: The Philadelphia Story." Aired as the first installment of a series on race in America, this particular segment chronicles the story of Bridget Ward, a thirty-two-year-old African American mother of two, and her attempt to move into a house in Bridesburg, a virtually all-white, working-class neighborhood in Philadelphia. Like many *Nightline* programs, "The Philadelphia Story" begins with an introduction delivered by the host, Ted Koppel, then moves on to a fairly lengthy (by television standards) news story introducing the key personae, events, and reactions regarding Bridget Ward and her ill-fated move to Bridesburg.

It is in this traditionally structured news story that we learn the basics of Ms Ward's experience. Just eight hours after moving into a handsome brick home in the neighborhood, she awoke to find hate graffiti ("leave nigger now" and "get out nigger") scrawled on her front steps and ketchup, presumably meant to signify blood, spilled on her porch. Almost immediately after she reported the graffiti on her steps to the local authorities, Ms Ward received a threatening letter. Signed by "posse" in a chilling reference to the history of lynching in America, the otherwise anonymous authors warned that they would "get" Ms Ward and her daughters unless they moved out of the neighborhood. It was only a short time later that she decided to move back out of Bridesburg.

The most striking features of this particular *Nightline* news segment, however, were the openly racist statements offered by some of the Bridesburg residents who were interviewed by the local and national media. In contemporary U.S. political discourse, race has long been a highly charged subject, and whites especially have considered it taboo in polite conversation, preferring to refer to race indirectly via euphemisms and code words (Lutz and Collins 1993, 254). However, in this *Nightline* segment, many Bridesburg residents spoke quite openly about their objections both to Ms Ward's presence and to racial integration in general. For example, consider some of the statements made by residents to the local media regarding the racial slurs scrawled on Ms Ward's steps.[4]

Neighbor #1:   *It's against the law, but if it gets them out, that's fine.*

Neighbor #2:   *I don't want them living around here.*

Passerby: *You're not wanted here. [voice* from the steps: yes we are!] *No you're not. We don't want our daughters and sons . . . Bluebirds don't mix with robins, you know what I'm saying?* [Speaking to someone on Ms. Ward's steps from his truck, covering his face with his hood to avoid the camera).

Beyond merely dismissing these statements and sentiments as more evidence of racism in America (though they clearly are just that), the question that needs to be asked at this point is: What cultural discourses render such statements intelligible and rational to those who produce them? What kinds of ideological resources are residents using to construct and interpret such statements about the relationship between race, crime, and neighborhood decay? Fortunately, the second half of the segment provides a rich source of data which can be used to discover answers to these questions. Picking up the story the day of Ms Ward's decision to move out of Bridesburg, *Nightline* assembled twenty white Bridesburg residents to comment on the events surrounding her arrival in the neighborhood. After informing the residents that Ms Ward had just come to her decision to move out, *Nightline* host Ted Koppel deliberately broadened the focus from the specifics of her case to more general questions about race and the politics of neighborhood. In essence, this segment asked of Bridesburg residents: What are you afraid of? Why do you care if a seemingly innocuous African American family moves in next door? The answers offered by the twenty white residents of Bridesburg in *Nightline*'s "town meeting" form the raw data for the following analysis, which will attempt to discover the ideological discourses that form the basis of their common sense concerning race, crime, and neighborhood decay.

"*When neighborhoods turn minority*": *Linking race and neighborhood decay.* During the course of *Nightline*'s town meeting, it became immediately clear that some of the assembled residents made a clear and explicit connection between the presence of African American families and the ensuing decay of white, working-class neighborhoods. As one older male participant (male resident #1) said, "when neighborhoods turn () minority, they, *they go down rapidly.*"[5] Other comments in the town meeting struck a similar theme.

Male resident #1:   The neighborhood she was leaving. What happened to that neighborhood? [TK: I haven't a clue.] It *went down* the toilet. That neighborhood's unlivable.

Male resident #2:   It's the truth. [TK: what's the truth?]. What he said about one () what you said about one () black family moving in, *just gets the ball rolling.*

Female resident #2:   In this city every neighborhood that wasn't affluent that became integrated *went downhill* and some have become war zones.

The interesting thing to note in these comments is the sense that neighborhood decay necessarily and inevitably accompanies racial integration. When one African American family moves in, this "gets the ball rolling." After that, the neighborhood goes "down" or "downhill" into inevitable decline, presumably due to the immigration of more African American families. In the end, the neighborhood decays into a "war zone" and becomes "unlivable." The theme common to all these statements is one of *momentum*—a sense that once "the ball" starts rolling "downhill," decline is inevitable. Residents emphasize this sense of inevitability through their recourse to physical metaphors—rolling, going down, going downhill—which imply that decay follows integration in much the same way that gravity works upon material objects.[6]

Encoded within these statements is a sense that Bridesburg, if integrated, will decay in a process that is as inevitable and unstoppable as gravity. However unsettling this equation of racial difference with neighborhood decay may be, an important task remains: discovering the cultural logic that underlies such damaging political discourses. Fortunately, the Bridesburg residents assembled by *Nightline* were quite explicit about the source of their common sense about race, crime, and neighborhood decay. According to some of the residents, the equation of African Americans with neighborhood decline emerged from their view of "the history of Philadelphia" since the 1950s.

"And that's the history of Philadelphia": A vocabulary of precedents. For some Bridesburg residents, "the history of Philadelphia" is basically an accumulation of urban stories that chronicle the decline of once stable, white, working-class neighborhoods into dangerous and decaying "war zones." As one resident claimed, "we've seen what happened in other neighborhoods, and we don't want it to happen here [in Bridesburg]. We're afraid of that." But what exactly do these urban stories describe? A look back at the introductory news segment in the *Nightline* program provides a clue. In order to present the residents' perspective on the politics of race and neighborhood, the producers gave two Bridesburg residents a video camera and asked them to provide a video defense of their opposition to racial integration. Shown during the broadcast, we discover that these two residents chose to film the streets of North Philadelphia, the neighborhood in which both had grown up during the 1950s and 1960s and one that now is home to mostly African American residents. Shot from inside their moving car (not once do the Bridesburg residents leave their vehicle), their video shows a row of abandoned buildings sprayed with graffiti and adjacent vacant lots littered with trash and broken glass. In short, their video shows the startling material face of post-Fordist urban devastation. Not incidently, the video also pauses to show a nearby group of young African American boys and girls standing in front of one of the decaying structures. In the audio voice-over, viewers hear the Bridesburg residents' narration as they drive through the streets of North Philadelphia: "it used to be rows and rows of well-kept () row houses here."

What is so startling in this short segment is the contrast the resident draws between his brief verbal description of the way "it used to be" and the images of decay framed by their home video. It is the fate of neighborhoods like North Philadelphia—neighborhoods that (in the words of Bridesburg residents) used to be "well-kept" and stable, that used to be mostly white and working-class, in short, that used to be like Bridesburg—that frightens Bridesburg residents.[7] These stories about the decay of neighborhoods like North Philadelphia into "war zones" form for many Bridesburg residents a "vocabulary of precedents" (Shearing and Ericson 1991,490) which prove that the associations between integration, crime, and neighborhood decline are quite real and quite frightening. In the end, according to some Bridesburg residents, this "history of Philadelphia"— a history in which stable white neighborhoods have been transformed into war zones by integration—teaches that if Bridesburg doesn't "want it to happen here," then the neighborhood should resist all attempts at integration. Therefore, by contrasting the way things "used to be" in once all-white neighborhoods in Philadelphia with the current condition of these same, now mostly African American neighborhoods, residents of Bridesburg attempt to justify their open hostility to (or at least their overt suspicion of) attempts at integration.

Underlying semantic dimensions: Order/chaos, white/black. Taken together, the statements offered by Bridesburg residents reveal a tight association between integration and neighborhood decay. Furthermore, this association is largely justified with reference to the "history of Philadelphia" which is said to chronicle the decline of many previously all-white neighborhoods after they were integrated in the 1960s and 1970s. Underlying these statements, however, is a cultural logic: a commonly held system of meaning. This cultural logic patterns and links these statements, making the sentiments expressed by Bridesburg residents intelligible and, from within the logic of the local system of meaning, even "reasonable." In order to interpret this cultural logic, the symbols used by the assembled residents can be usefully split into two clusters: those about Bridesburg, and those about black neighborhoods.

The first symbolic cluster—symbols about Bridesburg—invokes the imagery of order and stability. For white residents, Bridesburg is a place marked by continuity. As the president of the local civic association stated, it is a place "to put . . . roots down" and to "stay awhile." According to Ted Koppel, residents often describe Bridesburg as "the place time forgot," where "safety, stability, and family values" are said to still characterize everyday life. This verbal emphasis on continuity and stability is reinforced in the *Nightline* segment by the producers' choice of visuals. In one short part of the introductory news segment, we see a number of images designed to depict the friendly side of Bridesburg: here we see neighbors smiling and greeting one another, over here we see an elderly man gardening in his front yard, there we see a Little League baseball game. In the end, the visual juxtaposition of the elderly man with the children subtly reinforces the spoken representation of Bridesburg as a place where the social fabric is still intact, where people come to raise a family and to grow old with dignity.

The second symbolic cluster—symbols concerning African American neighborhoods—invokes quite different meanings. Unlike the representation of Bridesburg, black neighborhoods are portrayed verbally and visually as spaces of disorder. As we discovered above, Bridesburg residents describe neighborhoods with large populations of African Americans as unlivable "war zones" that have "gone down the toilet." These verbal constructions are echoed by *Nightline*'s one foray into a struggling black neighborhood, where the two Bridesburg residents filmed the streets of North Philadelphia from within the ostensible security of their moving car. The carefully chosen images of technicolor graffiti, abandoned buildings, and vacant lots, along with the telling inclusion of a group of young African Americans within the video frame, all serve to reinforce the spoken claim that "when neighborhoods turn minority" they degenerate into spaces of decay, danger, and disorder.

In the end, these residents differentiate between white neighborhoods like Bridesburg and African American neighborhoods like North Philadelphia along a single semantic dimension: *order/chaos*.[8] According to Bridesburg residents, white neighborhoods are spaces of order held together by a commonly shared code of morality, while African American neighborhoods are "unlivable" spaces of chaos where the social fabric has unraveled and where social disorder dominates daily life. Consequently, it is the articulation of this dimension of order/chaos with the racial dichotomy of white/black that structures many whites' opposition to integration. By associating "white" with meanings of order and stability and "black" with images of decay and chaos, these Bridesburg residents create a common sense about race, crime, and neighborhood that equates racial difference with social disorder.

As we have seen, the tenacity and power of this common sense about race and neighborhood decay derives in part from the fact that it is viewed as practical knowledge based on historical experience and, therefore, not as "irrational" or "prejudicial" in the folk sense of these words. In short, the urban stories that describe "the history of Philadelphia" teach white residents that the city can be practically divided into safe areas and chaotic "war zones" primarily by referring to the ethnic makeup of each particular neighborhood. As a result, racial cues have become, for many white residents, quick and easy ideological handles used to minimize risk within a symbolically charged urban environment. Put bluntly, this common sense urges whites to stick to white neighborhoods and to avoid black neighborhoods. In this way, interpersonal gossip and media stories that link crime to particular groups of people in particular parts of the city are used by many white residents as a means of "defining the extent of social exclusion and spatial avoidance which should be practiced in order to minimize exposure to risk" (Smith 1986,125). Therefore, the common sense about race, crime, and neighborhood decay has tremendous cultural purchase since it offers white residents a practical and simple way to navigate safely through an intimidating and complex urban landscape.

Finally, it is this articulation of racial difference with disorder that leads some Bridesburg residents to their astonishing ideological support for racial segregation and even the use of terror (e.g., racist graffiti and threats) to enforce this segregation. Within the cultural logic set up by the equation of white with order and nonwhite with chaos, many whites in places like Bridesburg have come to the conclusion that the presence of African Americans and other people of color in one's neighborhood will lead, seemingly only by virtue of their racial difference, to a long descent into chaos and disorder. If Bridesburg is to resist the fate that has befallen other once white neighborhoods in Philadelphia, this cultural logic concludes, it must patrol its racial and ethnic boundaries. As one Bridesburg resident cryptically told the local media: "nobody wants () mixed () people in their neighborhood . . . she [Ms. Ward] should've expected trouble."

Ideological Consequences: Displacing the Blame

All of this analysis leads us to ask a fairly straightforward question: What are the political consequences of this common sense that links "white" with "order" and "nonwhite" with "chaos"? In this section, I focus on the political consequences of this common sense about integration and neighborhood decay for members of white communities like Bridesburg. This is not to say that these urban stories about race and decay do not affect African American or Latino residents; the case of Bridget Ward clearly indicates that the stories whites tell about African Americans have very real and damaging consequences. But in this final section, I focus on how this cultural logic (which uses the language of race to explain the recent history of urban decay) serves to undermine white residents' ability to understand the economic forces that threaten the stability of *all* urban working-class communities.

First, the common-sense equation of racial difference with neighborhood decay recasts the recent history of urban economic restructuring as a story about race and integration. This is an unfortunate ideological development, for the recent history of economic instability clearly has played a major role in undermining the social fabric of many working-class communities across the United States. As David Harvey (1990, 1994) writes, the crisis of overaccumulation (stagnant demand and overproduction) experienced by U.S. capitalism in the early 1970s encouraged capital to experiment with new forms of economic and social organization that deviated from the postwar Fordist consensus (i.e., mass production and consumption, unionized labor, and Keynesian state intervention). One spectacularly successful method for restoring the potential for expanding profits has been the relocation of production facilities to more "business-friendly" (read "nonunionized" and "low wage") geographies. However, a crucial consequence of this dispersal of production to low-wage labor niches (both domestically and internationally) has been the absolute devastation of many working-class communities located in the traditional manufacturing centers of the United States. While the exodus of manufacturing jobs from U.S. cities has disproportionally affected African American communities (who were employed in disproportionate numbers in these industries),[9] many white blue-collar communities, also dependent on manufacturing jobs, also were devastated (Zukin 1991, 102). As high-wage, unionized factory jobs were relocated to other economic geographies, residents of working-class communities increasingly were forced to look for lower-wage service sector jobs or, if those were unavailable, forced to relocate themselves, undermining the stability so prized by working-class residents.

However, as we have seen, the common sense articulated by Bridesburg residents tells a different story. In this story, the destruction of working-class life is attributed instead to the racial integration of these neighborhoods—that is, to the increasing presence of African Americans and Latinos. Thus, this common sense about race and neighborhood decay serves as another dimension of working-class fragmentation. The dominant articulation of "nonwhite" with "disorder" establishes, in short, an ideological terrain that makes class-based links across racial lines extremely difficult. As Hall et al. write, "Although the black and white poor find themselves, objectively, in the same position, they inhabit a world ideologically so structured that each can be made to provide the other with its negative reference group, the 'manifest cause' of each other's misfortunes" (1978, 339). In the end, this common sense that explains the history of urban restructuring using the language of race and integration obscures the more fundamental story of the U.S. urban landscape since 1970 and thus serves to split working-class communities along racial lines.

Further, as Rose Brewer (1995) writes, the racist conclusion (implied within the cultural logic underlying the speech of some Bridesburg residents) that the disproportionate amount of crime, poverty, and unemployment within African American or Latino neighborhoods can be explained through their cultural or biological inferiority serves an important ideological function within the current economic and political climate. If poverty and unemployment within these neighborhoods can be recast as a matter of inferior cultural values (lack of thrift, honesty, work ethic, etc.), then neoconservative political claims, including the claim that government social support only encourages irresponsible social behavior, will have more political purchase. As a result, a common sense which blames neighborhood decay on the absence of family values (especially within the African American and Latino communities) serves to justify the current retreat of the state from previous political commitments to affirmative action and the expansion of the social wage. From within this political logic, poverty therefore becomes a moral issue and the poor (especially the African American and Latino poor) are blamed for their own suffering.

Logically, the daily anxieties and resentments that go along with life in a capitalist city (for example, the constant threat of unemployment, the withdrawal of the state from redistributive programs, and the increasing instability of modern economic and social life) should be focused upon restructuring corporations and the governmental policies that ease the transition away from welfare-state capitalism (Harvey 1985, 122). However, in their haste to differentiate themselves both spatially and socially from these stigmatized African American and Latino neighborhoods, the white middle and working classes seem more inclined to align themselves with the interests of urban and national elites who, in fact, are carrying out the process of economic restructuring. From within the cultural logic of this racially charged common sense (which blames impoverished African Americans and Latinos for their own poverty), the fear of losing one's own job and losing one's own house becomes rearticulated into a fear of the African American and Latino underclass and what they represent: the concrete manifestation of *what happens when things fall apart* (Hall et al. 1978, 333; Conquergood 1992, 135). As a result, this anxiety becomes twisted into overt political support for the neoconservative policies that privilege the interests of global corporations over the interests of local working-class communities. In Harvey Molotch's words, "[T]he fear of unemployment acts to make workers politically passive (if not downright supportive) with respect to land-use policies, taxation programs, and antipollution nonenforcement schemes which, in effect, represent income transfers from the general public to various sectors of the elite" (1976, 325). In the end, this "common sense" about the city (which separates the urban space into the hard-working and honest "us" and the criminalized and lazy "them") secures support for the reverse Robin Hood policies of contemporary American capitalism while concealing its most obvious negative manifestation—the plight of the poor—within a "blame the victim" ideology.

Conclusion

Common-sense ideologies, told and retold in everyday contexts, are productive. These systems of meanings, associations, and connotations generate the resources from which our identities and actions are constructed. It is within ideology that we learn who we are, how we *can* live, and how we *ought* to live. The ability to privilege a particular set of ideological resources over alternative ways of seeing and being (via articulation with social, economic, and political practices) is thus a component of any attempt to establish dominance within the social formation. In a positive definition of ideology, the terrain of meaning emerges from the shadow of the economy to become recognized as a crucial site of struggle within the social formation.

Furthermore, at its most "positive" and productive, ideology becomes invisible and natural. It becomes common sense: the collection of stories and tropes that contain the everyday knowledge we take for granted as describing "the way things are" and "how things fit." Storytelling in this way is revealed as a highly ideological practice, and those stories which are treated as natural and practical are potentially among the most ideological of all. When studying the ideological formations that coalesce around particular issues or events (e.g., race, gender, sexuality, colonialism, and so on), researchers would do well to listen carefully to the mundane, everyday stories told both within the media and in interpersonal networks. As the above analysis suggests, these mundane and practical stories often contain an ideological mother lode of linked and clustered connotations.

In the corner of the ideological terrain defined by the nexus of discourses about race and neighborhood, then, the above analysis of one *Nightline* segment suggests that for some white residents, certain city spaces have become charged with connotations of danger, crime, and drugs, which often can be coarticulated with discourses about race and poverty. Therefore, everyday stories about "good" and "bad" neighborhoods told in everyday contexts (the store, the front steps, the real-estate office) are revealed as a rich ethnographic resource for an investigation into the dominant "common-sense" connections made between discourses about race, crime, and urban geography. Finally, further analysis should attempt to uncover more complex and progressive stories about race, crime, and urban space—stories that link the conditions of these neighborhoods to wider social and economic inequalities. A project of *rearticulation*, therefore, should begin by uncovering, reconnecting, and publicizing these marginalized stories in new and interesting ways. In the end, the hope is that such a project of rearticulation could lead to alternative ways of "seeing" our cities and "being" within our neighborhoods.

Notes

1. To Gramsci (see Bennett 1981), struggles over signification occurred between distinct economic class alliances while to Barrett (1994, 252), ideological struggles occur on a variety of fronts, including the classic fault lines around how race and gender are to be signified within the social formation.

2. In this way, a positive definition of ideology can still account for the problematic raised by Marx and Engels in 1846—that ideas have historically worked to privilege some versions of "seeing" and "being" over others, creating dominant systems of representation.

3. As Shearing and Ericson (1991) suggest, common sense is produced and reproduced primarily via the stories, tropes, and metaphors that express everyday knowledge about "the way things are" and "how things fit." In this way, seemingly innocuous moments of daily discourse—storytelling, giving advice, trading aphorisms—are revealed as thickly political and ideological.

4. A complete transcript of *Nightline's* "America in Black and White: The Philadelphia Story" can be obtained from the author.

5. The use of the symbol () is meant to represent moments of pause or hesitation in the speech of individuals, as presented by *Nightline.*

6. Skogan (1990) and Conquergood (1992) have discovered similar metaphors of momentum and the inevitability of decay upon racial integration in their own ethnographies of white, working-class neighborhoods.

7. Wesley Skogan (1990) again uncovers similar constructions of urban history among his respondents in a working-class neighborhood in Chicago. According to one white resident, the increasing population of Puerto Ricans led to the decay of his neighborhood: "The Puerto Ricans are dirty. They throw garbage out their windows. They don't put trash into trash cans but throw it all over the alley, they don't keep up their property; it used to be a beautiful neighborhood, but it is all changed now."

8. This semantic dimension (Seitel 1974) was derived inductively, based on the scrutiny of the commonalities and patterns of co-occurrence among the residents' descriptions of "white" versus "black" neighborhoods.

9. Since African Americans historically have been disproportionally represented in low-skill manufacturing jobs, the loss of these industries or their relocation to the Third World have hit the black community particularly hard (Wilson 1978, 95). Moreover, the new jobs created by the service and information industries have either carried extensive education requirements or have located their operations in the suburbs, placing them both spatially and educationally out of the reach of a large segment of inner-city African Americans (Wilson 1987, 39–42). The result has been chronic unemployment in the inner cities, especially for young black males. For example, 37.1 percent of black male teenagers (aged 16–9) and 17.6 percent of young black men (20–4 years old) in the United States were unemployed in 1995 (U.S. Bureau of the Census 1996).

References

Barrett, M. 1994. "Ideology, Politics, Hegemony: From Gramsci to Laclau and Mouffe." In *Mapping Ideology*, ed. S. Žižek. New York: Verso Press.

Barthes, R. 1972. *Mythologies.* London: J. Cape.

Bennett, T. 1981. "Antonio Gramsci." In *Culture, Ideology, and Social Process*, ed. T. Bennett et al. London: Open University Press.

Brewer, R. 1995. "Knowledge Construction and Racist 'Science': Ideology, Political Economy, and Racial Inequality in the United States." *American Behavioral Scientist* 39: 62–73.

Conquergood, D. 1992. "Life in Big Red: Struggles and Accommodations in a Chicago Polyethnic Tenement." In *Structuring Diversity: Ethnographic Perspectives on the New Immigration*, ed. L. Lamphere. Chicago: University of Chicago Press.

Eagleton, T. 1991. *Ideology: An Introduction.* New York: Verso Books.

Hall, S. 1982. "The Rediscovery of Ideology: Return of the Repressed in Media Studies." In *Culture, Society, and the Media*, ed. G. Gurevitch et al. London: Methuen.

_____. "Signification, Representation, Ideology: Althusser and the Post-Structuralist Debates." *Critical Studies in Mass Communication* 2: 91–114.

Hall, S.; Critcher, C. Jefferson, T.; Clarke, J.; and Roberts, B. 1978. *Policing the Crisis: Mugging, the State, and the Law and Order.* New York: Holmes and Meier.

Harvey, D. 1985. *Consciousness and the Urban Experience: Studies in the History and Theory of Capitalist Urbanization.* Baltimore. John Hopkins University Press.

_____. 1990. *The Condition of Postmodernity: An Enquiry into the Origins of Cultural Change.* Cambridge, Mass.: Blackwell.

_____. 1994. "Flexible Accumulation through Urbanization: Reflections on 'Post-Modernism' in the American City." In *Post-Fordism: A Reader,* ed. A. Amin. Cambridge, Mass.: Blackwell.

Lutz, C. and Collins, J. 1993. *Reading* National Geographic. Chicago: University of Chicago Press.

Molotch, H. 1976. "The City as a Growth Machine." *American Journal of Sociology* 82: 309–32.

Seitel, P. 1974. "Haya Metaphors for Speech." *Language in Society* 3: 51–67.

Shearing, C. D. and Ericson, R. V. 1991. "Culture as Figurative Action." *British Journal of Sociology* 42: 481–506.

Skogan, W. 1990. *Disorder and Decline: Crime and the Spiral of Decay in American Neighborhoods.* New York: The Free Press.

Socio-Cultural Discourse in Mass Media Text: An Analytical Sample

Intermedial Location of Meaning in Muna Moto: A Metalanguage of Cultural Discourse

Boulou E. de B'béri

The Duala Cultural Metalanguage of Marriage

Some film analysts achieve a transparent dispositive of cinema-art in their analysis of black cinema. In those cases, they use, in part at least, psychoanalysis, structuralism, or post-structuralism as the paradigmatic frameworks rendering black cinema intelligible. They can, therefore, analyze an entire film, thousand of images, in twenty pages, as if these images were merely literal phrases. Given the space limits of this article, my approach is different. First, I use theory to analyze some key moments in *Muna Moto*. This approach differs from using film analysis to elucidate theory. Put in a different way, this article uses theories to explain the film. Second, I invite the reader to observe some specific cultural discursive articulations in *Muna Moto*. By cultural discursive articulations I mean the conditions under which a society produces specific meanings embodying specific cultural semiotic gestures. I suggest, for example, that one cannot analyze *Muna Moto* without thinking of the Duala's performative culture of marriage. Underlining this culture of marriage also requires an examination of the "hidden articulation" of this traditional performance. By hidden articulation, I mean the discourse beyond the structural economies of cinema-art—the dispositive of language, style, genre, or general dominant aesthetic of time and space. It is, however, at this hidden level of discourse that I situate the articulation of metalanguage in *Muna Moto*.[1]

Generally, the concept of metalanguage signifies an articulation occurring "with" or "after" denoted significations. The narrative process of self-referentiality whereby a film shows its own making procedures is called metalanguage. Metalanguage is further the vertical diacritical discourse occurring within (with or after) denoted narrative structures. For example, "within" the denoted level of the marriage in *Muna Moto*, specific diacritical cultural gestures can be decoded. These gestures manifest a vertical cultural semiotic that can be explained only within the framework of the Dualas' cultural articulation of marriage. In part at least, the performative frameworks proposed by Austin[2] can explain the modalities of this vertical discursive articulation. Nonetheless, it is through the figuration of "*Signifying*" in oral performance that I want to formulate the vertical diacritical discourse at the core of the articulation of metalanguage in the Duala's culture of marriage.

In Duala's oral performance, the figuration of *Signifying* refers to vertical diacritical frames of reference that allow endless dynamic possibilities of articulating new propositions, dispositions, enunciations, or meanings. *Signifying* is therefore similar to the Deleuzian and Guattarian "rhizome,"[3] or the Bakhtinian notion of "surplus."[4] In this article, I will use the notions of "rhizome" and "surplus" as two complementary conjectures allowing us to illustrate the exceeding potentiality of the figuration of *Signifying* in Duala's oral performance as displayed in *Muna Moto*.

Simply put, *Signifying* means the endless variation of oral cultural signification. In *The Signifying Monkey: A Theory of African-American Literary Criticism* (1989), Henry Louis Gates, Jr. analyzes this multileveled variation of significations in Black oral performances. Gates' study explores the relationship between African and African-American vernacular English and standard English. This comparative analysis of the notions of "black *Signifying*" and "standard English signifying" addresses a fundamental differentiation:

> The English-language use of *signification* refers to the chain of signifiers that configure horizontally, on the syntagmatic axis. Whereas signification operates and can be represented on a syntagmatic or horizontal axis, Signifyin(g) [in the Black Vernacular] operates and can be represented on a paradigmatic or vertical axis. Signifyin(g) concerns itself with that which is *suspended,* vertically: the chaos of what Saussure calls "associative relations," which we can represent *as the playful puns on a word that occupy the paradigmatic axis of language and which a speaker draws on for figurative substitutions.* These substitutions in Signifyin(g) tend to be humorous, or function to name a person or a situation in a telling manner. Whereas signification depends for order and coherence on the exclusion of unconscious associations which any given word yields at any given time, *Signification luxuriates in the inclusion of the free play of these vertically suspended associative rhetorical and semantic relations.* Jacques Lacan calls these vertically suspended associations "a whole articulation of relevant contexts," by which he means all of the associations that a signifier carries from other contexts, which must de deleted, ignored, or censored, "for this signifier to be lined up with a signified to produce a specific meaning." (49–50)

Put in a different way, in standard English, (s)ignification equals the juncture of signified and signifier, both referring to the concept: (image-sound); whereas in African vernacular, *(S)ignification* equals the vertical diacritical rhetoric related to the signifier that endlessly "regulates" its "fragments" or codes, depending on the specific cultural circumstances. It is through this African diacritical register of oral practice that I situate the metalanguage of the Duala's cultural performance of marriage.

In fact, the opening sequence of *Muna Moto* establishes the traditional performance of N'Gondo, the Duala tradition ritual, as a necessary narrative articulation, as a voice-over explains: "N'Gondo is the umbilical cord connecting

Duala people to their traditional virtues."[5] This establishing sequence displaying the hero of the plot, N'Gando—a name *Signifying* Cayman in the Duala language—connotes the metalanguage of this traditional diacritical meaning. Moreover, this establishing scene introduces us to N'Gando through close-up subjective images—a denoted metalanguage or self-reflective narrative—showing him on a pirogue pushed by high wind, then at the beach, and finally playing with his beloved, N'Domè—a name meaning Treasure.

The performance of the N'Gondo (the ritual), the meanings behind the names of N'Gando and N'Domè (Cayman, Treasure), and the images of the Wuri (Duala's littoral sea in which N'Domè and N'Gando play), which is a space in which the Dualas perform their traditional New Year ritual,[6] display specific semiotic gestures of Duala's culture. Specifically, this conjuncture prefigures the vertical articulation of the discourse at the core of this cultural performance. The conjuncture of cultural practices, significations of words, ritual, and spaces establishes the vertical diacritical metalanguage articulated in *Muna Moto,* as an experience chat is *"propre"* to the Duala people. Since this cultural performance occurs within specific vertical *Signifying(s)*, the "morphology of its experience"[7] remains unseized by any analysis based on the transparent economies of cinema-art because "thinking about the black concept of *Signifying* is a bit like stumbling unaware into a hall of mirrors: the sign itself appears to be doubled, at the very least, and (re)doubled upon ever closer examination" (Gates 44). This remark illustrates the ways in which African performance art, like Deleuze and Guattari's (1992) notion of "rhizome," eludes any analysis based strictly on dominant theories of cinema-art.

According to Deleuze and Guattari, the rhizome is like a "book-machine" assembling differences without necessarily losing or gaining anything and without giving more importance to one element over another, because it is a code that is inseparable from the cultural process of decoding inherent in it. In this case, the opening sequence of *Muna Moto* generates a process of meaning inherent to the Duala's culture. And it is only within this culture that one can understand the metalanguage—the encoding and decoding articulation—of the images the film displays, because according to Deleuze and Guattari, "there are no genetics without 'genetic drift.' The modern theory of mutations has clearly demonstrated that any code, necessarily operating in context of other codes, has an essential margin of decoding. That is, not only does every code *have supplementary signification capable of free variation*—a diacritical potentiality of signification—but a single segment may be copied twice, the second copy left free for variation. This involves not only translation between codes but a singular phenomenon we call the "surplus" value of code, or "side-communication" (Deleuze and Guattari 53).

This single opening "segment" of *Muna Moto* does nor portray a static decoding meaning of the Duala's culture. Rather, it is a ground for conjunctural investigation because the cultural code of marriage displays incessantly dynamic meaning or endless new forms of surplus. It is therefore a conjunctural space allowing us to see the "free margin of the [cultural] code," much as the molecular particles freed from their restricted role within the process of genetic transmission suggested by Deleuze and Guattari. The surplus value of the cultural code in *Muna Moto* empowers local environmental factors of the Duala people with the capacity to forge endless modifications and new codes that

> have an aleatory cause in the milieu of exteriority [such as cinema-art], and it is their effects on the interior milieus [—Duala's culture—], their compatibility with them, that decide whether they will be popularized, deterritorializations and reterritorializations, which "do not bring about the modifications; they do, however, strictly determine their [discursive] selection."
>
> (Deleuze and Guattari 54)

Jean-Pierre Dikonguè-Pipa is a Duala like myself. In applying the Duala's cultural code to critique the tradition of power—especially financial power—related to marriage in Duala, Dikonguè-Pipa not only observes the conditions of this power-structure, but also the articulation of its cultural semiotic gestures. In other words, Dinkongué-Pipa opens the Duala production of meaning to such endless diacritical assemblages that only the remaining cultural code—Duala's cultural semiotic gesture—is emptied to expose the structure of its authoritative constructs. Bakhtin underscores this articulation in arguing that critical quests of cultural expression especially history, are in fact quests for embodied experience transcending the subject's intention to reveal the discursive articulation beyond cultural production.

Intermediality as a Method of Analysis in Black Cinema

Jürgen E. Müller was one of the first to use the term "intermediality." In the late-1980s, Müller suggested that if "'intermediality' is the relationship between distinctive mediums, and that one of their functions is the historical evolution of these relationships, that implies that the 'monadic' conceptualization of singular kinds of media is unacceptable."[8] For André Gaudreault and François Jost, however, intermediality is imposed by media's interconnectivity. Modern communications technologies (computer, television, telephone) and institutional mergers in the fields of communication shifting disjunctive philosophies and interests have forced academics to revise their monophyletic theories. Gaudreault and Jost further observe that the evolution of technologies, especially with regard to visual representations, necessitated the establishment of new inter-disciplines such as Film, Television, and Media Studies. They propose to analyze this intersection of disciplines (intermediality) not as a revolutionary process or point of disjunction, but rather as a *"continuum space of interconnection,"* and *"variable duration"* (Gaudreault and Jost; my translation).

The notion of intermediality is an unavoidable methodological posture in the fields of social science, humanities, and arts today. Indeed, there have been multiple attempts to define its concerns prescriptively. One such attempt that shifts the concern of intermediality from the space of technological media to fundamental practices, such as cultural articulation, is the closing lecture of Eric Méchoualan at the 2000 Conference of Intermediality. Méchoualan suggests as follows:

> Intermediality [. . . should] also focus on all the "in-between" of arts and techniques; all this milieu where, somehow, this retreat operates, precisely. Not only the recent technologies such as video or internet, but also fundamental "Techniques" which constitute what has sometimes been referred to as view or memory or rumor. There lie some challenges which belong, I believe, to the order of what should concern us if we were to deal with intermediality.

Méchoualan's attempt to circumscribe the methodological space of intermediality is compelling, because he not only evaluates the intersections of the technological apparatuses observed earlier by Gaudreault and Jost but pushes the questions of intermediality within the surrounding modalities of human agency—"fundamental technique" as he calls it—transmitted by cultural performance using the arts of cinema, video, radio, or even telephone to endorse new conjunctural forms of expression. According to Méchoualan, collective memory constitutes one of the greatest achievements of contemporary technology, constituting a memory parallel to human memory.

This important observation shows how the notion of intermediality allows us to analyze the process of "transfer" of cultural semiotic gestures not merely within artistic practices, but within the social space of expression or fundamental social discourses, such as the traditional power-dispositive of the culture of marriage displayed in *Muna Moto*.

N'Domè and N'Gando love one another. However, the Duala's traditional dispositive of marriage—a complex *Doxa*—commands N'Gando to give a dowry to the family of N'Domè. N'Gando is a poor, young postcolonial boy living in the Depression. He survives by fishing in the Wuri and such other jobs as cutting and selling firewood.[9] As illustrated in film sequence #27, N'Gando and N'Domè promise one another to work together to secure a dowry.

This outline indicates social emergency as a practical articulation of Dikonguè-Pipa's cultural criticism that arises between the powerless working class and the traditional dispositive of power, the *Doxa*. Here, at the level of denoted metalanguage, Dikonguè-Pipa's self-reflexively indicates the unbalanced conditions within which N'Gando and N'Domè negotiate with their traditional dispositive. This powerful *Doxa* of the Duala's culture is, however, above both protagonists' communal love. Wherever they move, the "eye" that is the structure of this *Doxa* is always around them, even in the bush in which they have been hidden most of the time. In another words, *Muna Moto* shows how the structure of cultural *Doxa* circumscribes its social subject. Sequence #51 in particular displays this intermedial articulation between the feeling of the protagonists in *Muna Moto* and the structure of the Doula's *Doxa*. Here, N'Gando's friend argues that "we cannot support injustice our whole life. We have always complied, but now, it is over. You should go, you could have done that since the beginning." Not only does this exclamation suggest the ways in which the Duala's cultural *Doxa* subjugates people's determination, it also illustrates the result of any contradictory action against this *Doxa*. The final scene of the film in the Duala Central Prison supports this analysis.

Some scholars might analyze this articulation as a representation of the opposition between tradition and modernity. They may be right; however, this elementary opposition illustrates the unfamiliarity with the cultural discourse of the Duala people that this film displays. The examination of black cinema has been linked to two contradictory objects: (1) modernity as a site of contamination, hybridity, or cultural intersection in which social classes gain freedom or liberty from subduing subjects of power-tradition; and (2) archaic tradition as a site of cultural affirmation, or center of authenticity expressions, and racial purity. "At the most elementary level," argues Jude Akudinobi, "the opposite of 'modern' is 'ancient,' not tradition; [and] posting African [practice] as opposite to modernity [only] recasts the terms of reference and allows for [a] surreptitious western(ized) self-image" (26). Imruh Bakary suggests that "international audiences and writers within the North American and European tradition of film theory and criticism inevitably approached African film through what Teshome Gabriel has termed a 'cultural curtain.'" According to Bakary, the challenge is therefore to "understand African cinema on its own terms, and to identify the influences and discourses at work within it," because "what was to be confronted [is] a sophisticated [. . .] use of film technology and conventions to produce films articulating the very modern experiences of contemporary African societies" (4).

From this perspective, the Duala's cultural discursive articulation displayed in *Muna Moto,* beginning with their culture of marriage, and the social conditions of N'Domè and N'Gando, exposes *an intermedial ground for conjunctural investigation,* and not a decoding ground of the tensions between tradition and modernity. Further, intermedial analysis of those performed conjunctures allows us to understand their cultural discursive articulation, the meaning produced by the metalanguage within this specific Duala culture.

Thus, the suffering of N'Domè and N'Gando, before it is dichotomized as an illustration of the opposition between tradition and modernity, indicates a postcolonial social reality in which, for example, the working class is transformed into the "unworking" class as a result of colonialism, mismanagement, the statist bourgeoisie, and cultural customs that replaced colonial institutions.[10] This view of African societies, particularly the Duala's culture displayed in *Muna Moto,* illustrates the structural organization of this specific social *Doxa*.

In underlining this way of analyzing black cinema, I am once more indicating the potentiality of "surplus" as a diacritical figuration of *Signifying* in this Duala performance of the culture of marriage. Here, the surplus becomes a primordial articulation of connoted metalanguage allowing us to undertand the cultural *Doxa* displayed in *Muna Moto,* as well as the intermedial conjuncture opening new forms of meaning displayed in this film. Usually, surplus meanings escape even the most brilliant theorists operating within the paradigmatic frameworks of rationalism, and most broadly, those of conjectural theoretism. Bakhtin's idea of conjectural theoretism is generally an account for everything with no surplus, remains, or remainder, which I qualify as a transparent analysis of films. For example, Bakhtin would observe that erudite theoretists analyzing everyday life practices, such as marriage in *Muna Moto,* first transcribe the world into their own world system, that is, the dominant structural economy of cinema art which can handle and then overlook or deny whatever does not fit its Procustean structure. For Baktin, however, the experience that is often under the surface of these structural analyses lies in coming to terms with what exceeds the surplus of any conceivable structure. That surplus is most evident when we are dealing with everyday life practices of human beings, as in *Muna Moto.*

The notion of surplus illustrates the "becoming" conjunctural ground within which new forms of meaning emerge. In *Muna Moto,* besides the relationship of this cultural performance and its sophisticated use of narrative modalities and cinema conventions (e.g., the constant subjective camera and the complex spatial and temporal alternation of the plot), it is the conditions under which N'Domè and N'Gando negotiate with their cultural *Doxa* that explicitly indicates a new ground producing the meaning. Here, *Muna Moto* articulates the experiences of contemporary African societies with vertical diacritical *Signifying.* This experience illustrates how difficult an ontological phenomenon like love becomes subjugated to financial power or to the social *Doxa* controlling everyday life practices. In Africa today, love itself has became a commodity because behind the culture of marriage, the dowry is less a tradition than a privilege reserved for men capable of providing higher "treasure."[11] Here, the Duala meaning of N'Domè, "Treasure," more than a simple "name," becomes a conjunctural exposition displaying the intermediality between cultural semiotic gestures and social practices. I call this expression of cultural experience in *Muna Moto* a conjuncture— that is, a new form of meaning arising in the present analysis of *Muna Moto* almost thirty years after its first introduction in theaters.

This discursive analysis of some segments of *Muna Moto* posits one fundamental idea. In the Duala's cultural performance, the vertical rhetoric of Duala metalanguage invites any analyst to decode the *Signifying* articulation beyond the cultural discourse. I have focused my analysis on two such levels of *Signifying.* First is the metalinguistic meaning emerging within the articulation of the Duala's cultural practice of marriage, the space of traditional practices of N'Gondo, and the names of the film's protagonists. This metalanguage allowed me to underscore new forms of meaning arising within the specific cultural articulation Dikonguè-Pipa expresses in *Muna Moto.* Second is the subjacent conjunctural political criticism *Muna Moto* introduces in juxtaposing the Duala people's institutional dispositive of marriage and the social conditions of N'Domè and N'Gando. By outlining the intermedial space of discourse displayed by the film, I have argued that this political criticism posits the diacritical *Signifying* of the effect of power on human beings (N'Domè and N'Gando) and the social dispositive of marriage (the *Doxa* of Duala tradition). Here, I showed that one of the representative figures of this postcolonial bourgeoisie, the uncle of N'Gando, used his financial power to buy the love of N'Domè. However, the heart of this young girl was not for sale and therefore remains, *as a surplus of meaning,* attached to N'Gando, her true love.

The lesson that this analysis conveys is the following: *Muna Moto* uses the "technique" of cinema to display complex discursive articulation that is "propre" of the Duala's culture. Beyond its aesthetic devices (multiple temporalities of the plot and intersecting genres, combining as it does fictional and documentary footage), the film invites the analyst to examine the level of the "interrelatedness" of its multiple meanings. *No* master narrative meaning emerges from its articulation as a decoding finality, whereas a conjunctural ground for investigating new forms of meaning is here possible. And this articulation conjoining metalanguage or the commonly labeled *metanarrative* of film is intrinsically related to the location of meaning of this specific cultural discourse.

Notes

1. The reader who has never seen *Muna Moto* can read the summary annexed to this paper. I have reproduced a strict chronological summary of its plot; rather than achieving an entire analysis of the film, I have limited my investigation to certain specific scenes. That, precisely, is called discursive analysis. I do believe that image transcription in text, especially imaginative cultural transcription in academic texts like this article, still poses some ethical questions that I cannot debate here.

2. (See especially the well-organized second edition edited by M. Sbisá and J.O. Urmson). Austin, John Langshaw: *How to Do Things with Words* (Massachusetts: Harvard University Press, 1975.)

3. The rhizome is an underground or anti-disciplinary system that links some roots to other root systems in a disseminating structure. Here, I use this concept not merely to indicate the absence of an authoritative subject that is basic to rhizomic articulation, but also the potentiality of diacritical practices producing their own specific procedures, not limited, for example, to structural boundaries of cinema-art, however, in using cinema as a vehicle of expression. (See Deleuze, Gilles and Felix Guattari: *A Thousand Plateaus: Capitalism and Schizophrenia* (Brian Massumi, trans.), Minneapolis: University of Minnesota Press, 1994.

4. In Bakhtin's terms, the notion of surplus also opens the production of text (code) to such endless diacritical assemblages that only the remaining code is emptied from authoritative constructs, even from the producing site. Bakhtin underscores this framework in *"Problem of the Text,"* in which he uses himself as an example. The "quests for my own words are in fact quests for a word that is not my own, a word that is more than myself; this is a striving to depart from one's own words with which nothing essential can be said. I myself can only be a character and not the primary author. The author's quests for his own words are basically quests for genre and style, quests for an authorial position" (p. 49). This quotation defines Bakhtin's attitude toward the quest for transparency and autonomy and illustrates the ways in which the embodied experience, history particularly, transcends the subject's intention. (*The Dialogic Imagination: Four Essays by M. M. Bakhtin.* [Michael Holquist, ed., Caryl Emerson and Michael Holquist, trans.], Austin: University of Texas Press, 1981).

5. «*Le N'Gondo est le cordon ombilical qui relie le peuple à ses vertus originelles.*" (My translation).

6. Dualas' New Year has nothing to do with the Roman (Julian) calendar, but refers instead to specific natural signs generally occurring at the beginning of the long season of rain, between November and December. One of the main signs that launches the beginning of this collective gathering is the appearance of *M'Beatowe* in the Wuri, the sea. In Duala language, *M'Beatowe* is a sort of tropical lobster emerging from the sea once a year around the rainy season, a lobster so massive that one does not need a net

to pick it up but merely a basket. It is from this *M'Beatowe* that Portuguese navigators named the Wuri *"Rio dos Camaroes" (Camaron's Sea)*, from which the name Cameroon originated.

7. By morphology of experience, I follow Fabian in meaning discursive articulation "leaving aside the case of multilingual texts, which the Vocabulaire is not appearing in a given structure. The text, especially one that is based on a precarious literacy [precarious for both the creator and the analyst], must be creatively appropriated. Far from being just a decoding of graphic signs," analyzing such a film requires the knowledge of the articulation of oral performances "without which the writing would be a quaint example of literary incompetence (lacking orthography, misrepresenting morphological and syntactic structure), a caricature of speech (and, by implication, of thought)." (See Fabian, Johannes: "Commenting Kalundi's comments: Notes on the ethnography of translating the 'Vocabulary of the town of Elisabethville,'" *Journal of Language and Popular Culture*, Vol. 1, No.3, 2001, p. 12.)

8. Cited by André Gaudreault and François Jost (2000) in "Presentation," *Societies and Representations: La Croisées des médias* (www.cri.umonreal.ca). "Si nous entendons par 'intermédialité' qu'il *y* a des relations médiatiques variables entre les médias et que leur fonction naît entre autres de l'évolution historique de ces relations, cela implique que la conception de 'monades' ou de sortes de médias 'isolés' est irrecevable [. . .]. (See Müller, Jurgen E.: *"Top Hat* et l'intermédialité de la comédie musicale," *CINÉMAS*, Vol. 5, No. 1–2, 1994, p.219, my translation).

9. See sequences #19, 28, and 29.

10. See particularly sequence #17, in which N'Gando expresses his anger in the following word: *"White men with their modern ships took all fishes, thanks to the blessing and the help of our own fellows."*

11. See for example sequence #27, in which N'Gando's Uncle wants to convince him to pay the dowry for three other women. The same articulation is explicitly displayed in sequence #30, in which N'Domè's father appears to be subjugated by the money of N'Gando's uncle.

Works Cited

Akudinobi, Jude: "Tradition/Modernity and the Discourse of African Cinema," *New Discourse of African Cinema, IRIS*, No. 18, Spring, 1995: 25–37.

Austin, John Langshaw. *How to Do Things with Words*, 2nd edition (M. Sbisà and J.O. Urmson, eds.). Cambridge: Harvard University Press, 1975.

Bakary, Imruh. "Introduction" *Symbolic Narrative African Cinema* (June Givanni, ed.). London: British Film Institute, 2000.

Bakhtin, M. Mikhael. *The Dialogic Imagination: Four Essays by M. M. Bakhtin* (Michael Holquist, ed., Caryl Emerson and Michael Holquist, trans.). Austin: University of Texas Press, 1981.

Deleuze, Gilles and Felix Guattari. *A Thousand Plateaus: Capitalism and Schizophrenia* (Brian Massumi, trans.). Minneapolis: University of Minnesota Press, 1994.

Fabian, Johannes. "Commenting Kalundi's Comments: Notes on the ethnography of Translating the 'Vocabulary of the town of Elisabethville.'" *Journal of Language and Popular Culture*, Vol. 1, No. 3, 2001.

André Gaudreault and François Jost. "Presentation," *Societies and Representations: La Croisées des médias*. Montreal (www.cri.umonreal.ca), 2000.

Gates, Jr., Henry Louis. *The Signifying Monkey: A Theory of African-American Literary Criticism*. New York/Oxford: Oxford University Press, 1989.

Méchoualan, Eric. *Concluding Speech in Les Nouvelles sphères de l'intermédialité*. Montréal: Musée des Beaux Arts/Université de Montréal, 2000.

Müller, Jurgen E. «*Top Hat et* l'intermédialité de la comédie musicale." *CINÉMAS* Vol. 5, No. 1–2, 1994:211–220.

Appendix

The Sequential Plot of *Muna Moto,* 1975, 16mm, black and white, 90 minutes Director/Producer: Jean-Pierre Dikonguè-Pipa. *Muna Moto* is mainly composed of fifty-five sequences edited on multiple temporal levels. (A French version *of Muna Moto* is available in Ferid Boughedir *Le cinéma africain de A à Z.* Bruxelles, OCIC, 1987. Boughedir underscored sixty-three sequences/scenes of the film.)

1. Documentary footage of N'Gondo, the traditional ritual of the Duala people with their traditional clothes.
2. Close shot of N'Gando.
3. Flashback of subjective images: the Wuri, the pirogue, N'Gando and N'Domè play on the beach.
4. Flash forward on the N'Gondo: In Duala, a old man argues: "You, young men wake up . . ."
5. N'Gando looks at one lady.
6. Flashback: close shot on N'Domè
7. Flash forward: a man takes the lady with him.
8. Close shot: N'Gando endures some pain.
9. Collective gathering of N'Gondo juxtaposed with a dancing club with people clothed in European manner.
10. Flashback: N'Gando and N'Domè run on the beach. (They're happy.)
11. Flash forward: two men fight.
12. N'Gando dances with three women. (He would run away from them.)
13. Surrounded by a crowd, N'Domè holds a baby on her harms and looks at N'Gando.
14. N'Gando gravely challenges N'Domè, comes near her hands, and takes the baby before running away. N'Domè cries loudly, she and the crowd run after N'Gando. N'Domè and N'Gando fight, surrounded by the crowd.
15. Flashback: In the house of N'Domè, people drink wine, and the father of N'Domè gives his blessing, N'Gando is present and very happy. (It is the true beginning of the plot.)
16. N'Gando counts some money.
17. N'Gando is fishing with a borrowed pirogue. (It is interesting to notice his voice-over here: "White men with their modern ships took all the fishes, thanks to the blessing and the help of our own fellows.")
18. N'Gando and a friend argue in the bush. The friend says: "You don't even have the dot. It's your uncle who will pay the dowry of your wife."
19. (Parallel editing) N'Gando's uncle is drunk and screams after his four wives.
20. N'Gando and his friend in the bush.
21. N'Domè and N'Gando in the bush. (They mimic the future introduction of N'Domè to the uncle of N'Gando.)
22. N'Gando introduces N'Domè to his mother.
23. N'Gando and N'Domè in the bush. N'Domè says: "Even my mother-in-law has no privilege over me. I'm not sharing anything!"
24. N'Gando introduces N'Domè to his uncle. The uncle looks at N'Domè up and down, and foresees her expecting a child in touching her stomach.
25. N'Domè and N'Gando walk together. N'Gando says: "After slapping me in my face, I'm not paying your dot." N'Domè replies: "No problem! We will work together to pay' it . . ."
26. N'Gando does multiple tasks. In the bush he installs a partridge snare, cuts firewood, etc. N'Domè meets N'Gando in the bush. She brings water and foods.
27. N'Gando repairs a fishing net. His uncle comes and tries to convince him to marry three other women in exchange for N'Domè. N'Gando rejects this, and the uncle argues: "You're not able to pay the dowry . . ."
28. N'Gando and N'Domè in the pirogue.

29. N'Gando in the city's market. He purchases a bracelet for N'Domè.
30. N'Domè's father drinks whisky with N'Gando's uncle, who has brought some gifts. The father says: "I hesitate to accept you as my son-in-law because your nephew loves my girl." N'Domè's mother asks: "What is my girl going to say?" N'Gando's uncle argues: "Accept this, only the money contains the power today!"
31. N'Gando tuns on the beach.
32. N'Domè returns home and rejects the gifts of N'Gando's uncle. Her father begins slapping her.
33. N'Gando meets his uncle coming back from N'Domè's house. He offers the bracelet to N'Domè, but N'Domè's mother intercepts the gift, arguing: "If you want to marry my girl, bring the dot."
34. N'Domè and N'Gando in the bush. N'Domè asks N'Gando to make love: "If I'm not virgin, your uncle will refuse to marry me . . ." N'Gando rejects this proposition.
35. Diverse merchandise (cartons of whisky, bags of rice, etc.) is stocked in the front of N'Dome's house.
36. N'Gando and N'Domè lie idyllically on the beach (referring to sequences #2 and 33).
37. N'Domè painfully holds her stomach and throws up. Her mother asks her to tell the truth. N'Domè replies: "I'm pregnant, I didn't do it to disobey you . . ."
38. Flashback to sequence #36: N'Gando and N'Domè in the bush. (They're happy.)
39. Flash forward: N'Domè's mother suggests abortion, but N'Domè rejects the idea.
40. Back to sequence #16, but this time, N'Gando's uncle appears in the middle of the crowd, between N'Domè and N'Gando still holding the baby. (The last image of this scene is a close shot on N'Domè.)
41. Subjective flashback of N'Domè in the bush. (She imagines herself being trapped and captured by three men while she is pregnant.)
42. N'Gando cuts some firewood from a big tree.
43. In N'Gando's uncle's house, women gather to celebrate the marriage.
44. N'Gando with his friend (sequence #20) arrive at the house but are denied entry.
45. Subjective flashback to N'Gando performing his traditional childhood ritual. He views his dead father, arguing: "My son, would you disrespect your initiation? Shame on the young disregarding their origin!" N'Gando cries while viewing juxtaposed images of his uncle making love to N'Domè.
46. Flash forward: N'Gando and his friend in the bush.
47. N'Gando's mother happily holds a baby. N'Gando wants to take the baby, but his uncle interjects and takes the baby with him.
48. N'Gando, N'Domè, and the baby meet in the bush. N'Gando takes the baby on her hands. (He is happy.)
49. At the uncle's house, N'Gando brings a pair of shoes for the baby. The uncle rejects the gift. N'Domé protests: "It is not your baby!" N'Gando's uncle (here the husband of N'Domè) slaps her. N'Gando, ready to slap his uncle back, wants to intercede but declines and takes back the shoes.
50. Flashback to sequences #16 and 42: a policeman arrives in the middle of the crowd. He takes the child from N'Gando and gives him to N'Domè.
51. Subjective flashback of N'Domè: holding a suitcase, she walks with N'Gando and the baby on the beach, accompanied by a friend of N'Gando's who argues: "We cannot support injustice our whole life. We have always complied, but now, it is over. You should go, you could have done that since the beginning." N'Gando, N'Domè, and the baby get going, but they are trapped by the people of the village.
52. Subjective flash forward: N'Domè sees N'Gando, escorted by a policeman, coming from the courthouse.
53. Subjective image of N'Gando: he sees the city through the grids of the police car.
54. Flashback to sequences #2, 10, and 38.
55. Flash forward: N'Gando is pushed inside the jail yard. The last image on which the film closes is the *Prison Centrale de Doula* (Douala Central Prison).

Keywords for critical reading

By the end of this section the student should be able to define and provide a detailed example to illustrate their understanding of each of the following key concepts:

- Anecdote
- Audience commodity
- *a priori/ex posteriori*
- Content analysis
- Cultural practices/expressions
- Deductive/Inductive logic
- Empirical
- Epistemology
- Evidence
- Ideology
- Intermediality
- Research Design (Primary research; Secondary Research)
- Discourse (discourse analysis; promotional discourse; social discourse)
- Metaphysics
- Variable
- Theory

Key questions for critical learning

1. 'The result of the research process is neither theory nor data, but knowledge.' What do I mean by this statement?
2. Explain the difference between inductive and deductive logic.
3. What is the difference between a hypothesis and a research objective?
4. What is the difference between primary and secondary research?
5. Consider the following hypothesis: 'Increased exposure to violent cartoons leads to higher levels of reported aggression in teenagers.' What is the independent variable in this hypothesis?
6. Explain the difference between Immanuel Kant and David Hume's conceptions of knowledge.
7. Using a concrete example, such as a sitcom, a movie narrative, or any specific event you recently heard, viewed, or witnessed, outline how the notion of intermediality could allow you to see contradictory ideologies at work.
8. What role does the 'audience commodity' play in the shaping of sports news content?

Part 5

Media, Culture, and Society

Section Editor: Boulou Ebanda de B'béri

Introduction

Those studying the media and media content can only do so by taking into account the ways in which the meaning is 'represented' in mass media texts. Indeed, the content of mass media texts is composed of symbolic representation of ideas and images. And mass media texts cannot be a referent of one singular meaning, fixed in eternity and applicable in every culture. It should then be noted that the most striking question this section explores is the relationship between language, meaning, and representation. Differently put, the texts of this section explore the process and context of a specific kind of meaning-making entities. The first text uses straightforward examples, illustrating how human beings draw on language's phonological, syntactic, and semantic rules to communicate. This text shows that the meaning is not fixed because meaning is the mind of the people not in the texts, symbols, or words. It could then be said that human languages represent much of what the world is rather than a clear-cut idea of what the world has. The difference between 'to be' (e.g., how smart someone 'is') and 'to have' (e.g., how much smartness someone 'has') is enormous because it opens up the question concerning representation, or the process of meaning production, which is central to critical media studies.

The question of representation is of particular interest not only for the readers of this volume but for everyone—this question is at the centre of the ways in which human beings make sense of the world. And mass media texts tremendously contribute to this meaning-making process. Stuart Hall's essay, 'Encoding/Decoding', precisely tackles this meaning-making process in television texts. Written in the early 1980s, Hall's essay has become a must-read in media studies. It combines an understanding of television structures and how they function with both the network's meaning-making practices and with the wider social, discursive formations. In so doing, Hall suggests three ways of reading mass media texts, however, this formulaic application can only be taken as a starting point that allows us to re-open the apparently naturalized limits of signification (e.g., relative autonomy) and articulations of mass media texts. Essays by Richard Dyer and bell hooks closely outline the processes through which racial imagery becomes central to our modern society.

Both authors tackle the question of the representation by focusing specifically on the question of race. For Dyer, racial imagery of white people is central to the organization of modern world; this group of identity formation has been represented as if it was not a race but 'just' a group of people, whereas other colours are something else—usually case studies. This invisibility of whiteness as a racial representation defines the ordinariness, and helps those of that identity group to secure the position of power in our modern societies. While Dyer focuses on whiteness, bell hooks undertakes the examination of blackness, to see the ways in which black people represent, imitate, or apprehend whites system of domination. hooks concludes that the memory of racial apartheid plays an important part in black imagination, for the reason that black people associate 'whiteness with the terrible, the terrifying, the terrorizing'.

Linda Aldoory's and Shawn J. Parry-Gilles' writing moves from purely racial imagination to analyze the gendered ideology in Western feminist media theories. To do so, they mobilize the concept of 'intersectionality' to illustrate the complexity of feminist media research and to advance our understanding of stereotypical application on women, race, and ethnicity.

Dian K. Ivy and Phil Backlund look at the power of mediated communications and their effects on gender representation, focusing on television, advertisements, movies, and the articulation and perception of pornography. They conclude that it is important to critically decipher mass media productions that have the potential to influence us, because the more we understand what is the influencing us, the more ready we will be to dive into new relationships or to strengthen our existing ones.

Language, Representation, Meaning Production, and Reception

Language

Ronald B. Adler and George Rodman

The Nature of Language

Humans speak about ten thousand dialects. Although most of these sound different from one another, all possess the same characteristics of **language:** a collection of symbols governed by rules and used to convey messages between individuals. A closer look at this definition can explain how language operates and suggest how we can use it more effectively.

Language Is Symbolic

There's nothing natural about calling your loyal four-footed companion a "dog" or the object you're reading right now a "book." These words, like virtually all language, are **symbols**—arbitrary constructions that represent a communicator's thoughts. Not all linguistic symbols are spoken or written words. Speech and writing aren't the only forms of language. Sign language, as "spoken" by most deaf people, is symbolic in nature and not the pantomime it might seem. There are literally hundreds of different sign languages spoken around the world that represent the same ideas differently. These distinct languages include American Sign Language, British Sign Language, French Sign Language, Danish Sign Language, Chinese Sign Language—even Australian Aboriginal and Mayan sign languages.

Symbols are more than just labels: They are the way we experience the world. You can prove this fact by trying a simple experiment. Work up some saliva in your mouth, and then spit it into a glass. Take a good look, and then drink it up. Most people find this process mildly disgusting. But ask yourself why this is so. After all, we swallow our own saliva all the time. The answer arises out of the symbolic labels we use. After the saliva is in the glass, we call it *spit* and think of it in a different way. In other words, our reaction is to the *name*, not the thing.

The naming process operates in virtually every situation. How you react to a stranger will depend on the symbols you use to categorize him or her: gay (or straight), religious (or not), attractive (or unattractive), and so on.

Meanings Are in People, Not Words

Ask a dozen people what the same symbol means, and you are likely to get twelve different answers. Does an American flag bring up associations of patriots giving their lives for their country? Fourth of July parades? Cultural imperialism? How about a cross: What does it represent? The message of Jesus Christ? Fire-lit rallies of Ku Klux Klansmen? Your childhood Sunday school? The necklace your sister always wears?

As with physical symbols, the place to look for meaning in language isn't in the words themselves, but rather in the way people make sense of them. One unfortunate example of this fact occurred in Washington, DC, when the newly appointed city ombudsman used the word "niggardly" to describe an approach to budgeting. Some African-American critics accused him of uttering an unforgivable racial slur. His defenders pointed out that the word, which means "miserly," is derived from Scandinavian languages and that it has no link to the racial slur it resembles. Even though the criticisms eventually died away, they illustrate that, correct or not, the meanings people associate with words have far more significance than do their dictionary definitions.

Linguistic theorists C. K. Ogden and I.A. Richards illustrated the fact that meanings are social constructions in their well-known "triangle of meaning" (Figure 1). This model shows that there is only an indirect relationship—indicated by a broken line—between a word and the thing it claims to represent. Some of these "things" or referents do not exist in the physical world. For instance,

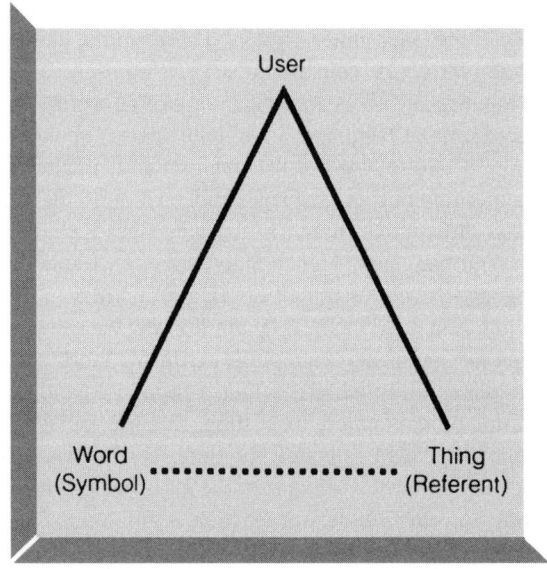

Figure 1 Ogden and Richards's Triangle of Meaning

some referents are mythical (such as unicorns), some are no longer tangible (such as Elvis, if he really is dead), and others are abstract ideas (such as "love").

Problems arise when people mistakenly assume that others use words in the same way they do. It's possible to have an argument about *feminism* without ever realizing that you and the other person are using the word to represent entirely different things. The same goes for *environmentalism, Republicans, rock music,* and thousands upon thousands of other symbols. Words don't mean; people do—and often in widely different ways.

Despite the potential for linguistic problems, the situation isn't hopeless. We do, after all, communicate with one another reasonably well most of the time. And with enough effort, we can clear up most of the misunderstandings that do occur. The key to more accurate use of language is to avoid assuming that others interpret words the same way we do. In truth, successful communication occurs when we *negotiate* the meaning of a statement. As one French proverb puts it: The spoken word belongs half to the one who speaks it and half to the one who hears.

Language Is Rule-Governed

Languages contain several types of rules. **Phonological rules** govern how words sound when pronounced. For instance, the words *champagne, double,* and *occasion* are spelled identically in French and English, but all are pronounced differently. Nonnative speakers learning English are plagued by inconsistent phonological rules, as a few examples illustrate:

He could lead if he would get the lead out.

A farm can produce produce.

The dump was so full it had to refuse refuse.

The present is a good time to present the present.

I did not object to the object.

The bandage was wound around the wound.

I shed a tear when I saw the tear in my clothes.

Phonological rules aren't the only ones that govern the way we use language to communicate. **Syntactic rules** govern the structure of language—the way symbols can be arranged. For example, correct English syntax requires that every word contain at least one vowel and prohibits sentences such as "Have you the cookies brought?" which is a perfectly acceptable word order in German. Although most of use aren't able to describe the syntactic rules that govern our language, it's easy to recognize their existence by noting how odd a statement that violates them appears.

Technology has spawned subversions of English with their own syntactic rules. For example, users of instant messaging on the Internet have devised a streamlined version of English that speeds up typing in real-time communication (although it probably makes teachers of composition grind their teeth in anguish):

A: Hey

B: r u at home?

A: yup yup

B: ok I'm getting offline now

A: no! why?

B: i need t study for finals u can call me tho bye

A: kbye

Semantic rules deal with the meaning of specific words. Semantic rules are what make it possible for us to agree the "bikes" are for riding and "books" are for reading; they also help us to know whom we will and won't encounter when we open doors marked "men" or "women." Without semantic rules, communication would be impossible, because each of us would use symbols in unique ways, unintelligible to one another.

Semantic misunderstandings occur when words can be interpreted in more than one way, as the following humorous headlines prove:

Police Begin Campaign to Run Down Jaywalkers

Prostitutes Appeal to Pope

Panda Mating Fails; Veterinarian Takes Over

Astronaut Takes Blame for Gas in Spacecraft

New Study of Obesity for Larger Test Group

Critical Thinking Probe

When Is Language Offensive?

See the official Web site of the Fighting Whites basketball team at http://www.fightingwhites.org/index.aspx. Do you agree with the rationale behind the team's name? How does it compare with athletic teams named after other ethnic groups (e.g., Indians)? Are there times when it is acceptable to use ethnic labels in a humorous way? What pragmatic rules govern the use of these terms?

Pragmatic rules govern how people use language in everyday interaction. Consider the example of a male boss saying "You look very pretty today" to a female employee. It's easy to imagine how the subordinate might be offended by a comment that her boss considered an innocent remark. Scholars of language have point out several levels at which the rules each person uses can differ. You can understand these levels by imagine how they would operate in our example:

Each person's self-concept
    Boss: Views himself as a nice guy.
    Subordinate: Determined to succeed on her own merits, and not her appearance.

The episode in which the comment occurs
    Boss: Casual remark at the start of the workday.
    Employee: A possible come-on?

Perceived relationship
    Boss: Views employees like members of the family.
    Employee: Depends on boss's goodwill for advancement.

Cultural background
    Boss: Member of generation in which comments about appearance were common.
    Employee: Member of generation sensitive to sexual harassment.

As this example shows, pragmatic rules don't involve semantic issues, since the words themselves are usually understood well by almost everybody. Instead, they involve how those words are understood and used. The reading on page 80 provides a good illustration of pragmatic rules: Is "shut up" an offensive attack or a statement of astonishment? It depends on the participants' understanding of when and how to use that expression. For another example of how pragmatic rules can shape understanding and interaction, see the Critical Thinking Probe on page 586.

The Power of Language

On the most obvious level, language allows us to satisfy basic functions such as describing ideas, making requests, and solving problems. But beyond these functions, the way we use language also influences others and reflects our attitudes in more subtle ways, which we will examine now.

Language Shapes Attitudes

The power of language to shape ideas has been recognized throughout history. The first chapters of the Bible report that Adam's dominion over animals was demonstrated by his being given the power to give them names. As we will now see, our speech—sometimes consciously and sometimes not—shapes others' values, attitudes, and beliefs in a variety of ways.

Naming

"What's in a name?" Juliet asked rhetorically. If Romeo had been a social scientist, he would have answered, "A great deal." Research has demonstrated that names are more than just a simple means of identification: They shape the way others think of us, the way we view ourselves, and the way we act.

At the most fundamental level, some research suggests that even the phonetic sound of a person's name affects the way we regard him or her, at least when we don't have other information available. One recent study revealed that reasonably accurate predictions about who will win an election can be made on the basis of some phonetic features of the candidates' surnames. Names that were simple, easily pronounced, and rhythmic were judged more favorably than ones that lack these qualities. For example, in one series of local elections, the winning candidates had names that resonated with voters: Sanders beat Pekelis, Rielly defeated Dellwo, Grady outpolled Schumacher, Combs trounced Bernsdorf, and Golden prevailed over Nuffer. Names don't guarantee victory, but in seventy-eight elections, forty-eight outcomes supported the value of having an appealing name.

The book of Proverbs (22:1) proclaims "a good name is rather to be chosen than great riches." Social science research confirms this position. In one study, psychologists asked college students to rate over a thousand names according to their likability, how active or passive they seemed, and their masculinity or femininity. The names Michael, John, and Wendy were viewed as likable and active and were rated as possessing the masculine or feminine traits of their sex. The names Percival, Isadore, and Alfreda were less likable, and their sexual identity was less clear.

Choosing a newborn's name can be especially challenging for people from nondominant cultures with different languages. One writer from India describes the problem he and his wife faced when considering names for their first child:

> How will the child's foreign name sound to American ears? (That test ruled out Shiva, my family deity; a Jewish friend put her foot down.) Will it provoke bullies to beat him up on the school playground? (That was the end of Karan, the name of a warrior from the Mahabharata, the Hindu epic. A boy called "Karen" wouldn't stand a chance.) Will it be as euphonic in New York as it is in New Delhi? (That was how Sameer failed to get off the ground. "Like a bagel with a schmear!" said one ruthless well-wisher.)

First names aren't the only linguistic elements that may shape attitudes about men and women. As the reading on the next page suggests, the choice of what last name to use after marriage can influence others' perceptions.

Credibility

Scholarly speaking is a good example of how speech style influences perception. We refer to what has been called the Dr. Fox hypothesis. "An apparently legitimate speaker who utters an unintelligible message will be judged competent by an audience in the speaker's area of apparent expertise." The Dr. Fox hypothesis got its name from one Dr. Myron L. Fox, who delivered a talk followed by a half-hour discussion on "Mathematical Game Theory as Applied to Physical Education." The audience included psychiatrists, psychologists, social workers, and educators. Questionnaires collected after the session revealed that these educated listeners found the lecture clear and stimulating.

Despite his warm reception by this learned audience, Fox was a complete fraud. He was a professional actor whom researchers had coached to deliver a lecture of double-talk—a patchwork of information from a *Scientific American* article mixed with jokes, non sequiturs, contradictory statements, and meaningless references to unrelated topics. When wrapped in a linguistic package of high-level professional jargon, however, the meaningless gobbledygook was judged as important information. In other words, Fox's audience reaction was based more on the credibility that arose from his use of impressive-sounding language than from the ideas he expressed.

The same principle seems to hold for academic writing. A group of thirty-two management professors rated material according to its complexity rather than its content. When a message about consumer behavior was loaded with unnecessary words and long, complex sentences, the professors rated it highly. When the same message was translated into more readable English, with shorter words and clearer sentences, the professors judged the same research as less competent.

Status

In the classic musical *My Fair Lady,* Professor Henry Higgins transformed Eliza Doolittle from a lowly flower girl into a high-society woman by replacing her cockney accent with an upper-crust speaking style. Decades of research have demonstrated that the power of speech to influence status is a fact. Several factors combine to create positive or negative impressions: accent, choice of words, speech rate, and even the apparent age of a speaker. In most cases, speakers of standard dialect are rated higher than nonstandard speakers in a variety of ways: They are viewed as more competent and more self-confident, and the content of their messages is rated more favorably. The unwillingness or inability of a communicator to use the standard dialect fluently can have serious consequences. For instance, speakers of Black English, a distinctive dialect with its own accent, grammar, syntax, and semantic rules, are rated as less intelligent, professional, capable, socially acceptable, and employable by speakers of standard English.

Sexism and Racism

By now it should be clear that the power of language to shape attitudes goes beyond individual cases and influences how we perceive entire groups of people. For example, Casey Miller and Kate Swift argue that some aspects of language suggest women are of lower status than men. Miller and Swift contend that, except for words referring to females by definition, such as *mother* and *actress,* English defines many nonsexual concepts as male. Most dictionaries, in fact, define *effeminate* as the opposite of *masculine,* although the opposite of *feminine* is closer to *unfeminine.*

Miller and Swift also argue that incorrect use of the pronoun *he* to refer to both men and women can have damaging results.

On the television screen, a teacher of first-graders who has just won a national award is describing her way of teaching. "You take each child where you find him," she says. "You watch to see what he's interested in, and then you build on his interests."

A five-year-old looking at the program asks her mother, "Do only boys go to that school?"

"No," her mother begins, "she's talking about girls too, but—"

But what? The teacher being interviewed on television is speaking correct English.

What can the mother tell her daughter about why a child, in any generalization, is always *he* rather than *she*? How does a five-year-old comprehend the generic personal pronoun?

It's usually easy to use nonsexist language. For example, the term *mankind* may be replaced by *humanity, human beings, human race,* or *people; man-made* may be replaced by *artificial, manufactured,* and *synthetic; manpower* may be replaced by *human power, workers,* and *workforce;* and *manhood* may be replaced by *adulthood.* Likewise,

- *Congressmen* may be called *members of Congress.*
- *Firemen* may be called *firefighters.*
- *Foremen* may be called *supervisors.*
- Policemen and policewomen are both police officers.

The use of labels for racist purposes has a long and ugly past. Names have been used throughout history to stigmatize groups that other groups have disapproved of. By using derogatory terms to label some people, the out-group is set apart and pictured in an unfavorable light. Diane Mader provides several examples of this:

We can see the process of stigmatization in Nazi Germany when Jewish people became vermin, in the United States when African Americans became "niggers" and chattel, in the military when the enemy became "gooks."

The power of racist language to shape attitudes is difficult to avoid, even when it is obviously offensive. In one study, experimental subjects who heard a derogatory label used against a member of a minority group expressed annoyance at this sort of slur; but despite their disapproval, the negative emotional terms did have an impact. Not only did the unwitting subjects rate the minority individual's competence lower when that person performed poorly, but also they found fault with others who associated socially with the minority person—even members of the subject's own ethnic group.

Language Reflects Attitudes

Besides shaping the way we view ourselves and others, language reflects our attitudes. Feelings of control, attraction, commitment, responsibility—all these and more are reflected in the way we use language.

Ethical Challenge

Sexist and Racist Language

One of the most treasured civil liberties is freedom of speech. At the same time, most people would agree that some forms of racist and sexist speech are hateful and demeaning to their targets. As you have read in these pages, language shapes the attitudes of those who hear it.

How do you reconcile the principle of free speech and the need to minimize hateful and discriminatory messages? Do you think laws and policies can and should be made that limit certain types of communication? If so, how should those limits be drafted to protect civil liberties? If not, can you justify the necessary protection of even sexist and racist language?

Power

Communication researchers have identified a number of language patterns that add to, or detract from, a speaker's ability to influence others, as well as reflecting how a speaker feels about his or her degree of control over a situation. Table 1 summarizes some of these findings by listing several types of "powerless" language.

You can see the difference between powerful language and powerless language by comparing the following statements:

> "Excuse me, sir, I hate to say this, but I . . . uh . . . I guess I won't be able to turn in the assignment on time. I had a personal emergency and . . . well . . . it was just impossible to finish it by today. I'll have it in your mailbox on Monday, okay?"

> "I won't be able to turn in the assignment on time. I had a personal emergency, and it was impossible to finish it by today. I'll have it in your mailbox on Monday."

Table 1 Powerless language

Type of usage	Example
Hedges	"I'm kinda disappointed . . ." "I think we should . . ." "I guess I'd like to . . ."
Hesitations	"Uh, can I have a minute of your time?" "Well, we could try this idea . . ." "I wish you would—er—try to be on time."
Intensifiers	"So that's how I feel . . ." "I'm not very hungry."
Polite forms	"Excuse me, sir . . ."
Tag questions	"It's about time we got started, isn't it?" "Don't you think we should give it another try?"
Disclaimers	"I probably shouldn't say this, but . . ." "I'm not really sure, but . . ."

Although the powerless speech described in Table 1 can often lead to unsatisfying results, don't assume that the best goal is always to sound as powerful as you can. Along with gaining compliance, another conversational goal is often building a supportive, friendly relationship; and sharing power with the other person can help you in this regard. For this reason, many everyday statements will contain a mixture of powerful speech and powerless speech. Our student-teacher example illustrates how this combination of powerless mannerisms and powerful mannerisms can help the student get what she wants while staying on good terms with the professor:

> "Excuse me, Professor Rodman. I want you to know that I won't be able to turn in the assignment on time. I had a personal emergency, and it was impossible to finish it by today. I'll definitely have it in your mailbox on Monday."

Whether or not the professor finds the excuse acceptable, it's clear that this last statement combines the best features of powerful speech and powerless speech: a combination of self-assurance and goodwill.

Simply counting the number of powerful or powerless statements won't always reveal who has the most control in a relationship. Social rules often mask the real distribution of power. Sociolinguist Deborah Tannen describes how politeness can be a face-saving way of delivering an order:

> I hear myself giving instructions to my assistants without actually issuing orders: "Maybe it would be a good idea to . . .;" "It would be great if you could . . ." all the while knowing that I expect them to do what I've asked right away . . . This rarely creates problems, though, because the people who work for me know that there is only one reason I mention tasks—because I want them done. I *like* giving instructions in this way; it appeals to my sense of what it means to be a good person . . . taking others' feelings into account.

As this quote suggests, high-status speakers often realize that politeness is an effective way to get their needs met while protecting the face of the less powerful person. The importance of achieving both content goals and relational goals helps explain why a mixture of powerful speech and polite speech is usually most effective. Of course, if the other person misinterprets politeness for weakness, it may be necessary to shift to a more powerful speaking style.

Powerful speech that gets the desired results in mainstream North American and European culture doesn't succeed everywhere with everyone. In Japan, saving face for others is an important goal, so communicators there tend to speak in ambiguous terms and use hedge words and qualifiers. In most Japanese sentences the verb comes at the end of the sentence so the "action" part of the statement can be postponed. Traditional Mexican culture, with its strong emphasis on cooperation, makes a priority of using language to create harmony in interpersonal relationships rather than taking a firm or oppositional stance in order to make others feel more at ease. Korean culture represents yet another group of people who prefers "indirect" (for example, "perhaps," "could be") to "direct" speech.

Affiliation

Power isn't the only way language reflects the status of relationships. Language can also be a way of building and demonstrating solidarity with others. An impressive body of research has demonstrated that communicators who want to show affiliation with one another adapt their speech in a variety of ways, including their choice of vocabulary, rate of talking, number and placement of pauses, and level of politeness. On an individual level, close friends and lovers often develop special terms that serve as a way of signifying their relationship. Using the same vocabulary sets these people apart from others, reminding themselves and the rest of the world of their relationship. The same process works among members of larger groups, ranging from street gangs to military personnel. Communication researchers call this linguistic accommodation **convergence.**

When two or more people feel equally positive about one another, their linguistic convergence will be mutual. But when communicators want or need the approval of others they often adapt their speech to suit the others' style, trying to say the "right thing" or speak in a way that will help them fit in. We see this process when immigrants who want to gain the rewards of material success in a new culture strive to master the prevalent language. Likewise, employees who seek advancement tend to speak more like their superiors: supervisors adopt the speech style of managers, and managers converge toward their bosses.

The principle of speech accommodation works in reverse, too. Communicators who want to set themselves apart from others adopt the strategy of **divergence,** speaking in a way that emphasizes their difference from others. For example, members of an ethnic group, even though fluent in the dominant language, might use their own dialect as a way of showing solidarity with one another—a sort of "us against them" strategy. Divergence also operates in other settings. A physician or attorney, for example, who wants to establish credibility with his or her client might speak formally and use professional jargon to create a sense of distance. The implicit message here is "I'm different (and more knowledgeable) than you."

Attraction and Interest

Social customs discourage us from expressing like or dislike in many situations. Only a clod would respond to the question "What do you think of the cake I baked for you?" by saying, "It's terrible." Bashful or cautious suitors might not admit their attraction to a potential partner. Even when people are reluctant to speak candidly, the language they use can suggest their degree of interest and attraction toward a person, object, or idea. Morton Weiner and Albert Mehrabian outline a number of linguistic clues that reveal these attitudes.

- **Demonstrative pronoun choice.** *These* people want our help (positive) versus *Those* people want our help (less positive).
- **Negation.** It's *good* (positive) versus It's *not bad* (less positive).

- **Sequential placement.** Dick and Jane (Dick is more important) versus Jane and Dick (Jane is more important). However, sequential placement isn't always significant. You may put "toilet bowl cleaner" at the top of your shopping list simply because it's closer to the market door than is champagne.

Responsibility

In addition to suggesting liking and importance, language can reveal the speaker's willingness to accept responsibility for a message.

- **"It" versus "I" statements.** *It's* not finished (less responsible) versus *I* didn't finish it (more responsible).
- **"You" versus "I" statements.** Sometimes *you* make me angry (less responsible) versus Sometimes *I* get angry when you do that (more responsible). "I" statements are more likely to generate positive reactions from others when compared to accusatory ones.
- **"But" statements.** It's a good idea, *but* it won't work. You're really terrific, *but* I think we ought to spend less time together. (*But* cancels everything that went before the word.)
- **Questions versus statements.** Do you think we ought to do that? (less responsible) versus I don't think we ought to do that (more responsible).

Troublesome Language

Besides being a blessing that enables us to live together, language can be something of a curse. We have all known the frustration of being misunderstood, and most of us have been baffled by another person's overreaction to an innocent comment. In the following pages we will look at several kinds of troublesome language, with the goal of helping you communicate in a way that makes matters better instead of worse.

The Language of Misunderstandings

The most obvious kind of language problems are semantic: We simply don't understand others completely or accurately. Most misunderstandings arise from some common problems that are easily remedied—after you recognize them.

Equivocal Language

Equivocal words have more than one correct dictionary definition. Some equivocal misunderstandings are simple, at least after they are exposed. A nurse once told her patient that he "wouldn't be needing" the materials he requested from home. He interpreted the statement to mean he was near death when the nurse meant he would be going home soon. A colleague of ours mistakenly sent some confidential materials to the wrong person after his boss told him to "send them to Richard," without specifying *which* Richard. Some equivocal misunderstandings can be embarrassing, as one woman recalls:

> In the fourth grade the teacher asked the class what a period was. I raised my hand and shared everything I had learned about girls' getting their period. But he was talking about the dot at the end of a sentence. Oops!

Equivocal misunderstandings can have serious consequences. Communication researchers Michael Motley and Heidi Reeder suggest that equivocation at least partially explains why men may sometimes persist in attempts to become physically intimate when women have expressed unwillingness to do so. Interviews and focus groups with college students revealed that women often use ambiguous phrases to say "no" to a man's sexual advances: "I'm confused about this." "I'm not sure that we're ready for this yet." "Are you sure you want to do this?" "Let's be friends" and even "That tickles." (The researchers found that women were most likely to use less direct phrases when they hoped to see or date the man again. When they wanted to cut off the relationship, they were more likely to give a direct response.) Whereas women viewed indirect statements as equivalent to saying "no," men were more likely to interpret them as less clear-cut requests to stop. As the researchers put it, "male/female misunderstandings are not so much a matter of males hearing resistance messages as "go," but rather their not hearing them as "stop." Under the law, "no" means precisely that, and anyone who argues otherwise can be in for serious legal problems.

Relative Words

Relative words gain their meaning by comparison. For example, is the school you attend large or small? This depends on what you compare it to: Alongside a campus like UCLA, with an enrollment of over thirty thousand students, it probably looks small; but compared to a smaller institution, it might seem quite large. In the same way relative words like *fast* and *slow, smart* and *stupid, short* and *long* depend for their meaning upon what they're compared to. (The "large" size can of olives is the smallest you can buy; the larger ones are "giant," "colossal," and "super-colossal.")

Some relative words are so common that we mistakenly assume that they have a clear meaning. In one study, graduate students were asked to assign numerical values to terms such as *doubtful, toss-up, likely, probable, good chance,* and *unlikely.* There was a tremendous variation in the meaning of most of these terms. For example, the responses for *possible* ranged from 0 to 99 percent. *Good chance* meant between 35 and 90 percent, whereas *unlikely* fell between 0 and 40 percent.

Using relative words without explaining them can lead to communication problems. Have you ever responded to someone's question about the weather by saying it was warm, only to find out that what was warm to you was cold to the other person? Or have you followed a friend's advice and gone to a "cheap" restaurant, only to find that it was twice as expensive as you expected? Have you been disappointed to learn that classes you've heard were "easy" turned out to be hard, that journeys you were told would be "short" were long, that "unusual" ideas were really quite ordinary? The problem in each case came from failing to anchor the relative word used to a more precisely measurable word.

Slang and Jargon

Slang is language used by a group of people whose members belong to a similar co-culture or other group. Some slang is related to specialized interests and activities. For instance, cyclists who talk about "bonking" are referring to running out of energy. Rapsters know that "bling bling" refers to jewelry and a "whip" is a nice-looking car.

Other slang consists of *regionalisms*—terms that are understood by people who live in one geographic area but that are incomprehensible to outsiders. This sort of use illustrates how slang defines insiders and outsiders, creating a sense of identity and solidarity. Residents of the fiftieth U.S. state know that when a fellow Alaskan says "I'm going outside," he or she is leaving the state. In the East End of London, cockney dialect uses rhyming words as substitutes for everyday expressions: "bacon and eggs" for "legs," and "Barney Rubble" for "trouble." This sort of use also illustrates how slang can be used to identify insiders and outsiders: With enough shared rhyming, slang users could talk about outsiders without the clueless outsiders knowing that they were the subject of conversation ("Lovely set of bacons, eh?" "Stay away from him. He's Barney").

Slang can also be age-related. Most college students know that drinkers wearing "beer goggles" have consumed enough alcohol that they find almost everyone of the opposite—or sometimes the same—sex attractive. At some schools, a "monkey" is the "other" woman or man in a boyfriend's or girlfriend's life: "I've heard Mitch is cheating on me. When I find his monkey, I'm gonna do her up!"

Almost everyone uses some sort of **jargon**: the specialized vocabulary that functions as a kind of shorthand by people with common backgrounds and experience. Skateboarders have their own language to describe maneuvers: "ollie," "grind," and "shove it." Some jargon consists of *acronyms*—initials of terms that are combined to form a word. Stock traders refer to the NASDAQ (pronounced "naz-dak") securities index, and military people label failure to serve at one's post as being AWOL (absent without leave). The digital age has spawned its own vocabulary of jargon. For instance, computer users know that "viruses" are malicious programs that migrate from one computer to another, wreaking havoc. Likewise, "cookies" are tiny files that remote observers can use to monitor a user's computer habits. Some jargon goes beyond being descriptive and conveys attitudes. For example, cynics in the high-tech world sometimes refer to being fired from a job as being "uninstalled." They talk dismissively about the nonvirtual world as the "carbon community" and to books and newspapers as "freeware." Some technical support staffers talk of "banana problems," meaning those that could be figured out by monkeys, as in "This is a two-banana problem at worst."

Jargon can be a valuable kind of shorthand for people who understand its use. The trauma team in a hospital emergency room can save time, and possibly lives, by speaking in shorthand, referring to "GSWs" (gunshot wounds), "chem 7" lab tests, and so on; but the same specialized vocabulary that works so well among insiders can mystify and confuse family members of the patient, who don't understand the jargon. The same sort of misunderstandings can arise in less critical settings when insiders use their own language with people who don't share the same vocabulary. Jeffrey Katzman of the William Morris Agency's Hollywood office experienced this sort of problem when he met with members of a Silicon Valley computer firm to discuss a joint project.

> When he used the phrase "in development," he meant a project that was as yet merely an idea. When the techies used it, on the other hand, they meant designing a specific game or program. Ultimately, says Katzman, he had to bring in a blackboard and literally define his terms. "It was like when the Japanese first came to Hollywood," he recalls. "They had to use interpreters, and we did too."

Overly Abstract Language

Most objects, events, and ideas can be described with varying degrees of specificity. Consider the material you are reading. You could call it:

A book

A textbook

A communication textbook

Understanding Human Communication

Chapter 3 of *Understanding Human Communication*

Page 91 of Chapter 3 of *Understanding Human Communication*

In each case your description would be more and more specific. Semanticist S. I. Hayakawa created an **abstraction ladder** to describe this process. This ladder consists of a number of descriptions of the same thing. Lower items focus specifically on the person, object, or event, whereas higher terms are generalizations that include the subject as a member of a larger class. To talk about "college," for example, is more abstract than to talk about a particular school. Likewise, referring to "women" is more abstract than referring to "feminists," or more specifically naming feminist organizations or even specific members who belong to them.

Higher-level abstractions are a useful tool, because without them language would be too cumbersome to be useful. It's faster, easier, and more useful to talk about *Europe* than to list all of the countries on that continent. In the same way, using relatively abstract terms like *friendly* or *smart* can make it easier to describe people than listing their specific actions.

Abstract language—speech that refers to observable events or objects—serves a second, less obvious function. At times it allows us to avoid confrontations by deliberately being unclear. Suppose, for example, your boss is enthusiastic about a new approach to doing business that you think is a terrible idea. Telling the truth might seem too risky, but lying—saying "I think it's a great idea"—wouldn't feel right either. In situations like this an abstract answer can hint at your true belief without a direct confrontation: "I don't know . . . It's sure unusual . . . It *might* work." The same sort of abstract language can help you avoid embarrassing friends who ask for your opinion with questions like "What do you think of my new haircut?" An abstract response like "It's really different!" may be easier for you to deliver—and for your friend to receive—than the clear, brutal truth: "It's really ugly!" We will have more to say about this linguistic strategy of equivocation later in this chapter.

Although vagueness does have its uses, highly abstract language can cause several types of problems. The first is *stereotyping.* Consider claims like "All whites are bigots," "Men don't care about relationships," "The police are a bunch of goons," or "Professors around here care more about their research than they do about students." Each of these claims ignores the very important fact that abstract descriptions are almost always too general, that they say more than we really mean.

Besides creating stereotypical attitudes, abstract language can lead to the problem of *confusing others.* Imagine the lack of understanding that results from imprecise language in situations like this:

A: We never do anything that's fun anymore.
B: What do you mean?
A: We used to do lots of unusual things, but now it's the same old stuff, over and over.
B: But last week we went on that camping trip, and tomorrow we're going to that party where we'll meet all sorts of new people. Those are new things.
A: That's not what I mean. I'm talking about really unusual stuff.
B: *(becoming confused and a little impatient)* Like what? Taking hard drugs or going over Niagara Falls in a barrel?
A: Don't be stupid. All I'm saying is that we're in a rut. We should be living more exciting lives.
B: Well, I don't know what you want.

The best way to avoid this sort of overly abstract language is to use **behavioral descriptions** instead. (See Table 2.) Behavioral descriptions move down the abstraction ladder to identify the specific, observable phenomenon being discussed. A thorough description should answer three questions:

1. **Who Is Involved?** Are you speaking for just yourself or for others as well? Are you talking about a group of people ("the neighbors," "women") or specific individuals ("the people next door with the barking dog," "Lola and Lizzie")?

Table 2 Abstract and behavioral descriptions

	Abstract description	Behavioral description			Remarks
		Who is involved	In what circumstances	Specific behaviors	
Problem	I talk too Much	People I find intimidating	When I want them to like me	I talk (mostly about myself) instead of giving them a chance to speak or asking about their lives.	Behavioral description more clearly identifies behaviors to change.
Goal	I want to be more constructive.	My roommate	When we talk about household duties	Instead of finding fault with her ideas, suggest alternatives that might work.	Behavioral description clearly outlines how to act; abstract description doesn't.
Appreciation	"You've really been helpful lately."	(Deliver to fellow worker)	"When I've had to take time off work because of personal problems"	"You took my shifts without complaining."	Give both abstract and behavioral descriptions for best results.
Request	"Clean up your act!"	(Deliver to target person)	"When we're around my family"	"Please don't tell jokes that involve sex."	Behavioral description specifies desired behavior.

453

2. **In What Circumstances Does the Behavior Occur?** Where does it occur: everywhere or in specific places (at parties, at work, in public)? When does it occur: When you're tired or when a certain subject comes up? The behavior you are describing probably doesn't occur all the time. In order to be understood, you need to pin down what circumstances set this situation apart from other ones.

3. **What Behaviors Are Involved?** Though terms such as *more cooperative* and *helpful* might sound like concrete descriptions of behavior, they are usually too vague to do a clear job of explaining what's on your mind. Behaviors must be *observable,* ideally both to you and to others. For instance, moving down the abstraction ladder from the relatively vague term *helpful,* you might come to behaviors such as *does the dishes every other day, volunteers to help me with my studies,* or *fixes dinner once or twice a week without being asked.* It's easy to see that terms like these are easier for both you and others to understand than are more vague abstractions.

Behavioral descriptions can improve communication in a wide range of situations, as Table 2 illustrates. Research also supports the value of specific language. One study found that well-adjusted couples had just as many conflicts as poorly adjusted couples, but the way the well-adjusted couples handled their problems was significantly different. Instead of blaming one another, the well-adjusted couples expressed their complaints in behavioral terms.

Confusing Facts and Inferences

Labeling your opinions can go a long way toward relational harmony, but developing this habit won't solve all linguistic problems. Difficulties also arise when we confuse factual statements with **inferential statements**—conclusions arrived at from an interpretation of evidence. Consider a few examples:

Fact	Inference
He hit a lamppost while driving down the street.	He was daydreaming when he hit the lamppost.
You interrupted me before I finished what I was saying.	You don't care about what I have to say.
You haven't paid your share of the rent on time for the past three months.	You're trying to weasel out of your responsibilities.
I haven't gotten a raise in almost a year.	The boss is exploiting me.

There's nothing wrong with making inferences as long as you identify them as such: "She stomped out and slammed the door. It looked to me as if she were furious." The danger comes when we confuse inferences with facts and make them sound like the absolute truth.

One way to avoid fact-inference confusion is to use the perception-checking skill described in Chapter 2 to test the accuracy of your inferences. Recall that a perception check has three parts: a description of the behavior being discussed, your interpretation of that behavior, and a request for verification. For instance, instead of saying, "Why are you laughing at me?" you could say, "When you laugh like that *[description of behavior]*, I get the idea you think something I did was stupid *[interpretation]*. Are you laughing at me *[question]?*"

Emotive Language

Emotive language contains words that sound as if they're describing something when they are really announcing the speaker's attitude toward something. Do you like that old picture frame? If so, you would probably call it "an antique," but if you think it's ugly, you would likely describe it as "a piece of junk." Emotive words may sound like statements of fact but are always opinions.

Barbra Streisand pointed out how some people use emotive language to stigmatize behavior in women that they admire in men:

A man is commanding—a woman is demanding.

A man is forceful—a woman is pushy.

A man is uncompromising—a woman is a ball-breaker.

A man is a perfectionist—a woman's a pain in the ass.

He's assertive—she's aggressive.

He strategizes—she manipulates.

He shows leadership—she's controlling.

He's committed—she's obsessed.

He's persevering—she's relentless.

He sticks to his guns—she's stubborn.

If a man wants to get it right, he's looked up to and respected.

If a woman wants to get it right, she's difficult and impossible.

The reading on page 97 illustrates how emotive language can escalate conflicts and make constructive dialogue difficult, or even impossible.

Critical Thinking Probe

Emotive Language

Test your ability to identify emotive language by playing the following word game.

1. Take an action, object, or characteristic and show how it can be viewed either favorably or unfavorably, according to the label it is given. For example:
   a. I'm casual.
      You're careless.
      He's a slob.

(Continued)

   b. I read adult love stories.
      You read erotic literature.
      She reads pornography.
2. Now create three-part descriptions of your own, using the following statements as a start:
   a. I'm tactful.
   b. She's a liar.
   c. I'm conservative.
   d. You have a high opinion of yourself.
   e. I'm quiet.
   f. You're pessimistic.
3. Now recall two situations in which you used emotive language as if it were a description of fact. How might the results have differed if you had used more objective language?

As this reading suggests, problems occur when people use emotive words without labeling them as such. You might, for instance, have a long and bitter argument with a friend about whether a third person was "assertive" or "obnoxious," when a more accurate and peaceable way to handle the issue would be to acknowledge that one of you approves of the behavior and the other doesn't.

Evasive Language

None of the troublesome language habits we have described so far is a deliberate strategy to mislead or antagonize others. Now, however, we'll consider euphemisms and equivocations, two types of language that speakers use by design to avoid communicating clearly. Although both of these have some very legitimate uses, they also can lead to frustration and confusion.

Euphemisms

A **euphemism** (from the Greek word meaning "to use words of good omen") is a pleasant term substituted for a more direct but potentially less pleasant one. We are using euphemisms when we say "restroom" instead of "toilet" or "plump" instead of "fat" or "overweight." There certainly are cases where the euphemistic pulling of linguistic punches can be face-saving. It's probably more constructive to question a possible "statistical misrepresentation" than to call someone a liar, for example. Likewise, it may be less disquieting to some to refer to people as "senior citizens" than "old."

Like many businesses, the airline industry uses euphemisms to avoid upsetting already nervous flyers. For example, rather than saying "turbulence," pilots and flight attendants use the less frightening term "bumpy air." Likewise, they refer to thunderstorms as "rain showers," and fog as "mist" or "haze." And savvy flight personnel never use the words "your final destination."

Despite their occasional advantages, many euphemisms are not worth the effort it takes to create them. Some are pretentious and confusing, such as the renaming of one university's Home Economics Department as the Department of Human Ecology or a middle school's labeling of hallways as "behavior transition corridors." Other euphemisms are downright deceptive, such as the U.S. Senate's labeling of a $23,200 pay raise a "pay equalization concept."

Equivocation

It's 8:15 P.M., and you are already a half-hour late for your dinner reservation at the fanciest restaurant in town. Your partner has finally finished dressing and confronts you with the question "How do I look?" To tell the truth, you hate your partner's outfit. You don't want to lie, but on the other hand you don't want to be hurtful. Just as importantly, you don't want to lose your table by waiting around for your date to choose something else to wear. You think for a moment and then reply, "You look amazing. I've never seen an outfit like that before. Where did you get it?"

Your response in this situation was an **equivocation**—a deliberately vague statement that can be interpreted in more than one way. Earlier in this chapter we talked about how *unintentional* equivocation can lead to misunderstandings. But our discussion here focuses on *intentionally ambiguous speech* that is used to avoid lying on one hand and telling a painful truth on the other. Equivocations have several advantages. They spare the receiver from the embarrassment that might come from a completely truthful answer, and it can be easier for the sender to equivocate than to suffer the discomfort of being honest.

Despite its benefits, there are times when communicators equivocate as a way to weasel out of delivering important but unpleasant messages. Suppose, for example, that you are unsure about your standing in one of your courses. You approach the professor and ask how you're doing. "Not bad," the professor answers. This answer isn't too satisfying. "What grade am I earning?" you inquire. "Oh, lots of people would be happy with it" is the answer you receive. "But will I receive an A or B this semester?" you persist. "You *could*," is the reply. It's easy to see how this sort of evasiveness can be frustrating.

As with euphemisms, high-level abstractions, and many other types of communication, it's impossible to say that equivocation is always helpful or harmful. As you learned in Chapter 1, competent communication behavior is situational. Your success in relating to others will depend on your ability to analyze yourself, the other person, and the situation when deciding whether to be equivocal or direct.

Culture and Language

Anyone who has tried to translate ideas from one language to another knows that communication across cultures can be a challenge. Sometimes the results of a bungled translation can be amusing. For example, the American manufacturers of Pet condensed milk unknowingly introduced their product in French-speaking markets without realizing that the word *pet* in French means "to break wind." Likewise, the naive English-speaking representative of a U.S. soft drink manufacturer drew laughs from Mexican customers when she offered free samples of Fresca soda pop. In Mexican slang, the word *fresca* means "lesbian."

Even choosing the right words during translation won't guarantee that non-native speakers will use an unfamiliar language correctly. For example, Japanese insurance companies warn their policyholders who are visiting the United States to avoid their cultural tendency to say "excuse, me" or "I'm sorry" if they are involved in a traffic accident. In Japan, apologizing is a traditional way to express goodwill and maintain social harmony, even if the person offering the apology is not at fault. But in the United States, an apology can be taken as an admission of guilt and may result in Japanese tourists' being held accountable for accidents for which they may not be responsible.

Difficult as it may be, translation is only a small part of the communication challenges facing members of different cultures. Differences in the way language is used and the very worldview that a language creates make communicating across cultures a challenging task.

Verbal Communication Styles

Using language is more than just choosing a particular group of words to convey an idea. Each language has its own unique style that distinguishes it from others. And when a communicator tries to use the verbal style from one culture in a different one, problems are likely to arise.

Direct–Indirect

One way in which verbal styles vary is in their *directness*. Anthropologist Edward Hall identified two distinct cultural ways of using language. **Low-context cultures** use language primarily to express thoughts, feelings, and ideas as clearly and logically as possible. To low-context communicators, the meaning of a statement is in the words spoken. By contrast, **high-context cultures** value language as a way to maintain social harmony. Rather than upset others by speaking clearly, communicators in these cultures learn to discover meaning from the context in which a message is delivered: the nonverbal behaviors of the speaker, the history of the relationship, and the general social rules that govern interaction between people. Table 3 summarizes some key differences between the way low- and high-context cultures use language.

North American culture falls toward the direct, low-context end of the scale. Residents of the United States and Canada value straight talk and grow impatient with "beating around the bush." By contrast, most Asian and Middle Eastern cultures fit the high-context pattern. In many Asian cultures, for example, maintaining harmony is important, and so communicators will avoid speaking clearly if that would threaten another person's face. For this reason, Japanese or Koreans are less likely than Americans to offer a clear "no" to an undesirable request.

Table 3 Low- and high-context communication styles

Low context	High context
Majority of information carried in explicit verbal messages, with less focus on the situational context.	Important information carried in contextual clues (time, place, relationship, situation). Less reliance on explicit verbal messages.
Self-expression valued. Communicators state opinions and desires directly and strive to persuade others.	Relational harmony valued and maintained by indirect expression of opinions. Comunicators refrain from saying "no" directly.
Clear, eloquent speech considered praiseworthy. Verbal fluency admired.	Communicators talk "around" the point, allowing others to fill in the missing pieces. Ambiguity and use of silence admired.

Instead, they would probably use roundabout expressions like "I agree with you in principle, but . . ." or "I sympathize with you . . ."

Low-context North Americans may miss the subtleties of high-context messages, but people raised to recognize indirect communication have little trouble decoding them. A look at Japanese child-rearing practices helps explain why. Research shows that Japanese mothers rarely deny the requests of their young children by saying "no." Instead, they use other strategies: ignoring a child's requests, raising distractions, promising to take care of the matter later, or explaining why they can or will not say "yes." Sociolinguist Deborah Tannen explains how this indirect approach illustrates profound differences between high- and low-context communications:

> . . . saying no is something associated with children who have not yet learned the norm. If a Japanese mother spoke that way, she would feel she was lowering herself to her child's level precisely because that way of speaking is associated with Japanese children.

Tannen goes on to contrast the Japanese notion of appropriateness with the very different one held by dominant North American society:

> Because American norms for talk are different, it is common, and therefore expected, for American parents to "just say no." That's why an American mother feels authoritative when she talks that way: because it fits her image of how an authoritative adult talks to a child.

The clash between cultural norms of directness and indirectness can aggravate problems in cross-cultural situations such as encounters between straight-talking low-context Israelis, who value speaking clearly, and Arabs, whose high-context culture stresses smooth interaction. It's easy to imagine how the clash of cultural styles could lead to misunderstandings and conflicts between Israelis and their Palestinian neighbors. Israelis could view their Arab counterparts as evasive, whereas the Palestinians could perceive the Israelis as insensitive and blunt.

Even within a single country, subcultures can have different notions about the value of direct speech. For example, Puerto Rican language style resembles high-context Japanese or Korean more than low-context English. As a group, Puerto Ricans value social harmony and avoid confrontation, which leads them to systematically speak in an indirect way to avoid giving offense. Asian Americans are more offended by indirectly racist statements than are African Americans, Hispanics, and Anglo Americans. Researchers Laura Leets and Howard Giles suggest that the traditional Asian tendency to favor high-context messages explains the difference: Adept at recognizing hints and nonverbal cues, high-context communicators are more sensitive to messages that are overlooked by people from cultural groups that rely more heavily on unambiguous, explicit low-context messages.

It's worth noting that even generally straight-talking residents of the United States raised in the low-context Euro-American tradition often rely on context to make their point. When you decline an unwanted invitation by saying "I can't make it," it's likely that both you and the other person know that the choice of attending isn't really beyond your control. If your goal was to be perfectly clear, you might say,"I don't want to get together."

Elaborate-Succinct

Another way in which language styles can vary across cultures is in terms of whether they are *elaborate* or *succinct*. Speakers of Arabic, for instance, commonly use language that is much more rich and expressive than most communicators who use English. Strong assertions and exaggerations that would sound ridiculous in English are a common feature of Arabic. This contrast in linguistic style can lead to misunderstandings between people from different backgrounds. As one observer put it,

> . . . [A]n Arab feels compelled to overassert in almost all types of communication because others expect him [or her] to. If an Arab says exactly what he [or she] means without the expected assertion, other Arabs may still think that he [or she] means the opposite. For example, a simple "no" to a host's requests to eat more or drink more will not suffice. To convey the meaning that he [or she] is actually full, the guest must keep repeating "no" several times, coupling it with an oath such as "By God" or "I swear to God."

Succinctness is most extreme in cultures where silence is valued. In many American Indian cultures, for example, the favored way to handle ambiguous social situations is to remain quiet. When you contrast this silent style to the talkativeness common in mainstream American cultures when people first meet, it's easy to imagine how the first encounter between an Apache or Navajo and a white person might feel uncomfortable to both people.

Formal–Informal

Along with differences such as directness-indirectness and elaborate-succinct styles, a third way languages differ from one culture to another involves *formality* and *informality.* The informal approach that characterizes relationships in countries like the United States, Canada, and Australia is quite different, from the great concern for using proper speech in many parts of Asia and Africa. Formality isn't so much a matter of using correct grammar as of defining social position. In Korea, for example, the language reflects the Confucian system of relational hierarchies. It has special vocabularies for different sexes, for different levels of social status, for different degrees of intimacy, and for different types of social occasions. For example, there are different degrees of formality for speaking with old friends, nonacquaintances whose background one knows, and complete strangers. One sign of being a learned person in Korea is the ability to use language that recognizes these relational distinctions. When you contrast these sorts of distinctions with the casual friendliness many North Americans use even when talking with complete strangers, it's easy to see how a Korean might view communicators in the United States as boorish and how an American might view Koreans as stiff and unfriendly.

Language and Worldview

Different linguistic styles are important, but there may be even more fundamental differences that separate speakers of various languages. For almost 150 years, some theorists have put forth the notion of **linguistic determinism:** the notion that the worldview of a culture is shaped and reflected by the language its members speak. The best-known example of linguistic determinism is the notion that Eskimos have a large number of words (estimated from seventeen to one hundred) for what we simply call "snow." Different terms are used to describe conditions like a driving blizzard, crusty ice, and light powder. This example suggests how linguistic determinism operates. The need to survive in an Arctic environment led Eskimos to make distinctions that would be unimportant to residents of warmer environments, and after the language makes these distinctions, speakers are more likely to see the world in ways that match the broader vocabulary.

Even though there is some doubt that Eskimos really do have one hundred words for snow, other examples do seem to support the principle of linguistic determinism. For instance, bilingual speakers seem to think differently when they change languages. In one study, French Americans were asked to interpret a series of pictures. When they spoke in French, their descriptions were far more romantic and emotional than when they used English to describe the same kind of pictures. Likewise, when students in Hong Kong were asked to complete a values test, they expressed more traditional Chinese values when they answered in Cantonese than when they answered in English. In Israel, both Arab and Jewish students saw bigger distinctions between their group and "outsiders" when using their native language than when they used English, a neutral tongue. Examples like these show the power of language to shape cultural identity—sometimes for better and sometimes for worse.

Understanding Diversity

Language and Perception

English speakers can often draw shades of distinction unavailable to non-English speakers. The French, for instance, cannot distinguish between house and home, between mind and brain, between man and gentleman, between "I wrote" and "I have written." The Spanish cannot differentiate a chairman from a president, and the Italians have no equivalent of wishful thinking. In Russia there are no native words for efficiency, challenge, engagement ring, have fun, or take care.

On the other hand, other languages have facilities that we lack. Both French and German can distinguish between knowledge that results from recognition (respectively, *connaitre* and *kennen*) and knowledge that results from understanding (*savior and wissen*). Portuguese has words that differentiate between an interior angle and an exterior one. All the Romance languages can distinguish between something that leaks into and something that leaks out of. The Italians even have a word for the mark left on a table by a moist glass *(culacino)* while the Gaelic speakers of Scotland, not to be outdone, have a word for the itchiness that overcomes the upper lip just before taking a sip of whiskey. It's *sgiob*. And we have nothing in English to match the Danish *hygge* (meaning "instantly satisfying and cozy"), the French *sangfroid*, the Russian *glasnost*, or the Spanish *macho*, so we must borrow the term from them or do without the sentiment.

Bill Bryson
The Mother Tongue

Linguistic influences start early in life. English-speaking parents often label the mischievous pranks of their children as "bad," implying that there is something immoral about acting wild. "Be good!" they are inclined to say. On the other hand, French parents are more likely to say *"Sois sage!"*—"Be wise." The linguistic implication is that misbehaving is an act of foolishness. Swedes would correct the same action with the words *"Var snall!"*—"Be friendly, be kind." By contrast, German adults would use the command *"Sei artig!"*—literally, "Be of your own kind"—in other words, get back in step, conform to your role as a child.

The best-known declaration of linguistic determinism is the **Whorf-Sapir hypothesis,** formulated by Benjamin Whorf, an amateur linguist, and anthropologist Edward Sapir. Following Sapir's theoretical work, Whorf found that the language spoken by the Hopi represents a view of reality that is dramatically different from more familiar tongues. For example, the Hopi language makes no distinction between nouns and verbs. Therefore, the people who speak it describe the entire world as being constantly in process. Whereas we use nouns to characterize people or objects as being fixed or constant, the Hopi view them more as verbs, constantly changing. In this sense our language represents much of the world rather like a snapshot camera, whereas Hopi reflects a worldview more like a motion picture.

Although the Whorf-Sapir hypothesis originally focused on foreign languages, Neil Postman illustrates the principle with an example closer to home. He describes a hypothetical culture where physicians identify patients they treat as "doing" arthritis and other diseases instead of "having" them and where criminals are diagnosed as "having" cases of criminality instead of "being" criminals.

The implications of such a linguistic difference are profound. We believe that characteristics people "have"—what they "are"—are beyond their control, whereas they are responsible for what they "do." If we changed our view of what people "have" and what they "do," our attitudes would most likely change as well. Postman illustrates the consequences of this linguistic difference as applied to education:

> In schools, for instance, we find that tests are given to determine how smart some-one is or, more precisely, how much smartness someone "has." If one child scores a 138, and another a 106, the first is thought to "have" more smartness than the other. But this seems to me a strange conception—every bit as strange as "doing" arthritis or "having" criminality. I do not know anyone who *has* smartness. The people I know sometimes *do* smart things (as far as I can judge) and sometimes *do* stupid things—depending on what circumstances they are in, and how much they know about a situation, and how interested they are. "Smartness," so it seems to me, is a specific performance, done in a particular set of circumstances. It is not something you *are* or have in measurable quantities. . . . What I am driving at is this: All language is metaphorical, and often in the subtlest ways. In the simplest sentence, sometimes in the simplest word, we do more than merely express ourselves. We construct reality along certain lines. We make the world according to our own imagery.

Although there is little support for the extreme linguistic deterministic view-point that it is *impossible* for speakers of different languages to view the world identically, the more moderate notion of **linguistic relativism**—the notion that language exerts a strong influence on perceptions—does seem valid. As one scholar put it, "the differences between languages are not so much in what *can* be said, but in what it is *relatively easy* to say." Some languages contain terms that have no exact English equivalents. For example, consider a few words in other languages that have no exact English equivalents:

- *Nemawashi* (Japanese) The process of informally feeling out all the people involved with an issue before making a decision

- *Lagniappe* (French) An extra gift given in a transaction that wasn't expected by the terms of a contract
- *Lao* (Mandarin) A respectful term used for older people, showing their importance in the family and in society
- *Dharma* (Sanskrit) Each person's unique, ideal path in life and the knowledge of how to find it
- *Koyaanisquatsi* (Hopi) Nature out of balance; a way of life so crazy it calls for a new way of living

After words like these exist and become a part of everyday life, the ideas that they represent are easier to recognize. But even without such words, each of the concepts mentioned earlier is still possible to imagine. Thus, speakers of a language that includes the notion of *lao* would probably treat older members respectfully, and those who are familiar with *lagniappe* might be more generous. Despite these differences, the words aren't essential to follow these principles. Although language may shape thoughts and behavior, it doesn't dominate them absolutely.

Summary

Language is both one of humanity's greatest assets and the source of many problems. This chapter highlighted the characteristics that distinguish language and suggested methods of using it more effectively.

Any language is a collection of symbols governed by a variety of rules and used to convey messages between people. Because of its symbolic nature, language is not a precise tool: Meanings rest in people, not in words themselves. In order for effective communication to occur, it is necessary to negotiate meanings for ambiguous statements.

Language not only describes people, ideas, processes, and events; it also shapes our perceptions of them in areas including status, credibility, and attitudes about gender and ethnicity. Along with influencing our attitudes, language reflects them. The words we use and our manner of speech reflect power, responsibility, affiliation, attraction, and interest.

Many types of language have the potential to create misunderstandings. Other types of language can result in unnecessary conflicts. In other cases, speech and writing can be evasive, avoiding expression of unwelcome messages.

The relationship between gender and language is a confusing one. There are many differences in the ways men and women speak: The content of their conversations varies, as do their reasons for communicating and their conversational styles. Not all differences in language use can be accounted for by the speaker's gender, however. Occupation, social philosophy, and orientation toward problem solving also influence the use of language, and psychological sex role can be more of an influence than biological sex.

Language operates on a broad level to shape the consciousness and communication of an entire society. Different languages often shape and reflect the views of a culture. Low-context cultures like that of the United States use language primarily to express feelings and ideas as clearly and unambiguously as possible, whereas high-context cultures avoid specificity to promote social harmony. Some cultures value brevity and the succinct use of language, whereas others value elaborate forms of speech. In some societies formality is important, whereas in others informality is important. Beyond these differences, there is evidence to support linguistic relativism—the notion that language exerts a strong influence on the worldview of the people who speak it.

Key Terms

abstract language *600*
abstraction ladder *599*
behavioral description *600*
convergence *595*
divergence *595*
emotive language *603*
equivocal words *596*
equivocation *605*
euphemism *604*
factual statement *602*
high-context culture *606*
inferential statement *602*
jargon *598*
language *585*

linguistic determinism *609*
linguistic relativism *611*
low-context culture *606*
opinion statement *000*
phonological rules *587*
pragmatic rules *588*
relative words *597*
semantic rules *588*
sex role *612*
slang *598*
symbols *585*
syntactic rules *587*
Whorf-Sapir hypothesis *610*

Activities

1. **Powerful Speech and Polite Speech** Increase your ability to achieve an optimal balance between powerful speech and polite speech by rehearsing one of the following scenarios:
   - Describing your qualifications to a potential employer for a job that interests you.
   - Requesting an extension on a deadline from one of your professors.
   - Explaining to a merchant why you want a cash refund on an unsatisfactory piece of merchandise when the store's policy is to issue credit vouchers.
   - Asking your boss for three days off so you can attend a friend's out-of-town wedding.
   - Approaching your neighbors whose dog barks while they are away from home.

Your statement should gain its power by avoiding the types of powerless language listed in Table 1. You should not become abusive or threatening, and your statement should be completely honest.

2. **Slang and Jargon** Find a classmate, neighbor, coworker, or other person whose background differs significantly from yours. In an interview, ask this person to identify the slang and jargon terms that you take for granted but that he or she has found confusing. Explore the following types of potentially confusing terms:
   1. regionalisms
   2. age-related terms
   3. technical jargon
   4. acronyms

3. **Low-Level Abstractions** You can develop your ability to use low-level abstractions by following these steps:
   1. Use your own experience to write each of the following:
      a. a complaint or gripe
      b. one way you would like someone with whom you interact to change
      c. one reason why you appreciate a person with whom you interact
   2. Now translate each of the statements you have written into a low-level abstraction by including:
      a. the person or people involved
      b. the circumstances in which the behavior occurs
      c. the specific behaviors to which you are referring
   3. Compare the statements you have written in Steps 1 and 2. How might the lower-level abstractions in Step 2 improve the chances of having your message understood and accepted?

4. **Gender and Language**
   1. Note differences in the language use of three men and three women you know. Include yourself in the analysis. Your analysis will be most accurate if you tape record the speech of each person you analyze. Consider the following categories:

      conversational content   conversational style
      reasons for communi-   use of powerful/
        cating   powerless speech

   2. Based on your observations, answer the following questions:
      a. How much does gender influence speech?
      b. What role do other variables play? Consider occupational or social status, cultural background, social philosophy, competitive-cooperative orientation, and other factors in your analysis.

For Further Exploration

For a more detailed list of readings about language, see the CD-ROM that came with this book, and the *Understanding Human Communication* Web site at www.oup.com/us/uhc.

Print Resources

Ellis, Donald G. *From Language to Communication,* 2nd ed. Hillsdale, NJ: Lawrence Erlbaum, 1999.

> The book covers a wide range of topics including the origins of language, a review of the field of linguistics, a look at the mental processes that govern language use, and how language operates in everyday conversations.

Rheingold, Howard. *They Have a Word For It.* Los Angeles: Tarcher, 1988.

> Rheingold has collected a lexicon of words and phrases from languages around the world that lend support to the Sapir-Whorf hypothesis. This entertaining 200-page compendium of "untranslatable phrases" illustrates that speaking a new language can, indeed, prompt a different world view.

Tannen, Deborah. *Gender and Discourse.* New York: Oxford University Press, 1995. *You Just Don't Understand: Women and Men in Conversation.* New York: Morrow, 1990. *Talking from 9 to 5.* New York: Morrow, 1994.

> *Gender and Discourse* provides a more scholarly look at the connection between gender and communication than Tannen's trade books. One chapter describes how social class interacts with gender to affect the interaction between men and women.

Wood, Julia. *Gendered Lives,* 6th ed. Belmont, CA: Wadsworth,2005.

> Chapter 5, "Gendered Verbal Communication," offers a good survey of the relationship between language and the way we think about men and women in society.

Feature Films

For descriptions of each film below and descriptions of other movies that illustrate language, see the CD-ROM that came with this book, and the *Understanding Human Communication* Web site at www.oup.com/us/uhc.

Jargon and Slang

Clueless (1995). Rated PG-13.

Cher (Alicia Silverstone) and her friend Dionne (Stacey Dash) are teen queens at a posh Beverly Hills high school. This film's opening line is "So, OK, you're probably like—what is this, a Noxzema commercial?" From beginning to end, the characters offer a clever, if exaggerated, illustration of how jargon and slang operate in youth culture.

The Nature of Language

Nell (1994). Rated PG.

Deep in the mountains of North Carolina, physician Jerome Lovell (Liam Neeson) discovers Nell (Jodie Foster), a young woman who has had no contact with the outside world for virtually her entire life. In her seclusion, Nell developed her own language. Lovell and psychologist Paula Olsen (Natasha Richardson) struggle to learn Nell's language and her unique way of perceiving the world.

Encoding, Decoding

Stuart Hall

Traditionally, mass-communications research has conceptualised the process of communication in terms of a circulation circuit or loop. This model has been criticised for its linearity—sender/message/receiver—for its concentration on the level of message exchange and for the absence of a structured conception of the different moments as a complex structure of relations. But it is also possible (and useful) to think of this process in terms of a structure produced and sustained through the articulation of linked but distinctive moments—production, circulation, distribution, consumption, reproduction. This would be to think of the process as a 'complex structure in dominance', sustained through the articulation of connected practices, each of which, however, retains its distinctiveness and has its own specific modality, its own forms and conditions of existence.

The 'object' of these practices is meanings and messages in the form of sign-vehicles of a specific kind organised, like any form of communication or language, through the operation of codes within the syntagmatic chain of a discourse. The apparatuses, relations and practices of production thus issue, at a certain moment (the moment of 'production/circulation') in the form of symbolic vehicles constituted within the rules of 'language'. It is in this discursive form that the circulation of the 'product' takes place. The process thus requires, at the production end, its material instruments—its 'means'—as well as its own sets of social (production) relations—the organisation and combination of practices within media apparatuses. But it is in the *discursive* form that the circulation of the product takes place, as well as its distribution to different audiences. Once accomplished, the discourse must then be translated—transformed, again—into social practices if the circuit is to be both completed and effective. If no 'meaning' is taken, there can be no 'consumption'. If the meaning is not articulated in practice, it has no effect. The value of this approach is that while each of the moments, in articulation, is necessary to the circuit as a whole, no one moment can fully guarantee the next moment with which it is articulated. Since each has

470   *Introduction to Media Studies*

its specific modality and conditions of existence, each can constitute its own break or interruption of the 'passage of forms' on whose continuity the flow of effective production (that is, 'reproduction') depends.

Thus while in no way wanting to limit research to 'following only those leads which emerge from content analysis', we must recognise that the discursive form of the message has a privileged position in the communicative exchange (from the viewpoint of circulation), and that the moments of 'encoding' and 'decoding', though only 'relatively autonomous' in relation to the communicative process as a whole, are *determinate* moments. A 'raw' historical event cannot, *in that form,* be transmitted by, say, a television newscast. Events can only be signified within the aural-visual forms of the televisual discourse. In the moment when a historical event passes under the sign of discourse, it is subject to all the complex formal 'rules' by which language signifies. To put it paradoxically, the event must become a 'story' before it can become a *communicative event.* In that moment the formal sub-rules of discourse are 'in dominance', without, of course, subordinating out of existence the historical event so signified, the social relations in which the rules are set to work or the social and political consequences of the event having been signified in this way. The 'message form' is the necessary 'form of appearance' of the event in its passage from source to receiver. Thus the transposition into and out of the 'message form' (or the mode of symbolic exchange) is not a random 'moment', which we can take up or ignore at our convenience. The 'message form' is a determinate moment; though, at another level, it comprises the surface movements of the communications system only and requires, at another stage, to be integrated into the social relations of the communication process as a whole, of which it forms only a part.

From this general perspective, we may crudely characterise the television communicative process as follows. The institutional structures of broadcasting, with their practices and networks of production, their organised relations and technical infrastructures, are required to produce a programme. Production, here, constructs the message. In one sense, then, the circuit begins here. Of course, the production process is not without its 'discursive' aspect: it, too, is framed throughout by meanings and ideas: knowledge-in-use concerning the routines of production, historically defined technical skills, professional ideologies, institutional knowledge, definitions and assumptions, assumptions about the audience and so on frame the constitution of the programme through this production structure. Further, though the production structures of television originate the television discourse, they do not constitute a closed system. They draw topics, treatments, agendas, events, personnel, images of the audience, 'definitions of the situation' from other sources and other discursive formations within the wider socio-cultural and political structure of which they are a differentiated part. Philip Elliott has expressed this point succinctly, within a more traditional framework, in his discussion of the way in which the audience is both the 'source' and the 'receiver' of the television message. Thus—to borrow Marx's terms—circulation and reception are, indeed, 'moments' of the production process in television and are reincorporated, via a number of skewed and structured 'feedbacks', into the production process itself. The consumption or reception of the television message is thus also itself a 'moment' of the production process in its larger sense, though the latter is 'predominant' because it is the 'point of departure for the realisation' of the message. Production and reception of the television message are not, therefore, identical, but they are related: they are differentiated moments within the totality formed by the social relations of the communicative process as a whole.

At a certain point, however, the broadcasting structures must yield encoded messages in the form of a meaningful discourse. The institution—societal relations of production must pass under the discursive rules of language for its product to be 'realised'. This initiates a further differentiated moment, in which the formal rules of discourse and language are in dominance. Before this message can have an 'effect' (however defined), satisfy a 'need' or be put to a 'use', it must first be appropriated as a meaningful discourse and be meaningfully decoded. It is this set of decoded meanings which 'have an effect', influence, entertain, instruct or persuade, with very complex perceptual, cognitive, emotional, ideological or behavioural consequences. In a 'determinate' moment the structure employs a code and yields a 'message': at another determinate moment the 'message', via its decodings, issues into the structure of social practices. We are now fully aware that this re-entry into the practices of audience reception and 'use' cannot be understood in simple behavioural terms. The typical processes identified in positivistic research on isolated elements—effects, uses, gratifications'—are themselves framed by structures of understanding, as well as being produced by social and economic relations, which shape their 'realisation' at the reception end of the chain and which permit the meanings signified in the discourse to be transposed into practice or consciousness (to acquire social use value or political effectivity).

Clearly, what we have labelled in the diagram (below) 'meaning structures 1' and 'meaning structures 2' may not be the same. They do not constitute an 'immediate identity'. The codes of encoding and decoding may not be perfectly symmetrical. The degrees of symmetry—that is, the degrees of 'understanding' and 'misunderstanding' in the communicative exchange—depend on the degrees of symmetry/asymmetry (relations of equivalence) established between the positions of the 'personifications', encoder-producer and decoder-receiver. But this in turn depends on the degrees of identity or non-identity between the codes which perfectly or imperfectly transmit, interrupt or systematically distort what has been transmitted. The lack of fit between the codes has a great deal to do with the structural differences of relation and position between broadcasters and audiences, but it also has something to do with the asymmetry between the codes of 'source' and 'receiver' at the moment of transformation into and out of the discursive form. What are called 'distortions' or 'misunderstandings' arise precisely from the *lack of equivalence* between the two sides in the communicative exchange. Once again, this defines the 'relative autonomy', but 'determinate-ness', of the entry and exit of the message in its discursive moments.

The application of this rudimentary paradigm has already begun to transform our understanding of the older term, television 'content'. We are just beginning to see how it might also transform our understanding of audience reception, 'reading' and response as well. Beginnings and endings have been announced in communications research before, so we must be cautious. But there seems some ground for thinking that a new and exciting phase in so-called audience research, of a quite new kind, may be opening up. At either end of the communicative chain the use of the semiotic paradigm promises to dispel the lingering behaviourism which has dogged mass-media research for so long, especially in its approach to content. Though we know the television programme is not a behavioural input, like a tap on the kneecap, it seems to have been almost impossible for traditional researchers to conceptualise the communicative process without lapsing into one or other variant of low-flying behaviourism. We know, as Gerbner has remarked, that representations of violence on the television screen 'are not violence but messages about violence': but we have continued to research the question of violence, for example, as if we were unable to comprehend this epistemological distinction.

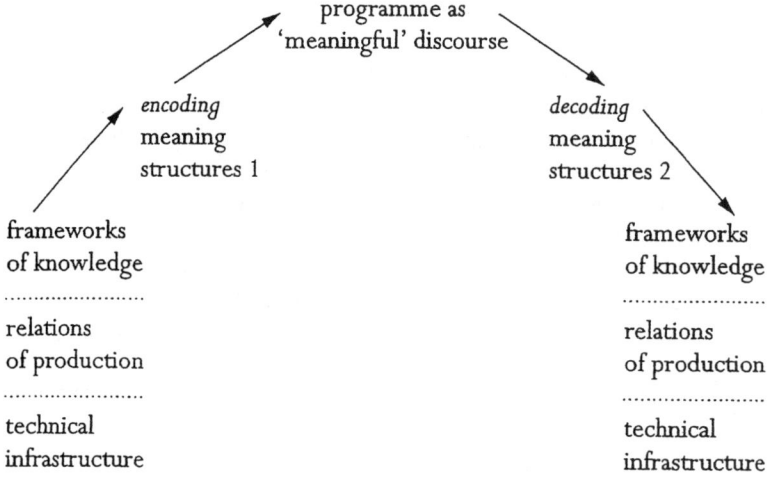

The televisual sign is a complex one. It is itself constituted by the combination of two types of discourse, visual and aural. Moreover, it is an iconic sign, in Peirce's terminology, because 'it possesses some of the properties of the thing represented'. This is a point which has led to a great deal of confusion and has provided the site of intense controversy in the study of visual language. Since the visual discourse translates a three-dimensional world into two-dimensional planes, it cannot, of course, *be* the referent or concept it signifies. The dog in the film can bark but it cannot bite! Reality exists outside language, but it is constantly mediated by and through language: and what we can know and say has to be produced in and through discourse. Discursive 'knowledge' is the product not of the transparent representation of the 'real' in language but of the articulation of language on real relations and conditions. Thus there is no intelligible discourse without the operation of a code. Iconic signs are therefore coded signs too—even if the codes here work differently from those of other signs. There is no degree zero in language. Naturalism and 'realism'—the apparent fidelity of the representation to the thing or concept represented—is the result, the effect, of a certain specific articulation of language on the 'real'. It is the result of a discursive practice.

Certain codes may, of course, be so widely distributed in a specific language community or culture, and be learned at so early an age, that they appear not to be constructed—the effect of an articulation between sign and referent—but to be 'naturally' given. Simple visual signs appear to have achieved a 'near-universality' in this sense: though evidence remains that even apparently 'natural' visual codes are culture-specific. However, this does not mean that no codes have intervened; rather, that the codes have been profoundly *naturalised*. The operation of naturalised codes reveals not the transparency and 'naturalness' of language but the depth, the habituation and the near-universality of the codes in use. They produce apparently 'natural' recognitions. This has the (ideological) effect of concealing the practices of coding which are present. But we must not be fooled by appearances. Actually, what naturalised codes demonstrate is the degree of habituation produced when there is a fundamental alignment and reciprocity—an achieved equivalence—between the encoding and decoding sides of an exchange of meanings. The functioning of the codes on the decoding side will frequently assume the status of naturalised perceptions. This leads us to think that the visual sign for 'cow' actually is (rather than *represents*) the animal, cow. But if we think of the visual representation of a cow in a manual on animal husbandry—and, even more, of the linguistic sign 'cow'—we can see that both, in different degrees, are *arbitrary* with respect to the concept of the animal they represent. The articulation of an arbitrary sign—whether visual or verbal—with the concept of a referent is the product not of nature but of convention, and the conventionalism of discourses requires the intervention, the support, of codes. Thus Eco has argued that iconic signs 'look like objects in the real world because they reproduce the conditions (that is, the codes) of perception in the viewer'. These 'conditions of perception' are, however, the result of a highly coded, even if virtually unconscious, set of operations—decodings. This is as true of the photographic or televisual image as it is of any other sign. Iconic signs are, however, particularly vulnerable to being 'read' as natural because visual codes of perception are very widely distributed and because this type of sign is less arbitrary than a linguistic sign: the linguistic sign, 'cow', possesses *none* of the properties of the thing represented, whereas the visual sign appears to possess *some* of those properties.

This may help us to clarify a confusion in current linguistic theory and to define precisely how some key terms are being used in this article. Linguistic theory frequently employs the distinction 'denotation' and 'connotation'. The term 'denotation' is widely equated with the literal meaning of a sign: because this literal meaning is almost universally recognised, especially when visual discourse is being employed, 'denotation' has often been confused with a literal transcription of 'reality' in language—and thus with a 'natural sign', one produced without the intervention of a code. 'Connotation', on the other hand, is employed simply to refer to less fixed and therefore more conventionalised and changeable, associative meanings, which clearly vary from instance to instance and therefore must depend on the intervention of codes.

We do *not* use the distinction—denotation/connotation—in this way. From our point of view, the distinction is an *analytic* one only. It is useful, in analysis, to be able to apply a rough rule of thumb which distinguishes those aspects of a sign which appear to be taken, in any language community at any point in time, as its 'literal' meaning (denotation) from the more associative meanings for the sign which it is possible to generate (connotation). But analytic distinctions must not be confused with distinctions in the real world. There will be very few instances in which signs organised in a discourse signify *only* their 'literal' (that is, near-universally consensualised) meaning. In actual discourse most signs will combine both the denotative and the connotative *aspects* (as redefined above). It may, then, be asked why we retain the distinction at all. It is largely a matter of analytic value. It is because signs appear to acquire their full ideological value—appear to be open to articulation with wider ideological discourses and meanings—at the level of their 'associative' meanings (that is, at the connotative level)—for here 'meanings' are *not* apparently fixed in natural perception (that is, they are not fully naturalised), and their fluidity of meaning and association can be more fully exploited and transformed. So it is at the connotative *level* of the sign that situational ideologies alter and transform signification. At this level we can see more clearly the active intervention of ideologies in and on discourse: here, the sign is open to new accentuations and, in Voloshinov's terms, enters fully into the struggle over meanings—the class struggle in language. This does not mean that the denotative or 'literal' meaning is outside ideology. Indeed, we could say that its ideological value is strongly *fixed*—because it has become so fully universal and 'natural'. The terms 'denotation' and 'connotation', then, are merely useful analytic tools for distinguishing, in particular contexts, between not the presence or absence of ideology in language but the different levels at which ideologies and discourses intersect.

The level of connotation of the visual sign, of its contextual reference and positioning in different discursive fields of meaning and association, is the point where *already coded* signs intersect with the deep semantic codes of a culture and take on additional, more active ideological dimensions. We might take an example from advertising discourse. Here, too, there is no 'purely denotative', and certainly no 'natural', representation. Every visual sign in advertising con-notes a quality, situation, value or inference, which is present as an implication or implied meaning, depending on the connotational positioning. In Barthes's example, the sweater always signifies a 'warm garment' (denotation) and thus the activity or value of 'keeping warm'. But it is also possible, at its more conno-tative levels, to signify 'the coming of winter' or 'a cold day'. And, in the spe-cialised sub-codes of fashion, the sweater may also connote a fashionable style of *haute couture* or, alternatively, an informal style of dress. But set against the right visual background and positioned by the romantic sub-code, it may connote 'long autumn walk in the woods'. Codes of this order clearly contract relations for the sign with the wider universe of ideologies in a society. These codes are the means by which power and ideology are made to signify in particular dis-courses. They refer signs to the 'maps of meaning' into which any culture is clas-sified; and those 'maps of social reality' have the whole range of social meanings, practices, and usages, power and interest 'written in' to them. The connotative levels of signifiers, Barthes remarked, 'have a close communication with culture, knowledge, history, and it is through them, so to speak, that the environmental world invades the linguistic and semantic system. They are, if you like, the frag-ments of ideology.'

The so-called denotative *level* of the televisual sign is fixed by certain, very complex (but limited or 'closed') codes. But its connotative *level,* though also bounded, is more open, subject to more active *transformations,* which exploit its polysemic values. Any such already constituted sign is potentially transformable into more than one connotative configuration. Polysemy must not, however, be confused with pluralism. Connotative codes are *not* equal among themselves. Any society or culture tends, with varying degrees of closure, to impose its classi-fications of the social and cultural and political world. These constitute a *domi-nant cultural order,* though it is neither univocal nor uncontested. This question of the 'structure of discourses in dominance' is a crucial point. The different areas of social life appear to be mapped out into discursive domains, hierarchi-cally organised into *dominant or preferred meanings.* New, problematic or trou-bling events, which breach our expectancies and run counter to our 'commonsense constructs', to our 'taken-for-granted' knowledge of social struc-tures, must be assigned to their discursive domains before they can be said to 'make sense'. The most common way of 'mapping' them is to assign the new to some domain or other of the existing 'maps of problematic social reality'. We say *dominant,* not 'determined', because it is always possible to order, classify, assign and decode an event within more than one 'mapping'. But we say 'domi-nant' because there exists a pattern of 'preferred readings'; and these both have the institutional/political/ideological order imprinted in them and have them-selves become institutionalised. The domains of 'preferred meanings' have the whole social order embedded in them as a set of meanings, practices and beliefs: the everyday knowledge of social structures, of 'how things work for all practical purposes in this culture', the rank order of power and interest and the structure of legitimations, limits and sanctions. Thus to clarify a 'misunderstanding' at the connotative level, we must refer, *through* the codes, to the orders of social life, of economic and political power and of ideology. Further, since these mappings are 'structured in dominance' but not closed, the communicative process consists not in the unproblematic assignment of every visual item to its given position within a set of prearranged codes, but of *performative rules*—rules of competence and use, of logics-in-use—which seek actively to *enforce* or *pre-fer* one semantic domain over another and rule items into and out of their appropriate meaning-sets. Formal semiology has too often neglected this practice of *interpretative work*, though this constitutes, in fact, the real relations of broadcast practices in television.

In speaking of *dominant meanings*, then, we are not talking about a one-sided process 'which governs how all events will be signified. It consists of the 'work' required to enforce, win plausibility for and command as legitimate a *decoding* of the event within the limit of dominant definitions in which it has been connotatively signified. Terni has remarked:

> By the word *reading* we mean not only the capacity to identify and decode a certain number of signs, but also the subjective capacity to put them into a creative relation between themselves and with other signs: a capacity which is, by itself, the condition for a complete awareness of one's total environment.

Our quarrel here is with the notion of 'subjective capacity', as if the referent of a televisional discourse were an objective fact but the interpretative level were an individualised and private matter. Quite the opposite seems to be the case. The televisual practice takes 'objective' (that is, systemic) responsibility precisely for the relations which disparate signs contract with one another in any discursive instance, and thus continually rearranges, delimits and prescribes into what 'awareness of one's total environment' these items are arranged.

This brings us to the question of misunderstandings. Television producers who find their message 'failing to get across' are frequently concerned to straighten out the kinks in the communication chain, thus facilitating the 'effectiveness' of their communication. Much research which claims the objectivity of 'policy-oriented analysis' reproduces this administrative goal by attempting to discover how much of a message the audience recalls and to improve the extent of understanding. No doubt misunderstandings of a literal kind do exist. The viewer does not know the terms employed, cannot follow the complex logic of argument or exposition, is unfamiliar with the language, finds the concepts too alien or difficult or is foxed by the expository narrative. But more often broadcasters are concerned that the audience has failed to take the meaning as they—the broadcasters—intended. What they really mean to say is that viewers are not operating within the 'dominant' or 'preferred' code. Their ideal is 'perfectly transparent communication'. Instead, what they have to confront is 'systematically distorted communication'.

In recent years discrepancies of this kind have usually been explained by reference to 'selective perception'. This is the door via which a residual pluralism evades the compulsions of a highly structured, asymmetrical and non-equivalent process. Of course, there will always be private, individual, variant readings. But 'selective perception' is almost never as selective, random or privatised as the concept suggests. The patterns exhibit, across individual variants, significant clusterings. Any new approach to audience studies will therefore have to begin with a critique of 'selective perception' theory.

It was argued earlier that since there is no necessary correspondence between encoding and decoding, the former can attempt to 'pre-fer' but cannot prescribe or guarantee the latter, which has its own conditions of existence. Unless they are wildly aberrant, encoding will have the effect of constructing some of the limits and parameters within which decodings will operate. If there were no limits, audiences could simply read whatever they liked into any message. No doubt some total misunderstandings of this kind do exist. But the vast range must contain *some* degree of reciprocity between encoding and decoding moments, otherwise we could not speak of an effective communicative exchange at all. Nevertheless, this 'correspondence' is not given but constructed. It is not 'natural' but the product of an articulation between two distinct moments. And the former cannot determine or guarantee, in a simple sense, which decoding codes will be employed. Otherwise communication would be a perfectly equivalent circuit, and every message would be an instance of 'perfectly transparent communication'. We must think, then, of the variant articulations in which encoding and decoding can be combined. To elaborate on this, we offer a hypothetical analysis of some possible decoding positions, in order to reinforce the point of 'no necessary correspondence'.

We identify *three* hypothetical positions from which decodings of a televisual discourse may be constructed. These need to be empirically tested and refined. But the argument that decodings do not follow inevitably from encodings, that they are not identical, reinforces the argument of 'no necessary correspondence'. It also helps to deconstruct the commonsense meaning of 'misunderstanding' in terms of a theory of 'systematically distorted communication'.

The first hypothetical position is that of the *dominant-hegemonic position*. When the viewer takes the connoted meaning from, say, a television newscast or current affairs programme full and straight, and decodes the message in terms of the reference code in which it has been encoded, we might say that the viewer is *operating inside the dominant code*. This is the ideal-typical case of 'perfectly transparent communication'—or as close as we are likely to come to it 'for all practical purposes'. Within this we can distinguish the positions produced by the *professional code*. This is the position (produced by what we perhaps ought to identify as the operation of a 'metacode') which the professional broadcasters assume when encoding a message which has *already* been signified in a hegemonic manner. The professional code is 'relatively independent' of the dominant code, in that it applies criteria and transformational operations of its own, especially those of a technicopractical nature. The professional code, however, operates *within* the 'hegemony' of the dominant code. Indeed, it serves to reproduce the dominant definitions precisely by bracketing their hegemonic quality and operating instead with displaced professional codings which foreground such apparently neutral-technical questions as visual quality, news and presentational values, televisual quality, 'professionalism' and so on. The hegemonic interpretations of, say, the politics of Northern Ireland, or the Chilean *coup* or the Industrial Relations Bill are principally generated by political and military elites; the particular choice of presentational occasions and formats, the selection of personnel, the choice of images, the staging of debates are selected and combined through the operation of the professional code. How the broadcasting professionals are able *both* to operate with 'relatively autonomous' codes of their own *and* to act in such a way as to reproduce (not without contradiction) the hegemonic signification of events is a complex matter which cannot be further spelled out here. It must suffice to say that the professionals are linked with the defining elites not only by the institutional position of broadcasting itself as an 'ideological apparatus' but also by the structure of *access* (that is, the systematic 'over-accessing' of selective elite personnel and their 'definition of the situation' in television). It may even be said that the professional codes serve to reproduce hegemonic definitions specifically by *not overtly* biasing their operations in a dominant direction: ideological reproduction therefore takes place here inadvertently, unconsciously, 'behind men's backs'. Of course, conflicts, contradictions and even misunderstandings regularly arise between the dominant and the professional significations and their signifying agencies.

The second position we would identify is that of the *negotiated code* or position. Majority audiences probably understand quite adequately what has been dominantly defined and professionally signified. The dominant definitions, however, are hegemonic precisely because they represent definitions of situations and events which are 'in dominance' (*global*). Dominant definitions connect events, implicitly or explicitly, to grand totalisations, to the great syntagmatic views-of-the-world: they take 'large views' of issues: they relate events to the 'national interest' or to the level of geopolitics even if they make these connections in truncated, inverted or mystified ways. The definition of a hegemonic viewpoint is, first, that it defines within its terms the mental horizon, the universe, of possible meanings, of a whole sector of relations in a society or culture; and, second, that it carries with it the stamp of legitimacy—it appears coterminous with what is 'natural', 'inevitable', 'taken for granted' about the social order. Decoding within the *negotiated version* contains a mixture of adaptive and oppositional elements: it acknowledges the legitimacy of the hegemonic definitions to make the grand significations (abstract), while, at a more restricted, situational (situated) level, it makes its own ground rules—it operates with exceptions to the rule. It accords the privileged position to the dominant definitions of events while reserving the right to make a more negotiated application to 'local conditions', to its own more *corporate* positions. This negotiated version of the dominant ideology is thus shot through with contradictions, though these are only on certain occasions brought to full visibility. Negotiated codes operate through what we might call particular or situated logics: and these logics are sustained by their differential and unequal relation to the discourses and logics of power. The simplest example of a negotiated code is that which governs the response of a worker to the notion of an Industrial Relations Bill limiting the right to strike or to arguments for a wages freeze. At the level of the 'national interest' economic debate the decoder may adopt the hegemonic definition, agreeing that 'we must all pay ourselves less in order to combat inflation'. This, however, may have little or no relation to his or her willingness to go on strike for better pay and conditions or to oppose the Industrial Relations Bill at the level of shop-floor or union organisation. We suspect that the great majority of so-called 'misunderstandings' arise from the contradictions and disjunctures between hegemonic-dominent encodings and negotiated-corporate decodings. It is just these mismatches in the levels which most provoke defining elites and professionals to identify a 'failure in communications'.

Finally, it is possible for a viewer perfectly to understand both the literal and the connotative inflection given by a discourse but to decode the message in a *globally* contrary way. He or she detotalises the message in the preferred code in order to retotalise the message within some alternative framework of reference. This is the case of the viewer who listens to a debate on the need to limit wages but 'reads' every mention of the 'national interest' as 'class interest'. He or she is operating with what we must call an *oppositional code.* One of the most significant political moments (they also coincide with crisis points within the broadcasting organisations themselves, for obvious reasons) is the point when events which are normally signified and decoded in a negotiated way begin to be given an oppositional reading. Here the 'politics of signification'—the struggle in discourse—is joined.

Note

This article is an edited extract from 'Encoding and Decoding in Television Discourse', CCCS Stencilled Paper no. 7.

Meaning and Race Matter

The Matter of Whiteness

Richard Dyer

Racial[1] imagery is central to the organisation of the modern world. At what cost regions and countries export their goods, whose voices are listened to at international gatherings, who bombs and who is bombed, who gets what jobs, housing, access to health care and education, what cultural activities are subsidised and sold, in what terms they are validated—these are all largely inextricable from racial imagery. The myriad minute decisions that constitute the practices of the world are at every point informed by judgments about people's capacities and worth, judgements based on what they look like, where they come from, how they speak, even what they eat, that is, racial judgements. Race is not the only factor governing these things and people of goodwill everywhere struggle to overcome the prejudices and barriers of race, but it is never not a factor, never not in play. And since race in itself—insofar as it is anything in itself—refers to some intrinsically insignificant geographical/physical differences between people, it is the imagery of race that is in play.

There has been an enormous amount of analysis of racial imagery in the past decades, ranging from studies of images of, say, blacks or American Indians in the media to the deconstruction of the fetish of the racial Other in the texts of colonialism and post-colonialism. Yet until recently a notable absence from such work has been the study of images of white people. Indeed, to say that one is interested in race has come to mean that one is interested in any racial imagery other than that of white people. Yet race is not only attributable to people who are not white, nor is imagery of non-white people the only racial imagery.

This essay is about the racial imagery of white people—not the images of other races in white cultural production, but the latter's imagery of white people themselves. This is not done merely to fill a gap in the analytic literature, but because there is something at stake in looking at, or continuing to ignore, white racial imagery. As long as race is something only applied to non-white peoples, as long as white people are not racially seen and named, they/we function as a human norm. Other people are raced, we are just people.

There is no more powerful position than that of being 'just' human. The claim to power is the claim to speak for the commonality of humanity. Raced people can't do that—they can only speak for their race.[2] But non-raced people can, for they do not represent the interests of a race. The point of seeing the racing of whites is to dislodge them/us from the position of power, with all the inequities, oppression, privileges and sufferings in its train, dislodging them/us by under-cutting the authority with which they/we speak and act in and on the world.

The sense of whites as non-raced is most evident in the absence of reference to whiteness in the habitual speech and writing of white people in the West. We (whites) will speak of, say, the blackness or Chineseness of friends, neighbours, colleagues, customers or clients, and it may be in the most genuinely friendly and accepting manner, but we don't mention the whiteness of the white people we know. An old-style white comedian will often start a joke: 'There's this bloke walking down the street and he meets this black geezer', never thinking to race the bloke as well as the geezer. Synopses in listings of films on TV, where wordage is tight, none the less squander words with things like: 'Comedy in which a cop and his black sidekick investigate a robbery', 'Skinhead Johnny and his Asian lover Omar set up a laundrette', 'Feature film from a promising Native American director' and so on. Since all white people in the West do this all the time, it would be invidious to quote actual examples, and so I shall confine myself to one from my own writing. In an article on lesbian and gay stereotypes (Dyer 1993), I discuss the fact that there can be variations on a type such as the queen or dyke. In the illustrations which accompany this point, I compare a 'fashion queen' from the film *Irene* with a 'black queen' from *Car Wash*—the for-mer, white image is not raced, whereas all the variation of the latter is reduced to his race. Moreover, this is the only non-white image referred to in the article, which does not however point out that all the other images discussed are white. In this, as in the other white examples in this paragraph, the fashion queen is, racially speaking, taken as being just human.

This assumption that white people are just people, which is not far off saying that whites are people whereas other colours are something else, is endemic to white culture. Some of the sharpest criticism of it has been aimed at those who would think themselves the least racist or white supremacist, bell hooks, for instance, has noted how amazed and angry white liberals become when atten-tion is drawn to their whiteness, when they are seen by non-white people as white.

> Often their rage erupts because they believe that all ways of looking that highlight difference subvert the liberal belief in a universal subjectivity (we are all just people) that they think will make racism disappear. They have a deep emotional investment in the myth of 'sameness', even as their actions reflect the primacy of whiteness as a sign informing who they are and how they think.
>
> (hooks 1992: 167)

Similarly, Hazel Carby discusses the use of black texts in white classrooms, under the sign of multiculturalism, in a way that winds up focusing 'on the complexity of response in the (white) reader/student's construction of self in relation to a (black) perceived "other'". We should, she argues, recognise that 'everyone in this social order has been constructed in our political imagination as a racialised subject' and thus that we should consider whiteness as well as blackness, in order 'to make visible what is rendered invisible when viewed as the normative state of existence: the (white) point in space from which we tend to identify difference' (Carby 1992: 193).

The invisibility of whiteness as a racial position in white (which is to say dominant) discourse is of a piece with its ubiquity. When I said above that I wasn't merely seeking to fill a gap in the analysis of racial imagery, I reproduced the idea that there is no discussion of white people. In fact for most of the time white people speak about nothing but white people, it's just that we couch it in terms of 'people' in general. Research—into books, museums, the press, advertising, films, television, software—repeatedly shows that in Western representation whites are overwhelmingly and disproportionately predominant, have the central and elaborated roles, and above all are placed as the norm, the ordinary, the standard.[3] Whites are everywhere in representation. Yet precisely because of this and their placing as norm they seem not to be represented to themselves *as* whites but as people who are variously gendered, classed, sexualized and abled. At the level of racial representation, in other words, whites are not of a certain race, they're just the human race.

We are often told that we are living now in a world of multiple identities, of hybridity, of decentredness and fragmentation. The old illusory unified identities of class, gender, race, sexuality are breaking up; someone may be black *and* gay *and* middle class *and* female; we may be bi-, poly- or non-sexual, of mixed race, indeterminate gender and heaven knows what class. Yet we have not yet reached a situation in which white people and white cultural agendas are no longer in the ascendant. The media, politics, education are still in the hands of white people, still speak for whites while claiming—and sometimes sincerely aiming—to speak for humanity. Against the flowering of a myriad postmodern voices, we must also see the countervailing tendency towards a homogenisation of world culture, in the continued dominance of US news dissemination, popular TV programmes and Hollywood movies. Postmodern multiculturalism may have genuinely opened up a space for the voices of the other, challenging the authority of the white West (cf. Owens 1983), but it may also simultaneously function as a side-show for white people who look on with delight at all the differences that surround them.[4] We may be on our way to genuine hybridity, multiplicity without (white) hegemony, and it may be where we want to get to—but we aren't there yet, and we won't get there until we see whiteness, see its power, its particularity and limitedness, put it in its place and end its rule. This is why studying whiteness matters.

It is studying whiteness *qua* whiteness. Attention is sometimes paid to 'white ethnicity' (e.g. Alba 1990), but this always means an identity based on cultural origins such as British, Italian or Polish, or Catholic or Jewish, or Polish-American, Irish-American, Catholic-American and so on. These however are variations on white ethnicity (though some are more securely white than others), and the examination of them tends to lead away from a consideration of whiteness itself. John Ibson (1981), in a discussion of research on white US ethnicity, concludes that being, say, Polish, Catholic or Irish may not be as important to white Americans as some might wish. But being white is

* * *

This then is why it is important to come to see whiteness. For those in power in the West, as long as whiteness is felt to be the human condition, then it alone both defines normality and fully inhabits it. As I suggested in my opening paragraphs, the equation of being white with being human secures a position of power. White people have power and believe that they think, feel and act like and for all people; white people, unable to see their particularity, cannot take account of other people's; white people create the dominant images of the world and don't quite see that they thus construct the world in their own image; white people set standards of humanity by which they are bound to succeed and others bound to fail. Most of this is not done deliberately and maliciously; there are enormous variations of power amongst white people, to do with class, gender and other factors; goodwill is not unheard of in white people's engagement with others. White power nonetheless reproduces itself regardless of intention, power differences and goodwill, and overwhelmingly because it is not seen as whiteness, but as normal. White people need to learn to see themselves as white, to see their particularity. In other words, whiteness needs to be made strange.

* * *

Notes

1. I use the terms 'race' and 'racial' in this opening section in the most common though problematic sense, referring to supposedly visibly differentiable, supposedly discrete social groupings.

2. In their discussion of the extraordinarily successful TV sitcom about a middle-class, African-American family, *The Cosby Show,* Sut Jhally and Justin Lewis note the way that viewers repeatedly recognise the characters' blackness but also feel that 'you just think of them as people'; in other words that they don't only speak for their race. Jhally and Lewis argue that this is achieved by the way the family conforms to 'the everyday, generic world of white television' (1992: 100), an essentially middle-class world. The family is 'ordinary' *despite* being black; because it is upwardly mobile, it can be accepted as 'ordinary', in a way that marginalises most actual African-Americans. If the realities of African-American experience were included, then the characters would not be perceived as 'just people'.

3. See, for instance, Bogle 1973, Hartmann and Husband 1974, Troyna 1981, MacDonald 1983, Wilson and Gutiérez 1985, van Dijk 1987, Jhally and Lewis 1992 (58ff.), Ross 1995. The research findings are generally cast the other way round, in terms of non-white under-representation, textual marginalisation and positioning as deviant or a problem. Recent research in the US does suggest that African-Americans (but not

other racially marginalised groups) have become more represented in the media, even in excess of their proportion of the population. However, this number still falls off if one focuses on central characters.

4. *The Crying Game* (GB 1992) seems to me to be an example of this. It explores, with fascination and generosity, the hybrid and fluid nature of identity: gender, race, national belonging, sexuality. Yet all of this revolves around a bemused but ultimately unchallenged straight white man—it reinscribes the position of those at the intersection of heterosexuality, maleness, and whiteness as that of the one group which does not need to be hybrid and fluid.

References

Alba, Richard D. (1990) *Ethnic Identity: The Transformation of White America*, New Haven: Yale University Press.

Bogle, Donald (1973) *Toms, Coons, Mulattoes, Mammies and Bucks: An Interpretive History of Blacks in American Films*, New York: Viking Press.

Carby, Hazel V. (1992) 'The Multicultural Wars' in Dent, Gina (ed.) *Black Popular Culture*, Seattle: Bay Press, 187–99.

Dyer, Richard (1993) 'Seen To Be Believed: Problems in the Representation of Gay People as Typical' in Dyer *The Matter of Images: Essays on Representations*, London: Routledge, 19–51.

Hartmann, Paul and Husband, Charles (1974) *Racism and the Mass Media*, London: Davis-Poynter.

hooks, bell (1992) 'Madonna: Plantation Mistress or Soul Sister?' and 'Representations of Whiteness in the Black Imagination' in *Black Looks: Race and Representation*, Boston: South End Press, 157–64, 165–78.

Ibson, John (1981) 'Virgin Land or Virgin Mary? Studying the Ethnicity of White Americans', *American Quarterly* 33(3): 284–308.

Jhally, Sut and Lewis, Justin (1992) *Enlightened Racism: 'The Cosby show', Audiences and the Myth of the American Dream*, Boulder: Westview Press.

MacDonald, J. F. (1983) *Blacks and White TV: Afro-Americans in Television since 1948*, Chicago: Nelson-Hall.

Owens, Craig (1983) 'The Discourse of Others: Feminists and Postmodernism' in Foster, Hal (ed.) *The Anti-Aesthetic: Essays on Postmodern Culture*, Port Townsend WA: Bay Press, 57–82.

Ross, Karen (1995) *Black and White Media*, Oxford: Polity.

Troyna, Barry (1981) 'Images of Race and Racist Images in the British News Media' in Halloran, J. D. (ed.) *Mass Media and Mass Communications*, Leicester: Leicester University Press.

van Dijk, T. A. (1987) *Communicating Racism*, London: Sage.

Wilson, C. J. and Gutiérrez, F. (1985) *Minorities and Media*, Beverley Hills: Sage.

Representations of Whiteness
in the Black Imagination

bell hooks

Although there has never been any official body of black people in the United States who have gathered as anthropologists and/or ethnographers to study whiteness, black folks have, from slavery on, shared in conversations with one another "special" knowledge of whiteness gleaned from close scrutiny of white people. Deemed special because it was not a way of knowing that has been recorded fully in written material, its purpose was to help black folks cope and survive in a white supremacist society. For years, black domestic servants, working in white homes, acting as informants, brought knowledge back to segregated communities—details, facts, observations, and psychoanalytic readings of the white Other.

Sharing the fascination with difference that white people have collectively expressed openly (and at times vulgarly) as they have traveled around the world in pursuit of the Other and Otherness, black people, especially those living during the historical period of racial apartheid and legal segregation, have similarly maintained steadfast and ongoing curiosity about the "ghosts," "the barbarians," these strange apparitions they were forced to serve. . . .

I, too, am in search of the debris of history. I am wiping the dust off past conversations to remember some of what was shared in the old days when black folks had little intimate contact with whites, when we were much more open about the way we connected whiteness with the mysterious, the strange, and the terrible. Of course, everything has changed. Now many black people live in the "bush of ghosts" and do not know themselves separate from whiteness. They do not know this thing we call "difference." Systems of domination, imperialism, colonialism, and racism actively coerce black folks to internalize negative perceptions of blackness, to be self-hating. Many of us succumb to this. Yet, blacks who imitate whites (adopting their values, speech, habits of being, etc.) continue to regard whiteness with suspicion, fear, and even hatred. This contradictory longing to possess the reality of the Other, even though that reality is one that wounds and negates, is expressive of the desire to understand the mystery, to know intimately through imitation, as though such knowing worn like an amulet, a mask, will ward away the evil, the terror.

Searching the critical work of post-colonial critics, I found much writing that bespeaks the continued fascination with the way white minds, particularly the colonial imperialist traveler, perceive blackness, and very little expressed interest in representations of whiteness in the black imagination. Black cultural and social critics allude to such representations in their writing, yet only a few have dared to make explicit those perceptions of whiteness that they think will discomfort or antagonize readers. James Baldwin's collection of essays, *Notes of a Native Son*, explores these issues with a clarity and frankness that is no longer fashionable in a world where evocations of pluralism and diversity act to obscure differences arbitrarily imposed and maintained by white racist domination. Addressing the way in which whiteness exists without knowledge of blackness even as it collectively asserts control, Baldwin links issues of recognition to the practice of imperialist racial domination. Writing about being the first black person to visit a Swiss village with only white inhabitants in his essay "Stranger in the Village," Baldwin notes his response to the village's yearly ritual of painting individuals black who were then positioned as slaves and bought so that the villagers could celebrate their concern with converting the souls of the "natives":

> I thought of white men arriving for the first time in an African village, strangers there, as I am a stranger here, and tried to imagine the astounded populace touching their hair and marveling at the color of their skin. But there is a great difference between being the first white man to be seen by Africans and being the first black man to be seen by whites. The white man takes the astonishment as tribute, for he arrives to conquer and to convert the natives, whose inferiority in relation to himself is not even to be questioned, whereas I, without a thought of conquest, find myself among a people whose culture controls me, has even, in a sense, created me, people who have cost me more in anguish and rage than they will ever know, who yet do not even know of my existence. The astonishment with which I might have greeted them, should they have stumbled into my African village a few hundred years ago, might have rejoiced their hearts. But the astonishment with which they greet me today can only poison mine.

My thinking about representations of whiteness in the black imagination has been stimulated by classroom discussions about the way in which the absence of recognition is a strategy that facilitates making a group the Other. In these classrooms there have been heated debates among students when white students respond with disbelief, shock, and rage, as they listen to black students talk about whiteness, when they are compelled to hear observations, stereotypes, etc., that are offered as "data" gleaned from close scrutiny and study. Usually, white students respond with naive amazement that black people critically assess white people from a standpoint where "whiteness" is the privileged signifier. Their amazement that black people watch white people with a critical "ethnographic" gaze is itself an expression of racism. Often their rage erupts because they believe that all ways of looking that highlight difference subvert the liberal belief in a universal subjectivity (we are all just people) that they think will make racism disappear. They have a deep emotional investment in the myth of "sameness," even as their actions reflect the primacy of whiteness as a sign informing who they are and how they think. Many of them are shocked that black people think critically about whiteness because racist thinking perpetuates the fantasy that the Other who is subjugated, who is subhuman, lacks the ability to comprehend, to understand, to see the working of the powerful. Even though the majority of these students politically consider themselves liberals and anti-racist, they too unwittingly invest in the sense of whiteness as mystery.

In white supremacist society, white people can "safely" imagine that they are invisible to black people since the power they have historically asserted, and even now collectively assert over black people, accorded them the right to control the black gaze. As fantastic as it may seem, racist white people find it easy to imagine that black people cannot see them if within their desire they do not want to be seen by the dark Other. One mark of oppression was that black folks were compelled to assume the mantle of invisibility, to erase all traces of their subjectivity during slavery and the long years of racial apartheid, so that they could be better, less threatening servants. An effective strategy of white supremacist terror and dehumanization during slavery centered around white control of the black gaze. Black slaves, and later manumitted servants, could be brutally punished for looking, for appearing to observe the whites they were serving, as only a subject can observe, or see. To be fully an object then was to lack the capacity to see or recognize reality. These looking relations were reinforced as whites cultivated the practice of denying the subjectivity of blacks (the better to dehumanize and oppress), of relegating them to the realm of the invisible. Growing up in a Kentucky household where black servants lived in the same dwelling with the white family who employed them, newspaper heiress Sallie Bingham recalls, in her autobiography *Passion and Prejudice*, "Blacks, I realized, were simply invisible to most white people, except as a pair of hands offering a drink on a silver tray." Reduced to the machinery of bodily physical labor, black people learned to appear before whites as though they were zombies, cultivating the habit of casting the gaze downward so as not to appear uppity. To look directly was an assertion of subjectivity, equality. Safety resided in the pretense of invisibility.

Even though legal racial apartheid no longer is a norm in the United States, the habits that uphold and maintain institutionalized white supremacy linger. Since most white people do not have to "see" black people (constantly appearing on billboards, television, movies, in magazines, etc.) and they do not need to be ever on guard nor to observe black people to be safe, they can live as though black people are invisible, and they can imagine that they are also invisible to blacks. Some white people may even imagine there is no representation of whiteness in the black imagination, especially one that is based on concrete observation or mythic conjecture. They think they are seen by black folks only as they want to appear. Ideologically, the rhetoric of white supremacy supplies a fantasy of white-ness. Described in Richard Dyer's essay "White," this fantasy makes whiteness synonymous with goodness:

> Power in contemporary society habitually passes itself off as embodied in the nor-mal as opposed to the superior. This is common to all forms of power, but it works in a peculiarly seductive way with whiteness, because of the way it seems rooted, in common-sense thought, in things other than ethnic difference. . . . Thus it is said (even in liberal textbooks) that there are inevitable associations of white with light and therefore safety, and black with dark and therefore danger, and that this explains racism (whereas one might well argue about the safety of the cover of dark-ness, and the danger of exposure to the light); again, and with more justice, people point to the Jewish and Christian use of white and black to symbolize good and evil, as carried still in such expressions as "a black mark," "white magic," "to blacken the character" and so on. Socialized to believe the fantasy, that whiteness represents goodness and all that is benign and non-threatening, many white people assume this is the way black people conceptualize whiteness. They do not imagine that the way whiteness makes its presence felt in black life, most often as terrorizing imposition, a power that wounds, hurts, tortures, is a reality that disrupts the fantasy of white-ness as representing goodness.

. . . Looking past stereotypes to consider various representations of whiteness in the black imagination, I appeal to memory, to my earliest recollections of ways these issues were raised in black life. Returning to memories of growing up in the social circumstances created by racial apartheid, to all black spaces on the edges of town, I reinhabit a location where black folks associated whiteness with the terrible, the terrifying, the terrorizing. White people were regarded as terrorists, especially those who dared to enter that segregated space of blackness. As a child, I did not know any white people. They were strangers, rarely seen in our neighborhoods. The "official" white men who came across the tracks were there to sell products, Bibles and insurance. They terrorized by economic exploitation. What did I see in the gazes of those white men who crossed our thresholds that made me afraid, that made black children unable to speak? Did they understand at all how strange their whiteness appeared in our living rooms, how threaten-ing? Did they journey across the tracks with the same "adventurous" spirit that other white men carried to Africa, Asia, to those mysterious places they would one day call the "third world?" Did they come to our houses to meet the Other face-to-face and enact the colonizer role, dominating us on our own turf?

Their presence terrified me. Whatever their mission, they looked too much like the unofficial white men who came to enact rituals of terror and torture. As a child, I did not know how to tell them apart, how to ask the "real white people to please stand up."

* * *

In the absence of the reality of whiteness, I learned as a child that to be "safe," it was important to recognize the power of whiteness, even to fear it, and to avoid encounter. There was nothing terrifying about the sharing of this knowledge as survival strategy, the terror was made real only when I journeyed from the black side of town to a predominantly white area near my grandmother's house. I had to pass through this area to reach her place. Describing these journeys "across town" in the essay "Homeplace: A Site of Resistance," I remembered:

> It was a movement away from the segregated blackness of our community into a poor white neighborhood. I remember the fear, being scared to walk to Baba's our grandmother's house, because we would have to pass that terrifying whiteness— those white faces on the porches staring us down with hate. Even when empty or vacant those porches seemed to say *danger*, you do not belong here, you are not safe.

Oh! that feeling of safety, of arrival, of homecoming when we finally reached the edges of her yard, when we could see the soot black face of our grandfather, Daddy Gus, sitting in his chair on the porch, smell his cigar, and rest on his lap. Such a contrast, that feeling of arrival, of homecoming—this sweetness and the bitterness of that journey, that constant reminder of white power and control. Even though it was a long time ago that I made this journey, associations of whiteness with terror and the terrorizing remain. Even though I live and move in spaces where I am surrounded by whiteness, there is no comfort that makes the terrorism disappear. All black people in the United States, irrespective of their class status or politics, live with the possibility that they will be terrorized by whiteness.

* * *

Meaning and Gender Matter

Women and Race in Feminist Media Research: Intersections, Ideology and Invisibility

Linda Aldoory and Shawn J. Parry-Giles

Introduction

Throughout the 1960s, 1970s and into the 1980s, many liberal feminists empha-sized the political, legal, and social inequalities that existed between women and men (Arneil, 1999; Whelehan, 1995). Feminists from this second wave of US fem-inism often treated gender and race/ethnicity as distinct categories, homogenizing 'woman', perpetuating dualist reasoning (black/white, masculine/feminine) of modernist thought, and further marginalizing women of colour (Fraser, 1989; Glenn, 1999). As a result, 'men of color stood as the universal racial subject', and '[w]hite women were positioned as the universal female subject' (Glenn, 1999: 3). Valdivia (1995) argues similarly that feminist work has centred largely on white women, and ethnic and race studies, while growing in number, have focused primarily on African-American men. In US popular culture and media, such homogenization and dualism depicted black women, for example, as 'all woman and tinted black', or 'mostly black and scarcely woman' (Gaines, 1988: 19).

We believe this homogenist and binary thinking reduces women and persons of colour to unproductive stereotypes, furthering the presence of sexism and racism in media studies. Instead, we encourage an emphasis on the differences among women in scholarship and in political practice. Other feminist scholars have also promoted a more 'multicultural feminism' (Shohat, 1998: 2), where 'the term "women" applies to differently situated individuals . . . who occupy a spectrum of identities as well as positions of power' (Valdivia, 1995: 9). Zinn and Dill (1996: 321–2) use the concept 'multiracial feminism' to impart 'race as a primary force situating genders differently'. They contend that the concept of 'difference' has replaced 'equality' as the central force in US feminist theory, demonstrating a significant shift in feminist scholarship and activism over the past two decades (p. 322).

Such commitments, which stem from third-wave feminism, moved many schol-ars toward developing what has become known as theories of '*intersectionality*'

(Valdivia, 1995; Zinn and Dill, 1996). Such intersectional commitments presuppose that studies of women should always be connected with considerations of race and class, characteristics that work together to define a person's particular subject position. West and Fenstermaker (1995: 11) suggest no one can 'experience gender without simultaneously experiencing race and class'. The main assumption is that race and gender are 'mutually constitutive' and 'relational' (Glenn, 1999: 9; McLaughlin, 1998: 85; Pellegrini, 1998).

We argue in this chapter that this move toward intersectionality makes media studies research more complex, more realistic, and more sensitive to cultural contexts, all of which are significant factors in improving media scholarship.[1] The goal of this chapter, then, is to review feminist media literature that works to disrupt (and in such cases perpetuate) such binary reasoning and interrogate the media as a complex system of gender, race and economics, which allows 'violence and inequities to continue' (Farrell, 1995: 643).

Similarly, we are attuned to issues of 'transnational affiliations' and 'diasporic nationalisms' related to 'gendering practices, class formations, sexual identities, [and] racialized subjects' (Grewal and Kaplan, 2001: 52). Such a 'multiplicity of relations' (Mouffee, 1992: 372) complicates matters of oppression and resistance as an individual can 'occupy both dominant and subordinate positions and experience advantage and disadvantage' because of race, class, gender and/or sexuality, as well as matters related to globalism, nationalism and localism (Weber, 2001: 105). We argue, however, that while feminist media scholars are making considerable progress in offering a more multicultural and global feminism in relation to progressing nations such as India, such research still often reflects the binaries of modernism and the hegemony of Western feminism that, well intentioned or not, can dominate feminist politics and scholarship. In the process, such scholarship often reinforces the power of elite white/anglo males and, in certain instances, elite white/anglo females while rendering certain women of colour in particular developing nations more invisible, particularly in relation to the African continent. As Flores and McPhail (1997: 115) warn, 'discourses [can] continue to maintain a binary opposition between the dominant and the marginalized, an opposition which may limit or obscure our understanding and comprehension of the complexity of difference, and preclude the possibility of moving away from the rhetoric of "us against them"'.

Specifically, we centre our attention on research that takes a cultural studies approach to feminism and the media, particularly to matters of media production, representation and audience reception (Henderson, 2001; Shohat and Stam, 1996). We note the ways that media production, representation and reception disrupt and/or perpetuate structures of domination. For example, some cultural studies scholars analyse media texts to study the ways that the media serve as sites of resistance for persons often oppressed within their local and/or global communities. Other studies examine whether specific audiences accept 'preferred' meanings offered by media producers, whether they resist or oppose the preferred meanings altogether, or whether they negotiate the preferred meanings that media producers generate. While media producers construct certain, preferred meanings in the media texts they produce, it is not necessarily the meanings received by audience members. Cultural studies scholars explore this meaning-making process from production through representation to reception and track the meanings that are created, negotiated and received, examining how such meanings change over time.

We define feminist research as scholarly work that critically examines gender and power relations and uses feminist theories as analytical frameworks. This chapter focuses on gender and race studies that have examined women and their interactions with, and representations in, the media. This limitation was necessary to construct a focused, relevant review of literature, but there are also weaknesses inherent in our delimiters. First, not all feminist media literature is represented here, and not all topics are represented. There is an emphasis on popular media, political communication, news and journalism in a US context most noticeably yet not exclusively. We are also aware that certain, critical areas of scholarship have been de-emphasized, particularly health communication, pornography, advertising, and new technology or internet studies from an appropriate multiplicity of international contexts. In this chapter we first detail themes that emerge in the research on intersectionality in media production, media representation and audience reception. We end with a discussion of the scholarly implications for feminist media research.

Media Production

In general, research on women, race and ethnicity in the context of media production has been limited, compared with the amount of research conducted on media representation. Media production is most often studied by feminists through ethnography that highlights women as producers of alternative media and through observational studies, surveys or interviews that examine women in media professions who struggle against racism and sexism to influence media production. Other studies accentuate the ideological influences that production has on media content.

Women Producing Media

Feminists have for decades challenged mass media portrayals of women by forming independent media sources and channels (Opoku-Mensah, 2001; Riano, 1994), or what Smith (1993: 61) calls 'women's movement media'. Riano (1994) argues that the process of creating alternative media forms make women the primary subjects of struggle and change in communication systems, by developing oppositional and proactive alternatives that influence language, representations and communication technologies. Using ethnography, researchers explore these media in order to illustrate how they offer alternatives to dominant meanings produced through media and how they construct sites of resistance (Baehr and Gray, 1996). Examples of this research include Byerly's (1995) historical description of the women's feature service in world news, Bhandarker's (1995) case study of female foreign news correspondents from developing countries, and Ruiz's (1994) examination of video and radio productions by Native Aymara women in Bolivia. These and other studies (Kawaja, 1994; Lloyd, 1994; Mensah-Kutin, 1994; Rodriguez, 1994) indicate that women working as cultural producers of media play crucial roles as conduits of social change. The authors integrate race, ethnicity, globalization and colonization into understandings of gendered media production. For example, Shafer and Hornig conducted a study of women journalists in the Philippines who were 'primary actors in using the press to hasten the downfall of President Ferdinand Marcos between 1982 and his exile in 1986' (Shafer and Hornig, 1995: p. 177). Rodriguez (1994) conducted ethnographic and participative research on women producing videos in Colombia. One video involved women from Ciudad Bolivar, a 'barrio' in Bogota, and their work with community day-care centres. A second video was produced by women working to transform a maternity clinic into a worker-owned institution because they were exploited as employees. Rodriguez found several significant changes in the women she worked with. First, the women began focusing on the nuances of their everyday lives. Second, the women who were originally enamoured with the media and popular culture became familiarized with production processes. Third, the women found themselves reconstructing roles of power among themselves, giving voice to some women who were invisible in the communities. Finally, the stories told on the videos were sources of collective strength and empowerment to the women.

In her edited book on women in grassroots communication, Riano (1994) offers a typology of media production efforts by women; she constructs four major frameworks: development communications, participatory communications, alternative communications and feminist communications. Development communications originate from outside the control of the community and are delivered through government, international development institutions, or non-governmental organizations (NGOs). In participatory communications, women are seen as participants in the process that enables them to take control of their lives and influence public policies through media production. Alternative communications is the development of means other than commercial media or vertical, one-way communication systems. Finally, feminist communications take on gender as a central, analytical dimension, where the main concerns are the ways in which gender influences the nature of participation and communication production and the mediation of gender in women's and men's experiences of subordination. Riano explains that these frameworks overlap and address issues of gender, race and globalization in different ways. Riano maps out this typology to counter prevailing myths of participation, communication and democratization while challenging how differences are ignored in current proposals of participatory communication.

Within the body of work on women-produced media are examples of partici-pative action research, where scholars assist participants in producing and analysing alternative media forms (Mensah-Kutin, 1994; Rodriguez, 1994; Stuart and Bery, 1996). Stuart and Bery (1996), for example, helped women in Bangladesh produce a video to increase awareness about domestic violence. The authors explain: 'In exploring less brokered forms of communication, we pro-duced programs with real people speaking from their own experience on issues of general concern' (p. 304). They argue that participative video enhanced the 'bottom-up' strategies used by global women's organizations.

Women Inside Mainstream Media

Feminist media scholars have also examined the ways that female professionals work to change policies and media content from inside popular media outlets. Much of the research has concluded, however, that in terms of overall numbers and distribution across and within specific occupations, women media workers are disadvantaged in the male-dominated field (Baehr and Gray, 1996; Creedon, 1993). Empirical research offers minimal evidence of a direct correlation between the number of women working in mainstream media and the increase in produc-tive representations of women. Baehr and Gray (1996) demonstrate that institutional and professional constraints inhibit progress for women in the male dominated media industry. They maintain that a specific women's perspective or aesthetic could radically transform discriminatory structures and practices in media institutions.

Production studies that intersect race and gender centre on the ideological con-straints and oppressive work practices for women. In her examination of the televi-sion series *Any Day Now*, aired on the US cable network Lifetime, Lotz specifically focuses on how executive producer Nancy Miller bisected race and gender for the two female characters on the show. Lotz finds through her observations and inter-views of the show's producers and writers that Miller's struggles with the network indicate 'how American society tries to separate aspects of identity into discrete categories, barricading the intersections that offer more complex understandings of identity in contemporary US culture' (Lotz, 2004: 295). Lotz explains that origi-nally the show was sold to the US broadcast network, CBS, who then cancelled production, citing fears that US audiences were not ready to see two female char-acters confront interracial friendship and racism. Miller adjusted the vision of her show at a time when drastic changes were taking place in the economics and com-petition between US broadcast and cable television stations. Seven years after CBS cancelled production, the cable network Lifetime—a channel targeting women— aired the drama with Miller as the producer. Miller still encountered challenges because Lifetime's executives did not wish to focus on character conflicts arising from racial differences between women. Lotz concludes that television networks are still maintaining a separation of identities in order to appease audiences. Even with niche networks such as Black Entertainment Television (BET) in the USA, relatively broad audiences are sought. According to Lotz, 'Voices such as Miller's may have difficulty receiving distribution because they recognize intersections more specific than those currently served by networks' (p. 299).

Ideological Influence of Media

Other media production studies focus on ideological influences in relation to matters of race, ethnicity and gender. Acosta-Alzuru's work on Venezuelan telenovelas is one of the most intricate and comprehensive examinations of the impact of media production on media content and audience reception. Telenovelas are Spanish language television shows featuring dramatic content and a continuous story line. In her study, Acosta-Alzuru interviews head writers, actors, and the producer of a popular Venezuelan telenovela, *El Pais de las Mujeres* (The Country of Women). Taking a cultural studies approach, Acosta-Alzuru also examines the content of the telenovela for its representations and interviews both male and female audience members in Venezuela. The author finds that the writer and producer of the show intentionally portray strong female characters who are often victims of patriarchal oppression. The producer wanted to show 'women's redemption and, in some way, use a flashlight to light the way for those who still don't know how to redeem themselves' (Acosta-Alzura, 2003: 274). Even though the producer and writers set out to honour Venezuelan women by presenting them as protagonists of their own stories, the head writer said he did not want a feminist telenovela. Acosta-Alzuru concludes that feminism is seen as a threat to the established social order in Venezuela. Thus, even though the producers develop story lines for female characters who are strong and who reflect real problems, the meanings presented still maintain the hegemonic ideals of womanhood. Such ideological commitments exhibited by the producers clearly impact the representations that circulate in media discourse.

Media Representation

Examining the intersectionality of gender, race and ethnicity has occupied the attention of scholars interested in the study of media representations, which communicate images of power and control (Fair, 1996), connect 'meaning and language to culture' (Hall, 1997: 15), and function as sources of 'desire, memory, myth, search, discovery' (Hall, 2000: 32). Grossman and Cuthbert (1996: 431) contend that the 'politics of representation is also always a politics of the material' and Rony (1996: 8–9) maintains that the media serve as a site where gender and race are represented as 'natural categories' in relation to the global, national and the local. While such representations can 'reinforce mental structures and images to constrain, dehumanize, and disempower particular individuals in both First- and Third-World cultures' (Heung, 1995: 83), they also 'can play a more coherent and transformative role in the social construction and reconstruction of difference, diversity, and dialogue' (Flores and McPhail, 1997: 107).

Representations as Mediated Stereotypes

One way that the media organize power is through stereotypical representations, which reinscribe social rules and roles that are often simultaneously sexist and racist (Fair, 1996)—troubling images that some believe are harder to detect in visual representations than in the written or spoken word (Wallace, 1990). Multicultural feminists commonly accentuate the sexualization of women in film, music videos, advertisements, news and other television genres. In the USA, scholars often attend to the ways in which black women are hyper-sexualized in the media (hooks, 1996). Wallace (1990) suggests that black women are more likely to be featured as performers in music videos or as fashion models than they are to be given roles with speaking parts. In hip-hop, for example, Perry charges that 'the visual image of black women . . . rapidly deteriorated into one of widespread sexual objectification and degradation', especially in music video images that are often controlled by record company executives (Perry, 2003: 137). Hooks explains that black women participate in such practices because 'the black female body gains attention only when it is synonymous with accessibility, availability, when it is sexually deviant' (hooks, 1992: 66). When black women are featured as lead characters in film, such sexualizations still persist. Bobo, for example, talks of Shug as the 'licentious cabaret singer' in the 1985 Steven Spielberg film, *the Color Purple* (Bobo, 1995: 73). Writing about Martin Lawrence's Fox television show, *Martin*, Zook (1999: 64) suggests that the relationship between Lawrence's character and his on-screen girlfriend, Gina, was really about 'power and patriarchal desire'.

The conflation of black women's sexuality and class with electoral politics is the subject of other media scholarship about the news media. Linking sexualization with drug use and welfare dependency, for example, Reeves constructs the image of the 'crack mother as an out-of-control black sexuality' that emerged during the presidential years of Ronald Reagan (1981–1989) (Reeves, 1998: 110). Vision of the black teen welfare mother were pervasive in US television news throughout the 1980s and 1990s—images that combined with black men as absentee fathers to further the '[r]acial coding parading as commonsense populism [which] associated blacks with negative [sexual] equivalencies . . . affirming the repressed, unspeakable, racist unconscious of dominant white culture' (Giroux, 1998: 46). Even the news media coverage of professionally successful black women can reflect overt sexualizations. Vavrus studied the news coverage surrounding Anita Hill's 1991 testimony before the US Senate Judiciary Committee concerning Clarence Thomas's Supreme Court nomination. She asserts that the press coverage of Hill's testimony 'pathologized her sexuality', as journalists and pundits debated, for example, one psychiatrist's view that Hill was 'diagnosed as erotomaniacal, a disorder characterized by the presence of sexual desire so strong that it overwhelms sufferers' (Vavrus, 2002: 63). Such constructions reflect the nineteenth-century ideology that women who entered the US public sphere and politics in particular were sexually provocative and promiscuous.

Sexuality and race also collide with colonialism, nationalism and class in other scholarship on media representations (Durham, 2001; Luthra, 1995; Parameswaran, 2001).Writing about US popular representations of Native Americans, Bird juxtaposes those found in the classic Western films of the 'squaw' that is 'sexually convenient', with the 'American Indian princess' as portrayed by Disney's *Pocahontas*—the non-threatening symbol of the 'virgin land' possessed by the white/anglo males (Bird, 1999: 72–4). Luthra intersects matters of colonialism, race, gender and sexuality when examining the US media coverage of Third World women over matters of population control during the Reagan administration. Within such coverage, Luthra contends, 'Third World woman' were depicted as 'mysterious, inaccessible, [and] oppressed', which helped justify 'foreign intervention in the international population arena'. Such images work to normalize First World power over women of colour and their sexuality to restrict the growing number of poor that might destabilize Western sovereignty (Luthra, 1995: 197, 211). Further emphasizing US international power, Parry-Giles and Parry-Giles (in press) focus on popular representations found in the US television drama, *The West Wing*, a fictional narrative about the US presidency. The authors emphasize how Russia is personified by a female leader whose sexual advances are decidedly rebuked by the white male political officials of the west wing, communicating a disgust and distrust of contemporary Russia attempting to rebuild its international prestige in the post-Cold War era.

In addition to accentuating women's sexuality, other critics note that Third World women or poorer women of colour in the USA and Britain are often portrayed as victims in need of Western benevolent aid. Fair shows that men are portrayed as 'producers' while women are depicted as helpless and dependent on international aid in US press coverage of famine in Ethiopia and other parts of Africa (Fair, 1996: 11–12). Parameswaran situates *National Geographic's* 1999 millennium issue in a globalized context as she examines the Western gaze toward women of colour and black women in the USA. She concludes: 'the *Geographic's* facile accounts of women as symbols, consumers, peddlers, and mute victims of global culture become the dominant narratives of femininity' (Parameswaran, 2002a: 300). Furthering such images of black women's disempowerment globally, Omenugha examines British newspaper coverage of 'African women', noting the common visual images of 'destitution, victimization, poverty, sickness, and wretchedness' (Omenugha, 2003: 15). Such transnational images deny women of colour a sense of agency, justifying international intervention and control in the increasingly global environment.

Images of Third World victimization are sometimes associated with 'primitive' visualizations—depictions that work in opposition to images of progress that often accompany characterizations of white/anglo women. When examining The Body Shop's advertising campaign entitled *Mamatoto*, for example, Grossman and Cuthbert note how non-Western women of colour are usually featured in outdoor settings, including a forest or desert surrounded by animals, as they bathe infants. Conversely, the images of white women in the same advertising campaign are mediated through computer-generated graphics that are highly stylized. Such differences, the authors suggest, 'informs and reinforces the ideological juxtapositions of progress and primitivism, science and folklore, knowledge and ignorance that discursively marks the boundaries between "us" and "them" throughout *Mamatoto*' (Grossman and Cuthbert, 1996: 438).

In some cases, feminist scholars juxtapose portrayals of Third World and First World women (Grossman and Cuthbert, 1996), while other scholars destabilize images of white/anglo female dominance, demonstrating how they are empowered in one context and disempowered in another (Durham, 2001). Durham, for instance, interrogates the ways that South Asian symbols of femininity (e.g. nose rings, mehndi, and bindis) are appropriated by white/anglo women and promulgated throughout US popular culture. As a result, Durham (2001: 213) suggests, 'The US mass media's presentation of Indian femininity as a substructure for White female sexuality serves to legitimate the hegemonic construction of Western superiority over Asian culture'. Willis reveals other ways that US white/anglo women are symbolized in dominant ways by studying how film and television drama commemorate their political contributions to the African-American civil rights movement (1950s and 1960s). Referring to white women as 'protofeminists', Willis suggests that they are portrayed as 'a medium for the transformation of racial consciousness of the men around her'. While such images can be read as productive on the one hand by writing white women into the activism of the civil rights movement, Willis accentuates the ideological ambiguity of the texts, concluding that 'the central focus on the progressive women downplays white resistance to integration in general' (Willis, 2001: 100, 113–14). Vavrus (2002) uses former US first lady Hillary Rodham Clinton as a case study, and contends that Clinton, 'a privileged white woman with fairly conservative politics . . . comes to be the poster child for feminism', communicating more restricted images of contemporary feminism. Thus, while white/anglo women are often imbued with power in a global context, such power is restricted in a US political context, demonstrating the contestation and complexities surrounding matters of domination and subordination as researchers seek to integrate intersectional perspectives in their media scholarship.

For many scholars, the stereotypes of women's sexuality, victimization, primitiveness and empowerment are often transported globally and locally through representations of women's bodies. Heung details how 'colonization operates by taking over land and bodies'. In assessing films by Asian and Canadian filmmakers, Heung says that for 'Asian women especially, ideologies of gender, race, ethnicity, and sexuality place their bodies under the burden of erasure while also marking them as receptacles of projected cultural meanings' (Heung, 1995: 90). Likewise focusing on the mediation of Third World women, Fair contends that 'women in Africa often . . . are depicted only in terms of their bodies . . . embodying inferior qualities of womanliness compared to their white Western counterparts' (Fair, 1996: 7). Juxtaposing the portrayal of women in India by centring attention on issues of age and globalism, Parameswaran demonstrates how the 'older Indian woman's body and posture announce her alignment with tradition'. Younger women's bodies, conversely, reflect 'an androgynous firm body' reflective of 'cosmopolitan modernity', communicating 'bold assertiveness, feminine youthfulness' against images of 'gentle passivity and the slack middle-aged body' (Parameswaran, 2002a: 291–2). Durham concludes that when white women's bodies replace those of Indian women in the mediation of South Asian culture, 'the cultural appropriation of Eastern cultures as trends, styles, or exotic sexual displays can be understood in terms of issues of imperialism and dominance' (Durham, 2001: 205).

Representations as Sites of Political Resistance

Even scholars who expend considerable energy isolating and destabilizing destructive images of oppression and submission also accentuate productive images of empowerment. As Durham suggests, historically oppressed communities and nations are making their presence felt in 'subversive ways'; Durham turns to India as a case study where its image is moving from one of 'swamis, gurus, or poverty-stricken laborers' to 'highly employable scientists, engineers, doctors' (Durham, 2001: 212). Bobo (1995) similarly insists that social movements, with clear connections to political activism, can do their work through media texts. Parry-Giles and Parry-Giles (in press) illustrate such political work by discussing how US civil rights organizations worked toward the diversification of television cast members in the late 1990s. Responding, at least in part, to such diversity calls, *The West Wing* places white women and people of colour in positions of political power. As a result, white women serve as presidential political and legal advisers, influential members of Congress, feminist activists, and as the president's press secretary. Women of colour, although less visible than men of colour in this presidential narrative, are still depicted as the National Security Adviser and the Secretary of Housing and Urban Development. While limited, such representations work to change the face of US television, demonstrating the potential impact of political activism. *The West Wing* also features significant debates over global feminist matters, including the trafficking of teen prostitutes worldwide, population control and abortion rights, and the complicit role of the US government in the violence against women in the Middle East. *The West Wing*, thus reflects the contention offered by Carter, Branston and Allan about television news, where 'privileged news celebrities' can 'allow a range of feminist debates to be articulated' with considerable emotion that might have previously been 'disallowed' (Carter *et al.*, 1998: 7–8).

Several scholars also indicate ways that representations of black women destabilize disempowered images previously discussed. In particular, several reveal how black women in music are taking greater control over their own image-making. Gaunt highlights BO$$, an African-American rap artist, who exudes images of independence and financial success that work against the typical sexualized or welfare mother stereotypes. In the process, she, along with other women in 'gangsta rap', co-opt 'the male voice and the male dress and use male privilege and space to deconstruct codes of gender identity as a sign of access' (Gaunt, 1995: 302). Further focusing on self-empowerment representations, Zook links another African-American rap artist and actor, (Queen) Latifah, to 'nontraditional representations of femininity, sexuality, and power' (Zook, 1999: 69), likewise prompting discussion about feminism and lesbianism. Latifah works with the activist group, Intelligent Black Women's Coalition; her voice and activism are reflected in the media representations of her, which resist the typical sexual victimization images that often pervade music videos in particular. Perry notes that feminism began to infiltrate hip-hop during the 1980s. The images that newer artists such as Alicia Keys and India Arie project in their songs and their videos evidence 'intelligence and integrity rather than expensive clothes, liquor, and firearms', defying visual sexual images that 'may be implicated in the subjugation of black women' (Perry, 2003: 140).

The disruption of historical images of colonization is also part of global political activism; media scholarship reflects such political commitments. Shohat and Stam urge that '[j]ust as the media can eroticize and "otherize" cultures, they can also promote multicultural coalitions'. In a contemporary context, they contend, the media is more 'multicentered, with the power not only to offer countervailing representations but also to open up parallel spaces for alternative transnational practices' (Shohat and Stam, 1996: 145). More specifically, Parameswaran (2001) demonstrates through the images of the 1996 Miss World pageant how local communities can impart influence in a global context, destabilizing the hegemonic control of the West and demonstrating that the media can serve as a site for counter-hegemonic causes. As Parameswaran and other multicultural feminists reveal, by integrating questions of race, gender, class, sexuality, globalism, nationalism, and localism, we see a much more contested terrain than previous scholarship generated during the second wave.

This contestation means, though, that certain women hold greater representational power than others in the mediated discourse of the global village. Parameswaran (2002a) showcases the polysemic images at work through her interrogation of *National Geographic*, which reflects the legacy of imperialism and juxtaposes women against women through representations of progress and disempowerment. Parameswaran illustrates how white/anglo women 'luxuriate in the freedom of pursuing ethnic culture and attractive Asian women express independence of style' as Asia is aligned with 'the vitality of modern progress'. Conversely, black women become 'the canvas on which the magazine etches poverty and disenfranchisement' in a US context while Africa, through its absence in the millennium issue, 'remains anchored to the amorphous state of extinction' (Parameswaran, 2002a: 313). While some scholarship on hip-hop accentuates the limited gains that US black women have made in the politics of representation, other multicultural feminists reveal the near invisibility of African black women in a global media context, illustrating the political work yet to be done. Cultural studies scholars who focus on audience reception are interested in understanding how people make sense of media and how media experiences affect daily life. While cultural studies scholars believe that the media can have potentially powerful effects, they also argue that audiences actively construct meaning when they interpret media. In fact, studies show that people use media to construct identities, gain knowledge and resist authority (Tracy, 2004).

According to Baehr and Gray (1996), questions of audience are never far away from any feminist work on the media. The number of studies on women's experiences with popular and mass media has increased over the past 20 years (Frazer, 1987; Gray, 1996; Gregg, 1992; Hobson, 1989, 1990, 1996; Press, 1990, 1991; Radway, 1984; Rakow, 1988; Seiter *et al.*, 1989), but there has been limited focus on interconnected experiences of women as gendered and raced subjects. The studies that connect race and gender often examine audiences for their differences in media consumption and reception. Cultural studies scholars also work to ascertain whether female audiences negotiate meanings from media texts or resist the preferred meanings offered by media producers.

Readings of Media as 'Different'

Many intersectional audience reception studies highlight difference in the ways that women of colour make meaning of media (Bobo, 1995; Harris and Hill, 1998; Munoz, 1994; Osborne, 2004). Bobo and others (Collins, 2000; King, 1988) suggest, for example, that black women face 'multiple jeopardy' because of their status as black and female, and, for the most part, because of a specific class hierarchy. Bobo contends that this multiple jeopardy is not additive, but rather an incremental process where racism is multiplied by sexism and then multiplied by classism (Bobo, 1995: 205). Reid (1989) argues that most studies of African Americans are based on the assumption that there is a relatively homogeneous black perspective and that most African Americans have similar views on political and social issues. Reid instead isolates the factors that lead to differences in attitudes toward television among young black women in London. She conducted a series of interviews with these women and found that gender, class and race influenced the viewing choices and attitudes towards television programmes. Darling-Wolf (2003: 153) similarly claims that there exists a theoretical recognition of the complexity of national and individual identity formation, but relatively few studies have attempted to determine how members of marginalized groups might experience processes of globalization.

In Darling-Wolf's study of Japanese women's meaning-making of popular Japanese media, a preference for Westerner's physical attributes was a significant element in the study's findings. Darling-Wolf spent eight months living in Japan and completed 40 interviews with 29 women ranging in age from 16 to 81. She found unanimous agreement among participants that white Western women presented in Japanese magazines and film were more physically attractive than Japanese women. She quoted one of the participants: 'That's the kind of beauty we pursue' (p. 166). However, Darling-Wolf also notes that this preference for white/anglo women's beauty did not mean that participants approved of white women's presence in the Japanese media environment. She argues that this racial hierarchy increases the alienation, remoteness and longing that the Japanese women feel toward representations of attractiveness in their favourite media (p. 167).

Negotiated and Oppositional Readings of Media

Many studies explore how certain audiences negotiate between meanings produced in media texts and meanings construed within the audiences' subjectivities. Tracy (2004), for example, found in her study of fourth-grade girls that racial and gendered identities, as well as friendship histories, affect and are affected by the girls' use of popular music. Tracy spent ten months and an average of three to four days a week with the girls in their school. She conducted group and individual interviews, observations, surveys and participated in school events. She concluded, 'While the girls negotiated their own identities when engaging with music in the lunch room and/or in their dance groups, dominant racial and gendered belief systems continued to affect their ways of seeing and being with others in other contexts' (p. 46). In Tracy's study, some participants claimed certain girls were 'acting black'; there was also gender allegiance against boys who wanted to interfere with the girls' dancing at recess. In arguing for the necessity of intersectional work, Tracy writes about one participant who identified herself as 'African American black and half white girl': 'If we were to judge Vanecia based on her skin color or gender alone we would most likely make assumptions that don't fully represent her day-to-day experiences' (p. 47). Durham (1999, 2004) also examines how gender, race and ethnicity interact with middle-school girls' readings of popular media in the USA. After conducting interviews and participant observations at one predominantly white school and one predominantly Latina school, Durham found that girls at both schools preferred mainstream media to Spanish-language media. While the potential for resistance was a subcurrent in her findings, Durham suggests that the girls accept the meanings preferred by their peer groups, in particular those reflecting heterosexual norms and behaviours. Durham (1999: 211) argues: 'The research indicates that while race and class were differentiators of girls' socialization and concomitant media use, the differences highlighted the ways in which their different cultures functioned to uphold different aspects of dominant ideologies of femininity'.

One of the most cited audience reception studies that integrates race and gender is Bobo's (1995) research on the representations of black women and the reception by black women of the US films, *Daughters of the Dust*, and *The Color Purple*. She describes her study as concerning not only the ways black women make sense of media texts but also with their battles against systematic inequities in all areas of their lives. Bobo conducted interviews with groups of black women and showed some of the groups the film, *The Color Purple*, and some of the groups the independent film, *Daughters of the Dust*. Bobo was particularly concerned about interpreting religious attitudes and beliefs, given the centrality of religion in many black women's lives. She also considered the differences between what she found and what other scholars maintain for marginalized groups. According to Bobo, 'If more contact was made with those who participate in a range of everyday activities and who watch and view a variety of cultural forms, then there would be a greater understanding of the ways in which audiences negotiate their existence [there would be] some attempts at control (p. 100). Bobo's participants noted the disparaging images of blacks in *The Color Purple,* yet still appreciated and enjoyed the film. By identifying with the women characters in the film, this audience felt that 'finally, somebody says something about us' (p. 101). Similarly, participants appreciated the film *Daughters of the Dust*, a story of four generations of black women, but also commented on the lack of reality in the film. Bobo concludes that 'black women cultural consumer's are part of an interpretive community, and, as such, are cogent and knowledgeable observers of the social, political and cultural forces that influence their lives (p. 204).

Other studies have featured telenovelas and their impact on gender, ethnic and feminine identity construction (Acosta-Alzuru, 2003; Munoz, 1994; Rivero, 2003). Rivero (2003) uses focus groups of Colombians, Mexicans, Puerto Ricans, Colombian Americans and Mexican Americans living in Texas to explore meaning-making of an extremely popular telenovela titled, *Betty*. Rivero argues that *Betty* creates a space for gender/cultural identification and provides a source of contestation regarding ideologies of female beauty. Similarly, Acosta-Alzuru (2003) finds that Venezuelan women described a Venezuelan telenovela as emphasizing qualities, rights and struggles of Venezuelan women; at the same time, these women denounced the idea that feminism was a useful tool. As the author put it, in the consumption of the telenovela, feminism is divorced from messages that seek to empower women and improve their living conditions because of the negative opinions that are socially constructed in Venezuela about feminism and its place in society. In Munoz's exploration of how women living in a Columbian barrio perceive and use telenovelas, she found that the women illustrate a sensibility that is expressed 'from a time and a logic that is not contemporary with those in the center of modernity' (Munoz, 1994: 97).

Colonialism and Cultural Imperialism in Audience Reception

Other research examines the connections among colonialism, language and media reception. Parameswaran (1999, 2002b) explores the social constructions of Western romance novels by Indian girls. She conducted group and individual interviews and participant observation over a period of four months with 42 young Indian women living in South India. She found some major themes that defined how these girls made meaning of their sexual and ethnic identities. First, the English-language medium of Western romance fiction reminded participants of the imported books and comics they read as children. Second, the romance novels was viewed as resources to improve English language skills. Third, reading Western romance novels was viewed as an expression of class privilege. Parameswaran concluded that the legacies of colonialism continue to prevail but that Western cultural forms in the Third World do not necessarily cause global cultural homogeneity. Such heterogeneity is dependent on factors such as language, the form of media, and the differences of class, gender and cultural capital.

Durham's (2004) work also articulates the relationship between media and girls of immigrant diaspora groups. She focuses on immigrant South Asian teenage girls and their media preferences and interpretations. She found through focus groups that the girls preferred Indian movies and music over US popular culture. Her conclusions bring together the impact of ethnicity, race and gender on sexual identity and media use: 'The cultural constraints on their lives—both the real restrictions imposed by their parents and the subtler cultural cues that tie female chastity to family honor and the preservation of Indian traditions and heritage—worked to facilitate a critical reading that must be distinguished from the sort of unthinking refusal to recognize the ideological content of media texts . . .' (p. 155). Such studies evidence the power of the local over the global.

Conclusion

In this chapter we have shown how theories of intersectionality have developed and can produce scholarship that highlights the complexity of political and personal identity. Such intersectional commitments produce research that is more sensitive and more realistic to women's everyday lives. Problems, though, still persist in studies of media production, representation and audience reception, particularly in the ways that certain characteristics defuse the political force of sexuality and race and perpetuate the monolithic stereotypes that disrupt political progress. Some scholarship also continues to reify the Third and First World binaries that third-wave feminism seeks to disrupt. For example, much of the current research has not yet developed a thorough and sensitive way to intersect race with sexuality. Pellegrini contends that through US films such as *Bar Girls* (1995), *Boys on the Side* (1995) and *Watermelon Woman* (1996), lesbian difference is articulated through racial difference, accentuating distinctions of race that blunts the level of intimacy expressed between women, ultimately promoting a sense of 'sisterly solidarity' instead. Pellegrini (1998: 254, 256) observes that moving 'from sexual difference to racial difference does not disrupt binaries but [simply] displaces them'.

Political (in)visibility is an on-going issue for women. Studies of middle- to upper-income white/anglo women situated in a US context are more common. McLaughlin offers an example in her analysis of the O. J. Simpson murder trial in the USA. She argues that the news coverage of this early 1990s trial and its outcome 'pitted race against gender, racial solidarity against domestic violence' as people either galvanized around the black male defendant as a victim of a racist prosecution or expressed solidarity with the white/anglo female murder victim of domestic violence. In the end the news media's concern over domestic violence was fleeting, showing the definitional force of race, masculinity and celebrity and the continuing challenge for feminists in 'overcoming the exclusion of women from representational space' (McLaughlin, 1998: 85, 89).

Obstacles also persist for women who labour in a persistently patriarchal institution of media production. Even as a more diverse community of women gain greater visibility in media production worldwide, the scholarship reviewed in this chapter reveals that the media perpetuate common stereotypes that further diminish women's power. Women's inclusion in media production therefore does not guarantee progress. Media stereotypes about gender and race and monolithic representations continue even as more women of colour work within media, produce alternative media, and gain more visibility in representations. As Casey *et al.* (2002: 48) predicted, media centre more on 'maintaining social and ideological systems' rather 'than changing them'.

An on-going problem is the hegemonic gaze of white, Western feminists, such as ourselves, toward women and issues from other racial, ethnic and colonized backgrounds. Grewal and Kaplan (2001: 54) explain the problem in these terms: 'in a transnational framework, US multiculturalists cannot address issues of inequities and differences if they presume the goal of progressive politics is to construct subjects, feminist or womanist, that are just like themselves'. Another concern is that a large percentage of the feminist scholarship is published in the West, which promulgates Western academic and feminist ideologies and offers privileged access to 'global village' media and scholarly outlets. At the same time, critiques are being raised about 'upper-middle class "Third World" women . . . unilaterally represent[ing] "other" working class sisters, or diasporic feminists operating within First World representational practices' (Shohat, 1998: 8). Writing from a Western location perpetuates the First/Third World juxtaposition, making transnational coalitions more difficult to sustain and normalizing First World dominance by reiterating its empowerments.

On a positive note, the research we reviewed demonstrates that theories of intersectionality are elevating the complexity of feminist media research and furthering commitments to understanding 'difference'. Such research is decidedly more global as multicultural feminists committed to counter-hegemonic gains are becoming more visible in scholarly projects. As Tucker insists, 'An elaborate web of discursive structures now enmeshes' race and feminism, 'along with many other related concepts and categories, in an inextricable field of multiple meanings, representations, and narratives that have put an end to an identity politics consisting of competitive individual, immutable, and categorically succinct entities' (Tucker, 1998: xi). We end with a call for additional feminist media research that further interrogates existing forces and constraints of dominant ideologies and attends to the intersectional complexities of gender, race, class, sexuality, nationalism and (post)colonialism.

Note

1. Our understanding of 'race' is guided by Winant's conception that 'The meaning of race is utterly variable among different societies and over historical time,' yet 'race is a significant dimension of *hegemony* that is deeply infused with power, order, and indeed the meaning systems of every society in which it operates'. Winant (1994: 2–3) concludes that 'Not only is the social racialized, but the racial is socialized, such that identity itself is, so to speak, color coded.'

References

Acosta-Alzuru, C. (2003) '"I'm Not a Feminist . . . Only Defend Women as Human Beings": The Production, Representation, and Consumption of Feminism in a Telenovela', *Critical Studies in Media Communication*, 20 (3), 269–95.

Antler, J. (ed.) (1998) 'Introduction', *Talking Back: Images of Jewish Women in American Popular Culture*. Hanover, MA: Brandeis University Press.

Arneil, B. (1999) *Politics & Feminism*. Oxford: Blackwell.

Baehr, H. and Gray, A. (1996) *Turning It On: A Reader in Women & Media*. London: Arnold.

Bhandarker, V. (1995) 'Female Foreign News Correspondents from Developing Countries Reporting from Washington, D.C.', in D. A. Newsom and B. J. Carrell (eds), *Silent Voices*. Lanham, MD: University Press of America, pp. 199–214.

Bird, S. E. (1999) 'Gendered Construction of the American Indian in Popular Culture', *Journal of Communication*. 49 (3), 61–83.

Bobo, J. (1995) *Black Women: As Cultural Readers*. New York: Columbia University Press.

Byars, J. and Dell, C. (1992) 'Big Differences on the Small Screen: Race, Class, Gender, Feminine Beauty, and the Characters at *Frank's Place*', in L. F. Rakow (ed.), *Women Making Meaning: New Feminist Directions in Communication*. New York: Routledge, pp. 191–209.

Byerly, C. M. (1995) 'News, Consciousness, and Social Participation: The Role of Women's Feature Service in World News', in A. N. Valdivia (ed.), *Feminism, Multiculturalism, and the Media: Global Diversities*. Thousand Oaks, CA: Sage, pp. 105–22.

Carter, C., Branston, G. and Allen, S. (1998) *News, Gender and Power*. London: Routledge.

Casey, B., Casey, N., Calvert, B., French, L. and Lewis, J. (2002) *Television Studies: The Key Concepts*. London: Routledge.

Collins, P. H. (1999) 'Moving Beyond Gender: Intersectionality and Scientific Knowledge', in M. M. Ferree, J. Lorber and B. B. Hess (eds), *Revisioning Gender*. Thousand Oaks, CA: Sage, pp. 261–84.

——— (2000) *Black Feminist Thought: Knowledge, Consciousness, and the Politics of Empowerment*. New York: Routledge.

Creedon, P. J. (1993) *Women in Mass Communication*, 2nd edn. Newbury Park, CA: Sage.

Darling-Wolf, F. (2003) 'Media, Class, and Western Influence in Japanese Women's Conceptions of Attractiveness', *Feminist Media Studies*, 3 (2), 153–72.

Durham, M. G. (1999) 'Girls, Media, and the Negotiation of Sexuality: A Study on Race, Class, and Gender in Adolescent Females', *Journalism and Mass Communication Quarterly*, 76 (2), 193–217.

——— (2001) 'Displaced Persons: Symbols of South Asian Femininity and the Returned Gazed in US Media Culture', *Communication Theory*, 11 (2), 201–17.

——— (2004) 'Constructing the "New Ethnicities": Media, Sexuality, and Diaspora Identity in the Lives of South Asian Immigrant Girls', *Critical Studies in Media Communication*, 21(2), 140–62.

Fair, J. E. (1996) 'The Body Politic, the Bodies of Women, and the Politics of Famine in the US Television Coverage of Famine in the Horn of Africa', *Journalism & Mass Communication Monographs*, 158 (August), 1–42.

Farrell, A. E. (1995) 'Feminism and the Media: Introduction', *Signs*, 20 (3), 642–5.

Ferree, M. M., Lorber, J. and Hess B. B. (eds) (1999). *Revisioning Gender*. Thousand Oaks, CA: Sage.

Flores, L. S. and McPhail, M. L. (1997) 'From Black and White to *Living Color*: A Dialogic Exposition into the Social (Re)Construction of Race, Gender, and Crime', *Critical Studies in Mass Communication*, 14 (1), 106–22.

Fraser, N. (1989) *Unruly Practices: Power, Discourse, and Gender in Contemporary Social Theory*. Minneapolis: University of Minnesota Press.

Frazer, E. (1987) 'Teenage Girls Reading *Jackie*', *Media, Culture and Society*, 9 (4), 407–25.

Gaines, J. (1988) 'White Privilege and Looking Relations: Race and Gender in Feminist Film Theory', *Screen*, 29 (4), 12–27.

Gaunt, K. D. (1995) 'African American Women Between Hopscotch and Hip-Hop', in A. N. Valdivia (ed.), *Feminism, Multiculturalism, and the Media: Global Diversities*. Thousand Oaks, CA: Sage, pp. 277–308.

Giroux, H. A. (1998) 'White Noise: Toward a Pedagogy of Whiteness', in K. Myrsiades and L. Myrsiades (eds), *Race-ing Representation: Voice, History, and Sexuality*. Lanham, MD: Rowman & Littlefield, pp. 42–76.

Glenn, E. N. 'The Social Construction and Institutionalization of Gender and Race: An Integrative Framework', in M. M. Ferree, J. Lorber and B. B. Hess (eds), *Revisioning Gender*. Thousand Oaks, CA: Sage, pp. 3–43.

Gray, A. (1996) 'Behind Closed Doors: Video Recorders in the Home', in H. Baehr and A. Gray (eds), *Turning It On: A Reader in Women and Media*. London: Arnold, pp. 118–29.

Gregg, N. (1992) 'Telling Stories About Reality: Women's Responses to a Workplace Organizing Campaign', in L. Rakow (ed.), *Women Making Meaning*. New York: Routledge, pp. 263–88.

Grewal, I. and Kaplan, C. (2001) '*Warrior Marks*: Global Womanism's Neo-colonial Discourse in a Multicultural Context', in M. Tinkcom and A. Vallarejo (eds), *Keyframes: Popular Cinema and Cultural Studies*. London: Routledge, pp. 52–71.

Grossman, M. and Cuthbert, D. (1996) 'Body Shopping: Maternity and Alterity in *Mamatoto*', *Cultural Studies*, 10 (3), 430–48.

Hall, S. (ed.) (1997) 'The Work of Representation', in *Representation: Cultural Representations and Signifying Practices*. London: Sage, pp. 13–64.

————— (2000) 'Cultural Identity and Diaspora', in N. Mirzoeff, *Diaspora and Visual Culture: Representing Africans and Jews*. London: Routledge, pp. 21–33.

Harris, T. M. and Hill, P. S. (1998) '*Waiting to Exhale* or Breath(ing) Again: A Search for Identity, Empowerment, and Love in the 1990's', *Women & Language News*, 21 (2), 9–14.

Henderson, L. (2001) 'Sexuality, Feminism, Media Studies', *Feminist Media Studies*, 1 (1), 17–24.

Heung, M. (1995) 'Representing Ourselves: Films and Videos by Asian American/Canadian Women', in A. N. Valdivia (ed.), *Feminism, Multiculturalism, and the Media: Global Diversities*. Thousand Oaks, CA: Sage, pp. 82–104.

Hobson, D. (1989) 'Soap Operas at Work', in E. Seiter, H. Borchers, G. Kreutzner and E. M. Warth (eds), *Remote Control: Television, Audiences, and Cultural Power*. New York: Routledge, pp. 150–67.

————— (1990) 'Women Audiences and the Workplace', in M. E. Brown (ed.), *Television and Women's Culture: The Politics of the Popular*. Newbury Park, CA: Sage, pp. 61–71.

————— (1996) 'Housewives and the Mass Media', in H. Baehr and A. Gray (eds), *Turning It On: A Reader in Women and Media*. London: Arnold, pp. 111–17.

Hooks, B. (1992) *Black Looks: Race and Representation*. Boston: South End Press.

────── (1996) *Reel to Real: Race, Sex, and Class at the Movies*. New York: Routledge.

Kawaja, J. (1994) 'Process Video: Self-reference and Social Change', in P. Riano (ed.), *Women in Grassroots Communication: Furthering Social Change*. Thousand Oaks, CA: Sage, pp. 131–48.

King, D. K. (1988) 'Multiple Jeopardy, Multiple Consciousness: The Context of a Black Feminist Ideology', *Signs: A Journal of Women in Culture and Society*, 14 (1), 42–72.

Lloyd, L. (1994) '*Speak* Magazine: Breaking Barriers and Silences', in P. Riano (ed.), *Women in Grassroots Communication: Furthering Social Change*. Thousand Oaks, CA: Sage, pp. 251–9.

Lotz, A. D. (2004) 'Barricaded Intersections: *Any Day Now* and the Struggle to Examine Ethnicity and Gender', in R. A. Lind (ed.), *Race/Gender/Media: Considering Diversity Across Audiences. Content, and Producers*. Boston, MA: Pearson, pp. 294–300.

Luthra, R. (1995) 'The "Abortion Clause" in U.S. Foreign Population Policy: The Debate Viewed Through a Postcolonial Feminist Lens', in A. N. Valdivia (ed.), *Feminism, Multiculturalism, and the Media: Global Diversities*. Thousand Oaks, CA: Sage, pp. 197–216.

McLaughlin, L. (1998) 'Gender, Privacy and Publicity in "Media Event Space"', in C. Carter, G. Branston and S. Allan (eds), *News, Gender, and Power*. London: Routledge, pp. 71–90.

Mensah-Kutin, R. (1994) "The WEDNET Initiative: A Sharing Experience Between researchers and Rural Women', in P. Riano (ed.), *Women in Grassroots Communication: Furthering Social Change*. Thousand Oaks, CA: Sage, pp. 221–34.

Mouffee, C. (1992) 'Feminism, Citizenship, and Radical Democratic Politics', in J. Butler and J. W. Scott (eds), *Feminists Theorize the Political*. London: Routledge, pp. 369–85.

Munoz, S. (1994) 'Notes for Reflection: Popular Women and Uses of Mass Media', in P. Riano (ed.), *Women in Grassroots Communication: Furthering Social Change*. Thousand Oaks, CA: Sage, pp. 84–101.

Omenugha, K. A. (2003) 'Photographs of African Women in British Newspapers: Graffiti?', *Media Report to Women*, 31 (2), 15–20.

Opoku-Mensah, A. (2001) 'Marching on: African Feminist Media Studies', *Feminist Media Studies*, 1 (1), 25–34.

Osborne, G. E. (2004) '"Women Who Look Like Me": Cultural Identity and Reader Responses to African American Romance Novels', in R. A. Lind (ed.), *Race/Gender/ Media: Considering Diversity across Audiences, Content, and Producers*. Boston, MA: Pearson, pp. 61–8.

Parameswaran, R. (1999) 'Western Romance Fiction as English-Language Media in Postcolonial India', *Journal of Communication*, 49 (3), 84–105.

────── (2001) 'Global Media Events in India: Contests Over Beauty, Gender and Nation', *Journalism & Communication Monographs*, 3 (2), 53–105.

────── (2002a) 'Local Culture in Global Media: Excavating Colonial and Material Discourses in *National Geographic*', *Communication Theory*, 12 (3), 287–315.

────── (2002b) 'Reading Fictions of Romance: Gender, Sexuality, and Nationalism in Postcolonial India', *Journal of Communication*, 52 (4), 832–51.

Parry-Giles, T. and Parry-Giles, S. (in press) *The Prime-Time Presidency: The West Wing and U.S. Nationalism*. Urbana: University of Illinois Press.

Pellegrini, A. (1998) 'Women on Top, Boys on the Side, But some of Us are Brave: Blackness, Lesbianism, and the Visible', in K. Myrsiades and L. Myrsiades (eds), *Race-ing Representation: Voice, History, and Sexuality*. Lantham, MD: Rowman & Littlefield, pp. 247–63.

Perry, I. (2003) 'Who(se) Am I? The Identity and Image of Women in Hip-hop', in G. Dines and J. M. Humez (eds), *Gender, Race, and Class in Media: A Text-Reader*. Thousand Oaks, CA: Sage, pp. 136–48.

Press, A. L. (1990) 'Class, Gender and the Female Viewer: Women's Responses to *Dynasty*', in M. E. Brown (ed.), *Television and Women's Culture: The Politics of the Popular*. Newbury Park, CA: Sage, pp. 158–80.

———— (1991) *Women Watching Television: Gender, Class, and Generation in the American Television Experience*. Philadelphia, PA: University of Pennsylvania Press.

Radway, J. A. (1984) *Reading the Romance: Women, Patriarchy, and Popular Literature*. Chapel Hill: University of North Carolina Press.

Rakow, L. F. (1988) *Gender on the Line: Women, the Telephone, and Community Life*. Urbana: University of Illinois Press.

Reeves, J. L. (1998) 'Re-covering Racism: Crack Mothers, Reaganism, and the Network News', in S. Torres (ed.), *Living Colour: Race and Television in the United States*. Durham, NC: Duke University Press, pp. 97–117.

Reid, E. C. (1989) 'Viewdata: The Television Viewing Habits of Young Black Women in London', *Screen*, 30 (1–2), 114–21.

Riano, P. (1994) 'Women's Participation in Communication: Elements for a Framework', in P. Riano (ed.), *Women in Grassroots Communication: Furthering Social Change*. Thousand Oaks, CA: Sage, pp. 1–29.

Rodriguez, C. (1994) 'A Process of Identity Deconstruction: Latin American Women Producing Video Stories', in P. Riano (ed.), *Women in Grassroots Communication: Furthering Social Change*. Thousand Oaks, CA: Sage, pp. 149–60.

Rony, F. T. (1996) *The Third Eye: Race, Cinema, and Ethnographic Spectacle*. Durham, NC: Duke University Press.

Ruiz, C. (1994) 'Losing Fear: Video and Radio Productions of Native Aymara Women in Bolivia', in P. Riano (ed.), *Women in Grassroots Communication: Furthering Social Change*. Thousand Oaks, CA: Sage, pp. 161–78.

Seiter, E., Borchers, H., Kreutzner, G. and Warth, E. M. (eds) (1989) 'Don't Treat Us Like We're So Stupid and Naïve: Towards an Ethnography of Soap Opera Viewers', in *Remote Control: Television, Audiences, and Cultural Power*. New York: Routledge, pp. 223–47.

Shafer, R. and Hornig, S. (1995) 'The Role of Women Journalists in Philippine Political Change', in D.A. Newsom and B. J. Carrell (eds), *Silent Voices*. Lanham, MD: University Press of America, pp. 177–98.

Shohat, E. (ed.) (1998) 'Introduction', *Talking Visions: Multicultural Feminism in a Transnational Age*. New York: MIT Press, pp. 1–63.

Shohat, E. and Stam, R. (1996) 'From the Imperial Family to the Transnational Imaginary: Media Spectatorship in the Age of Globalization', in R. Wilson and W. Dissanayake (eds), *Global/Local: Cultural Production and the Transnational Imaginary*. Durham, NC: Duke University Press, pp. 145–70.

Sloop, J. M. (2004) *Disciplining Gender: Rhetorics of Sex Identity in Contemporary U.S. Culture*. Amherst: University of Massachusetts Press.

Smith, M. C. (1993) 'Feminist Media and Cultural Politics', in P. J. Creedon (ed.), *Women in Mass Communication*, 2nd edn. Newbury Park, CA: Sage.

Stuart, S. and Bery, R. (1996) 'Powerful Grassroots Women Communicators: Participatory Video in Bangladesh', in D. Allen, R. R. Rush and S. J. Kaufman (eds), *Women Transforming Communications: Global Intersections*. Thousand Oaks, CA: Sage, pp. 303–12.

Tracy, P. J. (2004) '"Why Don't You Act Your Color?": Preteen Girls, Identity, and Popular Music', in R. A. Lind (ed.), *Race/Gender/Media: Considering Diversity Across Audiences, Content, and Producers*. Boston, MA: Pearson, pp. 45–52.

Tucker, M. (1998) 'Foreword', in E. Shohat (ed.), *Talking Visions: Multicultural Feminism in a Transnational Age*. New York: MIT Press, pp. xi–xiii.

Valdivia, A. N. (ed.) (1995) 'Feminist Media Studies in a Global Setting: Beyond Binary Contradictions and into Multicultural Spectrums', *Feminism, Multiculturalism, and the Media: Global Diversities*. Thousand Oaks, CA: Sage, pp. 7–29.

van Zoonen, L. (1999) *Feminist Media Studies*. London: Sage.

Vavrus, M. D. (2002) *Postfeminist News: Political Women in Media Culture*. New York: State University of New York Press.

Wallace, M. (1990) *Invisibility Blues: From Pop to Theory*. London: Verso.

Weber, L. (2001) *Understanding Race, Class, Gender and Sexuality. A Conceptual Framework.* Boston: McGraw-Hill.

West, C. and Fenstermaker, S. (1995) 'Doing Difference', *Gender & Society*, 9 (1), 8–37.

Whelehan, I. (1995) *Modern Feminist Thought: From the Second Wave to 'Post-Feminism*, New York: New York University Press.

Willis, S. 2001. 'Race as Spectacle, Feminism as Alibi: Representing the Civil Rights Era in the 1990s', in M. Tinkcom and A. Villarejo (eds), *Keyframes: Popular Cinema and Cultural Studies.* London: Routledge, pp. 98–118.

Winant, H. (1994) *Racial Conditions: Politics, Theory, Comparisons.* Minneapolis: University of Minnesota Press.

Zinn, M. B. and Dill, B. T. (1996) 'Theorizing Difference from Multicultural Feminism', *Feminist Studies*, 22 (2), 321–31.

Zook, K. B. (1999) *Color by Fox: The Fox Network and the Revolution in Black Television.* New York: Oxford University Press.

Pictures, Porno, and Pop: Gender and Mass Media

Diana K. Ivy and Phil Backlund

Case Study: A Day in the Life

It's 6:30 AM, the clock radio alarm goes off, and a couple of people on a morning talk-radio show are chatting away. Rey shuts off the alarm, rolls out of bed, and begins his morning routine. Over his usual bowl of cereal, he scans the local newspaper and the *Wall Street Journal*, reading stock indexes with interest and making a mental note to check the stock exchange later in the day. While shaving, he turns on the Weather Channel for a quick check of the local forecast, then switches to CNN for the latest headlines. CNN cuts to a commercial that irritates Rey—one in which a husband looks foolish in front of a young male stock analyst because his wife knows more about a certain kind of mutual fund than he does. Rey thinks to himself, "male-bashing again," switches off CNN, and channel surfs between other cable news sources, MSNBC and Fox News. Before he leaves the house, he checks his VCR and satellite dish setup to make sure the VCR will correctly record the network nightly news (which he tapes every weekday because he doesn't leave work in time to see the broadcast), as well as a few of his favorite television programs. If something comes up at work, he might not get home to catch these shows, so better to tape them than miss them.

On the drive to work, Rey tunes in his car radio and checks back with the talk-radio program. An air personality says, "Well, scandals are nothing new in politics . . ." Rey decides he's heard enough and is more in the mood to listen to a CD. About halfway between his home and the office, Rey puts the CD on pause and uses his cell phone to call ahead to the office and check in with his secretary so he can anticipate what will be happening when he gets there. She says it's pretty quiet, but that a few faxes did come in overnight; they're on his desk for him to read when he gets there. He cues up the CD again and notices he's reached that point in the drive where he passes a bank's digital billboard calculating increases in the national debt.

Rey arrives at the office; his secretary is on the phone so he swings by the central mailboxes and picks up his mail, including more messages and a couple of magazines he subscribes to. When he gets to his desk the light on his phone is blinking, indicating that he has voice mail messages. He takes off his coat, lays the mail on top of the faxes on his desk, and thumbs through the first couple of ads in one of his magazines. Then he picks up the phone and dials in his code to start listening to voice mail messages while, at the same time, punching the start-up key on his computer. The computer screen fires up and a mail icon with the statement, "You've got mail," appears. Once he's gone through the 10 or so voice mail messages and noted on his digital pocket recorder who to call back, he begins to read the interoffice e-mail. Later he'll log onto the Internet to read his other e-mail—the postings to an electronic bulletin board he subscribes to as well as messages from colleagues across the country, the occasional family member, and a buddy who's now working in Australia. Hopefully just before lunch he'll remember to use his Web browser to check the latest stock trends. He'd love to knock off early today to catch the newest Ah-nuld action film, but no doubt something would come up and his secretary would page him. There's nothing so irritating as somebody's beeper going off in a movie theatre. Too much going on, too many things and people to deal with, too little time.

HEY—wasn't technology supposed to SAVE us time? Do you think Rey, who is bombarded by media and surrounded by technological innovations, feels that they keep him informed and save him time or that they impinge on his time? Is Rey running the media or is the media running him? By the way, you probably think that Rey is some hot shot financial guy or corporate honcho—he's actually a high school principal, and this is an average day.

How much media and technology do you consume each day? What influence do they have on you? What messages about the sexes are communicated via the media you consume? That's the topic of this chapter.

Hot Topics

- Theories of media effects that show how consumers process mass media
- The impact of stereotypical depictions of women and men in advertisements on attitudes about the sexes
- Gendered messages in prime-time television shows and social issues programming
- Communication about the sexes via daytime soap operas and talk shows
- Gender-bending in film and how men's and women's film roles impact viewers
- The pervasive influence of pornography and the effects of its consumption on women's and men's attitudes and relationships
- Song lyrics and music video portrayals of the sexes

The Power of Mediated Communication: Effects on Our Lives

Probably no other force influences our daily lives more than media. Parents are hugely important, teachers have significant impact, friends affect us in profound ways—but we have come to believe that, over time, media have the strongest effect on us out of all possible influences. Consider how often you compare real life—work, family, relationships—to how these things are depicted in movies, television, song lyrics, and music videos. It's common to hear someone refer to something on television, such as, "I just don't trust that guy I went out with last night; he reminds me of Richard Fish on *Ally McBeal*," "My wife and I have arguments kind of like that couple on (pick a sitcom, any sitcom)," or "I felt like I was in a Hallmark card commercial." Media are highly influential in how they communicate messages *about* women and men.

Some argue that technology has made it easy for us to escape reality, meaning that media have allowed us to avoid connecting with one another. The claim is that, for many people, movies, television, the Internet, and music take the place of a social life and substitute for a roommate or spouse—a substitute that can be shut out with just the click of a switch. What do you think about that claim? Do various forms of media act as substitutes for something in your life?

A Bombardment of Media

You are literally bombarded with forms of mass communication every day and the effects of this bombardment are dramatic, as research documents (Comstock & Strzyzewski, 1990; Dambrot, Reep, & Bell, 1988; Lindlof, 1987, 1991; Press, 1991a). For example, one study found that over 11,000 magazines are currently published and distributed in the United States; the average American spends about 110 hours per year reading these magazines (Pratkanis & Aronson, 1992). Your modern existence is jammed full of mass communication every sunrise to sunset, but just how are you affected by it?

As a college-educated person, you are probably an above-average critical consumer of mass communication, meaning that you consciously select mediated messages to take in and to filter out. However, a great deal of mediated information is absorbed unconsciously, even by the most critical of consumers. Few of us have time in our busy lives to focus concentrated attention on all the mediated messages we receive in a typical day and make conscious decisions about their effects. This critical thinking process becomes a skill we use less often as we take in more and more mediated information. Just how this absorption affects us has been the subject of a good deal of attention among media researchers.

Theories About the Effects of Media Consumption

In the 1970s, media scholar Gaye Tuchman described how, as mass media grew "exponentially" during the years between World War II and the beginning of the

1980s, "so did study of the media" (1979, p. 528). Several theories have emerged that attempt to explain how media affect consumers.

Hypodermic Needle or Direct Effects Theory

This early theory viewed the mass audience as passively and directly consuming mediated messages. The imagery was that of a hypodermic needle that "injected" mass communication directly into the veins of its noncritical consumers (Vivian, 1999). This theory offered an inadequate, overly simplistic explanation of media effects because it ignored how other factors might influence the process.

Uses and Gratifications Theory

Media expert John Vivian (1999) describes the uses and gratifications approach as a theory that no longer viewed mass audiences as passive sponges, but rather as active "users" of media. Research has focused on how consumers are motivated to use various media and what gains, rewards, or "gratifications" they receive from such consumption (Palmgreen & Rayburn, 1985; Rubin, 1986). Media researchers have employed uses and gratifications theory to better understand such things as the uses people make of television news or commercial advertising (Rayburn, Palmgreen, & Acker, 1984), the pleasure people derive from soap operas (Lemish, 1985; Rubin, 1985), and children's music (Christenson, 1994).

Agenda-Setting Theory

This theory dates back to the work of Robert Park in the 1920s, who proposed that the media do not merely report, reflect, or dramatize what is important in society, media actually guide what we think is important. Vivian (1999) explains "the media create awareness of issues more than they create knowledge or attitudes. The media do not tell people what to think but what to think about" (p. 404). For an example of how this theory applies to gender concerns, consider talk shows. Many consumers of these shows believe that the issues raised constitute critical social, political, and economic concerns. In essence, viewers may be allowing a media outlet to set an agenda for what should be most important to them (Heaton & Wilson, 1995).

Cultivation Theory

This theory suggests that media consumption "'cultivates' in us a distorted perception of the world we live in, making it seem more like television portrays it, than it is in real life" (Bittner, 1989, p. 386). The media blur reality and fantasy, what life is really like and how it appears on television or in movies. Media scholar George Gerbner and various colleagues are among the most prominent researchers to use cultivation theory to better understand the relationships between the social reality of violence and crime to media's depiction of it (Gerbner, Gross, Eleey, Jackson-Beeck, Jeffries-Fox, & Signorielli, 1977; Gerbner, Gross, Morgan, & Signorielli, 1980). Gerbner, who began his investigations of television violence in 1967, contends that a typical American child will see 32,000 on-screen murders before she or he turns 18 (as in Vivian, 1999). To help you understand cultivation theory, just remember this easy example: Think about people who believe that romantic relationships are supposed to happen just like in Hollywood movies, happy endings and all.

Advertising: Selling a Product or Selling Sexism?

Advertising is a huge and pervasive industry. Estimates suggest U.S. advertisers spend over $150 billion *per year*, exposing the average person to about 1,800 advertising messages *each day* (Lazier & Gagnard Kendrick, 1993). Researchers contend that advertising has a powerful effect that goes well beyond the purpose of selling products to consumers. As media researchers Lysonski and Pollay (1990) point out, advertising "creates a pervasive and persuasive communication environment that sells a great deal more than just products. Through the use of imagery, the display of life-styles, and the exercise and reinforcement of values, advertisements are communicators of culturally defined concepts such as success, worth, love, sexuality, popularity, and normalcy" (p. 317). Do you think that gender should be added to that list?

A great deal of research has been conducted on the ways women and men are depicted in print and electronic advertisements, as well as the messages these ads communicate to media consumers. Media researchers Wells, Burnett, and Moriarty (1998) explain that *stereotyping* "involves presenting a group of people in an unvarying pattern that lacks individuality and often reflects popular misconceptions" (p. 49). Let's look at an overview of the various stereotypical portrayals of the sexes, including a few exceptions, and then consider the overall effects on consumers.

Babes in Bras: Female Depiction in Advertising

Programmatic research spanning two decades by marketing professors Alice Courtney and Thomas Whipple (1974, 1980, 1983, 1985) forms the basis for the claim that advertising has a major impact on individuals' views of gender in society.

Homemakers and Sex Objects

From the compiled results of numerous studies, Courtney and Whipple produced the following comprehensive list of female *gender-role stereotypes* in advertising, corroborated by subsequent national and international research (Kang, 1996; Lanis & Covell, 1995; Lin, 1997; Liu, Inoue, Bresnahan, & Nishida, 1998; Milner, 1994; Rakow, 1992):

1. Women in isolation, particularly from other women
2. Women in sleepwear, underwear, and lingerie more than in professional clothing

3. Young girls portrayed as passive and in need of help
4. Women as kitchen and bathroom product representatives
5. Women appearing more than men in ads for personal hygiene products (e.g., deodorants, toothpaste)
6. An abundance of women serving men and boys
7. Medical advertisements depicting male physicians interacting with hysterical, hypochondriacal female patients
8. Women more often depicted in family- and home-oriented roles than in business roles
9. Young housewives shown performing household duties, whereas older men act as product representatives who give advice to housewives
10. Women portrayed as decorative, nonfunctioning entities
11. Fewer depictions of older women than older men
12. Fewer depictions of minority women than minority men
13. Fewer women than men advertising expensive luxury products
14. Few women depicted actively engaged in sports
15. Ads overtly critical of feminist rights and issues

> A good man doesn't just happen. They have to be created by us women. A guy is a lump, like a doughnut. So first you gotta get rid of all the stuff his mom did to him. And then you gotta get rid of all that macho crap they pick up from beer commercials. And then there's my personal favorite, the male ego.
>
> Roseanne, actor & talk show host

Many manufacturers and advertisers still either ignore how the public feels about sexist ads or find segments of the market that like their ads and buy their products. One study compared magazine advertisements from 1979 to ads from 1991 to determine if depictions of women had been "modernized." The findings are disheartening: Stereotypical female depictions—including portrayals of women as weak, dependent, childish, domestic, irrational, subordinate, mentally feeble, and scantily clad—were actually more prevalent in 1991 ads than in 1979 ads (Kang, 1996). Although more ads now show women in business settings, the use of women as decorative objects—physically attractive but having nothing to do with the product being advertised—is on the rise as well (Lanis & Covell, 1995).

Killing Women Softly

Perhaps some of you are familiar with the work of Jean Kilbourne, particularly her educational films. Kilbourne's first film, entitled *Killing Us Softly*, was released in 1976; her follow-up film, entitled *Still Killing Us Softly*, was released in 1987. Both of these powerful films provide Kilbourne's commentary in tandem with example after example of ads reflecting female stereotypes, many of which Courtney and Whipple unearthed in their research. Kilbourne (1998) asserts that advertising presents women almost exclusively in one of two roles: housewife or sex object. Her examples include women pathologically obsessed with cleanliness and ridding their husbands' shirts of "ring around the collar," and thin, tall, long-legged mannequin-like women with perfect skin and no signs of aging. These portrayals have severe effects on women, as Kilbourne states: "A woman is conditioned to view her face as a mask and her body as an object, as *things* separate from and more important than her real self, constantly in need of alteration, improvement, and disguise. She is made to feel dissatisfied with and ashamed of herself, whether she tries to achieve 'the look' or not. Objectified constantly by others, she learns to objectify herself" (p. 129).

In particular, women of color fare poorly in ads, both in the quantity of depictions and the quality of the roles, according to Gail Baker Woods, author of *Advertising and Marketing to the New Majority* (1995). Woods reports that "Less than 20 percent of all ads with blacks feature black women. When they are seen, black women are often portrayed as 'jive'-talking, sassy 'sisters' or overweight, wise-cracking, church-going women" (p. 28). Hispanic, Asian-American, and Native-American women are less represented in advertisements than African-American women, who are less represented than white women.

One media analyst suggests that "Progress has been made in the 1990s, however there's still a disproportionate amount of gravity-defying breasts and giggly silliness in advertising . . ." (Fawcett, 1993, p. S1). Lazier and Gagnard Kendrick (1993) contend that it is "shocking to see the minuscule 'advancement' made in the imagery of women over a decade and a half." They then explore the question, "How can this stereotypical sexism survive given the incredible changes in women's social status?" (p. 206) They wonder, like we do, why stereotypical images of women still predominate in print and electronic media. Their conclusion is that ads

"reflect our current culture—one of the traditional balance of power (male). The ads reflect the critical components of culture—its stereotypes, its bigotries, its biases, its dominant values, its tendency toward the status quo, and the ongoingness of the traditional. The ads also reflect the ongoing confusion in our culture (by both men and women) of what women are"

(pp. 206–207).

An Exercise in Ad Analysis

Look at the billboard advertisement reproduced in Figure 1. Some of you might think there's nothing inherently wrong or sexist about this advertisement. The ad is simply catching the eye of motorists in Dallas, Texas, and effectively selling a product. However, others of you may look at this ad and think, "Not another scantily clad woman selling beer!" Using the following set of questions, analyze this ad; supply your own answers to the questions first, then we'll provide our perspective.

1. Who is the target audience for this product?
2. What's being sold here, beer? Sexuality? Leisure? Status?
3. Is there anything unusual in the fact that only a woman appears in this ad, given that men are the predominant beer drinkers in the country?

Figure 1

4. What is your interpretation of the clothing the woman is wearing (or lack thereof)?
5. Do you find anything sexist in her body position, meaning her prone position on the billboard?
6. What is your interpretation of the positioning of the beer bottle underneath the woman's body?
7. What is the meaning of the caption, "Tap into the cold, Dallas"?

Compare your answers with those of your classmates, particularly classmates of the opposite sex. This comparison will demonstrate how subjective a judgment of sexism can be.

Here's our interpretation of this advertisement: Since more men than women drink beer, it's safe to assume that this ad is geared more toward a male target audience rather than a female one. We think it's a sexist ad for many reasons, the main one being that it represents yet another attempt on the part of advertisers to use a woman's sexuality for profit. What's really being sold here is the woman and her sexuality, not beer (Hall & Crum, 1994). If that wasn't the case, then why not show just the beer bottle and the caption? The message to men is, "If you drink this brand of beer, you'll attract a woman who looks like this, who'll dress like this and lay down for you like this." What messages do women get from a huge billboard like this?

That interpretation is reinforced by the vulnerable position of the woman (in only a bathing suit) lying on her back with one arm up which conveys a sexual, submissive message. The fact that she is on top of a cold beer bottle suggests sexual imagery, if you want to go so far as to construe the neck of the beer bottle, intentionally placed underneath and between her legs, as a phallic symbol. Concerning the caption, one wonders if it is the beer that is to be tapped or the woman. Research shows that some men respond to sexual images of women in media with views that support sexual aggression and assault (Lanis & Covell, 1995; MacKay & Covell, 1997).

At this point you may disagree with us or wonder if we don't get out much. We realize that someone isn't likely to pull off a Dallas freeway to critique this billboard. Perhaps the argument could be made that, in isolation, this one ad isn't sexist. But what about the trend for advertisers to display women, typically in revealing attire, draped across the hoods of cars or posed in various suggestive positions with objects such as oversized beer bottles or shiny motorcycles between their legs? What's being communicated when sexist ads appear with such regularity?

Any Relief in Sight?

Some manufacturers have changed their approach to advertising products for female consumers—the operant word in this statement being *some*. Laura Zinn (1991), a *Business Week* writer, describes ads for women's products that show promise, such as Maidenform lingerie ads and Nike's women's athletic wear ads. Past Maidenform ads displayed the "Maidenform Woman," always a young, beautiful, thin woman who turned up in strange places wearing only her bra and panties. In efforts to change with the times, Maidenform launched a series of less sexist ads. One ad in the series depicted a baby chick, a Barbie doll, a tomato, and a fox, with the caption, "A helpful guide for those who still confuse women with various unrelated objects" (Zinn, 1991, p. 90). Since increasing numbers of women are making sports and exercise a significant part of their lives, Nike and Reebok ads in particular have wisely reflected the trend toward less sexist advertising. These companies have made serious, laudable, successful attempts to communicate to female consumers that they understand them and find them important, but they are the exception, not the rule.

A few other companies have made creative attempts to "clean up their advertising acts." Anheuser-Busch, for example, has been hugely successful with its reptile ads. The Swedish Bikini Team has disappeared from one beer company's ads. But when men and women appear together in ads, women still are too often portrayed less than fully clothed and in sexy, flirtatious, and vulnerable ways. We don't see sexism lurking at every turn, but we do worry about the prevalence of sexual images of women being used to sell all kinds of products—especially products geared to men.

Advertising's Effects on Women: Bodies, Sex, and Self-Esteem

Feminist media researchers Goldman, Heath, and Smith (1991) describe the harmful effects of stereotypical, idealized advertising images on female consumers. They contend that "a growing proportion of female viewers have grown antagonistic to the uninterrupted procession of perfect, but unattainable looks that daily confront them. Women don't have to be feminists to feel oppressed by images of perfection and beauty that batter and bruise self-esteem . . ." (p. 335). Lazier and Gagnard Kendrick (1993) express increasing concern about the results of media images of women: "Portrayals of women in advertising are not only potentially debilitating and demeaning, but they are also inaccurate. We do not have a demography of demigoddesses. Women today are considerably more than flawless decorative objects, dependent upon or defined by men" (pp. 200–201).

> Whenever I . . . turn on CV, I am reminded of the millions of women who have stringy hair, large pores, overweight figures, and rough hands.
> Warren Beatty, actor & director

Several studies across decades have been conducted on our culture's obsession with thinness, as reflected in advertising (Gagnard, 1986; Lee, 1995; Myers & Biocca, 1992; Silverstein, Perdue, Peterson, & Kelly, 1986). We won't go into detail on each, but the results are consistent and overwhelming:

1. Women receive many times more advertising messages about thinness and body shape than men.
2. The volume of these ads in prominent magazines and on television is staggering.
3. The trend toward severe thinness is inescapable in ads, creating an ever-widening gap between the weight of an "average" American woman and the "ideal."
4. Thin female models are perceived to be more attractive than average weight or overweight models in ads.
5. The majority of African-American models, including supermodels Tyra Banks and Naomi Campbell, are slim, although the thinness standard isn't as extreme among black women as for other racial and ethnic groups.
6. The pressure to be thin is not as great for men as for women, as evidenced by the greater number of average weight and overweight male models in ads in comparison to females.
7. Young women's images of their bodies become distorted when they are presented with images of ideal body shape. (Many simply believe that they cannot be "thin enough," and they suffer great self-esteem loss trying to achieve the unreal perfect body presented by the media. One survey found that a large percentage of fourth-grade girls reported being on diets.)
8. The term *heroin chic* was coined late in the 1990s to describe the gaunt, unhealthy look of many top fashion models. Kate Moss is the poster child for this look; she is also one of the top models in the world, admired by countless numbers of young women.

We've all heard the phrase "sex sells," but women's sex *really* sells, as television ads prove time and time again. Many women and men alike grow weary of women's bodies and sexuality, and to a lesser extent men's sexuality as well, being used in every possible way to draw a viewer's or reader's attention and sell a product—*any* product. One recent example is an ad for a new light bulb created by GE, called "Enrich." A man's voice—deep, rich, and sensual—slowly describes what attracts a man to a woman, all in physical terms, of course. As a thin, young, beautiful model wearing a sexy red dress that bares her shoulders and neckline walks toward the man in the frame, the ad encourages us to buy the new light bulb because the woman looks better for her man "in this light." What will it take to have a situation in which "sex *doesn't* sell?" Do you think it will ever happen?

Mixed Signals Create Confusion

People are confused by images in the media; at times, this confusion has consequences for their relationships and communication. Many men wonder if women want to be treated as equals and professionals, as traditional helpmates and caregivers, or as sex kittens because the media readily provide continuous, seemingly acceptable images of each.

One source of confusion is the cover pictures on women's magazines and the contradictory headlines describing the magazine's contents. Extremely thin female models, their breasts squeezed into outfits to create cleavage, appear on the covers of *Cosmopolitan*—opposite headings such as "How to Get Your Boss To Take You Seriously." In ads found in various print sources, the images of women create a paradox that is only compounded by reading the copy accompanying the ad (Jackson, 1991; Sullivan & O'Connor, 1988). For example, an ad meant to depict a typical day in the life of a professional career woman shows her dressed in a business suit with briefcase in hand, but the copy says she'd really like to be anywhere but at work; she's on the job, but actually thinking of her man.

Probably the best, and most insidious, example of mixed signal advertising has been perpetrated by the makers of Virginia Slims cigarettes, whose ads first emerged during the heyday of the women's liberation movement. The first television and print ads were done in sepia tones, to look like old-fashioned movie reels or still photographs. In the TV ads, a voice-over described how some women in history got into trouble for being rebellious and smoking. These ads then cut to modern-day images of women, accompanied by the motto (originally sung) "You've come a long way, baby, to get where you got to today!" The point was to illustrate how women's status has improved in American society. The 1990s versions of these ads could only legally appear in magazines and on billboards because of new laws restricting cigarette advertising. They depicted youthful, attractive women doing fun, active things (as active as you can be with a cigarette in your hand), while further employing the language of liberation. The paradox comes when you compare the visual images to the wording across the ads, such as "Now's your chance to tell the world just how far you've come" and the repeated sentence, just under the name Virginia Slims and next to the cigarette pack, "It's a *woman* thing." This ad campaign has long been criticized by health care officials and feminists alike who resent the fact that a tobacco company continues to ignore women's health issues and packages the product as though it epitomizes liberation, women's rights, and feminism. Is the company trying to convince young women that smoking equals liberation and that it's a "woman's thing" to smoke? What do teenage and adolescent girls think when they see these ads?

Studs in Suits: Male Depiction in Advertising

Just as there are female stereotypes in advertising, male *gender-role stereotypes* appear as well. More research has been conducted on the ways women are depicted in advertisements, but several studies provide interesting revelations about men in ads.

Corporate Success, Great Dad, and Bumbling Idiot

Studies in the 1980s showed that men were typically portrayed as dominant, successful professionals in business settings or engaged in fun activities in settings away from home (Courtney & Whipple, 1983). They were still portrayed this way in the 1990s, but a new trend presented men in decorative, nonfunctional roles that had no relation to the product being sold (Lin, 1997). Male depictions also began to include domestic tasks such as taking care of children, preparing family meals, and doing household chores (Craig, 1992; Kanner, 1990; Richmond-Abbott, 1992). One example is a television ad for a long-distance carrier in which a young man calls his mother while doing laundry, apparently for the first time. He says, "Mom, you said one cupful of detergent, right? Oh, one *capful*." At this point he looks at a sudsy washer and says "Gotta go, Mom."

While some think these ads realistic and humorous, others see them as male-bashing. A Hyundai ad from a few years ago was particularly memorable, if for no other reasons than its blatant role reversal and sexual innuendo—and the fact that it was hugely successful. The ad created twice as much awareness of the company than before. In it, two women critique men who get out of fancy sports cars, saying that one "must be compensating for a shortcoming." When a man arrives in a sensible Hyundai, one woman says to the other, admiringly, "I wonder what he's got under *his* hood." Researcher Philip Patterson (1996) views this ad as an example of what he terms *power babe commercials* in which "women enjoy the upper hand over men" (p. 93). He is critical of two prominent stereotypes of men in advertising, what he calls *Rambo* and *Himbo depictions*: "The image of men in advertising is either that of a 'Rambo,' solo conqueror of all he sees, or a 'Himbo,' a male bimbo" (p. 94). But reporter Bernice Kanner (1990) contends that male-bashing ads are on the way out. Kanner points to changing societal roles, in that as more women choose to work outside the home, domestic duties may be shared between wives and husbands. Kanner warns that "men have become too sophisticated as shoppers for advertisers to risk alienating them" (p. 20).

About two years after our first edition of this text came out, we got a letter from a professor whose class used our book and found an omission in the media chapter. They didn't see a list of male stereotypes that corresponded to the Courtney and Whipple list of depictions of women. So the class created one, and we think it's well worth printing here. According to Lynn Wells' students at Saddleback College in Mission Viejo, California (to whom we're grateful), male depictions in ads include the following:

1. Stud/Cowboy, like the Marlboro Man
2. Jock, who can perform in all sports
3. Handyman, who can fix anything
4. Young and "hip," as in a 7-Up ad
5. Handsome, ladies' man, as in beer commercials
6. Kind and grandfatherly, as in insurance ads
7. Professional, knowledgeable
8. Couch potato man
9. Blue collar worker, sometimes seen as a sex symbol
10. Androgynous, as in Calvin Klein ads
11. Romantic, coffee man
12. Fonzie type, Joe Cool
13. Helpless, as in the "Got Milk" commercials
14. Just a kid, who needs a woman to save him

What advertising types can you add to this list?

Media analyst Jennifer Nicholson, in a 1992 article in *Adbusters*, suggests that the societal roles of men and corresponding depictions in ads reflect a sort of male image schizophrenia. Nicholson explains: "By creating a variety of new male identities, advertisers gain access to a wider collection of pocketbooks. Whether the '90s man is actually changing is irrelevant—the point is to convince him that he's part of a market-driven trend" (p. 21). She cites varying depictions of men in television and print ads, including businessmen with babies strapped to their backs, dads preparing sack lunches before their kids go off to school, a "sensitive new age guy (SNAG)" who is "politically correct and even eligible to be called a feminist" (p. 23), men in Jockey underwear and Calvin Klein cologne ads, and scantily clad men working out in Soloflex commercials. The more varied the depictions of men in ads, the more messages are conveyed that there are diverse, nonstereotypical roles for men in society.

Advertising's Effects on Men

Most women prefer not to relate to men as though they were macho stereotypes. But then they wonder if men actually want such treatment, given that macho images of men still pervade many forms of media from magazine ads depicting rugged men in their pick-up trucks to infomercials pushing the latest exercise equipment. One study focused on views of magazine ads containing images of men that ranged from traditionally masculine to androgynous (Garst & Bodenhausen, 1997). Male subjects with traditional gender identities did not change their attitudes after viewing nontraditional depictions of men in ads. Men with nontraditional gender identities identified more strongly with androgynous depictions of men in ads, as well as with feminism and nontraditional views.

If you're a male reader, what's your reaction to an ad in which a scantily clad man is depicted as a sex object, as some would argue Calvin Klein, Versace, and other magazine ads do? Look at the new twist to Virginia Slims ads, for example. One depicts two women (one with the ever-present cigarette in hand) looking at each other, smiling a knowing smile, with a caption that reads, "What's the first thing we look for in a guy? A really great . . . um . . . personality." The guy in the ad has his back to them and is dressed in a t-shirt tucked into a tight pair of jeans. Another ad has a woman smoking and looking up at a man, laughingly, with this caption underneath, "Just because we laugh at your stories doesn't mean we believe 'em for a second."

Or how about the now-infamous Diet Coke ad from the early 1990s, in which a hunky, sweaty construction worker removes his shirt and downs a Diet Coke to the delight of the women working next door who watched the clocks for their "Diet Coke break"? As one female columnist wrote, "For a lot of us, this ad is sweeter than a thermos full of sugar substitute for a whole lot of reasons. Most obvious: It is so grand to take off the place mats and turn those tables" (Loohauis, 1994, p. 5C). For the guys, do you notice these ads more or in a different way than, for example, Victoria's Secret lingerie ads, which only recently began appearing on television? Do these ads make you feel bad about yourself in comparison to some stud women swoon over? Or do you find them refreshing and realistic because women show their "appreciation" of men?

Many scholars believe that men are the next targets for an all-out assault on self-esteem, mainly because the market for assaulting women's self-esteem—which forces them to buy products and services ranging from simple beauty remedies to full-scale plastic surgery—is saturated, profits maxed out. Research on American college students shows that "up to two thirds of young women and one third of young men experience significant dissatisfaction with their body size, shape, condition, or appearance in relation to most advertising campaigns" (Raeback-Wagener, Eickenhoff-Schemeck, & Kelly-Vance, 1998, p. 29).

Writer Ann Marie Dobosz explores this trend in an article for *Ms.* (1997). She explains, "There is an element of ad-inspired obsession with buying products and with measuring up to an unobtainable ideal of masculinity. Men's magazines have seen a conspicuous rise in ads for beauty and image products" (p. 91). She points to a significant increase in ads showing half-clothed male bodies, which encourage men to think of themselves as sex objects. Mass communication scholar Carolyn Lin (1997) agrees: "Rather than elevating both genders to more realistic portrayals, it appears that men, too, are getting caricatured in roles as sex symbols. This 'downgrading' of the traditional middle-class male image—from a breadwinner and responsible adult to simply a 'playmate'—is indicative of how advertisers are willing to sexually exploit men to market their products" (p. 247). You may find you have become so sensitized to sexually objectifying ads—of both men and women—that you hardly notice them any more. Since sexually objectifying female ads don't seem to be going away, do you think it's a form of equality to sexually objectify men in ads?

Worries About Young Consumers

It is possible for advertising to affect your self-esteem and gender-role identity, as well as your expectations for and communication with members of the opposite sex. But what about possible effects on people who have not yet developed the ability to critically analyze and selectively retain mediated information? Research continues to explore the impact of ads that accompany children's television programming, in terms of the numbers of male characters and the roles they enact, the lack of positive female portrayals, and the predominant use of male voice-overs in television commercials (see below). As cultivation theory suggests, these factors have the potential to reinforce for children conventional gender-role definitions, meaning that children may come to believe that life is supposed to be like it is portrayed in commercials. Advertising may also influence how children develop their own sex and gender identity and how they come to expect certain behavior from women and men (Kolbe, 1991; Macklin & Kolbe, 1984).

The Voice of Authority in Television Commercials

Voice-overs for ads represent unseen authorities or product experts, who typically greet the viewer, introduce the product or service, and conclude the ad with emphatic praise or a final sales pitch (Marecek, et al., 1978). Of the voice-overs for hundreds of American television commercials analyzed in three studies in the 1970s, researchers reported that more than 93 percent used male voices, while less than 7 percent used female (Culley & Bennett, 1976; Maracek, et al., 1978; O'Donnell & O'Donnell, 1978). In more current research, media analysts Allan

Recap

hypodermic needle theory, direct effects theory, uses and gratifications theory, agenda-setting theory, cultivation theory, stereotyping, female gender-role stereotypes, mixed signal advertising, male gender-role stereotypes, power babe commercials, Rambo and Himbo depictions, voice-overs and Coltrane (1996) found that women's voice-overs in American television commercials only increased by 2 percent from the 1950s through the 1980s, leading them to conclude that the "male bastion of authoritative voice continues unscathed" (p. 199). One study of television ads broadcast during Super Bowls from 1989 through 1994 produced interesting, if not predictable, results. Media researcher Bonnie Drewniany (1996) indicated that "One would hope to hear an equal number of male and female voice-overs, but the power of the male voice came across loud and strong 167 times, while the female voice was heard a mere sixteen times" (p. 89). International studies reveal similar trends: Twice as many male as female voice-overs occur in television commercials in Japan, and four times as many in Taiwan (Liu, Inoue, Bresnahan, & Nishida, 1998).

However, media researcher David Kalish (1988) contends that in the United States "advertisers are slowly becoming more flexible in their choice of voice-over artists" (p. 30). Even in Drewniany's (1996) Super Bowl study, 10 of the 16 spots using female voice-overs aired during the 1993 and 1994 games, which might be an indication of progress on this front. Celebrity women with distinguishable voices, such as Lauren Bacall and Kathleen Turner, have done television commercial voice-overs. But women who do voice-overs have a common vocal characteristic—their voices are low, deep, and husky, sort of a blend of masculine and feminine. Since things are improving *very* slowly in the area of voice-overs, do you think society still perceives masculine-sounding voices as having more credibility, particularly as product or service spokespersons?

Lessons from the Small Screen: Television and the Sexes

Ninety-eight percent of American households contain at least one television set; most homes have more than one set (Vivian, 1999). More than two-thirds of American television-viewing households are cable subscribers (Dominick, 1998). Former chair of the Federal Communications Commission Newton Minow (1991) reports that average household television viewing increased from two hours a day in the 1960s to over seven hours a day in the 1990s. When you consider that the latter figure equals about 49 hours of TV watching per week, this activity amounts to more than the average 40-hour work week. Video recording has greatly expanded television's impact by allowing consumers to tape and watch cable and network programming as well as films when convenient. Some experts estimate that more than 85 percent of American homes have VCRs and that many families own as many VCRs as television sets (Dorr & Kunkel, 1990; Krendl, Clark, Dawson, & Troiano, 1993). Once DTV (digital television) becomes available and affordable, that seven hours of viewing per day will increase (Goldberg, 1998). We've all no doubt seen futuristic ads in which someone handles all of life's needs (such as banking, purchasing groceries and clothing, and communicating with others) through the use of a telephone, television, and computer interface. Soon those won't be futuristic ads; they'll reflect reality. Since it's unlikely that exposure to programming will decrease any time soon, it seems reasonable that television's depiction of the sexes will continue to have an impact on the viewing audience.

Television: Mirroring Reality or Creating It?

Television is a rapidly changing industry; it's likely that some of the television shows we refer to in this chapter will be off the air when you read this material. But one thing will remain: a chicken-or-egg argument about whether the media merely reflect what is happening in society or actually create the issues and trends that then become relevant in society. Perhaps it's a bit of both.

On the "media reflect reality" side, one could argue that the economic pressures and changing lifestyles of young professionals in the 1990s are reflected in such sitcoms as *Friends* and *Working*. On the other hand, many media researchers support the "media drive or create culture" view, believing that television actually expands viewers' range of behaviors (Comstock, 1983; Larson, 1989). Probably the best example of this view was the hit series *Seinfeld*, which media scholars believe at once expanded language and created a whole new way of relating to friends, jobs, parents, lovers, and life in general. Yet another school of media thought contends that television programming, for the most part, neither reflects nor creates reality; rather, its exaggerated portrayals and overly dramatized situations are nowhere near the realities of most people's lives. (Maybe *Buffy the Vampire Slayer* is a good example of this perspective?) In this view, television programs and other forms of media serve purely as escapism and entertainment for consumers, as uses and gratifications theory suggests (Rubin, 1986).

The Changing Roles of Men in Prime-Time

To better understand depictions of the sexes in prime-time television programming, media researcher Marvin Moore (1992) conducted an extensive survey of family depictions in American prime-time television programming from 1947 to 1990. Moore analyzed 115 "successful family series," defined as prime-time programs that aired for more than one season (p. 45). Ninety-four percent of these television families were white and two-thirds involved the traditional family profile of a married couple, with or without children.

Moore found that men's roles were "exaggerated, with a large number of male single-parent portrayals and an emphasis on the family roles over work roles" (p. 58). (At the time, the program *Full House* was popular.) Moore points out that while such portrayals reflect positive roles for men, they may also create false images and distortions of reality. Moore might argue today that the male sportscasters (one who is in the throes of divorce) in the sitcom *Sports Night* are more the reality than Peter Berg's Dr. Billy Kronck on *Chicago Hope*, who decided to drastically cut his hours at the hospital so he can stay home and take care of his and Dr. Diane Grad's new baby daughter. (Interestingly enough, this is the plot line the show's creators came up with upon learning that the actor, Peter Berg, wished to more fully pursue a film acting and directing career.)

The Kinder, Gentler Male Character

Are there any depictions of men on television that are breaking new ground? Media scholar Stephen Craig (1992) argues that a feminized or reconstructed male has emerged in prime-time television programming. These male characters are not buffoons or wimps, but likable, masculine men who struggle as they learn about themselves, how to communicate with the women in their lives, and how to be better parents. Several highly successful shows have capitalized on this trend, including *Mad About You, Everybody Loves Raymond, Party of Five* (primarily in the character of Charlie), and *ER*. *ER* has remained the top- or second-rated show among viewers for several years as its lead characters Dr. Mark Green and Dr. Peter Benton continue to work on their roles as fathers. Dr. Doug Ross (in actor George Clooney's last two years on the show) curtailed his womanizing and returned to his love, nurse Carol Hathaway.

The expanded depictions of male roles are proving popular with male and female viewers alike. However, early responses of male viewers to such characters as Paul Buchman in *Mad About You* were none too positive, revealing a gender gap in TV-watching preferences. The female star of the show, Helen Hunt, tried to offer a reporter a reason for some men's negative reactions to the show: "I could get killed for this, but I've always believed that men struggle to see how they can fit relationships into their lives. For women, it *is* their lives. Why would someone want to be reminded of something they have trouble doing? *Cops* sounds a lot better than spending a half-hour watching a couple navigate their lives" (as in Parish Perkins, 1994, p. 7E). Craig (1992) explains that the changing male characterization is not a consequence of raised gender consciousness, but of the feminization of prime-time—a trend for prime-time programming to reflect the interests of female viewers who have departed daytime viewing to enter the workforce. Craig explains, "The 'enlightened' gender portrayals of prime time are more the result of the economic motivations of the producers, networks, and advertisers to reach (and please) working women rather than any morally-driven social consciousness" (p. 8).

The Non-PC Male Character

Another trend in male depictions in prime-time television is what media scholar Robert Hanke (1998) terms the *mock-macho sitcom*. These shows "address white, middle class, middle-aged men's anxieties about a feminized ideal for manhood they may not want to live up to, as well as changes in work and family that continue to dissolve separate gender spheres . . ." (p. 76). Shows like *Home Improvement* and the now-retired *Coach* mock masculinity in that they simultaneously present "male comic television actors who ridicule their own lack of self-knowledge" and men who are "objects of laughter" (p. 76). In each of these sitcoms the main male character is a devoted husband and father who is an equal partner with his wife, but who often goofs up and admits he doesn't understand women. This characterization is also termed the *playful patriarch* (Traube, 1992). Tim, "the Tool Man," and

Coach Hayden Fox are fairly macho male characters who, through situations and communication with others, often end up the butts of jokes. But, in the end, they learn valuable lessons and become better people.

Hanke (1998) also suggests that, disguised in humor, programs like these may send antifeminist messages to the mass audience. For example, Tim in *Home Improvement* often comes into conflict with wife Jill's views and has arguments with Karen, Jill's "feminist friend," Hanke contends that these exchanges provide "an opportunity for Tim Taylor to rebut feminist arguments and to make nonsense of feminist sense. Insofar as Tim's comic style includes tendentious jokes that make women the targets, these moments offer male viewers the pleasure of seeing the rational norms of feminist criticism subverted" (p. 80). Some politically incorrect characterizations seem to go too far, such as the character of the father in the sitcom, *Jesse*, whose 1998 reincarnation of Archie Bunker makes audiences wince.

Other male characters reflect blended roles, meaning that more shows than in past decades depict multidimensioned, complicated men. The epitome of this trend can be found in *NYPD Blue*'s Detective Andy Sipowicz, played by multiple–Emmy winner Dennis Franz. While Sipowicz has expressed sexist and racist attitudes over the years, frequented prostitutes during his prerecovery days as an alcoholic, and is quick to anger in his often brutal interrogation methods, his character also includes sympathetic dimensions. You'd probably call him a macho guy, but his emotional side, his subtle ways of responding to bittersweet moments endear the character (and the actor) to the viewing audience. He may be one of the most integrated, richly portrayed male characters in television.

The Slower-to-Change Roles of Women in Prime-Time

From *Xena: Warrior Princess, Buffy the Vampire Slayer, Sabrina the Teenage Witch, Ally McBeal's* short skirts, and the *Baywatch* women's cleavage, one might get the strong impression that June Cleaver and Lucy Ricardo are *long gone*. But are these extreme images rather than the average depiction of the female character on prime-time television? Research has found some fascinating, and at times depressing, trends about women and prime-time TV.

Glad to See the '80s Go

Marvin Moore's (1992) analysis of families in 1980s prime-time television was critical of some portrayals of women. He asserted that, while television programs depicted men in nontraditional roles, communicating that men have the freedom to choose different paths for themselves without societal sanctions, women's changing roles in society were largely ignored. Moore found that mothers and wives in family series were rarely identified as having occupations; they were predominantly home centered and supported by their male counterparts in the shows. The reality was that huge numbers of women entered the workforce during the '80s, to support themselves and subsidize the family income. Moore's primary example was the lead female character in one of the most successful sitcoms of the decade, *The Cosby Show's* Claire Huxtable. She was a successful lawyer, but rarely referred to her job and was only occasionally depicted in legal settings. Hanke (1998) offers the character of Jill Taylor on *Home Improvement* as an example of a '90s woman who chose to work outside the home, as Jill did in the show's second season, but who was rarely seen at her job and rarely discussed it with her husband.

A subsequent study to Moore's analyzed 10 of the most popular sitcoms in the United States from the 1950 to 1990, focusing on such variables as the depiction of equal sex roles, dominance of certain characters, stability of family relationships, and family satisfaction. The results detected, with some fluctuation across the 40-year span, a general decline in both the quantity and quality of female roles (Olson & Douglas, 1997).

Women Juggling Home and Work

However, in the decade of the '90s, the percentage of family profiles in TV shows that included and actually showed a woman working outside the home increased considerably. Several studies have examined how contemporary women are depicted in prime-time television, with specific regard for the portrayal of tension between a female character's personal life and her work (Atkin, 1991; Faludi, 1991; Japp, 1991; Vande Berg & Streckfuss, 1992). Although professional women are many more times central characters or significant family members in prime-time television programs than in decades past, they are still more likely to emphasize their love lives over their working lives.

> I went in and said, "If I see one more gratuitous shot of a woman's body, I'm quitting . . . " I think the show should be emotional story lines, morals, real-life hereos. And that's what we're doing. . . .
>
> David Hasselhoff, actor

Media and gender researcher Phyllis Japp (1991) explored this trend, explaining that the typical emphases for TV's working women are their relationships with men (and, for some, their relationships with their children) and the tension created when they juggle work and these relationships. While this tension constitutes a reality for many contemporary women, the personal and relational elements in television characters' lives receive more emphasis or "air time" than the professional, career-oriented elements. Current incarnations of this tendency can be found in *Suddenly Susan, Maggie Winters, Jesse,* and *Ally McBeal*, which all have as their original premise rebuilding life after a breakup with a man. In fact, we've never seen lawyers work as little as the ones in *Ally McBeal*. In the office, they are mostly depicted chatting amongst themselves about their latest interpersonal challenge or love affair. They are often seen in court, but rarely if ever are they seen actually preparing for trials. (We grant that this is a comedy, but the focus on the personal over the professional still sends a message.)

Even the 1998 rave sitcom, *Will and Grace*, deemed innovative for the platonic friendship relationship between its two main characters—one gay, one straight—included an early episode in which Grace, clad in wedding dress and veil, was in a crisis over her impending (and canceled) nuptials (Jacobs, 1998) Japp concludes that "Little cultural guidance exists for creating a credible, well-rounded image of a working woman, for such a character is necessarily a composite embodying cultural meanings of 'woman' and 'work', concepts that have long been on opposite sides in American cultural mythology" (p. 50). Similar sentiments emerge from the work of communication researchers Vande Berg and Streckfuss (1992) who surveyed female characters in prime-time television. They concluded that "television continues to present working women as lacking the competitively achieved occupational hierarchical power and status of male workers" and that female characters are defined through "stereotypically domestic, expressive, and socio-emotional roles" (p. 205).

One such portrayal can be found in the character of Daphne Moon in the hit sitcom *Frasier*. There was no pretense about this character's status; she was introduced to the show as a live-in housekeeper for the pompous Frasier Crane and physical therapist for Frasier's father. There are no lead female characters in this show; the supporting female characters include: (1) Frasier's co-worker Roz, who was pregnant during the 1998 season and now copes with single motherhood, a character whose sexuality is her main feature and who constantly struggles in relationships with men; (2) Lilith, Frasier's ex-wife who occasionally visits Seattle, typically when her latest marriage or romance has ended and she needs a sexual encounter with Frasier to restore her self-esteem; and (3) Maris, the unseen but peculiar and estranged wife of Niles, Frasier's equally status-conscious brother. The sitcom reached a milestone in 1998, being the first show to ever win five straight Emmy Awards for Best Television Comedy Series. Yet the female characterizations in the show won't win any awards for progressivism.

Breakthrough TV Roles for Women, in a Distant Galaxy

Scholars suggest that recent spin-offs of the *Star Trek* series broke new ground for female depiction. While untrue of the original series, most of the women's roles in the more recent shows were high-ranking officers, doctors, security specialists, engineers, and scientists. In fact, the January 1995 cover of *Entertainment Weekly* magazine pictured actress Kate Mulgrew, in full uniform as Captain Kathryn Janeway of the Starship Enterprise in the *Star Trek: Voyager* series, with a caption that read "Boldly Going Where Only Men Have Gone Before." In the interview that accompanied the cover, the actress expressed her view of the female-as-captain innovation in her show: "Women have an emotional accessibility that our culture not only accepts but embraces. We have a tactility, a compassion, a maternity—and all these things can be revealed within the character of a very authoritative person" (as in Kim, 1995, p. 16).

Media analyst Minh Luong (1992) asserts, *"Star Trek: The Next Generation* broke new ground by introducing women as senior commanding officers, as well as casting women in traditionally male-dominated occupational roles" (p. 1). Interestingly enough, this program, with its nontraditional female depiction and "enlightened" treatment of gender issues in occasional episodes, was the number one show on television among 18- to 49-year old male viewers (Svetkey, 1992). However, feminist media scholar Leah Vande Berg (1993) believes that, while roles have expanded for women in the *Star Trek* series, the roles are more "feminized" than "feminist." *Star Trek: The Next Generation*, in particular, Vande Berg claims, went "where primarily male, Anglo, heterosexual men have gone before" (p. 34).

Breakthrough Roles on Planet Earth

Certainly the characters of Roseanne Connor and Murphy Brown can be seen as groundbreakers for women's roles. The lead character in *Roseanne* was a contradiction—a challenge to the social norm of femininity, a struggling, outspoken, blue-collar worker, and a sarcastic, yet devoted wife, mother, and sister (Faludi, 1991; Rowe, 1990). Media author Susan Douglas (1995a) calls the actress Roseanne a "pioneer" who "ripped the veneer of flawlessness of TV motherhood and showed a household in which siblings scream at each other, parents disagree and have sex, and the doting mom yells to her kids, 'Go to your room and live in fear,' adding sardonically in an aside, 'To think I suckled them'" (p. 77). Douglas goes on to point out that *Roseanne* was one of the few primetime shows with a white cast to get high ratings from black audiences, citing statistics from 1993 in which *Roseanne* was the "only show with a white lead to be among the top 20 shows with both black and white audiences" (p. 77).

The central character in *Murphy Brown* has been studied for many reasons, primarily because she was one of the first strong, independent, career-minded, persistently single female characters (since *The Mary Tyler Moore Show*) who developed over time and seemed to defy stereotypes. At the same time, she was a recovering alcoholic and retained some unattractive, negative dimensions to her persona, like her abrasiveness with people. Bonnie Dow, in her 1996 book, *Prime-Time Feminism*, points out that *Murphy Brown* offered "validation of women's progress embodied in the power of the lead character and in its exploration of the costs of that progress" (p. 137). The show depicted a "progressive portrait of a professional woman," as well as "subtler themes about the lessons of liberation" (p. 137). As Diane English, co-creator of the sitcom, told a reporter, "I had never seen a strong, competent woman on television who also had the courage of her convictions, who wasn't trying to please everyone, who allowed herself to be rude and who didn't edit herself. These are traits you would normally find in a man. I really, basically, wrote Murphy as a man in a skirt" (Clark, 1993, p. 5C).

The character of Murphy Brown defied the corporate, scratching-to-the-top stereotype by becoming pregnant late in the run of the series. She approached single-mom challenges with humor, insecurity, and determination. In the final years of the series, she faced the challenge of breast cancer, treatment, and recovery, reflecting one of women's greatest fears. The show began to lose its audience and its appeal, as always happens, but the character of Murphy Brown will most likely be remembered as a groundbreaking role for women in prime-time television.

An important, if not controversial, breakthrough role came in the form of the character played by Ellen DeGeneres on the prime-time sitcom *Ellen*. Much has been written about this role and this show, as well as the courage of the actress-comedian to come out to the TV-viewing world, both in her personal life and in her on-screen persona. One reporter described it this way: "*Ellen* ended as inauspiciously as it began five seasons ago, just one year after it made history and a few short months after DeGeneres was hailed as *EW*'s [*Entertainment Weekly*] 1997 Entertainer of the Year. On April 30 of last year, 36.2 million viewers watched its lead character, Ellen Morgan, not only come out of the closet but become the first leading gay prime-time character *ever*, and a test case for the nation's tolerance" (Cagle, 1998, p. 28). No matter what your sexual orientation or your views on gay rights, it's hard to disagree that *Ellen* has had a significant impact on the television landscape.

Daytime Television: Not Just for Women Any More

Daytime television has its own viewing audience that includes a mix of people—full-time homemakers, teenagers (watching late afternoon programs), people who work part-time, college students (some of whom arrange their class schedules around their favorite soaps), shift workers home during the day, and others who use VCRs to record their favorite programs to watch at their leisure. In this section, we discuss two formats of daytime programming—soap operas and talk shows—with special regard for what these programs may communicate about women and men.

As the Culture Turns

Daytime dramas have been popular with radio and television audiences for many decades, and research on their effects dates back to the 1940s. An estimated 40 million viewers tune in daily to their soaps (Whitmire, 1996). One set of researchers views soap operas as extensions of childhood fairy tales; they suggest, "Dilemmas of identity, emotional anxieties, and other personal conflicts do not all reach resolution at the end of childhood. Thus, once grown up women have left behind the period when they may legitimately listen to fairy tales, other forms of popular culture are needed . . ." (Livingstone & Liebes, 1995, p. 157). A great deal has been written, primarily on the functions soap operas serve in society, predominant roles male and female family members play on soaps, communication between characters, and viewers' perceptions of the parallels between soaps and real life (Freud Loewenstein, 1993; Irwin & Cassata, 1993; Mumford, 1995; Scodari, 1998; White, 1995).

Before we go further in this discussion, let's address a popular misconception—that soap operas are watched exclusively by women. Daytime television programming has been, and still is to a great extent, targeted to the perceived needs and circumstances of women. This is understandable, given that over 67 percent of daytime viewers are women (Papazian, 1990). However, a study of the viewing behaviors of college students revealed that although the soap opera audience was predominantly female, it included a surprising number of faithful, male soap opera viewers (Lemish, 1985). Some of our male students reveal, albeit somewhat reluctantly, that they regularly watch certain soaps.

Gender and media expert Marlene Fine's (1981) research continues to affect subsequent investigations of soap opera viewing. Fine examined the kinds of relationships and interactions that take place within relationships that daytime soap operas regularly portray. She discovered that women wre most often portrayed in family settings, men were primarily depicted in professional settings, and men and women were most often portrayed in romantic heterosexual relationships. Fine concluded, "The general picture of soap opera relationships is one in which male-male relationships are professionally defined and female-female relationships are interpersonally defined. Men venture into the realm of intimate relationships almost solely through their encounters with women, and then generally through romantic involvements" (p. 101).

A Dose of Reality

Not only do soap operas affect viewers' perceptions of reality, viewers also may be prone to take cues from various forms of television programming about what to expect from members of the opposite sex as well as how to communicate with them. Fine (1981) determined that over 20 percent of the female-female and the male-female conversations in soap operas concerned romance, while only 3 percent of all male-male conversations focused on romance. Another finding showed that the fantasy world of the soap opera depicts women and men involved in intimate attachments and revealing their most intimate feelings to each another. Fine contends that this does not mirror real life where traditional sex roles separate men and women and where intimate thoughts and feelings quite often are expressed to friends rather than to romantic partners.

Media scholar John Fiske (1987), in his book *Television Culture*, discusses the contradiction between the depiction of male characters in soap operas and reality as follows:

> Women's view of masculinity, as evidenced in soap operas, differs markedly from that produced from the masculine audience. The "good" male in the daytime soaps is caring, nurturing, and verbal. He is prone to making comments like "I don't care about material wealth or professional success, all I care about is us and our relationship." He will talk about feelings and people and rarely express his masculinity in direct action. Of course, he is still decisive, he still has masculine power, but that power is given a "feminine" inflection. (p. 186)

This kind of depiction, Fiske suggests, is offered to please the primarily female audience of the daytime soap opera; thus, the soap opera man could be considered an economically derived creation. The problem then becomes one of separating reality from fantasy. If a woman expects men to behave and communicate like male characters on soaps, it's fairly safe to say that she will likely encounter some disillusion in her life. While the notion that someone would be so foolish as to assume that people will behave like television or movie characters may sound exaggerated or overstated, it's not all that outlandish. Probably more times than we'd like to believe, people compare their experiences and relationships to dramatic versions and become disillusioned when their own lives don't measure up.

Soap opera portrayals also have the potential to affect how people form expectations about sexual behavior. Media scholar Katherine Heintz-Knowles's research shows that "behavior performed by characters who are attractive, powerful, and popular is much more likely to be imitated by viewers" (as in Whitmire, 1996, p. A7). Her survey results revealed that 594 sexual behaviors were shown during a five-week period of soap opera programming, which averages to 6.1 behaviors per hour, compared to 6.4 such behaviors per hour in a similar survey in 1994. Of those sexual scenes, only 58 depicted discussions about contraception or the consequences of sexual activity.

Other studies have found that sexual activity depicted on television has not decreased and that it seems to be a predominant activity for unmarried partners and within extramarital affairs. Even given the rising societal concern about contraception, AIDS, and other sexually transmitted diseases, discussions or actions in the plot lines that show a concern for (or even an awareness of) these issues are almost nonexistent in both daytime and prime-time serials (Sapolsky & Tabarlet, 1991; Schrag, 1990). In attempts to caution or educate the public, a full-page newspaper ad purchased by Planned Parenthood displayed the headline, "They did it 9,000 times on television last year." The ad copy warned against viewing sex from a "Don't worry; be happy" mentality, one that stresses enjoyment without responsibility, pleasure without consequence.

Do you think that soap operas have a responsibility to educate the public or to depict characters acting responsibly on a variety of social issues? Or do you think that the public receives education in other forums, leaving television programming to fulfill an escapist function?

From Phil to Oprah to Jerry

Here are a few good questions for you: What do talk shows communicate to modern women and men? Are these shows examples of how men and women are supposed to talk to each other? (We *really* hope not.) Do these talk shows set an agenda for the viewing public?

Since there are between 20 and 30 nationally syndicated daytime (and a few prime-time) talk shows on the air (some of the more recent ones include *The Rosie O'Donnell Show* and *The Roseanne Show*), the popularity of these shows cannot be denied (Heaton & Wilson, 1995). Talk shows used to be primarily the province of women. Feminist author Naomi Wolf suggests that among the early effects of talk shows, "That daily act of listening, whatever its shortcomings, made for a revolution in what women were willing to ask for; the shows daily conditioned otherwise unheard women into the belief that they were entitled to a voice" (as in Heaton & Wilson, p. 45). These shows, particularly *The Phil Donahue Show* and *The Oprah Winfrey Show*, provided a platform for discussions of women's issues. Even though there are still more female than male viewers, corresponding to higher numbers of women at home during the day, the audience expanded during the decade of the '90s to include greater numbers of men.

The success of the slug-fest known as *The Jerry Springer Show* made this talk show one of the first to be aired as part of a national network's prime-time lineup. But many media scholars (as well as members of the public) are outraged by what they see on shows such as *Springer*. Media critics Heaton and Wilson (1995) assert: "As the number of shows increased and the ratings wars intensified, the manner in which issues are presented has changed. Shows now encourage conflict, name-calling, and fights. Producers set up underhanded tricks and secret revelations. Hosts instruct guests to reveal all. The more dramatic and bizarre the problems the better" (p. 45). The heightened competition and changing nature of the talk show led prominent hosts to retire (as was the case for Phil Donahue), move on to other things (like Geraldo Rivera did), or work to keep the quality of their shows high (as Oprah Winfrey made a decision to do in the late 1990s). Host Jenny Jones faced legal trouble when the events on one show resulted in the subsequent murder of one guest by another.

Gender Determinism and Agenda-Setting

Feminist media critic Roseann Mandziuk (1991) contends that talk shows seriously delimit gender boundaries. The intimate nature of talk programs corresponds with the cultural stereotype that women are supposed to be sensitive, nurturing, and responsive. This intimacy is exemplified by host-guest-audience relationships; the camera close-ups of tearful guests who are commended for their brave, emotional displays while recounting personal narratives on national television; the accessibility phone callers have to some shows; and the occasional personal disclosure or reaction of the host. The format also reinforces women's

Recap

feminized or reconstructed male, feminization of prime-time television, mockmacho sitcom, playful patriarch, social issues programming, news magazine shows existence, thus "genderizing" this programming. The spontaneity of discussion limited by interruptive commercial breaks mirrors the realities of women's multi-task existence. And the fact that there's never enough time to give full treatment to any issue sends a message, primarily to women, that "conversation is never finished" and that "there is always more to be learned, always another talk show to seek out of information on another day" (Mandziuk, 1991, p. 13).

Mandziuk also suggests that talk shows, particularly those aired during the day, may actually by instructing women what they should worry about; in other words, the programs serve an agenda-setting function. What are the possible ramifications of believing that "being a man trapped inside a woman's body" is one of the most critical issues facing contemporary women? While some topics may be deemed outlandish or trivial, such as a problem with a husband who likes to dress in women's lingerie or a girl who flirts with her sister's boyfriend, other topics may make some women wonder if they're *supposed* to be worried about these issues. A greater problem ensues when the larger, general public "ghettoizes" important issues, such as reproductive rights, sexual harassment, and child care, by labeling them women's issues rather than societal or human issues. As Mandziuk contends, "Precisely because they are talked about in the context of women's programming, issues which demand political solutions become personalized and hence are easily dismissed from being worthy of serious consideration as part of any public policy agenda" (p. 19).

Heaton and Wilson (1995) suggest, "The very same stereotypes that have plagued both women and men for centuries are in full force. Instead of encouraging changes in sex roles, the shows actually solidify them" (p. 45). The men on these programs are certainly not God's gifts to *womankind,* as Heaton and Wilson report, "Women viewers are given a constant supply of the worst images of men, all the way from garden-variety liars, cheats, and con artists to rapists and murderers" (p. 45). And the women fare no better: "If there is a man for every offense, there is certainly a woman for every trauma. Most women on talk TV are perpetual victims presented as having so little power that not only do they have to contend with real dangers such as sexual or physical abuse, but they are also overcome by bad hair, big thighs, and beautiful but predatory 'other' women" (pp. 45–46).

Have you ever considered the instructive potential or the agenda-setting function of talk shows? Perhaps you recall talking about particular shows in your college classes or in conversations with friends, dates, or your spouse. Have your perceptions about women and men—their gender-roles and issues—been influenced by one of these talk shows?

Lessons from the Big Screen: Film and the Sexes

Here's an interesting exercise: Imagine that you had to put together a time capsule, a snapshot of American life that represented your time on this Earth, something that future generations would stumble upon and use to better understand their heritage. No doubt you'd turn to media to help you fill the capsule; no doubt you'd include some movies. The question is: Which movies would you include and why? Going even further, if only three movies would fit in the capsule, which three would you make sure got in? Would you include films from different genres, such as a western, a romance, and a horror movie? Would you include a classic like *Casablanca,* a futuristic film like *Star Wars,* or a movie that depicts your version of typical American life? It's interesting to share responses to this exercise (and it makes for good dinner conversation). But what's most intriguing is people's answers to the question, Why did you pick that movie? Responses tend to reveal people's value systems; people pick certain films so that things they care most about in life can be communicated to future generations. What would your choices say to future generations about your view of the sexes? Would your choices reveal a patriarchal or an egalitarian, feminist value system?

According to film scholar Thomas Doherty (1988), "American motion pictures today are not a mass medium" (p. 1). He contends that the film industry caters to one audience—teenagers. Although Doherty made this statement a decade before the highest grossing movie of all time, *Titanic,* was released, that movie proves his point: The repeat business of teens and preteens put *Titanic* over the top. But when you consider how much wider the market and corresponding audience is for film nowadays via video rentals, pay-per-view services, and cable companies showing first-run movies soon after their initial theatrical releases, then the argument could be made that film is much more of a "mass" medium than it used to be.

Gender-Bending in the Movies

Film has the power to communicate gender roles. It may not be a blatant message about roles women and men play in society or about how we communicate in relationships; the more subtle messages that we see and hear repeatedly are more likely to sink in on some level and affect us. On the most basic level, if a subject is dramatized on the big screen, it's there for a reason; it has to be important, right? The potential effect on children is even greater, as the significant impact of Disney films on kids shows. Research shows time and again how various forms of media, including film, affects children's views of themselves, how male and female characters are supposed to behave, who are the good guys and who the bad guys, and so on (Hoerrner, 1996; Van Evra, 1990).

One phenomenon in film that stirs up a good deal of talk and controversy, not surprisingly, has to do with gender. Before we begin discussing that topic, here are a few questions for you to think about: Have you seen any movies that affected how you interact with members of the opposite sex, at work or in your social or family life? Was there a memorable movie that changed your views about women's and men's roles or that changed one of your relationships? Might it have been *Sleepless in Seattle, Forget Paris, Titanic,* or *You've Got Mail?* (Or were those simply "date flicks"?) Can movies affect you in this way?

One for the Capsule

For your textbook authors, one such memorable, outlook-altering movie was *Tootsie*, a movie that to this day conjures up confused but pleasant thoughts about gender roles. If you haven't seen this movie, rent it, but until then, here's a synopsis of the plot. Dustin Hoffman plays Michael, an actor who desperately wants work, but whose opportunities are limited because of his reputation as being "difficult." When his agent tells Michael that no one will hire him, Michael sets out to prove him wrong by auditioning for a role on a popular soap opera. The twist is that the role is for a woman, so Michael auditions in drag as an actress named Dorothy Michaels. After landing the part, Michael encounters a number of sticky situations because of his hidden identity. The stickiest situation arises when Michael realizes that he's falling for Julie, another actress on the soap, played in the movie by Jessica Lange. As Michael (via Dorothy) becomes good friends with Julie, he is confronted with how to admit the deception and still have a chance with Julie.

One amazing aspect of this movie is how Dustin Hoffman's portrayal of Dorothy, through the character of Michael, becomes real to viewers, so real that when Michael reveals his true identity in one of the final scenes, audiences are sad because they are going to miss Dorothy. Another fascinating aspect of this movie was that it fulfilled a fantasy for many people—walking in the opposite sex's shoes, seeing how they are treated, and getting to know an attractive member of the opposite sex without the hang-ups and pressures that often accompany romantic relationships. It was also intriguing to think about the opportunity of putting one's new-found insight into the opposite sex to work in a relationship. As Michael explained to Julie in the last scene of the movie, "I was a better man with you, as a woman, than I ever was as a man. I've just got to learn to do it without the dress."

The film *Tootsie* frames the rest of our discussion nicely, because it exemplifies the theme of *gender-bending,* a term referring to media depictions in which characters' actions belie or contradict what is expected of their sex. But our use of this term is not limited only to people who have masqueraded in films as members of the opposite sex. The example of *Tootsie* serves to start our thinking, but gender-bending doesn't necessarily mean actors in drag.

Buddies on a Dead-End Road

Thelma & Louise was a groundbreaking gender-bending film on many counts; one film critic termed it "a butt-kicking feminist manifesto" (Schickel, 1991, p. 52). It was an open-road, "buddy" film, but with female instead of male buddies (Glenn, 1992; Kroll, 1991). One of the most laudable effects of this film was that it sparked a great deal of discussion. In fact, it still sparks discussion. Although the film opened in May 1991, people still talk about it and film critics still write about it. One movie authority describes it this way: "*Thelma & Louise* came out swinging, an astounding, mind-blowing revisionist examination of the American Experience, an ode to beauty and freedom, a crash course in feminism, violence, and the loss of the American Dream. It was, above all else, a film that made you *feel*, like it or not" (Hoffman, 1997, p. 69).

Few people came out of theaters saying, "What a cute, fun little movie." Some people were outraged at what they perceived to be an inappropriate level of violence in the film, although only one person gets shot (the rapist). While the film contains violent images, critics maintained it had nowhere near the violence depicted in other films of the day. As one reporter explains:

> *Thelma & Louise's* filmmakers and stars countered that the real source of the outrage was the fact that the violence was directed at men. [Susan] Sarandon (aka Louise) said that the controversy showed "what a straight, white male world movies occupy. This kind of scrutiny didn't happen with that Schwarzenegger thing [1990's *Total Recall*] where he shoots a woman in the head and says 'Consider that a divorce!'"
> (Bowers, 1997, p. 74)

Female audiences for this movie had complex emotions. They cheered what they perceived to be "payback," especially in the scene with the trucker and his rig. At the same time, they felt odd to be applauding revenge, as Hoffman (1997) explains: "For some, it allowed an understanding as to why some women remain in abusive relationships and some women snap. For others, it was terrifying to realize that they themselves were applauding violent retribution, at least for the moment, in the dark anonymity of the theater" (p. 69).

Male Caricatures in Thelma & Louise

Besides the dominant images and "radical" behaviors of the leads, male characters in *Thelma & Louise* were portrayed in an atypical fashion for the movies. These portrayals led to claims of male-bashing, based on contentions that the male characters were unrealistic and exaggerated, particularly because they were repeatedly vanquished by the two women. One critic from the New York *Daily News* asserted that the movie justified violence, crime, and drunken driving and was "degrading to men, with pathetic stereotypes of testosterone-crazed behavior" (Johnson, as in Schickel, 1991, p. 52).

Film researcher Robert Glenn (1992) suggests that "Feminists have perpetuated a behavioral definition of sexism that has been fictionalized and lampooned for more than a decade in films and television. *Thelma & Louise* effectively reconstructs these identifiable caricatures in order to paint an extremely unflattering portrait of men as insensitive and ignorant savages who treat women as functional objects to be used and manipulated" (p. 12). From this viewpoint, the caricatures or overdrawn images of men in the film were created in efforts to further highlight the victimization of the two female characters.

What messages about women and men did audiences get from this movie? Some people came away thinking that women were winning some kind of war against male oppression, that they were retaliating against unacceptable male behavior in like fashion. This is a gender-bender message taken to an extreme. However, while believing that the movie made a significant statement about relationships between men and women in the '90s, some film critics and feminist scholars contend that *Thelma & Louise* was not a triumphant women's rights movie. They point out that the film depicts the desperation of women in modern times—women who counter the powerlessness they feel with some very isolated, extreme actions, but who, in the long run, are still out of power in a patriarchal system (Klawans, 1991; Leo, 1991; Shapiro, 1991). This theme is epitomized by the ending (which we won't give away for those readers who have yet to see it).

Descendants of Thelma & Louise

A few movies have followed in *Thelma & Louise's* blazing trail, such as *A League of Their Own, Waiting to Exhale, The First Wives Club, Boys On the Side,* and *The Associate.* While none of these depicts such a violent scene as the attempted rape in the first half-hour of *Thelma & Louise,* all contain female leads in tight-knit groups of friends who experience bad choices and disappointing relationships and who are rebuilding their lives.

The Communicative Power of Pornography

We usually don't begin our coverage on a topic with a disclaimer or apology, but this subject is different—*really* different. Pornography is a topic that continues to generate a great deal of research and writing, and there is no way we can do justice to that body of information in a short section within this chapter on media. Many books and articles offer insightful analyses of the pervasiveness of pornography in modern existence, its effects on how women and men are viewed in our culture, and its impact on everyday relationships between men and women. All we offer here is a snapshot—a highly condensed introduction to the topic—just to get you thinking about pornography, perhaps in a way you haven't before. If what we discuss here makes you angry or increases your interest to learn more, then we've done our job. Just realize that we barely skim the surface of the complexities of this aspect of media.

Multiple Definitions of Pornography: The Beginnings of Controversy

A specific, universally agreed-upon legal definition of pornography doesn't exist. In legal contexts, *obscenity* is the term used, but not all pornographic material meets the legal standard of obscenity (deGrazia, 1992; Tedford, 1993). Sometimes the term *erotica* is confused with pornography, although erotica differs in that it pertains to material that portrays sex as an equal activity involving mutual sensual pleasure, not activity involving power or subordination (Steinem, 1983; Unger & Crawford, 1996). Strictly speaking, erotic material isn't pornographic, but material that some deem pornographic may also contain erotica. (We told you this was a complicated topic.) Several scholars have offered descriptions of what the term *pornography* might encompass, even tracing the reference to its linguistic roots. In our view, researchers Neil Malamuth and Victoria Billings (1984) offer one of the clearest explanations of terms:

> Numerous attempts have been made to define pornography and to distinguish it from what some consider its more acceptable form—"erotica." The word pornography comes from the Greek "writings of prostitutes" (*porno* = prostitute and *graphein* = to write). In recent definitions, material has been classified as pornography when the producer's intent is to elicit erotic responses from the consumer, when it sexually arouses the consumer, or when women characters are degraded or demeaned. Pornography has been distinguished from erotica depending upon whether the material portrays unequal or equal power in sexual relations.
>
> (pp. 117–118)

Realize that some people would take two elements from the Malamuth and Billings definition—the "intent to elicit erotic responses" and the "sexually arouses the consumer" parts—and call them something other than pornography. In their minds, material that accomplishes these two purposes falls in the realm of erotica or sexual expression; it moves out of that realm and into pornography when it degrades or demeans people. But that can be a very fine line at times, can't it? If two people watch the same sexual scene in a film, for instance, one may find it sexually arousing while the other thinks the sexual activity is degrading—to the actors, to one sex or the other, or as a whole.

Definitions Born of Political Activism

Catherine MacKinnon and Andrea Dworkin are prominent activists on a variety of feminist fronts, especially in efforts against pornography. Each has written multiple books and articles discussing the serious negative effects of pornographic images on women's lives and American culture in general. MacKinnon (1993) argues, "It is not the ideas in pornography that assault women: men do, men who are made, changed, and impelled by it. Pornography does not leap off the shelf and assault women. It is what it takes to make it and what happens through its use that are the problem" (p. 15). MacKinnon and Dworkin made one of the most tangible contributions to the antipornography effort to date by trying to get a civil rights bill, in the form of an antipornography ordinance, passed in Minnesota in the 1980s. The definition of pornography in this bill was written from the standpoint of women's victimization, which is understandable given the very small numbers of men who are victimized in pornography. MacKinnon and Dworkin's definition is as follows:

> "Pornography" means the graphic sexually explicit subordination of women through pictures and /or words, including by electronic or other data retrieval systems, that also includes one of more of the following: (1) Women are presented dehumanized as sexual objects, things, or commodities. (2) Women are presented as sexual objects who enjoy humiliation or pain; or as sexual objects experiencing sexual pleasure in rape, incest, or other sexual assault; or as sexual objects tied up, cut up, mutilated, bruised, or physically hurt. (3) Women are presented in postures or positions of sexual submission, servility, or display. (4) Women's body parts—including

but not limited to vaginas, breasts, or buttocks—are exhibited such that women are reduced to those parts. (5) Women are presented being penetrated by objects or animals. (6) Women are presented in scenarios of degradation, humiliation, injury, or torture, shown as filthy or inferior, bleeding, bruised, or hurt in a context that makes these conditions sexual. The use of men, children, or transsexuals in the place of women is also pornography for purposes of this law.

(as in Gillespie et al., 1994, p. 44)

A 1994 issue of *Ms.* magazine contained a discussion of pornography by several prominent feminist researchers, authors, and activists, led by editor Marcia Ann Gillespie. The purpose was to air diverse views on the issue or as Gillespie stated, "to get feminists talking *to* instead of *at* each other—and listening; to get us thinking and sharing our thoughts and feelings and fears, our questions and concerns" (p. 33). In that discussion, Norma Ramos, attorney and antipornography activist, stated that pornography is "evidence of women's second-class status. It is a central feature of patriarchal society, an essential tool in terms of how men keep power over women" (as in Gillespie et al., 1994, p. 34).

> Coming to terms with women as real people and not as fantasies is part of growing up.
> Sting, singer/songwriter & actor.

Representing another viewpoint is Nadine Strossen, author of the book *Defending Pornography* (1995), and one of the most outspoken critics of anti-pornography efforts. In Strossen's view, "Pornography is a vague term. In short, it is sexual expression that is meant to, or does, provoke sexual arousal or desire" (p. 18). She goes on to critique others' definitions: "In recent times, the word 'pornography' has assumed such negative connotations that it tends to be used as an epithet to describe—and condemn—whatever sexually oriented expression the person using it dislikes. As one wit put it, 'What turns *me* on is erotica, but what turns *you* on is pornography!'" (p. 18). In her book, Strossen differentiates between pornography that is destructive and degrading and that which is merely sexually arousing. She still considers the latter pornography, but acceptable pornography.

Types of Readily Accessible Pornography

One other distinction in terminology is important before going further. *Hardcore pornography* depicts or describes intercourse and/or other sexual practices (e.g., oral sex, anal sex). In *soft-core pornography*, such acts are implied but not fully or explicitly acted out on a screen or displayed on a page. According to Malamuth and Billings (1984), "both soft- and hard-core pornography present women as animalistic and in need of control. Women also are portrayed as easily accessible objects intended for possession. This allows men to commoditize women and appropriate what women produce, undercompensating them or not compensating them at all" (pp. 122–123).

In the next few paragraphs, we present divergent viewpoints on pornography. But before doing so, we have some questions for you to consider: Before you dismiss or downplay this discussion because you don't believe yourself to be a consumer of pornography, think again. If you adopt a broad definition of pornography as material that provokes sexual desire, then what can be considered pornographic takes on a much wider frame, doesn't it? For example, do you consider television's *Baywatch* pornography? How about *Playboy* and *Penthouse* magazines? Are they somehow in a different, more acceptable category than *Hustler* magazine? If the depictions in *Playboy* are sexually arousing, then do they qualify as pornographic? How about the swimsuit issue of *Sports Illustrated*? (Uh-oh, we've just tread on some *really* sacred ground.) Believe it or not, there is considerable opinion that the swimsuit issue actually is soft-core porn, just packaged in a sports magazine to make it appear more socially acceptable (Davis, 1997). What about the stripping and dancing in so-called gentleman's clubs? Is this erotic, but not pornographic, even though it may be sexually arousing to the viewers? Do you see a difference between what is erotic versus what is pornographic?

We continue to go through this exact process as we struggle in our own minds as to what should and should not be considered pornographic. Here are more questions for you: Just because something might be pornographic, is it necessarily harmful, degrading, and dangerous for society? Does pornography serve some useful purpose? We have our own personal answers to all these questions, but what's most important for our discussion here is this: Concerned adults must deal with these questions and others about pornography carefully and thoughtfully. Sexually explicit, arousing material is all around us and available for our consumption any hour of the day, especially as *cyberporn* on the Internet (Burr, 1997; Robischon, 1998). What you consume, what you believe consenting adults have the right to consume, and what adults should protect children from consuming are very important decisions each individual should make.

Multiple Camps for a Complex Issue

As we've said, there are different ways of looking at the issue of pornography. One thing to remember is that the two main camps we discuss below aren't really opposing sides of the issue. It's similar to the debate over reproductive rights: The pro-life camp isn't really the opposite of the pro-choice camp. The pro-choice stance isn't really a pro-abortion or pro-death (the opposite of pro-life) view; it's about one's right to make decisions about one's body. Just as many people hold a mixture of views termed pro-life *and* pro-choice, one can be in more than one camp regarding pornography. The two main groups—antipornography and anti-censorship—both talk about the topic of pornography, but they talk about it in very different ways. The people do not consider themselves pro-censorship; the anticensorship people do not consider themselves pro-pornography. As journalist Maureen Dezell (1993) explains, "The American feminist movement's battle over censorship— those who favor legal limits on pornography versus those who oppose them—has escalated dramatically. Anti-porn feminists have won significant victories. Anti-censorship feminists—who've long maintained that it is

people, not books or pictures, that harm women, and that women have historically been targets of censure when censorship is condoned—find their ideological
opponents' growing influence alarming" (p. 2).

Voices from the AntiPornography Camp

Andrea Dworkin (1986), in an address before the Attorney General's Commission
on Pornography, stated the following (be forewarned about the language and
graphic descriptions):

> In this country where I live, every year millions and millions of pictures are being
> made of women with our legs spread. We are called beaver, we are called pussy, our
> genitals are tied up, they are pasted, makeup is put on them to make them pop out
> of a page at a male viewer. Millions and millions of pictures are made of us in pos-
> tures of submission and sexual access so that our vaginas are exposed for penetra-
> tion, our anuses are exposed for penetration, our throats are used as if they are
> genitals for penetration. In this country where I live as a citizen real rapes are on
> film and are being sold in the marketplace. And the major motif of pornography as a
> form of entertainment is that women are raped and violated and humiliated until we
> discover that we like it and at that point we ask for more.
>
> (p. 277)

Dworkin's descriptions may sound harsh, but many of us are shielded from such
degrading images of women. That doesn't mean those images don't exist; they
are readily consumed by people every day. In fact, the pornography industry is a
multibillion-dollar moneymaker—some estimates place it at $10 billion a year
(Peach, 1998; Steinem, 1997). With the pervasiveness and easy accessibility of
the Internet, coupled with the slow responses of governments to regulate what
appears in cyberspace, the porno industry is experiencing record success and
profits. How naive is it of all of us to think that the consumption of pornography
doesn't have some measure of an effect on us—our views of the sexes, our
expectations for how women and men ought to be treated and ought to behave
toward one another?

But don't get the idea that Dworkin is in favor of censorship; she and
MacKinnon believe that the pornography issue really has nothing to do with
censorship—it has to do with respect. As Dworkin explains in the 1994 *Ms.* discussion, "The mindset has to change. It's not a question of looking at a magazine
and censoring the content. It's a matter of looking at the social reality, the subordination of women necessary to create the magazine, and the way that the magazine is then used in the world against women" (as in Gillespie et al., 1994,
pp. 37, 38). Law professor and author Mari Matsuda (1994) commented about
the censorship issue, in relation to pornography: "We need to get away from
male-centered notions of free speech. We should say that pornography, sexual
harassment, racist speech, gay-bashing, anti-Semitic speech—speech that
assaults and excludes—is not the same as the forms of speech deserving protection. Why is it that pornography, which undermines women's equality, is singled
out for absolute protection?" (as in *Pornography,* 1994, p. 42). Gloria Steinem

holds a similar view, expressed in an article responding to the 1997 film *The People vs. Larry Flynt,* in which she asked the question "Why can feminists speak against everything from wars and presidents to tobacco companies, yet if we use our free speech against pornography, we are accused, in Orwellian fashion, of being against free speech? (p. 76)

Voices from the AntiCensorship Camp

Strossen (1995) describes herself as a feminist who is "dedicated to securing equal rights for women and to combating women's continuing second-class citizenship in our society," but she "strongly opposes any effort to censor sexual expression" (p. 14). She and other activists, including Leanne Katz, Executive Director of the National Coalition Against Censorship, believe that if you suppress women's sexuality, you actually oppress them. Strossen describes the position of many members of the anticensorship camp as follows: "We are as committed as any other feminists to eradicating violence and discrimination against women. But we believe that suppressing sexual words and images will not advance these crucial causes. To the contrary, we are convinced that censoring sexual expression actually would do more harm than good to women's rights and safety" (p. 14).

Performance artist Holly Hughes revealed her views of pornography and censorship in the same issue of *Ms.,* explaining that being a consumer of pornography doesn't mean that "I'm going to go out and do everything I see. To be anticensorship doesn't mean that you are not offended. But the antidote to speech that you find disturbing is more speech" (as in *Pornography,* 1994, p. 43).

Author Sallie Tisdale (1992), in an article for *Harper's Magazine* entitled "Talk Dirty to Me: A Woman's Taste for Pornography," provides an interesting, more personal glimpse into the anticensorship view. She describes her journeys into adult video stores, the fear and discomfort she feels while selecting porn tapes, and the bashful way she later views these films at home. She believes the tapes have educational value, that she learns a great deal about her own sexuality from them, and she's certainly not in favor of any efforts to censor her viewing pleasure. But she makes a distinction between viewing consensual sex in a film versus viewing violence against women or degrading images of them. She explains: "What I like about pornography is as much a part of my sexuality as what I do, but it is more deeply psychological. What I *do* is the product of many factors, not all of them sexually motivated. But what I *imagine* doing is pure— pure in the sense that the images come wholly from within, from the soil of the subconscious. The land of fantasy is the land of the not-done and the wished-for. There are private lessons there, things for me to learn, all alone, about myself" (p. 38).

While we would not put Malamuth and Billings (1984) in the anticensorship camp, they describe others' views that coincide with Tisdale's: "Some of those who see pornography as sexual communication interpret its function in light of consumers' needs. Accordingly, pornography affects only the realm of fantasy or provides desirable information often lacking in many people's sex education" (p. 118). In the view of one researcher Malamuth and Billings cite, porn may have "important positive instructional functions" (p. 119).

Where to Put Up Your Tent

If you're having trouble deciding which camp to align yourself with, you're not alone. Elements of both positions have merit, we realize. There are well-known, outspoken feminists who adopt what could be perceived as a middle position. One such person is Marilyn French, author of eight books including *The War Against Women* (1992). In the *Ms.* magazine discussion, French admitted that she viewed the Dworkin-MacKinnon ordinance against pornography as a form of censorship. She suggested: "There may be some of us who would defend the First Amendment rather than see these [pornographic] magazines end—I'm one of them. But the problem is never, never going to be solved unless we start thinking about what this stuff means to *men.* You cannot make a movie or write a book that defends the practices of the Holocaust or that exalts black slavery. But you can make a movie, you can write a book that shows any kind of torture, enslavement, or murder of women. How come?" (as in Gillespie et al., 1994, p. 36).

The Crux of the Matter: Pornography is Personal

We have two purposes in presenting this material on pornography to you: first, to help you better understand the complexities of the issue through a discussion of diverse viewpoints; and second, to challenge you to think about the role of pornography in your own life. Now before you start to think, "Hey, don't accuse me of looking at that kind of stuff," we realize, as we've said before, that many of you reading this text think of pornography only in a hard-core sense and that you choose not to consume it. But what concerns us more, as writers and teachers of gender communication courses, is the more subtle, soft-core porn that permeates our existence because even soft-core porn includes stereotyping of women as subordinate sex objects and men's playthings (Jensen, 1991).

The barrage of sexual images we consume daily—in song lyrics and music videos (as we explore in the next and final section of this chapter), television and film images, advertisements in magazines and newspapers, images in comic books, cartoon strips, and cyberspace—simply *have* to have some effect. No one is superhuman enough to be immune to the effects of these images. We really do believe, as research shows and our students confirm for us consistently, that the amount of sexual images we consume in mediated messages shapes our views of the sexes (Jansma, Linz, Mulac, & Imrich, 1997; Senn, 1993). Mediated messages affect how we believe we are supposed to behave toward one another, what we expect from each other in relationships (both pla-tonic and romantic), how we communicate our desires and needs (especially in sexual situations), and how much respect we develop for ourselves and others.

Here's an example to make this stance more concrete; you might think it an extreme case, but it involves a male student just like someone sitting in one of your classes. A few years back one of the TV news magazine shows did a story on a pornography-users' support group, a group of about 30 or so male students at Duke University that began as a small group of guys in a campus dorm having regular discussions about sex and the effects of pornography on their lives. The camera taped one of the weekly discussions, and the men's revelations were startlingly honest. Viewers at the time were shocked that pornography could so permeate these young men's lives, so debilitate their relationships with women and their feelings of self-esteem. One student's admission was particularly painful and memorable: He described a sexual encounter with a woman he was very interested in. They'd been out a couple of times but had not had sex. He was highly attracted to the woman and really wanted to be intimate with her, but described to the discussion group his embarassment over realizing that he was unable to become aroused and get an erection. He then explained how he enabled himself to function in the situation by imagining the woman beneath him as a pornographic image of a woman from a magazine. When he shut his eyes, tuned out the real person he was with, and vividly imagined the graphic magazine picture, only then did he become aroused. He was not only worried that this signaled his sexual future—that he was doomed to a life of being aroused not by real people, but by mediated images—but also mortified at the impersonal, at-a-distance way he behaved with the woman. He could not continue the relationship after this experience and had had no other sexual encounters at the time the group met.

What's your reaction to this story? Do you know people who seem to be more comfortable with pornography than with real lovers or with their own sexuality? Should sexual fantasy and reality blend, rather than exist as separate entities that debilitate one's ability to function? We worry on a macro or societal level about how pornographic images—hard- and soft-core—harm women and men, how they keep women "in their place," as sexualized commodities to be purchased and used for gratification, and how they add to the pressure men feel to be sexual performers. But we worry more on a micro level; we worry about people like the former Duke students who might now be considered as sex addicts. We wonder how some men can say that they respect their wives when they regularly frequent strip clubs or adult film houses, become aroused by the dancers or images, and then come home expecting to have sex with their wives. What's the role of pornography in these men's lives? And we cannot help but believe (as the research has begun to document) that the enormous problem of violence, such as date rape and sexual assault, that occurs between persons in romantic situations is somehow connected to the all-pervasive, ready-and-waiting-for-your-consumption pornography.

Sex and Degradation in Songs

Christenson (1993) discusses similarities and differences in the way men and women are depicted in song lyrics. He suggests that both sexes are often portrayed as emotional and dependent, stemming from "the natural tendency of popular music songs, no matter who is singing them, to take on a sad, bitter-sweet tone" (p. 15). But he does see persistent sex-role stereotypes and negative depictions of women in modern popular music. His insightful comparison of sexual imagery in songs by the Rolling Stones, Donna Summer, and Marvin Gaye with imagery in the songs of such 1980s and '90s groups as 2 Live Crew, Motley Crue, and Guns 'n Roses reveals a trend toward more explicit and graphic representations of sexual activity and more dramatically degrading images of and actions toward women.

> Basically I write for the females, because we go through the most Stuff. But even though I'm speaking from a woman's point of view, guys can relate, because they know the dirt that they do.
>
> Missy "Misdemeanor" Elliot, singer/songwriter

Popular culture researchers Harding and Nett (1984) asserted that rock music provided the most derogatory, sexist images of women among all forms of popular music. However, more recent opinion suggests that rap music has overtaken rock as the most misogynistic form (hooks, 1992; Leland, 1992). Although some rap and hip-hop artists focus on racial and political issues and attempt to show positive images of relationships in their music, other artists are notorious for their depictions of women as virtual sex slaves to men. A study of listeners' reactions to music revealed that subjects believed sexually explicit rap music to be more patently offensive than sexually explicit nonrap music (Dixon & Linz, 1997). The study's authors suggest that because rap artists tend not to use "softening strategies" (such as poor pronunciation of offensive words, excessive loudness of music to muffle explicit language, and double entendres to soften offensive ideas), the rap songs used in the study may have seemed more blatant in their offensiveness when compared to nonrap songs (p. 234). Some of the lyrics depicting men as brutal terrorizers and users of women communicate skewed, nonrepresentative images that do nothing to improve relationships between the sexes.

As examples, have you ever read the words to 2 Live Crew's "S & M" (sadism and masochism) and "Dopeman" by N.W.A. (Niggaz With Attitude)? On the rock front, have you ever really listened to the words in Nine Inch Nails' "Closer," Motley Crue's "Same Ole' Situation," or "Stone Cold Bush" by the Red Hot Chili Peppers? These are examples of lyrics on tapes or CDs that typically receive parental advisory labels (Christen-son, 1992). If you listen to any of these songs, you might be surprised, even appalled, at the language and brutal imagery the lyrics convey. Is it wise to say, "Oh the words don't really matter; it's got such a great sound, I just really like song"? If the words don't matter, if they don't communicate anything, then why aren't these songs instrumentals? Why include words at all if the words don't mean anything?

It's interesting to consider what effects song lyrics have on your perceptions or expectations of members of your same sex and the opposite sex. If you can easily remember the lyrics to a popular song (as opposed to formulas for your math exam), it's clear that they're permeating your consciousness on some level, right? So while we might not regulate our relationships according to what we hear depicted in song lyrics, those lyrics do affect all of us in some way. Do you think your own sex-role attitudes and gender communication can be shaped or affected by the messages contained in song lyrics? What about the effects of graphically violent and sexually explicit messages on noncritical consumers, meaning adolescents and children? Can children actually learn brutality through music? We can agree that music is not the sole or primary socializing agent of children, but along with violent, degrading images children view in other forms of media, it's safe to say that some popular music contributes to the problem.

> Women are really empowering themselves in politics and in every facet of life now. Music tends to represent what's going on with youth, and the youth of America felt really frustrated a few years ago, and you had these angry alterna-bands. Now you have a lot of females who are stepping up to represent women in America or women in the world, becoming role models for young girls.
>
> Sheryl Crow, singer/songerwriter

Sex Kittens and He-Men in Music Videos

What happens when visual images in music videos reinforce the messages of song lyrics? As one researcher put it, "Music videos are more than a fad, more than fodder for spare hours and dollars of young consumers. They are pioneers in video expression, and the results of their reshaping of the form extend far beyond the TV set" (Aufderheide, 1986, p. 57). Since MTV went on the air in 1981 and quickly infiltrated American households, the music video industry has skyrocketed (Vivian, 1999). So have profits in the music industry—an industry that wasn't floundering, but that wasn't booming either prior to the innovation of music video. Nowadays the music video industry has sparked so much attention and has become such a vehicle for boosting recording sales that popular music artists feel compelled to create and market videos to accompany their songs.

Sexes and Races in Music Video

As media scholar Joe Gow (1996) explains, although music video has been praised for its innovativeness, it has also been criticized for its stereotypical depictions of relationships between women and men and between people of different racial groups. In fact, not too long after music video was introduced into this country (having first emerged in Europe in the 1970s), researchers began to investigate the extent of sex-role stereotyping in music videos (Peterson, 1987; Seidman, 1992; Sherman & Dominick, 1986).

Music video researcher Richard Vincent (1989) found that music videos predominantly depicted women as decorations and sex objects and that female artists most often portrayed themselves and other women in their videos in seductive clothing, with Tina Turner and Madonna heading up this list. Media specialists Brown and Campbell (1986) assessed race and sex differences in music videos airing on MTV and *Video Soul,* a music video program broadcast by the Black Entertainment Television cable channel. Results revealed "indications of persistent stereotypes of women as less active, less goal-directed, and less worthy of attention" (p. 101). Women of both races were significantly less often portrayed in professional settings in comparison to men of both races, a finding corroborated by subsequent research (Seidman, 1992). Brown and Campbell concluded, "White men, primarily by virtue of their greater numbers, are the center of attention and power and are more often aggressive and hostile than helpful and cooperative. Women and blacks are rarely important enough to be a part of the foreground" (p. 104). Media researchers Sherman and Dominick (1986) found similar results; they concluded, "Music television is a predominantly white and male world. Men outnumber women by two to one" (p. 84).

Research in the 1990s found little evidence of increased sex equity in music video. Scholars Rita Sommers-Flanagan, John Sommers-Flanagan, and Britta Davis (1993) analyzed 40 music videos broadcast on MTV and found the following:

1. Men appeared in videos twice as often as women.
2. Men were significantly more aggressive and dominant in their behavior than women.
3. Women were significantly more sexual as well as subservient in their behavior.
4. Women were often targets of explicit and aggressive sexual advances.

The researchers concluded "we are still a very male-dominated culture" (pp. 751–752).

> I don't think having a naked woman strapped to a rack is sexist at all. And I don't think the fact that we pretend to slit her throat is violent. It's all show biz; it's entertainment. Can't everyone understand that?
> Blackie Lawless, member of rock band W.A.S.P.

Joe Gow's (1996) study of the 100 most popular MTV videos of the early '90s produced more bad news for women. In the videos he analyzed, five times as many men as women held lead roles. Women most often appeared performing their music for the camera (termed "posers" by Gow) or dancing while lip-synching the song, suggesting that "for women to star in music videos they had to affect an attitude or demonstrate physical talents, rather than exhibit the musical skills typically displayed by the men who appeared in lead roles" (p. 159). Thus, women's roles in these videos indicated "a much greater emphasis upon personal appearance" (p. 159). Men were most often shown performing in earnest in recording studios or on sound stages, but they also held several other lead roles in comparison to the narrow range of roles for women.

Music Video: Sex, Sex, and More Sex
Research on the sexualization of music video has focused on sexual content that degrades or demeans women, in particular. Perhaps you have seen the

documentary film *Dreamworlds: Desire/Sex/Power in Rock Video,* by Sut Jhally (1990), which explores music video's hypersexualized images of women. In many videos, especially rock videos, women appear as mere sex objects designed to please men—as "legs in high heels" according to Jhally.

The fact that so much sexual imagery and activity appears belies industry executives' attempts to "clean up" music video. In 1990, when MTV executives screened Madonna's "Justify My Love" video, they found images more common to triple-X-rated movies man to music videos, so they refused to air the video (Rich, 1998). This was a huge decision because Madonna was considered the "queen," a pioneer in the music video industry, a performer who helped make MTV as much as it helped make her. For the major television outlet for music video to censor her artistic expression was an enormous development (one that, needless to say, did not go over well with Madonna). However, slowly but surely, standards have evolved and videos continue to explore more sexual territory. As Gow (1996) contends, "It appears that the changes implemented by MTV executives in the late 1980s had little impact upon portrayals of women in the videos shown on the popular network . . ." (p. 160).

One team of media researchers compared rock, country, and Christian music videos for religious imagery and sexual imagery, which the study described as provocative clothing, physical contact, sexually suggestive dance movements, depictions of heterosexual and homosexual dating, using a musical instrument in a sexual way, and depictions of sadomasochism (McKee & Pardun, 1996). They found that sexual imagery was very prevalent; however, sexual and religious imagery in combination frequently occurred as well. Of the three types of music videos, country music videos contained the most amount of sexual imagery compared to rock or contemporary Christian videos. This finding contrasts with those of other studies, which have found that country music videos tend to contain more images of romantic love, including relationship endings, than sexual images (Porter, 1993; Wilson, 1996).

Is Seeing Believing or Is Hearing Believing?

Do music videos have an impact beyond that of song lyrics? As Desmond (1987) points out, "Music videos, with their capacity for both verbal and visual coding, and their tendency to dramatize the themes of lyrics, do add a potential for learning and arousal beyond the realm of music lyrics" (p. 282). While disagreement exists as to the exact added effects of visual images produced by music videos, there is considerable agreement that the combined visual and auditory channels have profound effects on memory and recall. And for some, this is a real concern when the lyrics and accompanying video images are sexist, racist, violent, and degrading. Calling it "concern" is an understatement for many feminists who believe that music videos and degrading song lyrics the music industry regularly distributes and profits from are among the most serious contributors to women's lowered status and violence against women in our culture.

Media scholar Susan Douglas (1995b), whose work we discussed in the section on prime-time television, describes her concerns about music video and its effects on future generations:

> What will be dramatically different for my little girl is that she will be less sheltered from images of violence against women than I was. Now the actual or threatened violation of women permeates the airwaves and is especially rampant on a channel like MTV. The MTV that initially brought us Culture Club, "Beat It," and Cyndi Lauper switched, under the influence of market research, to one of the most relentless showcases of misogyny in America. If MTV is still around in ten years, and if its images don't change much, my daughter will see woman after woman tied up, strapped down, or on her knees in front of some strutting male hominid, begging to service him forever. These women are either garter-belt-clad nymphomaniacs or whip-wielding, castrating bitches: they all have long, red fingernails, huge breasts, buns of steel, and no brains; they adore sunken-chested, sickly looking boys with very big guitars. Worse, they either want to be or deserve to be violated. Anyone who doesn't think such representations matter hasn't read any headlines recently recounting the hostility with which all too many adolescent boys treat girls, or their eagerness to act on such hostilities, especially when they're in groups with names like Spur Posse.
>
> (pp. 302–303)

Music video is a pervasive form of media, particularly in the lives of middle- and high-school and traditionally-aged college students. However, it is not as pervasive or intrusive into your day as music that you hear on the radio as you're driving to class or to work, or that you turn on instantly when you walk in the door of your dorm room or home. Turning on the television and tuning in to music videos implies more conscious choice and more action than merely listening to background music. But think for a moment about the whole effect—the very powerful effect of combining visual images with musical sound, a beat, and lyrics. Whether or not you actually watch every second of the average three-minute music video or really attend to the lyrics in a song, you still receive the message. Somewhere your brain is processing the information, sometimes on a conscious level, but most times on a subconscious level.

Do you think that taking in so many stereotypical, sexist messages has some effect on you? We encourage you to think about how the music you listen to and videos you watch (if you watch them) affect your view of self, your attitudes about sex roles in society, the expectations you form (especially of members of the opposite sex), and your gender communication within relationships.

Conclusion

You may not feel you have reached media expert status, but we suspect that you know more about the forms of media that surround you every day than you did before you read this chapter. When you think about the many media outlets and methods that have the potential to influence you, it's almost overwhelming. But rather than feeling overwhelmed by media influence, your knowledge can empower you to better understand the effects of media messages about the sexes. We hope that you not only have an increased knowledge about mass communication, but that you are able to more critically assess the role media play in your life. That critical assessment enables you to make thoughtful choices about just how much you will allow the media to affect you.

Think about whether you have some standards for romantic relationships between women and men, for example, and where those standards came from. Do your expectations reflect romance as portrayed in movies or between characters on television? When you think about communication between marital partners, do you think about your parents, your married friends, or married characters on soap operas or prime-time television shows? If you were to describe someone's relationship or use it as an example, would you mention a couple from real life or would you call it a "Mulder-Scully" or "Dharma and Greg" kind of pairing?

When you're feeling down, are there certain songs and musical artists that either help you feel your pain more fully or that help raise your spirits? Have you ever watched TV characters go through some trauma, such as the death of a loved one, an angry exchange between friends, or the breakup of an important relationship, and then later used how the characters talked about the experience in your own life events? We encourage you to take more opportunities to consciously decipher media influence, particularly in reference to gender communication. The more you understand what's influencing you, the more ready you'll be to dive into new relationships or to strengthen your existing ones.

Keywords for critical reading

By the end of this section the student should be able to define and illustrate their understanding of each of the following key concepts and notions:

- Anti-male bias
- Articulation
- Audience
- Blackness
- Encoding/Decoding
- Cultivation theory
- Cultural context; Cultural studies
- Erotica
- Feminism; Feminity; Feminized or reconstructed male
- Hypodermic needle theory
- Gender oriented artifacts; Gender determinism
- Indeterminacy of representation
- Intersectionality

- Ideology
- Invisibility
- Linguistic determinism; Linguistic constructions
- Masculinity; Male gender-role
- Meaning (denotation/connotation; making process)
- Memory
- Message (relative autonomy)
- Mixed signal advertising
- Mock-macho sitcom
- Preferred reading (Negotiated; Oppositional)
- Pornography (soft-core, hard-core, cyber-porn)
- Representation (representation of races; Representation of gender)
- Rambo and Himbo depictions
- Relative autonomy (message)
- Receiver orientation; Reception
- Self-fulfilling prophecy
- Semiotics of language and communication
- Sexist language, Sexual language
- Social construct; Social issues programming
- Stereotype
- Vocal properties
- Whiteness

Key questions for critical learning

1. What is the central difference between traditional mass communication research and Stuart Hall's position about the processes of communication?
2. What is the old view of representation? How is this different when compared to the new way of conceptualizing this notion?
3. Why can one system of representation not encompass the total spectrum of meaning-making process?
4. How does mass media's material instruments and social relations, specifically cultural structure, lead to the production of specific kinds of meaning?
5. Why are our social and cultural codes considered to be constructed?
6. What is the difference between the dominant hegemonic, negotiated code, and oppositional code positions?
7. What role do social and cultural discourses play in shaping our understanding of race and gender?
8. Following Dyer and hooks, why is it important to study whiteness?
9. Explain the difference between the notion of whiteness and blackness.

10. Explain the ways in which commercials use symbols or voice-overs to produce meaning.
11. Analyze an advertisement in the same way that Diana K. Ivy and Phil Backlund do. Explain if you are able to see it in different light.
12. How much of the media you consume can be classified as pornography? What is the role of pornography in your understanding of the sexes?

Part 6
Media and Politics in Canada

Section Editor: Evan Potter

Introduction

Talking about political communication in a democracy means talking about the 'politics of the news'. Politics always entails a struggle in democratic societies among citizens, the media, and politicians for control of what happens in public life—the public agenda. In an ideal democratic system, politicians send messages that promote broad deliberation and understanding; the mass media (owners, editors, journalists) ensure that the public interest is served by disseminating accurate information, providing a variety of perspectives, and framing messages responsibly; and citizens receive and analyze messages critically. Essential to a functioning democracy is the shared principle that communication should be open so that all political interests enjoy an opportunity to advance their causes, regardless of the popularity of their views. This requires journalists to be free from political and economic coercion when it comes to choosing and framing what is published or broadcast. However, over the last several decades there is increasing concern that due to changes in communications technology, greater economic concentration of media organizations, and the fragmentation of audiences, our democratic system is in danger of being manipulated by both the media and politicians to the detriment of citizens.

Darin Barney's chapter, 'Democracy and Communication Technology in Canada', argues that the growing mediation of politics through the expansion of the mass media and the rise of new communication technologies is not having the expected effects on the relationship between government and citizens. He points to the puzzling state of contemporary liberal democracies in which the explosion of information sources has not led to a rise political participation or civic knowledge. Paul Nesbitt-Larking examines the ownership structures within the mass media and the process of producing news and concludes that political information is being manufactured. As a result, he argues that there is no such thing as objective news because information is constantly going through a process of selective gate-keeping that frames information and primes audiences. Jonathan Rose focuses specifically on how the structural changes in the mass media are affecting the nature of political reporting and whether this serves democracy. Rose's examination of the role of negative advertising during the 2006 Canadian federal election illuminates the debate on the conditions under which negative campaigning can either help or hinder a political campaign.

Framing Political Discourse

Democracy, Technology, and Communication in Canada

Daniel Barney

The 2000 Canadian general election, understood at the time to be the country's first "Internet election," also featured the lowest voter turnout in the history of these contests at the federal level. Just 61 percent of registered voters turned out to cast ballots—when measured against the entire voting-age population, this figure drops to 55 percent (Johnston 2001, 13). Significantly, these numbers are less a blip than the continuation of a trend that has seen voter turnout in Canada drop precipitously and consistently from 75 percent of registered voters in the 1988 election to 71 percent in 1993, to 67 percent in 1997, and finally to the millennial level of 61 percent. This downward trajectory in this most basic form of political participation has occurred during the same period of time that formidable new information and communication technologies have come to occupy the Canadian political landscape and fairly saturate the Canadian political imagination. In its 1999 speech from the throne, the government of Canada articulated its goal "to be known around the world as the government most connected to its citizens" (Canada 1999); two years later it declared that it had "helped to make Canada one of the most connected countries in the world" (Canada 2001). This was no idle boast, as Canada does indeed rank highly among industrialized nations on most measures of Internet connectivity. It is also the case that, as political scientist Richard Johnston (2000, 13) has observed, recent electoral history "puts Canada near the bottom of the industrialized world turnout league tables . . . No other G7 country besides the US has turnout as low as Canada's."

Admittedly, voter turnout is neither the only nor, arguably, even the best measure of the health of a democracy, and many factors combine to determine its level at any given time. The suggestion here is certainly not that the explosive growth of new information and communication technologies directly correlates with the decline in voter turnout in recent Canadian elections. That being said, the fact of their coincidence is provocative. One of our deepest liberal democratic intuitions is that generalized advance in our ability to gather and share information, and to communicate with one another, invigorates democratic participation. This intuition has received forceful expression in relation to the computerized and networked information and communication technologies (ICTs) that mediate an increasing array of social, political, and economic activity in Canada. Information and communication, we believe, are foundational to democracy, and therefore technologies that facilitate these contribute positively to democracy's achievement and enhancement. How could a technology such as the Internet, which provides widespread instant access to increasing volumes of politically relevant information, and which enables direct, undistorted communication among citizens (and rulers) be anything other than complementary to informed, democratic deliberation and self-government?

The coincidence of the rise of the Internet and a historic decline in voter turnout does not invalidate the hypothesis that ICTs will enhance democracy in Canada. It does, however, raise the possibility that recent technological advances in information and communication capacity are not unambiguously or automatically beneficial to Canadian democracy, nor capable of overcoming other factors that may contribute to its current condition. Indeed, one of the nasty little facts of the coincident growth of mass democracy and mass media in the twenty-first century is that despite a dramatic trajectory of technological expansion in information and communication capacity, democratic participation has not improved significantly in quantitative or qualitative terms. As Bruce Bimber has written, documenting the absence of statistical evidence linking Internet use to increased political engagement (in its various forms) in the United States:

> Opportunities to become better informed have apparently expanded historically, as the informational context of politics has grown richer and become better endowed with media and ready access to political communication. Yet none of the major developments in communication in the twentieth century produced any aggregate gain in citizen participation. Neither telephones, radio, nor television exerted a net positive effect on participation, despite the fact that they apparently reduced information costs and improved citizens' access to information (Bimber 2001, 57).

While we must be sensitive to the technical attributes that distinguish new from previous mass media, we must also acknowledge the ways in which they may be the same. Similarly, we must be as open to the possibility that politics mediated by new technologies will aggravate the disconnection between information/communication and democratic engagement as we are to our intuition that they will mediate a democratic renaissance.

This suggests that the relationship between ICTs and Canadian democracy is more of a problem to be explored than a foregone conclusion. It is a problem that exists at a very basic philosophical level, a problem that has manifested itself historically in Canada, and a problem that surfaces in particular ways in the contemporary context of new ICTs. For many reasons that will become evident through the course of this investigation, the problem of democracy, technology, and communication crystallizes broader dynamics and questions of democratic citizenship, identity, power, and the public good. In this sense, democratic questions about technology and communication are something of a crucible, especially in the Canadian context.

This exploration of the relationship between ICTs and democracy in Canada will be framed by the three criteria set out for the Canadian Democratic Audit: public participation, inclusiveness, and responsiveness. Public participation is the sine qua non of democratic politics and government. Though participation can take many forms and be enacted in a variety of venues, the degree to which citizens take part in various processes of political expression, decision making, and governance is an indispensable measure of democratic legitimacy. Participation is an important concept for assessing the politics of ICTs in several respects. Have political processes surrounding the development and regulation of these technologies been participatory or not? Do ICTs provide means for improving or expanding political participation in Canada? And do ICTs enhance, or undermine, the socioeconomic equality that supports effective political participation?

Inclusiveness is the second Audit criterion, and it too is related to the core democratic principle of equality. Exclusivity, or privilege, is anathema to a democracy, wherein political participation must be at least available to, and at best undertaken by, as many citizens as possible without prejudice. A political order that formally or practically excludes significant segments of its citizenry from effective participation will be far less democratic than one that provides for inclusion of as many people as possible in the political process. This criterion is especially important in Canada, whose population exhibits multiple diversities that often correspond to systemic forms of disadvantage and exclusion. Here again, special questions are raised about ICTs. Has decision making surrounding their development and regulation included the diversity of views and interests of relevant constituencies in Canada? Do ICTs provide a means of effectively including a greater diversity of Canadians in political life? And have these technologies contributed to, or undermined, the socioeconomic basis of inclusion and political equality in Canada?

The third Audit criterion is responsiveness. It measures the degree to which various elements of the political system actually address, and are affected by, the needs, priorities, and preferences expressed by citizens in their participatory activities. In democratic polities, a diverse range of citizens participate not simply to lend the appearance of legitimacy to processes that may not *really* take their views into account; they participate so that political outcomes will reflect, at least to some degree, their duly expressed interests. In representative systems such as Canada's, the responsiveness of political agencies and institutions is a crucial measure of the democratic acceptability of a given regime. As with the criteria of participation and inclusiveness, ICTs have a special bearing on the question of responsiveness, and vice-versa. Has the development of ICT policy in Canada been sufficiently responsive to the diversity of interests at stake in it? Has the relationship between ICTs and globalization enhanced or diminished the capacity of Canadian governments to be responsive to their citizens? And has the use of ICTs by a variety of political actors made Canadian political institutions more responsive to public participation?

Taken together, the three criteria of participation, inclusiveness. and responsiveness focus the investigation that follows on three central questions:

- To what extent has the development of digital communication technology in Canada been subjected to democratic political judgment and control?
- What effect is the increasing mediation of political communication by digital technologies having on the practices of democratic politics in Canada?
- How do digital technologies affect the distribution of power in Canadian society?

These questions derive from an understanding that communication technology occupies a complex position in the universe of Canadian democracy. Communication and its mediating technologies are at once an object and an instrument of democratic practice in Canada. They also affect the material context in which democratic politics and citizenship take place. To concentrate on one of these questions to the exclusion of the others would be to tell only part of the story. I will return to consider the rationale that supports these questions later in this chapter. At this point, some added reflection is in order on the conception of democracy driving this investigation.

Democracy

Politics admits of many definitions, practices, and expressions. Nevertheless, at its core, politics involves collective judgment by citizens regarding common goods, and the engagement of authoritative collective action toward the realization of those goods. Insofar as it reflects this combination of judgment and action, the ultimate practice of politics is often specified as governing or government. (These terms are derived from the ancient Greek *kubernetes,* or "steersman," since to steer, one must form a judgment as to where the ship should go and take action to guide it there.) Politics, then, is not about strictly individual determinations of right and wrong conduct in personal affairs (the province of ethics), nor does it comprise simply those individual calculations of purely private self-interest that tend to guide economic behaviour in markets. Despite the many forms its constituent practices can take, genuine politics always has a public, collective character, it always involves judgment and action, and it always pursues goods identified as common.

Democracy is a particular manner of constituting the various practices of judgment and action that together make up politics. That is to say, democracy is a form of self-government. It casts the net of citizenship broadly, extending rights to participate in collective judgment (whether direct, delegated, or representative) on the basis of principles of equality, and deriving authority for sovereign acts from majoritarian consent. Within those parameters, existing democratic practices take many institutional and noninstitutional forms, which vary in the quality and degree of participation, deliberation, representation, inclusiveness, and legitimacy they embody. What unites these various practices as democratic is that each subjects matters pertaining to the common welfare to some manner of political judgment by citizens regarded as equals, and each maintains a discernible link between these judgments and the authoritative actions of government.

The stipulations set out above certainly allow for minimalist constructions of liberal democracy. For example, democracy can mean little more than periodic elections in which citizens who are formally equal express their private preferences by voting: a registration of consent that subsequently legitimizes the actions of a government. On its better days, however, democracy typically involves somewhat more. Even in representative democracies in which the main political activity for most citizens is voting in periodic elections, citizenship ought to exist as much between elections as it does during them, in the ongoing ability of people to contribute to common decision making in a meaningful manner. The word "meaningful" here means that, in a democracy, civic participation must be obviously connected to outcomes and it must be more than merely symbolic. Furthermore, even in liberal democracies that emphasize opportunity as the pivot upon which equality turns, there ought to be some recognition that not all people are equally *able* to take advantage of the citizenship opportunities afforded by their constitution. Thus, a robust democracy will seek out ways to equalize participatory ability so that it matches opportunity. Finally, while it is certainly possible for a democracy to serve as nothing more than a means of registering and aggregating private self-interest, a more substantial democracy will make the effort to orient its politics around civic deliberation on the common good, slippery though it may be. To adopt the language of one of democracy's great thinkers, Jean-Jacques Rousseau, democracy does not reside primarily in the combination of individual particular wills into the will-of-all, but rather in public-spirited generation of the general will.

Together, these stipulations give added substance to the criteria of participation, inclusiveness, and responsiveness used throughout this book. They construct an understanding of democracy that is neither radical nor foreign to the Canadian experience. Canadians understand their society to be democratic, and by that I think we can assume they mean more than that they get to vote occasionally. They probably mean that theirs is a political system in which *inclusiveness*, public *participation,* and *responsiveness*—the benchmarks of the Canadian Democratic Audit—are legitimate demands that citizens can reasonably expect will be met. This does not mean that Canadian democracy is perfectly or even sufficiently inclusive, participatory, and responsive. Rather, Canada is a democracy to the extent that serious deficits of inclusiveness, participation, and responsiveness are widely understood by its citizens to be illegitimate and intolerable.

Far from containing a Utopian standard that prejudicially disqualifies Canada as a democracy, this formulation arguably captures the kind of democracy Canada and Canadians imagine themselves as striving to be. The underlying question of this study is whether and to what extent our current encounter with ICTs contributes to meeting this goal.

These technologies, however, are not the only factor involved in securing a democratic political order on the terms outlined above. Indeed, the impact of ICTs on democracy can really be understood only in light of, or in relation to, a number of other conditions necessary to sustain a democracy. As I will discuss in further detail in Chapter 5, these conditions include not just a democratic constitution that distributes effective political power equally, but also an economy in which the material resources crucial to citizenship are distributed relatively equally, a culture in which the habits of citizenship are the norm rather than the exception, and a public sphere in which politics are conspicuous by their presence, rather than by their absence. Inclusive, participatory, responsive democracies require all of these conditions, whether or not technology is part of the picture. As I will argue in Chapter 5, however, when technology *is* part of the picture it has a significant impact upon the possibility of these conditions being met, and this has been especially true of ICTs in the contemporary period.

Technology

Canada is not only a democratic society. It is also an unambiguously technological society. Since at least the Second World War, Canada's commitment to democratic politics has been matched by a resolute commitment to the development of technology as a means to secure its material economic well-being. Statements from the government of Canada regarding "the challenge and the urgency" of constructing the "Information Highway" are but the latest manifestation of this enduring technological conviction (Industry Canada 1996, 3). But Canada's democratic convictions may be at odds with its technological commitments on a fundamental level, as a technological society may not be able to either support or withstand the sort of decision making and action described above as democratic, and still remain a technological society.

The tension between technology and democracy has three aspects. The first is that the complexity of technological issues can undermine the possibility of either intensive or extensive democratic consideration. Democracies do not demand expertise of their citizens as a condition of participation, but technological complexity can make demands that exceed the capacities of most citizens, thus reducing the efficacy of citizenship.

Second, even if the majority of citizens had the capacity to engage with complicated technological issues, their deliberations would most certainly undermine the conditions in which technology develops and is optimized. Democratic decision making tends to be slow, ponderous, risk averse, prone to reversals, lacking in clarity, easily seduced by superficial imaginings, and often irrational: qualities inimical to technological enterprise. It might not be to the material advantage of a technological society to subject technical determinations to genuine democratic consideration on a routine basis.

Third, modern technology tends to be universal rather than local, a quality that has been raised to high relief by new ICTs and their relationship to the phenomenon known as globalization. Technologies, especially those whose operation transcends national boundaries, challenge the applicability and enforceability of democratic political decisions and actions organized at the national level. Canadians have experienced this problem for a long time, especially in regard to communication technologies and policies: technologies that tend to transcend constraints of terri-torial space as a matter of their very design versus policies that are confined in their application to the territory over which the Canadian state is sovereign. Put simply, the democratic political authority of the Canadian state over broadcasting stops at the country's southern border, but radio signals originating from south of that border know no such constraint. Similarly, with regard to a technology such as the Internet, it could be argued that the wishes of the Canadian state— democratically derived or otherwise—are irrelevant to the terms under which this technology will be developed as a global phenomenon, and that Canada's only choice is whether or not it wishes to be part of the world connected by this tech-nology. In this case, for a society committed to technological development as a condition of its material progress, the choice is self-evident.

This suggests that a society that imagines itself as democratic has to be willing to pay the price of restraint, regression, and inefficiency in technological matters. It also raises the possibility that a society devoted to technological progress as a condition of its material prosperity may not be able to maintain a commitment to democracy that is anything more than rhetorical when it comes to technological matters. Technology recommends technocracy—rule by experts—over democ-racy. And technological matters are regularly given over specifically to experts intimate with the imperatives of science, management, and the market, regimes whose ends and practices are rarely accused of being particularly democratic and which typically shield technological issues from potentially obtrusive democratic consideration. Precisely this tendency prompted Ursula Franklin (1999, 121) to observe, radically, that in Canada "we now have nothing but a bunch of managers who run the country to make it safe for technology." There seems to be something deeply depoliticizing and fundamentally undemocratic about technology.

But that is not the whole story. Although democratic political deliberation can sometimes slow down technological innovation, technology is also irreducibly political. Far from being mere instruments or tools that accomplish their direct ends and nothing else, technologies also condition priorities, define possibilities, set limits on practices, constitute infrastructures and environments, and mediate relationships between individuals and between people and the natural world. As the American political theorist Langdon Winner (1995, 67) has written, when it comes to technology "the central issues concern how the members of society manage their common affairs and seek the common good. Because technological things so often become central features in widely shared arrangements and conditions of life in contemporary society, there is an urgent need to think of them in a political light." In a similar vein, Franklin (1999,120) characterizes questions concerning technology specifically as questions of "governance." For example, grain elevators are not simply instruments for handling grain. They also organize communities economically and spatially, and provide the material infrastructure for an entire way of living on the Canadian prairies. Their "progressive" replacement by high-throughput grain terminals is, consequently, radically restructuring communities and ways of living that grew up around the previous technology. The decision to replace the old elevators with the new terminals did not clearly emerge from an inclusive democratic political process that genuinely engaged and responded to the participation of those citizens whose lives are most affected by this technological change. Nevertheless, a technological moment such as this cannot be said to be without politics simply because its political aspect has been obscured by a perceived technological imperative. Technologies, in this sense, have a legislative character, insofar as they enable or encourage certain common practices and prohibit or discourage others. Technologies represent decisions about how we will and will not live together. Therefore no satisfactory meaning of the word "political" can exclude technologies and their effects.

Thus, technologies are political because they constitute widely shared social arrangements that frame a broad range of human social, political, and economic priorities and practices, and because they are artifacts in which power is embedded and through which power is exercised. Consequently, moments of technological change especially have the potential to be moments of intense democratic political contest, moments of deliberation over the character and needs of the common interest relative to the technology in question. These moments can also be sacrificed to the logic of depoliticization that is embedded in the technological spirit, which is often called forth by those who stand to benefit from insulating issues of technology from democratic political scrutiny. The history of the deployment of technologies of mass communication in Canada, and policy making surrounding this deployment, is replete with examples of this dynamic.

The political questions surrounding communication technology and policy in Canada have remained relatively consistent since at least the advent of the telegraph. They include questions about the following:

- the role of the state relative to the market in the distribution of communication resources
- the priority of either national-cultural or commercial-industrial objectives, and the tension between them
- the democratic imperative to ensure universal access to communication services throughout the country and the means to achieve it

- the liberal imperative of free expression in communication
- the structure of ownership and regulation in Canadian communication industries, including the possibility of state ownership
- the need to stimulate and secure domestic production and consumption of cultural content
- the role of public consultation in communication policy making
- the importance of separating control over carriage infrastructure (i.e., the pipes) from control over content (i.e., what goes through the pipes).

What is interesting about these enduring questions of Canadian communication policy historically is that, just as they begin to reach a point of settlement in relation to one communication medium, a technological change reopens them. Just when the politics surrounding the telegraph, for example, appeared to subside into normalization, the advent of the telephone repoliticized all the same old questions. It is also interesting to note the historical regularity with which technologically determinist arguments and rhetoric surface during times of technological change in communication—arguments and rhetoric often aimed at obscuring and depoliticizing the deeply political and highly contingent character of policy in this area. This strategy extrapolates from particular characteristics of the technology to specific policy choices that are presented as necessary outgrowths of the technology itself and, therefore, non-negotiable. This tactic is most often employed by those interests that have a great deal to gain in a particular configuration of technological change and a great deal to lose in political, and especially democratic, consideration of possible options.

A stark example is the "systems integrity" arguments used by telephone companies in the early and middle decades of the twentieth century to justify structuring the telephone industry in Canada as a natural monopoly. They argued that the technology involved in the successful construction and maintenance of a high-quality telephony system simply required that the system be controlled from end to end by a single entity, and ruled out other options from political consideration. The degree to which this technologically determinist argument became policy orthodoxy is suggested in *Instant world*, the 1971 report of a federal task force on telecommunications, which conceded that telephone companies had presented "powerful technical arguments for complete control of the public networks, including terminal devices and attached equipment. To maintain a high quality of service to all users, they must be able to guard against the technical pollution of the network from other signal sources" (DOC 1971, 156).

As we will see, there is no shortage of contemporary claims regarding the necessary connection between various technical aspects of new digital information and communication technologies and particular policy outcomes that are presented as non-negotiable. Interestingly, many of these—such as the suggestion that the technical properties of digital communication technologies demand competition and minimal regulation if they are to develop to their fullest potential in Canada—contradict the substance of earlier technologically determinist arguments such as those entailed in the "systems integrity/natural monopoly" thesis. This would seem to indicate that such arguments at. times of technological change are themselves deeply strategic and political, and that the extent to which they are accepted by policy makers reflects the distribution of political power in Canada more than it does any inherent technological necessity. Curiously, the surfacing of technologically determinist rhetoric in moments of technological change can be read as evidence of the essentially political character of those moments.

This is not to say that technologies do not constrain and condition political options. A strong tradition in the philosophy of technology-to which Canadians such as George Grant (1998) have made enduring contributions—asserts that something in the essence of technology prescribes a particular way of being in the world, a particular way of relating to our environment and to those with whom we share it, to the exclusion of other ways. In a society where technology is ubiquitous and technological progress is an overwhelming collective social project, certain ways of living recommend themselves, persuasively, at the expense of others. It is to this quality that Canadian political economist and theorist of communication Harold Innis (1995, xxvii) referred when he suggested that communication technologies do more than enable us to communicate, and emphasized "the importance of communication in determining 'things to which we attend.'" Innis's concern was primarily with how *all* communication technologies reorient the human experience of space and time, and consequently reorganize human priorities and practices. Different communication technologies accomplish this in different ways, but the fact that each of them alters our natural experience of space and time can be said to belong to their essence as technologies. A great deal distinguishes a telephone from an automobile and both of these from a pile-driver; indeed, among communication technologies alone, a great deal distinguishes a telephone from a radio and both of these from the Internet. Still, despite these distinctions, all of these devices share a quality as technologies, a quality that makes the world we inhabit a technological one that is very different than a nontechnological world might be (assuming that we can conceive of such a thing). One need only try to imagine what life would be like in a world *without* technology to appreciate that there is something about technology in general that, despite the specificities of particular technological instruments, shapes our world, our practices, and our attention.

This observation returns us to the tension between technology and politics in general, and between technology and democratic politics in particular. On the one hand I have argued that technologies, and moments of technological change, are deeply political and open to contestation. On the other hand, I have suggested that technology in general, and specific technologies in particular, have essential characteristics that act to condition and limit available political options. Can both of these claims be true? Part of the answer lies in recognizing that a number of elements combine to produce any technological outcome or effect, and that varying degrees of political intervention are possible relative to these elements.

Certainly, that which belongs to the essence of technology does not readily admit of political intervention, democratic or otherwise. But the practical outcome of a specific technology in the world is not wholly determined by its essence as a technology. A host of other factors—including design, situation, and use—also contribute to specific technological outcomes, and these typically exhibit considerable contingency, potentially leaving room for political determination.

Design refers to the technical configuration and orientation of a device's operation and application. Technological instruments are designed to do certain things in certain ways, and design choices can have serious political consequences. Referring specifically to the evolving design of the Internet and related technologies, American legal scholar Lawrence Lessig (1999, x, 3) has written that code builds "architectures of control" and so "code is law." In this sense, the effects of design are always political, and so too are the choices that precede design decisions, whether those privileged to make them recognize their political character or not.

Appreciation of the politics inherent in technological design immediately raises the question of democracy: if decisions about the design of technologies are political, then, in a democratic society, should they not be subjected to democratic deliberation? The answer is yes, but as Andrew Feenberg relates in the following passage, democratic participation at the fundamental level of design is far from the norm in modern technological societies:

> Technology is power in modern societies, a greater power in many domains than the political system itself. The masters of technical systems, corporate and military leaders, physicians and engineers, have far more control over patterns of urban growth, the design of dwellings and transportation systems, the selection of innovations, our experience as employees, patients and consumers, than all the electoral institutions of our society put together. But, if this is true, technology should be considered as a new kind of legislation, not so very different from other public decisions. The technical codes that shape our lives reflect particular social interests to which we have delegated the power to decide where and how we live, what kinds of food we eat, how we communicate, are entertained, healed and so on . . . But if technology is so powerful, why don't we apply the same democratic standards to it we apply to other political institutions? By those standards, the design process as it now exists is clearly illegitimate (Feenberg 1999, 131).

The democratic imperative attached to matters of technological design, and the failure of modern technological societies to observe that imperative, could not be expressed with greater force or clarity. Democratic intervention in technological design typically conjures images of excessive bureaucracy, inefficiency, and irrationality, each of which is presented as anathema to effective design and technological innovation. Democratic engagement with issues of technological design does not necessarily have to embody these negative qualities. Yet such charges have been used quite effectively to exclude citizens from participation in technological decision making, other than as isolated consumers choosing to buy or sell long after crucial design decisions have already been made. Canada's experience with the development of digital ICTs has been no exception in this regard. Questions of design have been readily referred to the expertise of scientists, engineers, and corporate executives, and evidence of democratic participation, inclusiveness, and responsiveness is conspicuous by its absence. Were the democratic audit of new ICTs in Canada confined to the matter of their design, its findings would be brief and unequivocally damning.

That being said, technological outcomes are not wholly determined by design. All technological instruments and practices are situated in complex social, political, and economic environments that strongly condition their possible elaborations in human practice. Whether the outcome of our encounter with ICTs is substantially democratic or not will depend to a great degree upon its social, political, and economic context. Of course, a great deal of contingency is at play in this respect. A democratic audit of these technologies and their prospects has to take these material conditions and contingencies into account, so much of the analysis that follows will be devoted in one way or another to this task. Subsequent chapters will, for example, pay close attention to the policy framework and economic conditions under which these technologies have been developed in the Canadian context, in an attempt to locate evidence of democratic success or failure.

Finally, a substantial portion of any technological outcome is constructed socially through the actual everyday uses to which institutions and people put a given technological device. The essence of technology challenges, but does not negate, human freedom; technological design favours, but does not determine, potential applications; and material situation conditions, but does not enforce absolutely, possible elaborations. Even George Grant (1986, 21), who clearly prioritizes the essential elements of technology, concedes that "the computer does not impose upon us the ways in which it will be used." Technological outcomes are linked crucially to use, and use admits a significant range of possibilities, many of which were not contemplated by design and some of which involve "democratic rationalizations" of technologies that were not intended for democratic use, or which are situated in conditions that are not otherwise democratic (Feenberg 1999, 12). Consequently, a democratic audit of new ICTs must also attend to the manner in which these instruments are actually used by political actors and institutions in the Canadian context, in order to determine whether these uses either reflect or encourage a democratic practice that is more, or less, participatory, responsive, and inclusive.

Communication and Democracy in Canada

In specifying the distinctly political nature of human beings, Aristotle singled out our capacity to communicate. A human being, he argued, "is by nature a political animal" precisely because human beings are unique in their capacity to communicate with each other about common issues "of good and evil, the just and the unjust" (Aristotle 1995, 1253a2-7). Politics, especially democratic politics, is impossible without communication. Deliberating citizens share information and communicate their opinions and reasons with one another; citizens communicate with elected and appointed representatives who, in turn, communicate with constituents; governing authorities, whether administrative or legislative, solicit information from subjects and communicate with them in various forms of service and command.

In mass societies, the bulk of significant political communication is mediated by technology. It is not just that democratic politics cannot exist without communication: contemporary democracies such as Canada could not function without communication technologies. They play an indispensable role in advanced political systems analogous to the role of transportation technologies such as railroads, highways, and airplanes in advanced economies. For this reason, the stakes in issues surrounding these technologies are very high. We all know how intense the politics of roads and railways can be, and indeed have been in Canadian history, a fact that attests to the centrality of these technologies to economic life. The centrality of ICTs to democratic political life has generated a similar history of intensive political contestation in Canada. To raise but one example, the history of state broadcasting in Canada cannot be understood outside its origins in an epic political confrontation between the Canadian Radio League and the Canadian Association of Broadcasters, one result of which was the firm establishment of mass communication as a public interest issue in Canada (Raboy 1990, 17-47). The collective amnesia that typically accompanies moments of technological change notwithstanding, contemporary debates surrounding the development and character of new ICTs are best understood as a continuation of this history of politicization.

As suggested earlier in this chapter, ICTs have a complex relationship with democratic politics in Canada. In the first place, these technologies serve as a crucial infrastructure for an increasing array of political activities in Canada. This fact requires that an audit of the democratic character of this new environment of political communication attend to the question of whether these technologies are, or are likely to be, successful in mediating democratic politics according to some of the standards set out in the foregoing discussion. That is to say, we must investigate *the effect that increasing mediation of political communication by digital technologies is having on the practices of democratic politics in Canada,* including the practices of government, political parties, and citizens.

Second, these technologies also play an increasingly central role in the social, political, and economic lives of Canadians—our shared arrangements for living together—even for those who opt out of using them routinely. In one way or another, we all live in the world as it is built by and around new ICTs. Therefore we must inquire into *the manner in which these technologies affect the distribution of power in Canada.* We must also understand the elaboration of these technologies as itself a public issue of the highest significance, and recognize that a society that fails to subject this matter to adequate democratic consideration undermines its own claims to being a democracy. As such, we must also inquire into *the extent to which the rapid and massive development of digital information and communication technology in Canada has been subjected to democratic judgment and control.* Together, these inquiries yield a provisional conclusion as to the inclusive, participatory, and responsive nature of this aspect of contemporary Canadian democracy.

It is tempting to begin this investigation with the obvious question of how Canadian citizens and institutions are using ICTs in their political activities. The meaning and significance of these activities, however, can be understood only in the context of how ICTs have been treated as an object of citizenship, and the role they have played in restructuring the political possibilities of the Canadian state. So discussion of the political uses of ICTs will be deferred until Chapter 4. Chapter 2 assesses the democratic character of recent policy making surrounding new information and communication technologies in Canada. The aim here is to assess the participatory, inclusive, and responsive qualities of policy making in this field. Chapter 3 examines the relationship between new ICTs and national culture and sovereignty in Canada. Issues of technology, culture, international capital, and national sovereignty walk hand in hand through the history of communication policy making, scholarship, and activism in Canada. These issues have gained prominence once again in light of the intimate relationship between digital communication technology and globalization. The question addressed in this chapter is whether these dynamics bode well, or ill, for the prospect of an inclusive, participatory, and responsive Canadian democracy.

This provides important context for Chapter 4, which examines the uses to which ICTs have been put by democratic actors in Canada, with specific focus on government, political parties, advocacy groups and social movements, and citizens. Here the intent is to gauge whether digital mediation enhances or undermines the practice of democratic citizenship, according to the criteria of participation, inclusiveness, and responsiveness. Under the heading "Digital Divides," Chapter 5 also provides context for the prospects of democratic uses of ICTs, by examining the role these technologies have played in establishing the material setting in which democratic citizenship might be practiced. Specific attention will be paid here to the relationship between ICTs and the distribution of power in Canada, and to the possibility of the latter's democratization. This chapter examines the digital divide in Canada, the political economy of ICTs, and the role of these technologies in the democratic public sphere. Chapter 6 offers some concluding reflections on the central themes of this portion of the Canadian Democratic Audit.

From Experience to Editorial: Gatekeeping, Agenda-Setting, Priming, and Framing

Paul Nesbitt-Larking

There is little mileage in reporting the safe arrival of aircraft, the continued health of a film star, or the smooth untroubled negotiations of a wage settlement.

— Peter Golding and Philip Elliott[1]

[to American journalists] Why not read a book—about welfare reform, about Russia or China, about race relations, about anything? Why not imagine, just for a moment, that your journalistic duty might involve something more varied and constructive than doing standups from the White House lawn and sounding skeptical?

— James Fallows[2]

For Noam Chomsky and Edward Hermann, the whole matter [of explaining news content] is just that simple: the New York Times *is* Pravda *(and the state apparently little more than a front for the ruling class).*

— Michael Schudson[3]

They've got us putting more fuzz and wuzz on the air, cop-shop stuff, so as to compete not with other news programs but with entertainment programs, including those posing as news programs, for dead bodies, mayhem and lurid tales.

— Dan Rather'[4]

Like any frame that delineates a world, the news frame may be considered problematic. The view through a window depends upon whether the window is large or small, has many panes or few, whether the glass is opaque or clear, whether the window faces a street or a backyard. The unfolding scene also depends upon where one stands, far or near, craning one's neck to the side, or gazing straight ahead, eyes parallel to the wall in which the window is encased.

— Gaye Tuchman[5]

Introduction

News, especially news on television, is at the intersection of politics and the media in Canada. Canada is renowned as a nation of news junkies, who consume vast quantities of information. Some two million of us watch the CBC news each night, and an almost equal number watch the CTV news. This is a substantial proportion of the 30 million inhabitants of the country. Politicians crave news coverage, any coverage if necessary, positive coverage if possible. For the people, television news plays a central role in defining politics. Politics here is much more than the daily interplay of politicians, parties, and pressure groups. It is also the realm of ideology and the broader policy perspectives that are generated from the logic of ideology. (This statement does not imply we should diminish the importance of politics in fictional entertainment.) The matter of how news gets made is critical to thinking about politics and the media in Canada. The nightly news broadcast is a commodity that results from a complex process of manufacture. There are other ways of putting this: Tuchman's book is called *Making News;* Altheide's is *Creating Reality.* Hall and his colleagues theorize "The Social Production of News."[6] They all suggest a process that is at once artificial and creative, rather than natural and functional. The manufacture of news is often compared to the workings of a sausage factory: We may enjoy the product, but the less we know about the process of production the better. If we did know a great deal, we might lose our appetite. But, the more we know about the process, the better able we are to dissect the product and extract the meat, while discarding the gristle. The news and how the news is manufactured, constitute the final stage of the encoding process. Encoding refers to the process by which that vast complex of human experience comes to be resolved down to particular texts. Both the broad political, ideological, and socio-economic forces that shape the context of news production, as well as the narrower microsociological forces at play in media enterprises have a role to play in the conditions of encoding. The news is produced as a series of texts: newspaper articles, radio broadcasts, and television programs. These texts are a complex manifestation of the effects of encoding. In order to be consumed, they are first decoded by the audiences who read them. However, there is no facile correspondence between the "intentions of the encoders" and the "readings of the decoders."

"Good Evening, Nothing Happened Today and That Was The News": The Manufacture of News

What constitutes the news is necessarily a matter of selectivity. The everyday world is extremely complex and multifaceted. That world has to be reduced to 18 pages or 22 minutes of a newscast. How do you tell the story of the world today in 22 minutes? The absurdity of the process of selectivity was illustrated by the ethnomethodological experiment of the California student radio station of the 1960s, which one night began and ended the six o'clock news with the statement: "Good evening, here is the six o'clock news. Nothing happened today." This statement told us two things: First, how much many of us have become news junkies, dependent upon the ritual and the habit of the news text, regardless of its content; and, second, how arbitrary is the choice of what makes news. The very absence of substance was sufficient to prompt us to reflect on the relevance of what might have "happened" had the broadcast told us anything.

Canadian newspapers and broadcasters operate in an advanced capitalist social formation in which a liberal-pluralist ideology is dominant, and in which the regulative and fiscal authority of the state, while still influential, is increasingly questioned. [Those who own and control the media have a vested interest in the maintenance of the current trends.] One does not have to subscribe to elite theory to believe this. Those who own and control the media might not think much about capitalism at all, or they might even have serious reservations about it. Nevertheless, their structured roles as leaders of the media require them to reproduce and enrich their corporations. For those media that remain in the public sector— they, like the CBC, are increasingly in jeopardy—the logic of the system applies regardless of the theoretical absence of bottom-line imperatives. In their book, *Policing the Crisis,* Hall and his colleagues argue that the social production of news is situated in a complex of political, economic, ideological, cultural, and situational/organizational criteria that complexly generate the stories.[7] Hall et al. take into account connections between police, crime statistics, and courts in urban USA and in the UK. We learn how these various agencies amplify, through framing, who become primary and secondary definers of reality. We also learn how the media amplify, through editorials, features, letters, and opinion pieces, and how common sense is appropriated. The work of the media and authorities in amplifying deviancy is situated in a political economy of class conflict, racialized divisions, and the politics of an incipient authoritarian populism. The work of Hall and his colleagues remains an exemplar of how to conduct socially and politically situated media analysis.

The manufacture of the news depends, in part, on the relations between the state and broadcasters. Both formal and informal factors influence what can be said, what is likely to be said, and who is going to get to say it. Factors include: the symbiotic relationship between the media, parties, and politicians; discretionary fiscal policy on the part of the state; executive, judicial, and regulatory agency laws and regulations about the media and their conduct; and news management techniques on the part of political actors. Canadian governments have the capacity, more or less, to regulate, legislate, initiate, inflate, and deflate. Governments, in addition to their awesome regulatory capacity, including regulation of fiscal policy, are among the biggest spenders, and government commissions can be of critical financial importance to the media. Political leaders use timed announcements, planned sound bites, discretion in leaking information, and trial balloons to manipulate coverage. Conversely, the media may use the threat of ignoring individuals or exposing hypocrisy or the workings behind the scenes to control politicians and party strategists.

State media agencies have their own rules of conduct with respect to the news-making process. Such rules have ramifications for the entire tenor of relations between state and media. The CBC journalistic policy statement of 1982, which has not changed in its fundamentals, stresses a liberal and pluralistic view of what constitutes objectivity in covering the news. (Although it is a private agency, the Canadian Press, in its stylebook, has the same conditions. CP realizes there would be political repercussions if it did not follow the accepted practice.) Legislation already exists at the federal and provincial levels to regulate the amount of time and space that can be bought by parties and politicians during elections and referenda. If parliaments wished it, these regulations could be applied to news programming. In fact, newspapers and TV follow their own guidelines with very little deviation. Because CBC covers television and radio, and its personnel are integral to the credibility of the stories they report, the CBC manual goes further than the CP style guide, insisting that its leading and most visible news personnel should sustain a public neutrality and avoid partisanship. The CBC confronted a serious challenge to this policy when one of its senior reporters was accused of failing to maintain his neutrality. The CBC and CP state that their coverage will be "comprehensive, objective, impartial, accurate, balanced and fair." Even a cursory examination on these concepts should alert us to the difficulties inherent in their pursuit. Full objectivity requires the kind of comprehensive apprehension of the world that is virtually impossible to attain. Objectivity in its purest sense implies no omission or distortion. The neo-liberal climate of government cuts and rationalizations in the private sector has resulted in cutbacks in the global reach of both the CBC and CP. Canada's major news agencies, far from becoming more objective, are, for economic reasons, becoming less objective. Whereas full objectivity is not attainable, impartiality implies merely an openness or disinterestedness. However, Canadian media have not been impartial. Instead, they have tended to attempt to achieve a balance that takes into account "all relevant viewpoints." Such viewpoints have rarely strayed far beyond a narrowly conceived centre. In a limited sense, working within this field of consensus is "fair." However, although journalists and organizations may follow the rules of enquiry, invite "both sides" of the issue to comment and verify their sources, they are likely to be operating from cultural and ideological foundations that are systematically biased against certain people, especially those deemed marginal. Even if they were somehow to overcome the implicit ideological limitations and cultural barriers of their social situations, the media would still lack objectivity, according to Edgar.[8] Edgar, working from fundamental philosophical principles, argues that journalism cannot be objective in its attempts to capture events because "that presupposes that an inviolable interpretation of the event as action exists prior to the report."[9] In other words, any interpretation of human action is, by definition, "biased." In offering a version of events, the news media open up interpretations according to the biases of journalists and readers. Critically, the original action is interrupted and overtaken by the mediated account. Other texts and meanings are interwoven in the version offered to the public. There is no solution to such bias other than the continued openness to interpretation and interrogation that comes with good journalism. "Journalism denies its own claim to truth when it forestalls rational argument through strategies that undermine the legitimacy of relevant disputants."[10] Schudson, in a sharp rebuke to professional journalism, argues that the essence of the problem of bias in the media is professionalism itself.[11] American news—and to some extent Canadian news—is negative, cynical, obsessed with strategy and tactics, and dependent on official sources. (These biases instill in the public an apathetic mindset toward politics as a spectator sport, in which politicians, media persons, and other talking heads obsess about "who is winning" or "what went wrong.") The media are not substantively biased in this respect, they are *irrelevant,* and that is far worse. Fallows echoes Schudson's argument.[12]

The propensity of the news media to adopt an ideologically and culturally bound perspective on objectivity narrows the realm of political discourse and privileges the power of the existing state and political regime. The fact that the news operates in a free enterprise capitalist environment is clearly related to the fact that the capitalist system is treated as normal and taken for granted. In most news programming, mention of business and finance is easily and readily identified with the needs of the community as a whole. [The country is said to suffer when labour goes on strike, and labour is said to be holding the country to ransom, but when capital strikes through disinvestment, it is regarded as an act of nature.] [Businessmen speak for something called "the economy," while labour leaders speak only for themselves.] They are regarded as irritants, outsiders, and deviants. Research by Knight and Hackett supports these contentions. Knight explains how the bias of the news media generalizes the interests of the middle and upper class as universal and natural to the society as a whole.'[13] Knight notes that, in reporting labour relations, there is scarcely any mention of capitalism, and the contradictory character of relations between employers and workers, whose interests are fundamentally incompatible (wages versus profits). Instead, the news media report on labour unrest as irrational outbursts by self-interested workers.[14] Knight's research included a content and discourse analysis of the *Toronto Star* and the *Globe and Mail* throughout the 1980 postal strike. Given the individualistic and abstracted nature of the news, labour unrest is invariably depicted as the consequence of union militancy rather than as the outcome of bargaining over fundamentally incompatible claims. ["Workers are said to make 'demands' while employers reply with 'offers.'"[15]] The principal findings of Knight's research include the following: Strikers are constructed as agents of social harm; the strike is explained largely in terms of the motives of the strikers, and accounts are dominated by stories of disruption and inconvenience. Hackett's findings parallel those of Knight.[16] Hackett focused on the CBC and CTV national news during the same time period. Whereas business is portrayed in a range of roles and enterprises normalized as a natural expression of "the economy," workers and trade unions are mentioned almost exclusively in the context of industrial unrest and strikes. According to Hackett: "The workers are portrayed as the active party, a group which must explain why it is so upset, what its 'demands' are, and what disruptive actions it might take in the future."[17] News values assume dominant interpretations of reality and so have no basis to explain strikes other than as explosive and dangerous occurrences. Hackett points out that the world of business generates less visual excitement than the depiction of labour. Business is what we take for granted and do not question. Business just goes on, and there is not much to be said about it, except to those who have a vested interest. Labour is also a matter of routine, and receives hardly any mention at all, general or specific. Only when labour is on strike does it become newsworthy. The term "strike" expresses its news value. A strike appears to be sudden, unexpected, unpredictable, violent, angry, personal, negative, and dangerous. These qualities make for great television news.

The owners of media enterprises are themselves members of the capitalist class and this is said to govern the way editorial staff is chosen and news gets made. However, not a great deal of overt pressure takes place—it is not normally necessary. But the news is entertainment, and if it's not good entertainment, advertisers will pull out and the media enterprise will make insufficient revenue. The acerbic comment of Dan Rather, presented at the beginning of the chapter, illustrates a prevailing mood among serious journalists. The need for advertising revenue results in a commodification of the news process in which entertainment value dominates. There must be conflict and drama, and news items must be short, easy to assimilate, and not too extreme in any way. The entire news show must be timed and structured into a flow that will ensure maximum audiences. Marvin Kalb, former CBS news correspondent and now an academic at Harvard University's Kennedy School of Government, identifies the growing pressures, throughout the 1980s, for TV news to be commercially successful.[18] Since it was discovered, in the late 1970s, that news could make a profit, the focus has become much more strongly oriented to entertainment, with shorter video clips, less in-depth coverage, and greater sensationalism. In Canada the impact of advertising and audience share on the news is evident everywhere. A recent example of the power of economic forces was the decision of the CBC to move the prime time news from 10:00 p.m. to 9:00 p.m. and then back to 10:00 p.m. again, in an effort to enhance market share. CBC's new 24-hour news channel, *Newsworld,* has extended the possibilities for Canadian news coverage. Although the CRTC did not allow the CBC to include satirical shows such as *The Royal Canadian Air Farce* on *Newsworld,* it raised no objection to the arguably farcical extended coverage of the infamous O.J. Simpson arrest and trial. It would be interesting to compare CBC news coverage in 1980 with 1990s to see what else has changed.

The entire output of the media is first conditioned by, and then conditions, the broader culture and the particular, dominant forms of ideology which emerge and decline through hegemonic struggle. There exist at any juncture elements of a broad and diffuse culture as well as partial appropriations in the forms of ideological projects, such as "the Common Sense Revolution" in Ontario. The capacity of ideologies to have an effect is conditioned by the extent to which they become part of the current "regime of signification";[19] that is, the particular combination of dominant and powerful cultural and ideological icons, texts, images, and messages by which the regime is reproduced and modified. The media are at the heart of this system of reproduction of the regime of signification, even when they are not always a key element or when, on occasion, they are out of step—either leading or following—in processes of cultural/ideological change. Political and socio-economic forces emerge in the media through specific practices of encoding, practices which are necessarily and intrinsically cultural and ideological.

In addition to the macrological conditions of encoding the news—the dominant political, economic and ideological/cultural forces described above—the organizational characteristics and imperatives of media organizations play a critical role in the process of encoding the news. State regulation of freedom of speech, the considerations of advertising in the competitive marketplace, and the degree of popularity of neo-liberal ideology all have the potential to shape the news product. Questions of the degree of concentration of media ownership and hierarchies of control existing *within* media enterprises are of potential importance in understanding the exclusion and inclusion of certain cultural and ideological viewpoints in the news. The personnel and the organizational structures and their requirements matter. A great deal of ink has been spilt in recent years in Canada on the former *bête noire* (pun intended) of media concentration, Conrad Black. Media organizations and their personnel are relatively autonomous, since, although they are linked to macrological structures of political, economic, and ideological power, they are never entirely determined or dominated by them. On the simplest level, we need to reject the view that there is some fixed and immutable truth out there, of which the news is a simple distortion. The philosophical work of Edgar on objectivity supports this view. Anthropologist [Clifford Geertz reminds us that social reality is constituted on the basis of a series of "partial truths." Stuart Hall says: "Once the [dominant] definitions come into play, [the media] can give enormous weight to one set of definitions, or one set of labels, and rule out of existence, rule out of reality, push to the margins, other kinds of labels, definitions and descriptions."[20] What causes news personnel to reinforce the dominant definitions is, on the whole, not conspiracy or coercion, but the application of the taken-for-granted and common sense in their practices. In other words, it is business as usual. As Hall points out, it would not do for media professionals to see themselves or to be seen by the public as in league with the rich and powerful, even though this may be the actual effect of their routine practices.

Todd Gitlin concurs with Hall, pointing out that it simply does not occur to media personnel to think outside the dominant frames of ideology of a given time and place: ("They fall into . . . pack journalism, not because they see themselves as agents of the ruling class or anything like that but because they are expressing their honest beliefs that the essential structures are as they should be, that the system is essentially a just one . . .) and that challenges to those ideas are freakish and not to be accorded legitimacy."[21] What are these basic beliefs? In a capitalist society, liberal possessive individualism is at the heart of most of them: that life is what you make it as an individual, and that people tend to get what they deserve. It used to be said in critical media analysis that the nuclear family was another standard accepted ideological credo, but this seems less true today. The image of the middle-class, middle-aged, White suburban couple with two children and a dog is changing, and the media are part of this change in the regime of signification. That there is social change in ideology and representation should alert us to the fact that the media do not support "the status quo." In fact, concepts such as "the status quo," "the powers that be," "the established order," and other such terms convey a false impression of society as entirely unchanging and lacking in dynamism.

How do journalists and editors fit their practices into the evolving cultural and ideological patterns of their time and place? Journalists and editors who conform to the prevailing trends tend to be successful. Mavericks and contrarians have to be exceptionally good in order to be successful. It is not impossible for journalists, directors, editors, and writers to be in advance of social change; but it is a decidedly risky strategy. Before we conclude that media personnel are little more than obsequious toadies, let us remember that they are people who, like us, need to look at themselves in the mirror each morning. Of course, there have been instances of interference, control, and manipulation by media owners and editors in Canada, and these should not be dismissed. There is also evidence of occasional manipulation by powerful advertisers, especially in dealing with small-market media outlets.

The production of news is a matter of planned and predictable patterns. Such patterns exert a strong influence on what is produced. Much news is planned in advance, and many stories are commissioned and/or expected. Data in Canada show that commissioned stories have a much greater chance of being aired on TV than non-commissioned stories. Schlesinger's British research demonstrates that the BBC news is also built largely around planned and predictable news."[22] Up to 90 per cent of news is planned the day before. There is too much coordination and expense to take unnecessary risks with the news. The news media operate with regular news beats and news categories. These include national politics, sports, city hall, the suburban beat, police, society and fashion, provincial parliament, religion, entertainment, finance and business, labour, real estate, education, and science. A certain balance of geographical coverage is important and, of course, focuses come and go, depending upon the trends of the moment. A series of stringers, reporters, correspondents, and assignment editors cover these beats, in combination with regular reports, files, and meetings. These places and events constitute the routine warp and woof of the news. Tuchman refers to stringers as the "fine mesh," reporters as the "tensile strength," and wire services as the "steel links" of the news matrix.[23] News media operate according to strict deadlines. This fact has a great bearing on the character of the news. What gets selected depends on the timing of the news-production process. Marginal stories and coverage may or may not be included, depending upon their technical readiness for dissemination. This gives strong advantage to those with the resources to meet and beat deadlines; they can influence the media by presenting copy that is acceptable for dissemination but too late for much immediate editorial interference. The CP manual states that deadlines, while important, should never compromise reliability. Nevertheless, this frequently occurs. Most news is ahistorical in its emphasis. There may be little in the way of background to a story, few developed themes, little discussion of serious research, and few links to other events and stories. There is little reference to broad socio-economic patterns and forces, and little historical contextualization. The news, in an attempt to be consensual and comprehensible, is often superficial and lacking in challenge. Time constraints and deadlines mean working to stereotypical formulae which may distort the news. Television news as a production raises considerations of presentation, style, personnel, camera angles, multimedia effects, such as graphics, each of which makes a difference to the presentation of reality. Within the predictable and planned nature of the news, the factor that operates to favour one story over another is "news value." The most essential components for news value are novelty and extraordinary characteristics. Hall et al. present us with the ideal type of good news. It is *"unexpected* and *dramatic,* with *negative* consequences, as well as *human tragedies* involving *elite persons* . . . [such as] heads of an extremely *powerful nation."*[24] It helps if the event is visually dramatic, conflictual, violent, novel, bizarre, whimsical, funny, scandalous, and far-reaching in its effects. The most important news is that which is close in spatial and cultural terms to the audience.[25] News items are called "stories," and this label is revealing: They are, to some extent, composites and fabrications—a construction where none existed before—with beginning, middle, end, heroes and villains, conflict and resolution. For a few months in 1998, the lead story on the CBC television news concerned events related to the APEC conference, a minor skirmish and fracas between police and protesters at the University of British Columbia and elsewhere in Vancouver, which resulted in scuffles, minor injuries, but no deaths. The story contained some of the most important elements of newsworthiness. As Alger puts it, the story had "flash, trash and crash."[26] The cliché "if it bleeds, it leads," came to mind as I watched the coverage. It involved conflict, violence, and drama with high emotions, including rage, fear, and shame; there was some great visual footage; and it captured perfectly that blend of the familiar and the bizarre which makes for the best copy.[27] Over the past few years, Canadian television audiences have grown accustomed to a stereotypical, narrow interpretation of radical and student protesters, notably in, British Columbia.

These are the same "troublemakers" previously seen hugging trees and pestering legitimate hunters. In other words, there is a framework for contextualization already in place. This story offers superb footage of tea-cosied and bearded skinny young men and women, with orange and green hair and nose rings, confronting pepper-spray-wielding, militaristic-looking, burly, middle-aged law officers. Putting aside for a moment the purely televisual attraction of the story, we need to ask why it made it to the lead item for so many nights. Why this story? We can certainly make a case for its importance and implications, not the least of which is the central issue of basic democratic rights in Canada, but why *this* story and not others? The job of the news media in making the news is to transform a complex series of events into a news package the audience can understand. This means that the story must be placed within a frame of meanings familiar to the audience. News personnel must take what is unexpected, novel, and unexplained, and dispense it in a manner that is both easy to understand and logical. In so doing, the news media clearly display their assumptions about both the audience and the wider society. The task of the media personnel is made easier in a number of ways. The use of stereotypes assists in rendering the unfamiliar explicable. Many newsmakers rely on their own instincts and gut feeling to get them through. An exploration of such taken-for-granted or common sense understanding on the part of most successful news people in Canada shows them to be moderately conventional, middle-class, and cautious. This is why the news is usually framed in such a way that what is stable, normal, decent, comprehensible, and predictable is anchored at the heart of the TV broadcast.

Dramatis Personae of the Great News Story: Lead Roles and Bit Parts

Many media professionals would object to the account just given. They would not recognize themselves in it and would state that by clearly and distinctly differentiating "facts" from "opinions," they offer news audiences both straight, mirror-like reportage and a broad range of popular opinion. Tuchman argues that it is difficult for media personnel to see themselves as embedded in a complex of structured relations that condition their output. Many, apart from their professional defensiveness, do not appreciate the point because their own frames of understanding and practices accustom them to assuming they are neutral. Tuchman points out that media personnel are very touchy about objectivity and have developed rituals of practice to defend themselves against attacks on their professional ethics.[28] Defensive strategies include the presentation of both sides of the story, especially if certain facts cannot be verified; the presentation of supporting evidence, i.e., stronger facts to back up weaker facts; the judicious use of quotation marks to separate expressed opinion from the reporter's own; the use of "expert" opinion; and the presentation of the most important facts—the five Ws—first in a story (this is especially true in print, where the inverted pyramid structure is used). The reality for Tuchman is that claims of objectivity, given the incredible pressures of deadlines, are mere rituals which cover news professionals against attacks on their bias. News professionals may appear unbiased, but are only being "fair" in a narrow sense. If the rule is that rioters, unemployed people, or foreigners do not get a voice, then it is quite objective to avoid them. It is also, of course, biased. If the rule is that the media give audiences their best attempt at the pure facts, this opens the media and their audiences to the possibility of being manipulated. Frequently, politicians put a misleading spin on a story. If the media were merely to report it, with no background or commentary, that spin would go unchallenged. The media, under these circumstances, are obliged to report not just the apparent story, but also the circumstances under which it took place, exposing the spinning practices of the politicians. Of course, this is not neutral either. The media cannot win here. Another convenient way of producing news in a hurry is to rely on experts. Despite the fact that the quoting of experts accentuates the tendency of the media to replicate a narrow range of significations, the idea "saves" journalists from the accusation of bias. If an expert said it, it must be true. The experts become the so-called "primary definers" (Hall) who set the agenda. Ideas outside of their primary definitions will be ridiculed and ignored. According to Tuchman, low status sources are portrayed as less reliable, more transient, and less relevant in order to defend the media against attacks of not being objective.

Behind the production of the news is a factory-like enterprise, the "sausage factory," introduced in Chapter Seven. Any factory depends upon the synergy of its personnel. In the introduction to the book, I offered the following itemization: the suppliers of the raw material, the builders of the machinery, the suppliers of liquid capital, the owners, the bosses, the workers, the semi- and unemployed, the state inspectors, preferred and general customers, and those affected by "externalities."

The suppliers of the raw materials of news are the people whose daily practices produce the requisite news value to be registered as eligible for inclusion. The general principle is that the more elevated the social status of the person, the greater the demand for raw material. Politicians, rich people, celebrities, and eccentrics feature prominently, while ordinary people, notably women, aboriginal people, poor people, and union members are of interest mainly as aggregates or collectivities. When it comes to collectivities of interest to the news media, the richer and better-organized interest groups, institutions, and corporations have better access. They can buy access through investment in sophisticated media relations personnel and public relations companies. Even without these commercial advantages, their views tend to be solicited more often. In the context of news values, these elite individuals and groups matter more than other people.[29] Elite persons are the primary definers. These include politicians, business people, academics, and experts, such as scientists. These people occupy a strategic position in the media because they define the basic parameters of the story. It is their reality that becomes the benchmark. Martin identifies secondary news sources as ordinary people, including oppositional groups, and "victims" in a story.[30] They provide filler to support the news narrative. Thus we get the familiar *vox populi* of "the man in the street," or the inevitable "how do you feel" question demanded of the victim at the crime scene. Martin's typology also registers those voices excluded from most news coverage as "tertiary" sources. These include aboriginal people and poor people. Based on their 1996 survey of the CBC *The National* news program, Austman reported that 84 per cent of news sources were men and 89 per cent were elite occupations. Those few cases in which women were granted access as sources tended to be in areas of "soft" news or social news items stereotypically related to women.[31] MediaWatch conducted a comparable survey of Canadian newspapers that discovered women were underemployed as sources of information, experts, and newsmakers. In their 1993 data, the percentage of women as sources, experts, or newsmakers in Canada's daily newspapers varied from 18 to 28 per cent.[32] Hackett and Gruneau say: "The gender imbalance in sources is strongly related to the media's long-standing focus on political and institutional authorities, who are still largely male."[33] Knight concurs with the analysis of Hackett and Gruneau adding the following useful insight about the reception of social movements, such as the women's movement:

> Social movements are not accorded such legitimacy as credible news sources as more formalized organizations, largely because they do not possess bureaucratic—institutional structures and are therefore assumed to be transient, less reliable, and simply less important.[34]

The builders of the news machinery are predominantly the technical operatives who make it possible for experience to be converted into editorial. Their routines are structured and determined for the most part by the media managers who orchestrate the daily-news gathering enterprise. The degree of political discretion or autonomy of such operatives is limited, although their work has distinctly political overtones. Deadlines and the demand for good news values shape the technological characteristics of newsgathering. The speed and expertise with which operatives record, edit, transcribe, splice, create a backdrop, and find persons willing to speak on camera condition the extent to which the vision of the media managers and directors can be realized. There has been no research into the political consequences of conformity, adaptation, and subversion among media technicians. It would be interesting to explore such issues in the context of evolving news-gathering techniques. Video and audio technique is intrinsic to the crafting of realistic effects in the new genres of faction, docudrama, reality television, and infotainment. Decisions about where to place a camera, when to pan or zoom, and how to introduce sound are critical to the achievement of political effect.

The suppliers of liquid capital are those who invest in and purchase the services of media enterprises. Many large media enterprises are public companies with many shareholders. They expect the corporation to be competitively profitable. They also expect conformity to the principles of liberal capitalism. Murdock states that "The routine practices of news production and the professional assumptions which support them are circumscribed by the general economic and political context within which news organizations are embedded."[35] The climate established by these expectations conditions the character of all programming, including news programming. If the viewing public favours infotainment, then the complaints of Dan Rather, Lloyd Robertson, and other senior journalists about the professional quality of news broadcasting are unlikely to be effective. Advertisers buy time during news broadcasts and in newspapers and, it is argued, buy the audiences that go with such media. Advertisers rarely attempt to interfere in the editorial policy of newspapers, but it does happen. What is of greater concern are the possibilities for self-censorship that exist among senior media personnel. If a large automobile manufacturer is a major advertiser, editors will think twice before running a story on a major recall of vehicles. The sheer necessity of running advertisements during news broadcasts changes the character of the program flow, thereby introducing subtle changes into the reception of the news. Although it is possible only to speculate about this matter, it is arguable that growing commercialization puts pressure on the average length of news items and reduces the possibility for the kind of extended coverage necessary to include a measure of analysis.

The principal owners of the media are able to dictate the tone and content of news coverage by selecting, promoting, and firing editorial staff. Owners, through their statements, set the tone for the overall pattern of coverage. Black and Radler of Hollinger/Southam are intolerant of dissent. They don't need to tell editors what to publish; their intentions are clear. On occasion, Black likes to write an editorial for his newspapers and thereby has an unedited outlet for his views. It seems unlikely that Izzy or Leonard Asper will feel so inclined now that CanWest Global has taken over most of the Hollinger and Southam empire.

The bosses are the editors, directors, and others who are in the employ of the owners and are answerable to the board of directors. They must be sensitive to the sensibilities of the owners. However, they are also media professionals who take pride in their craft. They are responsible for supervising the implementation of standard editorial control and for ensuring that accepted principles of objectivity, fairness, and balance are followed. It is possible for an editor to insist on scrupulous standards of professionalism that nonetheless implicate their media enterprises in biased and ideologically driven reportage. Schudson's assault on Chomsky and Hermann, which is extracted at the beginning of the chapter, is a much-needed corrective to their elite theoretical model of "propaganda."[36] As Schudson points out, the *New York Times* is not *Pravda,* and the differences are of critical importance. The editors of the *New York Times* are not told what to write, and they do not subscribe to any party line. They do not live in fear of publishing something that does not follow the correct party line. Although the spectrum of debate is limited, the American media are part of a national dialogue in which distinct voices and policy preferences are aired. Pat Robertson and Jessie Jackson are not the same. American papers must be attentive to their readers' interests. Nevertheless, editors of newspapers are usually promoted because of their success in meeting the expectations of owners, boards, and senior advertisers. They are accustomed to mixing with influential members of society, and are comfortable as members of the elite. Fallows would say that they are too comfortable in this role.[37] Editors and managers, therefore, are likely to be conventional and supportive of mainstream cultural and ideological values. Although they may tolerate dissent and diversity, it is always within their power not to do so.

The workers of the news media are the journalists and correspondents who do the news gathering and presentation. In many news organizations, senior reporters and presenters are better described as bosses than as workers. Senior news anchors in the USA command huge salaries and have become celebrities in their own right. In Canada, the ranks of such elite journalists are thinner, but a small number does exist. Journalists in Canada have been socialized to accept the principal cultural and ideological values, and tend to think within these parameters. Journalist education does little to facilitate critical and referential thinking. Canadian journalists are successful to the extent that they relate to prevailing norms and ideals and are able to articulate them. It is much easier to affirm the ideas and values of an audience than to challenge them. This does not mean, however, that journalists are mere mouthpieces of a single dominant ideology. There is diversity, doubt, and even dysfunction in the patterns of journalistic production, and there is space for journalistic creativity and contribution. Nevertheless, both Curran and Tuchman point out that news professionals tend to speak the language of the elites and institutional authorities. Journalists find it easier to go to accredited sources for information rather than to seek out a more difficult and less certain path to the truth. As Tuchman argues, such reliance on institutional authority shapes the news: "The New York City Police wire . . . does not carry stories about corporate crime, or does not carry stories about illegal takeovers or tax fraud."[38] The values and ideals of journalists are often apparent in what they choose to ignore, downplay, or ridicule. When it began in the late 1960s, the women's movement was the topic of extensive media ridicule, including news programming. Journalists are workers subject to the same processes of deskilling, downgrading, workplace alienation, and other forms of occupational oppression experienced by most workers. The craft of the journalist has been eroded by new communications technology, notably the word processor and satellite communications. These technologies have facilitated the downgrading of local reportage and have favored a bland and formulaic uniformity in style and presentation. The workplaces of journalists are increasingly regimented and regulated. The discretion and scope afforded to practicing journalists has been reduced considerably. A gap is emerging between those few journalists at the top, who are granted high salaries and occupational privileges, and the rest, who increasingly are subject to part-time, limited-term contracts in which "journalism" consists of little more than painting by numbers.[39]

The semi-employed and unemployed include lesser reporters, part-timers, and stringers, who are increasingly responsible for doing the groundwork of news reporting. There are few women working in newsrooms, but they predominate in the lower ranks. Martin says: "The business people who control news production, that is those who control the social definition of news—editors, wire service owners, newspaper owners, desk editors, reporters—are generally men."[40] While the situation has been improving somewhat, the proportion of women, ethnic minorities, and aboriginal people engaged in news production or who are called upon as experts or commentators remains low.

State inspectors are the official and unofficial monitors who ensure that the news media adhere to laws and regulations. In Canada, a number of government departments, such as Canada Post, Revenue Canada, Elections Canada, and crown agencies, such as the CRTC, conduct ongoing surveillance, intervention, and consultation at the federal level. There is also a number of provincial departments and agencies involved in the media in general and in the news media in particular. The courts are also implicated in the work of the media from time to time. The actions of these state agencies and persons have a direct bearing on the practices and texts of news production in Canada. In addition to this formal state intervention, a number of governmental, partisan and political organizations monitor the media and attempt to shape what becomes news.

Who are preferred and general customers? According to Smythe's logic, it is advertisers who are the customers of the media. However, it is more conventional to think of audiences as the consumers. In the construction or manufacture of news, the tastes and preferences of audiences must be kept in mind. All television programming, including news programming, is carefully tested prior to dissemination. Invited audiences and focus groups are tested for their reactions to formats, hosts, and content. Audiences vote with remote control devices or with their pocketbooks, in the case of daily newspapers. News media are obliged to pay attention to the numbers. With the proliferation of channels of information and the broadening range of media sources, it is now increasingly possible for news media to aim for a specific audience. General news broadcasts hope to appeal to a large number of viewers. In Canada, such broadcasts go out on CBC, CTV, and Global CanWest. Other channels offer local news, often action-oriented. A range of specialty channels offers news programming tailored to the interests of a particular market segment. There are broadcasts for those who want serious news commentary at the provincial, or federal level, or in the USA. There are news programs for women, aboriginal people, youth, and other demographic groups. In addition, Canadian cable and satellite television imports a range of infotainment channels from the USA.

Externalities occur when the process of manufacturing has an impact on those not directly related to producing or purchasing the commodity. An externality of a steel company might be pollution to the environment surrounding the plant. People not involved in the industry are nonetheless affected by it. Similarly, news programming largely dismissed the women's movement in the late 1960s and early 1970s. Epstein reports that NBC news would often finish a news broadcast with a "light" story poking fun at "women's libbers."[41] Tuchman makes a similar point in her work on media coverage of the women's movement.[42] Women in general continue to be affected by the extent of and nature of coverage in news programming. Since audiences regard the news as "a window on the world," the ways in which groups are portrayed is a matter of potential importance. Winter's careful research on the portrayal of aboriginal issues in Canada reveals the depths of the problem.[43]

Irascible Mr. Gates and the Gatekeepers

The process by which the complex mass of world events gets reduced to the 22-minute broadcast includes elements of "gatekeeping." Communication can be characterized as a flow, and the concept of channel connotes a kind of conduit or stream. The image of the gatekeeper is consistent with this metaphor of communication as flow. The gatekeeper is the person who controls the flow; reducing the huge gushes and tides of information to neat little cups of water that come out of the tap. The concept of the gatekeeper emerges in White's 1950 article, "The 'Gatekeeper': A Case Study in the Selection of News."[44] The originator of the term was sociologist Kurt Lewin.[45] White refers to the process of news selection as involving a range of players: "From reporter to rewrite man, through bureau chief to 'state' file editors at various press association offices, the process of choosing and discarding is continuously taking place."[46] White investigates the final and most important gatekeeper, the wire editor. This is the person who selects all national and international news to go on the front and "jump" (that is, continuation) pages. White asked one wire editor to record a week's decision-making, stating what he included and excluded from the wire and why. He called his wire editor "Mr. Gates." Mr. Gates rejected ninety per cent of what came to him. His grounds for rejection in the main were twofold: First, the incident was not worth reporting; second, the report was a duplicate and not as good as the one chosen. In exploring his criteria for rejecting stories as not worthy for inclusion, Gates apparently avoided radical material, sensationalized or insinuating accounts, stories with too many figures or statistics, and those he just found dull. There is something refreshingly frank about this description of acceptance and rejection. The criteria seem to complement a range of ideological and cultural prejudices with a dose of idiosyncratic arbitrariness in decision-making which approximates what journalists call "a good nose for news."

Gieber expanded White's project in 1956.[47] Gieber added to his list of gatekeepers persons other than news professionals, notably those informants at the source of the story and those readers of the story in the audience. Gieber discovered that wire or telegraph editors were highly conventional and task-oriented bureaucrats who minimized risk. These editors were passive, unconcerned with the work of the reporters, uncritical of the relative quality of the wire copy coming in, and lacking in any real perception of the audience. This bureaucratic mindset filtered down to the reporters, who seemed to be captives both of the bureaucratic needs of their superiors and, in a related manner, of the interests and perspectives of the high-powered sources they reported on. Gieber concluded that gatekeepers operate in an environment in which they are driven by the bureaucratic needs of the newspaper as well as the need to echo the outlook of the powerful. They come across as small-minded, conservative, and uncritical persons.

Who are the principal gatekeepers in the media? In terms of television, the owners and chief executive officers, if they wish; but more often, the presidents and vice-presidents of news divisions, managing editors or executive producers, news directors and, lower down the scale, assignment editors. Some of the more influential news anchors also play a gatekeeping role. In the newspapers, the executive editors, managing editors, and various section and area editors are the key gatekeepers. The concept of gatekeeping is less popular in media analysis today than it was in the 1950s and 1960s. Tuchman is only one of a number of scholars who find the concept unenlightening. In conversation with David Cayley, she says: "It seems to me the (gatekeeper theory) is a ridiculous theory, because newspeople . . . are not passive tollgate (keepers) . . . You didn't wait for me. You came down here (to New York to interview me). Newspeople are actively making something; they're having a say."[48] With respect to White's version of the theory, Tuchman has a point. If one tries to explain the manufacture of news in terms of the workings of passive and reactive sluice gates, then, clearly, it is an inadequate account. However, the kind of conventional and task-oriented passivity identified by Gieber is a vivid and plausible description of the constraints of working as a media professional. Passivity is, in fact, an extension of the very defensive strategies Tuchman so well describes elsewhere in her work. The concept of the gatekeeper contains within it the important factor of selectivity, regardless of which agents are most involved in making these choices.

French sociologist of the media Pierre Sorlin points out that "Absence or silence are also ideological."[49] In other words, what remains unspoken or unrecognized is as critical as what is spoken and recognized. Hackett and Gruneau have researched the issue of what is missing from Canadian news. Their findings alert us to the kinds of stories that do not make it into print or onto our screens. Corporate ties to political power, pollution, white collar crime, human rights abuses by countries with which Canada has extensive trading relations, and the exploitation of domestic workers in Canada are examples of major news items that were ignored or downplayed by the Canadian media in the 1990s.[50] In general, stories concerning the abuse of power by the powerful and the oppression of those who lack power are most likely to be ignored. A large number of important stories about women or poor people have been under-reported.[51] Hackett and Gruneau detect a general lack of depth in the coverage of social and political background forces. They draw particular attention to the inadequate coverage of stories concerning domestic violence against women.[52]

Agenda Benders? What Gets To Be Political?

The concept of gatekeeping is used to describe the range of controls over the channels of input into the media enterprise, and how the processes of selection take place. It implies a relatively uncreative and passive—if powerful—role on the part of the media professional. Agenda-setting, framing, and priming are terms used to describe the creative and deliberate packaging and presentation of reality. Gatekeeping studies are interested in the input process. Agenda-setting, priming, and framing studies are interested in the outputs. Lippmann, in his *Public Opinion,* first suggested there is a close connection between the political content of newspapers and the political ideas of the reading public.[53] Lippmann proposed that people's menu of issues for political discussion was to be found in the selections made by the media; that the press determine what people think about and talk about.

Shaw and McCombs conducted the best-known contemporary studies in agenda-setting, in the 1960s and 1970s. In a study of undecided voters in North Carolina in the 1968 presidential election, Shaw and McCombs found strong evidence of a close relationship between the political issues emphasized by the news media and the issues the voters regarded as important issues.[54] McLeod, Becker, and Byrnes studied the American presidential election of 1972.[55] They conducted a content analysis of two newspapers in Madison, Wisconsin, one liberal, the other conservative. The conservative newspaper devoted more space to American world leadership and the need to combat crime, while the liberal paper attended to the Vietnam War and honesty in government. Among older readers interviewed in the city, there was strong support for the hypothesis that each paper had set the readers' agenda. The rank ordering of issues among older readers of the papers was close to the order set by the paper in terms of its ideological tendency. Among younger readers, the relationship was present also, but was much weaker. In general, the researchers found the lower the political interest and the greater the dependency on the paper as a source of information, the stronger the influence of the agenda set. This finding supported the research of McCombs and Shaw. McCombs has recently updated his research findings on agenda-setting. An impressive array of studies in content analysis, survey research, and experimental studies now provides both internal and external validation to research findings in agenda-setting.[56] McCombs, refining his original ideas somewhat, reports that voters with high political interest combined with a high degree of uncertainty on the issues are the most likely to be influenced by the agenda set in the media.

In the Canadian context, Black and his colleagues, in the late 1970s, discovered some intriguing relationships between three small-town newspapers and the agendas of their municipalities.[57] The media paid more attention to the emotional and conflictual issues that met with the requirements of news value, while the councillors were more interested in routine budgetary and economic development matters. Although the agenda of the papers and the decision-makers diverged substantially in all three cases, there were some interesting examples of how the local paper could side with a faction on council or a group of local ratepayers to promote a particular issue. For instance, the anti-establishment mayor of Peterborough was able to provide consultants' reports and official papers to the *Peterborough Examiner* before they got to other council members and their businessman-development supporters.

A more critical investigation of the agenda-setting process shows it to be more than merely one-way. Katz's important research on the two-step flow indicates the importance of opinion leaders. The cultivation research project of Gerbner and colleagues stresses the long-term aspects of agenda-setting. Katz and Gerbner oblige us to reflect on the possibility that there is more going on in the agenda-setting process than the pure relationship between media and audience. In fact, such linear and monocausal thinking is always in need of critique. Fallows raises the important question of the nature of the content of agenda-setting.[58] His contention is that the media really do not set an agenda, other than their own limited version of the political game. Ordinary citizens are obliged to follow such idle insider speculation even though they would rather talk about the issues that matter to them, such as taxation and social programs. According to Fallows, journalists have become too rich, complacent, and too isolated from the lives of everyday Americans to be of much relevance. Their ignorance and indolence contribute to growing public cynicism about politics and the media in general.

Priming and Framing in the Construction of News

The classic assumption of agenda-setting research is that, although the media tell us what to think about, they cannot tell us how to think about it. Recent research in the field of framing argues the reverse: that the media do in fact tell us how to think about issues. McCombs and Shaw claim that "journalists' . . . perspectives direct attention toward certain attributes [of issues] and away from others."[59] Tuchman's explanation of framing suggests that we need to go beyond the simple fact that a picture has been painted for us to ask whose eyes are looking? Where are they looking and not looking? What are they really seeing? What are they missing, ignoring, or distorting? Whom are they standing next to as they look? What is their perspective? On the basis of these considerations, the naïve journalistic edict to report just "the facts" can often lead to distortion. To the extent that political leaders have become skilful in the presentation of themselves and events in which they have a stake, it is important for news professionals to offer a frame for analysis. Unless there is critical commentary on the manipulative tactics of the political actors being reported on, their frame will be dominant by default.

The practice of framing directs our attention to a limited set of attributes concerning an issue or person, and therefore away from others. The best way to conceive of framing is to join Tuchman in thinking metaphorically of a window on the world and the perspective it gives us. The concept of "priming" is often used interchangeably with framing. Priming encourages people to pay attention to some factors at the expense of others. To be primed means to be provided with cues as to what is important. A distinction can be drawn between the denotations of the terms. Whereas framing describes the manner in which the media conceptualize an issue or person in general, priming suggests a more targeted and focused attempt to condition audience and reader response. For example, a newspaper might frame an election as "the immigration election," even though it is about more than that. Readers might then be primed to regard immigrants as a social, economic, and criminal "problem."

Recent and comprehensive research by Iyengar and Kinder, employing experiments, surveys, and statistical records of media content and issues, finds evidence of framing or priming as they sometimes call it.[60] An example of what they mean is the propensity of television news to frame crime and poverty stories exclusively in episodic terms. Crime and poverty are presented as isolated and seemingly random incidents. Such a mode of presentation primes the audience to regard these issues in terms of individual responsibility and irrationality rather than in terms of social causality and explicable structural explanations. Canadian studies in priming include those of McQuaig and Knight and O'Connor. McQuaig's analysis is journalistic rather than academic, but is well researched and persuasive.[61] McQuaig offers an analysis of a particular edition of the Canadian television documentary *W5* in which the radical neo-liberal strategy of the New Zealand government of the mid-1980s is held up as a model for Canada as it confronts its debt crisis. McQuaig offers a skilful deconstruction of the program's frame of the New Zealand experiment as Canada's "only option," and refers to the negative consequences of the turn to the right in New Zealand that *W5* missed altogether. Knight and O'Connor conducted a detailed content analysis of the *Toronto Star* and the *Globe and Mail* throughout the early years of the NDP government in Ontario and their treatment of the NDP's industrial relations legislation.[62] The study records the pro-business framing of the issue during the two-year period leading up to the passage of the Ontario Labour Relations Act in 1993. Each newspaper identified the business view as the "general" one and associated labour and workers with violence, disruption, greed, anger, and demands. Strikes were associated with disruption, with business as the victim, regardless of the validity of the workers' claims. "Organized labour did have views . . . about how to tackle the issues of 'the economy.' What it lacked, however, was the same credibility and authority to speak for the economy that the media accorded organized business."[63]

It is apparent that substantial numbers of people employ strategies of resistance to encounter the media and their "preferred readings." Hall, when watching the news, operates on the basis of "another framework which tells me: 'When he says that, what he really means is. . . .' So I'm constantly *deconstructing* what the news media have constructed for me."[64] Hall is not alone in his skill and propensity to deconstruct. The discursive reasoning of ordinary members of audiences should not be underestimated. Graber supports this perspective and so does Fiske. Graber says that "Consumers . . . round out and evaluate news in light of past learning and determine how well it squares with the reality that they have experienced directly or vicariously."[65] Fiske refers to the propensity for news programming to be distant from people's everyday lives and therefore fail to connect with what viewers regard as relevant. They might watch halfheartedly, but not commit the information and insight to long-term memory.[66] Adopting a strong reader-oriented perspective, Fiske argues against the concept of preferred readings inherent in the textual structure, and therefore against the power of encoding as such.[67] This overstates the case in my opinion. Nevertheless, Fiske is justified in his insistence on the power of the social context of viewing and that meaning is never inherent merely in the abstracted act of watching the television screen.

Framing and priming suggest powerful tools in the hands of the media and their personnel to propose and prompt. However, there are limits to the extent to which the media can condition our responses. We have other sources of insight and information. The media do not always work in concert with those in positions of power and influence in Canadian society. In fact, there is an ongoing struggle for ascendancy between the media and the political actors.

There's No Business Like Snow Business: Politicians, Media Professionals, Sound Bites, and Photo Opportunities

Television has changed the character of political leadership everywhere. Canada's recent prime ministers provide excellent examples of the impact of the medium. As Taras explains, the relationship between television and prime ministers has been both symbiotic and subtle as it has evolved since the 1960s.[68] Modern styles of campaigning in Canada began with the Liberal Party in the late 1950s and early 1960s. A group of influential young liberals, including Martin Goldfarb and Keith Davey, began to import American-style electoral techniques into Canada.[69] By the election of 1974, the Liberals were employing basic media control techniques. These included restricting access to the prime minister to fixed announcements and the release of announcements from the Liberal Party so late that the media could not edit or comment on them. The media felt they were used in this election and were determined not to let it happen again. They became much cannier in 1979 and beyond.

American scholars Jamieson and Campbell, in their book, *The Interplay of Influence*, identify a number of ways in which politicians and the media seek to control each other, particularly in election periods.[70] Both media and politicians have had to learn how to play the game and manipulate coverage. Moreover, they must demonstrate the manipulative tactics of the other side, while keeping their own hidden. The principal tactics on the part of the politicians include attempting to control the gates, either by limiting information or by flooding so much that the media gatekeepers lack the time and resources to process the information. If the political agenda of the politician is heavy, rich in detail, and timed so late for media coverage that media organizations can add little commentary or editing, then the message of the political actor will emerge very much as the politician would like it to. If the political message is negative for the politician or party, a series of diversionary tactics can be employed. The announcement can be timed to avoid media coverage—late on a Friday afternoon in the summer is a good time—or any negativity can be concealed in the context of a larger, more positive announcement. If a party must report low figures in the polls, it may choose to announce these following a press conference in which there is enthusiastic endorsement of a new platform by a number of high-profile individuals. Politicians who wish to hide negative news may attempt to stonewall the media or "hide" from them. However, such strategies often backfire on the individual, making them look weak and indecisive. Among the first rules of public relations is never to say "no comment" to a journalist's probing question. "Spin doctors" are increasingly employed to "explain" events and issues to journalists and the media in ways that maximize the benefit and minimize the damage to a politician. Spin doctors are public relations experts who know how to convert disaster into salvation and modest success into supreme triumph. A good spin doctor is able to parlay a lackluster and pedestrian performance in a leadership debate into something that sounds much more purposeful and coherent. ("This is a candidate who has a statesmanlike grasp of the issues, who really knows how to listen to the people and who does not need to cover up his ignorance with flashy one-liners and negative put-downs.")

A major tool in the arsenal of a party or politician is control of access. When the status of the person or prestige of the party is high, the media crave access to information and insight and, conversely, fear denial of such access. Sympathetic media personnel are likely to enjoy a more favoured status. Such persons might be rewarded with a judicious "leak." These unofficial announcements made prior to the official statement give the chosen media and journalists a much-needed "scoop" and generate the impression that the newspaper or channel is "in the know." This kind of leaking is related to the concept of the "trial balloon" and is becoming more common in recent years. Many announcements made by Canadian politicians and parties are now known in advance, at least in their broad outlines. The trial balloon provides politicians with useful time and political space for plausible deniability. For example, a minister of finance who leaks details of a substantial tax increase in a forthcoming budget will monitor the response of general and interested publics. If the response is relatively muted, the minister can go ahead and implement the policy. If, however, there is an outcry, the policy can be adapted, modified, or even abolished in time for the formal announcement. Regardless of which way he or she will ultimately go, the minister will respond to journalists' questions with denials, evasions, and suggestions during the trial balloon period. The media themselves will not be neutral in this process. Attempting to balance their own editorial policy with their perception of the emerging public opinion on the issue, they will take editorial stances and report the news in certain ways that contribute to the unfolding decision.

Access to politicians can be controlled directly by press secretaries and other personnel. In media interviews and profiles, the more powerful politicians can insist upon editorial control and management of questions and image in the interview situation. This applies to television, radio, and newspapers. In organizing public meetings and other venues, the party and politician can make demands concerning setting, scripts, camera angles, editing, and other critical issues of appearance. Leadership debates are a complex forum for such negotiations. In American politics, the control of image has been a matter of critical importance since the 1960s. Today, a popular choice of genre among politicians is the chat show. Arsenio Hall, Larry King, and David Letterman have each provided powerful sites for the presentation of the political self by a succession of American candidates. In these contexts, the candidates appear relaxed, informal, familiar, and attractive. They are guaranteed an easy ride and are never ambushed with awkward questions. So far, Canadian politicians have been unable to make use of such opportunities since there is little of this kind of programming in Canada. A number of politicians have chosen to appear on the gently *Royal Canadian Air Farce* and seem to have benefitted from the exposure. Other Canadian politicians have been ambushed by *This Hour has 22 Minutes*, a more acerbic satirical show. While serious journalists continue to meet with politicians to discuss the issues in Canada, the trend seems to be to move away from the straight interview format of the past and toward the politics of image-making. How far the political culture and ideological mix of Canada will sustain these developments is an open and interesting question: Will Jean Chrétien, Joe Clark, Gilles Duceppe, Alexa McDonough, and Stockwell Day start appearing on *Open Mike* with Mike Bullard?

The world of instant communication has complicated the already-strained relationship between the media and politicians. Often television can be there to make the news by reporting on events as they unfold and then getting the immediate reaction of politicians to them. Sometimes, they can actually change the course of the crisis, drama, or conflict by strategically locating themselves in the flow of information. Taras illustrates this in his article, "The Mass Media and Political Crisis."[71] Taras notes that each team has its own experts, informants, and spin doctors. With skill in the management of access, leaks, plants, and other techniques, politicians can use the media effectively. Of course, in rolling the dice in this manner, a great deal depends on precise timing, impression management, and the presentation of face, and things can backfire.

I use the phrase "rolling the dice" advisedly. These were the three words that contributed to the failure of Prime Minister Mulroney at Meech Lake in the last-gasp meetings of June 1990. The phrase itself comes from a statement Mulroney gave to Susan Delacourt in June, 1990, about his intentions concerning the process of hard negotiation with other first ministers during the final days before the expiration of the time allowed to make a deal. The phrase was typical of Mulroney's discourse in that it was boastful and elitist. He probably did not mean to sound this way, but the phrase betrayed the "smoke-filled room" atmosphere of boys meeting behind closed doors that helped to scuttle the deal. More importantly, in that week-long, crisis-ridden series of meetings, the prime minister told the CBC that the failure of Meech portended the end of the country. The CBC was accused of contributing to the false sense of drama by their technique of hovering outside the Conference Centre in Ottawa and relaying Mulroney's impressions as if they were the gospel truth. If there was indeed a national crisis, then the CBC had a duty to follow the prime minister. But some argued that the critics of Meech Lake should have been allowed their say and that the CBC allowed itself to be too readily convinced by the crisis agenda of the prime minister.

While the media crave politicians and need them to generate their texts, the reverse is also true. The relationship can be described metaphorically as symbiotic. Politicians need the media in order to disseminate their views. Consequently, politicians must work within the parameters of news value and according to media schedules and preferences in order to be noticed. The media, feeling they had been conned in 1974 by the Liberal Party, covered the 1979 election campaign with greater resolve. They placed more of their tough-minded reporters on election coverage, and gave them instructions to report on party tactics, particularly media manipulation tactics. Attempts by the Liberal party and others to put a spin on something, or failure to release information until it was too late to broadcast without comment or editing, would now themselves be commented on. Additionally, the media sought broader and more independent sources of research to challenge what the parties gave them. All this led to a greater intensification of media commitment.

Despite their efforts to steer the agenda back to relevance, the media have been accused of narrowing and limiting the political debate through a range of routine news practices. In 1980 Fletcher said: "The most effective means for party leaders to reach the voters is to play by the media rules. In the television era, these rules inhibit thoughtful exposition of policies and promote simple and flashy promises and one-line put-downs of the opposition. Even when policies are effectively set out, the quips often grab the headlines. The sugar coating swallows up the pill."[72] Because reporters tend to know little of the issues, background, ideology, or workings of the parties, coverage is superficial. The media, making crude use of polls, resort to horse-race coverage, that is who is winning. Since the major parties tend to receive coverage, the media implicitly support the dominant political forces. There is too much emphasis on the leaders and their personalities and insufficient emphasis on parties and issues. These matters were of great concern to the authors of the Lortie Commission report of 1991. The media can exert influence by agenda-setting, that is, by identifying matters which should be on the public agenda, and/or through framing and priming, that is, identifying the appropriate criteria for evaluation of persons, policies, or actions. Although there is evidence of the power of priming, notably by accentuating the negative qualities of politicians and their ideas, agenda-setting does not seem to be a force in Canadian politics. In general, the media follow faithfully the agenda set by the parties and even, according to Fletcher, allow the parties to get away with empty sloganeering and vague promises instead of questioning their stands on issues. There is little evidence of the media attempting to get matters onto the political agenda when they are not already there in the broader public debate. The media can, however, limit and control the capacity of politicians and parties to promote their own agenda. As does any intelligent citizen, the media can multiply their sources of information and expertise. When politicians and parties attempt to rush their versions of events into print and onto air, the media can insist on adequate briefing time. If the politicians argue that there is no time, then the media can call their bluff and not cover the item in the news. Much depends upon who has the greater need at the time, the media or the politician. Media personnel can "just say no" to unreasonable requests and demands made concerning meetings, rallies, interviews, and debates. If necessary, the media can report on the unwillingness of candidates to face unscripted questions. In general, if politicians employ manipulative tactics, the media have an obligation to report on them. In the end, if all else fails, the media can threaten to ignore the politician or the party. Therein lies their ultimate weapon. The media have employed many of these tactics over the decades in Canada. Both Prime Ministers Trudeau and Mulroney were locked in struggles for ascendancy with the media, and both leaders felt the glare of concerted media scrutiny.

Vicious personal attacks have emerged in the media in the past few elections. These have been particularly challenging for inexperienced leaders. Some believe that Kim Campbell and John Turner were poorly treated. Fletcher is eloquent in his disgust at the treatment of Clark in 1979.[73] The media acted in excess of their role as watchdogs for public accountability in their coverage of these leaders and abused their role to mock and belittle individuals on a personal level.

How To Read The News

It is difficult to know how to read a newspaper or watch a television news program. What can we believe? Whom can we trust? Who is being honest? How do the everyday practices of news-manufacture shape the news text? The world of events and practices is not entirely arbitrary. Despite the fact that the news is manufactured, we can employ our skills as critical readers to assess the plausibility of the various claims, reports, and insinuations. Some versions of reality are more coherent, valid, and reliable than others. The following is a partial list of tactics and strategies to assist us as we slump in our chairs each evening to view the news or scan the newspaper over coffee in the morning:

The news is not a church service or elaborated instructions on how to use the safety features on an aircraft: You do not have to be reverential and you do not have to pay attention. Feel free to ignore the screen, glance at it, and do other things while it is on. Don't hesitate to turn it off for something better. Activities strongly recommended include: visiting political websites that relate to the news items of the day; reading a range of ideologically slanted newspapers and magazines, including those from other countries; talking and arguing with family, friends, room-mates, neighbours, workmates, cats and dogs, and anyone else who might listen; reading political and/or sociological theory or a fine novel. (Dostoevsky has much to teach us about politics.) To make these intertextual activities more interesting, a range of foods and beverages is often advisable.

Be on the lookout for slogans and clichés. If you get "action news," demand thinking news. If you hear a commentator say "it's obvious," explain to yourself why it is far from obvious. If you read a reference to "common sense," demand to know whose common sense and whose "uncommon nonsense"? If an article includes the comment, "according to political scientist Paul Nesbitt-Larking," it is of course *bound to be perfectly true in every way.* If any other expert is cited, you should not assume the comment, thought, or idea is unassailable. Think about what another "expert" might say. Whenever you read about "sources close to the prime minister" or "unnamed sources," take the remainder of the sentence as either rumour or a trial balloon.

Be alert to infotainment techniques. Distrust "specials" and cute "human interest stories." Be alert to grainy close-up visuals, lingering cameras, deep voices over, background music, especially emotional music, shaky, hand-held cameras. Once you have put the *Kleenex* away, think about what was going on and why the director wanted to elicit an emotional reaction to the story. If the cameras "walk" through studios and outside into the "real world," do not be fooled into thinking that this is the real thing. As Baudrillard says, it is entirely the opposite. With respect to news values, the "real world" is in fact a mere shadow version of the hyperreal construction that has been mounted in the studio.

In order to remind ourselves of the artificiality of news broadcasts, and that the world has been reduced to 22 minutes, it is useful to imagine Lloyd, Peter, or Sandy occasionally beginning with: "Good evening, nothing happened today and so, from all of us here to all of you there, have a safe and pleasant evening." In a similar fashion, it might be useful to regard the front page of the morning newspaper as a blank space.

It is a good idea to talk back to the television, and even to the newspaper if you are not in a public place. Not only is this therapeutic, but it can assist in ensuring that the flow of information is not one way. Good comments include: "No, it isn't," "Says who?", "Yeah, right!", "Everybody is not excited. *I'm* not excited," "You call that *bad* news?", and anything else that introduces a boundary of reflection between the news text and your response. This is not to advocate mindless naysaying, but rather to encourage critical refusal and a sceptical frame of mind.

What has been ignored, downplayed, or ridiculed? Don't let others gatekeep, set your agenda, frame or prime you. Why is there so little about Africa, Asia, or South America? Why does the death of a Canadian hiker receive front-page coverage, but not the death of fifteen Nigerian hikers? Light-hearted treatments of native issues or the use of native traditions, symbols, and icons might be genuinely funny and quite appropriate to the sensibilities of aboriginal peoples. Too often, however, what is sacred has been belittled and mocked in a thoughtless manner. Before laughing or smiling, think about who might be crying or frowning.

Whose voices are missing from the news report and whose voices are privileged? Who are portrayed as the good guys and the bad guys? Why are poor people, women, aboriginal peoples, immigrants, gays and lesbians, and other marginal groups ignored? Why are their stories and perspectives not taken seriously? Why do we not hear their voices? Why do "experts" in the Canadian media so often work for American think-tanks or conduct research at American or British universities? Why are Canadian experts underused? Why is business, a special interest group, assumed to speak on behalf of the general national interest, and why are its demands assumed to be in conformity with those of "the economy" in general?

What is said to be impossible? As we know, a key element of the construction of ideology is the declaration of what is possible or impossible. Gatekeeping, agenda setting, framing and priming contribute to ideological attempts to define the realm of the possible. Those who call for an end to world hunger, for global disarmament, deep reductions in levels of pollution, workplace health and safety, employment and wage equity, or for the elimination of violence against women are routinely dismissed as wide-eyed radicals or utopian dreamers. The media amplify such cynicism; at the risk of looking foolish and naïve themselves, they could refuse to be cynical and remain open to the possibility of change.

Ask why negative stories about the rich and powerful are not being told? Why is there not more about the connections between corporations and parties? Why are there so few stories about pollution? Why are tax evasion and white-collar crime not treated with the same contempt as other crimes?

Phone up, write letters, and complain in order to demand better news with more depth, stronger intellectual content, and greater attention to power and social change. Insist on knowing in detail what happens behind the scenes and how decisions are made. Refuse versions of "behind the scenes" that are little more than gossipy coverage of strategy and tactics of winning and losing. Demand deeper discussion of the issues and implications, and demand more politics; that is, genuine and sustained dialogue on the nature of the good society and how to achieve it. Require the media to present us with information that helps us to see the world differently and to think outside our boxes. Just say no to bad journalism, especially when it has been tarted up with technical bells and whistles. We need forums in which the full and frank exchange of views and perspectives can take place in a genuine, civil, open, equal, and free search for truth and meaning.

Conclusion

The process of news manufacture begins with the broad encoding of the ultimate news text by conditions of state regulation, the political-economic circumstances of ownership and control, and the shifting powers of representation inherent in culture and ideology. Illustrations of the impact of such macrological factors are evident in the news treatment of labour issues.

Institutional imperatives of ownership and control within news media enterprises exert a relatively autonomous impact on the emergence of news texts. Beats, schedules, advertising considerations, audience share, technical planning, and the existence of evolving news values shape the character of reportage and presentation. News currently favours unexpected, dramatic events that are negative and tragic and involve elite persons from powerful nations. If the story is visually compelling and involves conflict, violence, and anything that is bizarre, whimsical, amusing or diverting, so much the better. The corollary of "if it bleeds, it leads" is "if it thinks, it stinks." In other words, the news media have avoided material that involves deep social, political, or historical analysis. Items are selected and presented that are local, familiar, and based upon stock characters and stereotypical situations.

The news media shape news texts through processes of selectivity and preferential coverage, known as gatekeeping, agenda-setting, framing, and priming. Each of these concepts is useful but open to criticism: Gatekeepers do not just wait for the sluice to come down the pipes; the media are often too lazy and/or ignorant to set the agenda; and framing and priming are often trumped by the ready availability of competing sources of information and insight. Both media and politicians have a variety of tools at their disposal, and the question of ascendancy remains open.

The daily news is manufactured; it is to some extent an arbitrary construct. If we push this logic to its limit, we can argue there is no such thing as a good or bad news text, and that any version of "reality" is as good as any other. This is not my position. Some facts are incontrovertible and when the news media get them wrong, they stand in need of correction. There is a well-established range of philosophical, ideological, and cultural perspectives on most issues. When the news media ignore or misrepresent these positions, they require enlightenment. Certain individuals and groups routinely receive inadequate treatment in the media, notably those who lack socio-economic and political power. This too is unjust and should change. The news can be better. I hope that some of the recommendations made in the last section will enhance your viewing and reading experiences.

Notes

1. Peter Golding and Philip Elliott, "News Values and News Production," in Paul Marris and Sue Thornham, eds., *Media Studies: A Reader* (Edinburgh: Edinburgh University Press, 1996), 409.
2. James Fallows, "Why Americans Hate the Media," *Atlantic Monthly*, February 1986, 55.
3. Michael Schudson, *The Power of News* (Cambridge: Cambridge University Press, 1996), 4.

4. Dan Rather, quoted in Daniel C. Hallin, "Commercialism and Professionalism in the American News Media," in James Curran and Michael Gurevitch, eds., Mass *Media and Society,* 2nd ed. (London: Arnold, 1996), 243.

5. Gaye Tuchman, *Making News: A Study in the Construction of Reality* (New York: Free Press, 1980), 1.

6. *Ibid.;* David Altheide, *Creating Reality* (Beverly Hills: Sage, 1976); Stuart Hall, Chas Critcher, Tony Jefferson, John Clarke, and Brian Roberts, "The Social Production of News," in *idem., Policing the Crisis: Mugging, the State, and Law and Order* (London: Macmillan, 1980), 53–80.

7. *Ibid.*

8. Andrew Edgar, "Objectivity, Bias and Truth," in Andrew Belsey and Ruth Chadwick, eds., *Ethical Issues in Journalism and the Media* (London: Routledge, 1992).

9. *Ibid.,* 120, 121.

10. *Ibid.,* 128.

11. Schudson, *The Power of News.*

12. Fallows "Why Americans Hate the Media."

13. Graham Knight, "News As Ideology," *Canadian Journal of Communication* 8 (1982), 15–41.

14. Graham Knight, "Strike Talk: A Case Study of News," *Canadian Journal of Communication* 8 (1982), 61–79. Knight's research depends exclusively on a textual analysis of the news and he comments on the necessary limitations of this imputational approach (56).

15. *Ibid.,* 62.

16. Robert Hackett, "The Depiction of Labour and Business on National Television News," *Canadian Journal of Communication* 10 (1983), 5–50.

17. *Ibid.,* 44.

18. Dan Alger, *The Media and Politics,* 2nd ed. (Belmont, Wadsworth, 1996), 135.

19. Scott Lash, *The Sociology of Postmodernism* (London: Routledge, 1990), 4, 5.

20. Stuart Hall in David Cayley, "Making Sense of the News," *Sources,* Spring 1982, 127.

21. *Ibid.,* 128

22. Philip Schlesinger, "The Production of Radio and Television News," in Marris and Thornham, eds., *Media Studies: A Reader,* 416–23.

23. Tuchman, *Making News,* 22.

24. Hall et al., *Policing the Crisis,* 54.

25. Edward Jay Epstein, *News From Nowhere: Television and the News* (New York: Vintage, 1974). 164.

26. Alger, *The Media and Politics,* 144.

27. I was reminded of how many news broadcasts now call themselves "Action News." A curious experiment might be to launch a new program with the title: "Thinking News," or "Reflective News," or even "Armchair Enquiry." Would there be an audience for such programming? This concept might be stretched even further. Nike might promote a new line of clothing, replacing "Just Do It" with the slogan: "Take time to evaluate your potentialities," or Coca-Cola might come up with: "Coke is only one of a range of carbonated sucrose beverages, arguably no better nor worse than any of the others" to replace "Coke Is It." You can think of your own examples.

28. Gaye Tuchman, "Objectivity As Strategic Ritual: An Examination of Newsmen's Notions of Objectivity," *American Journal of Sociology* 77 (1972), 660–79.

29. Pierre Sorlin, *Mass Media* (London: Routledge, 1994), 74.

30. Michele Martin, *Communication and Mass Media: Culture, Domination, and Opposition* (Scarborough: Prentice Hall Allyn and Bacon, 1997), 243.

31. Angela Austman, cited in Robert A. Hackett and Richard Gruneau, *The Missing News: Elites and Blind Spots in Canada's Press* (Toronto: Garamond Press, 2000), 187–90.

32. *Ibid.*

33. *Ibid.*, 188.

34. Knight, "News As Ideology," 19.

35. Graham Murdock, "Mass Communication and the Construction of Meaning," in Roger Dickinson, Ramaswami Harindranath, and Olga Linne, eds., *Approaches to Audiences: A Reader* (London: Arnold, 1998), 207.

36. Schudson, *The Power of News*, 4–6.

37. Fallows, "Why Americans Hate the Media."

38. Tuchman in Cayley, "Making Sense of the News," 128.

39. Hackett and Gruneau, *The Missing News*, 79–98.

40. Martin, *Communication and Mass Media*, 240.

41. Epstein, *News From Nowhere*, 170.

42. Tuchman, *Making News*, 137.

43. James Winter, *Common Cents: Media Portrayal of the Gulf War and Other Events* (Montreal: Black Rose Books, 1992).

44. David Manning White, "The 'Gatekeeper': A Case Study in the Selection of News," in Lewis Anthony Dexter and David Manning White, eds., *People, Society, and Mass Communications* (New York: Free Press, 1964), 160–72.

45. Cited in *Ibid.*, 162.

46. *Ibid.*, 163.

47. Walter Gieber, "Across the Desk: A Study of 16 Telegraph Editors," *Journalism Quarterly* 33 (1956), 423–32.

48. Tuchman in Cayley, "Making Sense of the News," 126. Parentheses as in the original.

49. Sorlin, *Mass Media*, 94.

50. Hackett and Gruneau, *The Missing News*, 131–201.

51. *Ibid.*, 197–201.

52. *Ibid.*

53. Walter Lippmann, *Public Opinion* (New York: Macmillan, 1922).

54. Maxwell E. McCombs and Donald L. Shaw, "The Agenda-setting Function of Mass Media," *Public Opinion Quarterly* 36 (1972), 176–87; Donald L. Shaw and Maxwell E. McCombs, *The Emergence of American Political Issues: The Agenda-setting Function of the Press* (St. Paul, MN: West Publishing, 1977).

55. J. McLeod, L. Becker, and J. Byrnes, "Another Look at the Agenda-setting Function of the Press," *Communication Research* 1 (1974).

56. Maxwell E. McCombs, "News Influence on Our Pictures of the World," in Dickinson et al., eds., *Approaches to Audiences: A Reader*, 29–30.

57. Edwin Black, *Politics and the News: The Political Functions of the Mass Media* (Toronto: Butterworths, 1982), 193–203.

58. Fallows, "Why Americans Hate the Media."

59. McCombs and Shaw in Alger, *The Media and Politics*, 161.

60. Iyengar and Kinder, cited in Alger, *The Media and Politics*, 282–84.

61. Linda McQuaig, "Shooting the Hippo: Eric Mailing's Crusade to Bring the 'Debt Crisis' Home to Canada," *Canadian Forum*, April (1995), 10–15.

62. Graham Knight and Julia S. O'Connor, "Social Democracy Meets the Press: Media Coverage of Industrial Relations Legislation," *Research in Political Sociology* 7 (1995), 183–205.

63. *Ibid.*, 201.

64. Stuart Hall, quoted in Cayley, "Making Sense of the News," 126, 127.

65. Doris Graber, *Processing the News: How People Tame the Information Tide*, 2nd ed. (New York: Longman, 1988).

66. John Fiske, *Reading The Popular* (Boston: Unwin Hyman, 1989), 187.

67. *Ibid.*, 196.

68. David Taras, *The Newsmakers. The Media's Influence on Canadian Politics* (Toronto: Nelson, 1990), 119–79.

69. Christina McCall-Newman, *crits: An Intimate Portrait of the Liberal Party* (Toronto: Macmillan, 1983), 1–50.

70. Kathleen Hall Jamieson and Karlyn K. Campbell, *The Interplay of Influence: Mass Media and Their Publics in News, Advertising, Politics* (Belmont: Wadsworth, 1983).

71. David Taras, "The Mass Media and Political Crisis," *Canadian Journal of Communication* 18 (1993) 131–48.

72. Fred Fletcher, "Playing the Game: The Mass Media and the 1979 Campaign," in Howard Penniman, ed., *Canada at the Polls, 1979 and 1980: A Study of the General Elections* (Washington: American Enterprise Institute for Public Research, 1980), 319.

73. *Ibid.*, 318.

Mass Media Politics

Boundaries Blurred: The Mass Media and Politics in a Hyper-Media Age

Jonathan Rose and Simon Kiss

The media, we are told, are a vital link between citizens and government. Traditional ideals of the media see them as having a pivotal role in keeping government accountable and providing information to citizens about the health of the body politic. The centrality of the media is evident in the metaphors we employ in discussing their functions. When we speak of the media as a barometer of the citizenry or a watchdog over government, or even when we talk of muckraking journalism, we are suggesting that the media are an important link to how citizens get political information and how they understand the world around them. Canadian media scholar David Taras (1990) discusses the mass media through a number of different metaphors: media as watchdog, but also media as mirror and as distorted mirror. The former suggests that the media can be accurate reflectors of objective phenomena in the world; the latter grants more latitude to the interpretation of political life. All of these metaphors, however, assume a clear division between the mass media and the state. In this chapter we suggest that the metaphor of blurred boundaries provides us with useful insights into contemporary developments in the news media. In terms of structure, we see a blurring of boundaries between different media; between insiders and outsiders; between media and government; and between news and entertainment.

The media are, arguably, one of the most significant institutions in modern society. Timothy Cook goes so far as to suggest that newsmaking is now a central way for governmental actors to accomplish political and policy goals. "In that sense, the news media may well be an unwitting adjunct to power. . . . Making news, in other words, is not merely a way to get elected or reelected, to boost one's own ego or to be a show horse instead of a work horse; instead, it is a way to govern" (1998, p. 164). Other authors are equally emphatic in their claims about the centrality of the media in public life. Robert Hackett and Yuezhi Zhao suggest that "journalism is arguably the most important form of public knowledge in contemporary society. The mass media . . . have become the leading institutions of the public sphere"

(1998, p. 1). Canadian media scholar Paul Nesbitt-Larking (2001) makes a compelling case that the media are conduits for the creation of our culture. For him, the media shape and are shaped by our social practices, norms, and values. It is clear that conventional scholarship on the mass media sees a critical role for the news media in their support of liberal democratic values.

Democracy is premised on the ability of citizens to deliberate and reflect on issues. Early democratic theorists decried the fact that citizens did not have enough access to information. John Dewey, for example, argued that it was not that the public lacked ability but rather they lacked resources to have a public conversation (Dewey, 1927). The media, he believed, could be this conduit between the public and the governed. In the early days of the 20th century, the solution to the problem of creating an informed public was found in the mass media.

When one examines the media today, we find that few of these democratic obligations are met. Robert McChesney has called the current situation "a disaster for anything but the most superficial notion of democracy" (2000, p. 59). Ownership and the concentration of power has attenuated the public conversation. The news media's obsession with celebrity and the inane has not provided the fuel for the democratic fire. News is now virtually subsumed by entertainment so that discerning the boundary between the two is like drawing lines in the sand at the water's edge: boundaries are temporary, regularly wiped out, and continually shifting. Where we once could discuss separate spheres of news, politics, and entertainment, we argue that these are supplanted by boundaries that are increasingly porous, so that fulfilling important democratic functions is difficult if not impossible. This carries with it significant implications for the state of democratic debate. Despite the explosion in the type and number of media sources, there has not been an increase in their quality. Moreover, this explosion has not resulted in a better-informed public. This chapter explores the paradoxes of the modern media environment and raises questions about the relationship of the media to politics. Serious questions of accountability are also raised, given the relationships between journalists and their sources. The fact that the modern media have been marked by an adaptation of the codes, narratives, and styles of entertainment raises serious questions about the relationship between politics and mass media.

The Blur of Speed

In contemporary political life, the problem is not that we need greater access to information but arguably that we have access to too much information. For most of North America, where television sets reach over 90 percent of the population and, in Canada, where more than 70 percent of people have cable-TV access and 15 percent subscribe to pay TV (Statistics Canada, 2002), the issue is less one of access than of sheer volume. Some time ago Bruce Springsteen wrote a song where he lamented that there were "fifty-seven channels and nothing on." Now, in the age of satellite television, the choices are virtually infinite. One can choose sports channels, comedy channels, lifestyle channels, and channels for seniors, women, or children. David Taras (2001) calls these fragmentation bombs the biggest threat to national communities and the ability to create a public space. Each one of these speaks to a particular community defined by gender, age, hobby, interest, or any number of categories. The fragmentation of the public creates markets for advertisers rather than enabling a conversation of government with the people. The media hare become vehicles for producing specialized audiences of consumers rather than for producing debate among citizens.

Despite the explosion in the production of information, there is evidence that citizens are no better informed. In the United States, the world's most media-literate society, citizens lack basic knowledge of political issues. For example, a study at the University of Maryland (Kull, 2004) found that those tending to support President Bush were more likely than Democratic supporters to believe that Saddam Hussein had weapons of mass destruction and that the Iraqi government played a role in the terrorist attacks on September 11. This study *followed* the Congressional 9/11 commission, which categorically refuted these widely held beliefs. In Canada, the Dominion Institute regularly chronicles Canadians' lack of basic political knowledge. One poll found that Canadians were worse informed about basic historic facts than were Americans (Dominion Institute, 2001), suggesting that this lack of knowledge is not confined to the United States.

Todd Gitlin sees the proliferation of media not, primarily, as having a fragmentation effect—though he acknowledges that component—but rather as a flood, or an aural and visual tsunami. As the subtitle of his recent book suggests, this "torrent of images and sounds overwhelms our lives" (2001). Raymond Williams, the great cultural critic, was probably the first to observe this when he said, "What we have now is drama as habitual experience: more in a week, in many cases, than most human beings would previously have seen in a lifetime" (cited in Gitlin, 2001, p. 15). For Gitlin, the mass media torrent is indivisible. It is not that media fragmentation atomizes us but rather that the flood of media does not allow any critical reflection. The much discussed effects of the media are not to cultivate a more violent society (Gerbner, Gross, Morgan, and Signorielli, 1986), nor to create a bored society, as Neil Postman (1985) argues. Rather "media are . . . themselves the main products, the main transactions, the main effects of media" (Gitlin, 2001, p. 10).

Faced with this continuous flood of images and ideas we are forced to erect dams to protect ourselves. There is evidence to suggest that despite the plethora of media sources, we seek out media that merely confirm our own views rather than media that might challenge us. According to a Pew Research Center study, in the United States if you are Republican you will likely watch Fox, while if you are Democrat you will watch CNN (Kohut, 2004, p. 5). Apparently, your partisanship dictates what you watch. While some might point to the phenomenal success of Michael Moore's documentary film *Farenheit 9/11* as a counterexample, the National Annenberg Election Study found that virtually all Americans who saw the film were Democrats. They were therefore already convinced of the movie's main contention that George W. Bush acted improperly after the events of September 11, According to the study, "only a handful of Republicans saw the movie; they were too few for their attitudes to be measured with confidence" ("Farenheit 9/11 Viewers," 2004). Far from a free marketplace of ideas envisioned by early democratic theorists, modern media, though more plentiful and accessible than ever, have narrowed choices precisely because of their ineffable size and scope.

The speed and volume with which the torrent floods us also creates other problems besides the creation of filters. Susan Moeller (1999) argues that the flood of grisly images of disease, famine, death, and war has created "compassion fatigue," where the frames of the story result in a inured public whose sympathy and compassion are dulled. The media, in their attempt to deliver powerful images that pack a punch and speak to the audience, rely on formulas for these sorts of stories. They focus on stereotypical characters, the economic or cultural connection to the United States, and, of course, vivid and powerful images. This might explain the apparent rationale of newspapers around the world that on April 4, 2004, published pictures of the charred bodies of four Americans hanging from a bridge in Fallujah, Iraq. Such photos and styles of reportage do no service to informing the public but merely reinforce low levels of public efficacy and trust in elite institutions. The. photos and the blur of speed reinforce the idea that with traditional media, citizens are mere observers. Having been forced to respond to a 24-hour news cycle and having to interest a public that treats political information like any other commodity, the media may have been creators of this media flood.

The Blurring Between Government and Journalists

Historically, the media have viewed themselves as an independent watchdog on government power (Donohue, Tichenor, Olien, 1995). However, there is evidence to suggest that this role is changing. The relationship between political journalists and those they cover in the government has come under some scrutiny in Canada. A number of journalists have given up their role as supposedly independent political observers to become highly paid public relations practitioners for governments and cabinet ministers. Could it be that the watchdog has become the lap dog? One of the more high-profile examples is that of senior CBC radio correspondent Susan Murray, who left the press gallery to become the spokesperson for the Liberal Minister of Public Works, Scott Brison. A further example is the case of Drew Fagan, *The Globe and Mail's* senior parliamentary bureau chief, who left the newspaper to become a senior advisor to the Department of Foreign Affairs and International Trade (Martin, 2004, p. A18). Jim Munson, who was a reporter for CTV, moved to the Prime Minister's Office as Director of Communications under Jean Chrétien, after which he was appointed to the Senate in 2003.

Given the increasing complexity, intensity, and speed of contemporary political media, governments (and other institutions) require highly specialized knowledge that professional political journalists can often provide. The explosion of the hyper-media environment has also made the media more integral to government operations. In his exhaustive study of the centralization of Canadian political power in the office of the Prime Minister, Donald Savoie consistently cites the mass media as a cause:

> For the most part, [the media] is no longer just a narrator or an independent observer reporting and commenting on political events. It has become an important political actor in its own right. Television and its tendency to turn a thirty-second clip on the evening news to sum up major policy issues or, much more often, to report on something gone awry in government, have had a profound impact on government operations. The centre [of government], broadly defined, has become extremely sensitive to potential media-inspired developments it cannot control and to surprises, which can give rise to political problems and embarrassments.
>
> (1996, p. 39)

Although there has always been a crossover between the professions of journalism and public relations, it is worth asking whether or not this trend is increasing or becoming more problematic. There is no straight, empirical investigation of the claim that there are journalists who are leaving the profession in greater numbers to join the ranks of elite public relations firms. However, employment growth in the public relations profession has far outstripped that of journalism. The Statistics Canada census indicates that there were 13,470 journalists in the nation in 1991; this declined to 12,960 in 2001, for a decrease of 4 percent. The same survey, however, notes an increase of 16 percent in the number of Canadians practicing public relations, from 23,780 to 27,465 (Statistics Canada, 2001). While these data are stark, it should not be entirely surprising, given widespread public debate about strapped-for-cash newsrooms in institutions such as the Canadian Broadcasting Corporation. What makes the situation even more compelling is that it takes place against the backdrop of an exploding media environment that has resulted in a 500-channel universe. If the mass media are expanding at a rapid pace, but the professionals who work in that industry are experiencing severe cutbacks, then we must ask ourselves, who is producing the content that we consume in our daily lives? Perhaps public relations officials—whether they are government, industry, or otherwise—are gaining the upper hand in the production of political information.

This trend does raise other concerns about the potential reliability of political news media. Most news organizations have a segment of their staff on the political beat, working in close proximity to those in government. If some of those journalists are seeking to join the PR ranks of those they are supposed to cover, might it not colour their coverage? Don Martin, a senior columnist with the *National Post*, has raised questions about the practice of parliamentary correspondents joining the ranks of governments. He suggests a number of steps that could be taken to re-establish boundaries between governments and the journalists who cover them; for example, governments should institute a ban on hiring journalists for one year following an election campaign, as well as outright prohibitions on offering journalists patronage appointments to the Order of Canada and the Senate until a suitable cooling-off period has elapsed (Martin, 2004, A18).

A further example of this blurred boundary is the inevitable mixing of journalists, politicians, and commentators after election campaign debates. In the first minutes following live debates, the candidates, their political allies, their political staff, third-party observers, and supposedly neutral journalists all engage in a verbal brawl as they fight for a single news frame: "my candidate won." Watching this commentary, it is legitimate to ask: Who are the journalists? Who are the politicians? Who is independent and who is not? And, most importantly, who is accountable to whom for what they say? Instead, these situations appear to be a collective free-for-all, a ritual of producing political information engaged in by actors from all sides of the process.

Perhaps the most dramatic and controversial case of the blurred line between press and government was the use by the United States military of "embedded" journalists during the invasion of Iraq. In this case, journalists from Western media outlets were attached to specific military units to travel with them, even into extremely dangerous combat situations. In order to gain access to the front, journalists were required to sign an agreement with the Pentagon, foregoing their rights to sue the government in case of damages, and, perhaps more importantly, to agree to the military's standards of censorship, including not identifying "specific number of troops," "information regarding future operations," "rules of engagement," or "information on effectiveness on enemy electronic warfare," among other blanket categories (U.S. State Department, 2003).

The ethical implications of embedded journalists are a matter of significant debate. Some suggest that this practice guarantees biased coverage, pointing to the extraordinary sense of camaraderie that develops between embedded journalists and the military units they are stationed with (Laurence, 2003). On the other hand, there are those who argue that by embedding journalists, viewers and readers get a far clearer picture of the destruction caused by war. For example, John R. McArthur, publisher of *Harper's Magazine,* noted in an interview that embedded journalists with *The New York Times* and ABC News went so far as to display pictures of dead Iraqis. "Compared to the last war, that's 100 per cent more corpses. If you measure good war journalism by the extent to which it shows the violence and death, we are ahead of where we were 12 years ago" (quoted in Bedan, 2003, p. 34).

What is certain, however, is that the United States military considers media relations and the projection of images integral to the success of its operations. The guidelines issued by the Office of the Assistant Secretary of Defense for

Public Affairs regarding embedded journalists are quite clear on this point:

> Media coverage of any future operation will, to a large extent, shape public percep-
> tion of the national security environment now and in the years ahead. This holds
> true for the U.S. public; the public in allied countries whose opinion can affect the
> durability of our coalition; and publics in countries where we conduct operations,
> whose perceptions of us can affect the cost and duration of our involvement. . . . We
> need to tell the factual story—good or bad—before others seed the media with disin-
> formation and distortions, as they most certainly will continue to do. Our people in
> the field need to tell our story—only commanders can ensure the media get to the
> story.
>
> (U.S. State Department, 2003)

These examples indicate one important trend in contemporary political communications: in many ways, the media are no longer an independent institution.
Instead, they are integral to the political process, and they are inherently political
actors. The United States military has guidelines that emphasize the importance
of the media and communication strategies to their operations. Political journalists are crossing boundaries to work for governments. These contradict traditional conceptions of journalists and how journalists view themselves. In fact,
journalists will most often recoil at the allegation that they are "political." But if
we are right and today's media are inherently political, then a major question
best expressed by Timothy Cook must be asked: "If the media are now a key
intermediary institution, who elected reporters to represent them in politics and
how well is their power popularly checked?" (1998, p. 16).

The Blurred Line of Political Journalism

In the realm of hyper-media the very definition of what constitutes journalism is
now in question. No longer can we understand news media as simply news that
appears on television or radio, in print or over the Internet. But even the Internet
with its evolving structure and shifting modes of communication (i.e., from text
to pictures to video) is creating new forms of news dissemination. If every U.S.
presidential election brings with it a new innovation in political campaigning,
then surely the story of the 2004 presidential election was the growth of Web
logs, the stripped down Web sites known as "blogs." Essentially on-line diaries,
blogs can also chronicle the musings, gossip, and news of any political actor.
Because they are not constrained by editors, owners, or any pretense of balance,
and because of the immediacy with which stories can be published, blogs are a
challenge to traditional media. So, when mainstream news outlets refused to
publish stories of Bill Clinton's affair with an intern, Matt Drudge in his Drudge
Report (http://www.drudgereport.com), had no hesitation. Another leading
blog, "Wonkette" (http://www.wonkette.com), caters to Washington insiders. It
uses the format of listing links to mainstream media sources as well as creating
its own stories. The blog has become not just a filter in the media torrent but
also another source of journalism and another source for journalists. In Canada,

Warren Kinsella, who was a top Chrétien aide, uses his blog (http://www. warrenkinsella.com) to influence current political debates.

Blogs became an important part of the election cycle in the role they played in propelling Howard Dean from outside populist candidate to front-runner for the U.S. Democratic Party's presidential nominee. In this case, blogs supposedly enabled Dean's campaign to raise extraordinary amounts of money—$5 million per month in the second half of 2003, more than any other Democratic contender in history (Edsall, 2004)—and helped grassroots activists connect with each other, communicate with each other, and plan campaign events from the ground up.

Blogs also play an important role, not just in grassroots political organizations, but as alternate news sources. One prominent case in point occurred during the 2004 presidential election campaign, when CBS News mistakenly reported the existence of documents that supposedly proved President Bush had shirked his duties as a member of the National Guard during the Vietnam War. Within hours of the story being broadcast on the CBS nightly newscast, conservative bloggers had downloaded copies of the documents and raised serious questions about the documents' veracity. Forty-eight hours later, the controversy had spilled from the "blogosphere" into the mainstream media and quickly led CBS News to apologize and launch an internal inquiry into how the story had passed internal checks.

The importance of this incident lies in the increasing ability of bloggers to hold the mass media to account. Whereas the traditional media have often understood themselves to be the primary watchdog of government power, blogs allow citizens to hold the media to account in their political coverage. A common complaint levied against the political media is that they cannot be held accountable. Traditional means (letters to the editor, ombudsmen, etc.) are often too weak or too slow to respond to biases, slants, or outright errors propagated by the mass media.

Simple errors or biases within prominent newscasts in the midst of a campaign can quickly take on the status of what has been called congenial truths, a concept that William Fox applies to Canadian politics. Congenial truths are "a pact between the reporter and the reader, an understanding of reality that is mutually acceptable" (Fox, 1999). Fox discusses one Canadian congenial truth as our belief in Jean Chrétien as "le petit gar de Shawinigan"—we are willing to believe this as a congenial truth despite any evidence that might contradict it. In the case of the CBS newscast, above, the news story was a product of the congenial truth that President Bush had inappropriately avoided his military service; unchallenged, it would have substantially contributed to the strength of that truth within public debate. The interdiction by conservative bloggers was able to substantially alter the progress of the story. In this case, at least, blogs gave citizens a potentially powerful entry point into the 24-hour news cycle, subjecting mainstream journalists to real-time scrutiny, commentary, and accountability.

Blogs are important in other ways as well. Drezner and Farrell (2004) emphasize the role that political blogs played in United States Senator Trent Lott's political troubles in 2002. In that instance, videotaped comments made by Lott, in which he expressed sentiments sympathetic to segregation, were prominently discussed throughout the blogosphere, with liberal-minded bloggers expressing their outrage. The debate on-line became so fierce that the traditional media were forced to pick up the story, generating enough political pressure that Lott, at that time the Senate Majority Leader, was forced to resign. Moreover, Drezner and Farrell argue that blogs have significant advantages in the opinion-formation process, often shaping important political events early on. Whereas members of the traditional media must go through some basic processes of vetting and editing before their accounts can be put forward, these constraints are nonexistent for bloggers. It might be that blogs are the 21st-century version of the penny press in the 19th century (Tucher, 1994). In the Canadian context, bloggers could serve as early interpreters of key political events such as debates, throne speeches, budget speeches, or Question Period debates.

The Blurring of Entertainment and News

U2 singer Bono appears at the federal Liberal Party leadership convention that elects Paul Martin in 2004; Bruce Springsteen appears with U.S. Democratic candidate John Kerry in the last few days of the 2004 campaign. In both cases the photos and stories are front-page news. Just after the bombing of the World Trade Center. *Politically Incorrect* host Bill Maher is publicly chastised by White House spokesman Ari Fleischer for calling American politicians cowardly. In his rebuke, Fleischer says Americans "need to watch what they say, watch what they do. This is not a time for remarks like that; there never is" ("The *Salon* Interview," 2002). In 2003, country music stars The Dixie Chicks are pilloried in the press and have their music pulled from radio stations when they criticize George Bush's policy on Iraq. In all of these examples, the political views of celebrities become grist for the media mill. Our society has a longstanding fascination with the power of celebrity. That the potent combination of the mass media and capitalism has accelerated the growth of celebrity is not new (Gitlin, 1980). What has changed is that celebrities are now being sought out—or targeted—for their political views. In becoming the new pundits, they have demonstrated how news and entertainment cannot be separated.

One of the most significant political challenges to President Bush's reelection effort and to democratic debate came not from the traditional political media but from Michael Moore's feature film *Fahrenheit 9/11*. The impact of the film should not be underestimated. For example, the Saudi Arabian ambassador to the United Kingdom took the extraordinary step of publicly refuting claims made in the movie in an exclusive interview with BBC News. The movie is the highest-grossing documentary ever made, grossing approximately $119 million (U.S.) in ticket sales (Smith, 2004, p. 98). Shortly after the film's release, MoveOn.org organized thousands of private screenings of the film, offering private groups the opportunity to hear the filmmaker address the groups over telephone links. Moore was explicit in urging participants to support Democratic presidential nominee John Kerry (Gilgoff and Tobin, 2004, p. 38).

A similar story is found in the phenomenal growth of the satirical comedic news show, *The Daily Show with Jon Stewart.* This nightly comedy program mocks political actors and the political media simultaneously. The high point of Stewart's political influence, perhaps, came with a much publicized appearance on CNN's daily debate show *Crossfire.* On that show, Stewart publicly chastened the show's hosts and, by extension, the broader political media. On the American election night, many networks (CNN and CTV being two examples) seemed to throw in the towel and embrace celebrity/journalism when they broadcast Stewart's comedy show in the middle of electoral returns. Viewers who tuned in during the comedy show would find little difference between *The Daily Show*'s news-style presentation and a regular newscast. Both had attractive anchors sitting behind a desk and reporters filing stories about who might win, routinely interrupted by any electoral results that emerged. It was difficult to determine if comedy was co-opting the election or the election was simply material for a comedian. Either way, the line between entertainment and news was completely blurred.

Should the political warnings of a comedian be taken seriously? Perhaps in this case, there is little to fear. A study of over 19,000 respondents during the presidential campaign found that viewers of *The Daily Show* had higher levels of campaign information than did those who did not watch late-night comedy or those who watched other shows such as *The Late Show with David Letterman* ("*Daily Show* Viewers," 2004). There are no data to suggest that the show is a cause of increased political information; rather, it is more likely that the show's content requires a certain amount of political awareness on the part of its viewers to be successful. There are other, more general reasons to be cautiously optimistic about this development. First, in an age where youth voting is abysmally low, there may be positive benefits in seeing spokes-people more representative of that generation. Second, a poll of Canadians in 2000 suggests that 61 percent of Canadians have not very much or no confidence in the media (Canadian Opinion Research Archive, 2004). Hearing alternative voices might offset the apparently low esteem in which the media are held.

The theme of the blurring between news and entertainment has been addressed perhaps most successfully by Neil Postman (1985) in his book *Amusing Ourselves to Death.* In that work, Postman argues that the trend toward treating entertainment as news and news as a form of entertainment represents a powerful threat to democratic debate. He suggests that the threat to modern democracies is not from Big Brother, but from ourselves through our collective ennui. Though he did not live long enough to see the emergence and growth of reality TV, there is no doubt that Postman would see it as proof that television, in particular, is a medium completely unsuited for deliberation.

The growth of reality TV programming around the world is a strong testament to this idea. In the U.K., the final two candidates in the reality program *Pop Idol* "polled more votes than the Liberal Democrats in the general election" (Corner and Pels, 2003, p. 1). Each episode had more viewers than did the 10 o'clock news during the real election campaign. In Australia, more people watched the final episode *of Australian Idol* than the election debate. Even the treasurer acknowledged that "a lot of people would have turned on [the debate] to see how it was going then they'd start wavering with their finger on the remote control" (Symonds and Schultz, 2004). In the United States, the Showtime network had a reality TV show called *American Candidate* where viewers were invited to select the people's candidate. While candidates were not voted off the island *à la Survivor*, they were subjected to the same sort of competition where two individuals faced off to see who was the victor and who the vanquished. Lest anyone doubt the seriousness of this, the prestigious University of Virginia Center for Politics held an all candidates' debate with both entertainer Montel Williams and noted academic, Larry Sabato. The program was neither entertainment nor news but, with its blurred boundaries, a new hybrid of infotainment where you could not discern the expert academics from the talk-show host.

The growth of non-traditional media, whether in the form of blogs or as a response to why citizens are flocking to entertainment/news, gives us reason to examine what needs these other forms of communication are filling. Their popularity-stems from a craving for substantive political debate, alternative narratives, and news frames that are simply not being provided by traditional media. Instead, the traditional political media have become part of the political process, themselves political insiders. Rather than frowning on the intrusions of Jon Stewart and Michael Moore into the political process, we need to ask why they— and not traditional news—are capturing the imagination of viewers.

Is Public Journalism the Answer?

If the new forms of media are no longer able to provide the kind of information required in a democracy, then what ought to be done about these new blurred boundaries? Jay Rosen, one of the most vocal adherents of "public journalism" (sometimes called civic journalism) argues that what is needed is a new way of doing journalism that recognizes these blurred boundaries and uses them to construct a dialogue with the public. For Rosen, public journalism sees a radical transformation of the role of journalists in society. Public journalism asks journalists to address citizens as participants, not spectators; to help the public act on its problems, not just learn about them; and to improve the climate of public discussion (1999, p. 262).

It maintains some elements of impartiality while abandoning others. For example, the Canadian Association of Journalists has a "Statement of Principles" that lists fairness, freedom of speech, diversity, privacy, balance, and public interest as guiding principles. While public journalism would not abandon these ideals, it would recognize that journalists have an obligation to address compelling social problems and that often means taking sides in a public conversation. While this notion might subvert our traditional understanding of what journalists do, under public journalism the media provide a platform for meaningful deliberation and debate. By using newspapers as forums for public discussion, by allowing the public to frame issues put before political elites, public journalism changes the media from watchdog to participant. Newspapers (through on-line discussion boards) and television news (through town hall meetings) have begun to adopt some of the central tenets of this movement, but these are the exception, not the rule. Public journalism may offer a solution, as it respects citizens and sees the role of journalists as facilitating this great conversation with government rather than providing bite-sized and intellectually unfulfilling nuggets of news.

We have tried to show in this chapter that the mass media are undergoing tremendous structural changes. Since the boundaries surrounding media have become more open, this should be taken as an ideal opportunity to illuminate what media do and in doing so, shine a light on what that shows us about our own democratic practices and habits. A vibrant media is a necessary precondition for a vibrant democracy.

Questions

1. What are the ethical issues surrounding the military practice of embedding journalists?
2. Can you think of recent examples of "compassion fatigue" in the media?
3. According to the authors, how has entertainment media and news become increasingly blurred? Provide a recent example.
4. Why do you think there has been such an increase in the popularity of blogs and blogging?
5. What other forms of entertainment media can inform youth about political and news events?

References

Bedan, Audin. (2003, April 7). More skewed, very biased. *Maclean's,* 34.

Canadian Opinion Research Archive. (2004). Retrieved November 2, 2004, from http://www.queensu.ca/cora/trends/tables/Confidence-Media.htm

Cook, Timothy. (1998). *Governing with the news: The news media as political institution.* Chicago: University of Chicago Press.

Corner, John, and Dick Pels. (2003). The restyling of politics. In John Corner and Dick Pels (Eds.), *Media and the restyling of politics.* London: Sage.

Daily Show viewers knowledgeable about presidential campaign, national Annenberg election survey shows. (2004). Annenberg Center for Public Policy. Retrieved November 5, 2004, from http://www.annenbergpublicpolicycenter.org/naes/2004_03_late-night-knowledge-2_9-21_pr.pdf

Dewey, John. (1927). *The public and its problems.* London: Allen.

Dominion Institute. (2001). 5th annual Canada Day history quiz. Retrieved November 2, 2004, from http://www.ipsos-na.com/news/pressrelease.cfm?id=1255

Donohue, George. A., Phillip J. Tichenor, and Clarice N. Olien. (1995). A guard dog perspective on the role of media. *Journal of Communication, 45,* 115–132.

Drezner, Daniel, and Henry Farrell. (2004). The power and politics of blogs. Paper presented at the 2004 Annual Meeting of the American Political Science Association. Retrieved May 19, 2005, from http://www.utsc.utoronto.ca/~farrell/blogpaperfinal.pdf

Edsall, Thomas. (2004, January 7). Dean fundraising sets party record: Goal of matching Bush is still far off. *Washington Post,* A4. Retrieved November 7, 2004, from http://www.washingtonpost.com/wp-dyn/articles/A60457-2004Jan6.html

Farenheit 9/11 viewers and Limbaugh listeners about equal in size even though they perceive two different nations, Annenberg data show. (2004. August 3). National Annenberg Election Study 2004. Retrieved November 2, 2004, from http://www.naes04.org

Fox, Bill. (1999). *Spin wars: Politics and new media.* Toronto: Key Porter Books.

Gerbner, George, Larry Gross, Michael Morgan, and Nancy Signorielli. (1986). Living with television: The dynamics of the cultivation process. In Jennings Bryant and Dolf Zillmann (Eds.), *Perspectives on media effects* (pp. 17–40). Hillsdale, NJ: Lawrence Erlbaum.

Gilgoff, Dan, and Michael Tobin. (2004, July 12). Moore or less. *U.S. News & World Report,* 38.

Gitlin, Todd. (1980). *The whole world is watching: Mass media in the making and unmaking of the new left.* Berkeley, CA: University of California Press.

_____. (2001). *Media unlimited: How the torrent of images and sounds overwhelms our lives.* New York: Metropolitan Books.

Hackett, Robert, and Yuezhi Zhao. (1998). *Sustaining democracy: Journalism and the politics of objectivity.* Toronto: Garamond Press.

Kohut, Andrew. (2004, July 11). More news is not necessarily good néws. *The New York Times,* section 4, p. 5.

Kull, Steven. (2004, October 21). The separate realities of Bush and Kerry supporters. The PIPA/Knowledge Networks Poll, The American Public on International Issues. College Park, MD: Program on International Policy Attitudes, and Menlo Park, CA: Knowledge Networks. Retrieved from http://www.pipa.org

Laurence, John. (2003, March–April). Embedding: A military view. *Columbia Journalism Review.* Retrieved November 11, 2004, from http://www.cjr.org/issues/2003/2/embed-laurence.asp

Martin, Don. (2004, October 19). From media hack to ministry flack. *The National Post,* p. A18.

McChesney, Robert. (2000). The global media giants. In Robin Andersen and Lance Strate (Eds.), *Critical studies in media commercialism* (pp. 59–70). Oxford, England: Oxford University Press.

Moeller, Susan. (1999). *Compassion fatigue: How the media sell disease, famine, war and death.* New York: Routledge.

Nesbitt-Larking, Paul. (2001). *Politics, society and the media: Canadian perspectives.* Toronto: Broadview Press.

Postman, Neil. (1985). *Amusing ourselves to death: Public discourse in the age of show business.* New York: Penguin.

Rosen, Jay. (1999*). What are journalists for?* New Haven, CT: Yale University Press.

The *Salon* interview: Bill Maher. (2002, December 11). *Salon.* Retrieved November 5, 2004, from http://archive.salon.com/people/interview/2002/12/11/maher

Savoie, Donald. (1996). *Governing from the centre.* Toronto: University of Toronto Press.

Smith, Sean. (2004, October 24). Will Oscar listen? *Newsweek,* 98G.

Statistics Canada. (2001). *2001 census of Canada.* Census. Cat. No. 97F0012XCB01018.

_____. (2002, December 2). Television viewing, Fall 2001. *The Daily.* Retrieved from http://www.statcan.ca/Daily/English/021202/d021202a.htm

Symonds, Emma-Kate, and Jane Schultz. (2004, September 14). Idol moments defending PM. *The Australian,* p. 6.

Taras, David. (1990). *The newsmakers: The media's influence on Canadian politics*. Toronto: Nelson.

_____. (2001). *Power and betrayal in the Canadian media*. Toronto: Broadview.

Tucher, Andie. (1994). *Froth and scum: Truth, beauty, goodness, and the ax murder in America's first mass medium*. Chapel Hill, NC: University of North Carolina Press.

U.S. State Department. (2003, February). Public affairs guidance (PAG) on embedding media during possible future operations/deployments in the U.S. central commands [*sic*] (CENTCOM) area of responsibility (AOR), Sections, 4G1, 4G6, 4G9, 4G14. Retrieved November 7, 2004, from http://www.defenselink.mil/news/Feb2003/d20030228pag.pdf

The Politics of Advertisement

The Liberals Reap What They Sow: Why Their Negative Ads Failed

Jonathan Rose

In the 2004 election, the Liberal attack ads on Stephen Harper and the hidden Conservative agenda were effective because they were performance-validated by gaffes in the Conservative campaign. In 2006, the Liberals' attack ads blew up in their faces and became an object of comedic ridicule because the scary Stephen Harper depicted in them was nowhere to be seen. Instead, Harper was inoculated against the demonizing effects by his calm, measured demeanour during the Conservative policy rollouts in the first half of the campaign. By the time the Liberals delivered their negative ads to market on January 10, including the infamous "soldiers in the streets" spot, it was too late to portray Harper as scary. He was on television January 9 and 10, winning the debates in a quiet, reasonable tone of voice. Jonathan Rose examines the negative ads of the Liberals, Conservatives and NDP, and explains why some Worked and some didn't. He concludes with some recommendations for improving the environment of campaign advertising.

L'argument des intentions cachées de Stephen Harper avait fonctionné en 2004, en raison des impairs de la campagne conservatrice. Mais en 2006, les attaques des libéraux se sont retournées contre eux et les ont ridiculisés parce que le terrible Harper qu'ils dénonçaient brillait par son absence. Le chef conservateur s'est en effet immunisé contre toute diabolisation en manifestant une assurance paisible lors du dévoilement de son programme en première moitié de campagne. Et quand les libéraux ont lancé le 10 janvier leurs publicités négatives, notamment leur dérisoire message montrant des soldats envahissant nos rues, il était trop tard pour le dépeindre sous des traits menaçants. Les 9 et 10 janvier, il remportait les débats télévisés sans se départir de son calme. Jonathan Rose analyse les publicités négatives des libéraux, des conservateurs et des néo-démocrates,

Jonathan Rose teaches at Queen's University in the Department of Political Studies. jonathan.rose@queensu.ca explique pourquoi certaines ont mieux fonctionné que d'autres et formule des recommandations pour assainir les pratiques en la matière.

What a difference a year and a half makes. Writing here about the 2004 federal election I argued that the Liberals had successfully planted the seeds of doubt by engaging in negative advertising about Stephen Harper. The campaign was effective in part because it tied together Liberal claims of the Conservatives' "secret agenda" with the public's apprehension about Harper.

In the 2006 election, the Liberals attempted the same strategy of negative advertising. This time the negative ads harvested by the Liberals yielded a very different crop. The differences between the two elections highlight the different campaigns and also demonstrate the limitations of negative advertising. This campaign affords us an opportunity to scrutinize the usefulness of negative campaigning that was endemic to this election and to explore how campaign communications are conducted elsewhere.

The great cultural theorist Raymond Williams referred to advertising as a "magic system" where an attempt is made by the magic of advertising to relate an object with values to which it has no real reference. Successful ads—whether they are political or commercial—make this illusion work. But if the trick fails, it is exposed as the sham it is. In the 2004 election, the trick of negative advertising worked; this election it did not. What accounts for the change in fortune for the Liberals during this time? The calibre of the campaign, the plausibility of the ads, the timing of the ads and the role of the media all conspired to dull the impact of the Liberals' advertising campaign.

Only very rarely does advertising work in isolation to other factors. One of the reasons why the Liberals' negative ad campaign was successful in the 2004 election was that their campaign was virtually error free while the Conservatives' error-prone campaign reinforced the Liberals' message that Harper could not be trusted. Advertising is almost always an adjunct to campaign communications. The leaders' debates, media reporting about the national campaign and conversations at the proverbial water cooler all shape and reinforce the messages in ads.

The Liberal campaign in 2006 was marked by a series of missteps and communications blunders that affected how the ads were received. Some of them were gaffes that were controllable such as Scott Reid's infamous suggestion that the proposed Conservative child care allowance would be blown on "beer and popcorn." Or Rob Klanders, an Ontario Liberal organizer, whose puerile comment on his website about Olivia Chow was just embarrassing. In the last week of the campaign, CAW leader Buzz Hargrove, campaigning with Paul Martin, likened the National Citizens' Coalition to a "secret society" and implored Quebecers to vote Bloc over the Conservatives. Like the other blunders, that meant Martin was knocked off his message to mop up the damage left by someone else. In Hargrove's case it meant that Martin's sound bite that day was an *endorsement* of Stephen Harper's patriotism.

While some of these might have been avoidable, other issues that damaged their campaign could not have been foreseen. The RCMP investigation over increased stock-trading activity prior to the government's announcement on income trusts was just a case of bad timing for the Liberals. The Toronto shooting of a young woman on Boxing Day capitalized on the Conservatives' get-tough-on-crime agenda. All these took attention away from the Liberal claims that a Conservative government would be a scary prospect and directed attention to the Liberals' own failings.

A second reason that the Liberal advertising campaign was ineffective this time had to do with the plausibility of the arguments in the ads. Prior to Christmas, the Liberals ran a low key but positive ad campaign. The Conservatives, on the other hand, aired policy intensive ads on child care, taxes, seniors and crime—all planks laid out in their platform and reinforced by the campaign. The consistency between Harper's smoothly run campaign and policy-centred advertising made Liberal claims of Conservatives' secret agenda less plausible.

The agenda had already been set by the second half when the Liberals began their negative ads in earnest. It was this second half that was most noteworthy.

The now famous series of Liberal attack ads began on January 10, almost two weeks before election day. Each featured the out-of-focus face of Stephen Harper and was narrated by a female voice accompanied by a militaristic drumbeat. The camera pulled back to reveal a tightly cropped, sinister shot of Harper as the tag line is revealed. A subject of some derision in the press, mocked by political blogs and fodder for comedy programs, one of the infamous tag lines read, "No. We did not make that up. We're not allowed to make stuff up." In all the ads, the audio was reproduced in Courier font on the screen which reinforced the austere simplicity of the production values.

Liberal ads may have been "truthful" in that those that quoted Harper faithfully represented what he said, but they were not credible because of the chasm between the scary Harper in the ads and the cautious Harper in the campaign. Whether Harper had changed since 2004 or whether in this election he had done a better job of moderating himself, only time will tell. In elections, where image is often a replacement for reality, the reality of Harper did not match the image offered by the Liberals.

The Conservatives responded with negative ads such as "Can We Believe Him?" and "Entitlements," both of which reinforced doubts about Liberal ethics that were driven home by Harper in the pre-Christmas campaign and by the media coverage of the campaign. It wasn't that these two ads were any less negative than the Liberal ads but rather that, like any good ad, they successfully tapped into viewers' already held opinions—however latent—about the Liberal Party. More significantly they pre-empted the Liberal ads that followed and inoculated the Conservatives against the soon-to-be-aired Liberal ads.

The darker of the two, "Entitlements," was a machine gun volley of disparate images and quick shots. It began with Paul Martin saying, "The Liberal Party is not corrupt"—a mantra repeated in the background throughout the ad. Over this mantra was a visual of a front page of *The Globe and Mail* that read "Martin Liberals took illicit cash, probe told" followed by text and audio quotes from Justice Gomery saying "the heart of an elaborate kickback scheme" and "the culture of entitlement." The final element that refuted Martin's claim showed an exasperated David Dingwall appearing before a House of Commons committee saying, "I'm entitled to my entitlements." The effect of the authoritative claims of a newspaper and a judge, juxtaposed with a politician's denial, reinforced the primary claim of the ad: namely that voters couldn't trust the Liberals. The style of quick, rapid-fire shots added to the sense of urgency and chaos that the Conservatives wanted to create.

Because television is an audio-visual medium, it is not a surprise that this ad used both to knit together an argument. The associative logic of advertising is well suited to television where arguments and claims don't have to be graced with evidence to be plausible. What was "the heart of the kickback scheme" and who represented "the culture of entitlement" stated by Justice Gomery were left unsaid. The inference, however, was clear.

The failure of the Liberal ads may shed some insight into the degree to which Canadians are growing increasingly weary of negative advertising. While it is true that all parties used negative ads to some degree, the Liberals' flood in the last two weeks reminds us of the tipping point between reinforcement and redundancy. With 12 ads running at the same time on a similar theme of distrust for Harper, it is possible that the Liberal message lost its power.

Communication scholars call the phenomenon of being inured by repeated viewings of provocative images "compassion fatigue." The lawyers for the LAPD officers charged with the beating of Rodney King showed the tape of their clients' assault over and over again to inoculate the jury against the horrors of what they were watching. Arguably, the saturation of provocative ads by the Liberals unwittingly had the same effect. In early January, prior to the Liberal flood of ads, the Conservatives ran an ad called "They'll Go Negative" which primed viewers to expect the soon-to-be-shown Liberal ads. The claim made by the Tory ad dovetailed well with the substance of what would shortly be broadcast by the Liberals. The Conservatives followed the principle that less is more by using negative ads in a strategic and timely fashion. If elections are warfare, their ads were the precision guided bombs to the Liberals' carpet bombing strategy.

While the advertising data from this election are not yet known, we do know that in the last federal election the Liberals spent over 60 percent of their total campaign expenditures on advertising compared to around 41 percent for the Conservatives and New Democrats. If the proportion is the same for this year, it means that over $10 million was spent on advertising by the Liberals. In the two previous elections in 2004 and 2000, the Liberals out-spent other parties on advertising. There is no reason to think this trend would be halted in this election.

While these may be important reasons to explain the failure of the Liberal negative advertising, a more compelling reason may be found in the media reporting of the leaders themselves. According to the election media study by McGill's Observatory on Media and Public Policy, Paul Martin was viewed much more negatively by the press than any of the other federal leaders. Some of this negativity was reflected in the media's coverage of advertising. It also demonstrates the reality that the Liberals and Paul Martin were unable to convert the paid media of their advertising into positive earned media by the press.

The effectiveness of ads can be seen in two ways. First, ads may reinforce, change or affect public opinion by the claims they make. This is the ostensible purpose of advertising: to prime voters and attempt to agenda-set the campaign. Second, and perhaps more significantly, the impact of ads can be measured by media reporting of those ads. This earned media is arguably more significant than the paid media of the ads themselves as it provides context for understanding them. In this election, one of the important media narratives was the depths to which the Liberals descended in their advertising. News stories abounded that examined the Liberals' advertising strategy. Often those stories were more negative than the earned media on opposition party ads.

When political parties use negative advertising they straddle the fine line between drawing attention to the object of the ad and drawing attention to themselves, the communicator of the ad. If done correctly, the messenger should receive less press than the message. The Liberals got it wrong by making the sponsor of the ad the subject of the story. The earned media which should have been about the object of the ads was about the party that aired them.

All negative advertising is clearly not created equally. Negative political ads can be comparative and policy focused, personal and ad hominem, or implicitly negative. There are different criteria used by the media and voters to judge each of these kinds of ads. Ads which compare party platforms may be negative by the distinctions they draw between the policy differences. One of the most negative ads in the 2004 election played on the Conservatives' support for the Iraq war. While this drew much attention by the media, it was defended by the Liberals as making clear the policy differences between the two parties. Comparative ads that are negative allow parties to claim that the ads are warranted on the basis of drawing distinctions between party platforms. The same cannot be said for personal attack ads. The Liberal campaign relied almost exclusively on ads whose focus was their opponent's character, motives or actions. The series of closely cropped images of Stephen Harper's face that dominated the Liberal ads were seen as personal assault ads rather than the more favorably viewed comparison ads.

Building on the work of Anthony Downs, Samuel Popkin argues that voters use shortcuts to simplify the act of voting. These shortcuts can be dominant symbols found in ads, the opinion of a favourite columnist or a voter's perception of leadership. The negative ads used by all parties attempted to create these cognitive shortcuts either explicitly or implicitly. For example, the NDP in its ad "Gift" used a lump of coal and a boot to communicate implicitly what the Liberals were giving Canadians and what Canadians should give the Liberals. (It was the first time we've seen Christmas used in a political ad in Canada.) The

Liberals, on the other hand, explicitly labelled Stephen Harper as the condensation symbol for leadership and trust. This symbol as a frame failed because for many voters trust and integrity were ballot box questions directed at the Liberals and not the Conservatives.

One of the more common claims about negative advertising is that though no one likes it, parties have no option but to "go negative." The argument is that in a very tightly scripted race, political parties need to rely on negative advertising to distinguish themselves from other parties, to maintain the interest of voters and to create wedge issues for policy differentiation.

Some have feared that our election campaigns have become more Americanized and cite the increased use of negative ads as evidence of this. They argue that parties in Canadian elections routinely use negative ads, that elections are dominated by party leaders rather than parties and that the increased professionalization of campaigns is proof of this convergence. While there are similarities, the points of departure are perhaps worth mentioning. Much of the negative campaigning in the US is third party advertising and the courts' decision here to ban third party advertising as a reasonable limit on freedom of expression is a profound difference in our elections. The limit placed on campaign expenses and corporate and individual donations serves as a moderating influence on the always sticky relationship between money and politics. The recent changes to the *Elections Act* guarantee funding to political parties which suggests that in Canada, the state is willing to take a more interventionist role in the life of parties than in the US.

We are, however, like the US in that the state has little to say about campaign advertising. The experiences of other nations suggest that the state's involvement in regulating election advertising may go some way in enhancing the public debate that elections afford. An examination of those options might do much to inspire our imagination about what might be done here.

In Britain, election advertising by parties is prohibited. Instead political parties are given free time on national television in proportion to their electoral standing in the previous election. These party election broadcasts (PEBs) are several minutes in length allowing for a more nuanced and thoughtful discussion of a party platform. To be sure, some take the format of a "biopic," a political biography that extols the leader by glorifying his or her humble roots. Because they are longer they have the potential to be better vehicles than ads for providing information to the electorate.

PEBs do have several advantages over our election spots. First, because they are significantly longer than a 30-second spot, they make detailed arguments on policy areas. Second, because there are so few of them, they are more likely to be seen as credible sources of information. PEBs are based on the principle that less is more—something that our parties might be wise to heed. Third, because their allocation is based on electoral strength, minor parties, who under our system cannot afford network airtime, have access to public airwaves.

The German model is a hybrid of the British and Canadian systems, with a twist. Public television stations give political parties free airtime—similar to the

PEBs in Britain. Private stations sell airtime to parties as in Canada but at a lower rate than commercial advertising. The effect of this is to lower entrance barriers for smaller parties and to allow for longer ads, usually upwards of two minutes. In Germany the principle that underlies broadcasting ads is equal opportunity for all parties. If a station accepts ads from one party, it must accept them from all.

Even if we don't radically restructure our electoral process by banning election ads outright, we could civilize the process by limiting attack ads. Since the Canadian state already contributes campaign funding, it might be time to put on the agenda the regulation of campaign advertising.

Finland and Israel both have restrictions on the content of their ads. In Finland, comparative or critical party ads are allowed but negative ads targeted at a leader are prohibited. Such a rule would eliminate virtually all of the ads now broadcast by the Conservatives and Liberals. Israeli regulations adopted here would eliminate some of the more egregiously offensive ads. The Liberals' infamous 2004 election ad showing a tank and gun pointed at the camera would not be allowed in Israel where any military images are prohibited in political spots. It's not just ads that are regulated in Israel. Until a few years ago the very appearance of candidates or leaders was banned in news coverage during the latter part of elections. Imagine an election campaign devoid of the manufactured photo-ops so beloved by our political parties. The impact that this would have on the way leaders campaign and reporters file stories would be significant.

Election advertising performs a number of important campaign functions such as agenda setting, political mobilization, persuasion and, perhaps, changing voting behaviour. In this election, the advertising campaigns of all major national parties reflected the unclear nature of the ballot box question. The Liberal ads failed in part because the Liberal campaign failed. Moreover, this campaign reminds us that negative advertising, if used injudiciously and without the support of a strong campaign or positive media coverage, can fail on all of these counts.

Keywords for critical reading

By the end of this section the student should be able to define and illustrate their understanding of each of the following key concepts and notions:

- Blogs
- Congenial truths
- Democratic politics
- Earned media
- Embedded journalists
- Framing news
- Gatekeepers
- Infotainment

- Media agenda-setting; Media concentration
- Negative advertising
- Paid media
- Public journalism
- Priming audiences
- Spin doctors
- Technological determinism

Key questions for critical learning

1. Explain how voter advantage is gained through the use of negative advertisement—advertisements that denigrate or embarrass an opponent or that portray the opponent's policies in an unfavorable light.
2. How do you define the process by which the messages from the political campaign go directly to the audience through unfiltered placement in the media?
3. Explain the belief that technical force, including advances in communication (e.g., printing press, telegraph, television, and the Internet) is the main factor that drives social and cultural changes in society.
4. Why is the concentration of media ownership frequently seen as a problem of contemporary society?
5. Why is it important to have public or civic journalism? Enumerate the most important key roles of public or civic journalism in political communication.
6. What is the difference between experts ruling as opposed to 'ruled by the people'?
7. Explain the process by which the mass media determines what is on the public's agenda.
8. Discuss mass media practices of attaching journalists to specific military units and having these journalists travel with the solders, specifically into extremely dangerous combat situations.
9. What do you call the practice of directing the listener's, or reader's, or viewer's attention to a limited set of attributes concerning an issue or person, and therefore away from others?
10. Explain the difference between the process of encouraging people to pay attention to some factors relating to an issue rather than others and the notion of framing.
11. Why have 'blogs' become a challenge to traditional media?
12. Explain the process through which the news and entertainment become indistinct.
13. What are the main characteristics of public relations professionals and campaign strategists who are employed to 'explain' events and issues to journalists?

Permission Credits

This page constitutes an extension of the copyright page. We have made every effort to trace the ownership of all copyrighted material and to ensure permission from the copyrights holders. In the cases of any question or request for adjustment, we will be pleased to make the necessary corrections in future editions.

Adler, R.B. and F. Rodman, 'Language' in *Understanding Human Communication*, 9 ed. (New York: Oxford University Press, 2005). Reprinted by permission of the publisher.

Aldoory, L. and S.J. Parry-Gilles, 'Women and Race in Feminist Media Research: Intersections, Ideology and Invisibility', in *Mass Media and Society*, James Curran and Michael Gurevitch, eds. (Hodder Arnold, 2005), 336–55. Reprinted by permission of Edward Arnold (Publishers).

Barney, D., 'The Digital Mosaic: Democracy and Communication Technology in Canada', in *Communication Technology* (Vancouver: UBC Press, 2004). Reprinted with permission of the Publisher from *Communication Technology* by Darin Barney © University of British Columbia Press 2004. All rights reserved by the Publisher.

de B'béri, B.E., 'Intermedial Location of Meaning in *Muna Moto*: A Metalanguage of Cultural Discourse'. First Published in *Cinema and Social Discourse in Cameroon*, Alexie Tcheuyap, ed. (Germany: African Studies Series 69, 2005), 64–80. Reprinted by permission of the publisher.

Bélanger, P., 'Radio in Canada: An Industry in Transition'. From *Mass Communications in Canada, New Patterns in Canadian Communication, First Edition* by Attallah/ Shade. 2002. Reprinted with permission of Nelson, a division of Thomson Learning: www.thomsonrights.com. Fax 800 730-2215.

Berman, S., L.A. Shipnuck, and N. Duff, 'The End of TV as We Know It: A Future Industry Perspective' © IBM Institute for Business Values. Reprinted by permission of IBM.

Denham, B., A.C. Billings, and K.K. Halone, 'Differential Accounts of Race in Broadcast Commentary of the 2000 NCAA Men's and Women's Final Four Basketball Tournament', *Sociology of Sport Journal* 19 (2002). Reprinted by permission.

Downing, J.D.H., 'New Communication Research from Canada', *Journal of Communication* 52.2 (2002). Reprinted by permission of the International Communication Association.

Dyer, R., 'The Matters of Whiteness', in *White* (New York: Routledge, 1997).

Eid, M., 'Paul Lazarfield's Ideational Network and Contribution to the Field of Communication Research', *Communications: The European Journal of Communication Research* 29.2 (2004).

Feinstein, A., J. Owen, and N. Blair, 'A Hazardous Profession: War, Journalists, and Psychopathology', *American Journal of Psychiatry* 159.9 (2002).

Gasher M., and R. Lorimer, 'Communications Technology and Society: Theory and Practice" from *Mass Communications in Canada*, 5th edition, by Rowland Lorimer and Mike Gasher. © Oxford University Press 2004. Reprinted by permission of the publisher.

Gibson, T., '"I Don't Want Them Living Around Here": Ideologies of Race and Neighborhood Decay', *Rethinking Marxism* 10.1 (Spring 1998).

Grant, G., 'Thinking about Technology' from *Technology and Justice* copyright © 1986 by George Grant. Reprinted by permission of House of Anansi Press.

Greenberg, J., 'Opinion Discourse and Canadian Newspapers: The Case of the Chinese "Boat People"', *Canadian Journal of Communication* Vol. 25, No. 4 (2000): 517–37. Reprinted by permission of the Canadian Journal of Communication.

Hall, S., 'Encoding/Decoding' in *Culture, Media, Language: Working Papers in Cultural Studies, 1972–79*, S. Hall, ed. (London: Hutchinson, 1973; 1980).

Hamilton, S., 'Considering Critical Communication Studies in Canada'. From *Mass Communications in Canada, New Patterns in Canadian Communication, First Edition* by Attallah/Shade. 2002. Reprinted with permission of Nelson, a division of Thomson Learning: www.thomsonrights.com. Fax 800 730-2215.

Hardt, H., 'On Introducing Ideology: Critical Theory and the Critique of Culture', in *Critical Communication Studies* (London: Routledge, 1992).

hooks, b., 'Representation of Whiteness in the Black Imagination', in *Black Looks* (Southend Press, 1992).

Ivy, D.K., and P. Backlund, 'Pictures, Porno, and Pop: Gender and Mass Media', in *Gender Speak: Personal Effectiveness in Gender Communication* (New York: McGraw Hill, 2000).

Littlejohn, S.W., 'Communication and Media'. From *Theories of Human Communication* (with InfoTrac) 8th edition by Littlejohn/Foss. © 2005. Reprinted with permission of Wadsworth, a division of Thomson Learning: www.thomsonrights.com. Fax 800 730-2215.

Lowes, M., 'Sports Page: A Case Study in the Manufacture of Sports News for the Daily Press', *Sociology of Sport Journal* 14.2 (1997). Reprinted by permission.

McLuhan, M., 'The Tribal Drum' from *Understanding Media: The Extension of Man* (New York: McGraw Hill, 1964).

Nesbitt-Larking, P., 'From Experience to Editorial: Gatekeeping, Agenda Setting, Priming and Framing', in *Politics, Society and the Media* (Peterborough: Broadview Press, 2001). Reprinted by permission of Broadview Press.

Paré, D., 'Master of My Domain: The Politics of Internet Governance', from *Inside the Communications Revolution: New Patterns of Social and Technical Interaction*, R. Mansell, ed. (New York, Oxford University Press, 2002). Reprinted by permission of the publisher.

Rose, J., 'The Liberals Reap What They Sow: Why Their Negative Ads Failed'. Printed/reproduced with permission of the IRPP. www.irpp.org

Rose J., and S. Kiss, 'Boundaries Blurred: The Mass Media and Politics in a Hyper-Media Age'. From *Mass Communications in Canada, New Patterns in Canadian Communication, First Edition* by Attallah/Shade. 2002. Reprinted with permission of Nelson, a division of Thomson Learning: www.thomsonrights.com. Fax 800 730-2215.

Thussu, D., 'Approaches to Theorizing International Communication', in *International Communication and Change* (Hodder Arnold, 2000), 53–81. Reprinted by permission of Edward Arnold (Publishers).

Warschauer, Mark, 'Digital Resources: Content and Language' in *Technology and Social Inclusion: Rethinking the Digital Divide* (MIT Press, 2003). Reprinted by permission of MIT Press.

Weber, S., 'Introduction: Where in the World We Are?' and 'Television Set and Screen' in *Mass Mediarus: Form, Technics, Media*, A. Cholodenko, ed. (California: Stanford University Press, 1996). © Power Institute and Samuel Weber 1996. Reprinted by permission.